WRITING IN THE WORKS

WRITING IN THE WORKS

Susan Blau
Boston University

Kathryn Burak
Boston University

Houghton Mifflin
Boston   New York

Publisher: Patricia Coryell
Editor in Chief: Suzanne Phelps Weir
Senior Development Editor: Judith Fifer
Assistant Editor: Jane Acheson
Editorial Associate: John McHugh
Senior Project Editor: Rosemary Winfield
Editorial Assistant: Jake Perry
Art and Design Coordinator: Jill Haber
Photo Editor: Jennifer Meyer Dare
Composition Buyer: Chuck Dutton
Manufacturing Coordinator: Karen Banks
Marketing Manager: Cindy Graff Cohen

Front cover illustration: Robert Neubecker, Modern Media, Inc.

Printed in the U.S.A.

Library of Congress Catalog Card Number 2003109853

Instructor's examination edition: ISBN 0-618-69484-6

Student edition: ISBN 0-618-22211-1

1 2 3 4 5 6 7 8 9 - VH - 09 08 07 06 05

BRIEF CONTENTS

v

CONTENTS

PART I

The Writer's Craft

PART II
Assignments

Chapter 5   Memoirs: Writing a Narrative   135

Chapter 6 News Stories: Writing the Public Record 182

Chapter 11   Film Reviews: Writing Evaluations   370

PART III

Research and Documentation

PART IV

Grammar Handbook

Chapter 18   Common Errors   688

Chapter 19   Trouble Spots for Nonnative Speakers   710

THEMATIC CONTENTS

WRITING IN THE WORKS *motivates, inspires,* and *provides tools* to create writing projects for **courses**, for the **community**, and for the **workplace**.

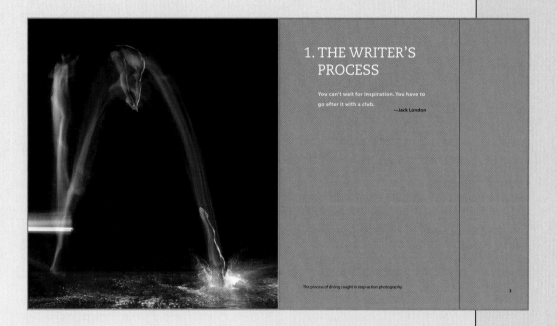

1. THE WRITER'S PROCESS

You can't wait for inspiration. You have to go after it with a club.

—Jack London

The process of diving caught in stop-action photography.

3

" The text . . . succeeds in treating students as writers, in providing them situations where they can write something meaningful to a real audience, in not abandoning the 'stalwarts' of freshman composition. . . . Blau and Burak have written an exceptionally innovative and teachable text."

—*Jose M. Blanco, Miami Dade College*

" . . . The 'teachability' of this text seems excellent . . . Overall I think the goals are accomplished because the text is engaging and consistently makes clear connections between the 'real' world and academic exercises."

—*Marti L. Mundell, Washington State University*

WRITING IN THE WORKS thoroughly grounds students in the *writing process*, from prewriting and document design through revision and peer review, with real-world examples and instruction in writing memoirs, editorials, news articles, public service projects, websites, and more.

six that you just love, that is so beautiful or wild that you now know what you're supposed to be writing about, more or less, or in what direction you might go—but there was no way to get to this without first getting through the first five and a half pages.

Questions for Discussion and Writing

1. Lamott writes, "The first draft is the child's draft, where you let it all pour out and then let it romp all over the place." In what ways does this describe your first-draft writing? In what ways does it differ? To what would you compare your first drafts?

2. Your friend is writing a first draft of a first college paper and has gotten stuck. Write an e-mail message to your friend, incorporating any advice from Lamott's piece that you think would be motivating.

REVISING

When I see a paragraph shrinking under my eyes like a strip of bacon on a skillet, I know I'm on the right track.

—Peter DeVries

Revision is the heart of the writing process, an opportunity to look with fresh eyes at what you have written. Some writers believe that this stage is where the real writing happens, where you can make changes that allow you to say clearly and precisely what you mean to say. Of course, you are revising during the entire writing process, not just at the end. You revise as you plan and write, as you choose one idea or word rather than another. However, the most significant revision usually occurs as you move from an early draft to a final one.

Make sure to leave enough time between an early draft and your final deadline to put the paper away for a while. Ideally, leave a day or two for end-stage revising. If you have just finished a marathon writing session, you will lack the perspective necessary to look at your writing with fresh eyes.

Revision consists of more than finding and fixing surface errors like typos or finding livelier synonyms for dull words. Changing words, checking spelling, and cleaning up grammatical and mechanical errors are all important end-stage writing activities, but they are not the essence of revision. Successful revision consists of truly rethinking your draft. You have to be willing to change your focus, reorder your thinking, lop off whole sections, and develop others, if necessary.

Five activities are key to successful revision: refocusing, reordering, adding, cutting, and editing.

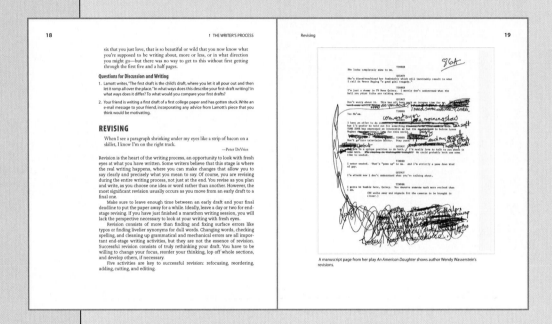

A manuscript page from her play *An American Daughter* shows author Wendy Wasserstein's revisions.

> **"Your textbook seeks to teach students that what they have to say is important and that they can write. . . . And more important, it seamlessly reminds them that, regardless of their chosen profession, they will always have to write, and the skills they master here will help them engage the world more intelligently."**
>
> —*Constantina Michalos, Houston Baptist University*

An **outstanding design** and **striking visuals** emphasize **visual literacy**, reinforced in Visual Literacy boxes in every writing chapter; in dynamic, intriguing photographs and illustrations throughout the text; and in chapter content that explores critical reading and critical viewing.

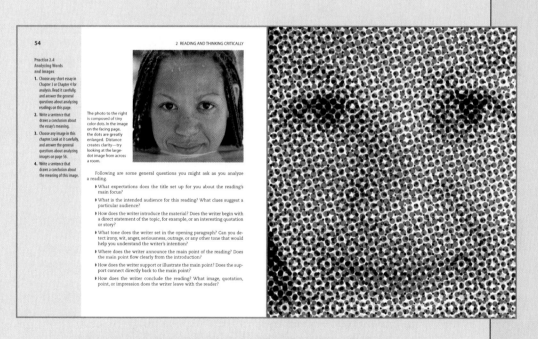

"The design layout is very effective. It gives the impression of being well-organized, uncluttered, and modern in its visual simplicity (with layout and type). The images are striking, and the tinted practice and sidebar sections are effectively set off from the main text."

—*Thomas Gerard McNamee, Eastern Oregon University*

The Two Fridas 177

Critical Questions

1. Where is your eye first drawn in the painting?
2. Observe the two images of Kahlo in the painting. What is revealed by the way that Kahlo positions these two images and the way that she uses color here? What do these images reveal about how she sees herself at this time?
3. What is the setting of this painting? What mood does the painting create? What has Kahlo done to reinforce the mood of this setting?
4. Much of Kahlo's painting is highly symbolic. What symbols can you see in this painting? What might they represent?

5. What is the story in this painting? What is the conflict?
6. Compare the photograph of Kahlo to the self-portrait. In what way is the painting interpretive? What do you think Kahlo is revealing about herself in the self-portrait?

Questions for Writing and Discussion

1. Images as well as words tell stories. What images can you think of in popular culture that tell stories?
2. If you were to paint a self-portrait, what symbolic items would you put in your hands?

178 5 MEMOIRS

WRITING IN THE WORKS
Interview with Antonya Nelson

Antonya Nelson

1. Your memoir, "All Washed Up" [see pages 153–155], reads a lot like a short story. It is sometimes hard for writers to imagine using a "real" event and making it into something that reads like a piece of fiction. For some, it is a matter of feeling bound by the events as they occurred, being loyal to every detail. Maybe you can help answer one question that is always on the minds of memoir writers: How do you take real life and make it into art? Do you ever feel the need to embellish?

Sometimes I like to pose the opposite question: how can you write about something that hasn't happened to you, that you know nothing or care nothing about, and turn that into fiction? That seems like the more challenging task, especially the not caring part. Ideally, finding fiction in one's factual life means locating a stance that will accommodate genuine feeling, on the one hand, without hurting genuine feelings, on the other hand.

2. Readers looking carefully at the way you craft your story notice your techniques of using parallel sentences, repeating certain phrases, and listing. Are you conscious of these techniques as you write, or are they part of your internal writing mechanism?

I'm pretty sure this is a matter of what we lovely call voice. I have an internalized rhythm that means something to me. It dictates how I write, how I pattern sentences, what vocabulary I choose, etc. I know what sounds good to myself. I'm sure I learned it reading books, reading aloud, bearing the spoken word when it's at its most seductive, and I'm sure I've attempted, pretty unconsciously, to channel that which pleases my own ear. I read aloud in the car too. Sometimes I just chat at the dog.

3. Much of the story happens "off-screen," and is revealed in the form of exposition. How do you decide when to let the camera roll and show the action in a scene rather than a "voiceover"?

Again, this has to do with some sense of being both writer and reader, simultaneously. I tell my students this all the time: imagine you are reading what you are writing. What do you want (need) to know (hear) next? Occasionally I've been aware of there being too much exposition in my work. I create separate files after I've finished a short story (on my computer) and copy the story over, then rename the file "X story, activated." The "activate" part is where I stop exposition, inasmuch as I can, and start creating either dialogue or action to do the same work. I'm trying to move further away from exposition in narrative. But that doesn't quite answer your question. I really do believe in the internalized sense of pattern and variation, of some monitor lodged behind the reader/writer's eyes or brain or heart that dictates when a line of dialogue needs to emerge, when a repeated background note needs striking, when a sentence containing only one word needs to fall. There.

4. Your voice in "All Washed Up" captures the essence of being eighteen and full of yourself, which is essential to the theme of the story. When you were learning the craft of storytelling, how did you go about finding a voice for yourself as a writer?

I imitated people for a long time. I still might be doing that. But I read enough people that the combo plate is pretty varied. I love Flannery O'Connor's precise humor. I love Carson McCullers' swampy psychotic emotional terrain. I love the scalpel-like descriptors of John Updike. I want David Sedaris' irreverence. I wish I had plot under control like Pete Dexter or Larry Brown or

At every step in the process, students practice writing, with Writer's Notebook suggestions, Peer-Editing Logs and suggestions for peer review and feedback, and Revision Checklists that emphasize writing as a continuous process.

WRITING AND REVISION STRATEGIES

Gathered here are three interactive sections for you to use as you write and revise your application essay and as you apply what you have learned to writing in other classes.

▶ Writer's Notebook Suggestions
▶ Peer Editing Log
▶ Revision Checklist

Writer's Notebook Suggestions

These short exercises are intended to jump-start your thinking as you begin to write your application essay.

1. Write a letter of recommendation for yourself.
2. You have been asked to go back to your former high school and give a useful two-minute speech to the senior class. Write the speech.
3. Describe your single best asset in one paragraph. Don't brag, but sell yourself.
4. List all the things you wish to accomplish in the next five years.
5. Give one example of a time you succeeded against the odds.
6. Write one paragraph explaining a disappointment and how it affected you.
7. Write about an experience that made you aware of a skill you have.
8. Write a paragraph about one goal you have. Be as specific as possible.
9. Link a personal experience with a career goal.
10. Create a visual image (a short video, a collage, a drawing) that communicates something about who you are.

Peer-Editing Log

As you work with a writing partner or in a peer-editing group, you can use these questions to give helpful responses to a classmate's application essay and as a guide for discussion.

Writer's Name _____

Date _____

1. Underline the essay's thesis. Make suggestions to strengthen it by rewording it or placing it elsewhere.
2. Put brackets around the introduction. Does the introduction announce the topic clearly?
3. If there is a prompt, has the introduction addressed the prompt specifically?
4. What development strategies does the writer use? Can you suggest specific places where narrative detail or supporting evidence might strengthen the essay?
5. Put brackets around the conclusion. What impression does it leave? Suggest ways for the writer to strengthen the final impression.
6. Put wavy lines under any application clichés the writer used; put check marks next to any language you find particularly fresh and appealing.

Revision Checklist

As you do your final revision, check to make sure that you

❏ Stated your thesis clearly and accurately
❏ Wrote an engaging and focused introduction
❏ Clearly answered the prompt, if there is one
❏ Organized the body of the paper in a logical pattern
❏ Used elements of narration, analysis, and argumentation where appropriate
❏ Wrote in a personal yet not informal voice
❏ Avoided application essay clichés
❏ Concluded with the impression you want to leave with your reader
❏ Wrote a memorable essay that reflects some aspect of your values, interests, and personality

> " I have high regard for Blau/Burak's efforts to provide a good selection of activities, journal prompts, and other questions for students to respond to readings."
>
> —*Lawrence Roderer,*
> *J. Sargeant Reynolds Community College*

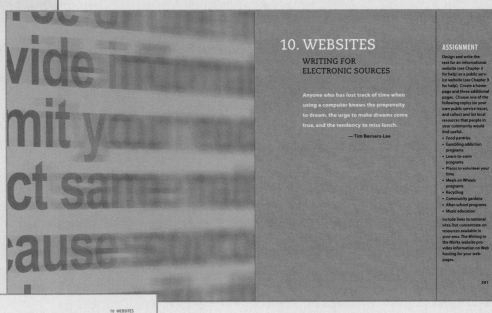

10. WEBSITES
WRITING FOR ELECTRONIC SOURCES

Anyone who has lost track of time when using a computer knows the propensity to dream, the urge to make dreams come true, and the tendency to miss lunch.

— Tim Berners-Lee

ASSIGNMENT

Design and write the text for an informational website (see Chapter 3 for help) or a public service website (see Chapter 9 for help). Create a homepage and three additional pages. Choose one of the following topics (or your own public service issue), and collect and list local resources that people in your community would find useful.

- Food pantries
- Gambling addiction programs
- Learn-to-swim programs
- Places to volunteer your time
- Meals on Wheels programs
- Recycling
- Community gardens
- After-school programs
- Music education

Include links to national sites, but concentrate on resources available in your area. The Writing in the Works website provides information on Web hosting for your webpages.

341

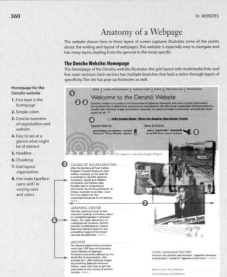

Text coverage reflects students' **use of the computer** throughout the writing process, from note-taking and drafting papers to design, layout, and revision, as well as writing for the Internet and finding, evaluating, and citing Web sources.

> "...the authors of this text do a first-rate job of explaining how students should evaluate their sources, reinforcing this as they talk about how assessment applies to various media and then by their use of questions and exercises."
> —*Joseph M. Schuster, Webster University*

WRITING IN THE WORKS fully covers how to **research** and **document** writing, in "Research Paths" content included in every writing chapter as well as separate chapters on research and documentation.

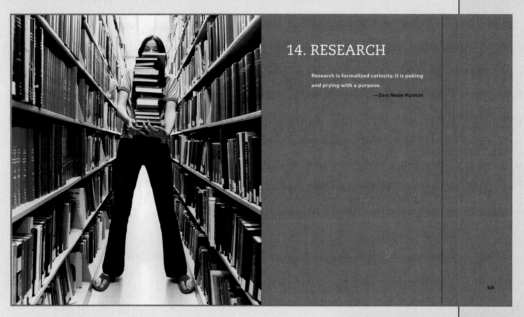

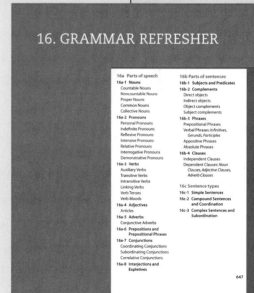

"I like the innovative method of having students conduct research, even in writing a memoir. This method helps students contextualize their life with events in the world."
—*Jose M. Blanco, Miami Dade College*

The text also provides a **Grammar Handbook**, with chapters on grammar, punctuation, common errors, and special help for nonnative speakers of English.

The **full supplements package** includes integrated websites for both students and instructors, Blackboard/WebCT courses, a special WriteSpace course exclusive to Houghton Mifflin, and Smarthinking tutorial service for students.

▶ **The Online Instructor's Resource Manual**, at www.college. hmco.com/english/instructors, includes a course overview, sample syllabi, chapter outlines, lecture notes, handouts, suggestions for class activities, technology ideas, and recommended resources by chapter.

▶ **The student website**, at www.college.hmco.com/english/students, includes chapter checklists and helpful weblinks; additional

readings not found in the book; "Springboard" exercises that help students further their writing practice; a special section on avoiding plagiarism; a Style Guide; a special section on publishing your work; and a bank of Audio-Visual Literacy exercises that provide practice in thinking and writing about movies, commercials, speeches, and other media. Website icons in the text indicate practices or links to websites that are also found on the student website.

▶ The **WriteSpace online writing program** provides more than 100 tutorial writing modules plus more than 2,000 exercises, and access to an online handbook.

▶ **Smarthinking online tutorial service** enables students to obtain personal assistance via phone or e-mail.

Additional HM resources include:

▶ **Student resource center** with additional support for coursework;

▶ **Adjuncts.com,** an online resource for adjunct instructors;

▶ Print supplements on teaching writing with computers and other resources for instructors.

PREFACE: TO STUDENTS

Earl Oliver wanted to weigh in on the issue of downloading music off the Internet, so he wrote a letter to the *San Francisco Chronicle*. The Pine Tree Neighborhood Group wanted to join a national campaign to provide teddy bears for children involved in police calls, so they wrote proposals and letters of appeal to get volunteers, donations, and support for their program. Salaam Pax wanted to share his experiences before and during the U.S. attacks on Baghdad in 2003, so he turned to his blog (web log) and wrote postings from Iraq that were read by thousands of people.

People write for all kinds of reasons. Some people, born under the writing star, write out of artistic impulse. Others, like Earl Oliver, the Pine Tree Neighborhood Group, and Salaam Pax, write in a public forum to effect change in the world. Sometimes the practical goal of earning money fuels the act of writing. Ask any engineer who has climbed the corporate ladder: the higher up you get in the company, the more you have to write. Successful people write, and people write to be successful.

WRITING FOR A LIFETIME

If you are reading this book, you are writing for a class in college, and your reasons for writing may seem obvious. You need a grade and credit for the course. Beyond that real and practical consideration, however, writing is a skill that you will use and develop over the course of your lifetime: in school, in your communities, and in your workplaces. The difference between being a *student who writes* and being a *writer* is that writers use their skills all the time, not just to express their ideas in academic assignments but also to create change, to share ideas in a public forum, to complete a work project, to earn money, and to communicate and connect with readers.

The writing assignments in this book have as their primary goal to help you become skillful and confident writers who write because they have something to say and an audience to whom they want to say it. The assignments themselves — essays, memoirs, editorials, film reviews, proposals, profiles, public service messages — are writing formats that you read and use every day and that may inspire you to write about ideas and issues that are important to you.

Being a writer also means keeping your reader firmly in mind. Readers of essays, reviews, proposals, and articles must be engaged, or even entertained, while they are informed or persuaded. People pay good money to read these formats when they are published in magazines, journals, books or on websites, and these readers can and do stop reading whenever they get bored or confused. Writing assignments that matter to you can help you to write directly on your reader's memory and to write with indelible ink.

PREFACE: TO TEACHERS

Writing teachers ourselves, we know that writing classrooms can be diverse and that each has its own character. Our interactions with our students change from semester to semester, often from class to class, and so do our materials and methods, depending on the needs — and the chemistry — of a particular group of students. At the same time, teaching writing is labor-intensive, requiring hours of responding to student texts and giving feedback, advice, and encouragement. We also realize that students do not learn to write by listening to us talk about writing; they have to become engaged in the process — generating writing, receiving feedback, and revising. Knowing all this, we set out to write a textbook that provides structure and interactivity for students, options and flexibility for teachers, and, we hope, exciting and engaging material for all.

Our approach in *Writing in the Works* is to treat students like *writers* rather than as *students who write*. This book offers serious writing tasks to do and provides students with important, satisfying, and practical reasons to write: to gain admittance to a program, to tell their own stories and the stories of others, to express their views in a public forum, to help improve the community or the world, and to learn and communicate their knowledge to their readers. These reasons are embedded in the assignments, the kinds of writing that students read and use in their daily lives both inside and outside the classroom: application essays, memoirs, news stories, film reviews, editorials and letters to the editor, proposals, public service announcements, websites, and magazine articles. We have discovered in our own writing classrooms that students are highly motivated to write these assignments, and through them, students learn the stalwart forms valued in writing classes: exposition, narration, argumentation, analysis, and persuasion. Students learn these academic skills in a context that makes sense to them and that has relevance to them. Also embedded in these assignments is a clear sense of audience; readers have to be engaged from the first to the final word of a piece of writing.

For teachers, the book is flexible. Assignment chapters and overview or reference chapters can be combined in a variety of ways, depending on your style, the course, and the needs of your students. *Writing in the Works* can be effective in courses in basic writing, first-year composition, advanced composition, or writing for the media. Each chapter offers options as well. You can choose from an array of interactive exercises, writers' notebook prompts, brainstorming and revising activities, and readings from student and professional writers. The readings are contemporary and topical and are drawn from such publications as the *New Yorker, Popular Science, Utne Reader, New York Times, Chicago Tribune,* and *San Francisco Chronicle* and from a variety of websites.

Writing in the Works has been in the works for a long time. Over twenty teachers have class tested this material during the past ten years. We have received feedback from our students, our colleagues, and, listening to their good advice, we have revised and revised again. What has remained constant, however, is the overarching aim of helping students see themselves as writers — writers who write to say something that matters to themselves and to their readers. Through years of teaching and writing experiences, we have learned that when students have a clear sense of purpose and audience for their writing, they are much more motivated. They understand that writing is not just an academic task but a craft practiced every day by people who care about communicating clearly and well.

DISTINCTIVE FEATURES

▶ **Engaging, Realistic Assignments**   Students' motivation and writing improve when assignments have a clear application to communication done in the wider world. These assignments include short articles, application essays, memoirs, news stories, editorials, proposals, public service announcements, websites, film reviews, profiles, and research articles.

▶ **Attention to Audience**   Students get the point about audience when they are writing something that could conceivably be published or posted for the world to see. Meaningful, contextualized writing assignments help students more readily understand the concept of audience and see themselves as writers in communication with real audiences. The "Markets" section on the website suggests places where students could possibly get published.

▶ **Connections between Academic Writing and Nonacademic Writing**   A theme of the book is the interrelationship and overlap between professional writing and the academic writing that will be asked of students in other courses. For example, the website has a "Springboard" feature for every assignment, linking the skills just learned to a similar academic type of writing across the disciplines.

▶ **Flexible and Teachable, with a Large Number of Practices, Activities, and Journal Prompts**   Teachers can use and adapt practices to suit the needs of their students. All help students apply new skills as they work on their main assignments.

▶ **Extensive Art Program with a Focus on Visual Literacy**   Real-world writing is often writing that combines the word and the image. *Writing in the Works* pays special attention throughout every chapter to the role of the image — how to analyze, use, design, and incorporate the image into the written text. The "Visual Literacy" feature in each chapter asks students to look at and analyze a variety of visual images: photographs, drawings, paintings, and cartoons. Chapter 9, "Public Service Messages," includes material on analyzing and developing documents that combine words and visuals, such as websites, posters, television storyboards, and brochures. Questions guide students to look closely and analytically at the paintings, illustrations, and photographs that accompany the assignment chapters. In addition, each chapter has an annotated example of the genre, which is a way to see the form visually.

▶ **Writing for the Web**   Chapter 10 presents techniques of writing for websites, a genre unto itself. In this chapter, students learn to think critically about websites and to evaluate them for clarity and usability. Web writing skills are integrated into the assignment chapters as students use websites for research, create websites to accompany their projects, and read and analyze essays, editorials, reviews, and articles from the Internet.

▶ **Critical Reading and Thinking**   Chapter 2, "Reading and Thinking Critically," introduces the skills of critical reading, including underlining, paraphrasing, summarizing, annotating, analyzing, and synthesizing. These skills are also then integrated into every chapter. Each chapter then has a section called "Anatomy of a __" (the blank is filled by the name of whatever genre that is the focus of that particular chapter). The Anatomy sections present (1) a brief reading already annotated to show the parts and elements of the genre in action, (2) an explanation of the elements that are annotated and how the elements work together in the form, and (3) an annotation practice that asks students to read another brief reading (another example of the form under discussion) and annotate it themselves. Following each reading are **critical reading questions,** which send students back to the text to do some focused analysis, and **questions for writing and discussion,** which ask students to think beyond the text and synthesize what they know and what they have learned.

▶ **Innovative Research Coverage**   Chapter 14 addresses research skills in depth, and then, since we believe researching is best taught contextually, every assignment chapter has a significant research component, called "Research Paths." Students learn to think about how a writer might apply research to a specific problem or inquiry, even in personal writing, memoir. Each chapter has an extended section on how the assignment might best be developed and investigated using a variety of sources, including direct observation, interviewing, and electronic and print sources. The Research chapter also helps students make distinctions between types of search tools and how to use the "invisible Web."

HOW TO USE *WRITING IN THE WORKS*

We developed *Writing in the Works* with the full knowledge that writing teachers most often pick and choose, customizing their courses to their own teaching styles and their students' needs. We have tried to provide a rich array of choices in writing assignments, bolstered by comprehensive information and instruction in separate chapters on the writing process, critical reading, research, documentation, Web writing, grammar, and style.

Part I: The Writer's Craft

The first two chapters, "The Writer's Process" and "Reading and Thinking Critically," lay the groundwork for many college-writing courses. These two chapters set up the writing process and critical reading activities that are woven throughout the assignment chapters.

Part II: Assignments

The assignment chapters are organized from least to most complex, from personal to public writing, making it easy for a teacher to select writing tasks appropriate for a particular approach. Each chapter presents a genre within one or more rhetorical modes, so, for example, students learn to write exposition though writing short articles and application essays. They learn elements of narration through memoirs and news stories; argumentation through editorials and commentary; persuasion through proposals and public appeals; and evaluation through film reviews. They learn to combine exposition, narration, analysis, and persuasion in writing profiles and trend features.

Each of the ten assignment chapters begins the way much real-world writing does, by giving students a writing task. The task is defined, its major elements presented, the research paths laid out, and the "anatomy" of that form of writing dissected. The readings provide contemporary and diverse models from student and professional writers as well as an interview with one of the writers, giving students an insider view of the writing process, the "writing in the works" for that piece of writing.

Following the readings are writing and revising strategies, including suggestions for journal entries, which often do double-duty as possible topics for the assignment. The "Peer Editing Log" and "Revision Checklist" help students acquire the analytic skills necessary for the essential task of revision.

Exercises   Each chapter is filled with many exercises from which a teacher can select. The first exercise in each chapter is called "Warm-Up Practice: Collaborative Exercise," and its purpose is to have students pool their collective understanding of the genre even before they have studied it in depth.

The exercise is a way to put students into the universe of that assignment and to help them realize how much they know already about application essays, memoirs, news stories, film reviews, editorials, and other writing in their everyday lives.

"Practice" exercises are sprinkled throughout the chapter, reinforcing the instruction they follow. Although they are brief and serve to provide a quick review of the concepts, far more exercises appear in the chapters than a teacher would want to assign. Some practice exercises ask students to work alone; others require collaboration; most can be used either way.

Part III: Research and Documentation

Two chapters are gathered here: "Research" and "Documentation." The research chapter provides in-depth discussion and general information about research methods through observation, interviewing, print sources, and Web sources. The documentation chapter shows students how to cite sources in the most up-to-date MLA and APA formats, and provides a student model documented clearly in both formats. Students might read these chapters for comprehensive understanding of research, or they might dip into all three chapters to find specific information for writing they are doing in the assignment chapters. Cross-references from the assignment chapters point students to the relevant sections.

Part IV: Grammar and Style Handbook

We include a practical grammar and style handbook at the end of the text. In keeping with our approach, the handbook is flexible, allowing students to use it in a number of ways: as a step-by-step guide to build grammar knowledge, as a reference handbook, or as a grammar review. The grammar chapters are filled with many brief exercises that students can use to check their progress. One of the grammar chapters focuses on trouble spots for nonnative speakers of English, which can be used equally well to teach grammatical concepts to basic writers.

The **style chapter** appears on the website for flexibility in integrating it into the classroom. The chapter presents the parameters of clean, clear, and concise writing style, complete with specific advice on what to do and what not to do to achieve this style. Some teachers like to use this chapter as an introduction; some use it as a culminating review of voice and style; others integrate it throughout the course.

THE SUPPLEMENTS PACKAGE

Supplements for the Student

▶ The *Writing in the Works* **website for students** provides support directly related to the book. The fully integrated website contains chapter review materials, practices, and web links (marked by an icon in the text, so students can go directly to practices and links on their own computers), as well as additional features not found in the text:

Further Readings are available for many of the chapters, extending the reading and critical thinking lessons to web documents and to networks of related links.

Audiovisual Literacy is a special section exclusive to the Web, with an introduction to critical thinking about audio clips, still images, and moving pictures.

The **Style Guide** helps you understand and improve your writing style.

Avoiding Plagiarism provides additional information on how to avoid inadvertently plagiarizing material found either online or in print.

Publishing Your Work explains the venues for bringing your words to a larger audience than just your classroom.

▶ **WriteSpace,** Houghton Mifflin's Blackboard-powered electronic writing program provides students with an extensive array of writing tutorials and assignments, more than 2,000 grammar and writing exercises, a series of diagnostic tests, and access to an easy-to-search digital handbook, Ann Raimes's *Keys for Writers*.

▶ **SMARTHINKING®** provides online tutoring in English (as well as in seven other disciplines). Students have three different kinds of support. *Live Help* provides access to 20 hours per week of real-time, one-on-one instruction from Sunday to Thursday, 9 p.m. to 1 a.m. Eastern time. *Questions Anytime* allows students to submit questions 24 hours a day, 7 days a week, for response by an e-structor within 24 hours. *Independent Study Resources* connects students around the clock to additional educational services, ranging from interactive websites to frequently asked questions.

▶ The **Student Resource Center** at the Houghton Mifflin website for students, **http://college.hmco.com/english**, provides additional support for coursework.

Supplements for the Instructor

▶ The *Writing in the Works* **Instructor Website** extends the book's lessons online, with tools for the instructor in the classroom and for sending home with the student, including a downloadable *Instructor's Resource Manual.*

▶ The *Instructor's Resource Manual* contains a course overview, sample syllabi, chapter outlines, lecture notes, handouts, suggestions for class activities, technology ideas, and recommended resources by chapter.

▶ *Classroom Management Systems* available with the text include Houghton Mifflin's Blackboard-powered **WriteSpace** course in Eduspace, an electronic writing program with gradebook capability and an extensive array of writing tutorials and assignments, more than 2,000 grammar and writing exercises, a series of diagnostic tests, and access to an easy-to-search digital handbook, Ann Raimes's *Keys for Writers.* To learn more about WriteSpace, visit **http://www.eduspace.com**

▶ A **Blackboard Course Cartridge** provides flexible, efficient, and creative ways for instructors to present materials and manage distance-learning courses. Instructors can use an electronic gradebook, receive papers from students enrolled in the course via the Internet, and track student use of the communication and collaborative functions.

▶ The **Web/CT e-pack** provides a flexible, Internet-based education platform containing text-specific resources to enrich students' online learning experience.

▶ The **Instructor's Resource Center**, located at the Houghton Mifflin website, **http://college.hmco.com/english**, provides numerous and varied sources of assistance, including **Adjuncts.com**, a site that is dedicated to helping adjunct faculty make the most of their teaching careers.

Additional print supplements are available on request:

▶ *Teaching Writing with Computers: An Introduction* Edited with an introduction by Pamela Takayoshi and Brian Huot, both of the University of Louisville, this book is an up-to-date resource on integrating technology into writing instruction. Essays cover (1) Writing Technologies for Composition Pedagogies, (2) Learning to Teach with Technology, (3) Teaching Beyond Physical Boundaries, (4) Teaching and Learning New Media, and (5) Assigning and Assessing Student Writing.

▶ *Finding Our Way: A Writing Teacher's Sourcebook* Edited and with an introduction by Wendy Bishop and Deborah Coxwell Teague of Florida State University in Tallahassee, this collection of essays is a unique and powerful guide for new or relatively new composition teachers. It addresses many of the unvoiced questions, challenges, and seldom discussed but crucial issues that arise for writing teachers.

▸ *The Essentials of Tutoring: Helping College Students Develop Their Writing Skills* Paul Gary Phillips and Joyce B. Phillips of Grossmont College have written this supportive and comprehensive guide for writing tutors. Covering the general guidelines of how to tutor, and the specifics of both sentence-level and essay-level tutoring, it can be used as a self-paced training program, in a classroom setting, in a formal tutor training class, or as a reference tool during the course of a tutoring session.

▸ *The Writing Teacher's Companion: Planning, Teaching, and Evaluating in the Composition Classroom* Rai Peterson wrote this volume to help instructors with organization of the course, assessment, classroom management, and selection of textbooks.

ACKNOWLEDGMENTS

Writing in the Works is brought to you by a cast of thousands: our own parents, teachers, and mentors who inspired us; the thousands of students we have taught over the course of our careers who have kept us honest and on-task; our generous colleagues, friends, and families, who have propped us up and taken up the slack. To all of them, we owe an enormous debt of gratitude.

Some individuals need to be thanked more personally. Our extraordinary colleagues in the 201 writing program have helped us create this writing curriculum, have uncomplainingly class-tested even the earliest drafts and have been generous in their praise and criticism, both of which are deeply appreciated. Ellen Davis, John Hall, Peter Rand, Cindy Anderson, Jenna Blum, Rose Cummings, Veronica Ellis, Leslie Goldberg, Jeff Mason, Midge Raymond, and Taline Voskeritchian are ideal colleagues and friends, and we are in their collective debt.

Others have lent their expertise by critiquing chapters, donating material to the book, and talking us out of trees. We thank Jack Falla, Tom Fauls, Leslie Goldberg, Garland Waller, David Maloof, Ellen Ruppel Shell, and Lou Ureneck for their sure voices and James J. McKeown, Jr., of McLennan Community College, for his close scrutiny of our final draft. We are also immensely grateful to our students who have allowed us to use their papers to enliven this book.

Our editors and friends at Houghton Mifflin believed in this project and helped give form and shape to our ideas. We thank the whole team but especially Chris Hyde who made the initial contact, Suzanne Phelps Weir who imagined the final project from our proposal, our wonderful and exacting first editor, Martha Bustin, and Judy Fifer, our vigilant second editor who took us down the home stretch. We could not have asked for a more supportive and creative art team: we are especially grateful to Sharon Donahue, photo editor, and Henry Rachlin, visionary designer.

The home fires kept burning during the three years we have been writing *WITW*, and for that and for so much more, we thank our husbands, John Shane and Paul Makishima.

We would like also to thank the many colleagues all over the country who wrote such thoughtful and useful comments as they reviewed this book in all of its iterations:

Jose M. Blanco, Miami Dade College
Mary Ann Bretzlauf, College of Lake County
Mark Browning, Johnson County Community College
Avon Crismore, Indiana University–Purdue University, Fort Wayne
Rachel Darabi, Indiana University–Purdue University, Fort Wayne
Cherie Post Dargan, Hawkeye Community College
Adenike Davidson, University of Central Florida
Julia K. Ferganchick, University of Arkansas at Little Rock
Gregory R. Glau, Arizona State University
Jack Jacobs, Auburn University
Meredith James, Eastern Connecticut State University
Millie M. Kidd, Mount St. Mary's College
Paul Lehman, University of Central Oklahoma
Mitchell R. Lewis, Elmira College
Alfred J. López, Florida International University
James J. McKeown, Jr., McLennan Community College
T. Gerard McNamee, Eastern Oregon University
Constantina Michalos, Houston Baptist University
Kate Mohler, Mesa Community College
Cindy Moore, St. Cloud State University
Ed Moritz, Indiana University–Purdue University, Fort Wayne
Marti L. Mundell, Washington State University
Charles Naccarato, Ohio University
Scott Oates, University of Wisconsin, Eau Claire
R. J. Osborne, Grossmont College
Victoria Ramirez, Weber State University
Gordon Reynolds, Ferris State University
Lawrence Roderer, J. Sargeant Reynolds Community College
Connie G. Rothwell, University of North Carolina, Charlotte
Mark Schaub, Grand Valley State University
Steven P. Schneider, University of Texas, Pan-American
Joseph M. Schuster, Webster University
Arvis Scott, McLennan Community College
Rhonda L. Smith, Jacksonville College
Pat Tyrer, West Texas A&M University
Xiao Wang, Broward Community College

Susan Blau
Kathryn Burak

WRITING IN THE WORKS

THE WRITER'S CRAFT

PART I

1. THE WRITER'S PROCESS

You can't wait for inspiration. You have to go after it with a club.
                                    —Jack London

The process of diving caught in stop-action photography.

THE WRITER'S PROCESS

Sometimes the hardest part of writing is getting started. Most of us have concocted a hundred ways to delay that moment. One person has to clean the room in which she writes; another has to have all his research done, notes organized, and virtual pencils sharpened; yet another works out of chaos, needing a cluttered desk in order to get started. Once we actually begin writing, other behaviors click in. One person cannot finish a sentence unless every word is spelled correctly and the sentence is grammatically perfect; another types madly, almost randomly, discovering what she means as she writes.

Ways of jump-starting the writing process are as individual as each writer. A friend tells this story about discovering her own writing process. Sara, a teacher and writer, took a six-month leave from teaching to research and write a series of articles. She woke up on Morning One, feeling enormous relief that she did not have to put on work clothes, gulp down breakfast, and drive twenty miles to her office through rush-hour traffic. A cup of coffee in hand, and still wearing sweats and a T-shirt, she sat down in front of her computer. Nothing. She got up, paced, sat down again. Panic set in. She decided to take the day off and not rush herself.

Day Two mirrored Day One. So did Day Three. By Day Four Sara dreaded getting up, so she lay in bed, trying to figure out the problem. It came to her that she had interrupted her lifelong habit of thinking and planning her day's writing as she showered, dressed, and drove. So she did just that. She showered, dressed, drove for twenty minutes around her neighborhood, got out of her car, reentered her house, took off her coat, sat down at the computer, and began writing.

Driving randomly around your neighborhood or campus may not be the best way for you to start a writing assignment, but most writers have their own rituals, whether they are as simple as having that second cup of coffee or as elaborate as Sara's. Discovering what works for you may be one of the most important first steps to becoming a comfortable and confident writer.

In these passages two students describe what they do after they get a writing assignment.

I react with a few instinctive ideas (oh, this, that, that, the other thing) and then forget about it for a few days. Probably in the back of my mind, some little neuron-slash-hamster is running inside the wheel of idea generation, churning out plethoric subconscious thoughts. Eventually one of those thoughts will be something neanderthalic—I'm not too smart—like "Paper. Thursday. Due," and off like a maniac I run to my computer. Although I claim to write nonstop till it's done, I really do take my fair share of breaks. "Oh, this comma is a good excuse to eat a cookie," or "Oh, that letter *Z* represents the time to check my e-mail," or "Ah this prose is so poetic I'll play guitar for half an hour." So things take a lot longer than expected, but this keeps my little hamster from getting too tired.

—Nathan Welton

When I enter my dorm room, I'm never focused on just my paper. I always seem captured by everything else in my room (computer, radio, food, bed . . . everything but the paper). In order to channel my energy to just the paper, I completely clear my desk, giving myself an open, fresh plain on which my thoughts will venture unimpeded. If this fails or the room does not act as a proper studying room, I bring my laptop/books into the lounge in hopes of finding it quiet; if not, I go downstairs to one of many other lounges and begin my work. I guess I have to "clean house" prior to working, as it also cleanses my mind of junk thoughts, off subject pondering . . . etc.

—Matt Sato

CHAPTER OBJECTIVES

In this chapter you will learn strategies for

▶ **Brainstorming**

▶ **Composing**

▶ **Revising**

▶ **Peer editing**

THE WRITING PROCESS

For most people, writing is a messy business—not straightforward at all. If you watch a videotape of a writer at work (which writing researchers actually do), you will see more seemingly random activity—and more emotion—than you might expect. Most writers, once they begin to write, jump from task to task. They may start writing and then back up and make a list. They may order their notes and then write a conclusion before writing the paper itself. They may spend an hour on a single paragraph or get the whole paper done in that hour. Writers also stretch, yell, grimace, pace the room, and laugh aloud.

Research also reveals that writers rarely move in a straight line from stage to stage in the writing process. Most of us do not first brainstorm, then draft, then revise, and then proofread. Instead, writers usually move both

Warm-Up Practice 1.1 Writing Rituals

1. Describe your own writing rituals. What do you do to get yourself primed for writing?

2. Interview a classmate about his or her writing rituals. Compare your rituals to your classmate's rituals.

3. Observe the writing ritual of someone you know—a friend, family member, or roommate, for example. Watch this person get ready to write. Take notes on your observations. Then interview the person and see if his or her perception matches yours.

Practice 1.2   Writing Processes

1. Describe your own writing process. You may want to consider the following questions.

   a. Do you start with an outline or a list?

   b. Do you write the introduction first, or the conclusion?

   c. When do you do your research: before you start, throughout the process, and/or after you've finished a first draft and know where the holes are?

   d. Does this process vary, depending on the assignment? If so, how?

2. Set up a tape recorder next to you as you write an assignment. Record the process aloud as you go, explaining what you are doing as you do it. (*"Now I'm stuck. I'm going back to read the assignment. Taking a break. Just got an idea. Wrote for fifteen minutes straight."*) Write a short analysis of your own writing process.

3. Discuss a classmate's writing process with him or her. Use the questions above, or come up with your own questions. How do your writing processes differ? How are they the same?

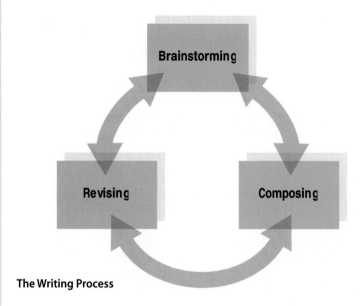

The Writing Process

forward and backward among stages, often revisiting earlier stages before advancing. This process, known as *recursive*, looks more like a circle than a straight line.

As the diagram suggests, to move forward you sometimes have to back up and reconsider a key idea, do a little more research, or think for a while about the meaning of a word. You can brainstorm at any part of the process, not just before you write; and while you are brainstorming, you are often also revising by editing out the workable ideas from the impractical ones (. . . *dumb idea, won't work . . . maybe I could go in this direction . . . that won't support the argument, but I might be able to use it later*). During revision, ideas can surface that redirect the whole paper or generate whole new sections.

One writing student explains her writing process for a literature class this way.

This past semester when I had to analyze books for my writing class, I would usually first write my introduction with a vague idea of the topic and somehow end the introduction with a thesis. . . . I'd usually write that on a Post-it Note to put on my computer because heaven knows I like to get off topic. Then I'd go through the books to be analyzed and pull out the important facts/quotes I want to include in my paper. I'm a pretty visual person, so I'd usually group quotes (etc.) from different books through webs or colored lists.

—Jenna Bouchard

BRAINSTORMING STRATEGIES

I write to find out what I'm thinking about.

—Edward Albee

Brainstorming opens the floodgates of your mind. When you brainstorm, you let all your ideas rush out unimpeded, bringing with them the flotsam and jetsam that get carried along. The process is akin to free association and works in a similar way. Bringing forth one idea stimulates a series of other ideas, even pulling long-forgotten details from your memory. Some of the ideas may be bizarre; others may be brilliant; some may be less than useful. As you come up with ideas, write them down so not to lose them. You will discover that the very act of writing can get your creativity flowing. Brainstorming collaboratively with a partner or in a group can also be helpful since you can build on each other's knowledge and backgrounds.

Brainstorming is useful

▶ When you begin to cast about for topics or ideas about topics

▶ As you start reading about and researching a topic

▶ When you need to refresh your thinking

▶ When you want to develop an idea

▶ If you become blocked

Since the purpose of this kind of unrestrained writing is to generate new thinking, be careful not to edit yourself in content or in form. Let the ideas flow. Later, you can consider which ideas to keep and which to reject.

Brainstorming also happens on the subconscious level. When you first get an assignment, read it carefully. Leave yourself time to think, talk, and read about your subject. Even if you do not begin to write immediately, you can be turning the ideas over in your mind and brainstorming both consciously and subconsciously. When it is time to write, you may find your words flowing more clearly than you had imagined they would because of the activity of your subconscious mind.

Knowing about some brainstorming strategies, and choosing the ones that work best for you, can help you generate ideas at any point in your writing process. Four useful strategies are keeping a writer's notebook, freewriting, clustering, and listing or outlining.

Practice 1.3 Keeping a Notebook

1. Buy a notebook of any size or shape. Carry it around with you all day for two days. Put it next to your bed at night. Write in it every time you have an idea for a writing assignment or for any writing you may want to do on your own. You can also use your notebook for recording

   - Snippets of your dreams
   - Funny or insightful comments made by friends or professors
   - Clever advertisements or tag lines
   - Quotations from your reading
   - Overheard conversations
   - Unusual events from the news or from your own observations
   - Original writing: descriptions of people, places, and events that interest you

   Write about anything that might work well in a piece of writing, but do not use your notebook as merely a log of your activities. Think of it as a collecting place for images, quotations, ideas, and bits of dialogue. Fill at least two pages each day.

2. Write a few paragraphs evaluating the experience of keeping a notebook for these two days.

Keeping a Writer's Notebook

Whether you use a binder, a black-and-white composition notebook, a reporter's spiral note pad, or napkins held together with paper clips, you should have a place to record random thoughts, overheard dialogue, and ideas that come unbidden in the midst of your daily life. Almost all writers keep this kind of notebook, also known as a daybook or journal.

Your ideas can incubate in a notebook. Once you write an idea on a piece of paper, you can return to it, alter it, expand on it, or, after reflection, discard it. Writing an idea inscribes it not only on the paper but also in your mind.

Having a notebook handy also helps you record and make conscious the kind of subconscious brainstorming discussed above. When you have a writing assignment, the assignment itself may retreat to the back of your mind as you go about your daily life. However, as you jog or shower or even as you talk with friends or attend a class, you may find yourself thinking about the topic or coming up with an approach or an idea for the assignment. As soon as possible, take out your notebook, and jot down your thoughts.

Similarly, you might wake up in the morning with a solution to a knotty writing problem that you were trying to untangle when you went to bed, or perhaps that you were not even consciously thinking about. By giving the matter a rest while you do, you can gain a new perspective. If you keep a notebook by your bedside, you can write a few notes while the ideas are fresh.

Freewriting

Athletes talk about "muscle memory." After repeating an activity numerous times, your muscles remember how to do that activity: how to ride a bike or whack a ball. Even after long periods of inactivity, your muscles can remember a previous action and help you recall its flow. So it is with writing. The physical act of forming letters with pen or typing them on a keyboard prompts your brain to recall the activity of writing: letters and words coming together. Writing can also help you retrieve memories of other words you have written, ideas you have formed, passages you have read, or experiences you have had. One idea leads to another.

Freewriting is the practice of writing without limitations and without a clear destination, using free association. It is writing to

This is the cover of the collected journals of Dan Eldon, internationally known photojournalist, who died at age twenty-two while documenting the 1993 famine in Somalia. Eldon had kept journals since age fourteen.

Practice 1.4 Freewriting

1. Try your hand at freewriting as it is described on pages 8 and 10. If you do not have a topic in mind or an assignment to work with, write about anything you know a great deal about: basketball, colonial America, global warming, cooking, chaos theory, or civil liberties, perhaps.

2. Read your freewrite. Circle any interesting ideas that might be useful to develop for later writings. Put a box around any phrases or sentences that might be keepers.

3. What was your response to the freewriting? Is it a technique you might find useful? Why?

discover meaning. Freewriting primes the writing pump, both physically and psychologically, and allows writers to capitalize on the physical aspect of writing, which is a real and important part of the process. The rules are simple.

▶ Write freely for a set period of time. Start with ten minutes, which allows you enough time to follow a train of thought but not so much time that the process gets tedious.

▶ Write everything you can think of about your topic on paper, or type it into your computer.

▶ Do not stop writing.

▶ Do not edit or censor your writing in any way.

▶ If you get stuck, write whatever comes to mind, even if you wind up writing, "I can't think of what to write" or "This is the dumbest thing I've ever done."

▶ After ten minutes, stop and read what you have written. But if you are on a tear, keep going. You may discover that everything you have written is garbage, or you may uncover some hidden gems.

▶ Underline or circle any ideas or good lines you think you can use—if not now, maybe later.

▶ Copy ideas for future writing into your writer's notebook.

When asked to freewrite about her writing rituals, one student realized that she had not thought about writing rituals before. The act of writing allowed her to reflect on her own writing practice, and she realized that keeping a writer's notebook might be a useful strategy:

> I've never really thought about my writing rituals *per se*. After pondering what my personal rituals are, I would have to say I do just that . . . ponder. When I find out about a writing assignment I usually start brainstorming immediately. I also seem to become more aware of the subject about which I have to write (i.e., I notice that subject in everyday life; I observe how that subject plays into my life). I tend to do this brainstorming and observing in my head, however. I think it would be far more useful for me to have a writer's notebook in which to jot things down. Sometimes the observations and ideas are so large in number that by the time I

actually sit down to write, I immediately get writer's block. It's as if my brain were clogged by my ideas.

—Arielle Greenleaf

Clustering

Clustering, also known as word webbing or branching, can be a powerful brainstorming technique. Like freewriting, it allows for free association of ideas, turning off the constant internal editing that can be so inhibiting.

Some writers believe that clustering allows them to bypass conventional, linear thinking and to have a direct line to memory and creativity. Writers who are more visual thinkers—screenwriters, advertising copywriters, and artists, for example—find that clustering opens up thinking in a way that listing or outlining cannot. Business managers and educational administrators also use clustering for problem solving, group process, and creating flow charts. Because relationships between ideas are created as the ideas themselves are produced, clustering allows you to generate a much more complex interrelationship of ideas than does a top-to-bottom list or outline.

The process of clustering begins when you think of a topic you want to explore.

- Write a keyword or a phrase in the middle of a page. This word or phrase becomes the physical and thematic center of your brainstorming session.

- Circle the word, and radiating out from it, write a series of associated words or phrases in quick succession.

- Circle each word or phrase, and connect it with a line to the previous and successive one.

- When you have run that string as far as it will go, return to the center, and begin again in another direction.

- When you finish generating ideas, look at your keywords, and draw lines to connect ideas that belong together.

The cluster on the following page shows how a student mapped out her ideas on good writing. The phrase "good writing" is the center of her web. After she created a line of association for each main idea, she began drawing arrows between ideas that seemed connected.

Clustering can also help you to break through writer's block, take notes during a lecture or while reading, and fix ideas in your mind as you study for an exam. For example, as you read a chapter in a textbook, you can put the key idea in a circle in the middle of a page. Then take notes radiating out from this key concept. Draw lines to show the relationship of the satellite

Practice 1.5 Clustering

1. Try your hand at brainstorming a writing assignment through clustering. If you have a writing assignment in mind, use that assignment as your starting point. If you do not have an assignment, write "college" at the center of the page. Give yourself ten minutes to do the clustering. When you are done, draw lines between words that belong together. Write the first paragraph of a paper that might come from this brainstorm.

2. Try using clustering as a note-taking technique. Since you have already read this far into Chapter 1, go back to the beginning, and create a study guide for the chapter up to this point.

3. Write a paragraph about your response to this technique. Was it useful? Will you use it again? Why?

Cluster Map on "Good Writing"

ideas. When you have finished the chapter, you have mapped the key ideas of a chapter in an easily accessible one-page study guide and have, most probably, gone a long way toward learning the material.

Listing and Outlining

Like freewriting and clustering, listing and outlining your ideas are good, quick ways to get them on paper for safekeeping and consideration. Once your ideas are on paper, you can rearrange, reorder, and develop them.

You do not have to create a formal outline with Roman numerals, capital letters, Arabic numbers, and lowercase letters, although you can if you find it helpful. Instead, you may want to write down your main ideas and then fill in the supporting points. Under each main idea, jot the information that supports, illustrates, expands on, or discusses that idea. Indenting each supporting idea will help you see the difference between equal, main points and subordinate, less important points or between your general ideas and the specific supporting information. (See page 20 for an example of a simple outline for an editorial.)

Outlines are particularly useful for organizing long papers with complicated structures. Outlining also makes good sense—and is a powerful organizational strategy—*after* you write your first draft, as a springboard into revision. Once you have a draft in hand, putting your ideas into outline form allows you to get an overview of your thinking. As you line up your main and subordinate points, you can easily see if your points are parallel, if your support is sufficient, and if your ideas proceed logically.

Whether you outline at the beginning, middle, or end of your writing process, make sure you think of the resulting structure as flexible. The outline should open up your thinking, not limit it.

[handwritten margin note: outline for revision]

COMPOSING

> The thing about writing is to stay in the chair.
> —Wallace Stegner

Getting yourself into the chair may be hard, but once you do, you will have an easier time staying seated if you have some idea of how to proceed. No matter the type of writing assignment, part of the process is doing some research, finding a focus, organizing your material, and writing that first draft.

Researching

Whether you are writing a researched article, a proposal to bring to a town meeting, a video script, or a personal essay, you have to gather information for your paper. Your research can take a variety of forms depending on the assignment. You can conduct traditional library or electronic searches for primary and secondary sources, or you can do fieldwork, which includes personal observations and interviews. Research for a memoir or a personal essay may involve searching your or another person's memory, or it may require reading magazines and newspapers to gain historical perspective and context. (See Chapter 14.)

Begin your research by reading widely and deeply. Go to the library or online, and read what others have said about your topic in journals, newspaper and magazine articles, interviews, or books. Read for information and inspiration. Also read other models of what you are writing. If you are writing a film review, a lab report, or a job application letter, you do not have to reinvent the format. Reading examples will give you a good sense of the variety of voices, styles, and structures others have used.

Remember to take careful notes on the ideas, quotations, and sources you consult as you gather your information. Part of the fun of research lies in becoming knowledgeable about a topic—becoming familiar with the experts, the theories, and the controversies. As you become more expert, you have to acknowledge your sources, giving credit to those whose words you have read or absorbed. (See Chapter 15.)

acknowledge sources

Reading and researching continue throughout the writing process. You can consult sources as you brainstorm, as you write your first draft, and as you revise. The more you learn about a topic, the more interesting it becomes to you. When you are interested in your topic, you communicate that interest to your readers.

Focusing and Developing a Thesis

Writing can be exploratory or experimental, but if you are writing for a public audience (a teacher, an editor, a producer), you have to know what point you are trying to communicate. Your main point provides the focus of your paper. This main point goes by many names: it can be called the *thesis* in an essay, a *theme* in a story, a *premise* in an argument, a *concept* in a proposal, or a *nut graf* in a feature article. No matter what it is called, your main point focuses your paper, organizes your ideas, and helps you communicate your thinking to your audience. The main point of a paper should be

- ❯ Substantive (not self-evident)
- ❯ Neither too broad nor too narrow for the scope of the paper
- ❯ Supported by evidence (facts, statistics, expert opinion, anecdotes, examples) in the body of your paper
- ❯ Engaging to your audience

A good way to find your focus for all your assignments is to summarize your main point in a single sentence. Ask yourself, "What is the point of this story (review, essay, proposal, report)?" If you cannot come up with a clear answer, try brainstorming: do more thinking, reading, talking, freewriting, or clustering. If you can come up with a clear answer, write the sentence on a note card or Post-it Note, and put it on the wall near your desk or on top of your computer. Writing your main point will help you clarify it, and keeping it in front of you as you write will help immeasurably to keep you on track.

Main pt. can shift

Often, your main point will shift as you develop your topic. You may not even discover your true focus until you have explored some side paths. Stay flexible as you draft your paper, and refine or redefine your main point. If you veer off and like the new direction, revise your sentence. You may arrive at the point of your paper just as you type the final sentence. That is fine. Rewrite your focusing sentence, and use it to drive your revision.

"Write about dogs!"

Your writing will be in focus if you know your point and communicate it clearly to your reader. On the other hand, nothing makes a reader's eyes glaze over more quickly than writing that rambles and lacks focus.

Organizing

Every piece of writing needs a beginning, a middle, and an ending as well as an organizing principle, a reason why this paragraph follows that one. A clear organization sets up expectations, even a sense of anticipation, for readers. Your job as a writer is to keep readers interested and moving forward. Ideally, readers should be drawn into your writing by your introduction, and they should keep reading because they are on a well-lit path that leads inevitably to your conclusions.

If you think about your readers being on a path, transitions are the signs that let them know where to go: straight ahead, around a corner, or off on a side trip. Transitions are words that link ideas within paragraphs and that link paragraphs to one another. Transitional words such as *first of all, then, next, on the other hand, interestingly,* and *however* signal your intentions and keep readers from getting lost. (See sidebar on p. 491 for more detail on transitions.)

If *you* are a bit lost in organizing your writing, try asking yourself these four questions. The answers can help you get back on track.

▶ What is the purpose of this writing? Is it going to *tell* a story or *report* on an event, *review* a book or *analyze* a poem, *argue* for building bicycle lanes in city streets or for getting an internship?

▶ What development strategies will best support my points? Some development strategies are examples, stories, definitions, analysis of causes and effects, facts, details, and comparisons. (See pages 74–86 for more details on development strategies.)

▶ Who is my targeted audience? You may be writing for a teacher or for a scholarship committee. If you are writing a news report, for example, it may be helpful to think of people reading over morning coffee or on a bus or train on their way to work. Always think of your readers as intelligent and interesting people.

In the assignment chapters, Chapters 3 through 13, you will see how considerations of purpose, development strategy, and audience will lead you to different organizational patterns. What is important is not which pattern you choose, but that you build a strong structure for your piece of writing.

Writing the First Draft

Your first draft can be messy and experimental, freeform and rough. Get your ideas on paper, and keep the ideas flowing. Try not to edit yourself or think that your worst writing critic is peering over your shoulder. The first draft is not the place to worry about grammar, spelling, and style—yet. You will have plenty of time later to revise and edit your paper.

Above all, stay in that chair.

In the following excerpt from her instructional book on writing, *bird by bird,* Anne Lamott reassures her readers about how messy a first draft can be.

Now, practically even better news than that of short assignments is the idea of shitty first drafts. All good writers write them. This is how they end up with good second drafts and terrific third drafts. People tend to look at successful writers, writers who are getting their books published and maybe even doing well financially, and think that they sit down at their desks every morning feeling like a million dollars, feeling great about who they are and how much talent they have and what a great story they have to tell; that they take in a few deep breaths, push back their sleeves, roll their necks a few times to get all the cricks out, and dive in, typing fully formed passages as fast as a court reporter. But this is just the fantasy of the uninitiated. I know some very great writers, writers you love who write beautifully and have made a great deal of money, and not *one* of them sits down routinely feeling wildly enthusiastic and confident. Not one of them writes elegant first drafts. All right, one of them does, but we do not like her very much. We do not think that she has a rich inner life or that God likes her or can even stand her. (Although when I mentioned this to my priest friend Tom, he said you can safely assume you've created God in your own image when it turns out that God hates all the same people you do.)

Very few writers really know what they are doing until they've done it. Nor do they go about their business feeling dewy and thrilled. They do not type a few stiff warm-up sentences and then find themselves bounding along like huskies across the snow. One writer I know tells me that he sits down every morning and says to himself nicely, "It's not like you don't have a choice, because you do—you can either type or kill yourself." We all often feel like we are pulling teeth, even those writers whose prose ends up being the most natural and fluid. The right words and sentences just do not come pouring out like ticker tape most of the time. Now, Muriel Spark is said to have felt that she was taking dictation from God every morning—sitting there, one supposes, plugged into a Dictaphone, typing away, humming. But this is a very hostile and aggressive position. One might hope for bad things to rain down on a person like this.

For me and most of the other writers I know, writing is not rapturous. In fact, the only way I can get anything written at all is to write really, really shitty first drafts.

The first draft is the child's draft, where you let it all pour out and then let it romp all over the place, knowing that no one is going to see it and that you can shape it later. You just let this childlike part of you channel whatever voices and visions come through and onto the page. If one of the characters wants to say, "Well, so what, Mr. Poopy Pants?," you let her. No one is going to see it. If the kid wants to get into really sentimental, weepy, emotional territory, you let him. Just get it all down on paper, because there may be something great in those six crazy pages that you would never have gotten to by more rational, grown-up means. There may be something in the very last line of the very last paragraph on page six that you just love, that is so beautiful or wild that you now know what you're supposed to be writing about, more or less, or in what direction you might go—but there was no way to get to this without first getting through the first five and a half pages.

Questions for Discussion and Writing

1. Lamott writes, "The first draft is the child's draft, where you let it all pour out and then let it romp all over the place." In what ways does this describe your first-draft writing? In what ways does it differ? To what would you compare your first drafts?

2. Your friend is writing a first draft of a first college paper and has gotten stuck. Write an e-mail message to your friend, incorporating any advice from Lamott's piece that you think would be motivating.

REVISING

> When I see a paragraph shrinking under my eyes like a strip of bacon on a skillet, I know I'm on the right track.
>
> —Peter DeVries

Revision is the heart of the writing process, an opportunity to look with fresh eyes at what you have written. Some writers believe that this stage is where the real writing happens, where you can make changes that allow you to say clearly and precisely what you mean to say. Of course, you are revising during the entire writing process, not just at the end. You revise as you plan and write, as you choose one idea or word rather than another. However, the most significant revision usually occurs as you move from an early draft to a final one.

Make sure to leave enough time between an early draft and your final deadline to put the paper away for a while. Ideally, leave a day or two for end-stage revising. If you have just finished a marathon writing session, you will lack the perspective necessary to look at your writing with fresh eyes.

Revision consists of more than finding and fixing surface errors like typos or finding livelier synonyms for dull words. Changing words, checking spelling, and cleaning up grammatical and mechanical errors are all important end-stage writing activities, but they are not the essence of revision. Successful revision consists of truly rethinking your draft. You have to be willing to change your focus, reorder your thinking, lop off whole sections, and develop others, if necessary.

Five activities are key to successful revision: refocusing, reordering, adding, cutting, and editing.

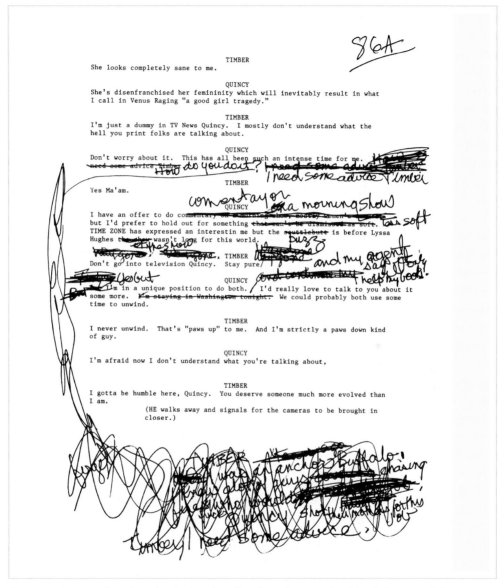

A manuscript page from her play *An American Daughter* shows author Wendy Wasserstein's revisions.

Refocusing

Remember the focusing statement that you wrote and taped to your computer? Check it as you finish your first draft to see if it is still accurate. If not, a good way to start your revision is to rewrite that one-sentence statement. Answer the question, "What is the main point (or thesis) of this paper?"

Assume that you are writing an issue-based editorial for the campus newspaper, and your focusing sentence is "The college administration should allocate more funds to the student escort service." Perhaps you began your paper by writing in general terms about money being allocated unfairly to student activities, or maybe you listed a few worthy groups that need more funding, the student escort service among them. Perhaps, as is often the case, you did not really figure out your thesis until you had written the whole editorial, and there at the end of the piece sat your main point—that the student escort service needs funding.

Once you have discovered your thesis, you can state it in a clear, bold opening sentence, such as "The student escort service is so underfunded that it compromises the safety of every student on campus."

Paste this sentence on your computer to help you refocus your editorial. Of course, you might have found your focus before this moment. In that case, you are ahead of the game. Jump to square two.

Reordering

Check to be sure that you have presented your ideas in the best possible order. Outlining can be extremely useful at this point. Look over your paper paragraph by paragraph, and outline what you have actually written.

The editorial about funding for a student escort service might look like this.

I.   Thesis: Student escort service is underfunded, which compromises student safety.

II. The budget is too small.
     A. $800 for advertising and staffing
     B. No money to purchase a van or pay for gas
     C. Statement from head of escort service about lack of $$

III. Other student activities have much larger budgets.
     A. Sports
     B. Outdoor club
     C. Debate society

IV. Call for action: We have to get more funding for the student escort service.
     A. Petition administration
     B. Elect new student government

Although this outline looks good, inspecting it more closely you notice that the second point of the thesis—underfunding the student escort service compromises student safety—is never developed. You can strike this phrase from the thesis, but you decide that a better choice is to add a section after III and before IV called "Student safety is compromised." You remember a story about a student who was frightened and a statement by the chief of campus police about student safety that you could use for support.

As you look over your outline, you rethink the effectiveness of the order of the points. You decide it would have more impact to cite the enormous sports budget *before* the miniscule one for the student escort service. You switch the order of II, the current budget of the student escort service, and III, the current budgets of other activities.

When you look at your call to action, you decide that petitioning the administration would be a more immediate way to muster the troops than waiting for the student government elections, which take place in two months. You switch the order of the final two points in order to leave your reader with your strongest point and something specific to do.

Your revised outline might look like this one. The highlighted areas show the changes.

   I. Thesis: Student escort service is underfunded, which compromises student safety.

 II. Other student activities have much larger budgets.

    A. Sports

    B. Outdoor club

    C. Debate society

 II. The budget is too small.

    A. $800 for advertising and staffing

    B. No money to purchase a van or pay for gas

    C. Statement from head of escort service about lack of $$

III. Student safety is compromised.

    A. Anecdote about sophomore girl who reported a stalker

    B. Statement from Chief of Police Robin Perez: "If even one student is frightened on this campus, we have to beef up security." (Personal interview, 2/19/04)

IV. Call for action: We have to get more funding for the student escort service.

    A. Elect new student government

    B. Petition administration

Adding

With a clear focus and a final-stage outline, you will know what you have to add in order to complete your revision. In the case of this sample editorial, the outline allowed you to see the hole in the argument: the lack of support for the idea that student safety is being compromised.

Another way to figure out what needs to be added is to take on the persona of an insistent reader who needs everything explained clearly, much as you did when you initially developed your ideas. Read the piece from this person's perspective, and ask yourself a lot of questions: *How do you know that? Can you give an example? What does that mean? Can you explain that in more detail? What is your evidence?* Do not let yourself get away with sloppy thinking, unexplained ideas, and unsupported generalizations.

Even better, find a real reader, a peer editor who is not as close to the piece as you are. Ask a classmate or a friend to give your piece a reader's response, telling you where a reader would get lost or bogged down or would need more information. If your college has a writing center, this is a good time to go there to get helpful feedback.

Cutting

Cutting, as the word suggests, can be a painful part of revising. Once you get those words down on paper, it is hard to press the delete key. But you may find that your writing becomes stronger when you cut unnecessary and irrelevant material. Less is usually more.

Cut on two levels. Cut on the *macro level* when you have figured out your focus, which you may discover during the initial brainstorming, during composing, or after writing the first draft. Examine every paragraph with that focus in mind. Does the paragraph relate specifically to the main point as support, illustration, or discussion? Even if you have written a brilliant passage, if it does not relate closely to your main point or if it is not a reasonable and interesting digression from the topic, you have to cut it.

Cut on the *micro level.* You may have smoothed out your sentences as you wrote them, but check again for clutter, for words and phrases that are confusing, redundant, or unnecessary. Cutting clutter rewards you with more elegant language, with cleaner and clearer sentences. As with any activity, the more you do, the easier it becomes. Soon you will notice and automatically cut bloated phrases, such as "in this modern world of today" and "at this point in time," and substitute the more direct "today" and "now." (See Style Guide on the website for more on identifying and removing clutter.)

Presidential speechwriter and author Peggy Noonan put it this way: "Remember the waterfront shack with the sign FRESH FISH SOLD HERE. Of course it's fresh, we're on the ocean. Of course it's for sale, we're not giving it away. Of course, it's here, otherwise the sign would be someplace else. The final sign: FISH."

An x-ray of this painting *Breezing Up* by Winslow Homer reveals details of his earlier draft. In his revision, Homer eliminated an additional passenger near the mast and two extra boats that he had originally placed on the horizon.

Editing and Proofreading

Most of the time, editing and proofreading are the final parts of revision. Go through the paper twice, first looking for places where you can enhance the style of your writing, and then correcting errors in grammar and mechanics.

Enhancing style does not mean adding linguistic flourishes to your writing but rather improving its sound, rhythm, flow, originality, and impact. Style is not an add-on to a piece of writing, but an integral part of it, the sum of all the choices you have made about words, sentence length, and paragraph structure. Often, reading your paper aloud will help you notice places where the sound, flow, or cadence could be improved.

Cutting clutter is one way to achieve a clean and elegant writing style. Other guidelines include using concrete nouns and muscular verbs, limiting the use of adjectives and adverbs, avoiding unintentional repetition, and developing an engaging voice. (See Style Guide on the website for more specific suggestions.)

Editing for correctness, often called proofreading, means correcting grammar, punctuation, and mechanical errors and checking for accuracy. Have you spelled names correctly? Are the dates right? Are all quotations exact, and have you cited their sources (documented them) precisely? (See Chapters 14 and 15.)

With proofreading, as with revision in general, fresh eyes see more. Put the piece away for a while, and return when you are not as close to the material. Another useful technique is to read each paragraph (or even the whole paper) from the bottom to the top. That way you isolate sentences from their context, allowing you to notice sentence structure problems, for example.

An old proofreading parlor trick demonstrates the difficulty of finding errors in context. See if you can find any errors in the following text.

> When I went to the deli,
> I asked for bagels and
> and cream cheese. "We're out,"
> said the clerk. I left
> empty-handed.

If you have not found the error in one reading, try reading the passage from bottom to top and see if the error is easier to find. Often, the eye skips over the repeated "and," correcting it automatically.

However you go about the final edit, aim for a result that is clean and error-free. Readers really do care, and so should you.

PEER EDITING

Even if you have enough time between an early draft and a final draft to gain some perspective, editing your own writing can be hard. Your ideas may be clear to you, but are they clear to a reader?

To find out how well you have communicated your ideas, work with a peer editor, preferably a classmate who has struggled with the same assignment and writing problems. The peer-editing process prepares you for many real-world writing situations. Authors of books and articles work with editors; proposal or report writers in community or workplace situations often write collaboratively, freely sharing ideas and criticism. Many writing classes use the workshop method, having students read and critique each other's writing.

As many writers have discovered, peer editing can be extremely useful, or it can be a waste of time, an unfocused gab session. A productive peer editing session

- Helps the writer strengthen the piece of writing
- Helps the editor strengthen his or her critical thinking about writing

To make peer editing work, and work well, you should understand the process and the roles of the writer and the peer editor.

The Process

Writing classes use peer editing in different ways. Some use peer-editing groups of three or four students; others use peer-editing pairs. Some students e-mail drafts to peer editors; others bring hard copies to distribute in class. Some students write comments directly on the papers they are critiquing; some use separate peer editing logs; and others just talk, letting the writer take notes. Essentially, the peer-editing process allows each writer to have a set period of time in which to get specific feedback on a piece of writing.

The Writer

1. Bring in (or e-mail) enough copies so that each peer editor has a copy of your paper.
2. Read the piece aloud, or let someone else read it aloud. Reading or listening to your own writing is an extremely useful technique. You can pick up problems in logic, word choice, structure, grammar, and voice that you did not "hear" when you read your writing silently. Reading aloud also allows peer editors to hear the cadences of your writing while they read along.
3. Identify areas that you would like to receive feedback on. You can do this by jotting down questions before the session or by asking questions during the session.
4. Listen carefully to the feedback you get. Be open to new ideas about how to develop your paper or support your points.
5. Be selective in the advice you accept. Not all that you hear may be useful. Filter the advice through your intentions for that piece of writing. If the advice conflicts with what you want to do—or with what other readers have said—you can decide not to follow it.

The Peer Editor

Respond as a reader, not as a teacher. Some students feel uncomfortable in the role of peer editor because, as they say, "I'm not a teacher." So do not respond as an expert in writing but as the intelligent reader you are. Tell the writer where the writing engaged you and where it lost you, where you were riveted by it and where your interest flagged. Point to sentences or images that worked well and those that seemed vague or confusing. This kind of reader response gives useful information to the writer.

Respond kindly and honestly. It should go without saying that criticism is meant to help, not inflict pain on the writer. Caustic comments undercut the process, but so does being dishonest. If you find a piece of writing weak or undeveloped, say so. Conversely, if the writing is strong and effective, let the writer know.

Be as specific as possible. "I loved it" and "It was boring" are not useful comments. "I felt as though I could see the mountains you describe in the third paragraph" tells the writer why you loved the writing. "You make the same point in the first three paragraphs" tells the writer exactly why you were bored. The more specific you can be, the more useful the writer will find your comments, and the stronger your own critical thinking will become.

Focus on specific aspects of the writing. All the assignment chapters in this book include peer editing logs that pose questions for your consideration. You can copy these logs and use them to write responses to the writer, or you can use them as guides for discussion.

One Student's Writing Process: Justin Lin

Justin Lin was writing a memoir—a story about an important event in his life. The drafts below show how he developed his memoir from an initial freewriting exercise, through peer editing, to the final draft. Note the significant changes and improvements he made as he received feedback and as his thinking about the topic deepened.

Freewrite   In brainstorming for the memoir assignment, Justin Lin did a freewrite on the following topic: "Write about a moment you remember particularly vividly. Include weather, a gesture, dialogue, sound, a scent, and a color."

A cold aura loomed through the night. As it grew stronger, it engulfed me like a tidal wave. I voraciously devoured the air as my eyes shot wide-open. Their eyes moved left to right . . . right to left. I caught my breath in complete blackness and scanned the bunk above to collect my thoughts. Light footsteps from around the hammocks surfaced. I heard squeaky mice-like chatter get closer. The odor of sweat, vomit, and mud from the older boys soon filled my nostrils. Their eyes focused in on the target. Crack! In an instant, a barrage of socks filled with rocks crashed from above—Whack! Thump!

"Stop it" he shouted. As I listened to this beating, I slithered into my covers. I shut my eyes and held my breath. Gritting my teeth together, I waited for it to end. Sweat on my forehead formed when I thought to myself, "What if I'm next?" "Stop it! I'm sorry . . . !" Felix cried. The pounding stopped just like that; I could not make out the perpetrators—four, five, or six of them fled back to their bunks. In sheer flashes, all the damage was done. The deafening silence in this cold . . . cold summer night that entwined with puppy-whimpers from above, kept me awake. "He was just a little kid . . . he was just a little kid," I repeated quietly.

Annotated First Draft   The peer editor annotated the first draft following the directions on the peer-editing log sheet on pages 30–32.

"I Was Just a Little Kid"

JUSTIN LIN

Puts you in the middle of a scene

The ninety-degree sun beat on his tan face. He had a scar across his right upper lip, most likely caused by a fight that seemed to stretch more and more every time he barked at us. "You imbeciles, get down and give me push-ups," he commanded. Down-up "sir one sir," down-up "sir two sir," we screamed back the count in unison until the hundredth push-up was completed. Sergeant Haines was not a very nice man—he just seemed bitter with his life. "Get up, dammit. **D** Get up," he screamed. "Sir yes sir," we screamed back while falling into formation. Sergeant Haines began lecturing us about life while we were enduring the desert heat in the peak of summer. "What does he know about life," I mumbled ✓ quietly while trying to catch my breath from the push-ups. This was the eighth **Conflict?** day out of this grueling ten-day ordeal.

While he yapped on and on, I drifted off into a daydream and tried to remember how I got myself into this predicament. My right brow lifted and I **IM** grinned as I recalled how stupid was I to let my Dad persuade me to endure boot camp. He made this Devil Pups Military Program sound fun, and convincingly he told me that it was a chance to become a man. Ever since I was ten he would say, "Justin, you will amount to nothing if you don't grow up." Repeatedly saying this to me, I naturally began to believe him—I was scared of growing up, but **Too much IM** in actuality I was more scared of not growing up.

✓ **Conflict** I jumped trains of thought to when he dropped me off. He was so proud. I do not believe I have ever seen my Dad stand as proud as he did on that day. I remembered his proud grin as he grabbed me to hug me. He whispered, "When you are done with this, you will be a man." Then he stepped into his Lexus and drove away. I saw the car whip a cloud of dust from the dirt roads. In moments he had stranded me at Camp Pendleton, imprisoned with malevolent juvenile delinquents and evil Drill Sergeants. I was thirteen years old, my dad's decision to send me to Devil Pups was just as wrong as my willingness to come.

End of setup? I'm not sure

"What the hell are you grinning for?" Sergeant Haines' beady eyes pierced mine. My pre-pubescent voice managed to squeal out, "Sir, nothing, sir." The older boys in my platoon snickered in the background, but I was too afraid to look. Sergeant Haines walked away, but I knew he was keeping his eye on me. I stood like a statue; my feet together making a forty-five degree V, my hands clenched together at pocket side, my head up with my eyes looking straightforward. We were drilled on staying in this form since the first day. My legs got tired the first couple days because each muscle had to be tensed up, but I got used to it. I could not even wipe the sweat running down to my eyebrows, but worse yet was a little dime-sized itch in the middle of my back. I could not scratch lest he would catch me and make the platoon do something horrible. I no longer could abstain from scratching. Just as I went to scratch, Sergeant Haines caught someone up the line sway back and stumble. The platoon was going to pay for making another mistake.

Narrative detail

Surprisingly, Sergeant Haines did not scream at us, but we all knew he had just about had it with our crap. He told us to face right and march on. The four rows of ten turned in accord and began to march. He took us to the track. "Two-hundred meter sprints, up and back . . . until I get tired," Haines said as he signaled us to begin. "Until I get tired . . . until I . . . get tired," rang through my ears as I paced myself. There was no doubt we would keep running until we vomited. I knew I would wear out fast, and I did not want to be the first one to stop. The day got hotter reaching well past a hundred. Sweat drops from my face hit the pavement and evaporated as I ran. "Left . . . right . . . left . . . right," I thought as I sucked in air. I finished three lines and then my mouth dried up—I started getting dizzy—I stopped—I leaned over and threw up all my breakfast.

Sergeant Haines ordered me to keep on running. I could not move. He signaled me to come to him. I hunched over and slowly dragged my legs to him. I reached him and I barely could stand in correct form—feet by my side, and hands clenched at my pocket-side. "You must be kidding me. . . . you ran half ass like that and couldn't even finish four. . . . Why?" he screamed at me. I was afraid of this man. I just wanted to crawl into a hole and never see his face again. I cleared my throat and said "Sir, I'm just a little kid, Sir." He scoffed back at me and said,

D "Little baby, if you want to be a man in this world, you need to suck it up."

"Sir, Yes, Sir!" I yelled.

Good detail He spat on the pavement and ordered me to do a hundred push-ups. I saw his spit sizzle and fry on the hot pavement, and I knew the pavement would burn my hands. I bit my lip. I knelt down. Feeling my hand melt on the pavement, my eyes stung a little as they started to water. The heat was unbearable—down-up . . . "Sir one Sir"—down-up . . . "Sir two Sir." Each tear ran down the bridge of my nose and splattered on the pavement and hissed away. I was too weak to do this . . . couldn't he see! I struggled for the third push-up. I felt his boot nudge me on the right side just before he kicked me. I fell down. My back burned on the pavement, so I began to get up. I stopped as he neared me. I had cried so much that I could only see Sergeant Haine's silhouette along with the bright beams of sun that outlined his figure. "You might as well stay down there," as he kicked me back down and walked away.

Summary Cuts, bruises, and burns can only hurt for so long. They at least heal.

I cried a little longer, but everyone was done vomiting, and Sergeant Haines called us to form together and march to the classroom. As we prepared for the graduation of the Devil Pups Program, the older kids that sat by me were whispering to each other about what had happened this afternoon. Later, I found out all this running was caused by my bunkmate, Felix. Felix was just as young as I, but shorter in height. I knew the older kids were upset about this and I knew something horrible would happen to Felix.

Summary The day was a blur because I was lightheaded from all the vomiting I had done from the running. I cried myself to sleep, and wished for the couple next days to come quickly.

Good detail

Vivid

A cold aura loomed through the night. As it grew stronger, it engulfed me like a tidal wave. I voraciously devoured the air as my eyes shot wide-open. Their eyes moved left to right . . . right to left. I caught my breath in complete blackness and scanned the bunk above to collect my thoughts. Light footsteps from around the hammocks surfaced. I heard squeaky mice-like chatter get closer. The odor of sweat, vomit, and mud from the older boys soon filled my nostrils. Their eyes focused in on the target. Crack! In an instant, a barrage of socks filled with rocks crashed from above—Whack! Thump!

"Stop it," he shouted. As I listened to this beating, I slithered into my covers. I shut my eyes and held my breath. Gritting my teeth together, I waited for it to end. Sweat on my forehead formed when I thought to myself, "What if I'm next?"

"Stop it! I'm sorry . . . !" Felix cried. The pounding stopped just like that; I could not make out the perpetrators—four, five, or six of them fled back to their bunks. In sheer flashes all the damage was done. The deafening silence in this cold . . . cold summer night was entwined with puppy-whimpers from above and kept me awake. "He was just a little kid. . . . he was just a little kid," I repeated quietly.

Peer Editing Log Sheet

Peer Editing Log

As you work with a writing partner or in a peer-editing group, you can use these questions to give useful responses to a classmate's memoir and as a guide for discussion.

Writer's Name ___**Justin Lin**___   Date **February 8**___

1. Bracket the introduction of the memoir. What technique does the writer use to open the story? Do you find it effective or could you suggest a better place for the story to begin?

   The writer is putting us in the middle of a scene, but the scene is interrupted by lots of telling—he seemed to be bitter with his life. This slows down the action of the scene. But the description of the sergeant—what he looks like, etc.—it's easy to picture him.

2. Put a line under the last paragraph of the set-up. How effectively has the writer set up the story? What other information or sensory details might help you better understand the events that follow?

   Not sure I can do this—the whole thing seems like set-up. I think the focus of the story is the nighttime beating and how this might have affected the writer, so everything that leads up to that scene seems like set-up, but it's hard to tell.

3. Box a section that presents the setting of the story. What details might make the setting stronger, more vivid, or more specific?

   The paragraph that starts "He spat on the pavement . . ." seems to give setting, but the whole description of the sergeant and what the "pups" were asked to do also seems to be setting for the violent scene at night. It's a place that's tough to be in. The spit sizzling seems exaggerated, almost like something you would see in a cartoon. Is that what you wanted? You might think about adding some more details of things you can see while you feel sick, how the yellow dust seemed sickly yellow, or what you stare at as you try not to think about your pain. You might be looking at the mountains way off in the distance, or the shade trees that are really far away from the place you are standing.

4. Write a sentence that expresses the theme of the story as you understand it. What images, language, events point to that theme? Does the title
also direct the reader's attention to the theme? If the title is weak, can
you suggest an alternative?

The father says, "When you are done with this, you will be a man."
This seems like part of the writer's theme, that he is just thirteen, but
looking for some kind of big change. He seems ready for a change.
The title "I Was Just a Little Kid," shows me that some kind of change
will take place, but I don't see it (the change) in the rough draft. Part
of the theme seems to be the writer's definition of what makes a
"man," what being "man" will mean to him after this experience.

5. Put a check next to the first place you notice the conflict beginning
to emerge. What is the conflict? What are the obstacles for the central
character? What is at stake?

I see two conflicts here: surviving the camp and the sergeant, and
impressing dad. The writer seems to want to make his father proud of
him and he has to get through the camp in order to do that. The conflict
becomes really clear when the writer says the father was wrong, and so
was he. What is at stake for the writer is his chance to become a man, at
least in his father's eyes, and also staying physically strong throughout the
ordeal. He is physically threatened, too, and part of what makes this story
interesting is the question of whether he will hold up through the pain.
Will he get really hurt—injured by the other "pups" or by the training
somehow?

6. What is your impression of the main character(s)? Suggest places where
the characters' actions and dialogue could be strengthened to develop
them more fully.

The main character is a mixture of frightened and willing. The writer
says, "my right brow lifted" when he thinks back on how he got to the
camp. It seems more like something somebody could see him doing. Not
something he could see. The main character could have some things he
does when he's nervous, like cracking his knuckles or biting his tongue
really hard when he wants to talk back but shouldn't.

7. Look at the narrative techniques the writer uses in the memoir. Identify places where the writer uses summary and places where the writer creates a scene through narrative detail. Identify places where the writer uses dialogue with a D and places where the writer uses internal monologue with IM. Which sections might be strengthened by *showing* through narration and dialogue rather than *telling* through summary and internal monologue?

I like the part where he drifts into the IM of saying how he got to the camp in the first place, but it seems like too much at one time and there might be more dialogue or description here. It seems like a lot of telling about the background, too much IM.

8. What kind of voice does the writer use to tell the story? Is it appropriate and consistent to the narrator's age and circumstance? How might the voice better reflect the narrator's character?

The voice is good in the story. It seems like the right age, especially the things he notices in the night scene when he can't see anything. These things seem childlike—the way the main character is inside even though he seems tough on the outside. Some sentences seem more like the adult talking—"desert heat in the peak of summer"—this is not a thirteen year old talking, obviously. It's the more grownup writer talking here. The voice is a good mixture of the two perspectives.

9. Bracket the conclusion. What technique does the writer use? Is the conclusion effective in leaving a last impression that fortifies the theme? Does the last paragraph add anything necessary to the story? Would the story be injured by cutting it?

This is hard to do because the last paragraph seems less like a conclusion than it does like the climax of the story. "He was just a little kid," is the conclusion somehow. It is the moment the main character sees how stupid it is to put these boys through all this just so they can be taught a lesson. He seems to realize something here, but there is too much packed into the image, and it doesn't seem to relate back to the theme of becoming a man in his father's eyes, which is the main conflict. The ending doesn't seem like an ending.

10. Comment briefly on the writing style. Put a "V" by places where the writing can be strengthened by substituting active verbs for "to be" verbs, a "T" where the writer could use a better transition. Put a * next to places where the writer uses interesting verbs and good transitions.

I like the way the story is written. I was interested in finding out what happened to him, and it kept me reading. I don't see any major problems with the style.

Final Draft Using his peer editor's comments and his own sense of where he wanted his story to go, Lin wrote this final draft.

Justin Lin
November 14, 2005

When I Was Just a Little Kid

I remembered his confident grin as he went to hug me. He whispered, "When you are done with this, you will be a man." Glancing down, I watched the summer sun hit his shiny leather shoes as he glided across the rocky path back to his Lexus. As he went to open the door, his new clean-cut hairstyle and facial features reflected off the window. Standing at the car door in his black suit, my dad turned to check on me one more time. In hindsight, there was nothing he could do to prepare me for the terror I would face in the last three days of Boot Camp. Then, he swiftly took his black coat off, placed his right leg into the car first and then maneuvered into the seat. He closed the door and drove away. I saw the Lexus whip a cloud of dust from the dirt roads. In an instant, he had stranded me at Camp Pendleton for the next ten days—imprisoned with juvenile delinquents and Drill Sergeants. I had once believed that I would be scared to grow up, but in actuality I was more scared of not growing up. I was thirteen years old, one of the youngest at the Devil Pup's Military Program, and my dad's decision to send me here was just as wrong as my willingness to come.

"What the hell are you grinning for?" said Sergeant Haines, with his beady brown eyes piercing mine. I snapped out of my daydream to notice the scar across his right upper lip. My prepubescent voice managed to squeak out, "Sir, nothing, Sir." The older boys in my platoon snickered in the background, but I was told never to fidget. I stood like a statue. My feet were together making a forty-five degree angle, and my hands were clenched together at my side pocket. My head did not drop, and my eyes were focused straight ahead into space. We were drilled to stand in attention since the first day.

Sergeant Haines' six-foot frame towered over me, and the momentary shade he created disappeared as he walked away. I knew he was keeping his eye on me. He was a lanky Caucasian, and if he wanted to hurt somebody with his shiny black boots, he would. Having already been seven days into boot camp, I knew better than to be caught off-guard. Just as I thought this, a cadet two rows in front of me fell to the black pavement. The cadet was disoriented and as he turned around to jump back into formation, I discovered it was my bunkmate, Felix. Felix was from South American descent. He was just as young as I, but shorter. He stood about five-feet tall, where I was five-feet, two-inches. Like me, he had come to Devil Pups to be a man but was falling short of the mark. Although he was my bunkmate, there was no time for me to get to know him.

Surprisingly, Sergeant Haines did not scream at us, but I knew he was irritated. He told us to face right and march on. The four rows of ten turned in accord and began to march. He took us to the track. "Two-hundred meter sprints, up and back . . . until I get tired," Haines said as he signaled us to begin. "Until I get tired . . . until I . . . get tired," rang through my ears as I paced myself. There was no doubt we would keep running until we vomited. The day got hotter reaching well past a hundred degrees. As I ran, sweat drops from my face fell . . . skipped from my wet-shirt to my dirty jeans and hit the track only to be evaporated. "Left . . . right . . . left . . . right," I thought as I gasped for air. Just as I turned the corner to finish the fourth line, my mouth dried up. I started getting dizzy—I stopped—I leaned over—I let the stomach acids leave my burning abdomen to pour onto the track.

From the side of the track, Sergeant Haines ordered me to keep running. I could not move. He signaled for me to come to him. I hunched over and slowly huffed-and-puffed my way towards him. When I reached him, I barely could stand in attention—feet by my side—hands clenched by my pocket-side.

"You must be kidding me . . . you ran half ass like that and couldn't even finish four. . . . Why?" he screamed into my left ear. My heart raced a little faster.

I cleared my throat and said, "Sir, I'm just a little kid, Sir."

He scoffed at me and replied, "Little baby, if you want to be a man in this world, you need to suck it up."

"Sir, Yes, Sir!" I yelled.

He spat on the pavement and ordered me to do a hundred push-ups. Watching his spit sizzle and fry on the hot pavement, I knew the pavement would burn my hands. I bit my lip. I knelt down. I felt my hands melt on the pavement, and my eyes stung a little as they started to water. Down-up . . . "Sir, one, Sir," down-up . . . "Sir, two, Sir." Each tear ran down the bridge of my nose—splattered on the pavement and hissed away. I was too weak to do this . . . Couldn't he see! I struggled and shook for the third push-up. I felt his black boot nudge my right side just before he kicked me. I fell down. My back cooked on the pavement, so I began to get up. I stopped as he neared me. With my swollen eyes, I could only make out Sergeant Haines' silhouette against the bright sun. "You might as well stay down there," he said, and with that, he kicked me back down and walked away.

Cuts, bruises, and burns can only hurt for so long. At least they heal.

I cried a little longer, but everyone had finished vomiting, and Sergeant Haines called us to form together. We marched to the classroom, so we could prepare for the graduation of the Devil Pups Program. While in class, the older kids who sat by me were whispering to each other. I listened closely as they talked about being upset with Felix for making us run. Intuitively, I knew something horrible would happen to Felix.

The rest of the day was a blur because I was lightheaded from all the vomiting I had done. I cried myself to sleep, and wished for the next couple days to pass quickly.

An eerie sensation loomed through the night. As it grew stronger, it engulfed me like a tidal wave. In a panic I voraciously devoured the air as my eyes shot wide-open. My eyes flickered anxiously—left . . . right . . . right . . . left. I caught my breath in the blackness and scanned the bunk above to collect my thoughts. My ears perked up to hear light footsteps surface around the hammocks. The squeaky mice-like chatter got closer. The odor of sweat, vomit, and mud from the older boys soon filled my nostrils. I saw their eyes narrow and focus in on their target. Crack! In an instant, a barrage of socks filled with rocks crashed from above. Whack! Thump!

"Stop it!" he pleaded, as the rocks pounded his flesh. As I listened to this beating, I slithered into my covers. I shut my eyes and held my breath. Gritting my teeth together, I asked God in a silent prayer to make it end quickly. With each swing, I felt my innocence slip away. I had never seen anything like this before. Sweat formed on my forehead when I thought to myself, "What if I'm next?"

"Stop it! I'm sorry . . . !" Felix cried. The pounding stopped just like that; I could not make out the perpetrators—four, five, or six of them fled back to their bunks. In an instant, all the damage was done. The deafening silence in this cold . . . cold summer night was entwined with puppy-whimpers from above that kept me awake. "He was just a little kid . . . he was just a little kid," I repeated quietly.

The sun's rays peeked through the little opening under the door. At any moment Sergeant Haines' boots would crunch on the gravel outside the door, and he would barge in screaming crude lines, flipping on the lights as he had done in the past mornings. I lay in bed for a moment and then I sat up. Indeed, it was a new day.

The door handle rattled a little and Sergeant Haines stomped in. This time I was ready for him. I stood in attention next to my already made bed. The sheets wrapped around the bed so tightly that even quarters could bounce off of them.

The last day was relatively simple. We marched for most of the day in preparation for the ceremony, "Left . . . right . . . left . . . right . . . skip step . . . halt . . . attention." We were prepared for the graduation. The American Flag, the Marine Corp Flag, and beside it the Devil Pups Flag, which the color guard held, danced and fluttered like butterflies in the wind. Before I knew it, I was seeing the same flags fly high during our graduation.

The day I had prayed for since I stepped into Camp Pendleton had come. I should have been filled with joy, but I wasn't. I should have felt as if I had conquered something, but I didn't. I should have become a real man, but I wasn't.

After the ceremony, my mom with her reassuring smiles and kisses came to retrieve what remained of the Justin she had left behind ten days earlier. Behind her, my Dad stood in his three-piece suit and leather shoes. As if he were a military cadet, he stood at attention, feet together making a forty-five degree V, hands clenched together at pocket side, head up with eyes locked into space. He extended his hand to congratulate me and saw everything he had wanted to see—himself. In the car ride out of Camp Pendleton, my dad, like a curious child, asked me questions about Devil Pups. I answered concisely, trying not to reveal the trauma I had endured. He asked the one question that has stuck out these past seven years, "How does it feel to be a man?"

I thought about what I wanted to say, "Dad, I'm thirteen years-old. I was just a little kid . . ."

Awake from the fleeting daydream, I wet my chapped-lips and gave him a fake half-smile. That day, I told him what he had wanted to hear. "Dad it's just a great feeling." The Lexus got onto the on-ramp of the freeway and drove home.

Critical Reading Questions

1. What connections can you see between the freewrite and the final draft?

2. Did the peer editor give any advice that you disagree with? If so, what advice would you have given instead?

3. What specific advice that the peer editor gave did Lin successfully integrate into the final draft?

4. Compare the introductions to the first draft and the final draft. In the first draft Lin begins the story with a scene at the Devil Pup's Military Program. In the final draft he begins earlier, in the car with his dad. What did Lin gain by changing the introductory scene? What did he lose? Which do you like better and why?

5. The peer editor comments that, in the first draft, he doesn't see the writer's change from being a kid to understanding what it means to be a man. Does Lin make this change more apparent in the final draft? If so, how does he make it more apparent?

6. The peer editor comments that the ending does not seem conclusive enough. Compare the endings of the first and final drafts. Which do you think is more successful and why?

READINGS

A short step away from thinking about your writing process is thinking about the time you first became aware of yourself as a writer—as a literate person able to read and write. Often a child's transition from preliterate to literate marks entry into the world of ideas and stories independent of adults. Writers often describe this rite of passage and how it influenced them to become writers. Sometimes a passion for writing and reading seems hardwired, part of the "original package." Sometimes a parent or teacher influences a child and helps foster a love for words. Sometimes life experiences, both wonderful and difficult ones, push people toward writing.

Literacy narratives reveal moments when people realize, usually for the first time, the power of words to shape their lives. Of course, writers are not the only ones to have these experiences; most of us do, as well. The three stories that follow are literacy narratives. Two are by well-known writers. Anne Lamott is a memoirist, a fiction writer, and a writing teacher. Stephen King is probably best known for books (and movies) such as *Misery, The Shining, It,* and *The Stand*. The third short piece is by a first-year college student, Caitlin Reynolds, who remembers how her early reading led to her first piece of writing.

bird by bird

Anne Lamott

In the introduction to *bird by bird*, her book about writing, Anne Lamott tells about her initiation into writing.

I grew up around a father and a mother who read every chance they got, who took us to the library every Thursday night to load up on books for the coming week. Most nights after dinner my father stretched out on the couch to read, while my mother sat with her book in the easy chair and the three of us kids each retired to our own private reading stations. Our house was very quiet after dinner—unless, that is, some of my father's writer friends were over. My father was a writer, as were most of the men with whom he hung out. They were not the quietest people on earth, but they were mostly very masculine and kind. Usually in the afternoons, when that day's work was done, they hung out at the no name bar in Sausalito, but sometimes they came to our house for drinks and ended up staying for supper. I loved them, but every so often one of them would pass out at the dinner table. I was an anxious child to begin with, and I found this unnerving.

Every morning, no matter how late he had been up, my father rose at 5:30, went to his study, wrote for a couple of hours, made us all breakfast, read the paper with my mother, and then went back to work for the rest of the morning. Many years passed before I realized that he did this by choice, for a living, and that he was not unemployed or mentally ill. I wanted him to have a regular job where he put on a necktie and went off somewhere with the other fa-thers and sat in a little office and smoked. But the idea of spending entire days in someone else's office doing someone else's work did not suit my father's soul. I think it would have killed him. He did end up dying rather early, in his mid-fifties, but at least he had lived on his own terms.

So I grew up around this man who sat at his desk in the study all day and wrote books and articles about the places and people he had seen and known. He read a lot of poetry. Sometimes he traveled. He could go anyplace he wanted with a sense of purpose. One of the gifts of being a writer is that it gives you an excuse to do things, to go places and explore. Another is that writing motivates you to look closely at life, at life as it lurches by and tramps around.

Writing taught my father to pay attention; my father in turn taught other people to pay attention and then to write down their thoughts and observations. His students were the prisoners at San Quentin who took part in the creative-writing program. But he taught me, too, mostly by example. He taught the prisoners and me to put a little bit down on paper every day, and to read all the great books and plays we could get our hands on. He taught us to read poetry. He taught us to be bold and original and to let ourselves make mistakes, and that Thurber was right when he said, "You might as well fall flat on your face as lean over too far backwards." But while he helped the prisoners and me to discover that we had a lot of feelings and observations and memories and dreams and (God knows) opinions we wanted to share, we all ended up just the tiniest bit resentful when we found the one fly in the ointment: that at some point we had to actually sit down and write.

5   I believe writing was easier for me than for the prisoners because I was still a child. But I always found it hard. I started writing when I was seven or eight. I was very shy and strange-looking, loved reading above everything else, weighed about forty pounds at the time, and was so tense that I walked around with my shoulders up to my ears, like Richard Nixon. I saw a home movie once of a birthday party I went to in the first grade, with all these cute little boys and girls playing together like puppies, and all of a sudden I scuttled across the screen like Prufrock's crab. I was very clearly the one who was going to grow up to be a serial killer, or keep dozens and dozens of cats. Instead, I got funny. I got funny because boys, older boys I didn't even know, would ride by on their bicycles and taunt me about my weird looks. Each time felt like a drive-by shooting. I think this is why I walked like Nixon: I think I was trying to plug my ears with my shoulders, but they wouldn't quite reach. So first I got funny and then I started to write, although I did not always write funny things.

The first poem I wrote that got any attention was about John Glenn. The first stanza went, "Colonel John Glenn went up to heaven / in his spaceship, *Friendship Seven.*" There were many, many verses. It was like one of the old English ballads my mother taught us to sing while she played the piano. Each song had thirty or forty verses, which would leave my male relatives flattened to our couches and armchairs as if by centrifugal force, staring unblinking up at the ceiling.

The teacher read the John Glenn poem to my second-grade class. It was a great moment; the other children looked at me as though I had learned to drive. It turned out that the teacher had

submitted the poem to a California state schools competition, and it had won some sort of award. It appeared in a mimeographed collection. I understood immediately the thrill of seeing oneself in print. It provides some sort of primal verification: you are in print; therefore you exist. Who knows what this urge is all about, to appear somewhere outside yourself, instead of feeling stuck inside your muddled but stroboscopic mind, peering out like a little undersea animal—a spiny blenny, for instance—from inside your tiny cave? Seeing yourself in print is such an amazing concept: you can get so much attention without having to actually show up somewhere. While others who have something to say or who want to be effectual, like musicians or baseball players or politicians, have to get out there in front of people, writers, who tend to be shy, get to stay home and still be public. There are many obvious advantages to this. You don't have to dress up, for instance, and you can't hear them boo you right away.

Sometimes I got to sit on the floor of my father's study and write my poems while he sat at his desk writing his books. Every couple of years, another book of his was published. Books were revered in our house, and great writers admired above everyone else. Special books got displayed prominently: on the coffee table, on the radio, on the back of the john. I grew up reading the blurbs on dust jackets and the reviews of my father's books in the papers. All of this made me start wanting to be a writer when I grew up—to be artistic, a free spirit, and yet also to be the rare working-class person in charge of her own life.

Still, I worried that there was never quite enough money at our house. I worried that my father was going to turn into a bum like some of his writer friends. I remember when I was ten years old, my father published a piece in a magazine that mentioned his having spent an afternoon on a porch at Stinson Beach with a bunch of other writers and that they had all been drinking lots of red wine and smoking marijuana. No one smoked marijuana in those days except jazz musicians, and they were all also heroin addicts. Nice white middle-class fathers were not supposed to be smoking marijuana; they were supposed to be sailing or playing tennis. My friends' fathers, who were teachers and doctors and fire fighters and lawyers, did not smoke marijuana. Most of them didn't even drink, and they certainly did not have colleagues who came over and passed out at the table over the tuna casserole. Reading my father's article, I could only imagine that the world was breaking down, that the next time I burst into my dad's study to show him my report card he'd be crouched under the desk, with one of my mother's nylon stockings knotted around his upper arm, looking up at me like a cornered wolf. I felt that this was going to be a problem; I was sure that we would be ostracized in our community.

10   All I ever wanted was to belong, to wear that hat of belonging.

In seventh and eighth grades I still weighed about forty pounds. I was twelve years old and had been getting teased about my strange looks for most of my life. This is a difficult country to look too different in—the United States of Advertising, as Paul Krassner puts it—and if you are too skinny or too tall or dark or weird or short or frizzy or homely or poor or nearsighted, you get crucified. I did.

But I was funny. So the popular kids let me hang out with them, go to their parties, and watch them neck with each other. This, as you might imagine, did not help my self-esteem a great deal. I thought I was a total loser. But one day I took a notebook and a pen when I went to Bolinas Beach with my father (who was not, as far as I could tell, shooting drugs yet). With the writer's equivalent of canvas and brush, I wrote a description of what I saw: "I walked to the lip of the water and let the foamy tongue of the rushing liquid lick my toes. A sand crab burrowed a hole a few inches from my foot and then disappeared into the sand. . . ." I will spare you the rest. It goes on for quite a while. My father convinced me to show it to a teacher, and it

ended up being included in a real textbook. This deeply impressed my teachers and parents and a few kids, even some of the popular kids, who invited me to more parties so I could watch them all make out even more frequently.

One of the popular girls came home with me after school one day, to spend the night. We found my parents rejoicing over the arrival of my dad's new novel, the first copy off the press. We were all so thrilled and proud, and this girl seemed to think I had the coolest possible father: a writer. (Her father sold cars.) We went out to dinner, where we all toasted one another. Things in the family just couldn't have been better, and here was a friend to witness it.

Then that night, before we went to sleep, I picked up the new novel and began to read the first page to my friend. We were lying side by side in sleeping bags on my floor. The first page turned out to be about a man and a woman in bed together, having sex. The man was playing with the woman's nipple. I began to giggle with mounting hysteria. Oh, this is great, I thought, beaming jocularly at my friend. I covered my mouth with one hand, like a blushing Charlie Chaplin, and pantomimed that I was about to toss that silly book over my shoulder. This is wonderful, I thought, throwing back my head to laugh jovially; my father writes pornography.

In the dark, I glowed like a light bulb with shame. You could have read by me. I never mentioned the book to my father, although over the next couple of years, I went through it late at night, looking for more sexy parts, of which there were a number. It was very confusing. It made me feel very scared and sad.

Then a strange thing happened. My father wrote an article for a magazine, called "A Lousy Place to Raise Kids," and it was about Marin County and specifically the community where we lived, which is as beautiful a place as one can imagine. Yet the people on our peninsula were second only to the Native Americans in the slums of

Oakland in the rate of alcoholism, and the drug abuse among teenagers, was, as my father wrote, soul chilling, and there was rampant divorce and mental breakdown and wayward sexual behavior. My father wrote disparagingly about the men in the community, their values and materialistic frenzy, and about their wives, "these estimable women, the wives of doctors, architects, and lawyers, in tennis dresses and cotton frocks, tanned and well preserved, wandering the aisles of our supermarkets with glints of madness in their eyes." No one in our town came off looking great. "This is the great tragedy of California," he wrote in the last paragraph, "for a life oriented to leisure is in the end a life oriented to death—the greatest leisure of all."

There was just one problem: I was an avid tennis player. The tennis ladies were my friends. I practiced every afternoon at the same tennis club as they; I sat with them on the weekends and waited for the men (who had priority) to be done so we could get on the courts. And now my father had made them look like decadent zombies.

I thought we were ruined. But my older brother came home from school that week with a photocopy of my father's article that his teachers in both social studies and English had passed out to their classes; John was a hero to his classmates. There was an enormous response in the community: in the next few months I was snubbed by a number of men and women at the tennis club, but at the same time, people stopped my father on the street when we were walking together, and took his hand in both of theirs, as if he had done them some personal favor. Later that summer I came to know how they felt, when I read *Catcher in the Rye* for the first time and knew what it was like to have someone speak for me, to close a book with a sense of both triumph and relief, one lonely isolated social animal finally making contact.

I started writing a lot in high school: journals, impassioned antiwar pieces, parodies of the writers I loved. And I began to notice something impor-

tant. The other kids always wanted me to tell them stories of what had happened, even—or especially—when they had been there. Parties that got away from us, blowups in the classroom or on the school yard, scenes involving their parents that we had witnessed—I could make the story happen. I could make it vivid and funny, and even exaggerate some of it so that the event became almost mythical, and the people involved seemed larger, and there was a sense of larger significance, of meaning.

I'm sure my father was the person on whom his friends relied to tell their stories, in school and college. I know for sure that he was later, in the town where he was raising his children. He could take major events or small episodes from daily life and shade or exaggerate things in such a way as to capture their shape and substance, capture what life felt like in the society in which he and his friends lived and worked and bred. People looked to him to put into words what was going on.

I suspect that he was a child who thought differently than his peers, who may have had serious conversations with grown-ups, who as a young person, like me, accepted being alone quite a lot. I think that this sort of person often becomes either a writer or a career criminal. Throughout my childhood I believed that what I thought about was different from what other kids thought about. It was not necessarily more profound, but there was a struggle going on inside me to find some sort of creative or spiritual or aesthetic way of seeing the world and organizing it in my head. I read more than other kids; I luxuriated in books. Books were my refuge. I sat in corners with my little finger hooked over my bottom lip, reading, in a trance, lost in the places and times to which books took me. And there was a moment during my junior year in high school when I began to believe that I could do what other writers were doing. I came to believe that I might be able to put a pencil in my hand and make something magical happen.

Then I wrote some terrible, terrible stories.

On Writing

Stephen King

Stephen King's writing memoir, *On Writing*, combines personal narrative with advice to writers. In the following excerpt, King tells how he made a sickly childhood year bearable by reading and eventually writing.

That year my brother David jumped ahead to the fourth grade and I was pulled out of school entirely. I had missed too much of the first grade, my mother and the school agreed; I could start it fresh in the fall of the year, if my health was good.

Most of that year I spent either in bed or housebound. I read my way through approximately six tons of comic books, progressed to Tom Swift and Dave Dawson (a heroic World War II pilot whose various planes were always "prop-clawing for altitude"), then moved on to Jack London's bloodcurdling animal tales. At some point I began to write my own stories. Imitation preceded creation; I would copy *Combat Casey* comics word for word in my Blue Horse tablet, sometimes adding my own descriptions where they seemed appropriate. "They were camped in a big dratty farmhouse room," I might write; it was another year or two before I discovered that *drat* and *draft* were different words. During that same period I remember believing that *details* were *dentals* and that a bitch was an extremely tall woman. A son of a bitch was apt to be a basketball player. When you're six, most of your Bingo balls are still floating around in the draw-tank.

Eventually I showed one of these copycat hybrids to my mother, and she was charmed—I remember her slightly amazed smile, as if she was unable to believe a kid of hers could be so smart—practically a damned prodigy, for God's sake. I had never seen that look on her face before—not on my account, anyway—and I absolutely loved it.

She asked me if I had made the story up myself, and I was forced to admit that I had copied most of it out of a funnybook. She seemed disappointed, and that drained away much of my pleasure. At last she handed back my tablet. "Write one of your own, Stevie," she said. "Those *Combat Casey* funnybooks are just junk—he's always knocking someone's teeth out. I bet you could do better. Write one of your own."

I remember an immense feeling of *possibility* at the idea, as if I had been ushered into a vast building filled with closed doors and had been given leave to open any I liked. There were more doors than one person could ever open in a lifetime, I thought (and still think).

I eventually wrote a story about four magic animals who rode around in an old car, helping out little kids. Their leader was a large white bunny named Mr. Rabbit Trick. He got to drive the car. The story was four pages long, laboriously printed in pencil. No one in it, so far as I can remember, jumped from the roof of the Graymore Hotel. When I finished, I gave it to my mother, who sat down in the living room, put her pocketbook on the floor beside her, and read it all at once. I could tell she liked it—she laughed in all the right places—but I couldn't tell if that was because she liked me and wanted me to feel good or because it really *was* good.

"You didn't copy this one?" she asked when she had finished. I said no, I hadn't. She said it was good enough to be in a book. Nothing anyone has said to me since has made me feel any happier. I wrote four more stories about Mr. Rabbit Trick and his friends. She gave me a quarter apiece for them and sent them around to her four sisters, who pitied her a little, I think. *They* were all still married, after all; their men had stuck. It was true that

Uncle Fred didn't have much sense of humor and was stubborn about keeping the top of his convertible up, it was also true that Uncle Oren drank quite a bit and had dark theories about how the Jews were running the world, but they were *there*.

Ruth, on the other hand, had been left holding the baby when Don ran out. She wanted them to see that he was a talented baby, at least.

Four stories. A quarter apiece. That was the first buck I made in this business.

Finally a Writer

Caitlin Reynolds

Student Caitlin Reynolds remembers a childhood steeped in books—and her first piece of writing.

My early childhood was filled with books. My mother was a fanatical photographer, and in many of my literally hundreds of baby photos, I can be spotted with a book in hand. Pictures overflow the family album: me sitting on my father's lap, cuddled up for a late afternoon read; me in the tub grasping my waterproof bath-time book. I didn't do any heavy reading at that point, just some stuff to get my mind working.

During my second year of life, my mother and I spent every afternoon wrapped up in her bed, forestalling our daily nap, reading stacks and stacks of *Sesame Street* books from a vast collection my mother had ordered through the mail. *The Case of the Missing Rubber Ducky* was my favorite of them all. We read it at least once, sometimes twice at my demand, before I would settle down. My exhausted, pregnant mother would attempt to sneakily skip pages, but I knew that book like the *Sesame Street* theme song, word for word. Even though I could not read the words myself, I knew exactly what they meant. Each of those books absolutely fascinated me, and even when we were not reading, I would muddle through them on my bedroom floor. I would turn the pages and stare at the pictures and the words and invent my own story and meaning.

This practice helped me when my kindergarten teacher exposed the class to our very first taste of writing. She assigned us to draw a picture and scribble a corresponding story below in the inch-thick, child-friendly lines. I remember anxiously contemplating what I would draw before settling on an elaborate scene of purple penguins distributed on some icebergs in the ocean; it was a true Crayola masterpiece.

Then came the most exciting part of all, writing my story. I had printed "Caitlin" and "Dad" to clarify preschool drawings, but never had I thought to write my own story. I confidently put my dull, yellow Ticonderoga #2 to the paper and scribbled my heart out. The final product looked as though I had strewn a series of short and long curly hairs across the page and traced each curve with as much precision as a five-year-old could manage. My teacher asked me to read my story to her while she printed the words above the scribble in a teacherly red pen. I have no idea what I told her I had written. I was too caught up in my inner celebration; I was finally a writer.

Critical Reading Questions

1. All three writers talk about reading as central to a writer's life. Is this true in your experience? Explain your answer.

2. As recounted in these childhood memories, King's home was not literary, while Lamott's and Reynolds's childhoods were steeped in books. How much influence do you think parents have on their children's development as readers and writers?

3. Lamott writes, "writing motivates you to look closely at life, at life as it lurches by and tramps around" (para. 3). What do you think she means by that line? Do you think that it is true?

4. King has said that writers cannot be "made," only "formed." What does he mean by this distinction? "The equipment comes with the original package," he has written. Do you agree or disagree? Explain your answer.

Questions for Writing and Discussion

1. Find a published writer whom you can interview. Focus your interview on how the writer started writing and on his or her writing process. On a college campus you should have many choices of professors who have published articles and/or books, but you can also go to a bookstore reading or a poetry slam. Write up your findings in a two- or three-page article.

2. Reread the literacy narratives above. Write a short piece about a time you were rewarded for your writing or wrote a piece that gave you pleasure.

3. Write a short piece in which you describe your family's attitude about books and your childhood initiation into writing.

4. Find a short passage that you think is poorly written. Write a page or two explaining why you think it is unsuccessful. Be persuasive.

5. Find a short passage that you think is well written. Write a page or two explaining why you think it is successful. Be persuasive.

6. Interview a person who is neither a teacher nor in a traditional writing profession like journalism. (The person could work in the field of business, medicine, social services, government, science, or entertainment, for example.) Find out how he or she uses writing professionally. Draw some conclusions from the information you gather. Write up your findings in a two- to three-page report. (You could do this assignment in collaboration with one or more classmates and poll your findings to come to your conclusions.)

7. Interview three students who are not in your writing class and who have different majors than your own. Ask about their attitudes about writing, how much writing they do in and out of school, and what their writing processes are. Draw some conclusions from the information you gather. Write up your findings in a two- to three-page report.

2. READING AND THINKING CRITICALLY

When you start reading in a certain way, that's already the beginning of your writing.

—Tess Gallagher

This x-ray image reveals something not visible on the surface: people hidden in a truckload of bananas that are being shipped from Guatemala to Southern Mexico.

READING AND THINKING CRITICALLY

Writers tend to be readers by nature and often write about the pleasures of reading. Novelist and journalist Anna Quindlen, for example, wrote the following.

> Reading has always been my home, my sustenance, my great invincible companion. "Book love," Trollope called it. "It will make your hours pleasant to you as long as you live.". . . I did not read from a sense of superiority, or advancement, or even learning. I read because I loved it more than any other activity on earth.
>
> —Anna Quindlen, *How Reading Changed My Life*

Although not everyone feels this "book love," many people turn to books to find information, inspiration, and possibly even "invincible companions." In your college classes, you need to read critically to understand the material thoroughly. And the texts that you read will not always be books. They can be online journal articles, websites, newspaper articles printed from databases, fellow students' papers posted on the class bulletin board, and other types of paper and electronic documents. To be a critical reader and thinker, you have to engage with the text, whatever form it takes. A critical reader

- Questions the author's authority
- Challenges or exhibits a healthy skepticism about the author's ideas
- Looks for patterns of meaning
- Makes connections between the text and other work
- Reads to understand a writer's explicit and implicit meanings—what is said and what is implied

Critical reading and critical thinking are lifelong skills, not just strategies to help you pass college courses. As you decode meaning, understand nuance, and uncover authors' intentions, you learn to identify language that is full of truth and wisdom as well as language that is full of half-truths and deception. Being a critical thinker helps you understand what people say and what they intentionally leave unsaid, essential knowledge in college and also in politics, in daily life, and in the workplace.

This chapter begins with ten general questions that provide an overview of critical thinking and reading skills. You can use the questions to begin thinking critically about any text you are reading. These skills are reinforced in later chapters. Chapters 3 through 13, the assignment chapters, contain annotation exercises and critical reading questions. Chapter 14 will help you evaluate sources and bias.

CHAPTER OBJECTIVES

In this chapter you will learn to

▶ read actively

▶ analyze and synthesize

▶ interpret irony and figurative language

▶ distinguish between fact and opinion

▶ determine the bias of sources

TEN QUESTIONS FOR CRITICAL THINKING AND READING

1. What genre (type of text) are you reading? Is the piece a story, a review, an argument, or a factual article? Does it conform to the expectations and conventions of its genre or vary from them?

2. Who is the intended audience? How do you know?

3. What is the topic of the piece of writing? Is it something you know about, or is the information new to you?

4. How credible is the writer? Is the writer an expert, a scholar, or an authority? Is the writer exploring ideas or authoritatively presenting information?

5. What is the writer's overall point (thesis)? What kind of evidence does the writer use to support this point? Is the evidence taken from credible sources?

6. What are the main points of each paragraph or section? Do they further support the thesis or digress from it?

7. What is the writer's conclusion? Does the conclusion flow logically from the evidence?

8. What kind of language does the writer use? Is some of the language nuanced, having more than one meaning?

9. What kind of voice does the writer use? Can you locate any irony, sarcasm, anger, passion, or pomposity?

10. Do you agree or disagree with the writer's ideas? How do you respond to the overall thrust of the piece of writing?

ACTIVE READING

Active reading exercises your mind and should also exercise your hand. When you read critically, plan to underline, box, or star passages and to write marginal notes. If the book is not yours, take notes, or photocopy the section you need and mark up the copy. As you read, annotate the text. Look for key ideas, subordinate points, evidence that supports the points, and the writer's conclusion. Also be alert for loaded language, for what is unsaid as well as what is said.

Active reading, by definition, disallows mental passivity. Engage with the text. Question what you are reading. Do not accept what you read as gospel or dismiss it out of hand. Weigh it against your own opinions and knowledge. Allow yourself to be convinced by a well-reasoned argument, but make sure the argument is bolstered by clear and convincing evidence. The following activities help fine-tune your critical reading skills.

▶ Underlining key points

▶ Paraphrasing

▶ Summarizing

▶ Annotating and making marginal notes

▶ Outlining or clustering

Underlining Key Points

Underlining key words and ideas as you read helps you concentrate on what you are reading and store information in your long-term memory. When you review the material, your underlining serves as a shortcut to key points. Be selective in what you underline. Weed out the essential from the nonessential; do not underline every word, only the words that convey important points.

While reading "How Bullets Tell a Tale" by Janet Rae-Dupree (see pages 94–95), one student underlined the following points. The underlining shows one way to highlight the essential information in these paragraphs.

Investigators have a tragic abundance of one kind of clue: "ballistic finger-prints," the scratches, dimples, bumps, and grooves that a gun leaves on a bullet and its shell casing. Like human fingerprinting, ballistics is all about matching: determining whether two rounds came from the same gun. It can be a powerful tool for crime-solving when investigators have a suspect's weapon and can compare a slug from the crime with one test-fired from the gun. Failing that, investigators can use it to link separate crimes, as in the Washington shootings.

To make a match, an examiner places the rounds to be compared inside a special double microscope that displays images side by side or overlaps them. Larger markings, such as the ridges on a bullet left by rifling grooves in the barrel, can be enough to show that the samples came from the same gun model. Shell casings like the one that Washington investigators have found can also be revealing because they can record the position and shape of the firing pin and, on semiautomatic weapons, the extractor and ejector that expel spent rounds.

Too much more underlining would make the strategy less useful since it would require rereading almost all the original text. You should be able to understand the essence of the two paragraphs by reading only the underlined words.

Paraphrasing

When you *paraphrase,* you put material that you have read into your own words. By paraphrasing passages as you read, you reinforce your understanding of the material. The first step in paraphrasing is to look up unfamiliar words so you have a thorough understanding of the writer's points. Then put the main ideas in your own language and your own sentence structure, making sure not to distort the meaning or add any details not in the original text. Put quotation marks around words or phrases you take from the original. Cite material you quote and material you paraphrase in your bibliography and in-text citations.

As you read new material, finding your own words to explain concepts helps you understand and "own" them. As you integrate quotations from print, electronic, or expert sources into your writing, you will often want to paraphrase them, saving direct quotations for especially articulate passages or original ideas.

The same student who underlined essential information in the Dupree piece about ballistics then wrote this paraphrase of the first paragraph.

Ballistics can help investigators solve crimes. Expert examiners can match the marks left on bullets or on the shell casings from a gun and tell if two bullets came from the same gun. They can fire a bullet from a suspect's gun and compare the results to a bullet from the crime scene, or they can tell if two bullets from the crime scene have come from the same gun. As in the Washington sniper shootings, they can also tell if bullets from different crimes came from the same gun.

This paraphrase recasts the original text in the reader's own words. By paraphrasing, the reader clarified the meaning, aiding both comprehension and memory. The paraphrase is about the same length as the original (ninety words, compared to eighty-nine words in the original). Paraphrases sometimes are noticeably longer than the originals, especially when you translate complex ideas into everyday language.

Summarizing

Summarizing boils a text down to its essence. A *summary* notes the important highlights, but it does not include examples, anecdotes, digressions, or elaborations that enliven or illustrate the writing. Most summaries are significantly shorter than the originals, perhaps a third or a fourth of the original length.

To write a good summary, you have to distinguish between the essential points and the nonessential points. Underlining or highlighting the topic sentence of each paragraph is a good way to begin writing a summary. Alternatively, you can make a quick outline, extracting the main point of each paragraph. As you write the summary, however, be sure to provide clear transitions so that the logic of the original piece is reflected.

A summary, like a paraphrase, should be in your own words. Put any material taken directly from the original text in quotation marks. Maintain the integrity of the original text. Do not change the intended meaning, interpret the text, or add your own opinions to a summary. The following paragraph summarizes the first two paragraphs of the Dupree piece about ballistics.

> Investigators use ballistics to help solve crimes. They can match the marks on a bullet or shell casing to a gun and determine if two bullets were fired from the same gun even in different crimes, as in the Washington shootings. Investigators use a double microscope to match bullets or shell casings from the same gun.

This summary reduces two paragraphs to one. It contains 56 words; the original contains 183. The summary provides the big picture, not a close-up.

Practice 2.1   Underlining, Paraphrasing, Summarizing

The rest of the Dupree article is reprinted below. Read it, and do the following.

1. Underline the key words and concepts.
2. Paraphrase the first paragraph in this excerpt.
3. Summarize the entire excerpt, including the first two paragraphs.

Then comes a more painstaking task: matching two rounds to the same weapon, based on the smaller marks left by microscopic imperfections in the gun's mechanisms. Individual lines inside the rifling grooves are one clue. "It's not unlike the lines left by a knife when cutting hard cheese," says John Nixon, ballistics expert at Athena Research and Consulting in Indiana. Because the markings appear different depending on viewing angle and lighting, Nixon says, there are "an infinite number of permutations." . . .

Besides comparing bullets and shells one by one, ballistics investigators can consult a national database. About 235 police departments are equipped with $100,000 stations linked to the National Integrated Ballistics Information Network, which stores the markings on bullets and shell casings as electronic signatures. It includes only ballistics data from crimes, although gun control advocates want firearms makers to test-fire all new weapons and deposit the data in the national system along with the weapons' serial number. But the 1968 federal Gun Control Act blocked any national gun registry, and the National Rifle Association opposes changing the law. States, however, can require gun makers to provide test-fired samples from new weapons. So far, only two have done so: New York and Maryland.

Annotation and Marginal Notes

Annotations are the marks you make on a piece of writing: underlining, high-lighting, bracketing, boxing, starring, numbering, drawing arrows between points, putting check marks in the margin. As you read, annotating aids your comprehension of the material, and it saves you time when you review the material later. You can productively annotate most texts by creating your own set of lines, boxes, or stars. Here is one system of marks.

✳ Star the overall point (thesis) of the piece.

Underline the topic sentence (main point) of each paragraph.

Next to each paragraph summarize | *Summarize*
its main point in a phrase or two.

Box the evidence that supports each topic sentence.

Put a wavy line under the conclusion.

Some readers use colored pencils, marking different elements in different colors.

You can annotate at any time in your reading and research, but annotating as you first read a text has the advantage of recording immediate impressions and keeping you alert and interactive. You cannot fall asleep—at least nodding off is more difficult—when your mind is engaged and you are marking the text in the systematic way you have devised. It is also useful to go back to a text and look for different elements on a second or third reading. For example, the first time through you might underline unfamiliar words or put question marks next to confusing passages. The second time you might mark main and supporting points to highlight the writer's argument and organization.

As you annotate, also make marginal notes, calling attention to and defining the points that the annotations mark. Interact with the text by writing questions, comments, and other responses. A "huh?" in the margin will remind you to go back and reread a confusing passage. Have a conversation, even if it is one-sided, with the writer.

Outlining or Clustering

Outlining, which you probably learned as a way to organize your thoughts before or during the writing process, is a useful reading strategy as well. By outlining a reading, you create a map of the writer's thinking, which helps you understand the main points and notice any detours or dead ends in the writer's thinking. More importantly, an outline reveals the writer's principles of division, that is, how the writer breaks down the topic into categories.

An alternate way to understand a writer's thinking is to create a visual map: a **cluster** or a word web. Put the writer's main point in the middle of a page, circle it, and as you read, take notes radiating out from this central idea. After you draw lines to show the relationship of the ideas to one another, you have created a visual map of the key ideas in a text. People who are visual thinkers often favor this strategy over outlining. (The technique of clustering is explained and illustrated in more detail on pages 11–12.)

Outlines of readings tend to be informal, quick sketches. Even if you do not produce an outline with Roman numerals and capital and lowercase letters, be sure to organize the outline so that you can visualize the relationships of ideas.

▶ Put bibliographic information (author, title, place of publication, publisher, date) at the top of your outline, so you will be able to find the original source.

▶ Begin the outline with the main point or thesis statement. If you cannot find a sentence in the text that presents the specific point, use your own words to summarize the main point.

▶ Link elements of the same importance (main points, supporting points) visually by aligning them in similar ways. Use numbers, bullet points, or indentations to show which ideas have similar weight.

▶ Be selective. As with a summary, the idea is to reduce a great deal of information to its essential points. You are creating an outline or sketch, not an oil painting.

Read Charles Fishman's essay, "Mighty Mice" (pages 96–97), and then read this student outline.

Title: "Mighty Mice" by Charles Fishman, *Fast Company Magazine*, June 2001, p. 147.

Thesis: Lab mice are indispensable in research.

1. Useful
Small and easy to care for
Reproduce quickly
Similar genes to humans

2. Long history in cancer research
Used by Clarence Cook Little when a student at Harvard
Little became president of U of Maine and Michigan
Founded Jackson Labs in Maine

3. Other medical research
Helped discover penicillin
Helped create vaccines (polio, rabies)
Helped understanding of human immune system

4. "Mice are big business"
Market for research mice more than $200 million a year
Human genome research will make more demand
Other research: Alzheimer's, AIDS, MS, cancer

This outline offers an overview of Fishman's main and subordinate points and the organization of his essay. As a reader, you can see the logic behind the writer's thinking. To prove his thesis that mice are indispensable in research, Fishman explains how they are useful in research, what their history is, and how they function in medical research and business. This brief overview also allows you to see what Fishman does not address, such as the ethics of animal research and the specifics of how the mice are used in experiments.

ANALYZING AND SYNTHESIZING

Analysis and synthesis can help you understand a piece of writing on a deeper level. When you analyze a text, you break it down into its component parts, which you can then examine more closely. Synthesis helps you connect the parts with other information to form generalizations or conclusions about the work.

Analysis

Analysis occurs on many levels when you read. You can analyze a writer's style by breaking it down into its component parts: vocabulary, sentence structure, grammar, and figurative language, for example. You can analyze the organization of a text, looking at how the writer structured the piece: chronologically, by order of importance, or by reasons that support an argument. In each kind of analysis, you have to decide on the principle behind the division. What categories can you use to divide a work into its parts? Often, you can find many possibilities.

Different kinds of materials require different criteria for analysis. You might analyze a memoir, for example, by looking at the narrative elements of character, setting, conflict, plot, and theme. On the other hand, you would analyze an editorial or argumentative essay by focusing on the individual points that support the argument and the kinds of evidence (facts, statistics, anecdotes, and examples) used to illustrate each point. You might analyze a photograph, a painting, or an ad in purely visual terms: how do the colors, shapes, or images create meaning?

Practice 2.2
Annotation and Outlining

1. Read one of these student application essays in Chapter 4.
   • "Smoke" by Jessica Polanski (page 118)
   • "That Other Part" by Nitya K. Venkataraman (pages 129–131)
   • "An American's Freedom to Choose" by Katie Robbins (pages 127–129)
   • "Yo Hablo Español" by Alexander Greene (on the website)

2. Annotate the essay by
   • Bracketing the introduction
   • Underlining the main point
   • Circling the topic sentences in each paragraph
   • Boxing supporting examples and anecdotes
   • Drawing an arrow between the main point and its support
   • Noting in the margin any questions or strong responses you have

3. Create a quick outline or word web of this essay.

Practice 2.3
Deciding on Principles of Division for Analysis

Decide on a principle you might use to divide each of the topics below for analysis. For example, to analyze a photograph, you might divide it into technical elements (composition), aesthetic elements (balance and harmony), and narrative elements (story and theme).

1. A cartoon
2. A novel
3. An advertisement
4. A textbook
5. A painting

**Practice 2.4
Analyzing Words
and Images**

1. Choose any short essay in
   Chapter 3 or Chapter 4 for
   analysis. Read it carefully,
   and answer the general
   questions about analyzing
   readings on this page.

2. Write a sentence that
   draws a conclusion about
   the essay's meaning.

3. Choose any image in this
   chapter. Look at it carefully,
   and answer the general
   questions about analyzing
   images on page 56.

4. Write a sentence that
   draws a conclusion about
   the meaning of this image.

The photo to the right
is composed of tiny
color dots. In the image
on the facing page,
the dots are greatly
enlarged. Distance
creates clarity—try
looking at the large-
dot image from across
a room.

Following are some general questions you might ask as you analyze
a reading.

- ▶ What expectations does the title set up for you about the reading's
  main focus?

- ▶ What is the intended audience for this reading? What clues suggest a
  particular audience?

- ▶ How does the writer introduce the material? Does the writer begin with
  a direct statement of the topic, for example, or an interesting quotation
  or story?

- ▶ What tone does the writer set in the opening paragraph? Can you detect irony, wit, anger, seriousness, outrage, or any other tone that would
  help you understand the writer's intention?

- ▶ Where does the writer announce the main point of the reading? Does
  the main point flow clearly from the introduction?

- ▶ How does the writer support or illustrate the main point? Does the support connect directly back to the main point?

- ▶ How does the writer conclude the reading? What image, quotation,
  point, or impression does the writer leave with the reader?

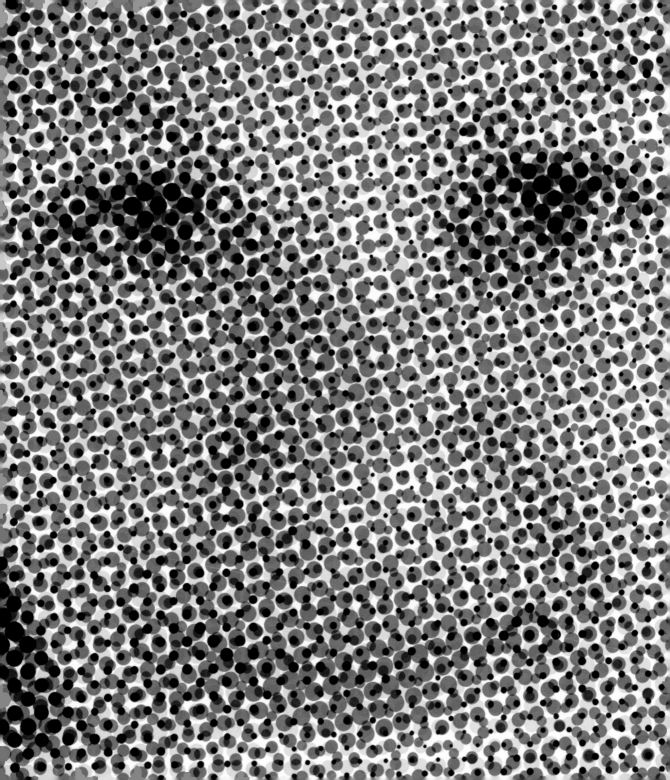

Nelson Mandela, South African leader, Nobel Peace Prize winner, and anti-apartheid activist.

Following are some general questions you might ask as you analyze an image.

▸ What kind of image is it: a photograph, painting, portrait, or computer-designed image?

▸ Where would you find this image? For what reason is it in public view? For example, is it for entertainment, information, self-expression, or sales?

▸ Where is your eye first drawn? What has the artist done to move your eye to this focal point?

▸ What tone or mood is created by the image? What elements in the image (line, color, shape, texture) create this mood?

▸ Does the image make you feel a new way about the subject? If the image is new to you, what impression does it create?

In the 2001 movie *Jurassic Park III*, actors were filmed against a simple backdrop. Later, artists created computer-generated images of a digital matte painting establishing a steep canyon.

Practice 2.5
Writing a Synthesis Sentence

Read either a set of essays or a set of film reviews, write summaries, and write a synthesis sentence.

1. Read the essays by Anne LaMott, Stephen King, and Caitlin Reynolds in Chapter 1. Choose one of these essays to consider in relation to the others.

   a. Read the essays carefully, underlining and annotating their main points.

   b. Write a sentence for each essay that summarizes its main points.

   c. Write a sentence that synthesizes the main point of one essay with the main points of the other two essays.

2. Read the two reviews of the film *Fight Club* printed in Chapter 11 (pages 399–404). Choose one of these reviews to consider in relation to the other.

   a. Read the reviews carefully, underlining and annotating their main points.

   b. Write a sentence for each review that summarizes its main points.

   c. Write a sentence that synthesizes the two reviews.

   d. If you have seen this film, add a sentence that draws a conclusion about the film from your own perspective

The purpose of analysis is to gain a clearer understanding of the individual parts so that you better understand the composition and meaning of the whole. Often, analysis leads you to make connections and uncover assumptions you might not understand or see on a first reading or a first viewing.

Synthesis

Synthesis helps you pull together information from different sources as well as integrate previously learned information with new information. This combination of old and new material may lead to original insights into the work. For example, perhaps you are a Quentin Tarantino fan and are reviewing *Kill Bill, Volume II*. Having seen *Reservoir Dogs*, *Pulp Fiction*, and *Kill Bill, Volume I*, you know that Tarantino's tone is often ironic; his characters are often larger-than-life caricatures; and stylized violence permeates his films. Knowing this, you can see how Tarantino reprises these themes in *Kill Bill* and where he deviates from them. By synthesizing what you know about the director with your insights into the film, you may come up with fresh insights and new conclusions.

Synthesis also occurs when you read many sources on the same topic, perhaps as research for an argumentative essay or editorial. As you read different views, you begin to notice patterns of thinking. By synthesizing the information you read, you build an understanding of the relationships among the ideas, deciding which you agree with, which you might challenge, which you might use to support your arguments, and which you will refute.

Here are some questions to ask as you pull together ideas from different sources.

▸ Where are the points of similarity? What main points about the topic appear in all or most of the readings?

▸ Where are the points of dissimilarity? Where do the writers disagree about the topic?

▸ What kind of interpretations do different writers present? For example, is one writer exploring a topic from a psychological angle and another from a historical or literary point of view?

▸ What aspects of the topic do different writers focus on? Is one writer looking at causes and another at effects? Is the writer identifying a problem, proposing a solution, or both?

Practice 2.7 Metaphor

Create a metaphor or simile for a person you see often: a bus driver, a cafeteria worker, a security guard, a dog walker, a professor. Use the metaphor to reveal your bias toward this person.

Example: My boss scuttled across the floor, his antenna alert for any fun we might be having.

Practice 2.8 Annotating Ironic and Figurative Language

Read the passages below, and underline the figurative language. In the margin write what that figure of speech suggests or implies. Next, bracket any passage that uses irony. In the margin write "irony," and explain what the author intends you to understand.

1. I was born in Tijuana, to a Mexican father and an American mother. I was registered with the U.S. government as an American Citizen, Born Abroad. Raised in San Diego, I crossed the border all through my boyhood with abandon, utterly bilingual and bicultural. In 1977, my father died on the border, violently.

   In the Borderlands, anything can happen. And if you're in Tijuana long enough, anything will happen. Whole neighborhoods appear and disappear seemingly overnight. For example, when I was a boy, you got into Tijuana by driving through the Tijuana River itself. It was a muddy floodplain bustling with animals and belching old cars. A slum that spread across the riverbed was known as "Cartolandia." In border-speak, this meant "Land of Cardboard."

   Suddenly, it was time for Tijuana to spruce up its image to attract more American dollars, and Cartolandia was swept away by a flash flood of tractors. The big machines swept down the length of the river, crushing shacks and toppling fences. It was like magic. One week, there were choked multitudes of sheds; the next, a clear, flat space awaiting the blank concrete of a flood channel. Town—no town.

   —Luis Alberto Urrea, *Across the Wire: Life and Hard Times*

2. Whew! Californians can rest easy these days, secure in the knowledge that the Justice Department has mobilized a crack team of enforcers to protect them from the danger in their midst. The Bush administration has instructed federal agents in the state to weed out a secret society of lawbreakers whose malfeasance is particularly insidious because they look so ordinary. They look like grandmas and promising young men and moms and dads and the girl next door. And they look like that because that's who they are.

   But the ones the feds are going after are sick. Not like "California sickos" (now that would be a project for the government to tackle), but sick as in cancerous, as in AIDS-afflicted. Sick as in throwing up after every bite, shaking, crying, painful chemo death-wish sick. The only thing that relieves their suffering—and there's precious little argument on this—is marijuana. A few puffs can bring blessed relief. It can mean a respite from pain, a meal digested.

   —Dianne Donovan, "Feds Are Busting the Wrong 'Drug Ring'"

3. For nearly a year, I sopped around the house, the Store, the school and the church, like an old biscuit, dirty and inedible. Then, I met, or rather got to know, the lady who threw me my first life line.

   Mrs. Bertha Flowers was the aristocrat of Black Stamps. She had the grace of control to appear warm in the coldest weather, and on the Arkansas summer days it seemed she had a private breeze, which swirled around, cooling her. She was thin without the taut look of wiry people, and her printed voile dresses and flowered hats were as right for her as denim overalls for a farmer. She was our side's answer to the richest white woman in town.

Her skin was a rich black that would have peeled like a plum if snagged, but then no one would have though of getting close enough to Mrs. Flowers to ruffle her dress, let alone snag her skin. She didn't encourage familiarity. She wore gloves too.   —Maya Angelou, I Know Why the Caged Bird Sings

4. Biff has a short, tight coat of fox-colored fur, white feet and ankles, and a patch of white on his chest roughly the shape of Maine. His muscles are plainly sketched under his skin, but he isn't bulgy. His face is turned up and pushed in, and has a dark mask, spongy lips, a wishbone-shaped white blaze, and the earnest and slightly careworn expression of a small-town mayor. Someone once told me that he thought Biff looked a little bit like President Clinton. Biff's face is his fortune. There are plenty of people who like boxers with bigger bones and a stockier body and taller shoulders—boxers who look less like marathon runners and more like weight lifters—but almost everyone agrees that Biff has a nearly perfect head.   —Susan Orlean, "Show Dog"

5. Once upon a time, a long time ago, a small miracle took place in the brain of a man named Solomon Linda. It was 1939, and he was standing in front of a microphone in the only recording studio in black Africa when it happened. He hadn't composed the melody or written it down or anything. He just opened his mouth and out it came, a haunting skein of fifteen notes that flowed down the wires and into a trembling stylus that cut tiny grooves into a spinning block of beeswax, which was taken to England and turned into a record that became a very big hit in that part of Africa.

Later, the song took flight and landed in America, where it mutated into a truly immortal pop epiphany that soared to the top of the charts here and then everywhere, again and again, returning every decade or so under different names and guises. . . .

Its epic transcultural saga is also, in a way, the story of popular music, which limped, pale-skinned and anemic, into the twentieth century but danced out the other side vastly invigorated by transfusions of ragtime and rap, jazz, blues and soul, all of whose bloodlines run back to Africa via slave ships and plantations and ghettos. It was in the nature of this transaction that black men gave more than they got and often ended up with nothing.

—Rian Malan, "In the Jungle"

6. The Apprentice, the NBC reality show starring Donald Trump as God, is the greatest show in the country, and maybe in the entire world, and, as I sit watching it in my spectacular apartment, just steps from legendary Amsterdam Avenue, the most desirable address in Manhattan, I feel that I am living out the American dream, and that writing about the show is the job of a lifetime, and will, if I work at it hard enough, make me a billionaire someday.

Well, maybe not. But this is the line of goods that Trump sells, and it seems that the sixteen contestants on the show, who are vying to win a job as the president of his companies, can't buy enough of it.   —Nancy Franklin, "American Idol"

Writers use various other types of figures of speech to imply meaning.

A simile is an explicit comparison between two unlike things using *as* or *like*:

> Now he would prowl the stacks of the library at night, pulling books out of a thousand stacks and reading them like a madman. . . . He pictured himself as tearing the entrails from a book as from a fowl.
>
> —Thomas Wolfe, *Of Time and the River*

Personification gives human qualities to nonhuman things:

> The mountains *glowered* in the distance.

Hyperbole is intentional overstatement:

> It would take us *forever* to climb the peak.

DISTINGUISHING FACT FROM OPINION

When someone begins a sentence with "It's a fact that" often what follows is an opinion, not a fact at all. "It's a fact that Dino's is the coolest club in town" is a fact only if you are talking about room temperature and have literally checked the temperature of every nightspot in the area.

Facts provide information that can be checked and definitively proved to be true not just once but repeatedly. That Saddam Hussein, the former leader of Iraq, was found hiding in a spider hole on December 14, 2003, is a fact. That the boiling point of water is 212 degrees Fahrenheit is a fact. That the planets revolve around the sun is a fact.

Opinions are subjective. They present a person's perspective, and they can change not just from person to person but also within the same person. That Saddam Hussein was the most evil despot in history is an opinion. That you should drink green tea made only with freshly boiled water is an opinion. That a person's astrological sign could control his or her personality and destiny on a day-to-day basis is an opinion as well.

Distinguishing fact from opinion is not as easy as it may seem, in part because writers often intermix the two, blurring the line between what is an indisputable fact and what is a subjective opinion. For example, if you wrote, "Saddam Hussein, the most evil despot in history, was found in a spider hole on December 14, 2003," you would be inserting your opinion into a fact.

Understanding the difference between fact and opinion allows you to see when opinion masquerades as fact and to hold writers accountable for clear and logical thinking. In your own writing, be careful not to blur the line between opinion and fact. Report writing (observation reports, lab reports, news reports, business reports) requires you to maintain as much objectivity as possible. You have to present facts—what you can verify

Did President Lyndon Baines Johnson really place a medal around the neck of Forrest Gump (Tom Hanks)? This shot from the 1994 film *Forrest Gump* shows how easily computer-graphics artists can manipulate digital images.

through your own observations or through research—and present opinions only in quotations from experts, participants, or observers. (See Chapter 6.)

DETERMINING THE BIAS OF SOURCES

A great deal of your reading requires you to extract information from sources. But not all sources are credible or reliable; some are biased, expressing only one side of an issue. Some information is misleading; some is just plain wrong; and some writers have agendas and want to convince you to believe as they do.

How do you know whether sources are credible and provide a balanced view, or if they are trying to manipulate you to believe their perspective? Sometimes it is obvious. A writer who represents a national tire company is going to have a different slant on tire safety than a writer representing a consumer advocacy group. Other times bias is more difficult to detect. For example, political campaigns now produce videos that look and sound like news reports, although the issues are clearly slanted toward the political views of

Practice 2.9 Distinguishing Fact from Opinion

Decide which of the following sentences present facts (F), which present opinions (O), and which intermix facts and opinions (F & O). Choose two sentences that intermix facts and opinions, and rewrite them to make them completely factual.

1. Noam Chomsky's lecture, "Iraq and U.S. Foreign Policy," drew an enthusiastic crowd to the student union last night.

2. The price to attend, a $10 donation, was not a problem for supporters.

3. Over two hundred college women attended sorority rush this year.

4. Many were unhappy when they arrived at noon on Saturday only to receive a blank sheet of paper that should have listed six sororities.

5. Jamnesty is a yearly event that raises money for an Amnesty International letter-writing campaign.

6. While enjoying music, eating delicious free cookies, drinking punch, and glancing at artwork, students strolled happily and received interesting information about many campus organizations.

7. After last night's hockey game, which the team lost 0 to 6, senior captain Scott Gomes argued with head coach Don Webster.

8. "Gomes told Coach that he should tell the players to keep their heads up," said teammate Joe Friendly, who witnessed the exchange.

9. Coach sarcastically retorted, "If you know so much, you should coach the game."

10. The argument dealt a serious blow to the team's ongoing struggle for unity and improved morale.

the candidate. In this and in all cases, it is important to be skeptical and consider the source.

You can go a long way toward determining whether a source is distorted by bias by researching the writer's background and the type of publication.

Writer's Background and Publication Type

▶ Can you assess the writer's expertise by looking at the writer's degrees or affiliations? What is the writer's profession? What else has the writer published?

▶ Can you tell whether the writer has a vested interest in this topic? Does the writer work for an organization that has a vested interest in the topic?

▶ Who published this information? Does it appear in a well-known journal, magazine, website, or newspaper? In a book published by a mainstream publishing house or university press? Is it self-published on a website?

Practice 2.10
Detecting a Source's Bias

Read the editorial "The 'Quota' Cry Doesn't Faze Me'" by Cynthia Tucker and the letter to the editor "Economic Status, Not Race, Should Be the Basis of College Admissions" (pages 245–247). These two pieces present different views of the 2003 Supreme Court decision to allow race to be a factor in college admissions.

1. What facts or details establish each writer's credibility? What research could you do to find out more?

2. What are the writer's biases? How do you know?

3. How fairly does each writer present his or her point of view?

4. What, if anything, detracts from the fairness of either piece?

▶ When was this information published? Is it recent?

▶ Is the work a classic in its field? Have any significant knowledge, discoveries, and theories been added to the field since it was published? (You can figure out the answer to these questions, in part, by reading other bibliographies in the same field and noting how often the source is cited and which other sources are most often cited.)

▶ What sources does this work cite? What is listed in its bibliography? Are these sources ones you have read about in other works?

The Way the Material Is Written

▶ Does the writer disclose a particular bias?

▶ Does the writer fairly present other viewpoints or conflicting information?

▶ Does the writer ridicule other points of view or attack people who disagree?

▶ Is the writer's thinking illogical or careless? (See pages 229–231 for more in-depth discussion of logical fallacies.)

▶ Does the writer furnish clear explanations and supporting evidence for his or her bias?

You can always use a writer's bias to understand one side of an issue as long as you understand where that writer is coming from—what assumptions and values the writer expresses.

ASSIGNMENTS

PART II

3. SHORT ARTICLES

WRITING EXPOSITION

I have made this letter longer than usual, only because I have not had the time to make it shorter.

—Blaise Pascal, *Lettres Provinciales* (1657)

ASSIGNMENT

Write a short expository (explanatory) article, one to three pages in length, that is appropriate for a magazine, website, newspaper, or newsletter. The article should explain one of the following.

- An idea
- A process
- An event
- A person
- A place

For ideas about possible topics, read the Writer's Notebook suggestions at the end of this chapter.

One image from a Pulitzer Prize–winning photo essay about teen stowaways on trains in Central America.

SHORT ARTICLES

Why is the sky blue? How deep is the ocean? Starting when you were very small, you have wanted the answers to hundreds of questions. You have asked for explanations not just of natural phenomena like the color of the sky and the depth of the oceans but also about made objects: how things are put together, how they work, what they are used for.

This curiosity about the world is reflected in the thousands of explanatory articles written every year. Pick up any magazine or newspaper, and you will find short expository articles that provide clear and brief explanations. These articles appear in all kinds of publications, and they make up most of the writing you find on the World Wide Web. They explain ideas, processes, events, people, and places. Some short articles, called sidebars, run as companions to longer pieces. A sidebar acts like a magnifying glass, offering a very close look at one aspect of a story, an aspect that most people might not know much about but that might interest them.

You might be surprised to learn that you have already written hundreds of these short articles in your career as a student. You may have explained the Coriolis effect in an earth science class, compared the British Parliament to the U. S. Congress for political science, or described the dyeing and weaving techniques of the Pueblo Indians for anthropology. In each case, you explained something in order to illustrate and communicate your knowledge of the subject.

Though they are brief, ranging from 100 to 750 words, these articles are not easy to write. As the Pascal quotation that opens this chapter implies, writing something short can be more of a challenge than writing something long. To write a short piece, you have to know the subject well enough to select only the most important details, and you have to organize your ideas into a concise, logical structure. Your focus must be laser-sharp.

Applications: School, Community, Work

Understanding how to organize and explain specific aspects of a subject can be useful to you in many college classes. On an exam, for example, you will often be asked to show your understanding of a topic by writing a short-essay answer. You might be asked to write a short article on a trend in society, the effects of a discovery, the explanation of a natural phenomenon, the

The Role of Captions

Look at the photos in this photo essay that begins with the chapter opener and continues in the images below. How are the images linked? How do they explain the experience of teenage stowaways on trains? Write a caption of three or four sentences for this essay. In your caption, try to capture the essence of the images as you interpret them. Then turn to the last page of the chapter, and read a caption that might go with the essay. Compare your impression of the photo essay and the impression that the caption imposes on the picture. What information is essential to add to photographs to complete the essay?

steps in a scientific process, or the definition of a term of social, scientific, or literary significance. No doubt, you have written many expository essays in your career as a student. The expository essay is quite similar to the expository article, although the essay usually combines explanation with a personal or philosophical perspective. As you can see, exposition is a useful skill to master as you write for school.

In community groups and workplaces, your skills at writing short articles might come in handy in several ways. A group might need a short, informative article describing itself and its activities for inclusion in brochures, fundraising letters, or newsletters. In the workplace, you might be called upon to write clear, concise directions for a process or to explain a course of action or a new policy or procedure.

Most informative websites are composed entirely of explanatory articles short enough to fill one screen without requiring the reader to scroll. The skills you learn in this chapter will help you write for a school, work, or personal website. You can combine your skills at writing short articles with the skills of planning and designing a website discussed in Chapter 10.

CHAPTER OBJECTIVES

In this chapter you will learn to

▶ create a clear thesis for a short article

▶ develop explanatory paragraphs using a variety of strategies: examples, illustrations, description, narration, definition, process analysis, comparison, classification, and cause and effect

▶ explain information clearly and concisely

UNDERSTANDING SHORT ARTICLES

Short expository articles reveal your command of the subject matter. Your readers expect to discover new information or new insights. As a writer of a short expository article for school, work, or publication, you take on the role of a teacher. Readers should know that they are in good hands, that you will inform them of your main point, and that the information will be interesting and perhaps even useful. In making your writing appeal to readers, the first steps are (1) to make sure your article has a thesis and focus and (2) to make sure you have an effective strategy mapped out for the clear development of that thesis.

Focus: The Explanatory Thesis

The thesis is your focus—the main point you want to make—stated explicitly and succinctly near the article's beginning. In a short article, the thesis could be a fact or a point that you are going to explain or elaborate on. It could go beyond simply stating a fact, presenting your interpretation of or theory about the topic. In either case, the thesis tells your reader what your piece will be about, and the rest of the article flows from this point.

As you settle on a topic, focus on an aspect of it, and develop your thesis or main point, consider the following guidelines. A good thesis is

▶ Substantive and sometimes arguable (not self-evident, overly obvious, and known by all)

▶ Neither too broad nor too narrow to be presented in the relatively brief scope of your short article

▶ Supportable by facts, statistics, details, testimony, evidence, anecdotes, or examples in the body of the paper

▶ Interesting and engaging to your audience

For example, a short article in the Readings section at the end of this chapter (pages 97–98) tells how mathematical models have been used to prove that *Tyrannosaurus rex* dinosaurs might have been slow runners. After asking, "Could it be the tyrant dinosaur, *Tyrannosaurus rex* was not the king killer we see in the movies?" the author states his thesis.

> New research hints that smaller, quicker creatures might have had the edge on the hulking dinosaurs.
>
> —Jeff Aaron, "*Tyrannosaurus rex:* No Longer King of Killers?"

If the writer does what he promises in this thesis, the rest of the article will lay out the new research and explain how the smaller creatures might have been more powerful than gigantic *T. rex.* The thesis does not just state a fact; it also poses a theory. The reader will want a good explanation about how smaller creatures might have "had the edge." The thesis sets out a promise to the reader that the rest of the short article delivers on.

Another short article in the Reading section (pages 94–95) explains the evidence that investigators can gather by examining bullets from crime scenes. This article's thesis sets out the general idea that the rest of the article will need to explain.

> Investigators have a tragic abundance of one kind of clue: "ballistic fingerprints," the scratches, dimples, bumps, and grooves that a gun leaves on a bullet and its shell casing. Like human fingerprinting, ballistics is all about matching: determining whether two rounds came from the same gun.
>
> —Janet Rae-Dupree "How Bullets Tell a Tale"

The major work of this thesis is accomplished with the phrase "ballistic fingerprints," which sets up an analogy, a comparison between human fingerprints and the prints a gun leaves on a bullet. Readers probably understand that fingerprints are unique patterns and are usually good evidence. Once stated, the thesis creates questions for the reader. How does this process work? How reliable is the science? The writer's next job is to anticipate and answer these questions.

Practice 3.2
A Thesis and Its Promise

1. Select a selection from the Readings section of this chapter (beginning on page 92), or choose a short explanatory article or sidebar from a magazine, and identify the thesis statement.

2. Write a sentence or two explaining what expectations the thesis sets up for the reading. What promise does it make that the reading then goes on to fulfill? What questions do you expect the reading to answer? Does it answer them?

Take care and time in crafting your thesis. Not only does it alert the reader to your central point, but it also helps you stay focused and organize your thinking.

Strategies for Developing Ideas

Once you have narrowed your focus and homed in on your thesis, consider how best to develop the ideas and support the thesis. Some effective ways to develop short articles include the following.

- ▶ Examples
- ▶ Description
- ▶ Narration (storytelling)
- ▶ Definition
- ▶ Process analysis
- ▶ Comparison and/or contrast
- ▶ Classification
- ▶ Causes and/or effects

Which development strategy should you choose? Your choice depends on what you are trying to accomplish in the article, what you discover in your research, and whom you have identified as your targeted audience. If you were writing about the Grand Canyon, for example, for a science class or a science publication, you might want to explain the process of the formation of canyons. For a travel article, you might decide instead to tell the story of your trip to the Grand Canyon, explaining the canyon from a visitor's perspective.

You might also combine a number of strategies in a single article. For an article about the history of jazz, you might define the musical genre in the first paragraph, tell the story of the first jazz performance in the second paragraph, and compare jazz to other musical genres like the blues, for example, in the third paragraph. As you read through the following information on each development strategy, think of the strategy as a possible way to develop an entire article as well as to develop an individual paragraph.

Examples Just as the thesis statement announces the topic and focus of your short article, the **topic sentences** announce—in general terms—the subjects of your paragraphs. Most paragraphs begin with clear topic sentences that provide overviews but often need to be supported by specifics. Perhaps the most common way to develop a topic sentences is to provide one or more examples.

Generalizations do not stick in a reader's mind the way specific examples can. You know the truth of this statement if you have ever remembered a

Practice 3.3
Using Examples
Develop one of the following
topic sentences for a short
expository article by giving
one or more examples.

• Applying to college is labor-
intensive.

• Recent films have been
innovative (or predictable).

• Small classes allow for
more (or less) student
participation.

• Large classes create more
(or fewer) opportunities
for class discussion.

• Contemporary music
expresses a variety of
emotions.

specific example from a lecture or book but cannot quite recall what point the example was illustrating. Presenting examples allows you to make your meaning clear. Using examples also forces you to refine your own thinking. If you cannot find an example, you probably have to think more or do further research about your idea.

The following paragraph is from a short article on bar codes. The first sentence is the topic sentence of the paragraph and sets up the general idea that bar codes are versatile and important ("Killer apps" is short for killer applications). The paragraph then uses a number of examples to support the topic sentence.

> The bar code is one of the killer apps of the digital economy. More than a million companies worldwide use the familiar UPC (Universal Product Code) symbols to identify consumer products. But the UPC symbol is just a subset of a much wider world of bar codes that are used for all kinds of identification and inventory control. FedEx, UPS, and the U.S. Postal Service use proprietary bar codes to move mail and parcels. NASA uses bar codes on the back of the heat-resistant tiles of its space shuttles to make sure the right tiles get in the right places. Researchers use tiny bar codes to track bees in and out of hives.
>
> —Charles Fishman, "Bar None"

Keep your reader in mind as you develop paragraphs by giving examples. Cue them in to your thinking by providing clear **transitions.** Words and phrases like *for example,* and *for instance* set up the reader's expectation that you are providing examples. In "Bar None," Fishman uses another useful transitional device, parallel structure, to signal transitions. Notice how he uses the exact same sentence structure for each example ("FedEx, UPS, and the U.S. Postal Service use"; "NASA uses"; "Researchers use").

Description   Describing a place or a person allows you to develop your point and at the same time add some color to your writing. Description requires close attention to sensory details: sights, sounds, scents, and textures. Well-written description—details that enhance a particular mood, for example— adds interest to your article. Through description, you can give your reader a better understanding of the physical qualities of your subject.

Sidebars that accompany a newspaper article about the architectural history of New England explain ten different house styles, describing some unique features of each. Note the description in this sidebar about the Queen Anne Victorian, a house style in use between 1870 and 1910.

> The most popular of the several Victorian styles, it is easily recognized by its turrets, elaborate wrap-around porches, and decorative shingles. Victorian architecture was a romantic rebellion against classical symmetry,

so doors, windows, porches, and towers were all deliberately off center. Renewed appreciation of the artisanship of this style has transformed the region's many surviving Queen Annes from tattered white elephants into lovingly restored and often wildly painted showpieces.

—Carol Stocker, "House Styles of New England"

Even if you never knew what a Queen Anne Victorian house looked like, this description of its architectural features—"turrets, elaborate wrap-around porches, and decorative shingles"—would help you recognize it. Stocker also draws your attention to the off-centered placement of doors, windows, and porches. The paragraph includes enough descriptive details to help you recognize a Queen Anne Victorian-style house when you see one.

Transitions used in descriptive writing vary depending on whether you are describing a person, a place, or a thing. Usually transitions for description draw the reader's attention to some kind of spatial relationship. Some common words and phrases are *next to, above,* and *underneath* for describing scenes. In describing people, writers often focus on a person's appearance from top to bottom: from hair to eyes, to mouth, to body, for example. Other descriptions focus on the most prominent features to the least prominent, or move from the big picture to the small details.

Narration (Storytelling)   Stories grab readers' attention and can help make an abstract or general point unforgettable. Narrative elements such as characters, conflict, surprise, and setting can all bring a short article to life and keep readers absorbed. In the short article on bar codes, for example, the author includes the following background story as he develops his topic, bringing some human interest to the article.

The format for the bar code came to Joe Woodland while he was at the beach in 1949. Woodland, who is now 80, had spent World War II working on the Manhattan Project. After the war, he returned to Drexel University to teach mechanical engineering. While there, a colleague of Woodland's, Bernard Silver, overheard the president of the Food Fair grocery stores appealing to a Drexel dean for help automating the process of grocery checkout. Silver and Woodland started brainstorming ideas.

Several months later, Woodland was vacationing on Miami's South Beach, pondering the problem and considering how Morse code might be used to solve it. Woodland idly stuck his fingers in the sand and pulled them toward him, raking a set of parallel lines that represented a kind of "long form" of dots and dashes. Those lines were the inspiration for the bar-code design that he and Silver ultimately patented.

—Charles Fishman, "Bar None"

**Practice 3.4
Using Description**

Choose one of the topics below, and brainstorm a list of descriptive details using some of your senses: sight, touch, smell, and sound.

• A comfortable room in your home

• An object you can see from where you are now sitting

• A swimming pool

• A computer keyboard

• A teacher, a coach, or a boss

This brief story of the invention of the bar code has many narrative elements: setting (1949, the beach), characters (Woodland and Silver), and surprise (the idle sand drawing that solved a problem). Most readers find stories to be engaging and satisfying ways to learn information.

As you tell a story, the usual transitions signal a time change. *Next, later,* or *a few months ago,* for example, help your reader situate the story in time. Even in the short narrative about the invention of the bar code, the writer breaks from the setting to give some background information and signals this time change with "After the war" and "While there." When he moves the story to a new setting, he does so with the clear transition, "Several months later."

Definition Some short articles are devoted exclusively to defining terms, trends, or phenomena, and many others include a few sentences or a paragraph of definitions. A basic definition puts a word or idea into a recognizable category and then explains how it is like or different from all others in that category. For example, the writer of an editorial defines the term *microcredit* in the first paragraph.

> These small loans, as little as $25, go to the poorest people, mostly women living on $1 a day or less. These loans could protect against terrorism by undermining the poverty that feeds social decay and destruction.
>
> —"Microprogress," *Boston Globe*

The writer puts *microcredit* into an understandable category, "a small loan," and distinguishes it from all other small loans by stipulating that it goes "to the poorest people, mostly women living on $1 a day or less."

If you choose to develop an entire paragraph or article through definition, you can also extend the definition with examples, description, narration, comparison and contrast, or causes and effects, for example. Look at how the following excerpt defines hip-hop music.

> In the early 1970s a musical genre was born in the crime-ridden neighborhoods of the South Bronx. Gifted teenagers with plenty of imagination but little cash began to forge a new style from spare parts. Hip-hop, as it was then known, was a product of pure streetwise ingenuity; extracting rhythms and melodies from existing records and mixing them up with searing poetry chronicling life in the 'hood; hip-hop spilled out of the ghetto.
>
> —"Kurtis Blow Presents: The History of Rap, Vol. 1: The Genesis"

In this excerpt, the writer begins with a narrative, telling the reader a little about hip-hop's history and the people who began to put together this hybrid form of music. Then the writer describes the unique blend of rhythm, melody, poetry, and urban experience that defines hip-hop.

Practice 3.5
Using Narration
Choose one of the topics below, and write a narrative paragraph, using a brief story from your own or someone else's life to support the topic. Be sure to help your reader by providing clear transitions.

• Allergies

• Books

• Music

• Learning to drive

• Exercise

Practice 3.6
Using Definition

In one or two sentences, write your own definition of one of the following words, putting it in its appropriate category and then showing how it is different from all others in that category.

• Techno music
• Cyberspace
• Terrorism
• Indie films
• MOO or MUD

One caution about using definition: try to avoid a lead-in like "According to the *American Heritage Dictionary*" or "Webster says." So many people have used this opener that it has become a cliché.

Process Analysis Process analysis is a natural development strategy for exposition. When you analyze a process, you explain how something works (a computer, a grading system, the electoral college), how something was accomplished (the Russian Revolution, the AIDS cocktail, the passage of Title IX), or how to do something (organize a walkathon, solve an algebraic equation, dissect a frog or a poem).

Process explanations isolate and describe each phase of the process, usually in chronological order, step-by-step. The following short article appeared in *Biography Magazine* as a companion to a profile of Dr. Michael Baden, a forensic pathologist who has written books about his work, most notably *Unnatural Death: Confessions of a Medical Examiner* and *Dead Reckoning: The New Science of Catching Killers*. Baden develops and organizes this article by explaining the process of doing an autopsy.

Most people don't have a To Do list that includes "witness an autopsy"—probably because they think it would be unpleasant. I, on the other hand, have always been intrigued by the procedure. Now that I have observed an autopsy, I can confirm that it's definitely not for the weak of stomach.

For the benefit of readers who are interested, here's what generally happens during a forensic autopsy:

The first step is to photograph the body. Trace evidence such as hair samples and nail scrapings (preserved by paper bags on the hands) are collected, and fingerprints taken. Descriptions of clothing and jewelry are recorded, then the items are removed. The body is laid out on its back on the steel autopsy table, X rays are taken and then the body is cleaned. The next step is to weigh and measure the body, and note any identifying marks (such as tattoos and scars).

The pathologist makes the first incision: from shoulder to shoulder, then straight down the torso to the pelvis. This is called the "Y" incision (though Dr. Baden says his looks more like a "U" with a tail). This provides easy access to all the internal organs, once the rib cage is lifted away. Next, internal organs—lungs, liver, stomach, kidneys, etc.—are removed, examined, and weighed. Tissue and fluid samples are taken for microscopic analysis.

The final step, perhaps the most difficult for a layperson to watch, is the examination of the head. An incision is made in the back of the head, from ear to ear, and the skin is brought forward over the face. An electric saw is used to cut through the skull, and the skullcap is removed. The brain is taken out, examined and weighed.

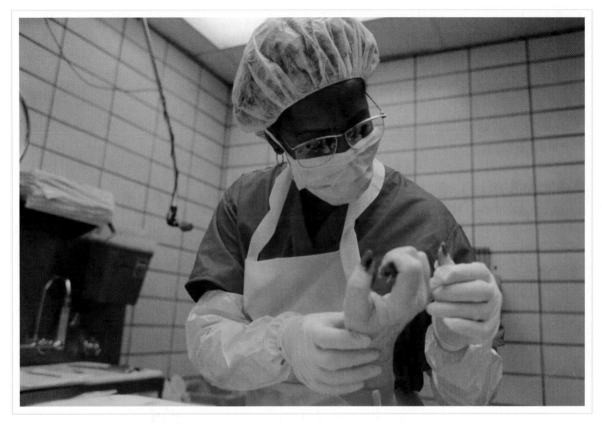

An autopsy in progress.

At this point, any organs that will not be needed for additional study are returned to the body cavity. Then the incisions are closed by the autopsy assistant (called the deiner), which leaves the body presentable for viewing at a funeral service. (The skull incision can't be seen when the head of the deceased is lying on the casket pillow.)

All samples and evidence are sent for laboratory analysis. When results are available (anywhere from several days to several weeks later), the medical examiner presents his final diagnosis in a written report.

—Noreen P. Browne, "Anatomy of an Autopsy"
(© *Biography* magazine, reprinted with permission)

Gruesome though it may be, the process of doing an autopsy fascinates many people, and Browne's description flows clearly from the first step to the last. Notice how she provides clear transitions as she guides her reader through the process: "The first step," "The next step," "The final step." Some writers

Practice 3.7
Using Process Analysis

1. Write a short paragraph about one of the following processes.
   - How to catch a cold
   - How to make an airline reservation
   - How to set up an e-mail account
   - How to diaper a baby
   - How to apply to college
2. Underline your transitions.

also begin with a general overview statement such as "Two ways to" or "You can do this process in six steps."

Comparison and/or Contrast Showing similarities between and among ideas, people, places, or objects can be useful in explaining points to readers and developing the topic of a short article. By comparing an unfamiliar subject to a familiar one, you can help readers gain a context or framework in which to learn about the topic. Similarly, by showing how things differ, you can help readers understand a new or unfamiliar idea.

How do you organize material when comparing two things? The two standard approaches are the block format and the point-by-point format. In the *block format,* you present all information about the first item, then move onto the second. In the *point-by-point format,* you alternate discussion of one item with discussion of the second item.

When you use comparison and/or contrast to develop your paragraphs or whole articles, make sure to lead your reader to a deeper understanding of the topic. It is not sufficient to point out similarities and differences; you also have to interpret them.

Comparison and contrast can be used alone or in combination. In the following excerpt from a short article about American impressionist painters, the author combines the two strategies.

> American impressionists such as John H. Twachtman, Childe Hassam, Theodore Robinson, and Mary Cassatt were influenced by the French painters in the 1890s and into the early 20th century. Like their French counterparts, they were interested in recreating the sensation of light in nature and used intense colors and a similar dab or fleck brushstroke, but they parted with the French painters' *avant garde* approach to form. The French artists rejected painting as a pictorial record of images, and made the details of their subjects dissolve into the painting, leaving the impression of an image rather than a record of an image. American impressionists, on the other hand, took a more conservative approach to representing the details of figures and form. The American artists were interested in capturing the specific subject, not just in representing the idea of a subject.
>
> —Kate Burak, "American Impressionists"

The writer clearly signals the comparison of American and French impressionist painters with the word *Like* in the second sentence. By listing specific concerns of American painters—recreating light in nature, using intense colors—the writer explains some of their similarities to the French painters. The word *but* signals the reversal, the contrast between artists from the two countries: the French painters experiment more with form; the Americans

Practice 3.8
**Using Comparison and/
or Contrast**

Assume that you are writing an article explaining the American educational system to someone from another country. Focus on the difference between high school and college or between elementary school and junior high school.

1. List three or four points of similarity and dissimilarity.

2. Develop one paragraph of comparison and/or contrast.

3. Underline your transitional words and phrases.

are more conservative. The comparison and contrast of French and American artists give the reader a deeper understanding and appreciation of the techniques and philosophy of impressionism, showing how each group of artists interpreted the form from its own national perspective.

When you compare items, use words and phrases like *similarly, like,* and *in the same way.* You can signal contrast, as this writer did, by using *but,* and also by using *however* or *on the other hand.* It is also fine to use the words *compare* and *contrast* to let your reader in on what you are doing. Sometimes the clearest transitions are the most obvious ones.

Classification   You can develop a paragraph or organize an entire piece of writing by dividing your information into mutually exclusive classes. The simplest classification system breaks information down into two categories—animals who eat meat and those who don't eat meat or vertebrates and invertebrates, for example. More complex topics break these categories into smaller subdivisions. A biology essay exam answer about invertebrates might include categories such as protozoa, sponges, jellyfish, flatworms, roundworms, and mollusks.

No matter how many categories you use, however, dividing and classifying information makes complex topics more manageable. Most books, for example, divide information into classifications that are reflected in their tables of contents. Each chapter explains and explores a discrete topic, which is itself often broken down into smaller categories.

Once you create your categories—two or many more—you can explore each category in turn. You could begin an article about kinship by classifying blood relationships: grandparents, parents, siblings, aunts and uncles, and cousins. Or you could classify kinship groups by age, gender, or marital status. Be careful not to create overlapping categories, such as grandparents and married people.

As a strategy for paragraph development, classification is a useful way to organize large amounts of information and provide an overview of what will follow. For example, in the introduction to *The Fourth Genre,* the writers divide and classify literature into the usual three genres: poetry, drama, and fiction. But their purpose is not to explain these three genres; instead they use this classification to define a new "fourth genre": creative nonfiction.

Creative nonfiction is the fourth genre. This assumption, declared in the title of this book, needs a little explaining. Usually literature has been divided into three major genres or types: poetry, drama, and fiction. Poets, dramatists, and novelists might arrange this trio in a different order, but the idea of three literary genres has, until very recently, dominated introductory courses in literature, generic divisions in literature textbooks, and categories of literature in bookstores. Everything that couldn't be classified in one of these genres or some subgenre belonging to them (epic poetry, horror novels) was classified as "nonfiction," even though, as Jocelyn Bartkevicius points out elsewhere in this collection, they could be classified as "nonpoetry" just as well. Unfortunately, this classification system suggests that everything that is nonfiction should also be considered nonliterature, a suggestion that is, well, nonsense.

—Robert L. Root, Jr., and Michael Steinberg, *The Fourth Genre*

The writers begin by setting up their definition of creative nonfiction; then they use division and classification, in an interesting way, to say what creative nonfiction is *not*. This combination of two development strategies—classification and definition—shows how to use these techniques to serve the purpose of your writing. Choose what works for you; develop your ideas as fully and creatively as possible.

You can cue your reader that you are using division and classification by using the words *divide* and *classify* as the writers do in the above passage. You might also want to introduce your ideas in an umbrella statement that includes a list of the categories you will discuss. A statement like "Poetry, drama, and fiction define traditional literature" alerts the reader that you will discuss these three genres. Such transitions help the reader understand how you are developing your ideas.

Causes and/or Effects   Another way to explain and develop concepts is to explore the reasons an event or trend occurred or to discuss its aftereffects. Exploring causes means finding out why something happened; exploring effects means finding out—or sometimes speculating about—what the results will be. Sometimes you can develop an idea by simply explaining causes, or sometimes by explaining effects; often writers use these two strategies in combination.

Cause and effect is a common development strategy for articles that explain science issues such as epidemics and the development of new medicines. College papers for history classes often ask for explanations of causes and effects of wars, of regimes toppling, of political changes, or of election upsets. This excerpt from a historical article about the Great Depression focuses mostly on causes.

The Great Depression was the worst economic slump ever in U.S. history, and one which spread to virtually all of the industrialized world. The depression began in late 1929 and lasted for about a decade. Many factors played a role in bringing about the depression; however, the main cause for the Great Depression was the combination of the greatly unequal

Practice 3.9
Using Classification

1. Work with a partner, and divide the following subjects into mutually exclusive categories: study-abroad programs, computers, films, gyms, relatives, college classes.

2. Make a list of categories you would use when writing about college classes for the following purposes.

   a. A registration pamphlet

   b. A letter home

   c. An article on grade inflation

   d. A source guide written by students to give helpful advice to other students

   e. A humorous editorial for your school or community newspaper

3. Write the introductory paragraph for any one of the five suggested pieces.

Practice 3.10
Using Cause and Effect

1. Choose one of these topics, and make a list of its possible causes.
   - The breakdown of the traditional nuclear family
   - The popularity of a specific musical style
   - The popularity of cell phones

2. Choose one of these topics, and make a list of its possible effects.
   - Cloning humans
   - Prohibiting alcohol on all public college campuses
   - Establishing an effective rapid-transit system for large cities

Practice 3.11
Using Development Strategies
Practice some of the strategies for developing a short article by writing several sentences on one or more of the following topics.

1. Give an example of what a learning disability feels like to someone who has one. Illustrate what the person experiences.

2. Write a short description of an unusual ethnic food that most people have not tried.

3. Write a concise narrative of a historical event in your community. Include character, conflict, and drama.

4. Define a term that many people have heard but do not fully understand, such as *Encryption*, the *infield fly rule*, or *postmodernism*.

5. Explain the process you go through when you dispute a traffic ticket.

6. Compare and/or contrast two college campuses.

distribution of wealth throughout the 1920's, and the extensive stock market speculation that took place during the latter part that same decade. The maldistribution of wealth in the 1920's existed on many levels. Money was distributed disparately between the rich and the middle-class, between industry and agriculture within the United States, and between the U.S. and Europe. This imbalance of wealth created an unstable economy. The excessive speculation in the late 1920's kept the stock market artificially high, but eventually led to large market crashes. These market crashes, combined with the maldistribution of wealth, caused the American economy to capsize.

—Paul A. Gusmorino III, "Main Causes of the Great Depression"

Even though this article explains the main causes of the Great Depression, the writer briefly alludes to the effects in the opening few lines. It was the "worst economic slump ever in U.S. history," and it "spread to virtually all of the industrialized world." These phrases remind the reader of stories about massive unemployment and breadlines caused by the Great Depression.

However, the main focus of the passage is on explaining two causes: the unequal distribution of wealth and speculation in the stock market. The writer introduces these two points at the beginning of the paragraph, then returns to each point and explains it in a bit more depth. Notice that the writer uses a clear transition: "the main cause for the Great Depression was."

RESEARCH PATHS

The more you know about your topic, the more clearly you can explain it to your reader. It is always a good idea to steep yourself in the subject. Gather as much information as you can from books, experts, magazines, and journals as well as from online sources. Sift through the information carefully, making sure that facts and statistics are corroborated by valid research and by other sources.

To begin researching your short article, your first impulse might be to do a quick keyword search on the Internet. Be careful when using this approach. Some websites are less reliable than others, and you can have a difficult time evaluating information if you do not know something about your subject. (See Chapter 14 for more on evaluating sources.) Instead, try finding and reading a range of articles specific to the subject; your reference librarian can help you locate them, or you can do online database searches.

Cast a wide net when you do your research. The best sources for one subject might not be the best sources for another. Using only a dictionary or an encyclopedia for the question about whether a tomato is a fruit or a vegetable, for example, would not lead you to such interesting information as the 1893 Supreme Court ruling that can be found on a website. On the other hand, you might find a website that offers information that contradicts authoritative sources and would thus not be a good source. With Web material, it is best to find at least two sources that agree on information.

When you use sources in your article, be sure to provide clear and accurate attribution. For a short article, you might integrate the source material and the attribution into the text of the article. For example, you might write, "The *Encyclopaedia Britannica* defines tomato as 'any fruit of the numerous cultivated varieties of *Lycopersicon esculentum,* a plant of the nightshade family (Solanaceae); also, the fruit of *L. pimpinelli folium,* the tiny currant tomato.'"

Academic essays call for more complete citation of sources on a Works Cited page. This source from a Works Cited page uses MLA style. (See Chapter 15 for more complete information on how to cite sources.)

"Tomato." Britannica Online. 2003. *Encyclopaedia Britannica.* 4 June 2003 http://www.search.eb.com/eb/article/eu=74730.

Another approach is to talk to people with experience in or knowledge about the subject area. For example, if you were writing a short article about violent video games, a preschool director might have good insights into how children play and socialize, as would a child psychologist or a pediatrician. Any of these experts could most probably direct you to recent articles and research about children and how they are influenced by games, toys, and media.

All writers consult experts, either online, in print, or in person. The care you take with your research and the depth of your exploration of a topic will result in writing that is authoritative and sure.

ANATOMY OF A SHORT ARTICLE

The writer of the following short article first uses two development strategies, narration and description, to introduce an unusual marine phenomenon. She plays with the elements of a mystery story—setting, characters, and plot—to gain the reader's attention and to set up the explanation. She then develops the remainder of the article through an explanation of cause

Practice 3.12   Finding Sources and Integrating Research

1. Choose one of the topics below, and list at least one website, one print source, and one expert you might consult to get information.

- Learning disabilities
- Ethnic food
- A historical event in your community
- Encryption
- The infield fly rule

- Postmodernism
- Disputing a traffic ticket
- Your college campus
- Types of diets
- Adrenaline rushes

2. This year's harvest yielded an abundance of tomatoes. To encourage consumers to buy tomatoes and boost the local economy, your local paper has asked you to write a short article explaining whether tomatoes are fruits or vegetables. Your research yields the following information. Select portions of the information, organize them, and write a three- to five-paragraph newspaper article that is appropriate for a local newspaper and is titled "Tomatoes: Fruits or Vegetables?"

California Tomato Commission says: "Botanically, tomatoes are a fruit. This is because generally, a fruit is the edible part of the plant that contains seeds, while a vegetable is the edible stems, leaves and roots of the plant."

—California Tomato Commission, "Tomato Facts"

any fruit of the numerous cultivated varieties of *Lycopersicon esculentum,* a plant of the nightshade family (Solanaceae); also, the fruit of *L. pimpinelli folium,* the tiny currant tomato. Tomato plants are generally much branched, spreading 60–180 cm (24–72 inches) and recumbent when fruiting, but a few forms are compact and upright. Leaves are more or less hairy, strongly odorous, pinnately compound, and grow up to 45 cm long. The flowers are yellow, 2 cm across, pendant, and clustered. Fruits vary in diameter from 1.5 to 7.5 cm or more and are usually red, scarlet, or yellow; they vary in shape from almost spherical through oval and elongate to pear-shaped. The fruit is a soft, succulent berry, containing two to many cells of small seeds surrounded by jelly-like pulp. Most of the tomato's vitamin C is found in this pulp. The tomato is used raw in salads, served as a cooked vegetable, used as an ingredient of various prepared dishes, and pickled.

—"Tomato," *Britannica Online*

Interview with Chef Michael of Chez Nous Restaurant: "Tomatoes are used as a vegetable in cooking."

Observation: Tomatoes grow on woody plants, like squash. Vegetables grow on woody plants.

Interview with produce manager, Jill Green, Star Market: "Tomatoes are never served in sweet dishes, the way fruits are."

Interview with middle-aged male shopper in Star Market: "In kindergarten I learned tomatoes are vegetables. But I have heard they are considered both a vegetable and a fruit."

Tomatoes are a type of berry. (*American Heritage Dictionary:* tomato: large, rounded and red or yellow pulpy edible berry of a widely grown tropical herb related to the potato. Berries are "fruits.")

Tomatoes appear on the food pyramid under "vegetables."

Fruit: a. the ripened ovary or ovaries of a seed-bearing plant, together with accessory parts, containing the seeds and occurring in a wide variety of forms. b. an edible, usually sweet and fleshy form of such a structure.

—*American Heritage Dictionary*

Vegetable: a. a plant cultivated for an edible part, such as the root of the beet, the leaf of spinach or the flower buds of cauliflower.

—*American Heritage Dictionary*

Nix v. Hedden, 149 U.S. 304 (1893): "As an article of food on our tables, whether baked or boiled, or forming the basis for soup, they are used as a vegetable."

—*Lawyers Weekly USA,* http://lawyersweeklyusa.com/nix_hedden.cfm

In 1893, the United States Supreme Court ruled the tomato was a "vegetable" and therefore subject to import taxes. The suit was brought by a consortium of growers who wanted it declared a vegetable to protect U.S. crop development and prices. Fruits, at that time, were not subjected to import taxes and foreign countries could flood the market with lower priced produce.

—University of Illinois College of Agriculture, http://www.ag.uiuc.edu/
~robsond/solutions/horticulture/docs/tomato.html

and effect. Thus she effectively combines three development strategies to present and clearly explain a dramatic phenomenon. Transitions make the article flow, and narration, description, and cause and effect all unfold within a simple, basic structure.

▶ An introduction, including a focusing thesis

▶ A body

▶ A conclusion

Oceanography:
They Came from the Bottom of the Sea

EMILY BERGERON

Introduction Narrative

It was June, a summer day like any other, when thousands of green invaders arrived at the Plaice Cove beach in Hampton, New Hampshire. The eerie green globs, which looked and felt like Brillo pads, were everywhere. Marine biologist Ellen Goethel was summoned to explain what they were, but she had never seen anything like them. She wasn't even sure if they were natural or man-made.

Create suspense

Goethel examined a few of them under a microscope. They consisted mostly of plant life, but krill, tiny plankton-like animals, were mixed in as well. She showed them to lobstermen, who said their traps were sometimes fouled with the things after storms. But the fishermen couldn't identify them either.

Transition

Now the mystery has been solved by plant biologist Arthur Mathieson and marine scientist Frederick Short of the University of New Hampshire. The

Definition

globs consist mostly of a seaweed called Chaetomorpha picquotiana. This seaweed proliferates when there is a rise in the amount of nitrogen and phosphorus in the water—often brought by sewage or lawn fertilizers. The seaweed forms rope-like masses that break into fragments. Wave action rolls these fragments around the ocean floor, mixing them with krill, shells, and sand, and ultimately creates the globs.

Body Process

Cause/effect

Their appearance on the beach required an unusual series of circumstances—heavy coastal rains, which probably carried the sewage and fertilizer into the ocean, then perfectly timed storms that formed the globs and guided them to Plaice Cove, where the geology is uniquely welcoming. It's not likely to happen

Conclusion

again soon, says Goethel. But if it does, there's nothing to fear: The globs are completely harmless.

Popular Science (September 2002), p. 31. © 2002 by Popular Science. Reprinted with permission.

Introduction

The beginning of a short article is an invitation to the reader. It often includes a sentence that attracts attention to the topic and may even present the thesis. This beginning section of a short article is necessarily brief, but it can quickly and deftly hook the reader. Bergeron's introduction gets the reader interested in the mystery of "invaders," the likes of which had never been seen before. The writer also gives us a good concise description, comparing the marine creatures to Brillo pads.

Your reader counts on you to state the main point. In a short article, this statement needs to appear early in the piece and to be clear and concise. Limit your thesis to something you can explain briefly but that still creates interest. The short article above tells us, "Now the mystery has been solved by plant biologist Arthur Mathieson and marine scientist Frederick Short of the University of New Hampshire." The reader should want to find out about the solution as well.

Body

After the opening section comes an organized explanation of the topic, with each element logically linked to those before and after. This part is the middle section, and it contains the substance of your piece. You have a lot of leeway and can be creative in how you develop the body of your article, choosing one development strategy or combining several.

Bergeron's article combines narrative and cause and effect to explain a phenomenon. The narrative makes an attention-getting opening. The explanation of the scientists' conclusions is concise and clear, showing how a confluence of circumstances created the weird globs.

Using Transitions Even in a short piece, readers like to see transitions, connections between ideas. Bergeron uses pronouns to point to things already discussed. Beginning by saying that "invaders" had landed on the beach, she refers to "them" and "they." She also uses a transition to show a passage of time and to connect the event with its explanation—the word *"now"* links the narrative beginning and the cause-and-effect explanation.

Good transitions act as road signs and guide readers through the article. Even in a brief piece of writing, readers can lose their way. Transitions provide the links that keep readers alert to sudden turns or connecting paths you might take. Remember to provide these links by using appropriate transitional words or phrases. You can think of transitions as having three main functions: to show changes in time, in space, and in logic.

▶ Time transitions like *then, after,* and *meanwhile* are used when the piece is reporting a process or another series of linked events. They link elements in a timeline.

▶ Space transitions like *under, above, behind,* and *near* act as directions. Usually found in articles that describe places or objects, they show connections between the component parts. They help move readers around in a space the way a camera would control and move the audience's point of view in a film.

▶ Logical transitions like *on the other hand, however, therefore,* and *likewise* emphasize the logical connection between ideas. For example, when you are comparing opposing ideas, you would explain one theory, then indicate that you are moving on to an opposing point of view with the phrase *on the other hand.* In writing an extended definition, you might conclude your article with a sentence that begins with *therefore.*

Conclusion

When you write short articles, you have neither time nor space for an extensive conclusion. Usually, one or two sentences suffice to wrap up your explanation and perhaps suggest the implications of the topic.

The short article about the unusual marine phenomenon begins by setting up a mystery: what are these odd-looking invaders? Are they plants or animals? Keeping to the spirit of the invader-from-the-bottom-of-the-sea tale, the writer concludes with reassurance: "It's not likely to happen again soon, says Goethel. But if it does, there's nothing to fear. The globs are completely harmless."

Genetics:
The Moistness of Your Earwax Is Controlled by a Single Gene—and That May Be More Important Than You Think

GUNJAN SINHA

OK, it's a geneticist's job to hunt for all sorts of genes. But now that Japanese researchers, led by Norio Niikawa at the Nagasaki University School of Medicine, are zeroing in on the gene that makes earwax, the question is: Who cares?

Well, it turns out earwax says a lot about a person. It comes in two varieties: moist and gloppy, or dry and flaky. (The wet kind is more common in Americans, Europeans, and Africans; the dry type more frequently found in Asians and Native Americans; both types are also found in chimpanzees.) A few years ago, epidemiologist Nicholas Petrakis at the University of California San Francisco found evidence suggesting earwax contains hints of a woman's risk for contracting breast cancer. Ears and breasts both contain apocrine glands, and women with too much apocrine tissue—and moist earwax—have a tendency to form breast cysts. Finding the gene that orchestrates apocrine development might one day help doctors predict a woman's risk of developing the disease. In addition, people who have moist earwax tend to have more pungent body odor. Armpits also contain apocrine glands, which secrete oily chemicals that stink-producing bacteria feed on. So the earwax gene might also clue researchers into ways to better fight B.O.

Annotate "Genetics: The Moistness of Your Earwax Is Controlled by a Single Gene—and That May Be More Important Than You Think"

1. In the margins, write the name of any development strategy or strategies you can identify in this short article.
2. Draw a line under the thesis.
3. Circle any transitions.
4. Identify examples of technical or scientific language with a *T* and examples of colloquial language (common words the average person can understand) with a *C*.

READINGS

Short articles and sidebars appear in a variety of publications, and they cover a wide range of topics. The first three readings demonstrate this range. The articles explain how suburbs have changed, describe how "bullets tell a tale," and report on the history of the laboratory mouse. The short student article about the *T. rex* reports on new research.

My Suburb

T. Coraghessan Boyle

Sometimes a magazine devotes an entire issue to exploring a theme. In April 2000 a variety of articles in the *New York Times Sunday Magazine* investigated how the suburbs have come to define the nation, or as the cover puts it, "How the new suburban majority is changing America." Sprinkled among the major articles are six short articles in which different writers describe and define their own communities. In the following short article, well-known fiction writer T. Coraghessan Boyle explains the changes he has seen in suburban life over the course of his lifetime.

Suburban rooftops

Lawns, shade trees, the boxy big car to take you to the mall, hay fever, drunks encamped in the undergrowth, skinny kids suspended over the narrow whirring tires of hurtling bicycles: this is my suburbia, the one stored away in memory. I grew up in northern Westchester, in Emery Hill Gardens, a development of look-alike houses built in the late 40's and early 50's. When I first came west, to L.A., and lived in Tujunga, my suburbia also included motorcycle gangs, killer dogs, dysfunctional cars up on blocks, chop shops and methamphetamine labs. My next destination—Woodland Hills in the San Fernando Valley—added garbage-addled coyotes into the mix, along with bull snakes, trapdoor spiders and one intrepid roadrunner (which bounced over a six-foot fence and skirted the blue tongue of the pool to give me a beaky sidelong glance).

But now, after a long and weary journey during the course of which I was forced to eat bad Chinese and worse Italian, not to mention having to buy my shoes at the mall, I have arrived in suburban heaven. These days, I live in an unincorporated area in the vicinity of Santa Barbara, surrounded by the lush growth only a hundred years of persistent irrigation can produce, four blocks from the mighty Pacific and only three from a quaint little village chock-full of *trattorie* and tourists. At night, from the front lawn, I can see the fat, luminous strip of the Milky Way overhead, and reflect on the humble place we suburbanites occupy in the grand scheme of things. The air is cool and pure, with a whiff of the ocean and focaccia on it, and on the coldest of February days I bow to the elements and shrug into a T-shirt at the beach.

Is this suburban life? What happened to the kids, the rich chlorophyll-laced scent of the newly mown grass, the smoke of the barbecue, the Tupperware parties and the sharp scintillating curses of all those overburdened fathers ringing out over the neighborhood first thing in the morning and last thing at night? I don't know. Bit lots, maybe. Fences. The mad growth of bougainvillea, pittosporum, hibiscus. Neighbors who aren't really neighbors at all. There's one of them now, the guy across the street coming down the steps to retrieve his morning paper with the stealth of a hunter. An instant, that's all it takes, and then he's gone, swallowed up in the shrubbery. I'm listening, listening right now, but I can't even hear a dog barking.

Critical Reading Questions

1. What techniques does Boyle use in the first paragraph to explain the suburbia of his childhood, both in New York and in California? What unites these two locations?

2. How would you characterize the "suburban heaven" Boyle describes in the second paragraph? What is his tone in this paragraph?

3. What is the main development strategy Boyle uses in the first two paragraphs?

4. How has Boyle structured the third paragraph?

5. How effective is the concluding line of this brief article? What do you think he implies when he says he "can't even hear a dog barking"?

Questions for Writing and Discussion

1. What points does Boyle make about how suburban life has changed? How do you think he feels about this change? Do you agree with his point of view?

2. How is suburban life portrayed in film and on television?

How Bullets Tell a Tale

Janet Rae-Dupree

The following sidebar appeared with an article about a sniper. The writer used the sidebar to explain how a number of shootings could have been conclusively connected by the impression guns leave on bullets they fire. At the time the article and this companion sidebar were written, two snipers, who were later captured, were at large in the Washington, D.C., area.

Investigators have a tragic abundance of one kind of clue: "ballistic fingerprints," the scratches, dimples, bumps, and grooves that a gun leaves on a bullet and its shell casing. Like human fingerprinting, ballistics is all about matching: determining whether two rounds came from the same gun. It can be a powerful tool for crime-solving when investigators have a suspect's weapon and can compare a slug from the crime with one test-fired from the gun. Failing that, investigators can use it to link separate crimes, as in the Washington shootings.

To make a match, an examiner places the rounds to be compared inside a special double microscope that displays images side by side or overlaps them. Larger markings, such as the ridges on a bullet left by rifling grooves in the barrel, can be enough to show that the samples came from the same gun model. Shell casings like the one that Washington investigators have found can also be revealing because they can record the position and shape of the firing pin and, on semiautomatic weapons, the extractor and ejector that expel spent rounds.

Then comes a more painstaking task: matching two rounds to the same weapon, based on the smaller marks left by microscopic imperfections in the gun's mechanisms. Individual lines inside the rifling grooves are one clue. "It's not unlike the lines left by a knife when cutting hard cheese," says John Nixon, ballistics expert at Athena Research and Consulting in Indiana. Because the markings appear different depending on viewing angle and lighting, Nixon says, there are "an infinite number of permutations."

Fragments. All of this is often more difficult with rifles than with handguns. High-velocity rifle rounds usually break into fragments, marring identification lines.

Besides comparing bullets and shells one by one, ballistics investigators can consult a national database. About 235 police departments are equipped with $100,000 stations linked to the National Integrated Ballistics Information Network, which stores the markings on bullets and shell casings as electronic signatures. It includes only ballistics data from crimes, although gun control advocates want firearms makers to test-fire all new weapons and deposit the data in the national system along with the weapons' serial numbers. But the 1968 federal Gun Control Act blocked any national gun registry, and the National Rifle Association opposes changing the law. States, however, can require gun makers to provide test-fired samples from new weapons. So far, only two have done so: New York and Maryland.

Critical Reading Questions

1. What is the thesis of this sidebar?

2. Reread the quotation by ballistics expert John Nixon. Why do you think the writer included this quotation?

3. How has the writer organized this sidebar? Can you suggest a different, or more effective, organization?

4. Although this short piece is explanatory in nature, its conclusion advocates for a particular position. What is this position? Is this an effective conclusion for the article? Why?

Questions for Writing and Discussion

1. Would readers be interested in this topic if it were not related to a current news story?

2. Research the Washington sniper story, and write a brief update on what happened or on where the case stands now.

Mighty Mice

Charles Fishman

Charles Fishman uses an entertaining voice to describe the use of lab mice in experimentation in this article from *Fast Company,* a magazine that covers business news in a style that appeals to leisure readers.

There is no category of Nobel Prize called "best supporting researcher." But if there were, it would surely be awarded to the unassuming lab mouse. Last year, the distinguished British scientific journal *Nature* concluded that 17 Nobel Prizes have been awarded for research in which a lab mouse was indispensable.

Why are mice so nice for biological research? They are small and easy to care for—and, in 12 months, a pair of mice can produce the equivalent of a century's worth of human descendants. Plus, "mice basically have the same genes as humans," says Joyce Peterson of the Jackson Laboratory, the premier breeder of research mice. "Mice have the same systems as humans, all the same little organs, plus a couple more. They get the same diseases for the same reasons."

The lab mouse has a long history. Clarence Cook Little was an undergraduate at Harvard College when he started breeding mice in his dorm room as a way of testing his theory that some kinds of cancer might be hereditary. Little became president of the University of Maine, and then the University of Michigan. Ultimately, he returned to research, founding the Jackson Laboratory as a cancer-research center, using money from auto moguls he met while in Michigan, including Roscoe B. Jackson, head of Hudson Motorcar Co.

Since then, the mouse has helped discover penicillin. Vaccines for a range of ailments, from polio to rabies, were developed using mice. Much of what scientists and physicians know about the immune system comes from working with mice—including techniques that have made the transplants of kidneys and hearts routine.

And mice are big business. The journal *Science* has estimated the total market for research mice at more than $200 million a year, in excess of 20 million mice. Manipulation of mice genomics has become routine, and the mapping of the human genome is expected to lead to an explosion of demand for mice to test new drugs, new theories about disease, and new methods of treatment.

Cutting-edge research on Alzheimer's, AIDS, multiple sclerosis, almost all kinds of cancer—even heart disease—relies on mice. "The mouse is in the vanguard of research," says Robert Jacoby, a veterinarian and research scientist who heads Yale University's Animal Resources Center. "The mouse is at the fulcrum of understanding how genes actually operate in whole living systems."

Critical Reading Questions

1. Make a list of the effects of the scientific innovation that is the lab mouse.

2. Comment on the style and voice in this short article. Does it sound like the kind of writing you would do for any class? Point out specific spots in the writing that you could use to defend your opinion.

3. Which development strategies does the writer combine here?

4. Does the writer need the quotation in paragraph 2? Could the writer have stated this as a well-known fact? Why use the quotation?

Questions for Writing and Discussion

1. What do you think about referring to the lab mouse as someone's "invention"?

2. Select and research another widely used device or item, and write a short history about its invention.

Tyrannosaurus rex: **No Longer King of Killers?**

Jeff Aaron

Jeff Aaron, a student in a first-year college writing class, was asked to write a short article for a target publication of his choice. Jeff chose to write his article on *Tyrannosaurus rex,* and he selected *Popular Science* as his target publication. He read a number of issues of the magazine beforehand to get a sense of its preferred style so that he could approach his topic in the magazine's characteristic way.

Could it be the tyrant dinosaur, *Tyrannosaurus rex* was not the king killer we see in the movies? New research hints that smaller, quicker creatures might have had the edge on the hulking dinosaurs.

Biomechanical studies using alligators and chickens, two relatives of bipedal dinosaurs, conducted by scientists John R. Hutchinson and Mariano Garcia suggest that tyrannosaurs didn't have enough exterior leg muscles to run. Starting with the assumption that tyrannosaurs were enormous, and that most animals, like elephants, with larger body mass have limited abilities to run, Hutchinson and Garcia used mathematical models to calculate the physiology of movement. Their research led them to conclude that tyrannosaurs' hind limb muscles would not support the animal in the activity of running. They say tyrannosaurs could not run but only walk, probably ten meters, top speed.

This notion that *Tyrannosaurus rex* sauntered into battle beleaguered by his massive size threatens to change the image of the beast. Combine this new conclusion with the probability that *T. rex* suffered from gout, a disease that would have caused great pain and deterioration of joints, and the image crumbles more. In 1997, *Nature* reported that scientists studying *T. rex* bones discovered in South Dakota theorize the giants were prone to the debilitating disease. This is not a surprise considering gout is commonly associated with diets high in red meat. Not only were these huge dinosaurs limited by their anatomy, they were also quite likely limited by chronic pain.

These bits of information turn the image of the tyrannosaurs upside down, implying small, quick creatures might have had the edge on the immense predators, who would have been left to find battles with somebody their own size—and speed.

Still some more subtle tools may have lain in the tyrannosaurs' arsenal. Tyrannosaurs may have used something other than massive size and brute strength to hunt: tiny bacteria. The teeth of a *T. rex* would have been packed tightly against the gums, causing tension between the lethal teeth and the relatively soft oral cavity. Such rubbing between tooth and tissue would have caused bleeding within the dinosaur's mouth. The blood of the predator, along with the blood and ragged flesh of wounded prey, would have provided a haven for bacterial growth. The vicious fighters could inflict even a small flesh wound in prey, which would have become infected, and the dinosaurs would have been able to track the victims by using their enhanced sense of smell, due to huge olfactory lobes, to locate a compromised animal. Quarry managing to escape with minor injuries would probably have died within hours, painfully, from massive bacterial infection.

Undeniably, though no creature ever had the awesome jaw strength of the tyrannosaurs. No one can dispute the well-known power of the four-foot-long jaw. So, even with a revised image as slow and in chronic pain, tyrannosaurs cling, at least for the moment, to their place at the top of the prehistoric food chain, as the most vicious of predators, massive teeth stained with their own blood, stalking across the Cretaceous plains.

Critical Reading Questions

1. What effect does using *we* have on the readers? Do you ever use *we* in academic articles? How is this article like and unlike writing for academic essays?

2. What evidence does the writer use to back up the theory that smaller animals might have had the advantage over the largest of the dinosaurs? Does the writer prove his theory?

3. Outline the article to identify main points, and identify the kinds of transitions the writer uses.

Works Consulted

Biewener, Andrew A., "Walking with Tyrannosaurs," *Nature*, Vol. 415, Feb. 28, 2002, pp. 971–973.

Hutchinson, John R. and Mariano Garcia, "Tyrannosaurus Was Not a Fast Runner," *Nature*, Vol. 415, Feb. 28, 2002, p. 1018.

Paul, Gregory S., ed. *The Scientific American Book of Dinosaurs*. New York: Bryon Press Visual Publications, 2000.

Rothschild, Bruce M., Darren Tanke, Ken Carpenter, "Tyrannosaurs Suffered from Gout," *Nature*, Vol. 387, May 22, 1997, p. 357.

Questions for Writing and Discussion

1. How does knowing your audience affect your writing? How does it affect your research?

2. What other audience might want to read this information about *Tyrannosaurus rex*? How might the article have to be edited for this audience? Rewrite one paragraph for a different audience or different target publication.

WRITING IN THE WORKS
Interview with Douglas Banks

Douglas Banks was a staff editor at *Fast Company*, a magazine that specializes in news and features from the world of business and commerce. The short articles on bar codes and laboratory mice were first published in this magazine. Banks is currently associate editor of the *Boston Business Journal*.

Douglas Banks

1. How do editors decide what topics to cover in short articles or sidebars?

After the writing process has already started, and you look at the material in an article, you might see an interesting point that would seem too much like a digression and turn that into a sidebar. An example is a recent company profile of Krispy Kreme in Fortune Magazine. *They ran a sidebar about the celebrities who own some of the company's franchise locations—an interesting point, but one that was off the main focus and probably not worth exploring in a larger format. Often in business journalism, where you focus mainly on companies and their performance in long articles, you might write short articles or sidebars about the people inside the company, the people with the vision, the innovators.*

2. Should writers try to express their own personal writing style or voice in short articles?

Whenever you write for any publication, you want to make sure you know the magazine inside and out. You want to internalize the style of the publication. And, when you write or edit short pieces you have to keep in mind that you don't have a lot of time to "clear your throat." You need to get to the point and get to it creatively and entertainingly. Newspapers like USA Today *have been writing short for a long time now, and readers are used to getting their information in quick bursts. The best writers give them both information and entertainment in that quick burst, and a particularly punchy lead or lively voice are two ways to accomplish that. You want to blend in with the overall style of the magazine, yes, but you also want to sell the short article almost the way you would when writing poetry. Every word counts in a piece that is as compressed as a short.*

3. Seasoned professionals have suggested that writing short articles is a good way to get started as a freelance writer. Would you say that's true?

Absolutely. The national magazines will often give recent college graduates or freelancers a chance to write shorts about microtrends—basically reporting news about what's happening in different fields, what's on the horizon. Your intimate knowledge of a publication will pay off when you write a query pitching an idea you might have about current trends. Obviously, your knowledge about what the magazine has covered before, whether they have covered similar subjects, and how they have approached similar topics will help you tailor your subject. Call the publication and ask whom you should contact, and whether an e-mail query is preferable. In your query, include information about your writing experience. That's where writing for your local or college paper can really come in handy. Editors like seeing clips of any previously published articles, even articles for your school or local newspaper. Your clips will show that you have an understanding of how to research and write, and that you are serious about your writing.

WRITING AND REVISION STRATEGIES

Gathered here are three interactive sections for you to use as you write and revise your short article.

> Writer's Notebook Suggestions

> Peer Editing Log

> Revision Checklist

Writer's Notebook Suggestions

You can use these exercises to do some start-up thinking and writing for your short article.

1. Explain a process you are familiar with, or choose one of the following.

   > Preparing yeast dough for bread

   > Pumping gas at a self-service station

   > Making coffee

   > Changing a flat tire

   > Starting a campfire

2. Research the origin of the three-ring circus, and write a paragraph about it, using narrative.

3. In three concise sentences, explain the historical background of any issue currently in the news.

4. Explain an unusual way of making money that most people don't know about.

5. Compare bottled water to tap water in several paragraphs. Write for a general interest publication.

6. Report on a small but remarkable episode in your school's history.

7. Write several paragraphs about postage stamps—their design, their price, or some other aspect.

8. Write the beginning of a short article related to sports. Choose your topic, or use one of the following.

> Explain the shape of a football.

> Describe the different tennis court surfaces.

> Report on the origin of synchronized swimming.

9. Explain the origin of Labor Day, Arbor Day, Kwanzaa, or some other holiday.

Peer Editing Log

As you work with a writing partner or in a peer-editing group, you can use these questions to give useful responses to a classmate's short article and as a guide for discussion.

Writer's Name_____

Date_____

1. Identify the explanatory thesis (underline it). Does it reveal the focus clearly? Why? What might make it stronger?

2. Identify any development strategies the writer uses by making a note in the margin.

3. Who do you think is the audience for this article? In what ways are the strategies appropriate or inappropriate for this audience?

4. Do you understand the writer's explanation of the idea, process, event, person, or place? Put a question mark next to any point that you find confusing or that needs more explanation. What other information might you need?

5. List the main points of the article. Can you suggest other points the article might cover?

6. Does the writer have a sense of the purpose of the article—as a school assignment, an article, or a website? Identify any places that seem too formal or too informal for the purpose. Put a check mark next to any material that seems at odds with the formal or informal approach, and make a note.

7. How well does the author use transitions? Write T where the writer could use a transition or might change a transition. Write a brief note to the writer.

8. Does the article come to a satisfactory conclusion? How would you suggest the writer improve the conclusion?

Revision Checklist

As you do your final revision, check to make sure that you

❏ Wrote an engaging opening sentence

❏ Stated your thesis clearly and accurately

❏ Explained your point using one or more of the development strategies appropriate to your purpose

❏ Used clear transitions keyed to the development strategies you used

❏ Wrapped up your explanation in a clear concluding sentence or two.

❏ Acknowledged sources

A caption you might use for this chapter's photo esssay.

Thousands of Central Americans, many of them teenagers, stowaway on trains each year and make a treacherous journey that often takes them thousands of miles from their homes. Sometimes they are looking for jobs, and sometimes they are looking for mothers and fathers who have left them behind. As their train passes the people who live along the tracks, the young migrants receive food from these subsistence farmers. Once in a while, the travelers find what they are looking for.

4. APPLICATION ESSAYS

WRITING FOR A SPECIFIC AUDIENCE

No matter which question, we are asking what is really important to you, who you are, and how did you arrive where you are.

—Delsie Z. Phillips

This image illustrates the importance of standing out among a crowd, as your application essay should.

Below are prompts taken from actual application essays. Choose one and write a five-hundred-word essay, or substitute a prompt from an application essay you are currently writing or are interested in writing.

1. Who speaks for our generation and what are they saying? If you answer "no one," why? What needs to be said?
   —Scholarship application

2. You have just retired. What would people say about you at your going-away party?
   —Scholarship application

3. In 500 words or less, describe any unusual circumstances or challenges you have faced and discuss the ways you have responded.
   —Transfer application

4. In 500 words or less, discuss your interest in your major, how your interest developed, and describe a related work or volunteer/community service experience.
   —Transfer application

APPLICATION ESSAYS

Just when you think you will never have to write another application essay, you decide to compete for a scholarship, study abroad, go to graduate school, or transfer to another college. Once again, in five hundred words or less, you must convince an unknown person or a committee to accept you into a program or choose you for a scholarship.

Getting started can be daunting if you are used to writing essays for classes in which the audience—your teacher—is a relatively known quantity. Application essays are written for faceless strangers. One student compared writing application essays to going to an interview and finding a one-way mirror. Her interviewers could see her, but she could not see them. Who were they? What mysterious elements made one application essay different from another? What made some of them winners?

Many students say they were never taught how to write application essays. They believe that some people have an intuitive sense of how to write outstanding essays and other people do not. The truth is that you can learn how to write application essays that will impress your readers. The keys are (1) to assess the rhetorical context for the essay (its purpose and audience) and (2) to understand the question that you are being asked, often called a *prompt,* so you can focus your essay. Even personal statements, which many applications ask for, can be more focused if you carefully consider the prompt and the specifics of your goal and audience.

Applications: School, Community, Work

The skills you need to write successful application essays are similar to those for writing in school, in the community, and at work. For example, analyzing a question on an essay exam or for a paper is much like analyzing a prompt for an application essay. Analyzing purpose and audience for the application essay is similar to the analysis you will do in writing academic essays for courses ranging from anthropology to zoology. The application is also a common form of writing in your community. You may often need to write applications—for instance, to work on local boards or to volunteer for community service projects. When performing a job search, you will find that job applications often ask for a personal statement similar to that required for entrance to college and graduate school and for scholarships and internships. In short, learning

Your Image and Style

When writing an application essay, you face what seems like a contradiction: writing in a formal voice while expressing your individuality. After all is said and done, you want your voice to make the strongest impression on the audience. How do clothes serve the same purpose? Think about business attire, and answer the following questions.

1. Is a business suit a kind of uniform?

2. When professionals dress for success, do they want to blend in with the crowd or do they want to stand out from it?

3. Think about the difference between women's business clothing and men's. Who has more choices?

4. In general, do women have more of a range of styles available to them than men? Does this spill over into writing? Do women have more flexibility than men in their formal writing voices?

to write excellent application essays is practical. It will help you in a broad and varied range of settings. The application essay is perhaps the most practical and useful of all essay formats.

CHAPTER OBJECTIVES

In this chapter you will learn to

▶ consider your purpose and audience

▶ analyze a prompt or question

▶ focus your essay

▶ develop your ideas, combining narration, analysis, and persuasion

Warm-Up Practice 4.1   Collaborative Activity

Your college has asked a group of students to participate in the admissions process. The administration has invited a select group of students, you among them, to read and evaluate application essays from high school seniors.

The admissions committee has set up the following grid. On this scale, 5 is the highest rating, and 1 is the lowest.

Focus	1	2	3	4	5
Organization	1	2	3	4	5
Clarity	1	2	3	4	5
Writing skills	1	2	3	4	5
Overall interest	1	2	3	4	5

1. Circle the appropriate number in each category for the following sample essay. The prompt for this essays was, "In your opinion, what is an educated person?"

2. Write a few comments justifying your evaluation.

USA TODAY Scholarship

A person is educated if they constantly strive to attain knowledge while simultaneously recognizing that they know very little about the nature of the universe. As a result, I am educated now, yet if I ever were to lose my desire to doggedly pursue knowledge and understanding, I would immediately be uneducated, despite the number of years of research and study that I have done during my life. Thus, to be truly educated, I must die devoted to understanding.

Vital to determining when a person is educated is understanding the nature of education. First of all, education is the pursuit of knowledge, not a goal that can be reached after a set number of years of doctoral study. Consequently, a person, no matter how much they know, can never stop learning because they have already attained "education." Instead, people are educated when they wholeheartedly devote their lives to understanding what they do not comprehend. As a result, I, a person with a strong will to understand, am more educated than a professor who dislikes his subject matter or a scientist who invents new technology, patents it, and then quits his job so that he/she can live off the patent's profits.

For example, in physics, my area of future studies, many men and women died always searching for more understanding. These people, like Einstein, Curie, and Bohr, are truly educated since they dedicated themselves to the pursuit of knowledge till death. Physics also has its share of people who nearly ended their education to experience a windfall of profits from minor discoveries. Ernest Rutherford, for instance, nearly dedicated his early life to making money from advancing radio technology. However, luckily for civilization, another scientist, Nobel Laureate J. J. Thomson, told Rutherford that he cannot serve God and Mammon at the same time. Rutherford immediately left the business of making money and within fifteen years earned a Nobel Prize and discovered the structure of the atom. He died committed to learning and understanding. Studying and advancing understanding till death is the unmistakable mark of an educated man.

Clearly, education is a constant pursuit, and the educated person devotes his entire life to this quest for knowledge. Thus, I know that I am educated as long as I never give up attempting to understand the universe. However, inseparable from this definition of an educated person, is the realization that no people, at least during my lifetime, can claim that they possess all knowledge and that their knowledge is irrefutable. Instead, educated people recognize how little they know when they gaze up at the night's stars, when they stare at the ocean, or even when they look at other people and animals. This complete uncertainty born out of not knowing how atoms could ever form mountains and life and of not understanding how the universe was born must lead the educated person to redouble his/her efforts to understand as much as possible. Moreover, this uncertainty must make the educated person have a mind open to new ideas and explanations. People like Einstein, for example, had to overcome the once accepted notions that distance, time, and speed are absolutes. Einstein, a model of an educated man, proved to society that its closed-minded explanations of the universe were wrong and that time, length, and speed are relativistic. Similarly, Galileo, a man committed to understanding, was excommunicated for his heretical belief that the earth revolved around the sun. Thus, the educated person is committed to the pursuit of knowledge, has a mind open to new theory, and never subordinates the truth to an authority's dictate.

Personally, I know I am educated as long as I remain tenaciously determined to understanding the world and to maintaining an open mind. Of course, this goal of remaining educated will lead me to Harvard next year and to a doctorate in physics in another university. However, these are just signs of an educated person. To be truly educated, I must be committed to learning my entire life and to making new discoveries in science, whether or not they contradict accepted theory. Education cannot be measured by the number of degrees a person has earned. Instead, education is a mind set that must last one's entire life. If, at the moment of my death, I am still dedicated to grasping misunderstood concepts, I can say that I am truly educated, as Einstein, Rutherford, and Galileo were before me.

—Essayedge.com

UNDERSTANDING APPLICATION ESSAYS

Essays of all kinds—application, academic, personal, and literary, to name a few—are defined by their purpose and their sense of audience. As you begin thinking about your essay, ask yourself some questions.

▶ Why am I writing this essay? What is its purpose?

▶ Who will be reading this essay? Who is my audience?

▶ What is my focus? What is the prompt/question asking me to do?

Purpose and Audience

As noted above, application essays are among the most practical of all pieces of writing. Their purpose is to get you a scholarship, internship, or assistantship, to get you admitted into a study-abroad program, or to get into another college or graduate school. The very factor that makes this form of writing practical, however, also makes it competitive. That factor is your audience—a person or panel of people who have the power to vote you in or out. Application essays are read by people who have not met you, who do not know what you might be capable of, and who are not familiar with your sense of humor or your personal style. This essay is their first impression of you.

Make no mistake: writing an application essay is entering a competition with a lot at stake. You will be judged by your writing. Unlike understanding teachers who might overlook typographical and grammatical mistakes, chalking them up to time pressures or the cold you had last week, the people who read your application essay have no personal interest in your success. They might be impressed by you, or they might not. In one of the worst scenarios, they might find it easy to forget you because your essay blends in with the hundreds of other applications in front of them.

How do you make your personal essay stand out positively from the rest? Readers of application essays have been interviewed on how they go about the selection process. They say that disorganized, unfocused, generic, and carelessly proofread essays go into the discard pile. They want useful information about you, and they also want a sense of your personality and style. They want to know that you have taken care with your writing, and they want to be engaged, interested, and even inspired. They want to know that you have given thought to *them*.

Finding Your Focus: Reading the Prompt or Question

The sooner you can find a focus for your essay, the clearer your thinking and writing are likely to be. Like an academic essay on a specific question or theme, the application essay has a built-in focal point: the question or, as many call it, the prompt. Read the question or prompt carefully. Pay attention to the rules or parameters of the application. If you make the mistake of forging ahead without reading the requirements, you may write a two-thousand-word essay when the prompt asks for five hundred words, or you may not fully address the question.

Purpose of the Prompt Pay close attention to the prompt. If you understand its purpose and the different categories that prompts fall into, you will find it much easier to find your focus.

No matter how it is worded, the purpose of the prompt is almost always to allow you to reveal something significant about yourself. In fact, the essay is an invitation to persuade your reader (the admissions team, the scholarship committee, the study-abroad program) of your worth. According to Delsie Z. Phillips, the acting director of admissions at Haverford College,

> No matter which question, we are asking what is really important to you, who you are, and how did you arrive where you are. The whole college application process is really a self-exploration, and the essay is a way to put your personal adventure into words. It is a summing-up, maybe a catharsis. You need not expose all of your innermost thoughts, but you must share some part of yourself.
>
> —Delsie Z. Phillips, "The Question of the Essay"

This is good advice even beyond the college application process. Your job in writing an application essay of any type is to find a way to "share some part of yourself," whether it is a part of your life experiences, of your values, or of your interests.

Types of Prompts The language of the prompt suggests ways to focus your essay. Most prompts fall into one of the following categories.

▶ Past experiences and achievements

▶ Future plans

▶ Values or personal philosophy

▶ Ability to analyze ideas

▶ General knowledge

Try to analyze what each kind of question is trying to elicit. Questions about your past experiences and achievements usually sound like this one from UCLA.

> What do you consider to be your most important personal and professional accomplishments to date?

Practice 4.2
Writing a Prompt

Students transferring into your college are stuck responding to a standard, dull essay question:"Why do you want to transfer to this college?" As part of a student recruitment team, you have been asked to come up with a prompt that allows for more creativity and still asks the basic question of why the student is applying to your college. Write a short memo to the dean of admissions suggesting a new question for transfer applications and explaining why it is superior to the old one.

Other prompts might be worded like this one.

> Describe an experience that has helped change your perspective. Describe a challenge you have met successfully.

These kinds of prompts ask you to focus on something that reveals who you are by relating and interpreting an experience. Remember that the word *describe* asks you to provide concrete details and to be specific about your experience.

Do not worry if you have not had any earth-shattering experiences. Small events such as winning a race or a prize, an unexpected friendship, or a setback are all fine topics for this kind of essay. One student wrote a memorable and compelling application essay on the unlikely topic of shopping for prom shoes. The important point is that you need to describe the event and then interpret it. Explain to your reader why the event is significant to you.

When an application asks about your plans, you can assume that the college or program wants to know whether your goals match its mission. In a sense, readers want to know whether they should invest in your future by giving you a scholarship, an internship, or an opportunity to study abroad. Your focus should be on convincing them that the fit is right. If you are applying for an internship in a political organization, for example, make sure you know and are in agreement with the organization's positions on major policies and candidates before you elaborate on the legislation you would sponsor in your future role as senator.

Questions about your values or philosophy can sound like this one from a scholarship application.

> If your education had no limits, you could stay as long as you wanted, and money were no object, what would you hope to get out of your time at college?

By asking you to strip away practical limitations, the question in effect is asking you to focus on and articulate your core philosophy about education. In your response, you should be honest as well as insightful about what you want from school.

Sometimes transfer or internship applications allow you to show your expertise in a subject. Such questions are opportunities to reveal your passion for and understanding of a subject of special interest.

> Describe how a work of art, music, dance, theater, or literature has inspired you.

Some questions ask you to analyze a quotation and relate it to your life.

Pearl S. Buck once said, "You cannot make yourself feel something you do not feel, but you can make yourself do right in spite of your feelings." Tell us about an experience where you felt that you did the right thing in spite of your feelings.

You will not be able to give a correct or incorrect answer to this analytical question, but you will have to be careful to stay on track and focus on having done the right thing when you did not feel like doing it. The important word in this question is *right*. You will want to take into consideration the moral issues suggested by the word as your form your answer. The prompt is not asking you to write about a decision that was "different" from other people's decisions or one that was "wrong." Reading the question carefully and analyzing its language and intent can help you come up with a focused and persuasive answer. Understanding what the question is asking can save you countless hours of frustration not just in writing application essays but also in answering questions wherever you encounter them.

Choosing a Development Strategy

Depending on the prompt and your topic, you can choose from a variety of approaches to develop your essay. Three basic approaches are narration, analysis, and argumentation. Each has strengths, and each can be appropriate for an entire essay or part of one.

Using Narration Narration, or telling stories, is probably the most reader-friendly genre, and most application essay writers use it. Stories allow you to be personal, even confidential, as you engage the reader's attention. The essential ingredients for a story are characters, setting, and conflict. Even if you do not use narration to develop your entire essay, consider starting with a story.

Application topics asking about your experiences or the people you have met lend themselves to narration. Try to tell your story with vivid description, well-selected detail, and maybe even some dialogue. In other words, you can summarize a story—"When I was in high school, I waited tables at the local greasy spoon"—or you can recreate a scene to make it more engaging and memorable.

"Pick up! Pick up!" Tony screamed, throwing three orders of burgers and fries onto the counter.

Practice 4.3 Analyzing Prompts

1. Analyze each of these typical application prompts. What are they asking? What might you focus on in an answer?

   a. Describe a personal experience that has profoundly changed your perspective on an issue of regional, national, or international importance. In what way has this event impacted your previous perspective? How will it change your approach to this issue (or similar issues) in the future?

   —UCLA, undergraduate application

   b. Why do you want to intern at the Office of Exhibits Central, and what do you hope to learn?

   —Smithsonian Museum, internship application

   c. Write a narrative about your life. This should include information about your accomplishments, family, educational experience, and outside activities. Be creative rather than philosophic. Remember that you are writing for a reader who knows nothing about you or your background.

   —Boston University, graduate application

   d. You have just completed your 300-page autobiography. Please submit page 217.

   —University of Pennsylvania, undergraduate school application

   e. Tell us about an opinion you have had to defend. How has this affected your belief system?

   —Cornell University, undergraduate application

2. Write the first fifty words of one of these essays.

The following opening, from an application essay about living abroad, uses narrative to draw the reader into the scene.

"Je deteste des Americains" [I detest Americans], said the old Swiss woman sitting across from me. Her face contorted into a grimace of disgust as she and her friend continued to complain that Americans had no culture, that they never learned another language, and that their inferior customs were spreading throughout Europe like an infectious disease. Each hair on the

back of my neck sprang to attention, as I strained to hear the woman's inflammatory remarks. I gripped my bag of McDonald's harder with each insulting phrase.

—Essay 32, Harvard, International Experience: Living in Switzerland," *Barrons*

The opening dialogue creates immediate tension. The reader wants to know who the Swiss woman is and how the writer responded to her angry outburst. The writer offers some description—the woman's "grimace of disgust,"

the hair on the back of the writer's neck, and finally the ironic detail of the "bag of McDonald's" gripped in the writer's hand. The introduction has characters, setting, and conflict, all the ingredients of a good story.

Using Analysis Even if you have chosen to tell a story, it is important to analyze the events—that is, to break them down into their parts in order to explain or interpret them. An application essay should not be creative writing that leaves the reader wondering. Instead, you want to show that you have understood the experience and its impact on your life, and that you can articulate its meaning.

One applicant wrote about a summer job "detasseling" corn—"removing the tassel from a corn stalk so that pollinization of the plant can occur and hybrid seed corn can grow." A variety of midwesterners, many of them students, do this work each summer. The writer's experiences with coworkers who were "different kinds of achievers" from people she had previously known led her to analyze her own experience of working under difficult circumstances, sometimes from sunrise to sunset.

> While discovering the strengths of so many different kinds of people, I also discovered some of my own strengths. . . . I realized that I am able to depend on my own inner resources. This discovery of my own physical strength and my ability to endure came as a revelation to me.
>
> —Celia E. Rothenberg, from *One Hundred Successful College Application Essays*

Other prompts call for analysis to be a major part of the essay. For example, prompts may ask you how a work of art or literature has inspired you or how you expect this internship (or scholarship or study-abroad program) to affect your future.

As part of brainstorming for an analytical essay, make a list or an outline of the points you wish to make, then cluster them into a few broad categories to organize your response. Make sure the major points are parallel and equal in importance, and that together all the points thoroughly explain the whole.

For example, if you are applying to study in France for a semester, a common prompt asks how you might benefit from such an experience. If you break down the experience of studying abroad into its component parts, you might brainstorm a list like the following.

> ◗ Visit great art museums
>
> ◗ Study French history with French professors
>
> ◗ Improve my ability to converse in French
>
> ◗ Learn about another culture
>
> ◗ Learn about another educational system

▶ Learn how to read French

▶ Broaden my perspective through travel

▶ Enrich my understanding of how another culture views my culture

The list could go on, of course, and encompass many other areas. The items in this short list could be sorted and organized into a few broad categories, each of which you could discuss briefly in your essay.

I. Education

    A. Learn about other educational systems

    B. Study French history with French professors

II. Language

    A. Improve my ability to converse in French

    B. Learn how to read French

III. Culture

    A. Broaden my perspective through travel

    B. Visit great art museums

    C. Learn about another culture

    D. Learn how another culture views my culture

With details, examples, and elaboration, this informal outline probably encompasses enough material for a short application essay. You could select and discuss only the strongest and most interesting points. No matter the exact points you cover, you will want to keep the wording of the prompt in mind and, in this case, discuss how you would *benefit* from the various aspects of the study-abroad program.

Using Argumentation In a sense, everything you write in an application essay is an argument in favor of your worth as a candidate. What you choose to write about and how you express yourself—your voice and style as well as grammar and vocabulary—together persuade your reader that you are an interesting and intelligent person who stands out among your peers.

Some essay prompts also require you to make an argument to support an opinion. In making this kind of argument, you claim a distinct position on an issue and present evidence that defends your position. For example, a prompt used by Cornell University was, "Tell us about an opinion you have had to defend. How has this affected your belief system?" For this application essay, you would need to state your position as well as your reasons for holding that view, the same way writers of editorials or opinion essays do. One student who was applying for a scholarship wrote about the controversial topic of federal funding for stem-cell research.

The federal government should fund stem-cell research because the government can make funds equally available to all scientists. If the government does not take the responsibility for research on stem cells, some private research group certainly will, limiting the amount of information available to scientists. Also, more researchers working on developing cures could speed remedies for chronic and deadly illnesses like diabetes and Alzheimer's.

—Chisom Aganabe, Scholarship application

The student takes a clear stand on a controversial scientific topic: that the federal government should fund stem-cell research. She supports her argument with two main points: that the federal government can make funds equally available to all researchers, and that having more scientists work on a problem can solve the problem more quickly. Another student might argue that stem-cell research is immoral or that there should be less government regulation of research. Whatever your opinion, make sure you state it clearly and support it specifically.

Combining Strategies You might write a fine application essay that is mainly narrative or analytic or argumentative. However, most writers combine these forms, using the techniques that work best to develop their ideas. Once you decide what you want to say, think about how best to say it and which forms can contribute to the quality of your essay.

You might combine all three genres. You could begin with narrative, telling a story that illustrates the point you want to make, then analyze the story, interpreting its meaning for your reader. Finally, you could argue for your acceptance by presenting compelling evidence to support your case. For an example of an essay that uses these three genres, read Jessica Polanski's "Smoke" on page 118.

RESEARCH PATHS

You have a clearly defined audience for your application essay: the person or committee in charge of evaluating applications for the scholarship, study-abroad program, admissions, internship, or college to which you are applying. It makes good sense to do some research about the goals and missions of your audience. Each has a different orientation; even though it might be tempting to recycle the same essay for all applications, tailoring the application to the specific audience is a much better idea.

If, for example, a scholarship is named after a prestigious alumnus, you should learn about that person. Find out what qualities the person embodied, who endowed the scholarship, and what prompted that person or group to endow it. You might want to begin your application with an acknowledgment of the person's contribution or importance, showing that you did your homework. Any group or organization that funds a scholarship—whether a religious group or a corporate one—wants to know that you have considered its reasons for offering the scholarship and that your values are harmonious with its values.

Since an internship application usually asks for a personal statement or a statement of purpose, become informed about the company or organization to which you are applying. You do not need to show comprehensive knowledge of the company's net profits or overall business plan, but you should be able to write convincingly about how your skills and abilities are a good fit for the work and how your values mesh with the company's values.

If you are applying to study abroad, know something about both the program and the country. Do you need to speak a foreign language? Will you be taking classes with native students? Will you be living in a dorm or with a family? Do not make the mistake that one student did when he wrote an essay about how much he wanted to learn about the English parliamentary system for his application to study at the University of Dublin in Ireland.

If you are seeking a transfer or admission as a graduate student, know the programs and the identities of the eminent professors. Check out a website; read the publicity; and talk to people who have gone before you. Gather as much information as possible, so that you can write from a firm base of knowledge about the school or program.

After attending an inspiring workshop with a writing professor, a student decided to apply for a fellowship to work with that professor. She began her application essay with a paragraph narrating her experience at the workshop. Too obvious? Maybe. But it was honest and heartfelt, and it worked: she got in.

All this advice boils down to one point: know your audience. Making an effort to research your audience will help you write a focused and successful essay in a confident voice.

ANATOMY OF AN APPLICATION ESSAY

Application essays usually follow a simple structure: introduction, body, and conclusion. Jessica Polanski wrote this essay to apply for a scholarship to a school of public health. Read the essay, which has been annotated, to see how all the elements work together. Then consider each element separately as it is discussed in the following section.

Practice 4.4   Research

1. Do some research to find a scholarship or internship you might be interested in applying for, and obtain application material. You can locate opportunities by doing a Web search, reading bulletin boards at your school, or talking to professors in your field of interest. Public and college libraries usually have books that list scholarships students can apply for.

2. After reading the application material, list the qualities that the scholarship or internship committee might be looking for in an ideal candidate.

3. In a brief paragraph, explain how your experience and education fit those expectations.

Smoke

JESSICA POLANSKI

Topic sentence

Introduction

As long as I can remember, someone in my house was always smoking a cigarette. My mother would have one smoldering in an ashtray next to her as she read the newspaper, while my father would be smoking in another room. He even smoked while he was changing clothes. He would be smoking as he rushed to get out of his overalls, coated with oil from the shift at Midas Mufflers and into his bartender clothes. I often wondered how he didn't catch fire.

Narrative details and examples

Cause

Topic sentence

Body

It was what I was used to; the smell of cigarette smoke was for me the smell of home. Smoking was what my hard-working mother, father, and grandparents did to relax.

Many people in my town in Pennsylvania are smokers. There were so many, in fact, that you routinely see the medical supply truck stop at three or four houses on the same block, delivering oxygen to elderly people, many of whom have emphysema—a preventable disease, one you only get from smoking. Everywhere you go you can see people with tubes leading from their noses, behind their ears, and over to portable oxygen tanks: in grocery stores, in cars, at Bingo and at my family reunions.

Effect (general examples)

Topic sentence

The first of my relatives to die of cigarette-smoking-related ailments was my grandfather, who succumbed to heart failure at 67. His doctors had been urging him to quit smoking for years. I remember him when he was near the end of his life, lying almost motionless on the hospital bed they installed in his living room, the way he would get my grandmother to prop him up with pillows and folded up blankets so he could smoke a cigarette. He was too weak to light up by himself.

Effect (specific examples)

Topic sentence

Conclusion

My grandmother died of cancer about two years later. It was then I finalized my decision to work in a field that would help people fight addictive behaviors. I'm not naïve enough to think that my grandparents didn't know smoking was bad for them. Who doesn't know that? Still, though the message was out there, it didn't get through to them. It didn't work on them. The fact that friends of mine are already hooked on cigarettes, despite all the information that's out there about the dangers, also makes me determined to work in the field of Public Health Education and concentrate on smoking cessation programs. I think I can make a difference: help inform and motivate people, and help them lead longer, and maybe happier lives. Receiving a School of Public Health scholarship will help me take my first step toward my goal.

Essay thesis

5

Writing a Thesis

Your thesis in an application essay is an explicit statement of your idea or interpretation of your topic. Make sure it also answers the prompt. Often you will state your thesis at the beginning of the essay, as either the first or last sentence of your introduction. However, if you are trying to build suspense or lead your reader to your main point by first presenting evidence, you might state your thesis farther into the essay. Whether you put your thesis in the first or last paragraph, make sure that you know, and that your reader knows, what point you are making in your essay.

You may begin drafting your essay without a thesis in mind. That is fine. Keep writing until you have exhausted the topic; then sit back and consider what you have written. You might even ask a friend to read your draft and to tell you what he or she understands the point to be. If you still have not identified the main idea of your essay, turn your paper over and write a one-sentence answer to the question, "What is your point?" The answer can become your working thesis.

In "Smoke," Jessica Polanski was addressing the question of why she wanted to enter the field of public health, and she decided to place her thesis in the very last sentence of the essay.

> Receiving a School of Public Health scholarship will help me take my first step toward my goal.

By waiting to state her thesis until the end of her essay, Jessica allowed the narrative details and specific examples in the first four paragraphs to build a convincing argument for her decision to work in public health. The essay would have had a different slant had she put the thesis first, before she explained and illustrated her personal experiences with the devastating effects of smoking.

Some writers like to give their thesis an argumentative edge to create some controversy. Although a thesis does not necessarily have to be controversial, a little tension or edge can be refreshing in any writing. A controversial statement or unusual point of view might wake up a reader who has been plowing through hundreds of essays on the same topics.

Introduction

The introduction is your first shot at making your essay stand out from the rest. Ideally, you will grab the reader's attention and keep it until the final word. One way to get the reader's attention is to create a scene in an engaging, personal voice, as Jessica Polanski does in her essay.

Jessica begins her essay with the phrase, "As long as I can remember." This narrative voice and the specific details that follow (her mother's cigarette smoldering in an ashtray, her father smoking while he took off his oil-coated coveralls) pull the reader into her essay. The reader observes the effects of smoking on people Jessica knows and loves. Even though Jessica does not present her thesis until the final paragraph, she begins her introduction with a clear topic sentence that does double duty. The opening sentence—"As long as I can remember, someone in my house was always smoking a cigarette"—both announces the topic of that paragraph and presents smoking as the focus of the essay.

An introduction that creates a scene, as Jessica's does, captures the readers' attention. Another good choice for an introduction is a relevant and interesting quotation.

As Robert Frost wrote, "Nothing gold can stay."

A simple and direct answer to the prompt can also serve as a good introduction.

What has led you to your major?
In junior high I discovered the art room was the only place I could be myself. Art has been my island ever since.

Why do you wish to study abroad?
Studying in Japan will help me understand what my father's mother, my *Obasan*, meant by *narai*, or what she called her habit.

However you begin, avoid an approach that a reader could find dull, long-winded, or pretentious. Help your reader like you and want to read what

---

Practice 4.6   *Analyzing Introductions*

You are helping your friends apply to your school by reading the introductions to their transfer applications. Write an e-mail message to each writer commenting on the effectiveness of these introductions. Make some suggestions to strengthen the introductions.

1. "I remember reading Tom Boswell in the *Post* and being mesmerized by Roger Angell's view of the '75 Series. The singular love of sport has been with me always. Never grasping the attraction entirely, I learned first the rules and the names and graduated to nuances. As I learned more, an understanding of sorts crept into the box scores."

   —Charles D. Haley, from "Essays on Sports and Activities"

2. "I chuckle to myself every time I think about this. I am perceived as a mild-mannered, intelligent individual until I mention that I am involved in riflery. It is interesting to watch someone's expression change. It is as if I instantaneously grew a pair of horns and a sharp set of claws. Believe me this gets worse; I am a member of the NRA. I try to tell these folks that I belong to the NRA to fire my rifle. 'Oh my God! You fire real guns? With real bullets?!?' they remark with a perplexed look on their face. Besides having horns and claws, I now possess a tail and leathery wings."

   —Essay Edge, "Opinion Essay," www.plantpapers.com

3. "Of the many ironies which exist in life, one stands out in my mind: the same information which you would like to attain from others is often the same knowledge they would least like to divulge. As competition continues to grow in all areas, many who strive for an advantage must act tactfully and follow Polonius's advice in *Hamlet* that states, 'By indirections find directions out' (II, I, L. 65). A perfect example comes to mind."

   —Essay 53, from "Beginnings and Endings," *Barrons*

you have to say. You can be creative or offbeat, but do not go overboard. Avoid getting too flowery or incomprehensibly philosophic. Write an introduction that would draw *you* in.

Body

The middle section of your essay, the body, should support your thesis and lead your reader to your conclusions. You can construct the body of your essay in a variety of ways. You can use narration to tell a story or use specific examples to illustrate your point. You can analyze an idea by examining its parts or discussing its causes and effects. You can present a logical argument and support it with evidence. Or you can combine these development strategies, as Jessica Polanski does in "Smoke." (See Chapter 3 for more discussion of development strategies.)

Jessica organizes the three paragraphs (paragraphs 2, 3, and 4) that make up the body of this essay in a clear and purposeful way. She develops her ideas using a cause-and-effect structure, but she also uses narration, analysis, and argumentation. In addition, Jessica organizes paragraphs 3 and 4 by focusing first on the general, then on the specific. In the very brief second paragraph, Jessica analyzes a cause of smoking: "hard-working" people like her mother, father, and grandparents smoke to relax. In the next two paragraphs she shows us the effects of smoking on people she knows. In paragraph 3 she uses narrative details to present a general, wide-angle view of the many people who smoke in her town. Through these details, she gives clear evidence to support her later argument that people need to be informed and motivated to stop addictive behaviors.

In paragraph 4 Jessica narrows her focus to people in her family who have died from smoking-related diseases. She presents specific narrative details of her grandfather's death. Here Jessica shows rather than tells. Relating a vivid scene in which her grandfather was propped up with pillows so that he could smoke as he was dying, she allows her reader to see the addictive nature of smoking and its horrible effects.

An effective essay structure does not have to be visible to the reader. In other words, you do not have to use the terms *cause* and *effect* to let your reader know you are organizing your ideas in this pattern. What is important is to consciously choose the organizational pattern that best communicates your good ideas and clear thinking.

Conclusion

The conclusion not only sums up your essay; it also provides a last glimpse of your personality. In an application essay, you want to convince your reader that you are the best candidate for the scholarship, internship, study-abroad program, or academic program. You want to be memorable.

Jessica's conclusion has an interesting structure. She begins the paragraph explaining how her grandmother's smoking-related death cemented her decision to help people fight addictive behaviors. Then she adds depth to her analysis by arguing that information about smoking may be well known but has not yet been effectively communicated. She cites another example to prove this point: many friends know the dangers, yet still smoke. This discussion sums up the points she has already made in the es-

SIDEBAR

Tips for Writing Application Essays

You want your reader to have a strong impression of you as a person, much like you would want an interviewer to see you. You want to stand out as a distinct personality, someone who is interesting, confident, capable, and professional. Most likely you would not go to an interview dressed in jeans or in a costume. Likewise, your essay should be written in a style and tone that fits the formality of the situation. Here are some tips to help you present yourself as an interesting, one-of-a-kind person while keeping your style and tone consistent with formal writing.

Write in a Personal Voice.

Aim to sound as if you are talking to another person in a formal setting. In other words, though you are not familiar enough with your reader to use slang or inside jokes, you are not addressing a large lecture hall either. One mistake writers make is to "institutionalize" their application essays, making them sound more like policy statements than personal statements.

> Utilizing coalitions built within family, friends, and acquaintances might be a way to succeed in the business world, but that is not what initiative is all about.

Here is the sentiment translated into more personal language.

> Many people use their family connections to succeed in business, but I have a different sense of initiative.

Try the following suggestions to achieve a personal voice in your essay.

1. Use the first person.   In a personal essay, the first person *I* is required, not optional.

2. Write in the active voice.   Make the subjects of your sentences the doers of the action. In other words, avoid the passive voice.

> *Passive:* "A scholarship was awarded to me."
> *Active:* "I received a scholarship."

The active voice is clearer and more appealing. (For more on active and passive voice, see the style guide on the *Writing in the Works* web site.)

3. Use your own vocabulary. Do not replace simple words with long or obscure words that you have found in a thesaurus. Inflated language is inconsistent with a personal voice.

> *Inflated Language:* My intransigent goal has consistently been to utilize my superlative business training for intromission to an appropriate salaried position.
> *Appropriate Language:* I want to use my business training on the job.

4. Use understatement rather than overstatement.
Modesty is more appealing than bragging. Avoid aggressive or pompous business-speak.

> *Overstated:* I have a proven record as someone who succeeds in anything he tries to do.
> *More Measured:* My friends sometimes make fun of my determination. Truthfully, since I am the only one in my family who has had the opportunity to go to college, I *am* determined to work hard and succeed.

say and leads the reader to her conclusion: she is "determined to work in the field of Public Health Education." Her final sentence, the essay's thesis, echoes the first sentence of the conclusion: she wants the scholarship so she can accomplish the goals she has just explained.

Some aspects of Jessica's personality emerge from this essay. She is sympathetic (she understands the reasons "hard-working people" smoke), and she is compassionate. She is determined and focused on her goal of

5. If possible, use few or no contractions *(I've, there's, haven't, would've).* Some readers do not find them appropriate in written works of importance.

Avoid Gimmicks

Creative writing and an engaging personal voice cannot take the place of having something substantial to say and a good focus. Give careful thought to your topic, trying several before settling on one, and avoid high-risk gimmicks. The problem with taking risks is that sometimes they fail miserably, and even the ones that are not total failures can be jarring to some readers.

1. Use sarcasm carefully. Relying on sarcastic humor is risky.

> Working hard for no money is the way I want to spend my professional life.

Starting an essay with this statement is provocative, but it also sets up a negative tone. The first impression your reader has of you is as someone who is angry and sarcastic.

2. Avoid application clichés. Clichés are predictable expressions that have grown so familiar that people no longer think of them as fresh or interesting.

> My eighth-grade teacher turned my life around.
>
> Education is the wellspring of knowledge.
>
> I am a people person.
>
> I want to help others help themselves.

When readers hear clichés, they tune out. If you find yourself using a cliché, revise the sentence and instead brainstorm fresh, original ways to make your point.

3. Reconsider experimental techniques. Writers will often try to brighten stories by writing in unusual points of view. One writer told a story from his dead grandmother's point of view, a technique that overshadowed the real point of the writing. Another writer began this way.

> Though I wanted to travel to 50 states on the rodeo circuit, I had to work at a copy store in my hometown, instead. The rodeo, it turns out, wouldn't even pay me enough so I could buy my books for college.

The essay concludes as follows.

> I know lots of kids have spent their summers in great internships that didn't pay, and volunteering to help people in exotic places. The fact is, that I don't look good on paper. If I said I spend more of my time at $6 an hour jobs making copies and serving coffee, and far less time studying while I'm at school, would I get the scholarship?

Though this approach offers a frankness that readers of application essays usually do not encounter, the material might be too jarring and personal. Offering something that makes the essay different can be a risky proposition. While you want to stand out, using gimmicks may alienate your readers and hurt your chances for success.

helping people live healthier lives. All in all, Jessica presents herself as someone whose personality and goals fit the profile of a serious candidate for a scholarship to a school of public health.

This kind of summary conclusion, especially with the somewhat unusual placement of the thesis as the final sentence, can be extremely effective, but so can other methods of ending an essay. You might choose a memorable quotation or image, or a metaphor or insight that will linger in your reader's mind. One student concluded his essay about the loss of a friendship by quoting Robert Frost.

> Reflecting on the friendship that TP and I once had, I can say that the saddest lesson that I learned from my transitory semester in high school is that the best things in life are often the hardest to preserve, the hardest to hold on to; in the words of Robert Frost, "Nothing gold can stay."
>
> —Josh Jacobs, from "Self-Portraits"

Another student, writing about his love of sports, concluded with this paragraph.

> A love of sport is a way to stir oneself through emotion—joy and humiliation and all else—in sets, quarters, or minutes. I love the escapism, the generation of stunning feeling that dissipates minutes after the fact. I revel in pre-game promises of championship, little bravado of airy summits comforting in its non-worth. I smile at grown men arguing over the amount of pine tar on a bat—and at myself for equally silly complaints. All 280 pounds of Jeff Ruland make me chuckle when he glides in, smoother than I could ever be, for a lay-up. And I am blindingly happy with green elbows streaking downfield for a tackle. Because real life has too few ways to act idiotic as it is, I need all of the sports I can get. I love every season like Jim Rice loves a low fastball.
>
> —Charles D. Haley, from "Essays on Sports and Activities"

The writer specifies how his love of sports affects his life, and he does it with some style. Notice how he creates a sense of balance and harmony with a series of sentences starting "I love" and "I revel" and "I smile," a technique known as parallel structure. The concluding analogy comparing his love of sports to Jim Rice's love of a fastball leaves the reader with a smile.

Leave *your* reader with a distinct memory of your writing and a clear statement of your personality, whether it is playful or serious. Above all, do not forget the importance of the conclusion. In a piece of writing as brief as an application essay, where every word counts toward making an impression, the ending is as important as the beginning.

African Eyes

STEPHANIE SHEEN

> The voyage of discovery is not in seeking new landscapes, but in having new eyes.
>
> —Marcel Proust

Those eyes. I've seen them before. The pleading stare from the child on the TV screen is so familiar. Her swollen belly peeks out from beneath the tattered shirt that she has long outgrown. Her face is soiled with a mixture of dirt and remnants of food. The commercial begins to fade as I close my eyes. The emotions return, and I am again in Africa.

Those same eyes looked into mine just months earlier. It was our last night in Samburu, Kenya, and we had been working all day. We had spent the week in this village through the CHOICE Humanitarian program working alongside the villagers in building schoolrooms, making bricks, hauling dirt, and teaching lessons in the schools. The preparation for the trip had begun almost a year before, however. It was an inaugural trip. Sixteen students were chosen to travel to Africa. The program emphasized "helping locally to help globally," so each of us had chosen a place to render service throughout the year. We each completed one hundred hours of service. I had worked at a local elementary school helping tutor children and reading to them three times a week. So here I was, an admittedly sheltered girl from Utah, in the middle of Africa. In addition to helping with physical tasks in the village, we had also been involved in cultural exchange activities—learning about the Kenyan culture while they learned about ours.

Since it was our last night, some of the villagers had invited us to their homes for dinner—a huge honor—and we accepted. As we reached the end of the long walk down the dirt road to their collection of huts, the sun was just setting on the African horizon. We stopped as we turned the corner to see all of the children of the village running towards us with wide smiles almost fighting to hold our hands. One young girl in particular stood out. She stood about waist high and looked at me smiling shyly. She reached up her hand and took mine. Wordlessly, we walked into the village together.

Some time passed as her mother prepared dinner. It had grown dark. We sat outside the mud-and-stick house that the little girl and her family called home. It was a one-bedroom hut that held the mother and her nine children. The little girl could only speak Swahili, and I could only speak English so she looked at me, studying my white skin and touching my straight, blonde hair. I set her on my lap and looked at her. Her tattered dress was hanging off her body. She made no attempt to swat at the flies that constantly buzzed by her head, frequently landing on her nose. Yet, as I looked at her, her eyes sparkled against her beautiful black skin. She seemed happy—and that puzzled me. This little girl lived in a house that barely kept out the elements. The other villagers often scraped together food for her family when their father who worked in the city to support them, had not sent money. But when they invited us to eat, they offered to kill their last goat to make a huge meal for us. Their generosity amazed me. This family was willing to give up everything they had to feed us and show their appreciation for what we had done for their village. I was on the verge of tears when the music began. The little girl slid from my lap, flashed me a smile, and pulled me from my chair onto the dirt floor outside the hut. Underneath the African moonlight with only a lantern to light the darkness, we danced. I held her little hand in mine as the music filled us both. We may have danced differently, but the feelings we felt were the same. We were one—me, the little girl, the music, and Africa.

5   The music subsided, and I relaxed back into my chair. My new friend twirled my ring between her delicate fingers and laid her head on my lap as I stroked her soft, fluffy hair. Her mother announced dinner, and we went into the hut cramped together but enjoying it all. They brought us all the food they had—a few *chapatis* and some sauce to dip it in. They kept nothing for themselves. We politely ate and thanked them profusely for the dinner. I was touched and yet saddened. They had given up their dinner in feeding us. The children would most likely not get to eat, and I knew that this wasn't the first time it had happened. I also knew it wouldn't be the last. We sat in the hut talking as the light of the lantern began to grow dim. The villagers walked us back to the school where we stayed.

As I scooped up my little Kenyan friend when we said good-bye, I could see the sadness, now, in her eyes. I felt the same. We had not spoken a word to each other, but I knew I was forever tied to this girl. Her wide eyes stared into mine, and I saw the dreams she held for what she could become. I had these same dreams when I was her age, yet I knew my circumstances had been much different and the opportunities afforded to me much greater. Coming to Africa to live and work with the people who make the country so beautiful was priceless.

Through the hours of service it took to get there and the hours of service rendered while there, I had come to see what I could become with a little work. I had seen the hero inside of me—the best part that resides in each of us that just yearns to get out. I had looked at service, at Africa, and at myself through those African eyes—eyes full of hope for a future that I may not see, eyes searching for whatever good may lie in things, eyes that see a need, eyes that have seen sadness and boldly dared to hope against hope.

The commercial ends and I switch off the TV. If only everyone knew what I knew. If only I could show everyone else those eyes.

Annotate "African Eyes"

1. Put a check mark next to the sentence where the writer first announces the focus of the essay.

2. Underline the thesis of this essay.

3. The author uses a frame device in her essay. That is, she starts in one scene, flashes back, and then ends with a reference to the opening scene, thus framing the story. Put brackets around the opening and closing elements of the frame.

4. Next to each of the six paragraphs in the middle of the essay, note how the writer developed that paragraph: narration, analysis, argument, or some other strategy.

5. In which paragraphs does the author generalize about her experience?

6. In which paragraphs does the author uses specific details?

READINGS

Katie Robbins wrote the first essay in this section as part of her transfer application from a community college. She takes a strong and controversial political stand, and she shows how her views have been shaped by current events and family tradition.

The last essay, "That Other Part," is Nitya Venkataraman's personal statement from her graduate school application. Like many application essays, this personal statement is about how a person shapes his or her identity. Using a narrative structure, Venkataraman sets her readers in the middle of a scene in her first-grade classroom. Venkataraman's essay is followed by an interview in which she discusses her thinking and writing process for application essays.

An American's Freedom to Choose

Katie Robbins

The rights to assemble peaceably and speak freely are two of the freedoms granted to citizens of the United States of America. These are only two of the reasons I am proud to call myself an American. As the threat of war against Iraq grew, I found myself taking advantage of my constitutional rights. As my involvement in the antiwar campaign increased, I found my respect and loyalty for the USA intensified as well.

Although I believe Saddam Hussein is a tyrannical dictator, deciding my position on how to remove him from power was a delicate matter. I was torn; maybe the inspections were an opportunity to find Hussein's weapons of mass destruction or maybe they were an excuse to gain control of the oil fields. Either way, I knew I detest war.

I began researching groups protesting the threat of war and joined my first protest. Arriving without a sign I stood at the street corner merely observing motorists. The majority against the war honked, waved, or extended a peace sign, while those in favor of the war gave thumbs down or shouted obscenities from their windows. Ironically, both sides were speaking out in the name of freedom.

I was prepared for protest number two with my sign and proper attire for a February afternoon in

French protesters express their views on the United States' war in Iraq.

New England. On this day the sentiments on both sides were more intense. Supporters of the war continued to shout from their automobiles denouncing the United Nations and encouraging George Bush. Those against beeped their horns longer, waving and smiling. Protest number three was a candle-light vigil that attracted 250 people. The evening breeze was light, and there was no support or opposition from passersby. The quiet seemed to reflect our message of peace.

5   Protest number four came the morning after the bombings officially began in Iraq. Again, I gathered my sign and proper attire; for even as March comes to a close there are no guarantees on Cape Cod. Beginning at a crosswalk on Main Street, Hyannis

we marched to Congressman Delahunt's office and spent the afternoon out front with our signs and flags. During those hours the opposition was quite hostile, but with each curse and piece of unwelcome advice, I waved a peace sign and a smile.

My grandmother protested for better schools; my father protested against the Vietnam War and, as an educator, for increased funding to public schools. As I continue to protest for peace, I am proud to follow in their footsteps as an American. It saddens me to know people consider my actions un-American and un-patriotic; however, I have tremendous respect for my country. I shall continue to exercise my rights and hold the ideals on which this country was founded in the highest regard.

Critical Reading Questions

1. How effective is the introduction in getting your attention and announcing the topic?
2. Where does Robbins establish the focus of the essay?
3. What is the thesis of this essay? Why do you think Robbins placed it where she did?
4. How has Robbins organized this essay? Identify places where she uses elements of narration, analysis, or argumentation.
5. Comment on the writer's style. Do you get a sense of her personality? What kind of person would you say the writer is?
6. What does the concluding paragraph accomplish? Is it persuasive?

Questions for Writing and Discussion

1. Making such a strong political statement can be risky. How well do you think Robbins handles the controversial nature of her topic?
2. Katie Robbins wrote this essay in March 2003, just as the United States entered Iraq and well before Saddam Hussein was captured. Do you think the essay is dated? Why?
3. How effective is this essay in revealing values that Robbins holds?
4. If you were peer-editing this essay, what advice might you give?

That Other Part

Nitya K. Venkataraman

I wasn't White, Black, or Mexican. But to a six-year-old, what's an "Other"?

White. Black. Mexican. Other.

I stared blankly down at the page in front of me and tried to answer a question that would echo throughout the rest of my life every time I sought to define an identity for myself.

The year was 1985 and the California Achievement Test was the most grown-up undertaking that had collided with my six-year old existence. And even though I promised my very Indian parents that my teacher said the test "didn't count," they had sailed to this country on the tide of education, and a test was a test was a test. I spent the week preceding the test doing math problems and taking spelling tests hosted by my mother around our kitchen table.

5   But what I'll never forget is the one question on the test that my mom never prepared me for.

I was giddy with excitement at the thought of answering multiple choice questions in a Scantron bubble format. With three newly sharpened No. 2 pencils, a gruff "good luck!" from my dad, a kiss from my mom, and my prettiest peach frock with puffed sleeves, I dismounted the bus and ran into my first-grade classroom, waiting for my first real test to commence.

I remained optimistic as we were instructed to fill in basic information about ourselves, feeling slightly worried that the California Achievement people might mistake me for someone else—my name amounted to "Nitya K. Venkatar," in a test-taking land where after the eighth Scantron box, the letters in your last name were irrelevant.

Sex: M or F? With little hesitation, I marked in the oval next to "F," giggling along with my classmates at the word sex printed on a test.

Birthday. That was easy: April 13, 1979.

So far, so good.

10   Ethnicity (Optional). I am: White. Black. Mexican. Other.

Our teacher told us that optional meant we didn't have to answer it. But part of my test preparation included the speech that I never skip questions (lest I lose points), and I assumed that if I thought and thought and thought hard enough, the right answer would come to me.

White? Black? Mexican? Other?

I knew I wasn't White. White was Stephanie, my best friend next door, and Peaches-and-Cream Barbie. It was the Pledge of Allegiance, potato salad, and the Nina, Pinta, and Santa Maria. White was my dad's boss. And I knew I wasn't any of those things.

15   I knew I wasn't Black. Black was the little girl across the street with hair that could be braided once a week and clipped at the ends with colorful, plastic barrettes. Black was Willis on "Different Strokes" and the kind lady with shiny, dark skin at the grocery store who told me I was as "sweet as brown sugar." Black was Stevie Wonder. And I knew I wasn't any of those things.

I knew I wasn't Mexican. Mexican was enchiladas and tacos and adios. It was the "Uno Dos Tres Qua-tro Cin-co Seis" song. Mexican was the man at the Farmer's Market in Berkeley who sold us fresh grapes every Saturday. And I knew I wasn't any of those things.

But Other. Who was Other?

I sighed, disheartened. After so much excitement, so much preparation, I was not going to be able to take the test. Ethnicity (Optional) didn't really apply to me. With a heavy heart, I collected my materials and tried to unobtrusively make my way to the front of the classroom to Mrs. Palmer's desk to tell her of this latest calamity.

"Mrs. Palmer, I don't think I can take this test." I showed her the question and I'll never forget the look that washed over her face.

20   "You're 'Other,' Nitya," she whispered with a kind smile. "You're a little bit special on this test."

I grinned, at the thought of being special, and pushed away all thoughts of confusion and unhappiness, even though something about bubbling in Other didn't exactly sit right with me. What was Other?

Was Other the plates and plates of sweets I ate every Diwali? The classical dance classes I took every weekend at the temple? The Hindi lullaby my mother sang to me before I slept?

On the way home, I overheard a Chinese girl on the bus telling the person sitting next to her that she "got to be an Other" on the test. And that is when I realized: Other was Chinese New Year and Egyptian pyramids. It was falafel, origami and Hindi lullabies. Other was the little piece of everyone that had been forgotten somewhere else.

Years later, multiculturalism became politically correct. Having a specific ethnic identity was beyond OK—it was chic, trendy, encouraged and evidenced in the Ethnicity(Optional) boxes, once reserved for White, Black, Mexican, Other.

25   Chinese New Year became Chinese-American. Falafel was Middle Eastern. Origami was Japanese-American. And Hindi lullabies? Well, they were Asian, Asian-American (Indian subcontinent included), and on special occasion, lucky enough to be considered Indian-American.

But what happened to Other? It was still there, lurking in the bottom right-hand corner of every Ethnicity (Optional) box, glaring at all the turncoats who had left it for their own identities. And yet, Other remained, proud to claim those without identity as its own.

As for me, I never really decided where I belonged. As much as I longed to bubble myself in as Asian-American, I always felt torn, like I was leaving Other behind. But Indian-American? Could I really be two things at once? Could I represent a culture of arranged marriages and another of sexual freedoms all at the same time? Was I Kulfi and apple pie? Bindis and blue jeans? Something in the picture didn't fit together.

As a newly defined Indian-American, I realized something that many hyphenated Americans recognize when their worlds collide: My identity lay not really in the Indian, and not really in the American, but more like that Other part.

The hyphen in between.

Critical Reading Questions

1. Is the opening scene effective in capturing your attention and pulling you into the essay? Why?

2. What is the thesis of this essay? Is the thesis stated explicitly? If so, where? If not, identify some details or sentences that lead the reader to the thesis.

3. From the details in the story, what do you know about the writer's family, history, and life?

4. The writer relies on many of the techniques of storytelling to organize her essay, especially the notion of central conflict. State the conflict in a sentence.

5. What is the writer's attitude towards multiculturalism? Support your answer with a specific line or two from the essay.

6. Comment on the writer's style and voice.

7. Does the fact that the concluding paragraph is only one sentence long and a fragment enhance or detract from the essay? What does the conclusion accomplish?

Questions for Writing and Discussion

1. One paragraph reads: "Years later, multiculturalism became politically correct. Having a specific ethnic identity was beyond OK — it was chic, trendy, encouraged and evidenced in the Ethnicity (Optional) boxes, once reserved for White, Black, Mexican, Other." What is your response?

2. What does the writer imply by the comment "after the eighth Scantron box, the letters in your last name were irrelevant"?

3. Would the committee remember this essay? What would they remember? Is it different from other essays you have read or written?

WRITING IN THE WORKS

Interview with Nitya K. Venkataraman

Nitya K. Venkataraman

1. What have you encountered as obstacles in writing essays for applications? What, for you, is the most difficult part of writing essays for applications?

The most difficult part of any application essay process, I think, is staying original and trying to say something old in a new way. We have a natural tendency to write what we think admissions committees want to hear, which sometimes makes essays generic and cookie cutter; as a result, we end up staying away from the stories and topics and anecdotes that make us unique and personal.

2. How do you imagine your reader when you write essays for applications? Does your version of that reader shape your style?

It sounds kind of funny, but I envision my reader as a member of an admissions committee who is surrounded by stacks and stacks of application essays (sometimes I even imagine them looking a little bit bored!). For some reason, when I think about the volume of generic essays these committees probably consume, I am forced to be creative, punchy, and take more chances with my writing, tone, and style.

3. How do you balance personal writing with the formality of an application essay? Or do you?

Application essays should be personal. In a lot of cases, this is your one and only opportunity to speak to the selection panel, so you need to paint a picture of yourself to a group of people who have never met you before. I always remind myself that real people are reading my essay, not robots. These people are human and they have hopes, dreams, ambitions, fears, etc. that are similar emotions to mine. Your essay is a chance to connect with the selection committee in a very personal way. Though the process may seem formal with rec-

ommendations and transcripts and multiple choice questions and resumes, your essay is the fun part where you get to show your selection committee who you really are.

4. We are calling your essay "a personal statement that was part of an application process for graduate school." Can you talk about your writing process?

My father told me once that all good writing starts in your imagination, and I remember that every time I start to put a body of writing together. I actually start well in advance and mull over the topic that I have been given (if it is a more open-ended "tell us about yourself" statement, I think about all the things in my life that have brought me to the point where I am applying to start something new) in my head. For days, weeks, and, on occasion, months, I travel around with a little notebook in my bag and just keep the application topic in the back of my head. When I think of good phrases I would like to use or things I would like to include, I jot them down as part of my brainstorming process so that when the right opening line hits me, I have a lot to work with. This particular essay started on the back of a McDonald's napkin.

5. Your essay has a definite narrative thread that makes the essay really engaging. You seem like a real person, an individual rather than a type. A mistake a lot of writers make when writing application essays is that they want to seem like a type, the right type, but a type nonetheless. What do you think you included to make yourself more of an individual, to help your reader remember you?

I think it's all in the details. My high school English teacher and my favorite college communications professor were big advocates of "show, don't tell." And in the end that all traces back to the details you decide to include. The details make it vivid and real and an experience that you share with your reader. Without the details, it's not personal, and you are not an individual. I wrote about the standardized test because I knew it was an experience that anyone could relate to, but the ethnicity optional box was a minute detail that changed my entire life. Without that small, poignant detail, I might have forgotten that I even took that test in 1985. The details are everything.

6. Would you say you enjoy writing application essays?

I do. I think that writing application essays is a good time to do some personal soul-searching. It is not necessarily a good time to put it in an essay and send it off to an admissions board, but it's a good time to remember what your goals are and why you are pursuing them. And in the middle of a mundane application process, it is a brief, shining opportunity to be creative and unique.

WRITING AND REVISION STRATEGIES

Gathered here are three interactive sections for you to use as you write and revise your application essay and as you apply what you have learned to writing in other classes.

▶ Writer's Notebook Suggestions

▶ Peer Editing Log

▶ Revision Checklist

Writer's Notebook Suggestions

These short exercises are intended to jump-start your thinking as you begin to write your application essay.

1. Write a letter of recommendation for yourself.

2. You have been asked to go back to your former high school and give a useful two-minute speech to the senior class. Write the speech.

3. Describe your single best asset in one paragraph. Don't brag, but sell yourself.

4. List all the things you wish to accomplish in the next five years.

5. Give one example of a time you succeeded against the odds.

6. Write one paragraph explaining a disappointment and how it affected you.

7. Write about an experience that made you aware of a skill you have.

8. Write a paragraph about one goal you have. Be as specific as possible.

9. Link a personal experience with a career goal.

10. Create a visual image (a short video, a collage, a drawing) that communicates something about who you are.

Peer-Editing Log

As you work with a writing partner or in a peer-editing group, you can use these questions to give helpful responses to a classmate's application essay and as a guide for discussion.

Writer's Name_____

Date_____

1. Underline the essay's thesis. Make suggestions to strengthen it by rewording it or placing it elsewhere.

2. Put brackets around the introduction. Does the introduction announce the topic clearly?

3. If there is a prompt, has the introduction addressed the prompt specifically?

4. What development strategies does the writer use? Can you suggest specific places where narrative detail or supporting evidence might strengthen the essay?

5. Put brackets around the conclusion. What impression does it leave? Suggest ways for the writer to strengthen the final impression.

6. Put wavy lines under any application clichés the writer used; put check marks next to any language you find particularly fresh and appealing.

Revision Checklist

As you do your final revision, check to make sure that you

❏ Stated your thesis clearly and accurately

❏ Wrote an engaging and focused introduction

❏ Clearly answered the prompt, if there is one

❏ Organized the body of the paper in a logical pattern

❏ Used elements of narration, analysis, and argumentation where appropriate

❏ Wrote in a personal yet not informal voice

❏ Avoided application essay clichés

❏ Concluded with the impression you want to leave with your reader

❏ Wrote a memorable essay that reflects some aspect of your values, interests, and personality

5. MEMOIRS

WRITING A NARRATIVE

If you want to write, you can. Fear stops most people from writing, not lack of talent, whatever that is. Who am I? What right have I to speak? Who will listen to me if I do? You're a human being, with a unique story to tell, and you have every right. If you speak with passion, many of us will listen. We need stories to live, all of us. We live story by story. Yours enlarges the circle.

—**Richard Rhodes**

ASSIGNMENT

Write a memoir, a true story about some part of your life. Your story can relate a single event or a series of closely linked events. Show a change of mind or heart, a discovery, a confirmation or contradiction of a belief, a disappointment, or a decision. Include the following narrative elements.

- Scenes full of detail and imagery
- Characters with motivation and depth
- Incremental, logical development of the plot
- Conflict and theme

Scattered throughout the chapter are other snapshots, each one a kind of memoir.

MEMOIRS

The first storytellers were cave dwellers. Painting on walls, they told stories of danger and survival. Scholars will argue forever about these first attempts to record images: Why paint on cave walls? Were the painters recording information so that others might know where to hunt or even how to hunt well? Or were they recording information that they themselves might otherwise forget—a "note to self" in charcoal, done by firelight? Maybe the pictures communicated bragging: "This wooly mammoth came from that direction. Little did I know that another, bigger wooly mammoth was headed toward me from over there." You could argue that cave art emerged because of the basic human need to record what happened—as a cautionary tale to the young, as a way to remember, as a way to say, "It mattered."

Stories wallpaper our daily lives without us being overtly aware of this fact. Newspapers and broadcasts tell us, sometime overwhelm us, with stories of day-to-day life. Cable news has made it possible to watch real-life drama unfold in real time. Music videos and commercials use true-life stories and fictional stories to get our interest. So much information comes to us in the form of narrative because people find stories irresistible and memorable. Good stories mark the memory; they leave footprints.

We watch movies and read fiction and nonfiction books because we like the feeling of getting lost in a story. Sometimes we do not care whether we remember details or whether the story has deep significance. But the best stories, the ones that leave marks, are well told and offer something beneath the surface action. These provide not just a record of what happened, but also a reason for listening to the story and understanding why it matters.

Memoirs are true stories, nonfiction narratives. They engage readers the way fiction does, by taking them into scenes. Films use the same techniques, creating scenes that *show* more than they *tell*. Think *pictures*, like the cave drawings and like the movies.

Your memoir is not private writing. You are telling a story that has to have meaning for your readers. People read to be entertained and informed, but with memoirs, people are interested in the fact that the story is true, that it really happened. Part of the appeal is the knowledge that same thing could happen to them, or that maybe in some way, on some level, it already has. This thematic connection with the reader gives memoirs their universal appeal.

Applications: School, Community, Work

Narrative writing can add color, provide evidence, and persuade readers in a variety of academic assignments. In English, sociology, psychology, or gender studies courses you might write personal narratives to examine your values or cultural identity. In a history or science class you might use narrative skills to compose oral histories or historical profiles that shed light on a social movement, discovery, medical breakthrough, or phenomenon. Narratives about you or about someone else reveal an insider's knowledge of time periods and cultural experiences.

You will also find narrative skills useful in writing for your community and your workplace. Because narratives are both engaging and personal, you can use them to persuade people when you write proposals, brochures, and letters for work or for community service. You have probably read many letters of appeal, for example, that begin with testimonials, true stories that relate personal or eyewitness accounts. Such stories often engage readers' emotions while establishing the writer's credibility. Similarly, you will often use narrative in newsletters, newspapers, or quarterly reports. Telling true stories is a useful technique in fundraising as well as in raising awareness about social, political, and cultural issues.

CHAPTER OBJECTIVES

In this chapter you will learn to

▶ write a nonfiction story using the techniques of fiction: character, setting, conflict, and theme

▶ "show" through detail, dialogue, and description

▶ write scenes that tell stories

UNDERSTANDING MEMOIRS

Storytelling invites your reader to enter a world you create. Although memoirs are true stories, memoirists borrow techniques from fiction writers to create scenes full of narrative detail—scenes that leave footprints in their readers' memories. Some inexplicable chemistry of the elements in a story gives it the power to get and keep readers' attention and to make an impression.

Warm-Up Practice 5.1
Collaborative Writing

This exercise is based on the game "Taboo," in which certain words are banned. The object of the exercise is to write descriptions without using taboo words. Here are some practice examples using the five senses.

• Describe the feeling of getting into a hot car on a summer day. Don't use *hot, heat, burning, sun,* or *melt.*

• Describe the sounds of waking up in the morning. Don't use *clock, ring, buzz, shower,* or *birds.*

• Describe the smell of Thanksgiving (or choose another holiday). Don't use *turkey, good, delicious, warm,* or *sweet.*

• Describe the look of a rainy day. Don't use *gray, drops, rain, water, puddle,* or *clouds.*

• Describe the taste of orange juice. Don't use *sweet, sour, fresh,* or *acid.*

In pairs or groups, create challenges like the ones above for another group. Exchange challenges, and write descriptions.

Compare these two versions of the same story.

Narrative A

Ironically, it was a beautiful day, and I felt quite relaxed as I rode the train from upper Manhattan, and we passed by the more run-down buildings. Suddenly we came upon a gruesome scene. A little boy had been hit by the train. A crowd of people stood around, as well as police and other rescue workers. Near me two men were playing a game of cards. This game of chance reminded me of the danger in the world: life is a game of chance. As I thought about it, I noticed the men pay attention to the poor dead boy for just a second, and then turn right back to their bridge game.

Narrative B

One afternoon in late August, as the summer's sun streamed into the car and made little jumping shadows on the windows, I sat gazing out at the tenement-dwellers, who were themselves looking out of their windows from the gray crumbling buildings along the tracks of upper Manhattan.

As we crossed into the Bronx, the train unexpectedly slowed down for a few miles. Suddenly from out my window I saw a large crowd near the track, held back by two policemen. Then, on the other side from my window I saw a scene I would never be able to forget: a little boy almost severed in halves, lying at an incredible angle near the track. The ground was covered with blood, and the boy's eyes were opened wide, strained and disbelieving in his sudden oblivion. A policeman stood next to him, his arms folded, staring straight ahead at the windows of our train. In the orange glow of late afternoon the policemen, the crowd, the corpse of the boy were for a brief moment immobile, motionless, a small tableau to violence and death in the city.

Behind me, in the next row of seats, there was a game of bridge. I heard one of the four men say as he looked at the sight, "God that's horrible." Another said, in a whisper, "Terrible, terrible." There was a momentary silence, punctuated only by the clicking of the wheels on the track. Then, after the pause, I heard the first man say: "Two hearts."

—Willie Morris, *North Toward Home*

Narrative A provides information about an incident but does not invite you into this world. The writing does not create a sense of place, nor does it put you in the middle of a scene. Though explaining can be important in making a vague point clear, when you write a narrative, you want to *show* all you can, rather than *tell*. You want to roll the tape, run the movie.

VISUAL
LITERACY

Snapshots

The illustrations in this chapter are personal photos—the kind that people keep on their refrigerators and in little frames on their desks or nightstands. These images take people back to places and times they want to remember always. Choose one of these pictures, describe what you see, and give that reasons that this photo might be important to its owner. Find a snapshot that is important to you, and write about the moment that it freezes. Write in present tense.

On the other hand, in Narrative B writer Willie Morris uses description to invite you into a scene and create a mood. The opening takes you to a specific moment, place, and mood, a late August afternoon on a train moving through the tenements of the Bronx. From this setting the story can progress.

People inhabit this setting. The narrator introduces himself as a train-rider, an observer of the scene about to unfold. Through his eyes you can see the tenement-dwellers and the tableau of the boy, the policemen, and the crowd. Then the writer shifts his and your attention to the four card players on the train. Morris creates many characters for such a brief story, but each plays a part in building the scene.

If you think of narratives as movies rather than still photos, you can see why something must happen in order for a story to develop. Even though the story is very short, Morris lets the tape roll to show a specific picture: an unforgettable scene of the tragic death of a small boy. Vivid pictures like this create the footprints.

Morris creates a setting and moves characters into it. Something happens there: a story filled with tension unfolds. By the end of the story, the meaning of this scene emerges. Even in a scene as brief as this one, you can see the elements of story: setting, character, conflict, and theme.

Setting

The setting is the time, place, and social or cultural context of a story. Most memoir writers establish the setting early in the piece to bring the reader more fully into the remembered place. Morris sets the mood for his commuter train with a sense of late summer and the hypnotic shadows of the train. The larger elements of the city and the impersonal way people sometimes treat each other in cities are also essential in understanding the meaning of the story.

Consider the setting of a rundown horse stable. Stables in general might make you think of the daily chores of farm life or the privileges of the wealthy. But the description of the horse stable at the Diamond D Ranch creates an "air of neglect."

No one at Diamond D knew how to properly care for horses. Most of the animals were kept outside in three small, grassless corrals. The barn was on the verge of collapse; our every entry was accompanied by the fluttering sounds of startled rats. The "staff" consisted of a bunch of junior high and high school kids willing to work in exchange for riding privileges. And the main source of income, apart from the pony parties, was hacking— renting out the horses for ten dollars an hour to anyone willing to pay. Mrs. Daniels bought the horses at an auction whose main customer was the meat dealer for a dog-food company; Diamond D, more often than not, was merely a way station. The general air of neglect surrounding the stable was the result more of ignorance than of apathy. It's not as if we didn't care about the horses—we simply didn't know any better.

—Lucy Greely, *Autobiography of a Face*

A story can also be set in a time. In the following example, a brutal winter becomes the setting for a story about finding shelter—in a literal and a figurative sense.

Winter was like a dark and endless tunnel I entered when I left the house for school. The clouds pulled themselves down around me, reducing clear sky to a place just above my head. I could almost touch those gray clouds that blotted out the sun for weeks and weeks on end. The cold was sometimes so intense that my nostrils would freeze, sticking together, and the coldness could transform the snow. There were days when it did not melt, or adhere to anything, but lasted as a fine powder that squeaked under my boots. The prowling winds skulked through the maze of buildings of the housing project where I lived, waiting behind corners to attack, to shoot icy blasts up my nose, down my throat. And then there was inside.

—Connie Porter, "GirlGirlGirl"

Character

You are the narrator of your memoir, and in telling your story you communicate how the experience affected you, how it mattered to you, and how it changed you. You introduce the other characters and show their actions and their personalities.

The people in your memoir are characters with needs, motivations, and choices. They can act and react, change or refuse to change. In Willie Morris's scene, the main characters are the card players who are as anonymous as the boy who is killed by the train. This anonymity helps express the theme of the story—namely, how impersonal tragedy can be. The true center of Morris's tale, though, is the speaker, the person who observes the action and understands the irony of the bridge player's comment, "Two hearts."

As a narrator, you need not explain your feelings or explain at length about the characters. Instead, you are a lens for the action. Your goal is to show, not tell. Rather than tell the reader what you are thinking through internal monologue or explain what a character is like, you reveal character through details or incidents. Rather than explaining, imagine how you would film such material. Keep asking, what is my movie showing now?

Not every character in your story has to be fully developed. Some minor characters will be in the story simply to move the plot along. The police officer with the big sunglasses that made him look like a bug, who gave you the speeding ticket on the fateful day you also got caught running a red light, will appear only for a moment. Still, all characters require careful attention. They

---

Practice 5.2
Description of Setting

1. Read the following description. What details does the writer use to create the feeling of the Fourth of July in a small town? What is the feeling he creates?

The Fourth of July

A young boy rides his bicycle in a serpentine pattern down the middle of a dusty street. Blue sky divides a broken pavement of clouds. The road out of town seems to stretch farther than usual before it fades out of sight between the fields of corn or soybeans, alfalfa or cotton. Near a railroad siding, the ringing against steel in the darkness of a repair shop. An old horse sleeps in a small corral behind the drive-in. The mail fails to arrive. A firecracker goes off in the alley.

—Verlyn Klinkenborg, "July"

2. Write a description of a place where you spent a Fourth of July.

Practice 5.3
Description of Character

In the following passage author David Eggers describes a trick his mother often did.

> She used to do a trick where it looked like she would be pulling off her thumb, when in fact she was not. Do you know this trick? Part of one's right thumb is made to look like part of one's left hand and then is slid up and down the index finger of the left finger—attached, then detached. It's an unsettling trick, and more so when my mother used to do it, because she did it in a way where her hands shook, vibrated, her neck's veins protruding and taut, her face gripped with the strain plausible attendant to pulling off one's finger. As children we watched with both glee and terror.
>
> —David Eggers, *A Heartbreaking Work of Staggering Genius*

Describe a character you know by writing a passage about one physical feature, gesture, or habit.

should be clearly drawn and have clear motivation. What they do comes logically from *who* they are.

Point of View

Art students will tell you that the most difficult assignment—and they are almost always given this assignment in a beginning drawing class—is to draw a self-portrait. Drawing yourself is complicated not only by the fact that drawing and studying the shape and shadows of your own face are very difficult, but also because objectifying yourself compounds the challenge. You are not used to looking at yourself from an emotional distance. Writing about yourself as a character is the same sort of challenge.

Writing a memoir requires a first-person point of view, a way of looking at things limited to only what you can see or feel or know. For example, when you rolled down the car window to see why the police officer was stopping you, you can't say your face was crimson red. How could you know that? You could feel the heat pulsing in your cheeks. Or you could possibly see your face reflected in the mirrored sunglasses the officer was wearing, but this point needs to be clear to your reader.

Your point of view might be limited to your knowledge and understanding at the time of the story. "I'm looking at the officer for some signal that he's not mad. All I see is me, my red-face, all guilty-looking, staring back at myself in his big, mirrored sunglasses."

You might also write in the first-person point of view that expresses an understanding of an event that has ripened with time.

> I looked at the police officer's face for some signal that he wasn't mad at me. I wouldn't find out until later that the officer was my mom's high-school sweetheart and a really nice guy. At that moment all I saw was me, my red face, all guilty-looking, staring back at myself in his big, scary, mirrored sunglasses.

You can't know what the officer is seeing (unless you see it too) or thinking. "He thought I was a stupid kid" is in a third-person point of view—*he*, not *I*, thought. You should remain in one point of view throughout a story unless you are experimenting with a special effect.

Dialogue

Dialogue allows the reader to hear the characters' voices, letting the writer reveal characters effectively through their own words. The challenge of using dialogue in a memoir is trying to stay true to your memory while selecting just

---

Punctuating Dialogue

Here are a few tips on the technical aspects of writing dialogue.

- Begin a new paragraph with each new speaker.
- Put quotation marks around each speaker's words.
- Periods and commas always go inside quotation marks.

  "All right," I said, "I'll walk with you."

- Place a question mark and an exclamation mark inside quotation marks if the quotation is itself a question or an exclamation. Place the question mark or exclamation mark outside the quotation marks if the sentence around the quotation poses the question or makes an exclamation.

  "When can we start walking?" she asked.

  When did you say, "I would rather drive"?

  "I want to go now!" she said.

- Use *said* or *says* for most attributions.

Practice 5.4   Dialogue

1. To understand how dialogue reveals character, write down an overheard conversation. Go to a public place—a café, a dining hall, a bus, a subway car, a lecture hall—and eavesdrop on a conversation. Write down as much of the conversation as you can in ten or fifteen minutes.

2. As soon as possible, rewrite the conversation, adding all the details about setting, appearance, gestures, and tone of voice that you remember.

3. Read over the conversation, and write a paragraph about what the speakers' language reveals about them. Rather than focusing exclusively on the content of the conversation, consider issues such as who dominates the conversation, how colorful or dull their words are, how expressive or monotonous their voices are, and what their verbal idiosyncrasies are.

   a. What can you tell about character from dialogue?

   b. Which pieces of dialogue would you choose to show a specific personality?

   c. Which sections of dialogue would you eliminate?

the right language to reveal character. The reader will not expect you to remember the exact words you uttered ten or five years ago or even a month ago, but the reader will expect you to recreate conversations as accurately as possible.

People have "signatures" in their speech—words, gestures, pauses, or subject matter that reveal who they are. Think about how people actually speak. One character might say "like" a lot or ramble from one subject to another. Another might pause often, be evasive, answer questions with few words, or repeat questions. Dialogue can highlight personality and emotion and create drama.

Conflict

The struggle, search, or mystery that drives the story forward comes from internal or external conflict. Conflicts can originate from inside (such as when you begin to outgrow a friend) or from outside (as when your parents say they are getting a divorce and that you must decide with whom you will live). Once introduced, conflict advances through scenes. The conflict gets more complicated as the main character encounters obstacles along the way. This development of conflict is the backbone of a narrative, and it must develop incrementally and logically.

A character requires motivation to grapple with a conflict and also needs a stake in the outcome, or something on the line. Think about telling a story about becoming so fed up with a frustrating boss that you quit your job. The story could center around your personal conflict: should you quit the job and suffer the consequences of unemployment? What is your motivation to quit? You may have been harassed or have felt intimidated. The stakes also need to be clear. If you quit, you have to change your lifestyle, live on less, or perhaps move home. Readers want to know why the conflict is important. The motivation and stakes create the tension and reveal the significance of the conflict.

Theme

Simply put, the theme is what your story is about: its point and its larger significance. The theme of a memoir provides insight into who you are, but at the same time it reveals something universal to which your reader can relate. Thematically, a story about moving to a new place could be about how you reinvented or transformed yourself. The theme of a story about winning over a difficult stepparent could be about gaining control, being out of control, being rejected, or being accepted. A story about meeting your Internet friend face to face could have the themes of trust and taking chances. The theme comes from your story, but it also reveals

Narrative Techniques

Stories need to move through time smoothly and logically. Sometimes, though, you want to pause the story, to show in very specific detail what is happening. Other times you might need to get from one time to another with a quick explanation rather than a descriptive scene. You can emphasize a moment or fast-forward over unimportant details by using these narrative techniques.

Summary: Tells

Summary can give you a chance to fast-forward over a period of time in order to advance the story to an episode or scene that you want to focus on. Summary won't offer pictures for your reader to remember, so you should keep it to a minimum, using it as a transition to connect moments and help your story flow.

> Later that night I called each member of my mother's family. I assured them that the accident was minor. At that point, nobody could know what would happen one month later.

Narrative Description: Shows

Narrative description puts you into a scene the way a camera would. Every detail you mention becomes significant to your reader. Detail slows down the movement of the story, focusing carefully on the moment. Use narrative description to emphasize dramatic and important moments.

Sophie stood shivering on the porch. Her eye liner was smeared, and her hair was slicked back by the rain. Her light jacket clung to her sharp, bony shoulders. As she started to speak, the thunder roared. I could see her mouth moving, but I couldn't make out the words.

Internal Monologue: Tells

Internal monologue is like the voiceover in a film. It is the script of what is going on in your head. Use it sparingly to add drama or help clarify a scene. Remember that this type of explaining won't create pictures your reader can remember.

> I wondered why my father would be up so late. Did he know about the argument? I wished I had one of those dads who works all the time and never pays attention to what's going on in the house.

Dialogue: Shows

Use dialogue to reveal character, not to provide information. You can combine full dialogue with summary to advance the dialogue. Write conversations or parts of conversations rather than speeches.

> "Where is car key?" I asked, opening the door.
> "In the ignition," she said.
> "You keep the key in the ignition?"
> "No, of course not," Mel said. "I wouldn't keep the key in the ignition. It's stuck."

a more universal truth that you and your readers share, even though you have not had duplicate experiences.

The theme you choose to reveal in your memoir depends on what actually happened, how it affected you, and what it helped you understand. Often stories about significant events in your childhood, for example, have to do with coming of age or experiencing a rite of passage as you leave some part of your childhood behind. It does not matter what theme you reveal in your story, as long as you make a point that has meaning for you as well as for your reader. Readers want to take something away with them and gain a greater understanding about the world, about people, and about life experiences.

One word of caution here: Do not confuse *theme* with *moral*. A moral reduces the entire meaning of your story to a boring and trite cliché, such as "you can't tell a book by its cover" or "easy come, easy go." Most memorable stories are about something deeper, more meaningful, and less clichéd. Surprising or unexpected twists, complex responses, and expectations turned upside down make for interesting and realistic themes.

Finding out what a story means can be a challenge. Sometimes you need to write the story several times before you see the meaning. Often

you will find clues in your language and the imagery you intuitively use.

For example, one student drafted a story about her embarrassment while dancing on the stage in middle school. The other students were talking, laughing, and making fun of her. It was a pivotal moment for her, but she could not figure out what the story was really about on a thematic level. When she reread her own language about her "flesh-colored leotard" and her "naked feet," she realized that she was writing about being metaphorically stripped of her dignity. With that insight, she was able to deepen her

Practice 5.5   Show, Don't Tell

One way to create scenes for stories is to adhere to the "show, don't tell" rule. Mark Twain advised writers, "Don't say the old lady screamed. Bring her on and let her scream." "Show, don't tell" is one of those rules that is easier to understand than to accomplish. But your memoir is a perfect place to practice the skill. If you want to evoke a feeling, description should lead your reader to that feeling. Look at the way Bernard Cooper evokes mood in the following piece, how he changes mood several times, and what he implies, through description, about the situation in the household.

> My mother and father and brother were asleep. It was quiet except for the ticks and groans of our Spanish house contracting in the cold. Degree by degree the temperature had dropped; November deepened. Undertones of orange were gone from the sky, the threat of rain sustained for weeks. What was to come was held in suspension, waited to happen: the blast of pain in my bother's chest, sensation drained from his fingers and toes, the blood in his body freed from its boundaries, leaving his lips, the ambulance attendants surging through our door, strangers in white who flanked a gurney, my father begging them not to use the siren—whatever you do, don't use the siren—afraid the sound would frighten his son.
>
> But none of this had happened yet. It was just after dawn. A pale light filled the hall. I stood in the doorway and stared at my parents sprawled in sleep. Their limbs were flung at improbable angles. Their mouths were slack. Beneath closed lids, eyes followed the course of dreams whose theme I tried to guess. But their faces—sunken in a stack of pillows, released from the tension of fear and hope—were emptied of all expression.
>
> —Bernard Cooper, "Dream House"

1. Choose a scene from your childhood, perhaps a place you often visited on holidays or vacations. Write a list of sensory details. Here are some prompts to get you started.

   a. What did you see? *The weather, somebody's clothing, a clock, a gesture, a hairstyle, the light, shadows, colors.*

   b. What did you hear? *Song fragments, voices, dialogue, footsteps, plastic rattling, metal grinding.*

   c. What did you smell? *The rain on the hot sidewalk, mildew, bleach, garlic, the hamster cage.*

   d. What did you taste? *Your own salty sweat, metal, sour milk, stale bread.*

   e. What did you feel or touch? *The wire of your braces digging into your cheek, your scratchy wool sweater, the smooth, cool surface of the closed door.*

2. Write a paragraph modeled on the description of the Cooper's house. Have in mind the overall impression you intend to create. Don't *tell,* but instead *show* that impression through well-chosen sensory details.

Practice 5.6   Using Narrative Techniques

1. Read this scenario.

   Fifteen-year-old Angela is arguing with her mother. She wants to wear a tight purple tube top to school. Her mother has forbidden her to wear revealing clothing and won't let Angela out of the house until she changes.

2. Write a short scene using all four narrative techniques. Write from Angela's point of view or the point of view of her mother, her father, her sibling, or her best friend, who is waiting to walk with her to school.

story, add language that emphasized her sense of exposure, and find more universal themes about vulnerability and violation.

Once you discover your theme, make sure to seed it into your story. Refer to it from the beginning. Even a short scene like Willie Morris's experience on the commuter train begins developing the theme in the first sentence. Morris is looking out at tenement-dwellers who in turn are looking at him. The idea that people look at each other without really seeing each other, which is hinted at in the first sentence, germinates and ripens throughout the story.

Practice 5.7
Researching a Time

1. Find a newspaper from
   September 10, 2001, and
   look at the headlines.
   What was the main story?
   What were the main
   concerns of Americans
   that day?

2. Choose a time in your
   own life, perhaps the time
   when your memoir will be
   set, and search the headlines for that time. What
   details from the larger
   world might you use to
   reveal some aspect of
   your life?

RESEARCH PATHS

Recalling the cultural and historical details of a time period can enrich the texture of a story. It can also help create a sense of place—not just a physical place, but also a place in time. Time-markers can provide a larger context for your story and help deepen your theme. One student, writing about a particularly disappointing moment that occurred in February 2002, used an image of American flags as a backdrop to her story. She described the flags as tattered from being displayed all winter after the patriotic awakening brought on by the terrorist attacks of September 11, 2001. Though the narrative had little to do with patriotism, the image added historical context and depth to her story about expectations and being let down.

Details from contemporary sporting events, advertisements, and popular television shows can add irony or humor and can help the reader understand characters in your story. Consult old magazines and newspapers to see which films were being reviewed, which books were on the best-seller list, which news stories were in the headlines, and which songs were popular. This research can help you gather details for your story and jog your memory about long-forgotten details. An interviewer once asked Pete Hamill, author of the memoir *A Drinking Life*, how he captured the Brooklyn of his childhood.

> You can get help with memory. You can look at old newspapers. You can listen to the music that was played. In my case, I got the Billboard lists for the different years I was writing about and made tapes. I went to oldies record shops like Colony Records on Broadway. I would be driving with the tape player on, and it would create whole rooms, you know? I think if you get the details right, if you get the thing very specific, it inadvertently becomes universal. There's always some detail that someone says, "Damn, the author knows what he or she is talking about. That was the kind of candy that was in the second row of the candy store in New York in a given year." Whether you are in New York or Tokyo, the sense of the specific makes it available and understandable. It feels true. You can't as a writer be wrong on those things. Otherwise, you'll get letters saying, "What do *you* know?"
>
> —Quoted in Carolyn T. Hughes, "A Thinking Life: A Conversation with Pete Hamill"

Pay attention to all the details you can gather from a source published on the date of your memoir. If you can, get a local newspaper or check the headlines on a This Day in History website for the place your story was set, and look at the weather for that day and the forecast for the next day. A brewing storm and an unusually warm February day can be authentic details and can possibly add thematic significance to your story.

Talk to your friends about what they remember about the time period. What were the trends? The gossip of the time? What music would have played on the radio?

ANATOMY OF A MEMOIR

You can structure your story in a number of ways. The most common is straight chronology, starting at the beginning and working your way through an event as it occurred. You can organize sections of your story by using flash-backs and flash-forwards. You might begin the story at the end as Bernard Cooper does in "Dream House" (in Practice 5.5), flashing forward and then moving back to the beginning. If you use this technique, be sure to provide clear transitions. Cooper tells us directly: "But none of this had happened yet." In effect, he restarts the story, using straight chronology this time.

Tinkering with the time elements of a story does not change the basic requirement of narrative order: that the story progresses incrementally, in steps. A typical narrative structure has a beginning, a middle, and an end, making up a *narrative arc*. A narrative arc provides a visual map of a story, showing how writers typically build up tension to a climactic moment and then allow the tension to decrease to the story's resolution. This structure can be—and is often—modified by skillful writers, as you will see in Antonya Nelson's memoir, "All Washed Up."

A classical story arc looks like this.

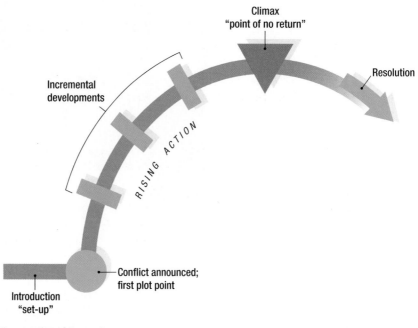

Conventional Story Arc

Some writers emphasize different parts of the story and may make their readers wait to begin the climb. Their story arcs might look more like this one.

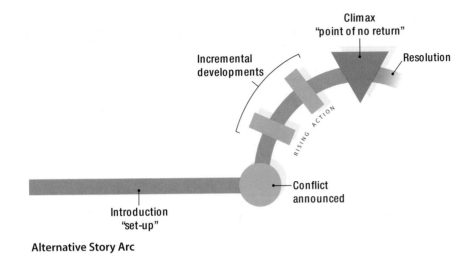

Alternative Story Arc

All Washed Up

ANTONYA NELSON

Set up — My boss that summer prided himself on having kissed all the waitresses. According to others, he had made them all cry. I swore that he would neither kiss me nor make me cry. — *Announcement of conflict*

This was a busy restaurant-bar in tourist-laden Telluride, Colorado. My job was to bus tables and wash dishes. I also played first base for the restaurant's softball team. At eighteen, I wasn't old enough to wait tables and serve drinks; at eighteen, I was still living in my parents' summer house, so my work felt casual. I had another job, at the local historical museum, where the crazy curator was constantly giving me pieces of the exhibits, like double-headed railroad spikes or articles of a prostitute's clothing. I would take the gifts home, then sneak them back the next day. At night, I worked at the restaurant.

Why mention? Effect? — Like the waitresses, I divided my time between the public front and the private kitchen. Like the waitresses, I was a girl. But, unlike them, I didn't feel superior to the bartenders (front) or the cooks (kitchen), nor did I receive tips. I was not only the worst-paid but also the youngest staff mem- — *Set up*

Set up — ber, which encouraged avuncular treatment from the men—the bartenders would send me shots of tequila, which I tossed down in between sending loads of steins through the Hobart. The waitresses liked to bestow advice—depilatory, pharmacological, chauvinistic. They thought I was pretty good at softball, and I didn't present a threat in the restaurant, stuck as I was elbow-deep in sludgy black water.

Theme — That busy kitchen combination of steam, grease, and tequila was heady and golden. The cooks fought with one another, dashed outside to get stoned, retreated to the walk-in to feed their munchies, and argued volubly about skiing or women or spices; about the bluegrass festival at the town park; about our boss, who was universally disliked but not universally understood. Some of these people intended to remain in the restaurant business. My status as temporary drudge made me stand out—that and a lack of humility. I was a college student; I had places to go when the summer ended.

First plot point — On the night that I was fired, James Taylor was singing in the park. He'd seen fire and he'd seen rain . . . My back was quacked from softball—a torqued swing had sent me into a cataclysmic spasm—and I couldn't haul the pony keg up from the basement. So I got one of the cooks to help, along with the drug-addled brother of my boss's silent partner; I recruited my own brother, two years younger, to haul the trays of beer steins to me from the front. I was still running the dishwasher. And I was still slamming shots. When the boss—nicknamed the Fireplug, two inches shorter than I, a dead cigar always between his lips—took me to task, I pointed out that I'd covered for myself rather than phoning in injured. Who cared if my brother wasn't on the payroll, or that No Man, the cook, had temporarily been away from his burners? But the Fireplug didn't see it that way.

I should have told him what I knew about the damage his vengeful staff had done behind his back. They'd contaminated pots of soup and tubs of dressing, thrown away dozens of plates and sets of cutlery, played bombs away with brandy snifters. They swindled and overcharged, sneaked in after hours to eat and steal, refused to wash their hands or scour the cutting surfaces, had sex in the walk-in. Flabbergasted and tongue-tied, attempting to say "I quit" before he said "You're fired," I didn't have the chance to rat on the others. I did, however, let him know that, as far as I was concerned, earning a college degree meant never having to work for someone like him again.

Telling Showing (details) — We'd been having this conversation at the sink. He turned to the busy kitchen and whistled it quiet. "Hey," he yelled. "How many of you went to college?" Everyone there raised a hand—even the dimwit brother of the silent partner.

"We're gonna miss you, First Base," my boss announced as he rocked forward and delivered a liver-lipped, ashtray-flavored kiss to my chin. Then he disappeared into the dining room. That's how he brought me to tears.

Conclusion

My own brother merely shrugged when I called to him from the back door. Already, he was rolling up his sleeves, eying my tequila nuggets. He'd been hired on the spot to replace me. Up the hill I stormed, back to our house, where my family sat around the kitchen table playing bridge and drinking gin, the front door closed against the "caterwauling" coming from the festival grounds—James Taylor's encore. My little sister was pleased to see me; she was terrible at bridge, and got dragged in only when no one else was available. A visiting cousin, between semesters at Baylor, was her partner. He's the one who started the pitying refrain that has become part of family lore: "Nobody gets fired washing dishes."

Introduction and Setup

The introduction hooks readers by providing a tease to tempt them to read the story. The beginning sets up the story by putting readers on the path that leads to the conflict. The introduction can be one, two, or more paragraphs— however long it takes to put the story into motion. Antonya Nelson sets up her story with a question: Could she keep her vow that her boss wouldn't kiss her or make her cry? Her readers immediately pay attention. Will she be able to do it?   *intro*

Beyond the attention-getting aspect of the introduction, the opening of a narrative gives the reader the essential information or the context for the story. Give your reader a sense of *who, what, where,* and *when*—news story elements, but in a narrative style. You can translate news elements into narration by thinking of *who* as character, *when* and *where* as setting, *what* as plot, *why* and *how* as conflict and theme.

Writers call the opening section the *setup* because it sets up the reader to understand the context of the story. Notice how long Nelson's setup is, how much time she spends describing her character and her placement in the story among her coworkers and her family.   *set up*

The setup leads to the conflict: when the main character's struggle becomes clear. In screenwriting, this moment is called "the first plot point," a descriptive term you might find useful. At the first plot point, the conflict comes into focus. Nelson's first plot point comes later than most, about one-third of the way through the story, in the line that starts "On the night that I was fired."   *Conflict*

Organize your story so the conflict is clear, or at least foreshadowed, at the beginning. You do not necessarily have to state the conflict directly in the first sentence. As always, common practice is a guideline, not a rule, and you may find yourself experimenting effectively with different kinds of leads and pacing in your story.

Rising Action

After the introduction, the hill-climbing starts. Known as the *rising action,* this part of the plot is made up of events that heighten the conflict. Stories can have many events or just one or two. The events are necessary to the development of the plot; they show the logic of the conflict as it develops. In "All

Washed Up," we need all the information that comes before Nelson's encounter with her boss. To see the logic in the climactic scene, we need to know that she's a bit arrogant, that she's a softball star, and that she has a relationship with the cooks.

Especially in longer stories, these plot developments can be charted along the narrative arc. Each time the character deals with a new obstacle, the conflict becomes more pronounced, and the struggle changes. These changes occur incrementally, one step at a time, in order for the plot to be well paced. Nelson loses her chance to argue with her boss and can respond only by telling him that she will have the edge on all the others because of her college degree. The tension mounts when his response, the next step in the arc, is to ask, "How many of you went to college?" It is a turning point for the naïve and overly confident Nelson when "Everyone there raised a hand—even the dimwit brother of the silent partner."

Having a character simply change does not make a good story; the steps are too steep and the story unconvincing. Another term some screenwriters use is the point of no return. By this point the character has changed in some small or big way. Something is different now, and the character cannot go back to the way he or she was at the beginning of the story. How could Fireplug have gotten away with kissing the young woman who "swore" he never would if he had not slowly disarmed her? His victory and her slight shift in self-image make logical sense.

pt. of NO return

Every single step of this incremental change over time does not have to be painstakingly recreated in your story. You could quickly summarize a scene or a string of conversations. Nelson does not tell us exactly what she said. She summarizes, writing "I did, however, let him know that, as far as I was concerned, earning a college degree meant never having to work for someone like him again," before she slows down the action and highlights the moment with a detail.

> We'd been having this conversation at the sink. He turned to the busy kitchen and whistled it quiet. "Hey," he yelled."

Resolution

All stories have to end, but all endings do not tie up all the loose ends. Figuring out where a memoir really concludes is sometimes hard; your life continues. If you get stuck for an ending, think about your theme. What moment in your story will point your reader back to the theme?

At the same time, avoid the temptation to end your memoir with a summary of a lesson learned. If you have told your story effectively, if you have allowed your story to unfold for your reader as it did for you, you should not have to tell what the experience meant to you. The reader should know.

If you find you have written a wrap-up conclusion in your first draft, see if you can cut the final paragraph. Writers often find that the next-to-last paragraph provides a much more satisfactory conclusion than the final one. That last effort to pull everything together, to be profound, to make sure the reader "gets it," can show its strain.

The best endings reveal how you have—or in some cases, have not—resolved the conflict. Nelson returns home to become an extra hand for bridge and watch the grown-ups drink gin. She's now branded as the one who "got fired washing dishes." The lesson she has learned, though clear, is implied through the parting image.

A Crest Side Story

MARISSA PETRARCA

Marissa Petrarca, a student, also wrote a story about her experiences working in a kitchen. Although her structure and story are different from Antonya Nelson's, they share some similarities with Nelson's. As you read "A Crest Side Story," note how the author organizes her memoir—the setup, the rising action, and the resolution.

The wafting food fragrances, brewing coffee, and powder from latex gloves permeated the air as I walked into the sprawling stainless-steel kitchen. The kitchen was empty at this time of day; the workers were slowly starting to trickle in for the dinner shift. I leaned against a sturdy-looking metal door, calmly waiting for my new boss and co-workers. Then, the door gave out from behind me, and I tumbled backwards, landing on the tile with a distinct thump. I looked up to find a young, unshaven man holding a vat of soup over me and watched as the cold liquid spilled onto my crisp, new apron. I was still lying on the ground, covered in pasta and carrots, when he stepped over me and walked towards the stove.

"Don't forget to shut the freezer door, soup girl," he demanded as I stood to brush myself off. As a member of the lowly kitchen staff of the Cedar Crest Nursing Center, I helped prepare and serve meals to the 250 ailing seniors who called it home. Sadly, most of the seniors would remain in the beige cinderblock building until the end of their lives, but for me it was just a way to earn some money in my senior year of high school.

From my first day, I saw that interaction between any nurse and kitchen worker was like watching the gang wars of *West Side Story*. The Sharks (nurses) roamed around in their crisp and pristine green scrubs, frowning whenever I'd wander onto their turf. They followed me around as I walked around the building, like a security guard tails a kid suspected of shoplifting. They made outrageous demands, arguing that Mrs. Massi absolutely needed a tuna sandwich, cereal, grilled cheese, and pudding along with her regular meal. They screamed and screeched when we insisted that a patient was not allowed a certain type of food, as they tried to get sweets for the diabetics, and milk for the lactose intolerant. We Jets of the kitchen staff started off the shift dressed from head to toe in immaculate white, although the uniforms were stained with red marinara sauce and black coffee grounds within the hour. We held dominion over the basement of the building and allowed no one to infiltrate the storage closets and staff lounges. When one of the former kitchen staff members returned to the Crest after nursing school, her old co-workers refused to talk to her.

"When you're a Jet, you stay a Jet," seemed to be the unspoken motto.

I always worked the dinner shift with two other aides and the chef. Rob, a 6 foot tall, 250 pound line-backer of a guy, was younger than I but was already considered a senior member of the staff, clocking more hours in a week than three aides combined. Patricia, a crazy-eyed forty-something brunette, was loud and certifiable. Her dilapidated maroon Chevy overflowed with random pieces of furniture that she found on the street, and she was constantly getting cryptic phone messages from gruff-sounding men whom she had "business" with.

And then, there was Mark. Mark, the chef and my boss, was a foul-mouthed, defiant guy, who had served time on a drug trafficking conviction. He wore a worn navy baseball cap at all times, removing it briefly to show us his prematurely bald 24-year-old head. He lived with his girlfriend Cathy in an expensive one-bedroom apartment, and his other girlfriend Katie paid all of his bills and debts. He dumped Katie over the phone when she cheated on him, arguing the he could not waste his time and energy on someone he could not trust.

He became defensive when we brought up his identical infidelity. "The two situations aren't even related, Soup Girl. Rob, why don't you and Soup Girl go do some dishes instead of being sneaky and listening to my conversation," Mark sneered.

Due to another unexplained indiscretion, Mark was not allowed to have a license and walked the mile to and from his apartment every day. On Mother's Day, Mark sent his mother a picture of him mooning her, with the title, "Crack a Smile Mom, Happy Mother's Day." I happily refused to look at the picture when he passed it around the kitchen.

Mark hated the nurses and swore at them until red in the face. Mark hated the slow kitchen staff members and fired them in the middle of the dinner rush. And being the king of the Jets that he was, Mark hated betrayal and disloyalty, whether it was with his girlfriend or with his workers.

Jo-Ann, a sweet rosy-cheeked nurse, had been a friend of my family for years. 10 Earlier that evening, Mark had neglected to turn off the oven, causing the charred main entrée to set off the building's fire alarms. Dinner was delayed two hours by the drill, and when Jo-Ann came to visit me on her late shift, I went into a diatribe about my job and my boss.

"The man has a prison record. He burns food every time I work with him. Plus, he's an arrogant, disgusting idiot, not to mention a jerk," I ranted, furious. "I wish . . ." I was stopped mid-sentence when I saw the flash of Mark's blue baseball cap dart past the open kitchen doors of the same color. Later, as Pat, Rob, and I washed the monstrous load of taupe plates, I imagined Mark, sitting in his air-conditioned office, cackling like a madman while scrawling a list of all the ways he could make my job miserable and punish my disloyalty.

For the next year that I spent at the Crest, Mark and I participated in a constant battle of wits, with the sole purpose of making one another miserable. He assigned me to take care of all of the most disgusting and painful tasks. He would make me stick my arm into the scorching water of the dishwasher to remove a mug that had gotten stuck in the gears. My hand would come out singed a bright pink from the heat, and to this day, I am able to use my bare hands as oven mitts. When I returned home every night, sweaty and exhausted, I was repulsed by food. As we started in on the dishes towards the end of every shift, the remnant food would gather on the long stainless steel belt and make a mushy soup of horrors. Corn, gravy, macaroni, bread, peanut butter and countless other things would mix together, forming a clumpy, putrid yellow-orange paste that would clog the garbage disposal, forcing me to reach my arm down into the muck to clear the clog. My arm would emerge covered with a sticky slime that stretched to my shoulder, and I would cringe as a smirking Mark would pull chunks of bitten leftover meat from my skin.

I secretly vowed to get him back, and was cheered on by Rob, my perpetual ally and co-conspirator. I would "accidentally" spill giant pots of pureed prunes all over Mark's newly-mopped floor, and watch as it formed sticky brown rivers in the grooves of the brick-red tile. I told nurses that Mark would give them a free dinner and watch as he attempted to control the throngs that ravaged our refrigerators. Rob would steal cartons of ice cream for us aides to eat on our breaks. Later, when we realized that we went to the same high school, Rob would leave weekly lists of sneaky ideas taped to the outside of my locker.

One humid, rainy June afternoon I drove towards the Crest, dreading the hours that I would spend in the kitchen. As I parked my car, and walked towards the building, I noticed Mark standing with an old man, speaking softly and nervously glancing in the direction of the Crest main entrance. I assumed that the man was one of Patricia's "buddies" trying to get Mark back in the business of dealing, so I pivoted on my food-stained white sneakers and turned towards the building's other entrance. As I glanced back over my shoulder, I became uneasy when I noticed the fearful look on my boss' face.

15   "Mark? Is everything okay?" I asked turning towards him.

"No," he replied tersely. "It's a Code Blue."

I stood back, dumbfounded and took a good look at Mark's friend. The silver-haired man, wearing striped pajamas that were probably a Christmas present from his absent children, was a patient. Blues meant that an Alzheimer's patient had gone missing, and the Crest reacted quickly by locking down the building as if it were a prison ward. The Alzheimer's patients were all housed in the Generations wing, a depressing labyrinth-like ward that kept its wandering, disoriented occupants within its confines. Code Blues were rare but dangerous; a bustling main road surrounded the Crest and one prior escapee had been found standing in the middle of a three-car pileup that he had caused.

"Those damn nurses," Mark fumed, before uttering other choice profanities. The only way to leave Generations was to pass through alarmed doors that had to be deactivated by a special employee code.

"They probably didn't even do a head count. They probably just turned it off and ignored it," said an agitated Mark, pulling off his cap and revealing tiny beads of sweat on his hairless forehead. Mark and I each gingerly took the patient's arms and led him back to the building. We were met at the door by the head nurse Betty, a heavyset disagreeable woman with the bedside manner of Nurse Ratchet. As she yelled at Mark for not notifying the proper departments, I suddenly heard myself start to speak, surprised at the words spilling from my own mouth.

"Mr. Lewis would have been in the middle of Scituate Ave. if Mark hadn't been 20
outside. This isn't the first time your nurses have ignored the alarm. Believe me
Betty, the proper departments will hear about that." As Betty sulked away, dragging Mr. Lewis behind her, I looked at Mark. He said nothing before walking back
into the building, and only patted me on the top of the head, mussing up my neatly
combed bun, the mandatory hairdo.

My display of loyalty proved to Mark that I was indeed "a Jet all the way." I
would come into the kitchen to find my juice already poured, desserts already
made, and the patient's dietary charts sorted neatly. Mark joined Rob and me for
our ice cream breaks, and would save us extra food for dinner. He still called me
Soup Girl, even when introducing me to his girlfriend Cathy. I accepted it as a necessary evil of working with Mark.

Then, one year after I had been named Soup Girl, it was time for me to leave for
college. I gave both Rob and Mark a ride home on my last day of work, the three of
us squeezing into my tiny black Suzuki Sidekick, a car more like an oversized Go-
Kart than a motor vehicle. After dropping Rob off, I drove Mark to Cathy's apartment, housed in a sprawling crème-colored resort with mauve shutters bordering
each window. As he got out of the car, he removed his baseball hat and stuck it in his
back pocket.

"So, you're going to college. Will we see you in four years then?" he asked.

"God, I hope not," I answered, smiling.

"Good."   25

I saw Cathy waving from the balcony, and waved back. Mark turned and started
walking up to the building's entrance. As I pulled out of the driveway, I heard Mark
shouting. As I turned to look in his direction, he smiled. "Thanks for the ride,
Marissa." Then he turned toward his unlikely home, disappearing into the enormous stone atrium.

Annotate "A Crest Side Story"

1. Bracket the lead. Note in the margin what it establishes about the main character and the situation.

2. Put a line under the last line of the setup. Where does the setup end and the narrative begin?

3. Circle setting details. Which details are particularly useful in helping you get a sense of the
   characters?

4. Put a star in the margin next to the climax. Then draw a narrative arc for this story. Identify the
   climax on the arc.

5. Bracket the story's resolution. Note in the margin what technique Petrarca uses. How is the
   story resolved?

READINGS

The memoirs in this section offer insights into the relationships between children and their parents, a topic that is familiar territory for memoirists. Proving that relationships can be complicated, students Karlene Barrett and Elaine Hom write about their mothers, while Henry Louis Gates, Jr. uses his father as a main character in his story about being a reluctant baseball player. Ashley Marie Rhodes-Courter has a slightly different take on the theme in her memoir about the day she was adopted.

Vacation
Karlene Barrett

Karlene Barrett and Elaine Hom have conflicts with their mothers, and both depict their youthful embarrassment about their mothers. Though the stories involve conflicts that are similar, the writers use different structures and styles to tell their stories.

Ever since kindergarten, the only vacation I took with my mother was our annual summer trip to San Clemente, a sweltering six-hour car ride to the Southern California coast. While vacations with my father and stepmother always promised getaways to Disneyland, fancy hotel rooms, San Francisco Giants games, speedboats on a lake, and expensive restaurant dinners, these things were, thanks to a complete lack of financial assistance from my father, non-existent luxuries in the life my sister and I had with our mother. She worked overtime to support us even in our normal, everyday lives, so this yearly trip (in which we stayed with friends, cooked our meals, and hung out at free beaches all day) was the only vacation she could afford, and my mother worked hard for it, looked forward to it with contagious excitement, and prepared months in advance.

And year after year after year, I single-handedly ruined it for her.

Usually by the third or fourth day, my mom was either angry or hurt, and I was always to blame. I normally guiltily defended myself with some weak protestation somewhere along the lines of: "Geez . . . don't be so sensitive!" or "What the hell did I do? Soooory . . ." But I always knew exactly what I did.

In San Clemente, we stayed with some friends my parents had made when they were still married, who had apparently chosen my mother's side of the battle. They had two daughters, Leigh and Kendall, who were, conveniently, more or less the same age as my sister and me. They both had tan, thin legs and curly hair so blonde it was almost white. They looked like Coppertone babies. We were best friends. Mr. and Mrs. Steffenson, as I had been calling their parents since I had learned to walk, were the storybook couple: tanned and athletic. He wore swim trunks and surfed every morning; she donned a bikini and laughed with her whole head tilted back. They were perfect.

And my mom was fat. Not just middle-aged-had-two-kids-slightly-overweight. Fat. *Her* swimsuit was the same one she had worn when she had first taught me to swim: a polka-dotted number with a little skirt, the kind you would see old ladies wear. *She* guffawed when she laughed, as I ducked my head, red-faced. And she *certainly* had no husband. I envied Leigh and Kendall their perfect parents. I knew they would grow to be just as perfect as the ones who bore them: wealthy, beautiful, and healthy. I had no one's shoes to fill but my mother's. And I was terrified.

"Who would want her?" I mused, knowing exactly why my father had left this graceless cow for my stepmother, a woman, who, if not always an enjoyable person, at least looked like one. At the supermarket in San Clemente, I secretly prayed the cashier would think I was Mrs. Steffenson's daughter, that this woman, who ordered her clothes from thin, shiny catalogs and had a bathroom stocked full of different hues of lipsticks and expensive looking bikinis, had given birth to me, and that some day I would grow up to look just like her. I mean, the resemblance was uncanny, I told myself as I squeezed her hand tighter to cement the cashier's impression of my identity. This was a pattern I repeated over and over again: betraying my mother without her knowing it in favor of someone more aesthetically pleasing.

At the beach, I would sit as far away from my mother as possible, hoping no one would connect me to the huge lady with glowing white skin, a giant sun-visor, and chubby ankles. I would dart away from my mother whenever she came near me or asked me to join her for a swim, but jump up and squeal with delight to play paddleball by the ocean with Mrs. Steffenson.

I thought I was being subtle, that my mother had no idea what was going on, but every once in a while, I had to throw off the hurt look I could see written on her face. On one particularly painful day for me (though no doubt more so for my mother), I at thirteen, jokingly told Kendall, in my mother's presence, that "you better try your hardest not to end up like my mom." I don't know why exactly these words came out of my mouth; I know that I didn't mean them as they ended up sounding, and that I honestly believed in my heart that my mother would laugh. I can't really remember the conversation that preceded this horrible state-

ment; my memory that was wiped away by the memory of my mother crying in the upstairs bedroom a few minutes later.

I defended myself in my usual idiotic way, with rolled eyes and protestations that "You didn't get it . . . that wasn't what I meant. . . . Geez . . . ." But my mother was too hurt to even listen or argue with me, and through her quiet tears, I saw that I had crossed the line and confirmed everything she thought about herself. It was the worst thing I could ever do. The worst I had ever done. It was my lowest moment. She forgave me of course; mothers always do, and we went on to have a decent rest of the vacation in which I tried my hardest not to flinch when she reached for me, to swim with her when she wanted to, and even to walk with her to the snack bar. But I suspect, though I am afraid to ask, that my mother has never forgotten that day. I wonder if she knows that I never have as well, that it haunts me as my worst, most painful memory.

My best memory, in fact, is somewhat related. It recalls an evening when I was around four when I went with my mother and father (still married) to a pizza parlor with some of their friends. For no reason other than I had seen it on a television show earlier in the day, as we were walking in, I wrapped my entire body around one of my mother's legs. She fell, and despite her not being hurt, I have never been yelled at, to this day, so much by my father in my entire life as I was that night. I was quickly forgiven, I'm sure, but the important part of that memory for me lies not in the fact that I was upset, or even that my mother fell, but that my father verbally and loudly defended my mother against me. There were so many years that I failed to hand her the field trip permission slips for fear she would want to chaperone, warned people about her weight before they saw her so I wouldn't have to note the surprise register on their faces, and hoped people associated my birth with a different woman than she to whom the credit (or blame) really belonged. I wish my father had been there to see through me, to scream at me, to punish me for what I was doing and thinking, to remind me what an incredible and strong person my mother was, and most of all, for her to hear someone standing up for her, defending her with vehemence and rage.

Our last summer trip to San Clemente was the summer before I left for college. Leigh and I had reluctantly agreed to join my mother and Mrs. Steffenson on the beach for one day. We had some shopping to attend to in San Diego now that we could drive, but our parents and the bright sun had convinced us that we could postpone our schedule for one day. I had, over the years, joined the ranks of the teenage girls who spent beach days sunning themselves in bikinis and darting into the water only for a quick dip to cool down and wash the sweat off before changing tanning positions. I was engaging in one of those quick dips when I saw her: my mother, who loved the ocean more than anyone I'll ever know; who still swam for hours as far out as I'd ever seen anyone go, as trusting of the waves as I'd ever seen anyone be. Floating, in her polka dot swimsuit, on the top of an unbroken wave, her feet pointed up at the sky, her arms at her sides, her eyes closed to the sun, her body responding only to the rocking motion of the sea. Weightless. And at that moment, I saw her as I'd like to hope she saw herself, despite all those summers of my poorly concealed embarrassment, condescension, and disdain. She was beautiful. She was triumphant.

Critical Reading Questions

1. Identify the lead of the story. Where does the setup end and the story begin? Do the lead and the setup provide essential information and foreshadow the conflict? If so, what information do they provide, and how do they foreshadow the conflict?

2. What is the conflict in this story? Where are you first aware of it?

3. The main character of this story is the narrator. How does she present herself in the story? Which scenes define her character? How does she change over time?

4. Barrett introduces you to the other characters in this story through concrete images and through their actions. What do you know about the following characters?

   a. When you picture the mother, what do you see? What kind of person is she?

   b. What do you picture when you think of Mrs. Steffenson? What does she represent to the writer?

   c. What kind of a person is the father? What do his actions reveal about him?

5. Instead of a single scene, Barrett moves her story forward through a number of connected scenes. What does she accomplish through this structure? Are there any scenes that you think could be eliminated? Why?

6. What stated and unstated themes can you find in this story?

7. How effective is the final image in the story? Do you find the conclusion satisfactory? Why?

Questions for Writing and Discussion

1. What motivated Barrett's transformation—her realization of her mother's true nature? Is it convincing?

2. Barrett has revealed an unflattering insight about herself: her disloyalty to her mother. How does this affect your feelings about her?

A Lesson from Pikachu

Elaine Hom

When I was eight, I told my mother that I hated being Chinese.

"I want to be white and have a normal family," I said to my shocked mother.

"Don't even joke about that," she snapped, smacking me across the back of the head. "You are who you are, and you can't change that. Nor should you want to."

But it was true. I hated my heritage. But only because it linked me to my very Chinese and very embarrassing parents. To me, they were as foreign as the subtitled kung-fu masters in my dad's prized movie collection. None of my friends had parents who had moved from another country when they were teenagers. They had normal parents who were born and raised in the good ol' US of A.

When my friends would come over, I'd cringe as they wrinkled their noses in disgust at the sights and smells of Chinese cooking. The worst was the fish. My mom would salt and dry fish in the windows to make *hom yiu*, a Chinese delicacy. To my Caucasian friends, the sight of the shriveled coelacanth-like creatures hanging from hooks attached to the ceiling was absolutely repulsive. It assaulted the senses even more when it was cooked. The dried fish was steamed with ginger and oil and it smelled like a putrid ginger-flavored death. I thought it was normal until I saw their reactions, and I began to feel repulsed too. In fact, I still can't eat *hom yiu* to this day.

Family outings consisted of my parents dragging my three siblings and me to Chinatown in Boston. To me, a trip to Chinatown epitomized my culture. Smelly, unkempt shops lined dirty streets filled with barbaric people and prostitutes on every corner. My parents often offered to have my friends come along with us on these trips, but I deftly made up excuses. "Kelly has swim practice," I'd fib. "Kristen has dance. Adele has flute. Oh, and Brittany has soccer." I didn't want them to see the filth that they would immediately connect to our family.

Things only got worse when my mother would chaperone school events. Words can't describe my embarrassment at her ridiculous accent. My friends would strain to understand her when she talked in her "fob" (fresh off the boat) accent. I remember when my fourth-grade class had a sewing project. My mom asked one of my classmates to bring her a yardstick but chose to refer to it as a ruler instead.

"Can you bring me that rulah?" she asked.

"The what?" asked the confused nine-year-old.

"The rulah." He stared at her in confusion. She pointed to it.

"Oh, you mean the 'yardstick,'" he said, almost condescendingly.

"Yes, yes, rulah, yahdstick, same ting." I was mortified when everyone started giggling at my oblivious mother.

High school arrived. We moved to a new town where the Chinese community was more accepted and established. But even at age fifteen, I continued to be embarrassed by my parents. My mother was still the tiny little vivacious Chinese woman with weird hats and far too much energy and excitement. My dad was still the dorky Chinese engineer who wouldn't dare be seen without his pocket protector and calculator. And I was still the awkward postpubescent teenager, trying to fit into a new town but unable to fit in at home.

I couldn't see how much my parents loved me and doted on me. I was too busy being a bratty teenager, embarrassed and hating them. It took a third person's perspective to convince me otherwise.

I had just settled into my new school as an avid member of the marching band. Columbus Day

Weekend was a huge event for my Italian-dominated town, and we had a great annual parade. As I put my band gear together, I saw my parents preparing the car.

"Where are you going?" I asked.

"We getting ready for parade," said my mom. "We want good spot to take good picture."

Inwardly, I groaned. Another event ruined by my ridiculous parents. I silently got into the car as they drove me to the band room.

"Are you excited for your first big parade?" asked my friend Maria as we put on our uniforms.

20 "I would be if my stupid parents weren't going to be there," I sighed. "I think they're more excited about this than I am."

"Your parents are coming?" she asked, surprised. "You're lucky. My parents haven't been to a single parade. They must really love you."

Startled, I didn't know what to say. She packed up her stuff and walked away. But she had said something I didn't even consider. My parents weren't out to embarrass me. They were there because they were proud of me and wanted to be a part of my life.

I thought about this the rest of the day. During the parade, I saw my parents waving and cheering as I went by blasting the Mickey Mouse theme from my saxophone. I recognized my mom's hideous green knit hat and my dad's gigantic outdated camera snapping pictures. Their faces blurred in the crowd as we marched by. We headed back to the buses and boarded, glad to be done with the march. I sat down next to my friend Daryl, who then tapped me on the shoulder and said, "Uh, Elaine . . ." and pointed out the window.

My mom was waving her arms outside, jumping up and down screaming "LING LING!" at the top of her lungs. Ling Ling is my parents' pet name for me, another embarrassing facet of my Chinese family. Her green hat clashed horribly with her hot pink sweater. And to make things worse, she was waving a gigantic Pikachu balloon she had bought me as a present. "I got you Pokemon!" she yelled. My dad stood behind her taking pictures of me in the bus. The image of her green hat bouncing in sync with the yellow Pikachu is forever embedded in my mind.

25 My first reaction was to cringe and hide, as I normally would have done. But then I thought about what Maria said. They loved me and were proud of me. I was terrible to them, and they still loved me. If they loved every little part of me, I had to love and accept every little part of them, including the weird quirks (such as buying a Pokemon balloon for a fifteen-year-old girl). I re-membered my mom's words from that day when I was eight. They were who they were and I couldn't change that. Nor should I want to. I opened the window, and waved back at them.

"Who *is* that?!" asked Daryl, laughing.

"That's my mom," I said with a grin. "That's my mom and my dad . . . and Pikachu."

Critical Reading Questions

1. How does Hom create a sense of setting for the story? Which details make the setting seem real?

2. Where does the conflict become clear?

3. Where is the turning point or climax of the story?

4. What kind of person is the storyteller?

5. Like the author of "Vacation," Hom gives a few details that help the reader imagine her mother. Without rereading, what do you see when you think of Hom's mother?

6. Hom's transformation comes from the outside, through a conversation with a friend. Is the dialogue realistic? How convincing is the conversation as a turning point?

Question for Writing and Discussion

1. How many young people struggle with some form of embarrassment over their parents? Is it unusual to overcome such feelings at a young age?

2. What helps young people accept their parents as separate and sometimes flawed characters?

Three Little Words

Ashley Marie Rhodes-Courter

Ashley Marie Rhodes-Courter was a high school junior at Crystal River High School in Florida when she won first place in the *New York Times Magazine's* Writing and Photography Contest for High-School Students. The judges said they were looking at craft or technical merit, or a "searing image," but for the most part, they said they looked for "works that moved us, that stayed with us, that made us feel we had caught a glimpse of the minds that created them."

I never thought three little words would have such an impact on my life, even though they weren't the words I was supposed to say. Every time I see the videotape, I cringe. It was one of those memorable occasions that families treasure, but this is one "treasure" I would rather bury.

It was July 28, 1998, my adoption day. I had spent almost ten of my twelve years in foster care; I was now living in my fourteenth placement. Some homes had lasted less than a week; few more than a year. So why would this one be any different? Before this placement, I had been in residen-tial care (the politically correct name for an or-phanage). Do you remember the movie *The Cider House Rules,* when the orphans try to smile in just the right way so they will be picked by the couple shopping for a child? While it wasn't supposed to be so obvious at the Children's Home of Tampa, prospective parents did act as though they were looking at puppies in a pet shop. For more than two and a half years I watched the few lucky dogs pack up their belongings, wave goodbye and exit the gate. I also saw them return—even after being placed with a family—with their tails between their legs. People made promises about "forever families," but often something went wrong. I don't know what families expected. Nobody is perfect, and children who have already been rejected by their parents—or at least feel they've been—are hoping that someone will love them no matter how they behave. I had been living with my new family for eight months. Everything seemed to be going well, but would that change after the papers were signed? And just because it was "official," did that mean they would not send me back if I didn't live up to their expectations?

My parents have two biological kids who are grown; they thought raising a daughter might fill their empty nest. I loved my new waterfront house, with my own room and a bathroom I didn't have to share. For the first time, I could have friends over, and my all-star softball team came to swim after our games. Overnights are forbidden in foster care, but now I had and went to slumber parties. I could use the phone anytime I wanted, and lots of the calls were for me. I had my first pet, a kitten named Catchew that slept on my bed. There were no locks on the refrigerator or scheduled mealtimes. I could help myself to as many boxes of macaroni and cheese, bowls of ramen noodles or grilled-cheese sandwiches as I wanted.

When I did something wrong, my pre-adoptive parents docked my allowance or cut back on TV or telephone time. In one foster home, I was beaten with a paddle, denied food, forced to stand in awkward positions, swallow hot sauce and run laps in the blistering sun. Other times, I was removed to a new home with a new set of rules and promises. Nobody really lives happily ever after, do they? So when was this picture-perfect story going to fall apart? Before or after the "finalization"?

5   You can see how terrified I am on the videotape as we enter the courthouse. My eyes seem to be searching for a way out as I am led into Judge Florence Foster's chambers. On one side of the conference table are the people from my old life; on the other, those who represent my new one. I am placed between Gay and Phil, who are about to become my new parents. Across the way are two representatives from the Children's Home, both therapists. They are happy for me, but that is their job. Mary Miller is smiling and holding a bouquet. She had been my volunteer guardian *ad litem* for four years and did the most to help me get a family.

"Our" side is also represented by Gay's father, Grampy Weisman; one of my new brothers, Josh, who is home from college and acting as the cameraman; and my new godparents, the Weiners, who have brought their three small daughters. The proceedings are delayed because the Department of Children and Families representative is late. He also held up the adoption by neglecting the paperwork for months. While the others chat, I am biting my lip and biding my time. Finally the representative arrives, and my attorney, Neil Spector, who is also Gay's cousin, begins the proceedings. I wait for my cue. But what am I supposed to do? Act as if this is the happiest day of my life? How can it be, when I am petrified that everything is a big fat lie?

After some legal jargon, the judge turns to me. "Nothing in life comes easy," she begins. "If it does, you should be suspicious." She may be trying to comfort me by saying that she knows I've overcome many hardships to get where I am. Instead, she just reinforces my fears that life with my new family is too good to be true. Because of my age, I have to consent to the adoption. After talking to my parents, the judge asks me, "Do you want me to sign the papers and make it official, Ashley?"

On the tape, it looks as if I am trapped center stage in the spotlight. Do I have a choice? I stare straight ahead, shrug my shoulder and mumble, "I guess so." In three words, it is done.

P.S. Almost five years later, I am still with my family. I didn't know then what I know now: some people can be trusted.

Critical Reading Questions

1. Identify where the setup ends and the narrative begins. What information does Rhodes-Courter give in the setup that helps put the story in context? How does she signal the shift from setup to narrative?

2. What is the conflict? Where do you first notice this conflict?

3. How does Rhodes-Courter reveal her character to you? What kind of a person is she?

4. Rhodes-Courter devotes two paragraphs to naming all the participants at the courthouse. What does she accomplish by doing this?

5. The author addresses the reader directly. Why? What effect does this have on the story?

6. Draw a narrative arc for this memoir. Is the structure conventional?

7. Note the places where Rhodes-Courter mentions the videotape in this story. What function does the videotape serve?

Questions for Writing and Discussion

1. Ashley Marie Rhodes-Courter talks about her bad experiences in foster care. Does she seem like a victim to you? Why?

2. The opening of this memoir gives the reader a kind of mystery to follow—what the three little words were. How important is this opening to getting and keeping your interest? Look at the openings for the other memoirs in this chapter and choose your favorite. Explain why it is your favorite.

Playing Hardball

Henry Louis Gates, Jr.

Henry Louis Gates, Jr., professor of the humanities and chair of the department of Afro-American studies at Harvard University, is one of the preeminent contemporary writers about literary and cultural theory. Gates publishes in the *New Yorker*, *Harper's*, and the *New York Times* as well as in scholarly journals. His books include *Loose Canons*, *Figures in Black*, *The Signifying Monkey: Towards a Theory of Afro-American Literary Criticism*, and his memoir *Colored People*, from which the following excerpt comes. Gates says he wrote his memoir about growing up in Piedmont, West Virginia, during the 1950s and 1960s to explain those times to his two daughters, who have grown up in a very different world. In this excerpt, Gates remembers his brief stint in Little League baseball and how it affected his relationship with his father.

Daddy worked all the time, every day but Sunday. Two jobs—twice a day, in and out, eat and work, work and eat. Evenings, we watched television together, all of us, after I'd done my homework and Daddy had devoured the newspaper or a book. He was always reading, it seemed, especially detective stories. He was a charter subscriber to *Alfred Hitchcock's Magazine* and loved detective movies on TV.

My brother Rocky was the one he was close to. Rocky worshiped sports, while I worshiped Rocky. I chased after him like a lapdog. I wanted to be just like him. But the five years between us loomed like Kilimanjaro. We were always out of phase. And he felt crowded by my adoring gaze.

Rocky and I didn't exactly start off on the right foot. When I was born, my parents moved my brother to Big Mom's house, to live with her and Little Jim, who was our first cousin and Nemo's son and the firstborn male of our generation in the Coleman family. It was not an uncommon arrangement to shift an older child to his or her grandparents', because of crowding. Since we had only three rooms, plus a tiny room with a toilet, my parents thought the move was for the best. And Big Mom's house was only a couple hundred yards straight up the hill. Still, it's difficult to gauge the trauma of that displacement, all these years later. Five years of bliss, ended by my big head popping out.

But Rocky was compensated: he was Daddy's boy. Like the rest of Piedmont, they were baseball fanatics. They knew who had done what and when, how much everyone had hit, in what inning, who had scored the most runs in 1922, who the most rbi's. They could sit in front of a TV for hours at a time, watching inning after tedious inning of baseball, baseball, baseball. Or sit at Forbes Field in Pittsburgh through a double-header without getting tired or longing to go home. One night, when I was seven, we saw Sandy Koufax of the Dodgers pitch one game, then his teammate Don Drysdale pitch another. It was the most boring night of my life, though later I came to realize what a feat I had witnessed, two of baseball's greatest pitchers back-to-back.

5   I enjoyed *going* to the games in Pittsburgh because even then I loved to travel. One of Daddy's friends would drive me. I was fascinated with geography. And since I was even more fascinated with food, a keen and abiding interest of mine, I liked the games for that reason too. We would stop to eat at Howard Johnson's, going and coming. And there'd be hot dogs and sodas at the games, as well as popcorn and candy, to pass the eternity of successive innings in the July heat. Howard Johnson's was a five-star restaurant in Piedmont.

I used to get up early to have breakfast with Daddy, eating from his plate. I'll still spear a heavily peppered fried potato or a bit of egg off his plate today. My food didn't taste as good as his. Still doesn't. I used to drink coffee, too, in order to be just like Daddy. "Coffee will make you black," he'd tell me, with the intention of putting me off. From the beginning, I used a lot of pepper, because he did, and he did because his father did. I remember reading James Agee's *A Death in the Family* and being moved by a description of the extra pepper that the father's wife put on his eggs the very morning that he is killed in a car. Why are you frying eggs *this* time of day, Mama asked me that evening. Have you seen the pepper, Mama? I replied.

An unathletic child with too great an interest in food—no wonder I was fat, and therefore compelled to wear "husky" clothes.

My Skippy's not *fat*, Mama would lie. He's husky.

But I *was* fat, and felt fatter every time Mama repeated her lie. My mama loved me like life itself. Maybe she didn't see me as fat. But I was. And whoever thought of the euphemism "husky" should be shot. I was short and round—not obese, mind you, but *fat*. Still, I was clean and energetic, and most of the time I was cheerful. And I liked to play with other kids, not so much because I enjoyed the things we did together but because I could watch them be happy.

But sports created a bond between Rocky and 10 my father that excluded me, and though my father had no known athletic talent himself, my own unathletic bearing compounded my problems. For not only was I overweight; I had been born with flat feet and wore "corrective shoes." They were the bane of my existence, those shoes. While Rocky would be wearing long, pointy-toed, cool leather gentlemen, I'd be shod in blunt-ended, round-toed, fat-footed shoes that nobody but your mother could love.

And Mama *did* love those shoes. Elegant, she'd say. They're Stride-Rite. Stride-wrong, I'd think. Mama, I want some nice shoes, I'd beg, like Rocky's.

Still, I guess they did what they were meant to do, because I have good arches now. Even today, I look at the imprint of my wet foot at a swimming pool, just to make certain that my arch is still arched. I don't ever again want to wear those dull brown or black corrective shoes.

What made it all the more poignant was that Rocky—tall, lean, and handsome, blessed with my father's metabolism—was a true athlete. He would be the first Negro captain of the basketball team in high school and receive "the watch" at graduation. (He was the first colored to do that too.)

Maybe Mama thought I was husky, but Daddy knew better, and he made no secret of it. "Two-Ton Tony Galento," he and Rocky would say, or they'd call me Chicken Flinsterwall or Fletcher Bissett, Milton Berle's or Jack Benny's character in a made-for-TV movie about two complete cowards. I hated Daddy for doing that and yielded him as unconquerable terrain to my brother, clinging desperately to my mother for protection.

15   Ironically, I had Daddy's athletic ability, or lack thereof, just as I have his body. (We wear the same-size ring, gloves, shoes, shirt, suits, and hat.) And like him, I love to hear a good story. But during my first twelve or so years we were alienated from each other. I despised sports because I was overweight and scared to death. Especially of baseball—hardball, we called it. Yet I felt I had no choice but to try out for Little League. Everyone my age did Little League, after all. They made me a Giant, decided I was a catcher because I was "stout, like Roy Campanella," dressed me in a chest protector and a mask, and squatted me behind a batter.

It's hard to catch a baseball with your eyes closed. Each time a ball came over the plate, I thanked the Good Lord that the batter hadn't confused my nappy head with the baseball that had popped its way into my mitt. My one time at bat was an experience in blindness; miraculously, I wasn't hit in the head. With a 3 and 2 count, I got a ball, so I walked. They put in a runner for me. Everybody patted me on the back like I had just won the World Series. And everybody said nice things about my "eye." Yeah, I thought. My tightly closed eye.

Afterward, Pop and I stopped at the Cut-Rate to get a caramel ice cream cone, then began the long walk up the hill to Pearl Street. I was exhausted, so we walked easy. He was biding his time, taking smaller steps than usual so that I could keep up. "You know that you don't have to play baseball, don't you, boy?" All of a sudden I knew how Moses had felt on Mount Sinai. His voice was a bolt out of the blue. Oh, I want to play, I responded in a squeaky voice. "But you know that you don't *have* to play. I never was a good player. Always afraid of the ball. Uncoordinated too. I can't even run straight." We laughed. "I became the manager of the team," he said. That caramel ice cream sure tasted good. I held Daddy's hand almost all the way home.

In my one time at bat, I had got on base. I had confronted the dragon and he was mine. I had, I had . . . been absurdly lucky . . . and I couldn't *wait* to give them back their baseball suit. It was about that time that Daddy stopped teasing me about being fat. That day he knew me, and he seemed to care.

Yes, Pop and I had some hard times. He thought that I didn't love him, and I thought he didn't love me. At times, we both were right. I didn't think you wanted me around, he told me much later. I thought that I embarrassed you. He did embarrass me, but not like you might think, not the usual way parents embarrass children in front of their friends, for example. He had a habit of correcting me in front of strangers or white people, especially if they were settling an argument between me and Pop by something they had just said, by a question they had answered. See, I *told* you so, he'd say loudly, embarrassing the hell out of me with a deliberateness that puzzled and vexed me. I hated him when he did that.

And despite my efforts to keep up, he and my 20 brother had somehow made me feel as if I were an android, something not quite a person. I used to dream about going away to military school, and wrote to our Congressman, Harley Staggers, for a list of names. I used to devour *McKeever and the Colonel* on Sunday nights and dream about the freedom of starting over, at a high-powered, regimented school away from home. Daddy and Rocky would make heavy-handed jokes about queers and sissies. I wasn't their direct target, but I guess it was another form of masculine camaraderie that marked me as less manly than my brother.

And while I didn't fantasize about boys, I did love the companionship of boys and men, loved hearing them talk and watching their rituals, loved the warmth that their company could bring. I even loved being with the Coleman boys, at one of their shrimp or squirrel feeds, when they would play cards. Generally, though, I just enjoyed being on the edge of the circle, watching and listening and laughing, basking in the warmth, memorizing the stories, trying to strip away illusions, getting at what was really coming down.

I made my peace with sports, by and by, and was comfortable watching Rock and Daddy watch sports. But I could never experience it with the absorption they were capable of, could never live and breathe sports as they did. Oh, I loved to watch all the tournaments, the finals, the Olympics—the ritual events. But my relation to sports was never as visceral and direct as theirs.

After I returned my Little League uniform, I became the team's batboy and then the league's official scorekeeper, publishing our results in a column in the *Piedmont Herald*, our weekly newspaper.

Much more than for sports, I had early on developed an avidity for information about The Negro. I'm not sure why, since Daddy was not exactly a race man. Niggers are crabs in a barrel: if he said that once, he said it to us a thousand times. My father was hard on colored people—and funny about it too.

Aside from the brief stint as a student in New Jersey, Daddy's major contact with Negro culture from Elsewhere had been in the army, at Camp Lee, Virginia. He used to tell us all kinds of stories about the colored troops at Camp Lee, especially blacks from the rural South. It was clear that the army in World War II had been a great cauldron, mixing the New Negro culture, which had developed in the cities since the great migration of the twenties and thirties, and the Old Negro culture, the remnants of traditional rural black culture in the South.

Camp Lee was where colored soldiers were sent to learn how to be quartermasters—butlers, chefs, and service people, generally. Because the Army replicates the social structure of the larger society it defends, almost all black draftees were taught to cook and clean. Of course, it was usually women who cooked and cleaned outside the Army, but *someone* had to do the work, so it would be black men. Gender and race conflate in a crisis. Even educated black people were put in the quartermasters.

Well, Camp Lee was a circus and my daddy its scribe. He told us stories about how he beat the system, or damn well tried to. The first day, he had raised his hand when an officer asked who knew accounting. How hard could it be? he responded when I laughed. Hell, all you had to be able to do was add and subtract. The one thing I knew, he said, was that an accountant had an office and everybody else had to do basic training. Now, which one would *you* have picked? For two years, he stayed at Camp Lee and avoided being shipped to the front. Everybody else would be processed, then shipped out to Europe. But Daddy became a staff sergeant, serving as secretary and accountant to the commanding officer, who liked him a lot. He sent for Mama, who took a room in a colored home in town. Daddy slept there too. Mama got a job in a dry cleaners. The pictures that I carry of them in my wallet are from this time, 1942.

The war wouldn't take Pop any farther than Camp Lee, but even that was an experience that stayed with him. There he encountered the customs and sayings, the myths and folklore, of all sorts of black people he had never even heard about. The war did more to recement black American culture, which migration had fragmented, than did any other single event or experience. "War? What is it good for? You tell 'em: absolutely nothing." Nothing for the Negro but the transfer of cultures, the merging of the old black cultures with the new. And the transfer of skills. Daddy was no "race man," but for all his sardonicism, he respected race men and women, the people who were articulate and well educated, who comported themselves with dignity and who "achieved." Being at Camp Lee, an all-colored world, he'd say a decade later, was like watching episodes of *Amos and Andy*.

Hard as Daddy could be on colored people, he was Marcus Garvey compared to *his* father. Pop Gates used to claim that the government should lock up all the niggers in a big reservation in Kansas or Oklahoma or somewhere, feed them, clothe them, and give them two names: John or Mary. Nobody would hurt them, he'd add plaintively when his children would either protest or burst into howls of laughter. Pop Gates *hated* to see black people in loud clothes, and he hated just as much our traditional poetic names, such as Arbadella or Ethelretta. Made-up names, he'd say. Shouldn't be allowed, he'd say.

I was more aggressive around white people than Daddy, and it didn't go down well with him— or anybody else. Especially my Coleman uncles. Daddy, as noted, would almost never take my side in front of others. And if he felt I had violated a boundary, he would name it publicly and side with the boundary. He would do so loudly, even with what struck my child's ears as a certain malice. It tore me up.

He was not always this way with me. At a Little League game when I was ten, I told off a white man, Mr. Frank Price, not for anything he'd done to me, but for the rude way he treated Mr. Stanley

Fisher, a black man in his sixties, who was maybe twenty years Price's senior. The details are murky, but Price had been rude to the older man in a way that crossed a line, that made the colored people feel he was a racist.

I do remember that I was unable to control myself, unable to contain my anger. I found myself acting without thinking. I felt the blood rushing to my face, and a flood of nasty words poured out of my mouth, just this side of profanity. Everybody on the first-base side of the Little League field over in Westernport looked up and froze in silence as I stood in front of that big-bellied man's fat red face and told him to leave Mr. Stanley alone. Then I turned to Mr. Stanley and told him not to waste his dignity on that trash: "Don't sweat the small stuff," I said. The colored held their breaths, and Daddy looked like a cat caught between two fighting dogs and not knowing which way to turn. Even Mr. Stanley's face showed surprise at this snot-nosed kid talking right up in some redneck's face. Mr. Stanley must have been more embarrassed by me than reassured.

Daddy stepped in finally, put his arm around my shoulder, and started woofing at Frank Price and giving him those dirty glares of his, all the while pushing me gently up the field toward Stanley and the colored men who always sat together on their lawn chairs out in right field. And we then all walked together up the dusty back road that bordered the Little League field like the rim of a crater, passing the new filtration plant, which made the whole place stink worse than the sulfurous chemicals that it had been built to remove, and all the old colored men were saying what an asshole Frank Price was and always had been, and how he had been rude to Stanley, and how nobody liked or respected him (not even white people), and how nobody within earshot should pay that motherfucker no mind.

Now, you know you are supposed to respect your elders, don't you? Daddy said to me much later, after we had bought a caramel ice cream cone, to go, at the Cut-Rate. And you know you are not supposed to talk back to older people, now don't you? And you know that Stanley Fisher can take care of himself? And you know that you can get in trouble talking back to white people, don't you? Don't you, boy? Boy, you crazy sometimes. That ice cream is dripping down your fingers. Don't let it go to waste.

Critical Reading Questions

1. Identify the introduction and the setup to this story. How does the focus on Daddy and Rocky set up the story to come?

2. Note some details of the setting of this story. What does Gates reveal to you about his childhood through these details?

3. How does Gates characterize the members of his family, including himself? Underline some of the description or dialogue in the story that reveals their personalities.

4. Mark the place where Gates's experience in Little League begins. Why do you think he takes so long to get to this part of the story?

5. Identify the place where the Little League story ends. Why do you think Gates continues the story for a number of paragraphs afterwards? What does he accomplish in those concluding paragraphs?

6. What is the essential conflict in this story? How is it resolved, or is it?

7. Underline a sentence that best expresses Gates's theme in this story, or put the theme in your own words.

Questions for Writing and Discussion

1. Sports is the means through which the young Skippy Gates tries to relate to his father and brother. How important is sports in the life of boys and in their relationships to their role models? Does sports play the same or a different role for girls?

2. Gates reveals a lot about himself that is not particularly flattering. He is fat, clumsy, and not particularly athletic. How do you respond to this kind of self-revelation? Why would a memoirist include such unflattering details?

The Two Fridas

Frida Kahlo

Frida Kahlo (1907–1954) was one of the most celebrated Mexican artists of the twentieth century. Her tempestuous marriage to painter Diego Rivera and a streetcar accident that left her permanently disabled and in pain are two details that she painted into many of her self-portraits. Kahlo painted *The Two Fridas* in 1939 at around the time of her separation and divorce from Rivera but before their second marriage. In the painting (on the following page), she shows herself split into two images. On the left, she wears European clothing that are splattered with blood that seems to come from a severed blood vessel. She holds a medical clamp in her right hand. On the right, Frida paints herself in traditional Mexican dress. She holds a picture of Rivera in her right hand. The two Fridas hold hands as they sit on a green bench, and both have their hearts exposed. Look carefully at the painting, and compare it to the accompanying photograph of Kahlo.

Critical Questions

1. Where is your eye first drawn in the painting?

2. Observe the two images of Kahlo in the painting. What is revealed by the way that Kahlo positions these two images and the way that she uses color here? What do these images reveal about how she sees herself at this time?

3. What is the setting of this painting? What mood does the painting create? What has Kahlo done to reinforce the mood of this setting?

4. Much of Kahlo's painting is highly symbolic. What symbols can you see in this painting? What might they represent?

5. What is the story in this painting? What is the conflict?

6. Compare the photograph of Kahlo to the self-portrait. In what way is the painting interpretive? What do you think Kahlo is revealing about herself in the self-portrait?

Questions for Writing and Discussion

1. Images as well as words tell stories. What images can you think of in popular culture that tell stories?

2. If you were to paint a self-portrait, what symbolic items would you put in your hands?

WRITING IN THE WORKS
Interview with Antonya Nelson

Antonya Nelson

1. Your memoir, "All Washed Up" [see pages 153–155], reads a lot like a short story. It is sometimes hard for writers to imagine using a "real" event and making it into something that reads like a piece of fiction. For some, it is a matter of feeling bound by the events as they occurred, being loyal to every detail. Maybe you can help answer one question that is always on the minds of memoir writers: How do you take real life and make it into art? Do you ever feel the need to embellish?

Sometimes I like to pose the opposite question: how can you write about something that hasn't happened to you, that you know nothing or care nothing about, and turn that into fiction? That seems like the more challenging task, especially the not caring part. Ideally, finding fiction in one's factual life means locating a stance that will accommodate genuine feeling, on the one hand, without hurting genuine feelings, on the other hand.

2. Readers looking carefully at the way you craft your story notice your techniques of using parallel sentences, repeating certain phrases, and listing. Are you conscious of these techniques as you write, or are they part of your internal writing mechanism?

I'm pretty sure this is a matter of what we loosely call voice. I have an internalized rhythm that means something to me. It dictates how I write, how I pattern sentences, what vocabulary I choose, etc. I know what sounds good to myself. I'm sure I learned it reading books, reading aloud, hearing the spoken word when it's at its most seductive, and I'm sure I've attempted, pretty unconsciously, to channel that which pleases my own ear. I sing aloud in the car too. Sometimes I just chat at the dog.

3. Much of the story happens "off-screen," and is revealed in the form of exposition. How do you decide when to let the camera roll and show the action in a scene rather than a "voiceover"?

Again, this has to do with some sense of being both writer and reader, simultaneously. I tell my students this all the time: imagine you are reading what you are writing. What do you want (need) to know (hear) next? Occasionally I've been aware of there being too much exposition in my work. I now create separate files after I've finished a short story (on my computer) and copy the story over, then rename the file "X story, activated." The "activate" part is where I stop using exposition, inasmuch as I can, and start creating either dialogue or action to do the same work. I'm trying to move further away from exposition in narrative. But that doesn't quite answer your question. I really do believe in the internalized sense of pattern and variation, of some monitor lodged behind the reader/writer's eyes or brain or heart that dictates when a line of dialogue needs to emerge, when a repeated background note needs striking, when a sentence containing only one word needs to fall. There.

4. Your voice in "All Washed Up" captures the essence of being eighteen and full of yourself, which is essential to the theme of the story. When you were learning the craft of storytelling, how did you go about finding a voice for yourself as a writer?

I imitated people for a long time. I still might be doing that. But I read enough people that the combo plate is pretty varied. I love Flannery O'Connor's precise humor. I love Carson McCullers' swampy psychotic emotional terrain. I love the scalpel-like descriptors of John Updike. I want David Sedaris' irreverence. I wish I had plot under control like Pete Dexter or Larry Brown or

Elmore Leonard. I long for the dreamy unstated business Mavis Gallant goes about. In short, I think I'm still an apprentice writer, whose voice, insofar as I could claim it, has the virtues of the mutt: mixed breeding.

5. "All Washed Up" is a funny story. The cliché among actors is that it's easier to make people cry than it is to make them laugh. Is it difficult writing funny stories?

I'm such a sucker for jokes, for laughter, for pranks and riddles and catchy puns, so grateful for anything that makes me crack a grin, that I'm just going to graciously accept the hidden compliment that question offered.

6. Was this memoir assigned to you? How was the length determined? Did you have to write to fit into a word count? If so, did this require editing? How do you edit your work to fit into a word count? Do you ever finish a piece and feel as if you want to guard it against editing, that you worked so hard to get it right that you couldn't cut a word?

The assignment was a general call that the New Yorker put out to its very large group of writers, inviting them to submit a thousand words on having been fired. It was very polite, as all dealings with that magazine are, and suggested that of course they assumed none of us had ever been fired from anything before, but, maybe, in case some clown in charge had somehow mistakenly let us go . . . I like a word count assignment. I like the way it creates form. Poets have forms to fall back on any time they like. Fiction writers can go flabby if they aren't careful. So the assignment really designated its own pacing, its own terms, its own limits. That was very nice. And I really like to be edited. The New Yorker edits and fact checks and is so incredibly careful that it's a real pleasure to be a part of their process of perfecting a piece. I don't object in the least. (The one line I wish they'd kept referred to the dishwasher as the "pearl diver," but nobody on staff had heard that expression, so they chucked it. Alas.) Plus, I was so pleased to have at that little idiot I once worked for.

WRITING AND REVISION STRATEGIES

Gathered here are three interactive sections for you to use as you write and revise your memoir.

▶ Writer's Notebook Suggestions
▶ Peer Editing Log
▶ Revision Checklist

Writer's Notebook Suggestions

You can use these exercises to do some start-up thinking and writing for your memoir.

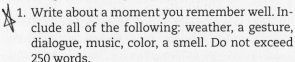

1. Write about a moment you remember well. Include all of the following: weather, a gesture, dialogue, music, color, a smell. Do not exceed 250 words.

2. Using the writing you did for the first question (or some other memory), change the voice. Use one of the examples in the chapter as a model.

3. Take any paragraph of memory writing and change it to present tense.

4. Write two different openings for a story about your first day at school or your first day on a job. Choose from the following types of openings.
   a. Start in the middle of action.
   b. Start by describing a photograph of that day (real or imagined).
   c. Start by seeing your reflection in a mirror or window.
   d. Start at the end.
   e. Start with dialogue.

5. Choose a day from your life you remember well, not necessarily because it was dramatic or important but because you can recall many of the details. Write a diary entry as if the day were yesterday.

6. Write a paragraph that combines internal monologue, dialogue, summary, and descriptive narrative.

7. Write about yourself in the third person.

8. Describe the weather on a day that was important.

9. Remember a phone call that was hard for you to make. Write the dialogue.

10. Describe someone who left an impression on you by describing a place in which that person belongs. How does the place represent the person?

11. Use the letter-to-a-friend technique: Write a letter explaining an event to somebody you know well.

Peer-Editing Log

As you work with a writing partner or in a peer-editing group, you can use these questions to give helpful responses to a classmate's memoir and as a guide for discussion.

Writer's Name _____

Date _____

1. Bracket the introduction of the memoir. What technique does the writer use to open the story? Do you find it effective, or could you suggest a better place for the story to begin?

2. Put a line under the last paragraph of the setup. How effectively has the writer set up the story? What other information or sensory details might help you better understand the events that follow?

3. Box a section that presents the setting of the story. What details might make the setting stronger, more vivid, or more specific?

4. Write a sentence that expresses the theme of the story as you understand it. What images, language, and events point to that theme?

Does the title also direct the reader's attention to the theme? If the title is weak, can you suggest an alternative?

5. Put a check mark next to the first place you notice the conflict beginning to emerge. What is the conflict? What are the obstacles for the central character? What is at stake?

6. What is your impression of the main character(s)? Suggest places where the characters' actions and dialogue could be strengthened to develop them more fully?

7. Look at the narrative techniques the writer uses in the memoir. Identify places where the writer uses summary and places where the writer creates a scene through narrative detail. Label places where the writer uses dialogue with D and places where the writer uses internal monologue with IM. Which sections might be strengthened by showing through narration and dialogue rather than telling through summary and internal monologue?

8. What kind of voice does the writer uses to tell the story? Is it appropriate to and consistent with the narrator's age and circumstance? How might the voice better reflect the narrator's character?

9. Bracket the conclusion. What technique does the writer use? Is the conclusion effective in leaving a last impression that fortifies the theme? Does the last paragraph add anything necessary to the story? Would the story be injured by cutting it?

10. Comment briefly on the writing style. Write V where the writing could be strengthened by substituting active verbs for "to be" verbs and T where the writer could use a better transition. Put an asterisk (*) next to places where the writer uses interesting verbs and good transitions.

Revision Checklist

As you do your final revision for your memoir, check to make sure that you

❑ Used an interesting, attention-getting opening

❑ Set up the story

❑ Created a setting that helps develop the mood of the story

❑ Presented a clear conflict

❑ Developed the conflict incrementally, in steps

❑ Presented a climax

❑ Described your characters

❑ Made your main character's motivation clear

❑ Explored a theme that has significance to you and your reader

6. NEWS STORIES

WRITING THE PUBLIC RECORD

Journalism is literature in a hurry.

— Matthew Arnold

Sergeant Jackie Milhomme, hugging her mother before her company, the 143rd Military Police, left Hartford, Connecticut, for training before the company's departure to Iraq.

Write a two- to three-page news report suitable for publication in your school paper, a local paper, or a newsletter or for posting on a website. Some suggestions for topics are the following.

- A speech, a public lecture, an open meeting, a fundraising event, a book or poetry reading, or a demonstration you have attended

- An accident or crime (robbery, burglary, vandalism) you have witnessed or one that allows you to interview people involved, or an incident with a report filed with police (the public has access to arrest reports at most police stations)

- An announcement of an upcoming event or series of events (the library's sponsorship of a film series, the town's acquisition of a new fire engine)

- An announcement for plans to do something in the community (build a new housing complex, institute a recycling program at the high school)

NEWS STORIES

You are a newspaper reporter. On Saturday night, June 17, 1972, you get a message that plainclothes officers from the metropolitan police department have caught five men who broke into an office building. The men were carrying bugging devices, forty rolls of film, and tear-gas guns. Several of them were removing ceiling panels, while the others were photographing files.

The circumstances of this crime and its implied espionage make it a natural news story. Even without knowing many details, all the elements that make a story interesting are present: characters, conflict, and mystery. As a reporter, you would jump at the chance to find out more. Who are the alleged burglars? What is their motivation? What is in those files?

Later that night, police and reporters are able to fill in some important blanks: The office is in the swanky Watergate building at 2600 Virginia Ave NW in Washington, D.C. The tenant is the Democratic National Committee (DNC). One of the burglars claims to have worked for the CIA. Another claims to have trained guerillas after the Bay of Pigs invasion failed to liberate Cuba.

This is the beginning of what is arguably the biggest scandal ever to involve the presidency of the United States, but you don't know that yet. What you know is that something suspicious happened: an event, a story with characters, conflict, setting, and themes. This story will grow and expand as the nation becomes aware of the context surrounding it and the intricacies of a monumental conspiracy. More characters will be added, and new information will become available as the context broadens and new conflicts emerge. On June 17, 1972, a defining period of American history begins, but for this moment, it is a story about a break-in—not an average burglary, but not a national scandal. Yet.

Five Held in Plot to Bug Democrats' Office Here
by Alfred E. Lewis
Washington Post Staff Writer
Sunday, June 18, 1972, page A01

Five men, one of whom said he is a former employee of the Central Intelligence Agency, were arrested at 2:30 a.m. yesterday in what authorities described as an elaborate plot to bug the offices of the Democratic National Committee here.

Three of the men were native-born Cubans and another was said to have trained Cuban exiles for guerrilla activity after the 1961 Bay of Pigs invasion.

They were surprised at gunpoint by three plainclothes officers of the metropolitan police department in a sixth floor office at the plush Watergate, 2600 Virginia Ave., NW, where the Democratic National Committee occupies the entire floor.

There was no immediate explanation as to why the five suspects would want to bug the Democratic National Committee offices or whether or not they were working for any other individuals or organizations.

Copyright © *The Washington Post*. Reprinted with permission.

Any time writers report events—publish news stories—they take part in creating the public record. Their stories will be read, trusted, and remembered by readers. A former publisher of the *Washington Post*, Phil Graham once said that news stories are the first drafts of history. The *Post* reporters writing, on June 18, 1972, about the attempt to install listening devices in the DNC offices were indeed writing the first draft of the opening chapter of a historical event that would culminate in the resignation of disgraced President Richard Nixon.

News stories have marked the beginning of many significant periods of history. Reporters have often uncovered scandals and initiated investigations that changed public policy by raising awareness about issues. Sometimes journalists' investigations have even led to major changes in laws. The revelation that tobacco companies knew that ingredients in cigarettes were addictive while claiming the contrary stands out as one example of reporting that had far-reaching effects.

Most news stories have a more local aim: to help people better understand what is behind the issues and events that affect them in their communities and at home. People read news stories because they want to know about events that will affect their everyday lives—how their tax dollars are spent, how secure they feel in their houses and on the roads, and how they view their civic leaders, their schools, and their health care.

Whether their scope is national or local, news stories attract people in part because of what they are at their core: *stories* with characters, conflicts, and themes, stories with mysteries, motivations, and details.

Applications: School, Community, Work

The skills discussed in this chapter—for example, writing concisely and organizing material in order of importance—are useful in a range of school, community, and workplace settings. You may use the skills in writing for your college or town newspaper; for newsletters at your workplace, church, or community group; or for the Web. You will also find that reading news stories, both new and old, helps you better understand events and their histori-

Warm-up Practice 6.1 Collaborative Exercise

Read the accounts of the *Titanic* disaster, on the following page, and compare facts as they were reported at the time.

1. Make a list of the most important facts.

2. Make a list of contradictions you find and details that surprise you considering how the story turned out.

3. Decide which details will be irrelevant to your readers.

4. Write a three-sentence summary of what happened, beginning with the most important details. Substitute your own words to make the summary sound more like contemporary news writing.

5. What differences do you notice between the style of this story, written and reported in 1912, and the style found in today's newspapers?

By Telegraf
Titanic In No Danger—Another Triumf [sic] For Marconi

(Special Dispatch to Daily News) New York, April 15

Officials are satisfied that there wce [sic] for alarm regarding the steamship Titanic, reported damaged by ice. The Titanic is now in latitude 41 degrees 46 minutes north and longitude 50 degrees 14 minutes west. The steamers Virginian and Baltic went to the rescue of Titanic. The Allan liner Virginian would reach her at 9:00.

— *Truro Daily News,* April 15, 1912

White Star Steamship Titanic Founders
With Loss of Over 1500 Persons
The Fateful Message

Cape Race Nfld, April 15th

The Steamer Olympic reports that the steamer Carpathia reached the Titanic's position at daybreak today but found boats and wreakage [sic] only. She reported that the Titanic had foundered at about 2:20 o'clock, a.m., in lat. 41.16 North and long. 50.14 west.

The message adds that all the Titanic's boats were accounted for and about 675 souls saved, crew and passengers, latter nearly all women and children. The report from the Olympic states that the Leyland liner Californian was remaining and searching the vicinity of the disaster. The Carpathia it was stated, was returning to New York with the survivors.

The White Star officers in New York concealed, as long as they could the terrible nature of this marine disaster, but the sad truth is before the world that the mighty leviathan of the sea has foundered with an enormous loss of human life.

The wireless advices [sic] receivd [sic] are that the WOMEN AND CHILDREN have mostly been saved, but, oh, what a loss of others. Experts do not believe that the Titanic in Latitude 41 degrees at this season of the year struck an iceburg [sic], but are inclined to the belief that a submerged wreck was the cause of the disaster. The ship foundered 420 miles east south east of Sable Island or over 500 miles from Halifax. Others think the big steamer struck submerged ice and was racing for Halifax when she sank.

Among the large passenger list, many of whom were Canadians, were New Yorkers of immense wealth returning after the winter in Europe, on this palatial liner on her first voyage across the Atlantic. It is feard [sic] that Mr. George Wright a prominent citizen of Halifax whose letters on many moral reform subjects have frequently appeard [sic] in the Nova Scotia Daily Press, is among the

A newspaper account of the *Titanic* disaster.

lost. President Hays of the Grand Trunk Railway and family, Montreal, were passengers on this ill fated steamer.

The city of Montreal has contributed many other prominent personages to this hart-rending [sic] disaster. In all probability the Titanic sank before any of the boats reacht [sic] her. The 675 passengers on board the Carpathia were probably pickt [sic] up from the Titanic life-boats. It will be found that the Titanic sank before any boat reacht[sic] her. The Carpathia got to the scene of disaster first and pickt [sic] up survivors. Later she was joined by the Parisian and Virginian and the three boats would cruise around looking for survivors who might be clinging to wreckage. As soon as they make careful search they will proceed to their respective destinations. The Carpathia goes to New York with the Survivors while the Parisian is heading for Halifax. There is no knowledge of any survivors being on board either of our boats.

— *Truro Daily News,* April 16, 1912

cal context. Your research skills are enhanced by finding and citing old news reports; they can be excellent research material for academic papers.

CHAPTER OBJECTIVES

In this chapter you will learn to

► write a clear, concise summary of an event in your community
► write with objectivity and balance
► structure a story using order of importance
► research using primary sources

UNDERSTANDING NEWS STORIES

The *Titanic* news reports illustrate the changes that have evolved as news writing has taken on a distinctive, immediately recognizable style. Today's readers have come to expect little or no overt opinion in news stories. They expect the most significant details of the story to appear first, so that they get a summary of events in the headline and first couple of paragraphs.

This form—summary first and detailed explanation following—developed during the Civil War, when reports from the battlefield were telegraphed to newspapers. Reporters wrote with the overriding need to summarize events as concisely and swiftly as the medium would allow. Since that time, other elements have become part of the distinct genre of news writing. Today people are getting news from television broadcasts and up-to-the-minute Internet sources, and news consumers try to judge the reliability of information by looking at how balanced the reporting is as well as how objective the coverage is and how newsworthy the topics are.

Newsworthiness

In choosing a topic for a news story, the first step is to figure out what makes a story newsworthy, of interest to readers of newspapers, newsletters, or websites. Sometimes this is obvious, as in the case of a fire that results in loss of life or a flood that destroys property. Other times newsworthiness is less obvious—perhaps a local doctor has decided to retire. To figure out the newsworthiness of a story, ask the following questions.

1. Is the story timely in some way? A timely story is about an event that has occurred recently, is related to trends, and concerns something in the public eye. Public attention might be tuned to gun violence, pollution, or taxes, for example. A story that follows up on or elaborates on current issues can be considered timely.

2. How many people are affected? A story may have more value if the issue affects a substantial number of people. Determining whether enough

**Practice 6.2
Testing for
Newsworthiness**

Sometimes stories need to be ferreted out. Here are a few situations in which newsworthiness might not be immediately obvious. Read these scenarios. For each scenario, list the story, the audience that would find the story interesting, and the news outlet that might publish the story (a local newspaper, a college newspaper, a newsletter, or a website).

1. When the university opens in the fall, it has too many students and not enough dorm rooms.

2. The town observatory announces its partnership with an observatory in China.

3. A restaurant has lost its liquor license.

4. A local florist has developed a new breed of orchid.

people will be interested depends on the story and on the publication. For example, the closing of a local hospital would affect more people than the closing of a single doctor's office. The way the community is affected is a factor in judging the value of stories, and so is the size of the newspaper that might print the stories. A small town paper might cover the closing of a single doctor's office, while a large metropolitan paper probably would not.

3. Is the story local? *Local* can be defined broadly as the area your newspaper covers, including anything your particular readers might find especially interesting and useful. A plane crash in Africa is a local story if five people from town were on the plane. A story about a new method of harvesting grain would be of special interest to a farming community.

4. Does the story involve something or somebody famous? The well-known person or place might be a celebrity only in your area (a high school coach with a great record, for example) or in a wider sphere (such as the coach of the Dallas Cowboys).

5. Is the story a novelty? Is it odd or striking because it involves human interest? Your story might not be timely, local, large in scope, or about a celebrity, but it might be newsworthy because it involves a novelty or some kind of human interest. The retirement of a doctor who ran a clinic to help people who were not covered by health insurance would be of great interest. The reasons for the doctor's retirement and the implications for the future of the clinic would certainly compel attention. In fact, many stories that generate compassion or empathy might be considered newsworthy.

Objectivity

Objectivity, the absence of the writer's personal biases, is another essential component of contemporary news stories. In the nineteenth and twentieth centuries newspaper writers were not as concerned about keeping personal opinion off the news pages, but today's readers, even readers of newsletters, look for news reports that make every attempt to be reliable. In the Watergate story, the writer is careful to note that "authorities described [the break-in] as an elaborate plot to bug the offices of the Democratic National Committee." The conclusion that the burglary was an "elaborate plot" was not the writer's, but was instead the conclusion authorities had reached.

Looking back at the story about the sinking of the *Titanic*, you find the statement: "the sad truth is before the world that the mighty leviathan of the sea has foundered with an enormous loss of human life." Today flowery statements like this do not appear in news writing. Opinions are saved for editorials, commentary, and columns in contemporary newspapers. The newspaper sections in which such material appears are now clearly marked as opinion.

Banishing "I" from a story—removing personal bias—is one of a news writer's most important struggles. It is a struggle because most journalists agree that true objectivity is almost impossible to achieve. Even the choices of what to report, whom to interview, and which details to include create some bias. Nevertheless, news writers try to make sure that their use of details creates color or interest in the story while they always keep their primary goal of objectivity in mind.

Balance

Though the writers of news stories should remain objective and make every attempt not to include their own opinions, they strive to report the perspectives of others. Every story worth reporting has more than one side to it. Just as readers expect news stories to be as objective as possible, they also expect news stories to be balanced and to show the differing sides.

The best way to achieve balance is to consult experts on both (or three or four) sides of the issue and to quote them carefully and accurately. You do not, of course, express your own opinion; for instance, you don't write "In my opinion soft drinks do not cause cavities." But you can express the idea in the form of a quotation from someone else.

> Dental cavities among teenagers and young adults are not linked to soft drink consumption, Virginia Tech researchers reported to the annual meeting of the American College of Nutrition. —Eurkalert.com, press release

Before using a quotation, make sure you understand whether a source has bias or a specific point of view. This point of view could be support for one side of an argument, or it could reflect promotion of an organization or product. If you had read the entire press release that included the above quotation, you would have found this statement: "The study of the data from that survey was supported by an unrestricted grant from the National Soft Drink Association." No link between cavities and tooth decay reported in a study paid for by soft-drink companies? You had better find a dentist to tell the other side of the story. A story for BBC News quoted the British Dental Association.

> There is a good evidence base to show that sweetened or carbonated drinks and pure fruit juices are linked to caries (tooth decay) and erosion

Photojournalism: How a Picture Tells a Story

Photographs work with news writing to provide a full record of an event. Some photographs, like those of abused detainees in the Abu Ghraib prison in Iraq, are themselves the news. Though the photos from inside the infamous prison were not intended to be a part of the public record, they became just that. Many people argue that photos depicting the treatment of prisoners initiated a wave of public opinion surrounding the war in much the same way that the photo of Kim Phuc, a Vietnamese nine-year-old burned by flames, changed opinions about that war. Facts in a news story can be persuasive, but photographs make us eyewitnesses to events.

Getting the right photo is a matter of luck and timing, but photojournalists also have to understand what is at the heart of a story before they can find the right image to tell it.

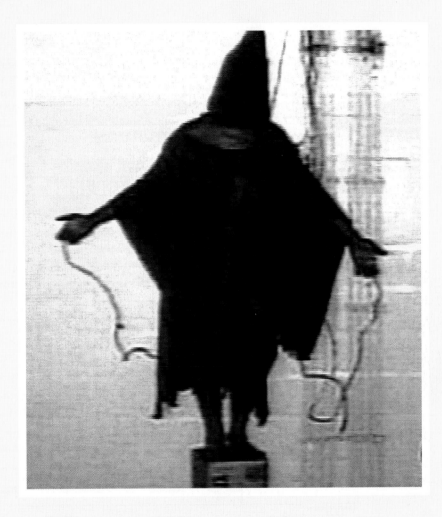

Critical Looking: Analyzing Photojournalism Using one of the photographs in this chapter, analyze the visual elements. Write about the following aspects.

1. The focal point: what elements does your eye see first?

2. The story in the image: what is the implied narrative? What is happening now? What happened before? Without reading the caption, what would you think is happening in the photo?

3. The implications of the image: what does the picture imply about the event? What kind of emotion is inside the image?

Take your own photographs to illustrate your news stories and write captions that expand the story. Name your subjects. Describe the context.

Practice 6.3 Newsworthiness and Balance

Examine the police report, to the right, which was filed in Kent, Washington.

1. Is the story newsworthy?

2. If you think it is newsworthy, whom would you would interview to get a clear picture?

MASTER CASE REPORT FORM		City of Kent Police	MASTER CASE REPORT NUMBER
MASTER INCLUDES ☐ SUSPECT FORMS ☐ EVIDENCE LOG ☐ ADDL PERSONS/VEH ☐ VEHICLE LOG ☐ ADDL PROPERTY REPORT ☐ MISSING PERSONS	KENT WASHINGTON	220 4th Avenue South Kent, Washington 98032 (253) 856-5800	08-5152

City of Kent Police
220 4th Avenue South
Kent, Washington 98032
(253) 856-5800

CASE SUMMARY

☐ RCW ☐ KCC ☐ NO CRIME — PRIMARY STATUTE 9A56040 — CRIME/INCIDENT TYPE THEFT 2 — PRIMARY COUNTS 0600270 /1 — 2ND 1 — 3RD 1

ADDRESS 1810 MAPLE LN — APT/SUIT M72 — BUSINESS NAME HOLLY GLEN COND — LOCATION IF NO ADDRESS — CITY KENT

OCCURRENCE DATE/TIME 4/28/3 1100 — DATE/TIME 4/28/3 1430 — REPORTED DATE/TIME 4/28/3 1510 — HOW TKN D

RPT OFFICER ID 23970 — LAST NAME, INITIALS GOODNER, AB — REVIEW BY ID # 92021 — LAST NAME, INITIALS PAGANWLL — CASE STATUS C

PERSONS/BUSINESSES

RP ☐ PERSON ☐ BUSINESS — NAME (Last, First, Middle) BALLANTINE, ROBERT — SEX ☐ M ☐ F W — RACE W — DOB (AGE) 6-4-39 — OCCUPATION/EMPLOYER —

ADDRESS 1810 MAPLE LN — APT/SUIT M72 — CITY KENT — STATE WA — ZIP 980 — HOME PHONE — BUS PHONE 2

IF PERSON WERE THEY (1P) INJURED? ☑ NO ☐ YES — INJURY RELATES TO ☐ FEL CRIME ☐ MIS CRIME — ☐ IND ACCID ☐ ACCIDENTAL — ☐ OTHER ☐ UNKNOWN — EXT-INJ — TAKEN TO — BY — STATEMENT ☐ YES ☑ NO

INVOLVED ☐ PERSON ☐ BUSINESS — NAME (Last, First, Middle) — SEX ☐ M ☐ F — RACE — DOB (AGE) — OCCUPATION/EMPLOYER

ADDRESS — APT/SUIT — CITY — STATE — ZIP — HOME PHONE — BUS PHONE

IF PERSON WERE THEY (1P) INJURED? ☐ NO ☐ YES — INJURY RELATES TO ☐ FEL CRIME ☐ MIS CRIME — ☐ IND ACCID ☐ ACCIDENTAL — ☐ OTHER ☐ UNKNOWN — EXT-INJ — TAKEN TO — BY — STATEMENT ☐ YES ☐ NO

PROPERTY

OWNER-LAST NAME, INITIALS ☑ SAME PERSON AS ABOVE SAME AS VM — GENERAL DESCRIPTION SEGWAY — WACIC NO

BRAND — MODEL — SERIAL NO — QTY 1 — $VALUE 5000 00 — BY

COLOR(S) BLK — PREMISE/AREA/ROOM TAKEN FROM — ADDITIONAL NOTES 2-WHEEL MOTORIZED VEH

OWNER-LAST NAME, INITIALS — GENERAL DESCRIPTION — WACIC NO

BRAND — MODEL — SERIAL NO — QTY — $VALUE — BY

COLOR(S) — PREMISE/AREA/ROOM TAKEN FROM — ADDITIONAL NOTES

OWNER LAST NAME, INITIALS — GENERAL DESCRIPTION — WACIC NO

BRAND — MODEL — SERIAL NO — QTY — $VALUE — BY

COLOR(S) — PREMISE/AREA/ROOM TAKEN FROM — ADDITIONAL NOTES

VEHICLE

INVOLVED — LICENSE — STATE — LIC-TYPE — YEAR — MAKE — MODEL — BODY — COLOR(S) — UNIQUE ID

VIN — R/O NAME ☐ PERSON ☐ BUSINESS — ADDRESS — APT/SUITE

CITY — STATE — ZIP — HOME PHONE — BUSINESS PHONE — DAMAGE TO VEHICLE

SUMMARY OF INCIDENT

RP/VM ROBERT BALLANTINE STATED THAT AT THE ABOVE DATE, TIME AND LOCATION HE HAD CHAINED UP HIS MOTORIZED TWO WHEELED WALKING MACHINE. BALLANTINE INDICATED THAT HE WAS THE ONLY ONE TO HAVE THE MACHINE IN SOUTH PUGET SOUND.

THE MACHINE WAS PARKED AND CHAINED AROUND 1130 ON 4/28/3 WHEN BALLANTINE RETURNED TO THE MACHINES LOCATION, THE CHAIN HAD BEEN CUT OFF AND THE MACHINE WAS GONE.

THERE ARE NO SUSPECTS — C-CLOSED ☐ ADDITIONAL NARRATIVE

OFFICER ID 23970 — LAST NAME INITIALS GOODNER, AB — DATE/TIME 4/28/3 1600 — APPROVE ID — LAST NAME INITIALS — DP BY

KPD121B 5/22/02 rev

Police report from Kent, Washington.

of dental enamel (loss of tooth surface.) We note that this new report appears to say nothing about the link between soft drinks and erosion.

—BBC News

Including the information from the study, the identification of the study, and the quotation from the dentists gives this story balance and allows the reader to uncover the truth. In order to give a full and factual account, you must gather quotes from many sides of the issues you are reporting. And you need to choose good quotations that further readers' understanding and give accurate information.

RESEARCH PATHS

In researching news articles, you will use both primary and secondary sources. In other writing assignments, your research often involves such secondary sources as print articles, information posted on the Web, and books. In news reporting, secondary sources are mostly used for background information, to provide context for your story.

Primary Sources

Using Interviews News reporting requires you to interview people and to observe places and events. This firsthand information gathering is called primary source reporting. As a news reporter, you have to go to where the news is happening; you have to attend fundraisers or talks and interview organizers or eyewitnesses. Make sure you get the full names and titles (chief of police, inspector, neighbor, high school teacher) of the people you interview, and check to be sure you are spelling the names correctly. You will find a list of interview tips on pages 426–430.

Using Observation Be your readers' eyes and ears. Make notes about the setting. "Telling" details add color and interest to your story. For example, the rainbow banners or the green T-shirts worn by protestors might show the groups' affiliation and unity. You might make note of the icicles clinging to the firefighters' hats; the severity of the weather during the fire could be well portrayed in that single, cinematic detail. The point is that you do not know what you might use until you begin writing. Make sure to watch the details carefully and take accurate notes.

Using Documents Locate public records like notes from city council meetings, birth and death certificates, court records, and marketing studies. (Some of these may be available online.) Libraries have many resources: indices,

On April 14, 2004, voters in Soweto, a residential area of Johannesburg, South Africa, waited for up to twelve hours to cast ballots in the national election. This was the third national election since the end of apartheid in 1994.

almanacs, telephone books, census data. Most important, libraries have librarians, and they can be a reporter's best tool.

Secondary Sources

Read what has already been published about your issue or about your story's topic. You might find some past stories on the Internet, or you may need to go to the library to read old papers on microfilm and microfiche. You can use LexisNexis, an online service with full-text excerpts of newspaper articles that is searchable by using keywords. (Find more suggestions on how to research your news article in Chapter 14.)

After flooding closed an interstate highway in Denver, Colorado, Shirley Farland was rescued, while Tom German found refuge on the roof of his car.

How to Use Quotations

Material you gather will sometimes have facts that are easy to double-check. In the following excerpt from a press release issued by the McDonald's Corporation, for example, you can find figures about earnings and about the number of stores the company plans to close.

> In fourth quarter 2002, the Company recorded $359.4 million of pretax charges ($298.8 million after tax) consisting of $298.2 million related to management's decision to close 719 underperforming restaurants (202 were closed in 2002 and 517 will close throughout 2003), primarily in the U.S.

Government officials seized Elian Gonzalez from the Miami home of relatives in April 2000 and reunited him with his father hours later at Andrews Air Force Base in Maryland. The boy had been rescued by fishermen when his mother's boat, fleeing Cuba, capsized in November 1999.

and Japan, and $67.2 million primarily related to the impairment of assets for certain existing restaurants in Europe and Latin America.

—McDonald's Corporate Financial Press Release

You might use the factual material gleaned from this press release to give your reader context for a story in your community, "The McDonald's on Western Avenue is one of 517 McDonald's restaurants that are scheduled to close next year, according to a company press release." This requires you to understand the source and translate it into easy-to-understand information for your reader. You must always cite the source of the information. These figures are

Using Quotations

After you have done some reporting, you have three ways to use material from interviews and other sources: full quotations, partial quotations, and paraphrases.

Full Quotations

Full quotations are usually a full sentence or two, transcribed exactly as spoken.

> *EXAMPLE:* "There is no evidence, at this point in time, that the accident was related to alcohol," said Ted Vargen, Wake County District Attorney.

Use full quotations for especially well-phrased thoughts or memorable language.

Partial Quotations

Selected material from an interview appears in a partial quotation, along with the attribution—the name of the source of the quotation.

> *EXAMPLE:* People became "hysterical, running out of the lab screaming," according to Marisol Boulanger, an eyewitness to the chemical spill in the chemistry lab on Tuesday.

Use a partial quotation to capture the power of a direct quote even though the full sentence may be too long, ungrammatical, or confusing.

Both full and partial quotations are most useful when they are clear, provide insight into a character, or help vary the information in a paragraph.

Paraphrases

Putting a quotation in your own language can help clarify meaning and can be a good way to make information more concise, easier to understand, or more relevant.

> *EXAMPLE:* Students were instructed in how to handle accidents in the lab, according to Boulanger.

Paraphrase long or wordy quotations or quotations where the language is fuzzy or vague, grammatically incorrect, or confusing.

Attribution for Quotations

- Always give the source or attribution, citing the speaker's full name and title.

  > *EXAMPLE:* "Pollution is causing asthma rates to soar," said Greg Spiro, head of Pediatrics at Faith Hospital.

- Follow a full quotation with the simple verb *said*.

- If you quote the same speaker later, use just the last name in the attribution.

  > *EXAMPLE:* Asthma is a major public health issue, according to Spiro.

- As a rule, do not start quotations with the attribution, as this tends to slow the story down. Instead, state the quotation and then cite the speaker's name.

- If you are using a quotation you found in another source, you must give attribution to the other source, citing the publication where it first appeared and identifying the speaker.

  > *EXAMPLE:* School board member Raisa Perez told the *Sun-Times* last Tuesday that more students would be left out of the free lunch program if budget cuts continue.

- Use quotations from other printed sources sparingly and only if you absolutely must. If possible, replicate the quotation by calling the source directly or by substituting a similar source and quotation that you collected.

More information on how to punctuate quotations appears on page 432.

not general knowledge like the date of the Normandy invasion or the fact that McDonald's serves not just hamburgers but milk shakes as well.

You can also quote statements that have harder-to-prove information, opinions, and claims. Would you use this quotation from a McDonald's press release in a news story, even though it reflects a claim?

> Jim Cantalupo, Chairman and Chief Executive Officer, said, "I am very excited to be back at McDonald's and I am absolutely convinced that we will regain our momentum."

Quoting the opinions or claims of sources can be a good way to illustrate the many sides of an issue. You might use a claim or opinion this way.

> McDonald's Corporation reported a loss this quarter for the first time ever. Still, company statements reflect a positive attitude. Jim Cantalupo, Chief Executive Officer at McDonald's, said he is convinced that the company will regain momentum, according to a company press release.

Do not use a claim or opinion as fact: "McDonald's will regain momentum in the future." This is a prediction, an opinion of the leadership of the corporation, but not a fact. Instead of stating claims as facts, use quotation and at-

---

Practice 6.4   Using Quotations

Read the following lead (opening paragraph) of a news story.

> College Park—A tornado blazed a 10-mile-long path of destruction through Central Maryland at rush hour yesterday afternoon, killing two Howard County sisters and injuring dozens of people while ripping the roofs off buildings and flinging cars through the air.
>
> —Michael Dresser and Alec MacGillis, "Tornado Kills Two UM Sisters"

Imagine that you were writing the news story to follow this lead, using the following notes gathered from interviews. Which quotations would you use as full quotations? As partial quotations? As paraphrased quotations? Which would you not include in your story?

1. The entire family is devastated. (Dr. Clifford Turen, family friend of Colleen Patricia Marlatt and Erica Patricia Marlatt who were killed when their car was lifted and thrown by wind)

2. The victims were sisters. (Turen)

3. The two students were killed when the storm picked up their car, which was heading in a westward direction, at a location near the East Hall residential dormitory on the main campus of the University of Maryland at University Park. The storm then threw the car into a tree located in the parking area of the East Hall. (Mark Brady, a spokesman for Prince George's County Fire and EMS)

4. I ran out of the dorm to see if anybody needed help. It was 75 feet up. I saw the car flying in the air. I could see the bottom of it. It dropped. It just hit the ground. (Jason Gleeber, 19, a student from Elkton)

5. Classes will be suspended today at the University of Maryland. We're in no position to conduct business as usual. (President C. D. Mote, Jr., U. of Maryland)

6. About 100 employees and customers were in the store. The storm hit and took the roof right off. It started out like it was going to be a strong thunderstorm and then you heard the wind start howling like I've never heard it before. You could then start hearing and seeing the skylights start shattering, and then the front windows started blowing in. (Eric Ziolkowski, College Park Home Depot manager)

Brandi Chastain celebrates the U.S. team's 5–4 soccer victory over China in the Women's World Cup Final in Pasadena, California, in July 1999.

tribution to show your readers that these are the opinions of the company leadership.

"We know we need to make changes," Cantalupo said, pledging to reveal more comprehensive turnabout plans by the end of March. "I think you're going to see a lot of changes at McDonald's in the weeks and months ahead."

—Associated Press, "McDonald's Loss Stems from Its Overexpansion"

Most important, always cite your sources in a news story.

ANATOMY OF A NEWS STORY

The early days of telegraphing news stories during the Civil War meant that reporters, who were aware that the telegraph lines could be destroyed in battle, had to dispatch the most important information first. The form of announcing a summary of the news, followed by the details in order of importance, is now identified as news style.

Technological advances have now made it possible for editors to "stop the presses!" with late-breaking news and insert or change front-page stories at the last minute. To make such changes as quickly as possible, editors rewrite the beginnings of stories, chop off the ends or the less important details, and disrupt the rest as little as possible. To accomplish this, they organize stories on an inverted pyramid: beginning with a news lead, which is a summary of the story, followed by quotations and details in descending order of importance.

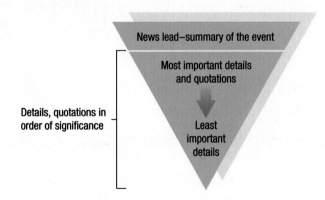

Search for New Mascot Halted at San Diego State U.

JESSICA ZISKO, *THE DAILY AZTEC*

Lead

A new mascot will not rally crowds during football season this fall, San Diego State University announced last week.   1

Citing disagreement over an "appropriate" mascot, University President Stephen Weber indefinitely suspended the group searching for a new Monty Montezuma, the former flame-throwing mascot some deemed culturally insensitive.   2

Who?
What?
When?
Where?

Why?
(angle)

A San Diego State University student proposed banning a new Aztec Warrior mascot for the school.

Body

Important details first

The group was unable to agree on which type of figure would best suit the campus. 3 Why? (angle)

"It's a question of what is appropriate, what makes most sense," said Steve Schnall, committee member and Athletics director of marketing and promotions. "There wasn't a clear-cut favorite." 4 Quotation

Weber rejected two ideas proposed by the committee. The <u>one that received the most support</u> was an Aztec Eagle Warrior, which would have been portrayed by a person wearing an eagle headdress. 5 New developments

The <u>other was a more playful figure</u>—an animal called "Zuma the Puma," said committee member Josh Miller, who represented Associated Students. The group thought the animal would appeal to families, he said. 6

San Diego <u>State has been without a mascot since May 2001, following</u> a <u>national debate over whether the bare-chested, flame-wielding Monty was demeaning to Native Americans.</u> 7 Facts

The controversy was ignited in fall 2000 by the Native American Student Alliance, which complained about the mascot and the use of Aztecs as the campus nickname. 8 Background context

Weber retained the name Aztecs but promoted Monty to an ambassador, a figure that met citywide criticism for his appearance when introduced in January. The ambassador visits local elementary schools to teach about the Aztec culture. 9

Body

Less important details

The nine-member volunteer committee of faculty, staff, alumni and students had been working since April to develop a new mascot. Last semester, they held a public forum to solicit ideas from the community and met several times to discuss designs. · 10 · **More background**

In total, the group considered about 50 different concepts, Schnall said. Campus officials hoped to debut the new figure at the start of the 2002 football season on Sept. 14. · 11 · **Details**

"The process has run its course and the contents that have come forward are not satisfying the goals we had established early on—that we would have a unifying, spirit-raising symbol of the university," university spokesman Jack Beresford said. · 12 · **Quotation**

Miller said he would have preferred Weber not suspend the group, but instead ask the members to brainstorm new ideas for a mascot. · 13 · **Counter-quotation**

He said he did not find out the committee had been abolished until he received inquiries from the media about his reaction. · 14 · **(balance)**

Critics get the last word

"I was shocked," he said. "We did all this work. We sat down with (Weber) and now he's just chickening out." · 15 · **Commentary from a source**

The Lead and the Inverted Pyramid

Most news stories are frontloaded, built with a summary first, followed by an explanation and a list of details in descending order of importance. This structure, commonly known as the inverted pyramid, is the traditional order of news stories.

The lead should be concise, but full of detail, like a telegram. It is a brisk summary of the most important elements of the story: who, what, when, where, and how. Imagine that you are paying by the word. In this historic telegram from December 17, 1903, relaying news of the first flights at Kitty Hawk, Orville Wright sends the news of the brothers' success home to their father. He includes the most important information: "four flights," "average speed" of "thirty one miles" per hour. He includes the time element: "thursday morning." He emphasizes the significance of the flights ("with engine power alone") and gives lots of significant detail, all of it in few words. Think of this economy when writing your lead.

A news lead is a little like poetry in that every word counts; each word must be precise and packed with meaning. Choose the best subject and the best verb you can, and remember that the lead not only summarizes the event, but must also capture readers' attention and get them to read on. The lead in the "Search for New Mascot" story includes who and where (San

A telegram from Orville Wright to his father, 1903.

Diego State University), what (new mascot won't be unveiled), and when (announced last week). The story also comes with a past conflict and thus a controversy that is left unresolved, all the more appealing to readers.

Most leads focus on what happened: the highway was closed due to an accident; a total smoking ban in local bars starts today; a new mascot will not rally crowds. Sometimes the more important details lead you to focus on the who, where, or when of the story.

▶ Mae Jemison, the first woman in space, spoke about the future of satellite technology in a lecture last night at the student union. *(The emphasis is on communicating who.)*

▶ Howard University will be the recipient of a National Merit Fellowship for its work with gifted high school students. *(The emphasis in on communicating who.)*

▶ Two years after pleading guilty to manslaughter, a Westbridge man took his own life. *(The emphasis is on communicating when.)*

▶ San Francisco will be the site of the new Japanese Internment Camp Museum, the Human Rights Watch announced today. *(The emphasis is on communicating where.)*

You might also find yourself covering "soft news" rather than "hard news." Make sure the tone of your writing suits the subject matter. A fundraiser for the local animal shelter that involves a pet beauty contest, for example, should be reported in a playful way, perhaps even delaying the news for a sentence or two:

> Maribel, a three-year-old Australian Terrier, took the crown in a hotly contested "Most Beautiful Pet" pageant this year, but she jumped into Lansley Lake before she had a chance to collect her sash.
>
> Eighty dogs and cats and a parrot competed in the Third Annual Westerly Animal Shelter Paws and Claws Day yesterday to help raise $4,200 to pay for new cages, according to organizers.

Use the delay—a sentence or two of attention-attraction—when it seems appropriate, and make sure to get to the who, what, where, when lead paragraph as soon as possible.

Angle

The angle of a news story tells the *why* or *how* of the event. When deciding on an angle, the writer goes beyond the facts to reveal the event's significance. You can often find the angle by locating the story's central tension or conflict. The reasons for the search for a new mascot at San Diego State University, for example, are key in the story. Your readers need to know background—that the old mascot was called "culturally insensitive." Without knowing this, they would not have the full story.

In writing about the closing of a McDonald's in your community, your job is to reveal how the loss of the restaurant will affect the town, why it is closing, and what the significance of the closing is. *How* and *why* questions sometimes require analysis and interpretation. Many times, events can be looked at more than one way. A store employee might tell you that the store is closing because of consistently bad health department ratings, while a company representative might tell you the reason is corporate cutbacks. In doing more research, you might realize that the McDonald's is not the only store scheduled for closing in the Western Avenue area. Then your angle might reflect the trend. The same story reported by different three writers might have three different angles, or three different ways to describe how the event fits into a bigger picture, a context. This sense of bigger picture is what explains the significance of the event. This context is revealed in the lead and explained through the rest of the story.

Consider these three possible leads, with different angles, for a story about the closing of a McDonald's.

> ▶ The McDonald's restaurant on Western Avenue will be closing, the company announced yesterday, after two years of bad ratings from the Board of Health.

Fifteen thousand people gathered in 1991 in front of KGB headquarters in Moscow to watch the toppling of the statue of Feliks Dzerzhinsky, head of Cheka, the first Soviet secret police force.

- The McDonald's on Western Avenue will be one of 517 McDonald's restaurants to close nationwide this year in an effort to boost earnings, according to a company press release.

- Another Western Avenue business will close next year, adding to the number of vacant and boarded up businesses just three blocks from the new Alden Mall. McDonald's Corporation announced the closing of its Western Avenue restaurant yesterday.

Though the news is based on the same event, the interpretation of the significance can result in three different stories: one about cleanliness in this restaurant and perhaps others, one about the bigger story of the McDonald's Corporation's financial troubles, and one about a pattern in an area of town. Each involves some tension or conflict.

Practice 6.6
Finding an Angle

Write down some possible angles for each of the following stories.

1. You go to a book signing at your local bookstore. The author, who is originally from your town, has written a book about his hunting expedition in Africa. Animal rights activists urging people to boycott the reading are picketing outside. Inside the store people are waiting in a long line to have the author sign copies of the book.

2. Your college administration has banned student parking on campus. Administrators say that students should ride bikes or take public transportation, such as the new campus shuttle service sponsored by a tobacco company. You go to a meeting at which students are protesting the ban. Outside a group of environmental activists is rallying in support of the administration.

3. A man is robbed at gunpoint at ten o'clock in the morning on a busy city street. No one goes to his aid. He is not hurt physically, but his wallet and all his jewelry have been taken. It is the fifth such robbery in two months.

The angle may be easy to determine for some stories. For others, you may have to think hard to find a context. In writing about a fundraiser, you might compare this year's results to last year's and ask why the amount raised went up or down. What was different about this year? You might ask about patterns in your news stories. Was there another accident like this one? Are these accidents common? What provoked the city council to vote a certain way? As you think about angle, go beyond the facts, and think about what the event means.

The Body of the Story

Though the lead is the most important part of the news story, the body of the story explains background and provides readers with a balanced picture. Using the inverted pyramid structure as a guide, you will arrange the information so that the details you consider most significant appear early or "higher up" in the story. Keep in mind that balance is achieved by providing quotations and counter-quotations, almost like a debate or dialogue.

The mascot story considered earlier is organized this way.

1. Begin with the news: the search for a new mascot is suspended.

2. Follow with the angle or context: reasons for the search or background that led up to the new developments.

3. Fill out the story with reactions or quotations that reflect different perspectives. Sources include the university president, a university spokesman, and search committee members who agree and disagree with the decision to suspend the committee.

Notice that the story includes information about the fifty contenders for new mascot, including "Zuma the Puma," and plenty of background information about the controversy and its history. The body of the mascot story offers a good overview with lots of specifics. Though the same news story might be written in different ways by different writers, some points about the body of the story will remain constant.

News stories are arranged so that the paragraphs flow logically but can also easily be shuffled and rearranged. Paragraph 8, for example, could follow paragraph 2, but the logic of the entire news story does not depend on it. The writer might have used the final quote, a negative comment, earlier in the story. This might have shifted the focus to the criticism of disbanding the committee. Jessica Zisko instead elected to focus on the point that no one could agree on an appropriate mascot.

Ending the News Story

The structure of the news story evolved because of the technology of disseminating news to the public as quickly as possible. For much the same reasons, news stories do not have "conclusions" that summarize or tie up all the loose ends. As news was updated, the tops of stories changed and the bottoms were chopped off, leaving the other stories on a page intact. Instead of changing the whole page, printers were able to change one paragraph of a late-developing story. Since stories were written in descending order of importance, what comes last should be the least important—and most expendable—detail. Traditionally news writers have spent little time thinking about the ends of news stories for this reason. Stories seem to fade out rather than conclude. But notice that the writer of the mascot story ends the story with a quotation that might influence the reader. Nowadays, many news stories end with a quotation, fact, or statistic that shapes the impression of the story. In the case of the mascot story, for example, the ending does have power; critics of the decision to suspend the mascot committee have the last word, the parting impression left on the reader.

Practice 6.7   Deciding on the Heart of the Story

Write a news story based on the quotations that follow. First, decide what is at the heart of the story. Then write a lead that has an angle. Write three to five paragraphs of a body for this story, incorporating paraphrases, partial quotations, and full quotations. You don't need to include all the information, but choose elements that provide a summary of the news and a balanced view.

> Pine Tree Brook bridge was a gathering place for students on their way home from school. These students often hung around smoking and drinking. Since the bridge was removed, we don't have the same amount of garbage and vandalism in our neighborhood.
>
> —Larry Tompson, resident of Harland Court, one of the streets that leads to the bridge

> Figures on crime rates since the bridge was removed are inconclusive.
>
> —Henry Morrison, Chief of Police, Jamestown

> I have decided to replace the Pine Tree Brook bridge since it provides access to Jamestown High School and recreational fields. We need more routes for foot travel to and from school and less driving and parking congestion on the school grounds.

> The bridge will be replaced by the opening of school in September.
>
> —Mayor Hailey Goode, written statement released yesterday

> My two children have suffered back problems due to the long walk with their 20 to 30 lb. backpacks to the main entrance. My daughter also carries her cello and my son his hockey equipment. The bridge over Pine Tree Brook will provide them with a shorter walk to school. I'm grateful that it is being replaced.
>
> —Lisa Stromberry, German Road resident

> Too many students from other towns are enrolled in our public schools. Our tax dollars should support education for our children, not children from other towns. That's why the parking lot is so full of cars. That's why they drive to school. They aren't from here.
>
> —Berte Langer, Tax Collector for Jamestown.

> The Pine Tree Brook bridge was removed in 2001 during a construction project, and then never replaced. I'm not sure why it wasn't replaced.
>
> —Gerry Wasserman, Department of Public Works, Jamestown.

Cox's Chilling Tales of Stamina Recounted

JEFFREY CARSON

World renowned swimmer Lynne Cox discussed her recently released memoir *Swimming to Antarctica: Tales of a Long Distance Swimmer* last night at Brookline Booksmith. Roughly 60 people, from adolescents to elderly, packed the Coolidge Corner bookstore's Writers and Readers Room to listen to the swimmer's anecdotes, challenges, and emotional responses to the accomplishments of her illustrious career.

"Whenever she's in the water, she seems to break a record and push the limits of endurance," says Richard Gregg, Brookline Booksmith's events director. The talk is one of a series of book readings by authors organized by the bookstore each week. The hour-long discussion and question and answer session was followed by a signing of *Swimming to Antarctica*, which was released on January 13 by the publisher Knopf.

Cox held the crowd's attention by telling the tales of her early days as a swimmer, including her world record time crossing the English Channel in 1972 at the age of 15, to her most recent project, navigating the 32-degree waters off Antarctica during the summer of 2002. "All my swims were about human endurance and reaching out," says Cox, whose most important achievement was swimming across the Bering Sea and International Dateline from Alaska in 1987, thus breaking down the political barriers between the Soviet Union and the United States near the end of the Cold War. Not long after that swim President Ronald Reagan signed a treaty with Russian President Mikhail Gorbachov to open the borders between the U.S. and Soviet Union.

The International Swimming Hall of Famer and former *LA Times* Woman of the Year was quick to compliment all her coaches, friends, and acquaintances for helping her endure times of great difficulty while she swam. While she was crossing Cook Strait in 1975 off the coast of New Zealand, she was reminded of a sheep farmer she met who expressed his confidence in her abilities before the challenging swim. She even felt inspired by the dolphins that swam along with her off New Zealand. Cox described distance swimming as being "in between two different worlds. You're buoyant on top and there's this whole other world in the water below."

Looking back on her career, the 46-year-old said, "What do you do when you reach your highest goal in life at 15? I started out doing firsts; now it's about opening borders." The success in her early life led her to bigger and better ac-

Lynne Cox, swimmer.

complishments later on; she is the first person to swim through the Strait of Magellan, the Bering Sea, the Cape of Good Hope, and Cook Strait.

"All of us need to have dreams, big and small," she says, a belief that has been the mantra of her career. After breaking the world record for the English Channel a second time in 1973, she felt the need to expand her horizons to more daring tasks. "I can't just go to a gym [to work out]. I feel I need a focal point," she said.

The former New Hampshire native kept the crowd entertained with her light-hearted humor throughout the talk. She opened by thanking the audience "for braving the cold."

Cox did not say specifically what her next swim would be other than the fact that the possible locations she is considering for swims are very risky. Outside of swimming she is in the process of writing a children's book about the ocean.

Annotate "Cox's Chilling Tales of Stamina Recounted"

1. Draw a line under the lead.
2. Write *who, what, where,* and *when* next to information in the story that answers those questions.
3. Write *angle* next to the information that explains context.
4. Write *para* next to paraphrased quotations.
5. Circle the sources.

READINGS

The following news accounts reflect the "snapshot" quality of daily news that is compiled immediately following events. In some cases, the timeliness of the story shows its flaws: We don't have the full picture yet. News reports lock themselves into a moment. That quality of instant information, particularly when the story is brand new, is what attracts people to news and is also what makes it highly perishable. Regardless of whether today's news is tomorrow's litter box liner, news stories are indisputably the first records of historical moments.

U.S. under Attack

Charles M. Madigan, *Chicago Tribune*

People can tell you exactly where they were when they heard the news that the World Trade Center had been attacked on the morning of September 11, 2001. This event is indelibly stamped into millions of peoples' minds. Newspapers issued special editions that came out that same evening, and they sold out quickly. The voracious appetite for news about the event seemed unsatisfied in the first few days. You have probably read many accounts of that day from a fuller perspective. As you read one of the first accounts of the attacks, notice the limitations of the initial reporting.

Terrorists in at least three hijacked airliners staged a coordinated attack on the nation's financial, military and government centers Tuesday morning, devastating the World Trade Center in New York and the Pentagon in Washington and setting off a national panic as bewildered citizens raced for safety from a determined, but as yet unknown, enemy. Although there were no early estimates, authorities feared a heavy loss of life in the attacks. One New York police official said thousands of people may have been killed or injured in the attacks.

Both towers of the huge World Trade Center, which houses some 50,000 workers, were destroyed after they were hit by two airliners that had been hijacked earlier in the day. Smoke billowed from the burning buildings, which collapsed at midmorning. The Federal Aviation Administration ordered all commercial airliners grounded. Financial and government centers were shut down and evacuations were underway all across the country.

The FAA said at least five planes operated by American Airlines and United Airlines were reported to have crashed or were "in trouble." The

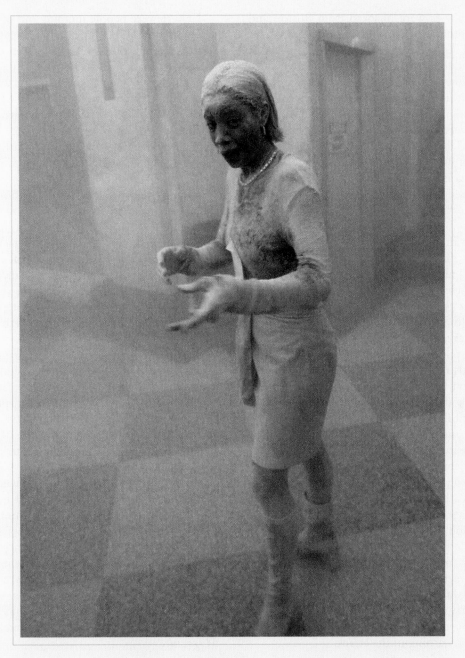

A woman, covered with ash from the World Trade Center on September 11, 2001.

American planes were hijacked from Boston and Dulles International Airport in suburban Washington and flown into the Trade Center towers. It was believed the attack on the Pentagon involved a United airliner. American Airlines reported it had lost two airliners, which had been carrying 156 people.

There were also reports that another airliner, a United 757 bound from Newark to San Francisco, flight 93, which was scheduled for a stop in Chicago, crashed outside of Pittsburgh. The plane crashed in Somerset County, just north of a small airport. It was not immediately known whether the plane was trying to land or what role it played in the terrorist attacks.

5   United officials said they were also "deeply concerned" about one of its flights from Boston to Los Angeles. Later in the morning, United reported that that plane also had crashed. United confirmed that it had lost UA 93, a Boeing 757, from Newark to San Francisco with 38 passengers, two pilots and five flight attendants on board. It also said it lost UA 175, a 767, bound from Boston to Los Angeles with 56 passengers, two pilots and seven flight attendants.

President Bush, on a trip to Florida to push his education initiative, boarded Air Force One in heavy security and headed back to Washington. The president ordered "a full-scale investigation to hunt down the folks who committed this act."

"Today," the president said, "We have had a national tragedy."

"May God bless the victims, their families and America."

In New York, Mayor Rudolph Giuliani ordered an evacuation of the lower part of Manhattan in the wake of the attack. The mayor asked people to try to remain calm and said there had been an enormous loss of life. He said there was no threat or warning of the attack.

"There were people jumping out of the World   10 Trade Center. It was a horrible, horrible situation," Giuliani told local broadcasters.

The attack began at about 8:45 a.m. EDT, well after the beginning of the work day, when an airliner slammed into the north tower of the World Trade Center. About 18 minutes later, a second plane crashed into the south tower. Within an hour of the second collision, the south tower collapsed in billowing clouds of dust. The north tower soon followed.

Even as the nation watched in horror as the twin towers erupted in flame and were engulfed in smoke, a third plane circled and then smashed into the Pentagon in Washington, sending a black cloud of smoke into the sky and setting off evacuations and panic across Washington. Many Pentagon workers were said to be trapped in the smoking wreckage and fire that followed the attack.

Virtually all federal agencies were evacuated by midmorning. Agents armed with machine guns patrolled the White House grounds. The attack crippled commercial, financial and governmental agencies around the nation. In Chicago and in other major cities, police were put on a high state of alert and disaster and fire services were shifted to a high state of readiness.

Military jets were scrambled to guard the skies against any further attacks. Commercial airliners that were already in flight were diverted to Canada, as were inbound flights from Europe. There was no way to estimate the number of casualties caused by the wave of terrorist assaults.

"This is perhaps the most audacious terrorist   15 attack that's ever taken place in the world. It takes a logistics operation from the terror group involved second to none. Only a very small handful of terror groups is on that list," said Chris Yates, an aviation expert at *Jane's Transport Magazine*.

While the source of the attack was unclear, it came three weeks after Saudi dissident Osama bin Laden warned that he and his followers would carry out an unprecedented attack on the United States for its support of Israel, according to an Arab journalist.

Abdel-Bari Atwan, editor of the London-based al Quds al-Arabi newspaper, said Islamic fundamentalists led by Bin Laden were "almost certainly" behind the attacks. American officials had no immediate comment about responsibility for the horrific assault, other than to note that it came without warning.

The New York attack came eight years after terrorists bombed the towers, killing six people and injuring more than 1,000.

"Everyone was screaming, crying, running, cops, people, firefighters, everyone," said Mike Smith, a New York City fire marshal. "It's like a war zone."

20   Hours after the attack, the World Trade Center buildings in New York and the Pentagon in Washington were still aflame. Coverage of the attacks and the ensuing panic were telecast around the world. As the morning passed, the nation slowly shut down.

Dazed workers, many coated with thick dust from the collapsing buildings, wandered in the streets of Manhattan as emergency workers, firemen and police searched for those who were injured.

There was an immediate response from world capitals.

In Moscow, Russian President Vladimir Putin expressed deep sympathy over the "terrorist act. This terrible tragedy." British Prime Minister Tony Blair branded the attack "the new evil in our world. . . . It is perpetrated by fanatics who are utterly indifferent to the sanctity of human life, and we, the democracies of this world, are going to have to come together and fight it together."

"I send my condolences to the president, the government and the people for this terrible incident. We are completely shocked. It is unbelievable," said Palestinian leader Yasser Arafat.

Critical Reading Questions

1. Why does the story use vague phrases like "terrorists in *at least* three hijacked airliners" and United officials were "deeply concerned about one of its flights from Boston to Los Angeles"? Do you usually see this kind of uncertain reporting in newspapers?

2. What background details help shape a reader's understanding of the story?

3. Look closely at paragraph 14, which begins, "The attacks began. . . ." Does this paragraph capture the drama of the attacks? Why?

4. As a reader who knows more of the details about the attacks, read the lead and comment on it: Does it fully summarize the event?

Questions for Writing and Discussion

1. You might remember seeing the video of the second plane hitting the World Trade Center. How does having film and still photos of an event affect public opinion? Give an example of other photos that represent important events.

2. What role does the daily newspaper play in delivering news to you? Do you read the newspaper to get information about important national or international events?

Scary Formula: Old Buildings, Timeworn Prank
Colleges adding sprinklers and boosting punishment for false alarms

Matthew Reilly, Newark *Star-Ledger*

This story was part of an award-winning package of reports put together on deadline following a fire in a dormitory. It supports the main news story about a deadly dormitory fire at Seton Hall University. Stories like this one help explain the context of an issue or news event. In this case, the writer is evaluating whether the reasons the Seton Hall fire turned deadly are present at other schools in the New Jersey area. This kind of story, a companion to a news story, is also called a "reaction story" because the reporter collects comments about the subject. You might write a reaction story in response to news in your community.

Hoping to avoid the nightmarish loss of students to fire, college administrators across New Jersey say they have taken pains to ensure fire safety on their campuses, from retrofitting older buildings with modern equipment to harshly penalizing the students who pull false alarms.

Even so, many of the state's older dormitories, like the Seton Hall University building where three students died in a smoky blaze yesterday, are not equipped with sprinkler systems. Nor are they required to be. Because fire codes have evolved over time, older buildings must add sprinklers only when they undergo large-scale renovations.

Adding to the danger is a common difficulty on college campuses: Because there are so many false alarms, some students ignore the warnings, riding them out in their rooms. At Rowan University in Glassboro, George Brelsford, assistant vice president for residential life and student services, said six of the school's 11 residence buildings have sprinkler systems, including a pair of buildings more than 70 years old.

"Whenever there's a renovation, the building has to be brought up to the most recent issue of the code," Brelsford said. "I have two buildings, from 1927 and 1929, and we did a re-work of them two years ago and sprinklers were added."

5   The last dorm fire on the Rowan campus, where about 2,400 of the school's 10,000 students live, was six or seven years ago, he said, and was confined to one room by the sprinkler system that extinguished the flames.

Some older buildings, dating from the 1950s, do not have sprinklers, Brelsford said, because they have not been renovated and are still under the fire code in effect at the time of their construction. However, the university has gone beyond those earlier code requirements to upgrade fire safety systems in those buildings, he said.

"What we have done is hard-wire all rooms with smoke detectors and put heat and smoke detectors in hallways and common areas," he said. "These buildings are above and beyond what the original code was." He said flame-retardant materials are used whenever possible.

The school runs formal fire drills at least twice a year but also treats any alarm, from a malicious false alarm to a simple smoke condition, seriously. Students who ignore fire alarms are subject to punishment.

The College of New Jersey in Mercer County has added sprinkler systems to all but two of its 14 residence buildings. Three dormitories built in 1931 were retrofitted for sprinklers when they were renovated in 1992, spokeswoman Sue Murphy said.

Chief Joseph Zuccarello of the Rutgers Uni-   10

versity Fire Department said his firefighters chased down 107 malicious false alarms last year.

"Every college and university has a hassle with false alarms," Zuccarello said. "It's amazing. The students go away for winter break and we don't have any false alarms, and the minute they come back in the dorm, the alarms start transmitting for one reason or another."

At least once a year, the chief said, university officials inspect every dorm room for items such as candles, halogen lamps, cooking appliances, extension cords longer than 6 feet, overloaded outlets, and posters fixed to the ceiling. All of those items are prohibited in residence halls.

All dorm furniture, from mattresses to desks, is fire-retardant, Zuccarello said.

Michael Massaro, a 19-year-old sophomore at Rutgers, said he inadvertently has tested the university's fire safety measures on occasion. In October, a smoke alarm alerted him to the melting, smoking remote control he had left on a lamp in his room.

15   Last year at Tinsley Hall, where he lived, the residents were fined a total of $2,000 to cover the installation of new fire alarms after some 15 false alarms there, he said.

Jamaal Lowery and Jed Herb say it can get awfully cold in their dorm room at Kean University in Union Township, and they had resorted to using an open oven to keep their suite toasty.

But since a fire erupted in their 28-year-old dorm Monday night, they have made sure the oven stays shut.

Lowery was getting ready for bed at 12:30 a.m.

Monday in his room at Sozio Hall when the fire alarm went off. He looked out into the hall and saw smoke pouring out of the trash chute. Lowery ran outside, but noticed that some of his fellow students did not follow.

"They hear the alarm all the time and just figured it wasn't a real fire," said Lowery, 21, a sophomore from Pleasantville.

20   Kean officials believe someone threw a cigarette down the trash chute. The blaze caused minimal damage, said Robert Cole, a university spokesman.

Herb, 19, a sophomore from Lacey Township, said he had been across the quad, at Rogers dorm, when he saw fire trucks roll in.

"I thought it was a false alarm, but no one picked up when I called our room," he said. "People don't pay attention to that kind of stuff."

The roommates estimated 10 fire alarms have been pulled at Sozio Hall since the beginning of the school year.

At Ramapo College in Mahwah, many students said it's not uncommon for residents to stay inside during alarms.

25   Tiffany Patterson, a 21-year-old senior who now lives in campus apartments, said she got tired of fire alarms going off twice a week when she lived in their dorms. Rather than trudge outside, she hid in the shower.

"I usually stayed in my room most of the time because I assumed they were false," she said. "Nobody wants to go outside at 3 or 4 in the morning."

Critical Reading Questions

1. Is this story organized in inverted pyramid style?

2. How important is the context or background in making this information newsworthy to readers?

3. Evaluate the sources in this story. Are they good sources? Is their public image at stake? Can you think of other sources the writer might have consulted?

4. Is this story useful to a reader? Does it offer information that furthers a reader's understanding of a larger issue?

Questions for Writing and Discussion

1. Does writing about tragic situations serve the public good?

2. What sort of stories currently in the news might serve as springboards for reaction stories?

Student News Report:

Twenty-five Percent of Students Plagiarize

Grace Lin, *The Daily Free Press*

Grace Lin was a reporter for her university newspaper when she was assigned to get local reaction to a survey claiming that 25 percent of college and university students report plagiarizing. Her job was to take the news of the survey and show its significance on her campus, Boston University. This is the same sort of story you might write for the assignment in this chapter if you choose to write about the release of a study or investigation.

Twenty-five percent of students report plagiarizing online sometimes to very frequently, according to a recent survey, but the problem has stayed steady over the past few years at Boston University (BU), Provost Dennis Berkey said this week.

The study, done by two professors at the Rochester Institute of Technology (RIT), shows that 25 percent of students surveyed at nine colleges reported plagiarizing online sometimes to very frequently.

Professor Patrick Scanlon, a professor in the Department of Communication at RIT, said coverage of Boston University's lawsuit against online term paper mills in 1997 incited his interest to conduct the study, published last year in the Journal of College Student Development.

BU has a history of taking legal action against companies that promote plagiarism, including influencing a law that prohibits the sale of term papers in Massachusetts through a lawsuit more than 25 years ago.

5 Yet despite the high percentage of college students who plagiarize and the boom in Internet use, problems with plagiarism have not increased. Both the RIT study and BU faculty said the problem has remained the same for the most part.

However, plagiarism is still a major problem. Eighty percent of the 100 annual cases of academic misconduct involve plagiarism, Berkey said. "What is increasing is the fraction of those cases involving either direct copying and pasting of online text or prohibited collaboration among classmates," Berkey said.

College of Communication (COM) professor Kathryn Burak said the Internet has only exacerbated a problem that already existed.

"I have taught at BU since 1990, and I think the Internet has made plagiarism a problem everywhere," Burak said. "But plagiarism was around before the Internet, too."

She added that most students plagiarize out of desperation and can easily avoid it simply by talking to their professors.

10 The College of Arts and Sciences (CAS) Academic Conduct Code defines plagiarism as "any attempt by a student to represent the work of another as his or her own," including copying other students during a test and restating the work of someone else.

It goes further to include "collaboration with someone else in an academic endeavor without acknowledging his or her contribution."

COM's statement about plagiarism describes it as the most serious academic offense a student can commit and can result in probation, suspension or expulsion.

Although past cases show colleges rescinding degrees years after they were granted and a board revoking the license of a Massachusetts physician eight years after receiving his M.D. degree, students said such severe consequences do not always deter others from plagiarizing.

College of Engineering (ENG) senior Bethany King said she encountered plagiarism among her classmates in a logic design class. At the last minute,

10 students turned in the same circuit using a shared folder on the network in the computer lab due to the overload of work that week.

15 "Plagiarism is a problem in ENG," King said. "People get away with it all the time but I think it eventually catches up with them on tests because they don't know what they're doing."

She said the extensive amount of collaborative work ENG students do is "acceptable to some extent," supported by ENG's conduct code that has nearly the same in wording as CAS's definition on plagiarism with the addition that collaboration is permissible if it is "specifically permitted."

"A lot of times we'll share problems on an assignment instead of doing them all because it's so time consuming and pointless," King said. "However, I think that a lot of people have crossed the line when they do collaborative work."

The concern with plagiarism has called upon universities such as BU, Duke University and most University of California schools to use a new service known as turnitin.com, whose "products and services help educators and students maximize the Internet's educational potential by making it a safe place for research and learning," according to the site. The site checks assignments submitted by students with content on the Internet as well as previously submitted work by other students to turnitin.com.

Berkey said many teachers at BU are using turnitin.com, in addition to providing clear statements on the definition and consequences of plagiarism in course syllabi. However, BU students said turnitin.com is a pointless and added burden.

20 "I use turnitin.com for BI 108, and we were told it is used to prevent lab groups from collaborating," said CAS freshman Kelly Miller. "The site is effective for research papers and critical essays, but for lab reports, I don't think it's a good idea."

"We're all performing the same experiment and getting similar data, and when you have 603 students in a biology course writing about photosynthesis, I'm sure some ideas and exact wording will appear in more than one report," she said.

However, Beena Thomas, a freshman in the Sargent College of Health and Rehabilitation Sciences, said she feels turnitin.com is pointless for writing classes as well.

"It was just one more unnecessary thing to worry about because sometimes it would not work and we would have to worry about not handing it in on time, and there would be controversy because if we didn't use the site, it would affect our grade," Thomas said. "Professors know when students plagiarize; they don't need a website or computer to tell them."

Scanlon said he feels there is too much emphasis on tracking plagiarism. "This problem has been with us for quite a while, and its roots are really not technological, at all, although clearly the Internet has exacerbated the problem," he said. "Still, I'd like to see educators focus on being educators, not amateur detectives."

Critical Thinking Questions

1. The issue of plagiarism has been talked about on college campuses for a long time. How does Lin update the subject? How does she make the news seem recent?

2. Who are Lin's sources? How many points of view do her sources represent?

3. Is Lin's definition of plagiarism important to her report? Why?

4. What does the twenty-five-year-old history of her school and term paper sales add to the story?

5. Lin reports that the plagiarism at Boston University has "stayed steady." Does this tell you how much plagiarism is reported there? What does this statement tell you?

Questions for Writing and Discussion

1. How seriously do you take surveys that report people's claims of misconduct? Do you think people are honest in such surveys?

2. If not a survey, how would you, as a researcher, get a measurement of a trend like plagiarism?

3. Do the findings of the survey surprise you? Did you expect the number of students admitting to plagiarism to be higher or lower? Why?

WRITING IN THE WORKS
Interview with Grace Lin

The story Grace Lin wrote for her college newspaper was actually her second report on plagiarism. The first story announced the findings of the study, while this second story shows the reaction to the news at her school—the local angle on a national story. In the following interview, Lin talks about writing for her school paper in general and writing the plagiarism articles in particular.

1. What made you decide to write for the college paper?

I wanted to get experience in news writing. I had done some in high school, but I wasn't very committed to the school newspaper, and I only did some special assignments for them. I was really intimidated when I first went to the *Daily Free Press* informational meeting because there were so many people there, but I knew that I had to start somewhere if I wanted to start getting experience in writing.

2. What has surprised you about your news writing experience?

How much fun it is and how much passion I have for it. After my first article made the front page and I started doing other articles, I knew that this is what I am good at. It is really satisfying knowing that you have put all that you know about a certain topic into writing and then seeing it in print and knowing that others are reading it too. Of course, there are days when sources aren't good and you just can't write a good article that you are happy with, but there are other days when you produce something you are really proud of. I was also surprised at how easy interviewing people can be. I have never been someone who talks easily with people; I stutter and forget things I wanted to say. At first I was so intent on getting every word people would say that I wouldn't have a flowing conversation and wasn't very confident about how the interview went after I finished talking to people. Then I realized how much easier the interviewing is if you just listen and ask any questions that come to mind. After I started doing that, interviewing became fun and so much easier to do.

3. How difficult was the plagiarism article? What was your process for researching the assignment?

The funny thing about my first plagiarism article was that I know it was meant to be some extra article that would be tucked somewhere in the newspaper where no one would really pay attention. I mean, who really cares if a study is done on students and plagiarism? The night the *Daily Free*

Press called me about it, they asked if I was sure I wanted it because everyone had been turning it down. So I did some research on the Internet and found out really interesting facts like about BU's history of lawsuits against paper mills, and how the study I was doing actually stemmed from those lawsuits. I know I definitely impressed my editor because he had never heard about that either, and I ended up turning in an in-depth article that went beyond what they expected out of a topic like this.

The hardest part about doing the plagiarism article was my follow up article [included in this chapter], which was supposed to be more focused on how BU is affected by plagiarism, and the first article was more about the study done at RIT and what some students at BU thought about it—a basic reaction story. My editor wanted me to make the story local to BU and get stories and the "nitty gritty" about what is really done when it comes to cases that are reported and missed. That follow up article was really challenging because this issue is highly sensitive and you know administration is definitely not going to make themselves look bad and tell you what really goes on if it is a much greater problem than they are allowed to say. I did get confirmation that there are probably a lot of missed cases, but that's the most I could get from deans.

The other really hard part was getting specific stories of people who knew about plagiarism at BU. Again there are confidentiality issues and most students are uncomfortable talking about such issues because it could have some bad effects on themselves and the people they mention. I can remember how much I dreaded doing that follow up article because I was on time constraints, and it was right around spring break, so people were inaccessible. It was also an open-ended topic, meaning that there wasn't a specific story or lead I could easily write about—I had to come up with that myself, so it took me a while to figure out what exactly I was supposed

to research on. But in the end both articles made front page, and I know that both articles were a huge step for me in learning about what news writing and reporting is all about.

4. Do you read newspapers?

I get the *New York Times* daily e-mail on their top stories, so I scan through the stories every day, but typically only read the stories I'm interested in. What I do read are magazines—I've always read them from cover to cover, even the articles that don't have relevance to me. My friends have always made fun of me because they usually look through magazines for pictures but don't really read the content as much as I do. At home I read the Spotlight section of the *Rocky Mountain News* very often because I am very familiar with the columnists and have read the section for years, but I would have to admit that I don't read the news sections often unless there is a story on the front page that pops out at me.

In January 2003 I went to a panel where the editor of a local magazine was speaking and one of the things she said that I will always remember is that if you want to write for a newspaper, read newspapers, and the same with magazines. She said that too often she will ask candidates wanting to do an internship at her magazine what they read, and a lot of them don't have any answer. So I make it an effort to read as many newspapers and magazines as I can because you can learn so much by getting used to the style of writing and how a writer will approach a subject.

5. What kind of editing do your articles get? Do you ever disagree with your editors on their changes? Did you have any interaction with editors when you were writing the plagiarism article?

The editors at the *Free Press* are very good at what they do. The editing they make is mostly making sentences more concise to cut out unnecessary words because they have limited space, and changing wording so that something is clearer. It's interesting to see what they decide isn't necessary because that's always the hardest part for me. Sometimes quotes get cut out entirely, so I feel slightly bad because the time and effort sources used to help me goes to waste. The only bad experience I had once was with an editor who was in for my usual editor, and the final article came out with incorrect information. I was really mad because she changed some major facts and misquoted someone else. She had no idea what the topic was about and had assumed that her edits still kept the information the same, but they definitely hadn't.

I was supposed to see how my editor would edit my first plagiarism article, but I came in right when they were about to start a meeting. So my editor just sent me his comments after he edited it. He told me that he made very few edits and commended me on my writing and reporting. That same night I got an offer to do a very prestigious assignment, so he must have really liked my article, and later on he also proposed the follow up article.

WRITING AND REVISING STRATEGIES 🖥

Gathered here are three interactive sections for you to use as you write and revise your news story.

▶ Writer's Notebook Suggestions
▶ Peer-Editing Log
▶ Revision Checklist

Writer's Notebook Suggestions

You can use these exercises to do some start-up thinking and writing for your news story.

1. Read today's newspaper. Make a list of newsworthy topics that are covered in the hard-news stories, not the features or commentaries.

2. Brainstorm a list of topics you could cover, either as follow-up stories or as related topics.

3. Choose two stories in today's newspaper. Read them carefully, and figure out their angles. See how many other angles you could approach the stories from. Generate at least three other angles for each story. Write a lead sentence for each of the new angles you created.

4. If your city or town has two competing newspapers, read the same story in both papers or read the same story in your local paper and one of the national papers like the *New York Times*, *Washington Post*, *San Francisco Chronicle*, or *Chicago Tribune*, all of which you can find online. Compare the coverage of the stories, looking at the headlines, the leads, the angles, and the writing. Analyze any difference that you find, and note instances of bias or lack of objectivity, if any.

5. Using the topic of today's lead story in the newspaper, interview two friends and find out their opinions on the topic. Write a three- to four-paragraph news story on local reaction to this event, integrating at least two quotations from your friends.

6. Write a short news story about a trend you observe, and explore the implications, effects, and/or causes by talking to people directly affected. (A weather pattern, poor turnout at elections, and parking problems are some examples.)

   • Report the trend in the lead.

   • Get reactions and quotations from people.

   • Investigate whether the trend shows up in other places.

7. Write a lead paragraph for the following story. Set it in the present time, and write it for tomorrow's paper.

In Verona, Italy, the teenage children of two feuding families fall in love. Juliet Capulet and Romeo Montague, with the help of the local friar, Friar Lawrence, escape from their homes and plan to meet at a remote family tomb and then marry secretly. Juliet arrives first. She takes a powerful sleeping potion as she waits for her lover. When Romeo shows up, he mistakenly believes that Juliet has committed suicide, takes out his knife, and kills himself. When Juliet wakes up, she sees her dead lover and, tragically, kills herself with the same knife.

8. Think of a fairy tale you remember well, or reread some of your old favorites. Choose one—such as *Cinderella, Hansel and Gretel, Little Red Riding Hood,* or *Snow White*—and rewrite it as a news story, with today's date.

9. Write a letter home or to a faraway friend about your life this week, using news story form and structure. Make sure that your lead summarizes the news, that you have a clear angle, and that you organize your information in order of importance. Don't make anything up.

10. Write an "anniversary" story. Follow up on a story that was happening a year ago. Report any new developments or ongoing issues.

Peer-Editing Log

As you work with a writing partner or in a peer-editing group, you can use these questions to give useful responses to a classmate's news story and as a guide for discussion.

Writer's Name _____

Date _____

1. Underline the lead. Put check marks by the who, what, where, when, and (if included) how. What is missing, if anything? What is the angle?

2. Is the topic of the story newsworthy? Is it interesting to readers? Why would readers find the topic useful?

3. Is the story objective and free of the writer's personal viewpoint? Does the writer seem to be advertising, promoting, or lecturing in the news

story? Label any spots that seem biased or promotional with *OBJ?* (for *objectivity*).

4. Number the sources (1, 2, 3). Do the sources reflect different perspectives on the topic? Could the writer use an opposing or different view?

5. Are quotations attributed to sources? Note any problems with quotations by writing question marks in the margin. Look for quotations that are too long or too confusing. If you can suggest that the writer paraphrase or use a partial quotation, make a note in the margin.

6. Does the story sound like something you might hear on the evening news? Is the style formal? Circle any words or phrases that jump out as inconsistent with the voice of news reporting.

7. Does the body of the story reveal enough about the background of the story? Do you have questions about why or how the event happened?

8. Are paragraphs arranged to show order of importance? Draw arrows if you think some paragraphs might be rearranged.

Revision Checklist

As you do your final revision, check to make sure that you

❏ Chose a newsworthy, timely topic

❏ Wrote a concise lead including who, what, where, when, and perhaps how or why

❏ Included a clear angle

❏ Provided background information to give a full picture and organized according to importance of information

❏ Used correctly attributed quotations from several sources

❏ Organized the story by order of importance

❏ Balanced your reporting to show several sides of an issue and remain objective

❏ Consulted good sources

7. EDITORIALS

WRITING ARGUMENTS

An effective editorial has two ingredients . . .
a position and a passion.

—Richard Aregood

ASSIGNMENT

Choose a local issue on your college campus or in your community, or choose a global issue that is in the news and that interests you. Read as much background information as you can on the topic: news articles, editorials, columns, letters to the editor, websites, and journal articles. Decide what your position is on this issue, and write a persuasive letter to the editor, a column, or a guest editorial for a specific newspaper or online news site.

This image of graffiti on a wall in New York City makes a public statement about eliminating AIDS.

EDITORIALS

I n fall 2003 the Recording Industry Association of America (RIAA) brought lawsuits against 261 people, including a twelve-year-old, for what some people called sharing music on the Internet and others called piracy. All over the country people reacted strongly to the lawsuits, some by writing letters to the editors of newspapers. One professional musician wrote to the *San Francisco Chronicle*.

> By escalating their prices, thus wringing every possible profit from their loyal customers, and also by ignoring talented, creative performers while foisting shallow, manufactured stars on the listening public, the record companies have made their own bed. Now they should be made to lie in it.
>
> —Earl Oliver, Letter to the Editor

Newspapers ran editorials on the issue of file sharing, and some editorial writers, like this one from the *Dayton Daily News* in Ohio, put the issue in a different light.

> Perhaps the intimidating lawsuits will get more parents involved in an important discussion about the ethics and risks of file-sharing. In truth, it's safer and more honorable to buy music in a record store than to get it for free online. The sooner parents understand and communicate that, the better off both they and their children will be.
>
> —*Dayton Daily News*, "File-Sharers Must Get Used to Heat"

Web loggers (more commonly known as "bloggers") also entered the debate.

> I just wonder what all the resources that the RIAA is throwing at this from a legal perspective could do if they were funneled to discovery of new talent or new distribution channels. They don't seem to understand that trading of the files "is a GOOD thing." Exposure is half the battle, especially for the majority of little bands out there. Sure, the big manufactured talent gigs will suffer, but that's flawed design.
>
> —Joseph Lorenzo Hall, cited in "We Don't Need Your Stinkin' Amnesty!"

File sharing and RIAA's lawsuits prompted a national conversation about ethics, intellectual property rights, living in a digital age, corporate greed, and parental guidance. These conversations occurred privately in homes, schools, and workplaces and publicly in the press and on the Web.

When you take your argument to a public forum, you become a voice in the public debate of an issue. Writers of letters to the editor, columns, and edi-

Commentary through Photography

The photographer is making a comment using only a picture. What is she implying? What is the tone of each photograph? What effect do the words shown in the photographs have on your impression of the meaning of the photographs?

torials share a common purpose: they argue for change in opinion or social policy. And they reach a broad audience: the readers of that newspaper or website or the listeners to a radio or television broadcast.

For this assignment, you will be writing your opinions in the form of letters to the editor, columns, or guest editorials. Guest editorials, which are written by people who are not on the newspaper staff, often appear on the op-ed page opposite the newspaper's own editorials. You will be writing from your own informed perspective. As you enter the public debate and share your

well-reasoned argument in a letter, column, or editorial, you will be taking part in the shaping of public opinion.

Applications: School, Community, Work

The skills involved in writing your opinion piece will transfer well to other settings. In college you write argumentative essays in many of your courses: an essay for or against genetically modified food in your biology or nutrition course, for example, or a position paper on welfare reform for a sociology or political science class.

As a member of a community group, you might write a letter to convince your neighbors to create a coalition to protect wetlands. You might write an opinion piece for the local newspaper to sway public opinion on this or other issues that are important to the community: perhaps tax relief, extra funding for schools, or election of local officials.

As a worker you might write an argument for changes in your workplace: better conditions for workers or a pay raise for part-time employees. You might write a letter on behalf of your company in response to criticism or an article arguing for legislation that would affect your profession.

CHAPTER OBJECTIVES

In this chapter you will learn to

▶ craft a strong argumentative thesis

▶ consider and counter opposing viewpoints

▶ support your thesis with well-reasoned arguments

UNDERSTANDING ARGUMENTS

Persuading someone to your way of thinking requires strategy. After all, we all have a built-in resistance to change, especially when change affects our values or beliefs. To overcome readers' resistance and persuade them to shift their perspectives or accept new ways of thinking, you can appeal to logic, emotion, and ethics, the classical ways to sway public opinion. The original Greek terms for these appeals are *logos, pathos,* and *ethos.* Most arguments—whether in formal debates, advertising, or opinion pieces in newspapers, on radio, and on the Web—use these appeals either alone or in some combination.

Using Logical Appeals

When you present a logical argument, you appeal to the reader's intellect and sense of reason. Using logic you create a path of evidence for your reader that inevitably leads to your conclusion. To get your reader to follow you from point to point, your argument must be clear and supported by objective evidence: facts and statistics.

For example, an editorial titled "An Obesity Epidemic" asserts that "Overweight children . . . are the victims of an epidemic of childhood obesity in the United States." The writer provides evidence to support this assertion by citing statistics such as "The percentage of overweight young people has increased from 4 percent in 1963 to 15 percent in 1999" ("An Obesity Epidemic," *Boston Globe*, 27 May 2003).

By making a reasoned argument or using facts and statistics to support your points, you make a logical appeal to convince your readers that your views are valid.

Using Emotional Appeals

Because using emotion to sway opinion has often been done manipulatively, the appeal to emotion has garnered a bad reputation. Sunlit children running through fields of flowers do not make a compelling argument to vote for Candidate X. However, if you use emotion appropriately, especially in combination with a logical appeal, you can speak to readers' hearts as

**Warm-Up Practice 7.1
Collaborative Activity**

Bring copies of local newspapers and the most prominent regional newspaper to class. Read the editorials and the signed columns on the facing page. Working with a group, select a topic of interest, pool your knowledge, and discuss your various responses to the issue.

1. Write an individual two- to three-paragraph response to the issue, stating your point of view.

2. Compare your response to the responses of others in your group. Note the similarities and differences in your views. Which arguments are the most compelling?

well as their minds, evoking anger at injustice, sadness at tragedy, or outrage at inequity.

Using emotion to support your points involves marshalling subjective evidence, such as opinions, anecdotes, and personal observations. An emotional appeal appears in "Make Chris Take His 'Meds,'" an editorial that supports legislation requiring California courts to take a person's mental illness into consideration before sentencing. To vividly illustrate the plight of mentally ill homeless people, the editorial tells the story of one man.

> Meet 22-year-old Chris Hagar, who is now locked up in the Sacramento Mental Health Treatment Center. Since age 15 Hagar has cycled in and out of six jails and mental hospitals, tormented by paranoid schizophrenia. He'd steal food from mom-and-pop grocery stores and promptly get arrested. He'd assault his parents and others. He'd break into a car to escape shadowy stalkers.
>
> —Alex Raskin and Bob Sipchen, "Make Chris Take His 'Meds'"

Even these few details of Chris's life evoke anger at the injustices he has had to face and sadness at the tragedy of his life.

Using Ethical Appeals

Although the word *ethics* suggests a moral code of behavior, the term *ethical appeal* actually refers to the writer's credibility. To be swayed by your argu-

---

Practice 7.2
Identifying Logical, Emotional, and Ethical Appeals

Read the following passages. For each, identify what type or types of appeal the writer is making: logical, emotional, or ethical.

1. "The First Amendment protects not only those whose ideas Americans like but, more important, those whose ideas they abhor."

—*New York Times* Editorial

2. "Technology is driving America's economy and our way of life. Whether in creating technologies or using them on the job, practically every employee of every company will need the skills that math and science provide."

—*Baltimore Sun* Editorial

3. "A homeless Orlando couple with too little money to maintain a bank account must pay a fee and forfeit 3 percent of their meager earnings simply to cash a paycheck."

—*Orlando Sentinel* Editorial

4. "As a professor at a liberal arts college, I must take a stand and refuse to take any more responsibility for student failure. If students plagiarize, it is not because my assignment was not creative enough."

—Laura Tropp, Letter to the Editor

5. "An average of 78 percent of the convicted felons in that program stay clean and sober for one year or longer. Re-arrest rates for those participants after release is almost two-thirds lower than for non-participants."

—Jim Gogek and Ed Gogek "Drug War Solution Between Legalization, Incarceration"

6. "As a veteran of family reunions, I can tell you they are often fractious affairs. Folks get their feelings hurt."

—Cynthia Tucker, "Jefferson's Kin Ought to Accept Black Relatives"

ments, a reader has to trust you and know that the evidence you cite is accurate, valid, and reliable.

One way to establish credibility is to use authoritative sources to support your positions. For example, your argument will be strong if you cite the surgeon general's warning about the effects of smoking rather than quote an actor who plays a doctor on a television show. Similarly, the Centers for Disease Control and Prevention is a better source for information about the latest flu epidemic than your runny-nosed roommate. You create your credibility, in good part, by clear and accurate attribution of your sources. Tell your reader who your sources are and why they are especially suited to speak to a particular subject.

Another powerful way to establish your authority and your credentials is to cite your own experience. Mark Edmundson, who wrote an editorial entitled "How Teachers Can Stop Cheaters" (on the website), is identified as "professor of English at the University of Virginia." The reader knows that he writes from experience. In the same way, if you have worked for a particular cause—raising money for cancer research or housing the homeless—using information you have learned from your experience can be germane and persuasive.

Avoiding Pitfalls in Logic: Fallacies

As you argue your position, you have to be careful not to commit an error in logic. Logical errors, commonly known as fallacies, weaken your argument considerably. On the other hand, if you can detect logical pitfalls in the work of people whose views differ from yours, you have a perfect way to deflate an opposing argument. You can sharpen your skills in logic by searching out fallacies in your own and other's thinking.

Circular Argument   In a circular argument the end of the argument restates the beginning.

Pornography should be banned because it is obscene.

This statement says circularly that pornography is pornographic.

Post Hoc Fallacy   *Post hoc* is short for the Latin term *post hoc, ergo propter hoc,* which means "after this, therefore, because of this." You cannot logically assert that phenomenon A causes phenomenon B simply because B occurred after A.

Because a snack-cake company advertises aggressively during Saturday morning cartoon shows, obesity rates have risen among children.

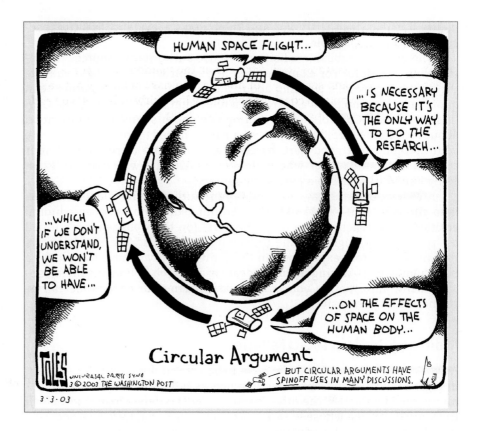

Perhaps the obesity rate among children has risen at the same time as the advertising campaign aired, but you cannot truly assert that the campaign *caused* the increase.

Ad Hominem Fallacy *Ad hominem*, Latin for "to the man," means an attack that targets a person rather than that person's views or arguments. Ad hominem attacks ignore or sidestep the issue at hand.

> Professor X dresses like a clown. How could anyone take his economics theories seriously?

Attacking Professor X does not build an argument that convinces your reader that his theories on economics are flawed.

Hasty Generalization A hasty generalization is a conclusion formed from only one or two examples. One case does not prove a point.

Airbags are not worth the risk because my friend was seriously injured when an airbag opened.

You could cite this example to illustrate that the cautions that come with airbags should be taken seriously, but not that the risks of airbags outweigh the benefits. When you also consider how many lives airbags have saved and note that injuries are much less frequent and less fatal with airbags, you avoid this hasty generalization.

The Either-Or Fallacy The either-or fallacy oversimplifies a complex issue. It uses language that polarizes discussion into two extreme and mutually exclusive positions, leaving no room for nuances, other options, complexities, or the existence of common ground.

The school budget crisis can be solved either by reducing the teen center's hours of operation or by raising users' fees by $100.

This statement suggests that the budget crisis has only two possible solutions. Many ways exist to cut costs and raise money other than these two specific suggestions.

RESEARCH PATHS

Because opinion pieces concern broad public issues that reach far beyond personal preferences, research is an essential step in choosing a topic for your opinion piece. Using print, electronic, or expert sources will deepen your understanding of the issue and help you find the evidence you need to present your position to a public audience.

Choosing a Topic for an Opinion Piece

You will sometimes be writing an opinion piece on a topic for which you already have a "position and a passion." Other times you might need to do research to prompt your thinking. Research can help you discover what is being debated in the public arena and decide what issues interest you.

Consider something you care about that is currently in the news or can be tied to recent events in your school, your community, or the world. Read the papers, listen to and watch the nightly news, log on to a reputable news website, and talk about current issues with friends and teachers.

Once you decide on an issue, make sure that your topic is *arguable*. Arguable means that good points supported by solid evidence can be made on more than one side of the issue. You could not write much of an opinion piece, for example, asserting that ethnic or gender discrimination is illegal. Who could argue with that? However, if you wrote a piece that argued that

---

Practice 7.3
Identifying Fallacies

Identify the fallacies in these statements.

1. America—Love It or Leave It!

2. My dog was killed by a speeding car. We have to lower the speed limit in residential neighborhoods.

3. Women can't be allowed to go to war because they are too feminine.

4. Of course, being wealthy, he wouldn't know much about welfare reform.

5. You're either part of the problem or part of the solution.

6. Whenever I wear my lucky hat, I ace a test.

Practice 7.4
Researching Other Fallacies

Select one of the following common fallacies, research its meaning, find or create examples, and present your findings to the class.

- Non sequitur
- Fourth term
- Red herring
- Slippery slope
- Begging the question
- Appeal to the bandwagon
- Poisoning the well

Practice 7.5
Brainstorming for a Topic

1. List local or global issues about which you have opinions, preferably strong ones. Look at the editorial topics in your college, community, or city newspaper for ideas. Try to generate at least ten possible topics.

2. Choose one of the issues you listed, and make it the focal point for a freewrite. Write the topic on the top of a page; then write as many different positions on this issue as you can imagine. Do not worry about logic, clarity, or grammar at this point. Just get your ideas down on paper. Write nonstop for ten minutes.

3. Alternatively, choose one issue you listed, and make it the focal point of a clustering activity. Write the issue in the center of a page, circle it, and see how many points of view you can generate radiating out from this topic. (See Chapter 1 for more information on freewriting and clustering.)

Practice 7.6   Narrowing Topics

Choose one of these topics, and break it down into three or four narrower topics, as in the example on global warming. See if you can also find a local angle as you narrow the topic.

• Drug testing for athletes
• Airport security
• Film censorship
• Internet fraud
• New technologies

ethnic or gender discrimination exists in college admissions policies, you would certainly have an arguable position.

Narrowing Your Topic

Social, political, economic, scientific, and cultural issues tend to be sprawling and multifaceted. People can spend years studying them. For example, global warming, airport security, book censorship, and the conflict in the Middle East are huge topics. But each can be approached in numerous ways: by examining history, reporting on current developments, citing anecdotes from a particular place or instance, noting a technological development, pointing to a change in trends, or looking through the lens of a certain discipline, such as sociology or psychology.

One way to narrow your topic and find a specific focus for your opinion piece is to break the topic down into its component parts. Find the aspect of the topic that affects you and people in your community. Stay local, and be specific.

For example, assume that you have decided to write about global warming, a huge topic that interests you. As you read for background, you discover that people have focused on a number of specific solutions to global warming, including regulating automobile emissions, preserving green space, adding more-efficient mass transportation, and making buildings more energy efficient. Any one of these topics will narrow your focus. If your college or community is about to begin construction on a new building, you can further narrow your topic to that very specific and local issue: persuading the builder to use solar panels or photovoltaic cells in the building, for example.

Print, Electronic, and Expert Sources

To argue persuasively in a letter, column, or editorial, you have to know about the topic you have chosen and its background. Inform yourself by reading back issues of newspapers, magazines, and journals in libraries or online. You can also talk to expert sources—people who know your topic well.

▶ Many big-city newspapers publish indexes that organize previously printed articles by topics. Most college libraries keep at least the *New York Times Index* in their reference section and often have microfiche copies of editions going back many years. Check your college or local library to see what indexes are readily available to you.

Protesters hold up a 24-foot screw in New York's financial district, making clear their position about the accounting fraud charges that were brought against the bankrupt telephone company Worldcom in 2003.

▶ Many colleges and universities subscribe to the powerful online database LexisNexis and provide it as a resource for their students. The news section of this database catalogues thousands of periodicals from twenty or more years ago and from all over the country and retrieves information using keywords, writers' names, or article titles. The reference section gives biographical information, information from polls and surveys, quotations, and facts from the *World Almanac*.

▶ In addition to researching your chosen issue in newspapers and periodicals, you will often want to go to other sources for deeper information. For example, if you are writing about a scientific breakthrough like cloning, a social issue like homelessness, or an economic issue like Social Security, you will need to read journals, books, textbooks, and public documents. (For more information about consulting sources, see Chapter 14.)

▶ Another research path takes you to experts. Take advantage of your college or university community. Professors spend their lives becoming expert in their fields, and most are more than willing to pass on their knowledge and their sources of information to students. For background information on current issues in science, psychology, politics, economics, medicine, law, or a variety of other topics, you can consult your teachers. If you know other professionals or practitioners in a field related to your issue, they can also be useful sources. (See the tips for interviewing on page 426–430.)

Whether you search at the library or on your computer or consult with experts, good research is key to forming your opinion and developing your argument. As you read, collect supporting evidence—facts, statistics, public opinion polls, anecdotes—for all sides of the issue. So that you can later review and document your sources, take careful notes or make photocopies of all that you read and consult.

Every print source you use needs clear attribution. Make sure to note author, title, place of publication, publisher, date, and page number for all print sources. For Internet sources, copy the URL accurately. For interviews, note the time, date, and place of your interview as well as the correctly spelled name, title, and affiliation of your source. Published opinion pieces in newspapers always attribute information to sources within the

SIDEBAR

Evaluating Evidence

Check your supporting evidence for reliability, timeliness, accuracy, and relevance.

Reliability

Does the evidence come from a person who is an authority in the field?

- What are his or her credentials?
- Is this person cited in other sources?

Does the evidence come from a reliable study?

- Who funded the study?
- Was the study sponsored by a government, university, or commercial source?

Timeliness

Is the information up-to date?

- Has it been published in the last few years?

- Have there been more recent studies that make this one outdated?

Accuracy

Is the information correct?

- Have you found a second source to corroborate facts and figures, especially for information found on the Web?
- Have you double-checked your transcription of this information?

Relevance

Does the information support your point?

- Does the evidence specifically address the point you are making?
- Have you tied this evidence clearly to the point?

text, and academic papers require this information on a Works Cited page, so it is essential to be accurate and thorough in keeping track of all your sources. (See Chapter 15 for specific information on different documentation systems.)

ANATOMY OF AN OPINION PIECE

Letters to the editor, columns, and editorials have to sway opinion through the clarity of their arguments. A clear structure for your opinion piece will showcase your clear thinking and help your reader understand and be persuaded by your argument. Read this annotated editorial to see how all the elements work together; then consider each element separately as it is discussed in the following section.

A Blackout for the Blind

BOSTON GLOBE

Introduction

Hundreds of sightless people in Massachusetts are being cut off from essential information since the termination last summer of Newsline, which allows the blind to listen to audio editions of daily newspapers.

Background Information

The Baltimore-based National Federation of the Blind, a nonprofit advocacy group, introduced the service in 1995 and offered it free to subscribers with the help of a significant federal grant. Newsline provides more than 90 daily newspapers to blind and disabled listeners by converting digital text into computer speech. Users merely make a toll-free call and punch in their identification number

In July, however, the lines went dead for the state's estimated 1,300 users. The federal grant had dried up in March. The nonprofit Massachusetts Association for the Blind appealed for pledges to blind runners in the Boston Marathon, but those funds bought only four months of service at a cost of roughly $3,500 per month.

Chester Darling, a prominent local attorney who lost most of his vision due to macular degeneration, said he tried to subscribe individually but was told by *Anecdote* the National Federation of the Blind that the service could be provided only on a state-by-state basis at a cost of roughly $40,000 annually.

"Every day I listened to those papers religiously," said Darling. "I devoured that *Testimonial*
thing. I felt like a human being. I could talk to my colleagues."

A degree of shortsightedness is keeping Newsline from its users. Dawn *Argument*
Neubeck, Newsline's program manager, estimates that the system requires $1.5 *Source*
million to $2 million to operate nationally. It can't without a reliable source of
revenue, she says. True enough, but it also seems that Newsline could allow for *Counter-*
longer grace periods. Utilities, after all, don't cavalierly cut off disabled clients. *argument*
The National Federation of the Blind exists to promote "self-confidence and *Analogy*
self-respect" among the blind. Cutting off sources of news can hardly advance
that mission.

Body   Ideally, a private sponsor would step forward with sufficient funding to re-
connect Newsline until the state provides money for this service. Thirty-four *Fact*
states provide public funding for Newsline, and a bill to do just that in Massachusetts is currently in the Senate Ways and Means Committee. Lawmakers
should realize that Newsline's promise extends beyond the current subscriber
base. Joseph Collins, executive director of the Massachusetts Association for the *Argument*
Blind, says that 35,000 legally blind individuals live in the state and the number
of "print impaired" people is more that double that figure. Newsline should also
be marketed to disabled people who can see but can't turn pages.

For short money and meager reasons, thousands of the blind and disabled are *Thesis*
Conclusion being denied a window on the world.

An Argumentative Thesis

The specific point that you assert in your opinion piece is your thesis, a
sentence or two that states your position on an issue. There is no one right
thesis; there are defensible and nondefensible theses. In other words, intelligent people with differing viewpoints can make very different but equally
valid points about an issue. Responses to the Recording Industry Association of America's lawsuits (discussed earlier), for example, showed a range
of positions. One writer thought that greedy record companies created the
problem; another felt that the lawsuits unintentionally provided an opportunity for parents to talk to their kids about ethics; and yet another felt that
the RIAA should use the money spent on lawsuits to discover new talent or
better distribution channels. Each position has validity and can be put forth
and supported with logic and evidence.

This is not to say that all positions are equally valid and logical, only that most issues are complicated. The more complicated an issue, the more ways there are to look at it. Your position on an issue can fall anywhere along the continuum between the two extremes of pro and con, or it even can be a compromise between the extremes.

A common and effective pattern for argumentative writing is to announce your thesis and then prove it. Thus the most common placement for a thesis is in the first paragraph. An equally effective strategy, however, is to state your thesis after you have presented your arguments so they carefully lead your reader to that conclusion. In the annotated editorial "A Blackout for the Blind," the thesis is the final line of the piece.

> For short money and meager reasons, thousands of the blind and disabled are being denied a window on the world.

In this instance, the writers presented their reasons first; then they clinched their argument with the thesis statement. Note that even though the thesis appears at the end of the editorial, the writers still announce their two main points "short money" and "meager reasons." No matter where it is placed, the thesis should present your position in clear and unequivocal terms.

Introduction

An effective introduction for an opinion piece rouses curiosity, strong feelings, or both in your reader. Without much space to waste in a letter, column, or editorial, you have to hook your reader right away. Your introduction—the first paragraph or two of your piece—should bring the reader right into your topic. Questions, stories, quotations, facts, definitions, analogies, and direct assertion of the thesis can all be effective ways to draw a reader into your opinion piece. Make sure your introduction cues your reader into the issue and your position.

In "A Blackout for the Blind," the writers hook the reader's attention and announce the issue with two facts that show a cause and its effect: because a news service for the blind was terminated last summer, "hundreds of sightless people in Massachusetts are being cut off from essential information." A straightforward introduction like this one wastes no words as it clearly presents the issue.

Background Information

As you plan your opinion piece, you have to decide how much background information your reader needs in order to understand your position on an issue. If your issue is current and well covered in the news, sometimes all

Practice 7.7
Crafting a Thesis

Assume that your state legislature is considering a bill to make driving tests mandatory every time you renew your driver's license. According to the bill, mandatory road testing will reduce the number of accidents caused by young, inexperienced drivers and by older drivers whose eyesight and reaction time have diminished.

1. Make a list of four or five arguments on this topic, considering pro, con, and some positions in between.

2. Put the arguments in order of strength, saving the best argument for last.

3. Choose the position that you think is most compelling, and write a thesis that promotes that position.

4. Edit your thesis so it is written as economically and clearly as possible.

Practice 7.8   Assessing Introductions

Read the following introductions. Identify the techniques (questions, stories, quotations, facts, analogies, thesis statements) that the writers use, and evaluate their effectiveness.

1. "In a society infested with junk foods, schools ought to be havens for healthy eating. A bill before the Legislature would insure that vending machines in public schools offer foods and drinks that are as nutritionally sound as those in the school breakfast and lunch programs."

   —Editorial, *Boston Globe*

2. "Let's explore the role of the modern athlete in wartime. By this I don't mean let's pull off his pads, hand him an M-16 and a Gurkha knife and drop him in the middle of the Hindu Kush. But who doesn't wonder about the relevance of our all-pros and home run kings, now that U.S. soldiers in Afghanistan and firefighters in New York are engaged in real conflict, as opposed to the weekend wars-without-death we watch in stadiums?"

   —Sally Jenkins, "As Many Soldier On, Athletes' Relevance Fades Away"

3. "On any given day, about 50,000 severely mentally ill homeless people roam California's streets, rummaging through trash bins, doing battle with invisible demons and occasionally inflicting harm on very real citizens. They do so largely because laws crafted decades ago put their 'civil right' to be free ahead of society's right to compel them to be treated."

   —Alex Raskin and Bob Sipchen, "Make Chris Take His 'Meds'"

4. "Some say that all acceptance notices come in big envelopes; so you can tell right away if you'll be attending your favorite college next year. Unfortunately, many high schools currently have a grading system that increases the chances that their top students will be receiving the smaller envelopes from their colleges. This disadvantage stems from the weighted grading system that some high schools don't use, and should use."

   —Aaron Rasmussen, "Schools Need Weighted Grading"

you need is a brief reminder. If the issue is complicated or not well known—for example, some little-known aspect of foreign policy or local politics—you need to provide enough background and context for the reader to understand the issue.

Your research should help you find relevant background information, but do not try to include the complete history of the issue or a comprehensive overview. Define the out-of-the-ordinary terms, and summarize the important points for your reader. In a summary, you have to find the most concise way to put the issue in context.

Because it focuses on an issue that has not had wide coverage in the mainstream press, "A Blackout for the Blind" devotes two paragraphs to background information. Paragraphs 2 and 3 bring the reader up-to-date with a quick summary of the events leading up to the termination of Newsline.

Acknowledgment of Opposing Views

To make a convincing argument, you have to acknowledge opposing views and refute them, even briefly. Sometimes a single sentence that might begin "Granted" or "Still" states the opposition's strongest argument with a brief refutation to disprove that argument.

An Iraqi man sits in front of a mural in a Baghdad suburb in May 2004. The mural comments on American abuse of prisoners at Abu Ghraib prison. Compare this image with the photo of this Abu Ghraib prisoner in Chapter 6's Visual Literacy feature on Photojournalism: How a Picture Tells a Story (p. 191). Note how this image editorializes and the one in Chapter 6 *reports* on the Abu Ghraib prison scandal.

Practice 7.9   Providing Background Information

Assume that you are writing an opinion piece about changing your college's entrance requirements. You might be advocating making entrance requirements more stringent or less stringent, or you might have a new idea about attaining gender or ethnic equity. Assume that your reader has no knowledge of the current admission standards.

1. Write as brief a paragraph as you can that provides the background information your reader will need in order to understand the issue.

2. Choose two editorials from your local paper, and identify the background information presented in them. Note how much information is provided and where it appears.

**Practice 7.10
Acknowledging
Opposing Views**

Choose one of these opinion statements and anticipate counterarguments by creating a list of opposing views. After you have generated a list of four or five con arguments, arrange them so that the strongest argument is first.

• Academic cheating can be stopped by having students endorse an honor code.

• Pulling vending machines out of schools will not make kids eat less junk food.

• Internet file sharing is no different from taping music from the radio or from a friend's CD.

• Drivers over seventy years old should have to take a driving test every two years.

• Drivers under age twenty-one should have to take a driving test every two years

Note that the annotated editorial uses the phrase "True enough" to grant that Newsline requires a reliable source of revenue before going on to suggest that the organization could have allowed "for longer grace periods." To bolster this counterargument, the writer compares Newsline's action to utilities that "don't cavalierly cut off disabled clients." It is a good strategy to anticipate objections to your position by creating a list of arguments others might have and to address the ones you think are the strongest.

When you acknowledge and dispense with your opposition's possible arguments, you enhance your credibility and build strength for your position. You show that you understand and have thoughtfully considered the opposing views.

Well-Supported Arguments

What will convince your reader best are thoughtful, well-supported arguments. You can draw on or combine appeals to logic or to emotion or you can use credible sources to make your arguments strong. For example, paragraph 7 of "A Blackout for the Blind" includes the argument that the state should provide money for the service. To support this argument, the writers cite two facts: that thirty-four states already provide public funding for Newsline and that "35,000 legally blind individuals live in the state." These facts prove that a precedent exists for state funding and that an audience exists for the service.

As you write your opinion piece, keep your audience clearly in mind. Though your opinion piece might help some readers confirm already-held opinions, thinking of your audience as the unpersuaded will help you marshal your strongest arguments. As you know, insulting, *ad hominem* attacks do not convince. Write "any idiot who believes such-and-such," and you have lost your intended audience immediately.

Think of your audience as made up of intelligent people whose views differ from yours, and consider their arguments respectfully and thoughtfully. Figure out what it means to believe differently from what you believe. If you can understand other people's positions, you will be in a position to argue ethically, logically, and passionately to change their minds.

Saving your strongest argument for your closing is an effective persuasive technique. It is good practice to leave your reader thinking about the most compelling reason to support your position.

Supporting material for your arguments can come in a variety of forms. This kind of evidence, as mentioned earlier, can be used to appeal to logic or to emotion. Evidence that comes from reliable sources, of course, adds to the credibility of your arguments.

▶ *Facts* state objective reality. That you have blue eyes or brown eyes is a fact. That you are attractive is an opinion based on that fact. Your factual supporting evidence should be accurate and unadulterated by opinion.

▶ *Statistics* are numerical data, which often seem to have the weight of irrefutable analysis behind them. Statistics can be slippery, however, and can be skewed or misinterpreted to fit the desired outcome, so you have to be careful to choose reputable sources.

▶ *Examples* and *anecdotes* illustrate your point. An example provides a single case, and an anecdote tells a story. You have to be careful not to generalize from a case or story, however, and commit the hasty generalization fallacy discussed earlier. Relevant examples and anecdotes often provide vivid support for an argumentative point.

▶ *Testimonials,* stories of experts or witnesses, provide excellent support for arguments as long as the source is well positioned to speak to the issue.

The stronger your support, the stronger your argument. The more variety of support you use, the more you demonstrate the truth behind your position. To set forth a convincing argument, amass a great deal of evidence, enough to convince your most skeptical critic.

Conclusion

Your purpose in an opinion piece is to persuade others to change their minds and/or to take action. You can use a range of techniques to end your piece persuasively. A powerful quotation, an anecdote, or a vivid descriptive passage can help a well-made point linger in your reader's mind.

Many editorials include a *call to action* in their conclusions. Columns and letters often include specific suggestions for actions also, but sometimes the call to action is implied rather than stated. If your editorial persuades the reader to change positions on an issue, your call to action can be a suggestion to support legislation or a political candidate, as it does in the annotated editorial. In "A Blackout for the Blind," the call to action is in the next-to-last paragraph, asking lawmakers to vote for a current bill to provide state funding for Newsline. In the last paragraph, the conclusion, the writer, sums up the editorial's argument with the thesis statement. Whatever you decide to do in your conclusion, make sure it brings home your point and leaves your reader at least thinking about, if not acting on, your ideas.

End the Hands-off Policy
on Cell Phone Users

PAUL MULSHINE

Not too long ago I was driving along minding my own business when the car next to me suddenly swerved into my lane. Not only was the jerk cutting me off, but he didn't even have the decency to signal.

I blew my horn just as the bozo was about to push me into the weeds. When he looked over, I realized why he hadn't signaled. His right hand was holding his cell phone. His left hand was dialing it. He would have needed a third hand to work the blinkers. If he'd had a fourth, it could have been usefully employed on the steering wheel.

This is among the reasons I fully support New York's ban on the use of cell phones while driving. I fervently hope New Jersey adopts such a ban as well. I would write into the law an exception for any Eastern deities who have driver's licenses, since some are said to have as many as six hands. But we two-handed mortals are not up to the task of using a telephone while driving.

This rather obvious point is lost on the many radio talk-show hosts and other self-proclaimed conservatives who have opposed cell phone bans in New York and in the New Jersey town of Marlboro on what they mistakenly believe to be principles of individual liberty. I consider myself something of a scholar on the question of liberty, and I can assure them that the principles they are citing do not exist.

The classic work on the subject is by John Stuart Mill. It is titled, appropriately enough, "On Liberty." Here is the relevant passage: "The individual is not accountable to society for his actions, in so far as these concern the interests of no person but himself."

Note the "but" in that sentence. You can yap all day on your home phone and you are affecting no one but yourself—and, of course, the person on the other end of the line, presumably a consenting adult.

But when you get into a 2-ton vehicle and direct it down a public road, your cell phone use concerns not just you but the thousands of other drivers you will soon be menacing. Many of those drivers, moi for one, have not in any way consented to be run off the road so that your conversation can proceed more smoothly.

Art student Nick Rodriques wears one of his sculptures that comments on how cell phones can isolate us from one another.

The cell phone defenders argue there is no evidence that using a cell phone while driving is any more dangerous than using the radio, drinking coffee or eating. Nonsense. As I've noted, we humans have but two hands. A minimum of one should always be on the steering wheel. If you wish to adjust your radio or sip your coffee, you can do so with your free hand at a time of your choosing, presumably a time when you are going down the road in a straight line. You set the schedule.

But if you have a cell phone, your schedule is being set by someone who is not in your car. Your phone can ring at a time when you should be using your turn signals, adjusting your wipers, turning on your headlights, concentrating on braking, or all of the above. And you have just a few seconds to answer it.

Once you start yapping, you have just one hand free for as long as you talk. Does the typical cell phone user say, "Excuse me, I have to put the phone down so I can employ my turn signal so Mulshine will know that I am about to dispatch him into the weeds"? If so, I've never seen it. In my experience, cell phone users have a harder time staying in their lanes than even drunks.

Any true conservative would see the cell phone as Mill would have seen it, a device that should be used sparingly for fear of causing offense or injury to others. That cell phones have changed driving behavior for the worse is obvious even if you accept for the sake of argument the mistaken contention that they are no worse than radios, coffee or screaming kids. All of those other distractions were there already. With the roads getting more crowded by the day, we don't need another distraction.

I think I can make that point best with this rather disturbing sight I encountered one day upon leaving Star-Ledger offices in Newark. A car came barreling through the intersection in front of the building. It is a corner packed with pedestrians and cars leaving the parking lots, but this clown sped right through without slowing down. As the car got closer, I saw the driver had a cell phone in his right hand. Was his left hand on the wheel? I fear not.

He was picking his nose.

Annotate "End the Hands-off Policy on Cell Phone Users"

1. Put brackets around the lead. In the margin write the name of the technique Mulshine uses in the lead.

2. Underline the thesis.

3. Circle the sections where Mulshine acknowledges opposing views and refutes them.

4. Put brackets around the conclusion. In the margin write the name of the technique Mulshine uses in the conclusion.

5. Put a wavy line under phrases and sentences that get your attention, either positively or negatively. Indicate your assessment with a plus or minus sign.

READINGS

The following letters, columns, editorials, and political cartoons demonstrate how some issues are debated in the public sphere. The first two readings, an editorial and a letter to the editor, show different views of the 2003 Supreme Court decision to allow race to be used as a factor in college admissions. Next is an op-ed piece by a student on weighted grading. A column explores "the role of the modern athlete in wartime," and Pulitzer Prize–winning editorial cartoons focus on the national response to the terrorist attacks of September 11, 2001.

The "Quota" Cry Doesn't Faze Me

Cynthia Tucker

Cynthia Tucker is the editorial page editor of the *Atlanta Journal-Constitution* and often appears on Jim Lehrer's *News Hour*. She won the 2000 American Society of Newspaper Editors Competition for Best Commentary. Tucker wrote the following opinion piece after the 2003 Supreme Court decision to continue using affirmative action in college admissions.

O ccasionally, critics of affirmative action will try to persuade me to drop my support for affirmative action programs, contending that such efforts taint me and other black professionals with assumptions of incompetence. No matter how talented or accomplished I may be, they say, some will always wonder whether I was given good jobs simply because I'm black.

With the Supreme Court's recent ruling backing affirmative action in college admissions, that argument is once again making the rounds. Indeed, Justice Clarence Thomas, who disagreed with the court's majority, holds the view that affirmative action taints its beneficiaries.

In his dissent, he quoted black abolitionist Frederick Douglass to make the point:

"And if the negro [sic] cannot stand on his own legs, let him fall also. . . . Let him alone! . . . Your interference is doing him positive injury."

5   Thomas is a complicated man. He was admitted to Yale University's School of Law with a boost from affirmative action, yet he has fought having those same benefits extended to others. Perhaps Thomas knows that many people perceive his success as the result of preferential treatment (With scant judicial experience, would he have been appointed to the U.S. Supreme Court if he were white?) and he struggles with that burden.

I don't.

There is no doubt that my career received an assist from affirmative action efforts. To hire me right out of college, The *Atlanta Journal* suspended its usual rule of requiring a few years of solid experience at another daily newspaper. The newspaper did so as a remedy to years of legally sanctioned discrimination, which barred blacks from professional jobs at Southern newspapers, and years of restrictive social custom, which barred most women.

But they suspended no other rules for me. I was expected to write stories that were clear and concise, with names spelled correctly and numbers that added up. I was expected to stalk politicians trying to evade reporters, decipher budget documents and locate official records.

I had to work hard, since I lacked experience and didn't know what I was doing. But there were experienced reporters and editors around—white men, given the times—who were more than happy to help me when I came to them for advice. I learned the trade, and I like to think I'm pretty good at what I do.

Are there those who think I'm in my job only because I'm black? Are there critics who suspect I'm just filling the newspaper's political correctness quota? Of course there are. I hear from them frequently.

But I know better, so I'm not troubled by what they think. And I doubt that many other affirmative action beneficiaries allow themselves to be limited by the prejudices of their critics.

Over the last two decades, the biggest group to benefit from corporate affirmative action efforts has been white women, many of whom know what it's like to be highly competent but subject to old-fashioned stereotypes about their skills. However, no woman who has ever succeeded, whether in medicine, law, architecture, journalism or some other field, allows the prejudice of others to define her.

Nor do successful blacks, who have been subject to the slander of inferiority for the 400 years—well before the term "affirmative action" became part of the political lexicon. Less than a decade ago, two whites, Richard Herrnstein and Charles Murray, wrote an 845-page screed, "The Bell Curve," arguing that blacks are intellectually inferior. I don't know a single black engineer, neurosurgeon or molecular biologist who lost sleep over it.

Black professionals who entered elite colleges through diversity efforts have not been defined by the misperceptions of others, either. According to "The Shape of the River," an exhaustive study published in 1998, those students have done well, many going on to graduate schools and prestigious careers.

I'll likely receive missives from my critics claiming this column is just more evidence of my incompetence, more proof that I'm in this job only because I'm black. They can believe what they like.

But I'll keep writing.

Critical Reading Questions

1. Why do you think Tucker begins her editorial by acknowledging the opposing views? How effective is this lead in grabbing your attention?

2. Do you find Tucker a credible source? Why?

3. How effective is Tucker's use of the personal voice in this editorial?

4. What is Tucker's thesis? Where does she first state it?

5. Where does Tucker provide the background information? Is it sufficient for you to understand the topic?

Questions for Writing and Discussion

1. How does Tucker support her thesis? What are her main arguments?

2. Identify places where Tucker appeals to logic. Where does she appeal to emotion?

3. Tucker ends her piece with the line, "But I'll keep writing." Discuss the effectiveness of this line as a clincher for her argument.

Letter to the Editor:

Economic Status, Not Race, Should Be Basis of Affirmative Action

Lisa Wehran

The *Columbus Dispatch* published this letter to the editor in response to an earlier letter supporting "race-based admissions" to college. Recent high-school graduate Lisa Wehran argues against this position.

I respond to Alicia D. Smith, who recently wrote a letter to the editor, "Race-based admissions essential to learning." Is affirmative action righteous and just?

I am a recent high-school graduate who was constantly stressed out about grades while in school. However, as many of my classmates and I were anxious about the college-application process, I couldn't help but think: Would all of our hard work be overlooked simply because we would not meet the colleges' particular "quota" or help them become a "diverse" campus?

The United States is a country of equal opportunity, a country of freedom and equality of all people. However, if colleges are giving extra points for being of a particular race, then all applicants are not given an equal opportunity.

Children in America often are taught that it is what's inside that matters the most. And although they might have worked prudently during high school, their racial background may go for or against them when it comes to that college application.

5 Colleges and universities should start by abolishing the question of race on applications. The admissions officers should be colorblind when judging the thousands of applications.

The question of race on an application should be replaced by a question of economic status. A low-income family might not have had the resources to provide their children with such things as an SAT preparation course, tutoring and quality teachers to boost their chances of getting into college.

The race or ethnicity of a low-income family should not play a role in the college-admission process, therefore giving all students an equal opportunity at a higher education.

Group preference demeans the ability of minority students. It insults the intended beneficiaries by subtly telling them that without being given an extra boost, they otherwise would not be accepted.

If colleges were to give me a boost simply for being a woman, I would feel offended that they did not believe I had comparable credentials to my male counterparts.

10 I feel sympathy for the numerous minority students who truly deserve a spot at a prestigious school. Affirmative action seems to cause the whole race to lose credibility for its achievements.

Each child has the same potential to succeed as the next, and any student's hard work always should pay off.

Critical Reading Questions

1. Lisa Wehran identifies herself right away as a recent high-school graduate. How effective is this opening in setting up her position?

2. What is Wehran's main argument? Where does it appear in the letter? Is this an effective placement? Why?

3. Where does Wehran use logic, and where does she use emotion to make her arguments?

4. How convincing do you find this letter?

Questions for Writing and Discussion

1. Though the two pieces above are about affirmative action, each writer looks at the issue through a different lens and writes from a different point of view. Discuss the strengths and weaknesses of the two arguments.

2. Write a reply to Wehran, responding to her points about affirmative action in college admission policies.

Which of the two editorials on affirmative action would cartoonist Mike Keefe be most likely to agree with?

Schools Need Weighted Grading

Aaron Rasmussen

Aaron Rasmussen originally wrote this opinion piece for a classroom assignment. Then he sent it to his hometown newspaper, *East Oregonian*, where it was published on the Opinion page.

Some say that all acceptance notices come in big envelopes; so you can tell right away if you'll be attending your favorite college next year. Unfortunately, many high schools currently have a grading system that increases the chances that their top students will be receiving the smaller envelopes from their colleges. This disadvantage stems from the weighted grading system that some high schools don't use, and should use.

The weighted and unweighted systems both have their strong and weak points, but the real problem isn't the weighted grading system, it is the differences and incongruities caused by the two different systems coexisting.

Some schools adopted the weighted grading system because it gives an incentive for students to take more challenging courses. A weighted grading system is a style of grading that gives more than four points on a 4.0 GPA scale to an "A" in Advanced Placement (AP) and honors classes. Unweighted systems give four points to an "A," three points to a "B," two points to a "C," and so on. So, a student with straight As who took AP courses throughout high school, could achieve up to a 5.5 GPA in some weighted grading systems.

Likewise, if that student got some Bs in some classes, but maintained As in AP courses, he or she could receive a weighted 4.0 GPA. This student could appear to have the same GPA as another student who got all As, even in AP courses, but had a school with an unweighted grading system. This type of confusion allows some students with inferior performance in high school to enter universities in place of better students with unweighted grades.

For example, UCLA and UC Berkley's median entering GPA for freshmen is over 4.0, a GPA impossible to attain by any students from schools with unweighted grading systems, according to a study by the University of Maine. 5

GPA isn't the only thing that places students in universities, and the other important number isn't the student's SAT score. A student's rank in class (RIC) along with GPA is more important than SAT scores for acceptance consideration at private universities, according to the Center for Research and Evaluation at the University of Maine. The SAT's decline in importance has been especially noticeable recently as the College Board tries to rework the test to be fairer, examine different aspects of the high school experience and prevent the University of California from completely dropping the SAT from its admissions criteria.

With the diminution of the SAT's status as a reference point, class ranking is even more important, and weighted grading systems can wildly vary the class ranking of some students.

When one study re-ranked a weighted-grade class according to an unweighted system, the 11th student became the valedictorian.

Consider this: Private universities chose students with weighted grades 76 percent of the time over students with unweighted grades when given nearly the same transcripts. Yet nearly half of U.S. high schools still use unweighted systems. These schools need to change as soon as possible to a weighted system sparing any students an unnecessary injustice as well as improve the high school's reputation.

10   Changing an entire grading system is not easy. It takes hard work and a lot of time to do it, and are some of the reasons not all schools have changed over to it. But receiving a rejection notice after four years of work because of circumstances beyond a student's control isn't easy either.

Critical Reading Questions

1. How does Rasmussen engage the reader's interest in the first paragraph?

2. What is the specific argument that Rasmussen puts forth in this piece? Rasmussen defines the difference between "weighted" and "unweighted" grading systems. How important is this background information for the reader? How clear is his explanation?

3. Identify appeals to logic and to emotion in this piece. How well does this evidence support the thesis?

4. Where does Rasmussen cite sources to build credibility, and where does he seem to be speaking from his own knowledge? How convincing are his arguments?

5. What does Rasmussen want his reader to think or to do after reading this piece? Is the call to action feasible?

Questions for Writing and Discussion

1. When he wrote this piece for class, Rasmussen titled it "Straight A's Are for Rejects." Why do you think the newspaper changed the title to "Schools Need Weighted Grading"? Which title do you like better?

2. In your opinion, how fair is the college admissions process? Do you think that a consistent weighted grading system in high schools will make the process more equitable?

3. What do you think would be the fairest way to admit students to college?

As Many Soldier On, Athletes' Relevance Fades Away

Sally Jenkins

Sally Jenkins, former writer for *Sports Illustrated* and current sports columnist for the *Washington Post*, has written five books. Perhaps the best known is *It's Not About the Bike: My Journey Back to Life*, which she coauthored with Tour de France bicycling champion Lance Armstrong. In this prize-winning column from *The Washington Post* written in October 2001, Jenkins focuses on the role of athletes in wartime.

Let's explore the role of the modern athlete in wartime. By this I don't mean let's pull off his pads, hand him an M-16 and a Gurkha knife and drop him in the middle of the Hindu Kush. But who doesn't wonder about the relevance of our all-pros and home run kings, now that U.S. soldiers in Afghanistan and firefighters in New York are engaged in real conflict, as opposed to the weekend wars-without-death we watch in stadiums?

What's written on the wall of a gym at West Point is not as true as it once was. It was said by Gen. Douglas MacArthur, when he was superintendent at the academy in the early 1920s: "Upon the fields of friendly strife are sown the seeds that, upon other fields, on other days, will bear the fruits of victory."

When we watch Miami versus Florida State, or the Giants and the Redskins, we are perhaps watching future servicemen, should we ever need a national draft again. But more likely, we are simply watching football players and part-time recording artists. This is not a slur against them; it is merely the reality of a cultural shift that we have all participated in.

Athletes are not obliged to do any more or any less than other men and women between the ages of 20 and 30, who aren't asked to do a whole lot either. They have fewer responsibilities and obligations than ever before—almost none, in fact.

5   This is not to say athletes should or could be doing more, or that they are unimportant. But they are, for once, in context. As a culture we've chronically over-rewarded and over-praised them beginning when they are young. We're not doing that now. We see them for exactly who they are. The war in Afghanistan and at home provides context. If you were wondering why Barry Bonds's home run record or Michael Jordan's comeback lacked the emotional resonance either might have had otherwise, context is the answer. Ballplayers are great, and great ones are especially great, but they aren't nearly as moving or reassuring at the moment as national guardsmen, welders, doctors and plebes.

Originally, games were formalized for the purpose of fitting young people for power. Amateur and collegiate competition—from which all pro leagues grew—has its roots in the old British public school belief that the responsibilities learned on a rugby field prepared a young man for assuming larger responsibilities later on. The V-7 training programs during World War II operated on a similar principle, that there was a valuable correlation between competition and fitness for military service.

This is not just cliche. When athletes become soldiers themselves, they often exhibit extreme valor. Ted Williams served his country twice, flying missions in World War II and again in Korea. Angelo Bertelli, who won the Heisman Trophy at Notre Dame in 1943, participated in a number of invasions as a Marine. Nile Kinnick, who won the Heisman at Iowa in 1939, was killed while trying to land his disabled fighter plane in the Caribbean. Capt. Waddy Young, an all-American end at Oklahoma in 1938, went down with his B-29 on a bombing raid over Tokyo.

Many of the top commanders who emerged from the service academies were athletes, including Dwight Eisenhower, James Van Fleet and Omar Bradley, who played football together at Army. Don Whitmire, who commanded the Seventh Fleet during the evacuation of Vietnam, was among the greatest linemen in Naval Academy history. Gen. George Patton always favored football players as his commanders in the Third Army, because he thought they understood mobility, quickness and how to be aggressive in an intelligent way. And that's just the short list.

But this central mission, games-as-preparation-for-responsibility, has eroded. The only vestiges of it remain at the service academies. Games are now played for their own sake, not as preparation for other careers, but as careers in and of themselves. Today's athletes "never had any cause to think of anything other than themselves," says Jack Clary, author and historian of football at the Naval Academy. Nor have the rest of us.

10   When the great Naval Academy running back Napoleon McCallum was a senior in the early 1980s, he expressed frank ambivalence that he had a service commitment to fulfill when he could have been on an NFL playing field. "Can't I just buy them a missile or something?" he asked. McCallum was joking, but his superiors were not amused. At the time, I thought they were being

humorless. Not anymore. They must have viewed McCallum's joke as a summation of the modern mercantile anti-ethic.

Military service is not about easy exits or buying your way out of commitments; it's all about doing certain things so no else has to: eating food you don't want to eat, going places you don't want to go. McCallum regretted the remark and went on to serve without complaint.

The days of Williams giving up at-bats to become a fighter ace are clearly over. What would happen if our home run kings were called up in a draft now? Some of them would serve gallantly, no doubt. But we have the sneaking suspicion that some of them would phone agents. And the agents,

cell antennas waving, would set up meetings with military commanders, and haggle over what their clients would do, and for whom.

Ironically, athletes are our most able-bodied citizens—they represent the most extreme examples of human physical capacity. But while their bodies and their celebrity are ever-expanding, their purpose has atrophied. It is shrinking. They are great for morale, and they are stalwart volunteers at fundraisers and relief centers. But asked what the role of an athlete is in a time of national crisis, Michael Jordan replied succinctly, "We're entertainers. We're supposed to play."

They used to be the troops. Now they sing to the troops.

Critical Reading Questions

1. Jenkins begins her column with an invitation to the reader, "Let's explore the role of the modern athlete in wartime." How effective is this opening in pulling you into the column?

2. How would you describe Jenkins's voice in this piece?

3. Explain the "cultural shift" Jenkins alludes to in paragraph 3.

4. What background information does Jenkins provide? How important is this information in building her case?

5. What is Jenkins's central argument? Where does she state it? Identify places where Jenkins presents counterarguments to opposing views.

6. Where can you find appeals to reason, to emotion, and to authority in this column?

Questions for Writing and Discussion

1. Jenkins writes this about athletes: "As a culture we've chronically over-rewarded and over-praised them beginning when they are young." Do you agree?

2. What do you think the role of the athlete should be in modern times? Should it be different in wartime?

Political Cartoons

Clay Bennett

Winner of numerous prizes, including the Pulitzer Prize in 2001 and 2002 and the Society of Professional Journalists' Prize for editorial cartooning in 2001, Clay Bennett is the editorial cartoonist for the *Christian Science Monitor*. The process of creating a cartoon, according to Bennett, combines creative right-brain and analytical left-brain activities. He explains his process on the Society of Professional Journalists' website (http://www.spj.org): "You begin with the more analytical left brain—researching a story, establishing facts, and then formulating an opinion based on those facts. Once you form an opinion, you narrow your focus to the single point you wish to make in that day's cartoon."

Bennett won first prize in the National Population Cartoon contest run by the non-profit organization Population Media Center for this cartoon, "Be fruitful and multiply."

Be fruitful and multiply...

Now divide.

For Halloween, 2004, Bennett drew this cartoon, "Intelligence," responding to leaks in the national intelligence gathering.

In 2002, Bennett drew "Traffic Jam," commenting on the stalled Middle East peace process.

Critical Reading Questions

1. Find the focal point, the place where your eye is first drawn, of each cartoon, and explain how it suggests the cartoon's intent.

2. How important are the words in each cartoon? How do the visuals and the few printed words play off each other?

3. What is Bennett's thesis in each cartoon?

Questions for Writing and Discussion

1. Editorial cartoons can get dated quickly as new events eclipse old ones. Do any of these cartoons seem dated to you? Which issues are still very much in the news?

2. If you were to draw a political cartoon that represented your views on any of these issues—population control, national intelligence, the Middle East process— what would you show?

3. How much impact do you think political cartoons have in shaping public opinion?

WRITING IN THE WORKS:
INTERVIEW WITH AARON RASMUSSEN

Aaron Rasmussen

1. How did you decide on the topic of weighted grading for your editorial? Did you have some personal stake in the topic?

My high school had an incredibly low percentage of students going on to four-year colleges, in the neighborhood of 10 percent for my graduating class. When I wrote the piece, I was in the second semester of my freshman year at college, so the issues of high school were still on my mind. I was bitter about the poor quality of my high school and the ignorance of the administration when faced with students with high goals. Although Boston University was my choice as a school, a number of my friends applied to top-ranked schools and were rejected. Rather than resent my high school, I wanted to try and improve it for the better students.

2. Were you clear about your position when you began writing this piece? Did your position change or get clarified during the writing process?

My position changed drastically from the time I selected the topic to the time I started writing. I originally hated the idea of a weighted grading system. I believed the system made it too easy to achieve high rankings for undeserving students. Although I didn't lose that belief after my research, I found that the admissions process already favored a weighted system. While it may not be the best system, the greatest benefit to students is for high schools to change over to it. The writing process made me more comfortable in my utilitarian decision to support a system about which I had reservations. Collecting, analyzing, and organizing the facts convinced me that it was best for schools to switch to the weighted system.

3. What made you decide to submit this piece for publication in your hometown newspaper? How did you go about it?

There were a number of reasons that went into my decision to submit my piece to our regional newspaper. The first was that I was also submitting a proposal to the district school board at the same time, urging the board to change over the grading system. I tried to time the printing of the piece so that it was in newspapers the week before the board looked over my proposal. School boards are very sensitive to public opinion, especially that of the parents, so it was an attempt to influence their decision. My second reason was that I wanted to see if I could get an example of my writing published as a test of my own abilities as a communicator. The third reason was that I seem to remember getting a grade I disagreed with on the piece, and I wanted to prove that it wasn't such a bad article, to the professor as well as myself.

4. I know that the editors changed your title from "Straight A's are for Rejects" to "Schools Need Weighted Grading." What other changes did they make? Did you like the changes the editors made?

At the time I was annoyed with the change from my original title. I thought the original was catchy and fun. At the least "Schools Need Weighted Grading" is a very accurate title, but it seemed so flat. I still prefer the original title, but I understand the reasons behind the change. The target audience of the newspaper probably responded much better to the printed title. The original title is more appropriate for a younger demographic. The editors made two other changes, one was very minor; the other doesn't make sense. I don't remember the first, but the second was a change in the last paragraph to "It takes hard work and a lot of time to do it, and are some of the reasons. . . ." I have no idea why the previous word (probably "which") was changed to "and" after the comma. The sentence doesn't make any sense now. As can be expected, I'm not a big fan of that last change.

5. What kind of response did you get when you published this as an op-ed piece?

I got a large response to the piece. While I was attending a friend's graduation ceremony, a number of parents mentioned that they had enjoyed the article and found it very informative. A former substitute teacher told me that he thought it was an important article. That was especially enjoyable because this was the same teacher that made me do push-ups during class in middle school for being a pain. The response that makes me proudest is that the school board decided to change the unweighted grading system of our high school to a weighted grading system.

6. If you could revise this piece one more time, would you? What would you say differently?

I would definitely revise the piece. Paul Valery said, "A poem is never finished, only abandoned." This holds true for any art. I don't think you can ever revise too many times, as long as you give yourself enough time in between revisions to take a fresh look at your work. I would take out every "a lot" in the piece—it's far too conversational. The last line of the lead needs to be in a different paragraph, and all of the paragraphs need to be broken up a little more. Paragraph length didn't seem critical until I saw the piece in newspaper format. The long blocks of text are intimidating to readers. Beyond that, it could do with some sentences tightened and the rhythm within some sentences improved.

WRITING AND REVISING STRATEGIES

Gathered here are three interactive sections for you to use as you write and revise your opinion piece.

▶ Writer's Notebook Suggestions

▶ Peer-Editing Log

▶ Revision Checklist

Writer's Notebook Suggestions

Many writers informally jot down their ideas and refine their thinking in notebooks that they keep handy. This compilation of suggestions for writing and thinking can be used to generate ideas at any point as you write your opinion piece.

1. Write an e-mail message to convince a friend to transfer to your college. Think about what would best convince him or her to make such a big change.

2. Cut out political cartoons or opinion pieces that attract your attention, and paste them into your notebook.

3. Make a list of issues that appear on the editorial page of a local newspaper during the course of a week. Star the ones you find interesting.

4. List policies at your college that you think should change. Choose one, and write a letter to the college president arguing against the policy or for a revised policy. Remember to consider the president's point of view.

5. Write an e-mail message to the student government president taking a stand on a campus controversy.

6. Read an editorial in today's local or school newspaper. Write the lead and thesis of a letter or column in response to the editorial, furthering the writer's argument or disagreeing with the editorial.

7. You've been hired as a speechwriter for a candidate running for the student senate. The candidate has been asked to deliver a ten-minute speech on a proposed 5 percent tuition hike. Outline a draft of this speech for your candidate, taking a stand for or against the hike.

8. The president of your college or university has asked you to serve as student consultant for a speech that proposes a 5 percent tuition hike. Write an outline for the president's speech, aiming to convince students of the importance of raising tuition.

9. Draw a political cartoon that presents your opinion on an issue about which you feel strongly.

Peer-Editing Log

As you work with a writing partner or in a peer-editing group, you can use these questions to give useful responses to a classmate's opinion piece and as a guide for discussion.

Writer's Name
_____

Date
_____

1. Identify the lead. Did it get your attention? Why? What might make it stronger?

2. Underline the thesis in the paper you are reading. Is the writer's opinion clear? Could you suggest better wording?

3. Do you understand the issue the writer discusses? What other information might you need?

4. Put a star next to the main points of the writer's argument. Do they support the thesis? Can you suggest other points the writer might consider?

5. How effectively does the writer appeal to the reader's heart or mind? Are there places that could use facts, statistics, opinions, anecdotes, or testimonials?

6. Can you identify any problems with logic? How could the writer solve those problems?

7. Does the writer effectively acknowledge opposing views? Are those opposing views countered well?

8. Does the writer end strongly? Is there a call to action? What might make the conclusion more effective?

9. Comment on the writer's voice. Is it appropriate for the kind of opinion piece? Are there places where the writing bogs down? Could you suggest some places to insert stronger verbs or livelier language?

Revision Checklist

As you do your final revision, check to make sure that you

❏ Wrote an engaging lead

❏ Stated your thesis clearly and accurately

❏ Provided necessary background information

❏ Acknowledged and refuted counterarguments, if necessary

❏ Made clear points that supported your argument

❏ Used facts, statistics, examples, anecdotes, or testimonials to support your arguments

❏ Appealed to your reader's intellect and emotions

❏ Did not commit any fallacies in logic

❏ Wrote with clarity and conviction

❏ Concluded strongly, perhaps with a call to action

8. PROPOSALS

WRITING FOR YOUR COMMUNITY

When you sit down to write, you must have one clear goal in your mind. What is the ONE thing you want your reader [or] funder to remember?

— Garland Waller

ASSIGNMENT

Write a three- to five-page proposal that suggests a fresh way to help solve a local, community, or global public problem. Your proposal might take the form of a grant proposal, a letter requesting funding or other support for a program, an editorial or article that proposes a solution to a specific problem, or an Internet petition that lobbies for a specific change. Organize your proposal into three sections.

- Problem
- Solution
- Benefits

Proposals are often written by teams such as groups of citizens or staff members. You can make this a group project and experience the kind of debate and compromise that goes into the process of effecting social change.

Walkers raise money for breast cancer research.

PROPOSALS

A community group in a small town has taken on a project called Teddy Bears on Patrol. The group will provide teddy bears to the local police department. Police officers, in turn, will give the bears to upset or traumatized children who may have been involved in traffic accidents or domestic violence.

A high school student in a suburban community has helped found the Teen Action Board. The group's goal is to address the issue of sexual assault among high school students. With other teens around her state, she has created the See It and Stop It campaign. The campaign's primary focus is on using teen peer groups to help recognize and stop behavior that can escalate to date rape.

A young woman who grew up in foster homes has spearheaded a campaign to create the Bridges to Independence program to provide transitional housing for eighteen-year-olds who are no longer eligible to live in foster homes. These young adults will be able to stay in this safe environment while being mentored in seeking jobs, filling out college applications, and learning independent living skills.

All of these projects began when individuals or groups identified problems: children traumatized by violence, the alarming incidence of teen date rape, the high rate of homelessness among eighteen-year-olds no longer in the foster care network. The solutions to these problems are all being addressed through specific actions: comforting children with teddy bears, creating a public awareness campaign, and creating transitional housing for eighteen-year-old former foster children.

Community service proposals offer plans to solve these kinds of problems. The purpose of any proposal is to persuade readers to take some action: to donate time or money or to create a program, plan, or public service campaign. Proposals have to provide readers with compelling and logical reasons to take the suggested action. Most proposals identify a problem, suggest a feasible solution, and present the benefits of the solution.

Writing proposals is enormously useful work, and the ability to write successful proposals is highly prized. This chapter focuses on proposals concerning public issues. You will have the opportunity to think about problems in the public arena that you believe need to be fixed and work to find real solutions to those problems. Research will help you discover

How Images Persuade

Study these posters from the website that accompanies the "See It and Stop It" campaign.

- What is the focal point of each poster?

- What emotions are conveyed by the central photographs? How are these emotions communicated to the viewer?

- What emotions do the visuals appeal to?

- How do the words on the posters enhance the visuals? Would the visuals be effective alone?

- What message is the poster presenting to the viewer?

- How persuasive do you find these posters?

261

Warm-Up Practice 8.1
Collaborative Activity

Assume that your college has just received a donation from a wealthy alumnus to fund a community service project. The college president has created the President's Service Commission to decide which project should be funded. The commission has asked student groups, including yours, to come up with ideas for worthy projects. All the groups will present their ideas to the commission.

1. Create a list of at least five projects that would benefit your college or local community.

2. Choose the one project you think is most important, and prepare a brief position statement that
 • States the problem the funding will solve
 • Proposes how the money will be used
 • Predicts the benefits to the group and the community

3. Present your proposal to the President's Service Commission. You have only five minutes for your presentation. Keep in mind that the audience includes all the other groups advocating for their projects to be funded.

which solutions have been tried in the past and which are feasible in the present.

The problems you choose are up to you. They can be local to your college campus, perhaps student safety after dark. They can involve your town or city, such as groundwater pollution caused by lawn fertilizer or rock salt de-icer. Or the problems might be global, like hunger or disease in Third World countries. Whatever problem you choose to help solve, you will engage in a valuable process—one that helps create change in some aspect of community life, whether local or global.

Applications: School, Community, Work

Because many school, community, and work situations call for writing proposals, knowing how to write successful ones is a skill well worth learning. Many academic courses require students to use the basic proposal form—problem, solution, benefits—to write papers. A sociology professor asks students to identify a current social problem and propose two or three solutions, showing the benefits of each. Other courses require students to write proposals for major research projects, presenting the problems they plan to address and the way they will research the topics. In honors programs and graduate school, students propose topics for their theses.

Communities unite to solve problems all the time, and many of these efforts begin with proposals. For example, a citizen's action committee in a town or city that wants to help homeless people writes a proposal to the civic leaders who allocate money. Community leaders have written proposals to rezone land for conservation purposes and to fund local mentoring programs for troubled teens. Very often, citizens propose solutions to local problems in letters to the editor and guest editorials in community newspapers.

In the workplace, proposal writing and problem solving go hand-in-hand. Businesspeople write proposals inviting investors to fund projects. Scientists propose research to foundations or corporations in return for income to pay researchers' salaries and obtain equipment. An independent filmmaker might propose a documentary to the National Endowment for the Arts or write a letter to private funders. Nonprofit organizations have proposal writers on staff writing to foundations to obtain grants that support their work. Educators write proposals to conference committees, hoping for an opportunity to share research, and they propose their ideas for articles and books to editors and publishers.

CHAPTER OBJECTIVES

In this chapter you will learn to

► find solutions to identified problems

► support your solutions with good reasons

► research and tailor your writing to a specific audience

UNDERSTANDING PROPOSAL WRITING

As in "Teddy Bears on Patrol," the "See It and Stop It" campaign, and "Bridges to Independence," a community service project often begins with a specific problem. Once you identify a problem, you have to come up with a feasible solution, then inform and persuade readers to accept your proposal.

Identifying a Problem

Unfortunately, it is not all that difficult to identify a worthwhile issue for your proposal. Think about global problems like pollution, hunger, human rights violations, and underfunded medical research, or local problems like homelessness, lack of college scholarships for underprivileged students, and the need for bicycle lanes in your community. Find a problem that matters to you.

Tackling a huge problem can be overwhelming, however. How can you find solutions to world hunger or war or global warming when scientists and politicians around the world have failed? One way to create a manageable topic is to keep it narrow or local. Keep your goals realistic and feasible. For example, human rights violations are a vast global problem but one that you might be interested in helping to solve. To define the problem more narrowly, select a particular aspect or perhaps even a particular case.

One student group wanted to help eradicate human rights violations. The students began searching the Web using the keyword "human rights violations." They discovered countries in which people are still enslaved. As they continued their search, they found the Christian Solidarity International (CSI) organization, which is actively working to end slavery in Sudan. They decided to narrow their focus to creating a public awareness and fundraising campaign in their communities. Helping CSI end slavery in Sudan became the focus of their community service proposal.

Formulating a Clear and Feasible Solution

When you write a proposal, you are not lodging a complaint but are instead presenting a plan of action. In an editorial or other opinion piece, you iden-

Practice 8.2
Identifying a Problem for Your Proposal

Writing a proposal about a public issue allows you to suggest ways to make life better for yourself and others in your school, in your community, or in society at large. Often proposals originate in anger at injustice, unfairness, or lack of understanding. It is useful to begin thinking about proposing changes in public policy by determining what things anger you enough to want to devote time and energy to finding a solution.

1. Make a list of five things in your personal life that make you angry.

2. Make a list of five things about college life that make you angry.

3. Make a list of five things in society that make you angry.

4. Look over your fifteen items, and star those you think you could change.

5. Choose the item that most interests you,

6. Write that item on the top of a piece of paper and brainstorm ways you could effect that change.

Children trick-or-treating
for UNICEF.

tify a problem and write an argument to change people's minds or behaviors.
But proposal writers go one step farther; they present a clear and feasible
solution, a plan that is doable.

Formulating a preliminary plan on how to solve the problem helps you
focus your thinking and research. You may refine or even change your approach as you gather information. But generating ideas early in the process
and putting them into clear language helps you see their possibilities as well
as their limitations. Once you have a plan in mind, test its feasibility by asking these questions.

▶ Does this plan actually solve the identified problem?

▶ Can this plan be accomplished with the resources I have or can get?

▶ Can this plan be accomplished within the time I have?

▶ Has this plan been tried before?

No simple blueprint exists for coming up with a creative solution, though it is always useful to begin by researching the issue. Read about the issue. Find out what has been done in the past. Talk to other people about the problem and past solutions. Freewrite to discover what you think about the issue. In other words, coming up with a possible solution starts with analyzing the problem.

Let's say you read a newspaper article about the lack of interest in environmental issues, especially among low-income city youth. Being an environmental activist, you decide that you want to ensure that today's young people become educated and involved. You think that the first step could be to involve urban kids in outdoor adventures. One plan is to provide city youth with outdoor experiences, taking them on biking, hiking, and camping trips. What resources would you need to implement this plan? You might come up with this list.

- Volunteers from your campus outdoor club
- Support from parents and teachers
- Donations of bikes and camping equipment from local businesses

What activities will help kids understand the importance of preserving wilderness? What equipment will you need? Are enough people willing to work with you so that you can get the program running by summer vacation? The answers to those questions will help you decide on the feasibility of your plan.

Providing Reasons

Why should your reader accept your proposal? You have to provide compelling reasons, and you have to think about the possible downsides so as to counter possible objections. Generate as many reasons as you can, more than you will be able to use, to make sure you have considered all possibilities. Weed out the weak reasons, and select the ones that will be most persuasive.

One way to generate reasons is to analyze the problem. Break the problem down into its parts, and consider the different aspects. Working on the environmental education proposal, for example, you might think about what would compel parents, teachers, local businesses, and volunteers to support outdoor adventures for low-income city kids. Your list might be similar to this:

1. Provides lessons in personal responsibility, achievement, and environmental awareness.
2. Helps kids develop practical skills and have fun.
3. Keeps low-income city kids away from gangs, drugs, and violence.

**Practice 8.3
Creating Feasible Solutions**

Create a feasible plan to help solve one of the following problems. List some resources you might need to accomplish that plan.

- Commuter students on your campus do not feel that they are part of campus life.
- The arts budget has been cut in elementary schools in your community.
- Summer residents of a beach community abandon their pets at the end of tourist season.
- On your college campus or in your town, three people have been robbed while waiting for a bus over the past year.
- The local food pantry will run out of money next month.

Practice 8.4
Providing Reasons

1. Reread the six reasons for supporting outdoor adventures, and put them in order from strongest to weakest. Give reasons for your decisions.

2. Think of the different audiences: parents, teachers, local businesses, volunteer group leaders. Which of the reasons would you use to persuade each of these audiences? Explain your decisions.

3. What objections might someone have to any of these reasons?

4. What other reasons can you think of to support this proposal? Try to come up with at least three more.

4. Provides guidance from supportive adults.

5. Helps kids get individualized attention.

6. Boosts self-esteem while kids learn about their role in protecting the environment.

—Rachel Kleinman, "Trips for Kids Proposal"

RESEARCH PATHS

Facts, statistics, and studies show the seriousness and scope of your problem. Anecdotes and quotations can add a human face to your proposal. To be fully prepared to present your solution, you have to research two things: your audience and your issue.

Researching Your Audience

Who has the authority to grant what you are seeking? This is the person or persons to whom you address your proposal. You might propose a change that requires support from the college community—for example, a student volunteer program to mentor local schoolchildren, collect used books for a literacy program, or help feed the homeless people in your area. You should be able to find the person in the college administration who is responsible for that area, perhaps a dean or director.

The community group working on the Bears on Patrol proposal might decide to target community leaders to sponsor a fundraiser or local toy stores to donate teddy bears. Proposals to help solve global social problems, like slavery in Sudan, can be directed to one of a number of nonprofit organizations already engaged in that area. In this case, the students addressed Christian Solidarity International, an organization working specifically in Sudan. You can often find the names of heads of organizations in a telephone directory, a Web search, or a simple phone call.

Familiarize yourself with the group that will read your proposal. Knowing the assumptions, philosophy, and history of your audience helps you understand possible obstacles. Why would audience members resist your proposal? Why would they embrace it?

Persuading someone to say yes to a proposal requires some understanding of an organization's work. The mission of an organization or agency is the top priority of its administrators, so you need to show how your proposal fits with that mission. Most organizations and foundations have mission statements that you can study on their websites or in their promotional materials. Before you write your proposal, make sure you have thoroughly researched the organization's mission and philosophy.

You also have to do some research around past efforts to solve the identified problem before you can propose your approach. Sometimes it is useful to interview a person in the organization, especially in the publicity department, to find out what the organization has accomplished and to see how it has targeted specific issues or particular populations. Become an expert on the group or individual who will read your proposal, and present yourself as someone who is not just knowledgeable, reasonable, and logical but also useful to the organization.

Researching the Issue: Facts, Statistics, and Studies

Facts, statistics, and studies make the abstractions of your ideas concrete and give context to the issues. In their research about the problem of slavery in Sudan, for example, the students found statistics from Amnesty International and the United Nations on the number of civilians who have suffered as a result of civil war in Sudan.

> Civilians are the ones who suffer the most. Amnesty International estimates that more than two million people have died so far in the South alone. According to the United Nations, 700,000 are considered to be under a threat of death and 4.5 million have been driven away from their homes.
>
> —Dana Benjamin, Joanna Mayhew, Alexandra Mayer-Hohdahl, and Peter Myers, "Proposal to Help End Slavery in Sudan"

These numbers, from highly reputable sources, show the scope of the problem and the context in which the enslavement of civilians occurs.

In an article about Bridges to Independence, the writer lists studies that prove that "homelessness and foster care intersect at that alarming point in social research where the problem is clearly documented."

> A 1988 study of homeless persons in Lexington, Kentucky determined that 16 percent had been in foster care, more that four times the rate for the general population. A federally funded study by Westat, Inc. in the late 1980s found that 25 percent of the emancipated youth had experienced at least one night of homelessness. A 1997 study of Wisconsin discharged foster youth indicated that 12 percent reported at least one experience of street or shelter homelessness.
>
> —Susan Kellam, "Give 'Em Shelter"

Practice 8.5
Researching Your Audience

Solve these research problems.

1. You want to write a proposal to post nutritional information in the student union or cafeteria. Find the name and e-mail address of the person in charge.

2. You want to send a letter supporting a proposal to create a food pantry in your hometown. Find the name and e-mail address of your local representative in the state legislature.

3. You want to locate a local environmental group. Find the names of the environmental groups active in your area. Get contact information for one group.

4. You are interested in finding out more about national service, and you know that AmeriCorps has a number of programs. Find the name and local contact information for at least one AmeriCorps program.

5. You are proposing that a local elementary school set up an e-mail pen pal program, pairing American students with kids from Europe, Asia, and Africa. Find out whether such a program already exists. Provide the names of existing programs and contact information.

6. Explain how you found the answers to each of these problems: whether in a print source or online, or by asking a knowledgeable person.

In a proposal for a child-care center at Northwestern University, writers use statistics to reveal the costs of private babysitting to help put the benefits of providing quality child care at the university into context. These statistics help make the abstract idea that child care is expensive more concrete.

> The combined impact of market forces and government regulation brings the total costs (with taxes) of hiring a full-time babysitter to $25,000, at a minimum. Those listed with employment agencies have salary expectations of $350–$500 per week, often with room and board expected as well. The pressure to provide health insurance adds further to the total cost of employment.
>
> —"Proposal for On-Campus Child Care at Northwestern University"

Facts, statistics, and studies go a long way toward making the issues understandable and putting the problem in a context. But how do you go about finding them?

First, consider who knows about the statistics. Who would know how many civilians have died in Sudan, the number of homeless people who have been in foster care, or how much it costs to provide daycare for children? Chances are that some international agency, government group, or university has researched many of the topics you will write about.

Digging up statistics relies in part on your intuition and common sense. Wouldn't Amnesty International know about global human rights violations? Wouldn't social scientists study homeless populations? Wouldn't a university have considered the costs of daycare centers? You can try Internet searches for organizations with expertise on the issues you are writing about, or you can enter the name of the issue in a search engine and see which groups or agencies have studied the problem. As always, make sure your sources are reputable and credible. (See Chapter 14 for specific criteria on evaluating sources.)

Researching might also include contacting people or groups involved in similar projects. For example, Teddy Bears on Patrol projects can be found in many towns across the United States. The citizens' group that decided to institute the program in its community e-mailed other groups across the country and got some useful ideas. One idea was to ask the local Eagle Scouts to adopt Teddy Bears on Patrol as a merit-badge project.

In researching your topic, look for places your plan might run into problems. One student group proposed a seemingly simple solution to feeding the local homeless population: pack up leftover food from student dining halls and bring it to homeless shelters. However, they discovered a serious impediment to this plan when interviewing the head of food services. He told them that the college was legally responsible for the quality of the food and that anyone who got sick could sue for damages. If the group had submitted the proposal before thoroughly researching the plan, this group would have been turned down immediately. Instead, the students altered their proposal to include a release form from the shelter absolving the college of legal responsibility, showing that their plan was fully developed down to the last detail. This kind of care in researching helps prepare you to face any hesitations your audience might have about accepting your proposal.

Researching the Issue: Anecdotes, Quotations, and Visuals

Your research will help you find facts, statistics, and studies that provide logical support for your reasons. But the most persuasive reasons often combine logical and emotional appeals. Anecdotes, quotations, and visuals can provide the human face of an issue and bring home your point more compellingly. The "Bridges to Independence" article focuses on one young woman's story.

> A terrified young woman in Los Angeles walks into a lit office building because she has nowhere else to go. She's a decent kid and knows what it is like to be out there, having spent the better part of her 18 years bouncing between temporary homes. Later, after 18 months in transitional housing to dust herself off, and acquire the skills necessary to live independently, she emerges with a part-time job, her own apartment and a twenty-yard dash toward a nursing diploma.
>
> —Susan Kellam, "Give 'Em Shelter"

The proposal to fund the environmental education program for low-income youth includes a number of quotations from kids who have been on such trips. One elementary school student wrote this after a trip.

> I like how you took time out to ride with us people, and thank you for not giving up on me. And I like how you said, "Keep on going Edric."
>
> —Rachel Kleinman, "Trips for Kids Proposal"

A number of proposals include photographs that illustrate the issue. Turn to the "Foster Parrots Proposal" on pages 274–277 to see pictures of the abandoned parrots this group has rescued. Focusing on an individual example, telling a story, or giving a voice or face to a problem helps persuade a reader already hooked by facts and statistics. Logic and emotion combine to create a powerful case for any proposal. It is well worth the work to research your proposal issues as thoroughly as possible.

Practice 8.6
Generating Research Ideas

Choose one of the proposals below. Make a list of the kinds of research that would help you show the seriousness and scope of the problem. What facts, statistics, studies, anecdotes, quotations, and/or visuals would you want to find? First review this example.

Example: Creating a hotline for troubled teens.

• Data on how many hotlines exist in nearby areas

• Anecdote about how a hotline has helped a specific teen

• Quotation from a counselor

• Quotation from a teen who was helped

• Studies about the usefulness of hotlines

• Expert opinion from psychologist about effectiveness of hotlines

• Costs of operating a hotline

Choose a proposal from this list.

• Creating an antiviolence campaign on your campus

• Raising money for a local homeless shelter

• Advocating for twenty-four-hour public transportation

• Lobbying against using live animals in science classrooms

• Creating a public awareness campaign about juvenile diabetes

ANATOMY OF A PROPOSAL

Proposals come in many forms: formal grant proposals, letters to agencies or funders, editorials or articles that propose solutions to problems, and public petitions that lobby for change. "Stopping Teen Dating Violence" by student Jessica Hollander launched the See It and Stop It campaign in Massachusetts during the fall of 2003. Read the annotated article, noting the way Hollander presents the three typical elements in a proposal: problem, solution, and benefits.

Stopping Teen Dating Violence

JESSICA HOLLANDER

Intro: Problem Statement

Everyone would like to believe that sexual assault or domestic violence happens only to someone else, somewhere else. We think of the perpetrator or even the victim as a faceless person one reads about in the papers. — *Summary of problem*

Unfortunately, statistics show otherwise. One in five female high school students in Massachusetts report being physically and/or sexually abused by a dating partner. Think of five teenagers you care about. Your daughter. Your little sister. Your best friend. Chances are they'll be affected by dating violence. It can be physical, emotional, or sexual. It starts with power and control. It starts early in our lives. And it happens everywhere. — *Statistic*

When I was a sophomore in high school, I learned this the hard way. An old boyfriend and close friend, one whom I not only trusted but believed I loved, snuck over to my parents' house in the middle of the night. Like many young girls do too often, I sacrificed my own personal safety in the pursuit of what I thought was "romance." That night I sacrificed much more. — *Personal Story*

When other students hear my story, they are surprised because I am not how they pictured a "typical" survivor. I lived in an affluent neighborhood, attended one of the best public school systems in the country, in a city that not only promotes but demands social awareness. I have a wonderful, caring, and intimate family and friends.

Because I was so convinced that I was immune to these dangers, so certain that this individual would never consider hurting me, I ignored the warning signs, my very own intuition telling me something was wrong. I learned the hard way to follow your instincts and speak up, whether it's for your own safety or the safety of a friend. My friends and his friends ignored the signs too.

Teens need to be given more tangible tools, phrases, and words in our own language that we can use. And we need to have the confidence to know that if something in a relationship *looks or feels wrong*, it probably is.

The Teen Action Campaign is the long overdue vehicle to provide such tools to teens. For the past two years, I have been working with other teens from across the state to create the "See it and Stop it" campaign. We chose to launch in October for Domestic Violence Awareness month.

Because friends are such a major influence in teens' lives, the focus on by-standers is one of the main strengths of the campaign. Seeitandstopit.org asks teens to recognize the warning signs, be it jealousy, possessiveness, etc., in their friends' relationships and prevent them from escalating into a hazardous situation. The actions can be small, but can have a powerful impact.

We must all accept responsibility for the overwhelming presence of sexual assault and domestic violence in today's world. This is not *just* a woman's issue. Men of all ages must encourage each other *not* to be a man that women fear, *but instead* be a man that women can trust.

Those of us who helped create the "See it and Stop it" campaign are convinced that our generation has the power to speak up and change attitudes about gender violence before it becomes entrenched. But it takes resources and the support of everyone in our lives: parents, educators, faith-based leaders, philanthropists and government.

We had the help of the best experts and research in the country and the pro bono support of Hill Holliday Advertising, which took our ideas and made them into TV, radio, outdoor, print ads, posters for schools and our website. We were supported by local philanthropists and corporations who shared our belief that we can end relationship violence as we know it. As we launch in Massachusetts, we've learned our campaign will be picked up nationally, by the Ad Council and Family Violence Prevention Fund.

After my assault, my friends and I became vigilant in our daily activities to prevent such tragedy from occurring again. Simple things, like checking in with one another at parties, staying in groups, calling one another, and saying something out loud when something didn't feel right, became automatic.

Such precautions and social awareness can make the world a safer place for all of us. Check out our campaign, so the next time you see it, you'll know it. You just might speak up and do something to stop it.

Margin annotations:

- Concept behind campaign
- Concept behind campaign
- Solution
- Body: Solution
- Call to action
- Support for campaign
- Return to Personal Story
- Conclusion
- Benefits

Introduction: Background and Problem Statement

No matter what form it takes, the opening of your proposal should hook your reader's attention, establish your credibility, and make a strong first impression. It should also present and summarize the problem and provide the background information your reader needs to understand the seriousness and scope of the problem.

Jessica Hollander begins her proposal to stop teen dating violence by dispelling a common belief, that "sexual assault or domestic violence happens only to someone else, somewhere else." To prove her point, Hollander cites the statistic that "one in five female students" reports abuse by a dating partner. The human face she puts on this statistic is first hypothetical, "Think of five teenagers you care about" and then quite specific: Hollander herself was abused by someone she dated. By the end of the first section, the first five paragraphs of the piece, Hollander has defined the problem of teen dating violence, has provided context and facts to establish the scope of the problem, and has established her own credibility as someone who cares deeply and personally about this issue.

Body: Solutions

The main text of the proposal presents the solution. You can address one or more of these questions.

▶ What is your concept?

▶ What is your specific plan?

▶ How will your solution help create a plan or program or change people's attitudes or behaviors?

▶ Are there costs? How will you cover them?

The middle section of Hollander's article begins by presenting the concept behind the campaign: teens have to be given "tangible tools" and gain the confidence to speak up against potential abuse. Since peer groups are a strong influence among teens, the campaign's approach is to focus on educating friends to identify warning signs of abuse and to speak up when they see excessive jealousy or possessiveness.

Once she establishes the goals and concept of her plan, Hollander provides ways to support this effort. To end domestic violence, men and women have to work together. To end domestic violence, young people have to "speak up and change attitudes."

Since this is a proposal to bring an already-established program to public awareness, Hollander describes the pro bono support it has received and the various aspects of the public service campaign: "TV, radio, outdoor, print ads, posters for schools and our website." By going to the website, readers can see how the concepts have been put into practice. (Two posters from this campaign appear on page 261.)

Other kinds of proposals require different elements in the solution section.

▶ If your solution is to establish a new program, such as an after-school arts program in a poorly funded school, explain how the program will work. If there are costs involved, list them.

▶ If you are solving a problem through a publicity campaign, such as a campaign to create awareness about health or human rights issues, explain the campaign, describe the publicity materials you plan to develop, and explain the intended impact.

▶ If your solution is a local project, such as creating transitional housing or instituting a recycling program, present your arguments and back them up with research. If your research has turned up a similar project—a neighboring town's or a local college's recycling program—describe it.

No matter how you develop the body of your proposal, remember that you are selling your solution. Describe your vision. Be positive, optimistic, and specific. *This* is what we will do, and *this* is how we will do it. Show your readers that your plan of action is visionary and thorough and that it helps solve the problem you have identified. Be brief. You are selling the concept, not describing every single detail of your plan. When writing a proposal, write concisely but with impact.

Proposal Design

Substance is more important than style, but how your proposal looks on the page is almost as important as what it says. The writing, of course, should be clear and free of typographical and grammatical errors. Here are some general guidelines on presenting your proposal in a professional manner.

- Use white space in the document to create visual appeal. Too much text on a page is hard to read. Keep paragraphs short.

- Limit yourself to one text typeface and one contrasting typeface for titles and subtitles, so that the document does not look cluttered or overly designed.

- Use twelve-point type, since it is the easiest to read.

- Use clear headings, with clear contrast to text type (boldfaced or in a contrasting typeface) to set off different sections and subsections.

- Use bullet points to summarize or list items. Make sure the sentence construction in the bullet points is parallel.

- Use visuals such as graphs, charts, and photographs to break up long text passages and add to the visual appeal of the proposal.

SIDEBAR

Conclusion: Benefits

End by emphasizing the way the proposal will benefit the reader and the general public. What is in it for them? Be persuasive and specific as you present the benefits. Also, be specific about what you want the reader to do. If you want readers to fund a project, make sure you have clearly presented the amount of money you need. If you want your readers to take action—support legislation or organize a charity bike ride, for example—explain exactly what steps you wish them to take. If you want readers to use your publicity campaign, explain your materials, the concept, and audience you are targeting. You might even want to create prototype materials to accompany your proposal. (See Chapter 9.) All these possible approaches have a common goal: to convince the reader of the benefits of accepting your proposal.

The last two paragraphs of Jessica Hollander's article comprise her conclusion. Notice how she brings the issue back to the specific and the personal. "After my assault," she writes, and then describes how she and her friends changed their behavior. Her suggestions are clear and specific; they could serve as models for how to put this plan into action: "checking in with one another at parties, staying in groups, calling one another, and saying something out loud when something didn't feel right." The benefit, "making the world a safer place," is clearly articulated in the final paragraph. The piece ends with a call to action: check out the website and become proactive; by speaking up you may be able to stop violence before it begins.

However you decide to end your proposal, make sure your reader knows how the community would benefit from the plan. If you want readers to do something, be clear, specific, and persuasive in your call to action. The conclusion gives you a final chance to motivate readers.

Foster Parrots Proposal

Karen Lee

Program: Parrot Sanctuary and Rescue Operations
Amount of Request: $10,000

Foster Parrots Ltd. is a 501(C)(3) nonprofit organization that is dedicated to the rescue and sanctuary of abused, unwanted, and languishing companion parrots. We currently care for over 180 parrots at our Rockland, Massachusetts, facility. Though we never turn away a bird in an emergency situation, we have nearly reached full capacity and may soon be forced to accept only those birds that are facing the immediate threat of euthanasia.

We are well aware that many other parrot rescue facilities are experiencing similar overcrowded conditions or have been forced to close their doors to new arrivals altogether. Clearly, we are seeing the start of a parrot overpopulation crisis. As parrot rescue facilities continue to sprout up nationwide only to find themselves swiftly overwhelmed by the immensity of the task at hand, parrot rescue is guaranteed to become a well-known presence in our society.

Unfortunately, we also predict that widespread euthanasia of unwanted parrots will soon become as commonplace as that fate is for our unwanted cats and dogs. IT IS ALREADY HAPPENING. Parrots now outnumber dogs as the second most popular pet in America. We are putting tremendous effort into curbing the tide of tragedy and preventing mass euthanasia from becoming the solution to the unwanted parrot problem.

In an effort to protect parrots both domestically and in their natural habitat, Foster Parrots acts as an educational resource to the local community as well as on a national scale. Some of our programs are as follows.

- **Grade School Education Program** By visiting grade school classrooms with several of our "ambassador birds," we are able to teach children about responsible pet selection and ownership. We also discuss habitat preservation issues as we learn about our ever shrinking rainforests and other amazing yet fragile ecosystems that support parrots and other endangered wild life.

- **Virtual Adoption Program** Available to school classrooms and individuals, for a token donation people are invited to "virtually adopt" a

parrot featured on our web site. Adoptive parents will receive a photo of their bird, a biography, geographical distribution information, and periodic updates.

- **Tufts University Selective Student Program**   By volunteering at Foster Parrots Ltd., students at the Tufts University School of Veterinary Medicine are able to earn college credits while getting hands-on experience in avian care.

- **24-Hour Advice and Information Resource**   By making information and emergency assistance readily available via our 24-Hour Hotline and our Internet web site, we hope to assist people in making the best choices regarding the welfare of their pet birds or in selecting a particular parrot as a pet in the first place. In addition to keeping the public abreast of issues facing pet birds in America, our website provides information on the various birds at Foster Parrots Ltd., outlines our strict requirements for adoption and provides opportunities for "virtual adoption." Visit our web site at www.fosterparrots.com.

- **Rapid-Response Rescue**   Time is of the essence when assistance is needed to retrieve an escaped parrot or to provide rescue services to birds in abusive or unwanted situations. Neither the MSPCA nor the Animal Rescue League of Boston is prepared to help when there is an escaped bird in New England. Foster Parrots Ltd. is available as an emergency parrot rescue resource.

To continue our work, we must procure adequate funding. As a true no-kill rescue facility, we are well aware that many of the residents here will be with us for life. This is a responsibility we gladly accept, for we are vehemently dedicated to improving the lives of these once unwanted parrots.

General operating support of $10,000 from the Foundation would ensure the availability of funds for medical care, food, and supplies and help strengthen our local rescue efforts, community education programs, and national parrot welfare campaigns. Our feeding expenses alone now total over $1,200 per month.

The success of our efforts will be measured in the ability of Foster Parrots Ltd. to maintain high standards of care within our sanctuary and improve in areas where we may fall short. Our success will also become apparent as our efforts to educate people about parrots start to impact the currently accepted standards of parrot care, breeding, and marketing.

We hope that the Foundation will find our work to be a valuable contribution as we continue to preserve the lives and the dignity of these intelligent and sensitive creatures. We thank you for taking the time to review our proposal and learn about our organization.

Annotate "Foster Parrots Proposal"

1. Bracket the introduction.

2. Put a wavy line under the phrase that explains the organization's mission.

3. Underline the sentences in the introduction that define the problems that this organization is working to solve.

4. What solution is presented in the body of this proposal? Rank the programs presented in the bullet points on a scale of 1 to 5, with 1 being the program that you think would be most persuasive to a potential funder.

5. Find one example of logical appeal and one of emotional appeal in this proposal. Mark them *L* or *E*.

6. Bracket the conclusion.

7. Put a wavy line under any sentences or phrases that discuss the benefits of this proposal.

8. Underline the specific request made in the conclusion.

READINGS

The readings show the variety of forms that proposals can take: a neighborhood group proposing a partnership with a teddy bear manufacturer to help local police calm traumatized children; a student-written proposal to help end slavery in Sudan; and a funding request for an independent documentary film about the impact of custody decisions on children in abusive homes. These proposals have one thing in common; they are proposing feasible solutions to important social problems.

911 Bears Program Proposal

The Pine Tree Neighborhood Group

The Bears on Patrol campaign is a national effort to provide local police with teddy bears that will help comfort children who are caught in traumatic situations. Citizens in the small town of Milton, Massachusetts, created a neighborhood group to bring this national program to their community. They called their version the 911 Bears Program. As a first step, they decided to write a proposal asking a national manufacturer of teddy bears to partner with the program and create low-cost, child-safe teddy bears.

To: The American Teddy Bear Company
From: Pine Tree Neighborhood Group

Problem

Red lights flashing, strangers in uniforms, voices you can't recognize. Imagine how terrifying an emergency situation is to children who may have witnessed a traffic accident or violence in their own homes. Now imagine you are the police officer trying to assist that frightened child— a situation police encounter surprisingly often. Last year alone, police officers in our quiet, suburban town with a population of 25,000, reported that they made over 500 calls involving children. This figure is typical, as police officers find children on the periphery or in the center of one out of every five calls they answer. Officers can tell you the toughest part of their job on those calls was trying to get the children to trust them. They admit that more than firearms or handcuffs or radios, what they could use most at those moments is a teddy bear. Police also find the bears useful when comforting elderly people. We don't have to tell you about the universal appeal—and power to comfort—of teddy bears since Vermont Teddy Bear is the largest maker of handcrafted teddy bears in the United States.

Community groups across the nation are organizing drives to collect bears for "Bears on Patrol" programs, hoping to help police comfort children in crisis. A search on the Internet will reveal links to programs in California, Washington, Kansas, Arkansas, Iowa, Georgia, Michigan, and many other states—essentially, coast to coast. These programs are well established too, with some of them originating as far back as 1990.

One community near ours with a "Bears on Patrol" program keeps a stockpile of 500 bears stored at the Hanson, Massachusetts police head-quarters. Police officer Mark Vigneau said the bears "keep the kids' minds off the stress and make it a whole lot easier to get them to let us help." Officer Vigneau told a local paper about how one bear actually helped him respond to a child in a medical emergency. The child was having an asthma attack: "The child had a hard time breathing but was crying, which was scary because his condition could have become worse," Vigneau said. "The most important thing was keeping the child calm, and the bear helped." (*The Quincy Patriot Ledger*, "Bears on Board," Joe McGee, January 15, 2002)

Solutions

Our town is currently starting up what we call a 911 Bears Program, our version of Bears on Patrol. We project our program will require a start-up supply of 500 bears, which will need to be replenished yearly. Our fear is that enthusiasm for the program will wane as keeping supplied with bears will mean continually asking for donations of bears. Additionally, the bears we might collect will have to be child-safe: no buttons or parts that might endanger a toddler. Finding safe bears is an obstacle we are encountering as we assemble our program. That is why we are approaching you at Vermont Teddy Bear Company. We would like to propose that you produce a low-cost, child-safe bear that we can purchase to help establish our program as well as keep it going.

The Importance of Child-safe Bears   As our group started planning collections and bear drives, the president of a local ambulance company approached us with her concern that children might be given bears that could have pieces small children could swallow. She added that bears collected by toy-drives might have sat in musty places like attics or basements, collecting allergens that could be aggravate some medical emergencies, citing a child in the middle of an asthma attack as an example. Though most Bears on Patrol programs collect bears from the public, we think this might be unsafe, and that is why we have looked for a high-quality product, one such as a Vermont Teddy Bear. These new bears would be stored wrapped, thus keeping them clean.

The Availability of Low-Cost Bears   Some groups have been able to encounter a close-out sale, or have made deals to get bears at wholesale prices through drug store chains such as CVS. These are usually one-time deals, with the organizers having to find a new supplier of quality bears to replenish supplies. If you become a partner with Teddy Bears on Patrol programs across the country, communities will be able to purchase bears all the time.

Benefits

Once you manufacture these child-safe, low-cost bears, you can produce a teddy bear for all the Bears on Patrol programs across the US, thus linking the American-made Vermont Teddy Bears with comfort for children in crisis, as you have before, but on a much larger and more powerful scale. Vermont Teddy Bears were associated with helping children during the September 11 tragedy, when you gave hundreds of bears to children who lost loved ones in New York, Pennsylvania, and Washington, D.C. Your company has also made national news when your president, Elisabeth Robert, was honored by the Small Business Administration at a national ceremony in Washington as one of the nation's 53 most outstanding leaders of small businesses. Already widely known for your hand-made, quality teddy bears, you can expand your leadership into nationwide community service by providing a bear that will patrol with police officers.

Your partnership in this cause will assure communities that they will be able to get new bears of an excellent quality at low-cost whenever their supplies dwindle. Bears will be available to police departments into the future, with a minimum of organizational effort, thus making the programs easy to maintain, and the Bears on Patrol programs permanent additions to community policing. More communities will be able to get involved, helping an even larger number of children through crises.

In return, Vermont Teddy Bear Company will broaden its name recognition and be immediately associated with helping children through crises. The headline can read: Police armed with Vermont Teddy Bears Help Children Across the U.S.

Conclusion

Children are often innocently and unwittingly wedged deep inside situations involving police intervention. The sad statistics about children involved in domestic violence and abuse, for example, are undeniable. Children find themselves in need of help, perhaps even rescue, by police officers in other dangerous situations like car accidents and house fires. Police are often the first to arrive on the scene of medical emergencies like the asthma attack described earlier. These crisis moments may seem rare and uncommon, but they aren't, as police describe 20–25% of their calls involving children in some way. This does not even account for calls that might involve the elderly, the mentally handicapped, or other adults who might be calmed with a bear.

Vermont Teddy Bear Company can make an enormous contribution by becoming partners with communities that want to put a teddy bear in every police car.

Works Consulted

LeDu, Jessica. "Teddy Bears Used by Police to Calm Traumatized Victims." *Kansas State Collegian*, September 19, 2000.

McGee, Joe. "Bears on Patrol." *Quincy Patriot Ledger*, January 15, 2002.

United States Small Business Administration. "Elisabeth Roberts Chosen SBA's Small Business Person of the Year." Press release, January 28, 2004.

Critical Reading Questions

1. What technique do the writers use in the introduction to capture readers' attention? How effective do you find the introduction in capturing attention and defining the problem?

2. What kind of research did the writers do to establish the problem statement?

3. What kind of research did the writers do to learn about their audience? Where does this research become apparent?

4. How clearly stated is the solution? Explain the solution in a sentence. Is it feasible?

5. How do the writers explain the benefits for the community? For the manufacturer?

6. Identify appeals to logic and to emotion. How do the writers establish their own credibility?

7. What techniques do the writers use in the conclusion? What final image is left with the reader? How effective is this conclusion?

Questions for Writing and Discussion

1. If this group consulted you and asked for ideas to strengthen the proposal, what suggestions would you make?

2. Assuming that Vermont Teddy Bears agreed to this proposal, how might you get public attention focused on the Bears on Patrol program?

3. What other programs might help police comfort children caught in crisis situations?

Proposal to Help End Slavery in Sudan

Dana Benjamin,
Joanna Mayhew,
Alexandra Mayer-Hohdahl, and
Peter Myers

This student group proposed a media campaign to increase public awareness of the plight of enslaved people in Sudan. The students created this poster as an illustration of the public awareness campaign they describe in the proposal.

DANA BENJAMIN, JOANNA MAYHEW
ALEXANDRA MAYER-HOHDAHL AND PETER MYERS

BOSTON UNIVERSITY

May 7, 2005

Christian Solidarity International
870 Hampshire Road, Suite 7
Westlake Village, CA 91361

Dear Sir or Madam:

While researching nonprofit organizations, we came across Christian Solidarity International, and your case immediately sparked our interest. We feel that our campaign will raise awareness for the problem of slavery in Sudan.

In the following proposal, we have put together a public-service campaign for both print and television.

Sincerely yours,

Dana, Joanna, Alexandra, and Peter

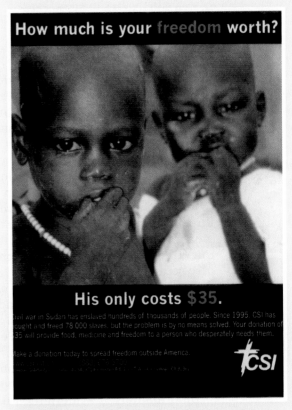

This poster accompanied the students' proposal for Christian Solidarity International.

DANA BENJAMIN, JOANNA MAYHEW
ALEXANDRA MAYER-HOHDAHL AND PETER MYERS
BOSTON UNIVERSITY

Proposal: A Public-Service Campaign for Christian Solidarity International to Raise Awareness of the Problem of Slavery in Sudan

1. Problem

The United Nations Universal Declaration of Human Rights states, "No one shall be held in slavery." However, slavery is still an every-day threat for a number of people around the world. Sudan, Africa's largest country, cannot provide complete protection for its inhabitants. A war-torn nation for decades, Sudan has become a scene of ethnic and religious discrimination.

The mainly black and Christian south regularly faces the Islamic north in bloody battles. Civilians are the ones who suffer the most. Amnesty International estimates that more than two million people have died so far in the south alone. According to the United Nations, 700,000 are considered to be under a threat of death, and 4.5 million have been driven away from their homes.

In addition to these overwhelming statistics, a new trend in warfare has appeared in the north's strategy. Soldiers, equipped with the most modern arms supplied by the northern government, regularly raid villages in the south. They are not only looking for loot: they are also searching for slaves.

Tens of thousands of children and women are abducted, forced to walk several days to the north, and then sold into bondage under conditions that go against all human rights. These slaves are mistreated physically and psychologically. Severe beatings, rape, female genital mutilation, death threats, torture, and forced conversion to Islam are the norm. The stories and testimonies they bring back, along with the bruises and scars, are proof enough.

Unfortunately, the international community has turned a blind eye to what is happening in Sudan. Their intervention is needed to stop the northern regime, based in Khartoum, from leading a so-called Jihad against the south. A sanction against companies doing business with or in Sudan had been considered by the United States, but this sanction has been forgotten in the midst of the antiterrorist work it is now involved in. In September 2001, the United Nations Security Council lifted its sanctions. Sudan is now to become part of the "civilized" world, even though such barbaric actions are still taking place.

Slavery and the actions of the Sudanese government remain a crucial violation of human rights. It is essential for the international community to react to this violation and apply pressure on the Khartoum regime to make sure it stops its inhuman warfare strategies. In addition, it is important to lend our support to nonprofit and nongovernmental organizations that fight slavery, CSI being one of the only ones to do so in Sudan.

2. Context

It is impossible to determine exactly how many people have been enslaved since the beginning of the civil war in Sudan. Yet the slave trade has been documented over and over again by journalists—from *Newsweek*, *Time*, *ZDF*, and *3-SAT*, to name but a few—especially over the last years, when the organizations involved in Sudan have brought them into the country.

Today, CSI is one of the few nongovernmental organizations that remain in Sudan. A similar American organization, Christian Freedom International, was recently forced to discontinue its practice of buying back the slaves' freedom because of international pressure and criticism. Indeed, it has been said that organizations such as CSI only end up helping the slave traders to make more money. Still, CSI continues its work and is thinking of expanding its program.

Actions at a more global international level include the proposed Sudan Peace Act, which would stop companies that do business with Sudan from receiving any U.S. capital. However, this treaty now faces an uncertain future, as the United States is looking for allies among Islamic states to strengthen its fight against terrorism.

3. Research

Since 1995, over 78,000 black Sudanese slaves have been liberated through the CSI-sponsored "Underground Railroad." In this slave-redemption program, CSI pays networks of Arab retrievers a fixed rate of

50,000 Sudanese pounds—currently the purchase price of two goats or $35—for every slave freed and returned. Once returned, CSI provides food, medical aid, and education to the former slaves (www.csi-int.ch).

According to CSI, over 200,000 Sudanese are believed to currently be in bondage. Slavery is clearly defined in international law as a "crime against humanity." The U.S. State Department, several U.N. Special Rapporteurs, and many human rights organizations have implicated the government of Sudan in the revival of black slavery in Sudan. CSI's ultimate goal is nothing less than the abolition of slavery in Sudan.

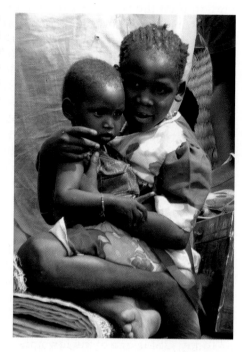

Recently, CSI joined forces with the American Anti-Slavery Group and the National Black Leadership Roundtable to begin a project for documenting liberated and missing Sudanese slaves. The new documentation project aims to enable governments, human rights organizations, and the general public to better understand the extent of Sudan's revived slave trade. Sound documentation of this scourge of Sudanese slavery is essential for its complete abolition and the reunion of slaves with their families.

The documentation project is underway, and according to CSI, preliminary analysis of interviews with over 1,200 liberated slaves reveals that more than 70 percent of females over the age of twelve were raped while in bondage and over 15 percent of boy slaves older than six years were sexually abused by their captors or members of their masters' households. Over 80 percent reported they had witnessed the execution of at least one slave by their mujahadeen captors or by their domestic masters. The same percentage said that they were forced to convert to Islam.

This documentation process, while extremely important, is also very costly. We believe that our new campaign proposals will effectively result in a significant increase in monetary support. This support can then be directed to the documentation program and other areas, but it will be aimed at aiding CSI reach its ultimate goal: to end slavery in Sudan.

The opponents to CSI have only one complaint: by buying back slaves in Sudan, CSI is funding slave traders to buy more ammunition to perform further raids and thus increase the slave trade. However, this argument is easily refuted. CSI argues that all available research suggests that the number of slave raids has decreased since CSI began its slave-redemption program in 1995.

4. Solution and Analysis

Our campaign is targeted at the middle-aged American workforce. Usually, this segment of the population has expendable income to give to charity. Though the ads that we will be presenting may not seem target-based, their placement has been strategically planned for the middle-aged American businessperson.

To reach this target group effectively, we plan on putting our public-service announcement in *Newsweek*, the *New York Times Magazine*, *Time*, and the Sunday editions of various newspapers. In addition to publications, these advertisements will be placed on subways and buses.

Although appealing to both intellect and logic, our campaign focuses predominantly on an emotional appeal, using testimonials and pictures of Sudanese slaves. The more personal and truthful the ads are, the more likely the audience is to identify with the cause and invariably contribute to freeing the very people they see.

Our campaign consists of both print ads and television commercials. In the latter, the use of testimonials will bring people closer to the cause CSI is advocating. In both formats, we use emotion-evoking pictures and the slogan "How much is your freedom worth?" These common aspects of the ads help create an image of the organization and a sense of urgency for the cause. The dark backgrounds of both ads aid in creating the serious mood that accompanies CSI's cause. If we were to use twenty different slogans with catchy words and bright colors, the message would not be communicated nearly as urgently or effectively.

We also predict that our ads will create publicity for CSI, resulting in discussion around the business community. Once CSI has established itself, we plan to integrate a cause marketing campaign, which would consist of a letter of appeal sent to large companies and their employees. Cause marketing links a nonprofit organization and a large company, forming a symbiotic relationship that results in publicity for both. There is a lot of potential for the bright future of CSI, and with our campaign, we feel that this potential will be reached and surpassed.

Critical Reading and Critical Viewing Questions

1. What are the visual design elements of this proposal in terms of the use of white space, headings, and typeface? How effective are they?

2. What techniques do the writers use in the introduction (the problem section) to focus readers' attention on the problem?

3. By the end of the introduction is the problem clearly defined? Summarize the problem as you understand it.

4. What kind of research have the writers done? Where do they appeal to emotion and where to logic?

5. What solution do the writers propose? How feasible is this solution?

6. What benefits do the writers hope will emerge from this proposal? Can you suggest other benefits that might accrue?

7. What are the design elements of the poster in terms of composition and color?

8. How does the visual image work with the language of the poster?

Questions for Writing and Discussion

1. How persuasive do you find this proposal? If you were in a position to work on this campaign, would you? Why?

2. How persuasive is the poster? To what does it appeal?

3. How do human rights issues like this one in Africa affect people in other parts of the world?

Proposal for *The Silent Screams: Court Ordered Abuse of Children*

Garland Waller

Garland Waller is an award-winning producer, writer, and director of nationally syndicated and local television programs and films. Her first independent documentary, *Small Justice: Little Justice in America's Family Courts*, has received national attention and was named Best Social Documentary at the New York International Film and Video Festival and the Key West Indie Film Festival. Waller wrote this proposal to fund a follow-up documentary. She has sent it to a number of potential funders, including some national foundations dedicated to promoting peace and justice.

Dear Sir/Madam:

I am requesting support to conduct research, write and produce a one-hour documentary that explores an issue of national importance. It is a little known secret that men who sexually abuse their children are MORE likely to get custody of their kids than non-abusive men. In fact, men with histories of sexual abuse are more likely to ask for custody. But the problem lies in the family courts. *The Silent Screams: Court Ordered Abuse of Children* shows how the family courts in America systematically send children in contested custody cases to live with a physically or sexually abusing parent. The goal of this program is to expose what in any other country we would call human rights violations.

This general topic was explored in my award-winning one-hour, independent documentary, *Small Justice: Little Justice in America's Family Courts*. The focus in that project was on mothers who were victims of domestic violence and their courtroom trials. This documentary won the "Best Social Documentary Award" at the New York International Independent Film and Video Festival and was selected by the Key West Indie Film Fest as a winner. *Small Justice* was also shown at the NOW National Conference in 2002 and in 2003. The Museum of Fine Arts in Boston and the Boston Film and Video Foundation have screened *Small Justice* to shocked audiences. In addition, it has been used in numerous court cases across the country. Most recently, *Small Justice* (as well as *Antwone Fisher*) received the "Award for Media Excellence" from the internationally respected Family Violence and Sexual Assault Institute.

I am seeking grant money to make a follow-up documentary on the impact of family court decisions on the children who have spent months, years, or entire childhoods with abusers. Many of these children have come of age and are now free to talk. In fact, three interviews have already been shot.

The working title for this documentary is *The Silent Screams: Court Ordered Abuse of Children*.

The following problems and issues will be addressed in this proposed project:

- Judges are awarding custody of children to men who physically and sexually abuse those children. New research from the Department of Justice, from the Wellesley College Centers for Research on Women, and Justice for Children supports this. What people are now realizing is that if a man beats his wife, sexually abuses his child and then asks for custody, he has more than a reasonable chance of being granted custody. According to the American Judges Foundation on Domestic Violence and the Courtroom, batterers have been able to convince judges and legal authorities that they deserve shared custody in approximately 70% of challenged child custody cases. This statistic is more troubling because numerous studies show that batterers are twice as likely to seek custody.

- Children are suffering in record numbers. The National Organization of Women (NOW), the National Institute of Justice at the Department of Justice, Justice for Children, United for Justice, the Battered Mothers Testimony Project of the Wellesley Centers for Research on Women, the Massachusetts Children's Council and the Leadership Council are just a few of the advocacy groups that are researching the issue or going to court on behalf of child victims.

The question must be raised in the public forum, "Why are judges giving abusers custody?" The widespread use of Parental Alienation Syndrome (PAS) is being used in courts by fathers with histories of domestic violence and/or child abuse. Dr. Richard Gardner coined the term and did "research" which experts now know is purely anecdotal. ALL the books on PAS are self-published. Yet this theory, taught in legal education seminars around the country, influences the outcome in thousands of custody cases. (It is important to note here that Professor Waller got the last recorded interview with Dr. Gardner before his suicide.) Because of the widespread use of PAS in custody cases, the courts often turn children over to abusers.

Budget Estimate and Time Line

The estimated overall budget for this one-hour documentary project is $175,000. This money will be spent over a two-year period when research and production will take place. Professor Waller has already begun shooting this project, but she can go no farther until there are additional funds. (She has used her savings to pay for the initial shooting.)

Research and development has already begun. Initial photography has begun. Interviews have been shot with three women who grew up in homes where, because a judge ignored their pleas to be protected from their fathers, they were raped and assaulted from childhood until they left home. The interview with Dr. Richard Gardner is complete (his last before he committed suicide) as are three interviews with women who were sexually abused and beaten by their fathers. Interviews are in line for a 14-year-old girl whose father, a felon, is seeking full custody. Despite substantial forensic evidence of sexual abuse, the judge has agreed to unsupervised visitation.

The project will be completed by January 2005.

In Conclusion

Recently the public became aware that members of the Catholic Church hierarchy had protected pedophile priests and ignored the words and needs of children. What people do not know yet is that judges, guardians *ad litem*, even some social service agencies whose mandate is to protect children, are not providing the protection that is expected from the justice system. This documentary will be the voice for children who have been silenced by the courts. It will focus public awareness on the failure of the judicial system to protect the children who have endured years of torture and abuse because of a flawed legal system.

Critical Reading Questions

1. How does Waller define the problem in her introduction? Who does she blame for this problem? How effective is she in getting your attention?

2. How does she establish her credibility? (Note that this excerpt does not include the section that presents the qualifications of all the people who will work on the project.)

3. What kind of research does Waller integrate into this proposal? Where does she appeal to logic and where to emotion? How persuasive is her research?

4. How does Waller define the solution to the problem? How feasible is the solution that she presents?

5. In her conclusion Waller refers to the scandal of pedophile priests. Does this reference strengthen or weaken her argument? Explain your answer.

6. What are the benefits Waller sees accruing from this project? Do you agree?

Questions for Writing and Discussion

1. If you represented the foundation, would you fund this proposal? Why?

2. How effective is the documentary film medium in bringing social ills to light? What documentary films have you seen that accomplish this goal?

3. What would you expect to see in a film like the one described in this proposal? What would be effective and appropriate? What would you avoid?

WRITING IN THE WORKS

Interview with Garland Waller

Garland Waller

1. How much proposal writing do you actually do as an independent filmmaker?

A producer's life is writing and rewriting. You are either writing grants to foundations to try to get money or to broadcasters to try to get money. Your goal is to get your show made and seen by some particular audience. If I had to assign percentages, I would say that 75 percent of my day is writing and 25 percent is on the phone, talking about ideas, trying to sell an idea, getting someone excited and committed to an idea. I have heard some students say, "I don't want to write. I just want to produce." Good luck. Most of them will have a hard time. If they can't write, they will have to create partnerships with people who can write. It's the nature of the producing beast. You just plain have to write.

2. You wrote this proposal to get funding for a follow-up film to your first documentary *Small Justice*. Both films have David-and-Goliath aspects to them, an independent filmmaker taking on a huge adversary, the American judicial system. How do you locate funders willing to take on these kinds of projects?

I have found funders to be just as scared of controversy as the "Big 4" [networks]. I have perhaps become more jaded since beginning work on these documentaries. I am jealous of Michael Moore and Errol Morris because they produce controversial documentaries, but they are stars; they are proven, and they are therefore safer in the eyes of people with money. Ken Burns isn't controversial, but he's another one who gets money easily. It's a tough business, and don't let anyone tell you other-

wise. The trick is to make funders understand why your program is important. If you can't do that through your writing, you will never get a dime because the chance of a face-to-face to beg for money is pretty slim.

3. You have obviously done a great deal of research on the topic of custody battles in family courts both for your first film and this one. How much research do you need to do before you propose a project? On the average, what percentage of the project is doing research before you start to look for funding?

I do an enormous amount of research before I get anywhere near a camera. I find out who the key people are that I should interview, what they will say and why and who will say just the opposite. I think about where I will shoot them, how much access I will have to them, what makes their story different from any other story on the planet. I make sure I have spoken to experts who agree and disagree with my primary experts, and I read books and journals, both old and new, so that I can know the scope of the issue. I read traditional papers like *The New York Times*, but I also read *Mother Jones* or *Alternative Medicine* . . . whatever the nontraditional source might be. In terms of percentages, before I start shooting, I would say 90 percent of the project is research before shooting. Ten percent is booking. That's the easy part.

4. How did the topic of abusive fathers getting custody of their children first come to your attention?

A close friend of mine, a paralegal named Diane Hofheimer, told me that more and more of her divorce cases involved child sexual abuse. She told me that more domestic violence played a role in custody cases. SHE was the one who put the pieces together. It was early on in what I would now call a "movement." I was lucky to get the story before anyone else did. I trusted her, but I also did an enormous amount of research before I committed to the project. I found out she was right. There was a link, but no one in the media had covered the story. In fact, they still haven't. And it's shameful, and it reveals just how terrified mainstream media is of true controversy.

5. Would you say your film has had any effect on the problem?

I am so lucky to know that *Small Justice* has been used in courtrooms as evidence and has also been used to raise money for women who have been jailed for protecting their children from abusers. It has been shown at the NOW National Conference twice. It has won an award for media excellence from the Eighth International Conference on Family and Domestic Violence. It was shown to a packed room of lawyers, advocates, and professors at the Battered Mothers Conference in New York. The word is getting out and one day, someone from the mainstream media will do this story and get a lot of credit. How many loving mothers will have to go to jail before that happens is anyone's guess. It's very sad.

6. When you are proposing a project, how careful is your tone? Do you ever feel yourself trying to maintain restraint? Obviously, after you have started to research a project, you have some strong opinions about it. In general, would you say passion is good fundraising technique?

I have to be careful with my tone because basically I get very emotional about this topic. It scares people, so I have to be much more of a TV person than

an advocate. Mostly when I pitch to funders, I try to help them see what they will get out of it. I find that companies or funders rarely do things because it's the right thing to do. They need to understand what they get out of it. To me, that's part of what all TV producers have to understand. Frankly, all the producers I know do understand that. Them's the rules.

As for passion and fundraising, you've got to have some fire in your belly. If you are not excited by your project, no one else will be. But . . . and this is a big but, you had better have your ducks in a row. You need to have done your homework, have a nice production package that is easy to read and makes sense. Otherwise, you will never get in the front door.

7. Your proposal will be read by students who will be writing their own proposals to help solve problems in their communities. What proposal writing advice can you give them?

When you sit down to write, you must have one clear goal in your mind. What is the ONE thing you want your reader/funder to remember? One of the problems writers often face is that they want to tell too much. It is important to keep to your topic, build on the reason for it, and make the writing as seamless as possible. Read it aloud if necessary. Does it flow?

Also, you must use your knowledge of the world around you. The more you read, the better writer you will be, and the better treatment or documentary you will write. You can tie in world events or pop psychology, it doesn't matter, as long as you are able to make your idea come to life and the reader can see the relevance of that topic to today's world.

WRITING AND REVISION STRATEGIES

Gathered here are three interactive sections for you to use as you write and revise your proposal.

▶ Writer's Notebook Suggestions

▶ Peer-Editing Log

▶ Revision Checklist

Writer's Notebook Suggestions

You can use these exercises to do some start-up thinking and writing for your proposal.

1. Write a one-page proposal aimed at the US Postal Service recommending a commemorative stamp design. Choose a person or event you think worthy of a stamp, and make an argument for it.

2. You want to organize a fundraising barbecue to support a homeless shelter if your local chapter of the Salvation Army will sponsor it. Write a brief letter to the Salvation Army proposing this idea.

3. Talking with friends, you realize that each of you knows someone battling smoking or who has a smoking-related disease. You are irate that cigarette company advertisements target young people and poor people. Write a short letter to the American Cancer Society proposing that they pitch their next efforts to keep junior high kids from smoking.

4. Choose an editorial in today's paper. Write a letter to the editor proposing a solution to the problem discussed in the editorial.

5. Write a letter to your boss or former boss proposing improvements in the workplace. Consider your audience carefully.

6. You learn that your college is trying to recruit students from abroad to help create a more international student body. You decide to write and shoot a short promotional video to help recruitment efforts. Write a one-page proposal pitching your ideas to your college president and asking for funding for your project.

7. Write an e-mail message to a former professor proposing a feasible change to the course syllabus.

8. Valentine's Day is approaching. Write a proposal to your sweetheart.

Peer-Editing Log

As you work with a writing partner or in a peer-editing group, you can use these questions to give helpful responses to a classmate's proposal and as a guide for discussion.

Writer's Name _____

Date _____

1. Who is the specific audience for this proposal? What do you know about this audience? Can you make any suggestions on how the writer can more effectively tailor the proposal to this audience?

2. Bracket the introductory section. Does the introduction hook the reader? Can you suggest ways to strengthen this section?

3. Underline the problem statement. Can this statement be clarified? Does it need more support?

4. Underline the solution presented in the body of the paper. Is the solution feasible? What might make it more appealing or more doable?

5. Point out places where the writer has considered possible objections to the proposal. Can you suggest other points the writer might consider?

6. Mark places where research appeals to logic (facts, statistics, studies, graphics) and to emotion (anecdotes, quotations, visuals). Are the sources credible? Does the proposal need more or different kinds of support?

7. Bracket the conclusion. Underline sentences that explain the benefits of the proposal. Are these benefits clearly stated? Can you suggest other possible benefits?

8. Look at the overall design of the proposal. Could the writer use white space, headings, or different typefaces to help organize the proposal and make it more visually appealing?

9. Put a wavy line under writing that could be more concise, clear, positive, or specific. Can you make suggestions to strengthen the writing?

10. Does the proposal persuade you? If not, what else might the writer do to win you over?

Revision Checklist

As you do your final revision for your proposal, check to make sure that you

❏ Chose a specific audience for your proposal and tailored your writing to that audience

❏ Wrote an introduction that engages your reader

❏ Stated the problem clearly in the introduction

❏ Provided some background or contextual information

❏ Included research that shows the scope and seriousness of the problem

❏ Attributed your research clearly to credible sources

❏ Presented a clear solution to the problem

❏ Provided the necessary details to show the feasibility of your solution

❏ Explained the benefits of your solution to your audience

❏ Designed the proposal visually so that it is clear and easy to read

❏ Wrote with language that is concise, clear, positive, and specific

9. PUBLIC SERVICE MESSAGES

WRITING APPEALS

Creativity is a continual surprise.

—Ray Bradbury

ASSIGNMENT

Find a nonprofit group or organization in your community that offers information or services that could benefit the public. This organization will be your client. Develop a portfolio of three public service messages and one pitch letter introducing your work to this new client. Your aim is to serve your community by raising awareness of an issue, initiating a new behavior or attitude, or changing a behavior or attitude. Choose from following type of public service messages.

- Print advertisements for magazines, newspapers, posters, or billboards
- Brochures
- Storyboards and scripts for television commercials
- Websites

Smokey Bear ads were created by the War Advertising Council and were among the first public service announcements.

PUBLIC SERVICE MESSAGES

In 1944, after shells fired by a Japanese submarine exploded in an oil field in Santa Barbara, California, forests along the Pacific coast seemed particularly vulnerable to large-scale fires. With professional as well as volunteer firefighters serving in the war, the Forest Service decided to recruit the American public in a campaign to prevent forest fires. To attract attention and get the message out, they created a bear to head the campaign. Their bear became the most recognized image in public service advertising: Smokey Bear, also known as Smokey the Bear.

The Smokey Bear ads were among the first public service advertisements (PSAs). Created by the War Advertising Council, the ads combined illustrations and catchy phrases to raise awareness and encourage civic vigilance. Smokey was not the council's only effort. It produced many awareness-raising ads that promoted good citizenship along the way, including an entire campaign urging discretion to support the war effort: the "loose lips sink ships" campaign. To entice women unaccustomed to working outside their homes into the workforce, the council introduced Rosie the Riveter, now an icon for the power of women.

Combining words and images proved to be an excellent way to raise awareness and marshal the public into civic action, so good that advertising campaigns that spread messages about public welfare are still used today. The War Advertising Council became the Ad Council, a group that today pairs advertising agencies with nonprofit groups and government agencies to promote positive social change.

The Ad Council is not alone in informing the public about important issues through advertising. Many groups and organizations also use advertising to inform and help people. Their public service advertisements (called public service announcements when they are broadcast) cover a great range of topics: raising awareness about the risks of skin cancer, promoting public transportation as an alternative to driving, discussing health issues like disease prevention, and informing the public about social issues like homelessness and environmental issues like conservation, to name a few.

Some now-classic campaigns produced through the Ad Council are as memorable for their catchy language as they are for their images. The promotion of seatbelt use introduced us to the crash test dummies: "You could learn a lot from a dummy." McGruff the Crime Dog told us to "Take a bite out

Evaluate the Visual Element of a Public Service Advertisement

Choose a public service advertisement in this chapter, or find one on your own, that has good text but weak visuals. Write a memo to the sponsor of the ad.

1. Analyze the visuals, including where the viewer's eye is drawn first, second, third. Include any connotations or meanings that might be inconsistent with the aim of the ad. Include your assessment of any visuals that might create confusion or a mixed message.

2. Make recommendations on how to revise or improve the visuals. What would work better?

---

of crime." The importance of providing scholarships to minority students was emphasized: "A mind is a terrible thing to waste." "Friends don't let friends drive drunk" showed us how to prevent drunk driving. Nonprofit groups compete to have their messages placed in broadcast airtime and print space. Radio and television stations are required by law to allot time for these ads, and other media also clear time or space for public service advertising. The amount of space is limited, however, and only the best PSAs get chosen: those with the most creative, appealing, and relevant combinations of words and pictures.

You are exposed to these and other media messages constantly through billboards, posters, print ads, television commercials, and websites. It is impossible to get to work or school in the morning without seeing or hearing requests for your attention, time, and money. You can learn to think more critically about the validity and worth of the thousands of messages you are exposed to each day by analyzing the way words and pictures work together. Visuals have become increasingly important in writing. In evaluating a message—any message—what you see can be as important as what you read.

Applications: School, Community, Work

As you create your own public service messages, you will continue the Smokey Bear tradition of getting attention for civic action. You will find many opportunities to design posters and flyers to alert people about events in your community. In community groups, at school, and in the workplace, blood drives, clothing drives, and fundraising events are always in the works. A college group might be interested in raising awareness about sweatshops. Your student government might side with striking custodial workers, and you might need to develop materials explaining the conflict to students.

Your town library is most likely perpetually collecting used books or trying to recruit volunteers. Churches and synagogues have annual events and

Warm-up Practice 9.1
Collaborative Activity

Collect examples of public service advertisements from magazines, and grade them using the following scorecard. Award the PSA one point for every box checked.

Public Service Advertisement Scorecard

- ❏ The ad attracted my attention.
- ❏ The ad kept me interested; I did not stop looking at it because I was offended, confused, or bored.
- ❏ The ad provided information that was new to me.
- ❏ I believed the ad.
- ❏ I would read the ad again.
- ❏ I would read more information about the topic.
- ❏ I would act on the information.
- ❏ After reading, I remember the message.
- ❏ I would tell my friends and family about the message.

_____ Total PSA score

Compare your totals to those of your classmates. Collect and examine the ads with the highest scores and the lowest scores, and decide which factors the best have in common and which factors the weakest have in common.

ongoing projects like food pantries. Schools, scouts, animal shelters, and hospitals are a few more good places to find clients who need your expertise. National nonprofit groups like Big Brothers Big Sisters and the March of Dimes run local campaigns to raise awareness as well as to solicit donations and volunteers.

A good way to serve your community is by collecting information about resources on a webpage. The page can list and link to places with more information and provide phone numbers and names of resources people might not otherwise find. Information can be provided about how to find music programs for children, for example, how to learn to swim, or how to register to vote.

Thinking about how words and images work together can help you design brochures and websites for use in the workplace as well. Attracting attention and delivering a clear message succinctly are the aims of all advertising. Businesses need to inform the public about their products and services and to provide accurate and useful information to customers and clients in brochures, flyers, and websites.

CHAPTER OBJECTIVES

In this chapter you will learn to

- ▶ analyze the role of visual design in information
- ▶ consider audience and purpose in designing public service messages
- ▶ combine images and words to create messages that serve your community

UNDERSTANDING PUBLIC SERVICE MESSAGES

Writers in the information age cannot ignore the significance of the visual components of a message. When it comes to getting readers' attention and making information clear, what we see on a page is arguably as important as what we read. The relationship of pictures and words is particularly important in advertising. Knowing how to use the few seconds' attention an individual might give a public service advertisement before losing interest and moving on involves understanding what kind of people make up the audience, what might attract and hold their attention long enough for them to receive the message, and how a suggestion can carry meaning.

Most people do not set out to read ads, especially ads with lots of copy. The challenge for the designers of public service ads lies in making messages about "what's good for you" interesting reading.

Creating Public Service Material for a Specific Audience

Creators of public service advertisements understand that their messages are mini-arguments asking people to adopt or change behavior and attitudes. They are aware of not only the general reluctance of people to listen to "what's good for them," but also the specific obstacles that lie between a message and a particular audience. Sometimes PSAs need to be serious and somber. Other times PSAs attract the attention of a resistant audience with humor.

Your understanding of purpose and audience is important in designing PSAs. As in all forms of advertising, you can speak to a broad audience or a more specific one, but you need to have a sense of the people at whom you are aiming your message. You need to pin down exactly what you want your PSA to achieve.

The writers and designers working on PSAs have a clear sense of *who* their intended audience is before they start to think about *how* to deliver the message. They might have a number of different audiences in mind and create different campaigns to target these different audiences, but they know, for example, whether they are pitching their material to children, teenagers, men between eighteen and twenty-four, affluent middle-aged businesswomen, or senior citizens.

For your PSA, you will have a variety of messages and audiences to choose from. For example, if you are interested in helping the Red Cross with blood donations, you can choose from a variety of target audiences.

- First-time donors who might hesitate due to fear
- Businesses that might sponsor blood drives at their offices during work hours
- College-age donors who are healthy and have time to donate
- People between the ages of thirty and fifty who are busy but are motivated to help
- People between the ages of thirty and fifty who find lots of excuses
- Retired people who have time and are interested in civic involvement

Where you decide to place your PSAs—in which publications, in what neighborhoods, on which modes of public transportation, or at which television or radio stations—depends on *whom* you are aiming to persuade. The group you are working for, your client, may have ideas about whom they want to target.

To assess how you will talk to an identified group, first think about where your target group is most likely to go for information, so that you can place

**Practice 9.2
Finding Your Target
PSA Audience**

1. Generate a list of possible target groups, like the one on page 301 for blood donations, for public service advertisements designed to solicit donations to the Every Child Is a Reader program, which gives new books to children in low-income school districts.

2. Decide where you would place the PSAs to reach each target group on your

your message where they will encounter it. In your community, which publications do women read frequently? What places would attract the attention of retired people? Would college students visit the same places? A poster in a coffee shop near a college would be likely to be seen by college students. A poster in a women's fitness center would be seen by women. But what about ads in the sports and business pages of the newspaper? Would these be good places to address a specific or a general group? Who would be exposed to a poster at the public library? A billboard on the interstate?

Thinking about the means of delivering your message dovetails with thinking about your audience. The most important part of making a persuasive statement is knowing who makes up the audience and how to speak directly to it. You must understand the rational as well as the emotional motivators.

Images in Public Service Advertisements

In all advertisements, public service advertisements included, visuals work in conjunction with the words as you simultaneously speak to one person and reach out to many. The images are so important to the text that the teams of writers and designers who create advertisements face a chicken-or-egg question: Do they work on the words, then on the pictures? Or the pictures first, then the words? The answer is that they need to work on the words and pictures simultaneously. Each is important in creating meaning in an advertisement. Good text will not have appeal without good design that attracts attention, while readers will find a poorly written message easy to ignore. Still, what the reader sees is without a doubt the first step in comprehending your message. The design of a PSA motivates people to read the text. The design delivers the first impression.

Images can work on many levels, calling on associations we all share to make sense of them. In the split seconds it takes your retina to record a picture, you have already started to decipher the meaning and to respond both intellectually and emotionally. You see a photograph of sunglasses with one smashed lens, for example, and you think of something fragile that has broken. You may think about bad fortune or bad choices, accidents, damage, or loss. If that is what the sunglasses look like, what about the eye? The face? Pictures really can be worth thousands of words. When that image is partnered with a headline that states "Friends Don't Let Friends Drive Drunk," the image tells a terrible story and leaves a lasting impression.

Images can be photographs and illustrations, and words too. In fact, some ads are words only. The typeface—its size and shape—can be the image. Sometimes the absence of a photo or an illustration delivers a powerful message.

The billboard on page 303, which uses only type, exemplifies architect Mies van der Rohe's design principal that "less is more." The ad is more pow-

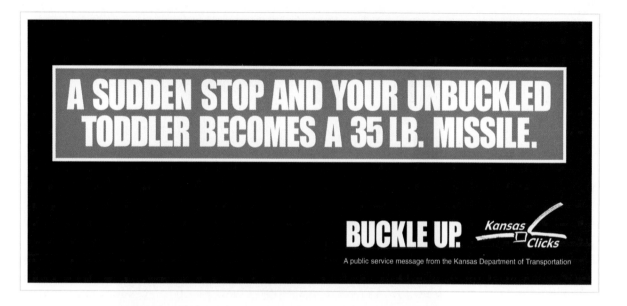

A SUDDEN STOP AND YOUR UNBUCKLED
TODDLER BECOMES A 35 LB. MISSILE.

BUCKLE UP.

Kansas Clicks

A public service message from the Kansas Department of Transportation

erful without a picture because it lets the viewer imagine his or her own child in the car. When the type is the imagery, the choices of typeface, size, and colors are crucial decisions. In the case of a billboard, the designer and the copywriter also have to factor in how much time motorists have for reading. Any single ad competes with thousands of other nonprofit as well as for-profit appeals. The first step in getting the message across is attracting attention. When images and words work together, they create a distinct impression. The first impression of any ad is its visual appeal. Design—the choices about which text type and size and which illustrations or photos to use, and how the ad is arranged in the space—is the most significant aspect of attracting attention.

Analyzing the Visual Images in Print Ads Understanding design of an ad is like understanding any artwork. You need to break it into components to understand the whole thing. Without thinking about the words, isolate just the visual part of the ad "A Tan Never Fades," on the next page.

1. What do you see? This question is deceptively simple. The key is in describing the choices the designer has made.

    a. Does the imagery surprise you in some way?

    b. What is the point of view or the camera angle?

    c. How close or far away are you from the image?

    d. What is missing in the image?

    e. Which colors dominate the image?

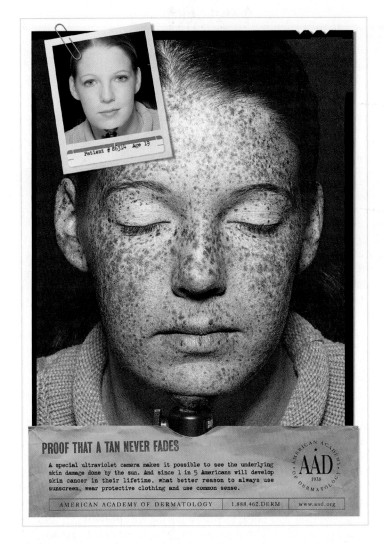

2. Think of the text as an image. Where do the words appear? Do the words dominate the ad, or does the illustration or photograph dominate?

3. When you look at this ad where does your eye go first, second, third?

4. Without reading the text or headline, or without listening to the words in the case of a commercial, how does the image make you feel: sad, uncomfortable, nervous, guilty? Peaceful, happy, relaxed? Other emotions?

5. What do you think is the designers' goal?

6. How is the goal achieved?

Sample Analysis In this public service advertisement produced for the American Academy of Dermatology, the contrast between the two images of the face immediately catches the viewer's eye. The imagery is both surprising and mysterious. It creates a question in the viewer's mind about the face marred by splotches. How can the same person look attractive in one photo and scarred in another?

The dominant and larger image is a black-and-white photo that has the look of a scientific document. The snapshot attached to the top also makes this image look like a doctor's case file. The woman's eyes are closed in the larger photo, which helps depersonalize her. She is a case, not an individual.

In contrast, in the snapshot her eyes are open and she is revealed as a person, a young woman, not just a case number. The urge to compare the images is irresistible, and your eyes travel back and forth between them.

The designer uses the contrast to show a powerful image of the invisible damage beneath the surface of skin. By showing the ultraviolet image, the designer makes something abstract (that the sun might damage your skin) seem very real.

Practice 9.3
Analyzing Visual Images

Analyze the visual in this public service advertisement using the questions presented on pages 303 and 304. Is the image successful in capturing attention and expressing the point?

Text in Public Service Advertisements

Anybody who has ever written an ad will tell you that it is a lot like writing poetry. Every word matters. The text, known as *copy*, needs to be spare, concise, and evocative because people resist reading the messages in ads. Your job as a copywriter who is writing a public service advertisement is to compress a great deal of information into a few words in order to deliver the message before the audience loses interest.

Understanding the audience is critical to the choices you make. Think about talking to one person and at the same time to a crowd. Each ad is a personal appeal that just happens to be broadcast to thousands. You will be walking a fine line between attracting the attention of thousands and possibly offending individuals in the group.

Analyzing the Text in Public Service Advertisements Analyzing the text in PSAs is much like analyzing any piece of writing. You have to pay attention to words in their contexts, think about their nuances, and find verbal clues that suggest whether the piece is intended to be funny, ironic, poignant, or angry. If you can, try to isolate the language, keeping it separate from the images as you do your initial analysis.

Poetry and Advertising Copy

Why do we remember so many advertising slogans through the years? Advertising copywriters often use poetic techniques to create language that stays in our minds—often pleasingly, but sometimes also annoyingly. A few poetic techniques copywriters use effectively are metaphors, similes, alliteration, onomatopoeia, rhymes, hyperbole, repetition, rhythm, and parallel constructions.

Metaphors and Similes

Metaphors and similes compare unlike things.

A sudden stop and your unbuckled toddler becomes a 35 lb. missile.

Make your children superheroes. Teach them how to dial 911.

Alliteration

Alliteration is the repetition of a beginning sound.

Hopeless, hungry, hidden

Onomatopoeia

Onamatopoeia is the re-creation of sounds.

*Every time the cash register goes **ka-ching**, we'll donate part of the sales to helping keep the parks clean.*

Rhymes

Rhymes are words with the same end sound.

Imagination and inspiration in education: Art in the schools.

Hyperbole

Hyperbole is exaggeration.

In the time it takes to get your child vaccinated, you could watch half a television commercial.

Repetition, Rhythm, and Parallel Construction

Copywriters also use repeated words or phrases and songlike rhythms created by patterns of syllables.

Freedom. Appreciate it. Cherish it. Protect it.

Practice 9.4
Finding a Main Point in Text

You have been asked to comment on the new "Math Is Power" campaign, focusing mainly on the text and how well the words clarify the ad's main point. Write a brief memo to the head copywriter assessing this ad from a textual perspective.

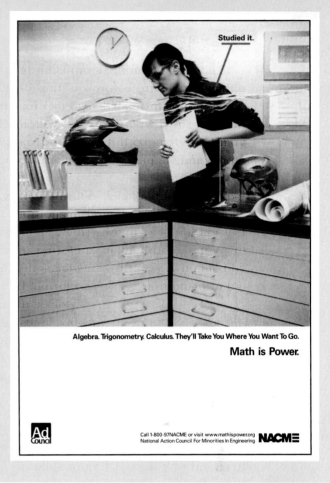

Studied it.

Algebra. Trigonometry. Calculus. They'll Take You Where You Want To Go.

Math is Power.

Ad Council

Call 1-800-97NACME or visit www.mathispower.org
National Action Council For Minorities In Engineering **NACME**

1. What words do you read or hear? Do you notice any particular word choices? Does the writer use a familiar phrase or cliché to draw attention to the ad?

2. Are any of the words meaningful to a specific audience and not to a general audience? Is the writer addressing *you* in the ad?

3. Are there any literary devices? Can you identify any poetic techniques? Does the ad use characters? Does the ad tell a story?

4. What is the tone of the ad?
   a. Authoritative: does the ad seem to lecture the audience?
   b. Plaintive: does the ad seem to express or solicit sadness?
   c. Angry: does the ad use outrage?
   d. Solicitous: does the ad ask for consideration?

   Does the ad have a tone other than these four?

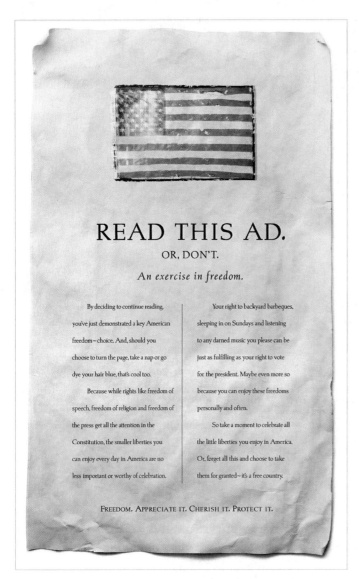

READ THIS AD.

OR, DON'T.

An exercise in freedom.

By deciding to continue reading, you've just demonstrated a key American freedom~choice. And, should you choose to turn the page, take a nap or go dye your hair blue, that's cool too.

Because while rights like freedom of speech, freedom of religion and freedom of the press get all the attention in the Constitution, the smaller liberties you can enjoy every day in America are no less important or worthy of celebration.

Your right to backyard barbeques, sleeping in on Sundays and listening to any darned music you please can be just as fulfilling as your right to vote for the president. Maybe even more so because you can enjoy these freedoms personally and often.

So take a moment to celebrate all the little liberties you enjoy in America. Or, forget all this and choose to take them for granted~it's a free country.

FREEDOM. APPRECIATE IT. CHERISH IT. PROTECT IT.

Sample Analysis This ad begins by challenging the reader to read on, a kind of generic in-your-face plea for attention. To illustrate the theme of "an exercise in freedom," the writers offer readers the option not to read on—an equally valid choice.

The ad copy addresses the reader directly, using the second-person pronoun *you*, and makes the reader part of the ad. The tone is chatty, saying that deciding to dye your hair blue would be "cool, too." The language suggests that the person talking is an open-minded individual.

Mixing formal and folksy language, the speaker is articulate enough to say "the smaller liberties you can enjoy every day in America are no less important or worthy of celebration" than the larger ones, and at the same time can tell you that you can listen to "any darned music you please." This speaker also uses alliteration: "backyard barbecues," "sleeping in on Sundays." The designers rely mostly on the text to deliver a complicated message. The ad seeks not just to rekindle an awareness the reader already has, but also to evoke action. Exactly what the ad wants us to do—"Freedom…Protect it"—remains vague and open to interpretation.

USING HUMOR

Something every schoolchild learns before junior high is that joking can be a great way to get attention. A companion lesson, often learned at the same time, is that jokes come in many forms, some of them more appropriate than others for the context. Often PSA writers and designers use different kinds of humor to get attention and make a lasting impression. Humor can break down

The physical changes that come with age make senior citizens more likely than other age groups to be involved in automobile crashes.

In terms of miles traveled, the accident rate of drivers age 65 and older is exceeded only by drivers age 24 and younger.

So remember, use common sense and courtesy whenever you're behind the wheel. That's...

Safe not sorry
A program of the Kansas Department of Transportation

For more information contact the KDOT Bureau of Traffic Safety at 785-296-3756 or on the Web at www.ksdot.org

Practice 9.5   Analyzing Text

1. Read and analyze the text in this ad.
2. Evaluate the ad. Will it reach a clearly defined audience? Will the audience heed the message? Why?

barriers between the message and the audience. To get people to think about a frightening topic, colon cancer, for example, the American Cancer Society created Polyp Man, a comic figure in an overstuffed red suit (see page 314).

Sometimes humor works well, and other times it crosses the line and offends the audience. If you decide to use humor, keep in mind that offensive humor can turn off your audience, resulting not just in an ineffective ad, but in a counterproductive one. Remember, your client's image is at stake.

Types of Humor

Irony is one of the most commonly used forms of humor in advertising. When you use irony, you rely on parallel logic—two-track thinking that leads to a surprising or counterintuitive outcome. Jokes work in a similar way: You set up a word or a situation, then deliver the opposite of what the audience expects, that is, the opposite of the literal meaning. Playing with your audience's expectations and assumptions can be a good way to get people interested in your message. One television ad for a fuel assistance program showed a mother dressing her daughter in snow pants, mittens, and a ski hat right before tucking her into bed for the night. The ad played on the assumption that the child was going out to play in the snow, not going to an icy bed in an unheated house. In a more humorous context, jokes often twist assumptions in the same way.

A British ad to raise awareness about the dangers of driving while using a cell phone uses visual irony. The two messages—in contrasting colors—work together to illustrate the multitasking involved in using a cell phone while operating a car. The image is a trick played on the reader.

> **You are more
> It's hard to
> likely to crash your
> do two things at
> car while talking
> the same time.
> on a cell phone.**

This ad is based on a British public service advertisement called "mobile madness."

Another example, a print ad designed to raise awareness about child-hood obesity targeted at parents, includes a picture of a boy eating a candy bar, a can of generic soda pop next to him, with his face lit up by the glow of a computer screen. A large dog sits next to the boy. The headline reads: "The fleas on his dog eat a more balanced diet than he does." This statement reveals an ironic possibility, not necessarily a fact but a notion that captures attention. Does it go too far? Sometimes the advertiser must ask, "When have I crossed the line?"

Double entendre, like irony, plays with the meaning of words. When you use double entendre, your words have a second level of meaning, and the message resides in the double play of meaning. Double entendres may not be laugh-out-loud humor, but as with irony, your assumptions shift. An ad for a homeless shelter uses a play on the homonyms *grate* and *great*. The image is of a homeless man sleeping on a run-off grate, with the headline: "Imagine waking up in the morning and feeling this grate." That everybody understands the cliché of "feeling this great" after waking up is essential to the point. What kind of appeal does this ad make? Certainly, it rallies guilt in the audience, a put-yourself-in-somebody-else's-shoes kind of appeal.

Exaggeration, or in poetic terms, hyperbole, is another kind of humor. The audience understands that the claims are incredible and waits for the payoff or the explanation. A television commercial shows people making outrageous claims: "I lifted a car out of a river today." "I used my x-ray vision to free somebody who was trapped in a collapsed building." "I ended a drought." Then each person says: "I taught a child to read." In this example, the exaggeration is subtly comical.

Another kind of irony, satire mocks assumptions and notions about people and institutions. Television ads to promote the USA Freedom Corps use satire to mock the "superstar complex" that some actors and athletes are accused of having. In these ads, the celebrities allow themselves to be made fun of to encourage people to volunteer their time.

RESEARCH PATHS

Your first step in understanding how to relay a message is to interview the group for which you are designing your PSA. Understanding its mission will help you create a public service message. The group will most likely be able to offer you the most current and relevant information that you can use to become familiar with issues and previous campaigns. For example, this mission statement from Big Brothers Big Sisters of the Tri-State (West Virginia, Ohio, and Kentucky) clarifies the organization's goal.

> The mission of Big Brothers Big Sisters of the Tri-State, a non-profit agency, is designed to provide guidance and companionship to youth from single parent homes through the provision of an adult Big Brother Big

Sister volunteer. This is done through recruiting, screening, counseling and supervision by a professional staff. The concept of our program is based on the premise that a child, in order to grow into responsible adulthood, needs a positive relationship with a mature adult figure. Where this influence is lacking, the child is handicapped in reaching his or her potential. Our clients are children needing friendship, affection, advice and guidance. They may be emotionally deprived, in trouble at school, or just a lonely, unhappy child in need of a meaningful relationship. If the problems of the child are so severe that they require professional help exclusively, Big Brothers Big Sisters service will not be a consideration.

The mission statement informs you that Big Brothers Big Sisters' goal is to help children reach their full potential by giving them an adult mentor who will commit to a "meaningful" relationship. Knowing this can help you design an ad that fits the organization.

Your client group might have ideas about whom it is trying to attract and why. In marketing, breaking down a group into a profile of age, neighborhood, income, education, and gender is called *demographics*. Your client will probably be able to give you a good overview of the demographics it is targeting with its message.

Web Searches

Your public service materials need to include up-to-date and quality information, facts, and statistics from authoritative sources. Do not make the mistake of doing a Web search without carefully evaluating your sources. Some organizations with special interests might post misleading or even inaccurate numbers. Look for information that comes from unbiased sources such as universities and government agencies. Even these sources can offer information that has a slant. The best advice is to avoid clear advocates of a particular opinion. A site that argues for gun control might not be the best place to get statistics on the number of gun-related homicides last year, for example. A government site might be more objective.

Information from the census and other studies can be useful in raising awareness about issues that affect the public. You can also find these on the Web. Good sources for locating statistics and other information are state department of public health sites. Much data, including census information you may find useful in creating PSAs that resonate with your audience, can be found at "The US Government's Official Web Portal" at www.firstgov.org.

By using official statistical sources like the census, you can create an argument that has authority. You can find out how many people are homeless in Michigan, or how many women in your community identify themselves as single parents, information that could be useful in revealing a rise or fall in numbers or a pocket of need in a community.

Print Sources

If you find news stories citing a study or statistic that comes from another source, track down the original source. Checking to see if you can get the same information in two sources helps verify it. Going to the source of a statistic, fact, or study is the best way to double-check it. For example, if you find a news article that refers to a study done by the researchers at Arizona State University, locate the actual study. You can use specialized databases like ERIC (Educational Resources Information Center) and LexisNexis to find studies, or librarians can help you find these primary sources.

Experts as Sources

Combine research methods: Start by searching the Internet, but make phone calls too. Most websites include a contact section that offers a phone number. Contacting a group or agency that specializes in your topic could be a good way to get current information and insider sources. Explain that you are working on a project to raise awareness for a particular issue. People might be more inclined to answer your questions if they know what you want to accomplish. Do not forget to ask if there is anyone else you could call. No phone call will be a dead end if you gained another possible contact.

Take notes while you talk on the phone. Always ask for the name of the person who gives you information. If you make another call, you will have a name to mention. ("Mr. West at the Awareness Office gave me your number.") You will have the name in hand for follow-up calls as well. (See Chapter 14 for more on interviewing.)

IMPORTANT: Keep notes about the origins of all facts and claims. Write down the information and source, and cite the source in small print in the text of your ad. Be sure to check facts; get the information from two different sources to make sure it is valid.

ANATOMY OF A PUBLIC SERVICE MESSAGE

As you begin to write and design your public service advertisement, you will need to consider how to attract and persuade your audience. PSA designers and writers use what they call a "persuasion path," a series of steps the reader or viewer will take to arrive at the advertisers' desired destination. Three steps on the path are as follows.

- ‣ Attract attention and generate interest: the headline and visual images
- ‣ Provide reasons: the body
- ‣ Call to action: the conclusion

humorous photo helps with
a serious issue—makes
getting attention easier

Colon Polyps
AMERICAN CANCER SOCIETY

play on "go bad"—
double entendre

Headline

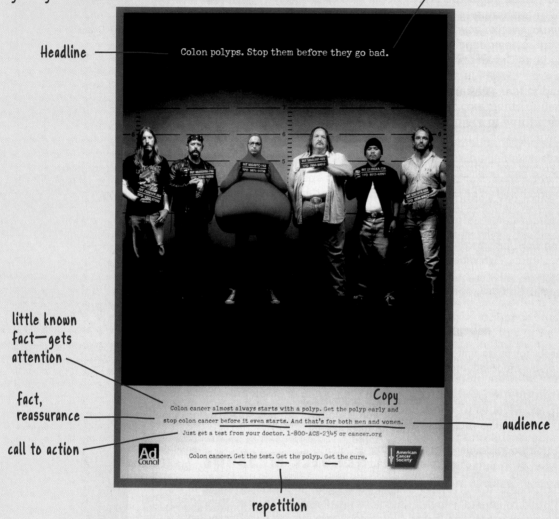

little known
fact—gets
attention

fact,
reassurance

call to action

(Image text: Colon polyps. Stop them before they go bad.)

Copy

Colon cancer almost always starts with a polyp. Get the polyp early and stop colon cancer before it even starts. And that's for both men and women.

Just get a test from your doctor. 1-800-ACS-2345 or cancer.org

Colon cancer. Get the test. Get the polyp. Get the cure.

audience

repetition

1. This attracts attention by providing information that most people probably didn't know.

2. This gives people a logical reason to think that this ad is useful. It also provides a sense of reassurance to a frightening proposition—the possibility of cancer.

3. Here the copywriters emphasize the audience.

4. This provides a sense of conclusion. It answers the question, "Now what do I do with this information?"

Elsewhere in America

FEEDING CHILDREN BETTER, AMERICA'S SECOND HARVEST

attention-
grabbing text
creates a
mystery

photo seems
torn out of a
magazine

Irony,
layout
emphasizes
the elements

Direct address
"you"

Copy, Call
to Action

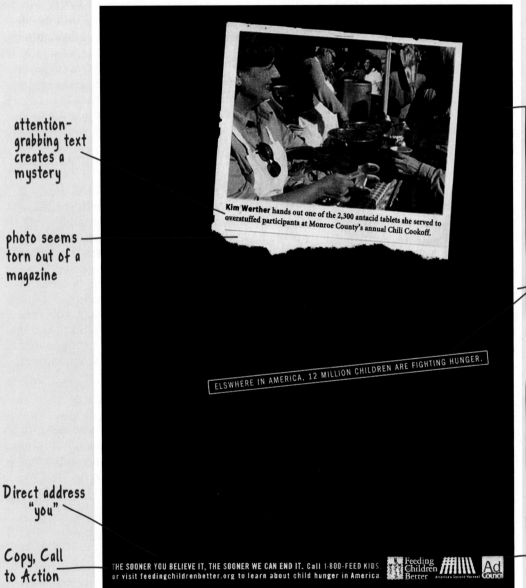

Kim Werther hands out one of the 2,300 antacid tablets she served to overstuffed participants at Monroe County's annual Chili Cookoff.

ELSWHERE IN AMERICA, 12 MILLION CHILDREN ARE FIGHTING HUNGER.

THE SOONER YOU BELIEVE IT, THE SOONER WE CAN END IT. Call 1-800-FEED KIDS, or visit feedingchildrenbetter.org to learn about child hunger in America.

Feeding Children Better
America's Second Harvest

Ad Council

Headlines and Visual Images:
Attract Attention and Generate Interest

A headline, like all titles, gives readers an entry point into a public service advertisement. Unlike headlines in news stories, however, PSA headlines do not necessarily appear at the tops of pages. Sometimes a headline is in the middle or even at the bottom of the PSA. What distinguishes it as a headline is not placement but rather function; it calls attention to the PSA, generates interest or intrigue, creates readers' attention, and announces or suggests the topic. You can also identify a headline by its appearance; it is usually large, in boldface or contrasting type, and set apart from other text.

Some ads have only headlines and no other text. Other ads have no headlines, like the Feeding Children Better appeal. In that ad you can see how art directors often do not differentiate among headlines, text, and tag lines and sometimes create "headless" ads in order to make them seem fresh and contemporary.

Still, headlines have an important function. Good headlines create a sense of intrigue or mystery, attempting to involve the reader in the message or present a mystery the reader will want to solve. Combined with the visual, the headline in the colon polyp PSA invites readers into the text, where they will find answers to the puzzles of the headline. Colon polyps are not a topic most people are automatically drawn to, unlike "Look Years Younger" or "Make More Money." Though the headline would not work on its own, it works in partnership with the image to give a full (and humorous) message.

In their quest to get people to read or listen to their message, advertisers consider that the audience has a natural reluctance to pay attention and is perhaps even skeptical about the information. In both the headline and the text, writers try to draw in audiences by appealing to their emotions and their intellects.

Appealing to Hearts and Minds

Ads that get attention appeal to hearts and minds, emotions and intellect. Appealing directly to the audience's emotions in order to attract attention is probably the most commonly used strategy in creating the images and text in public service advertisements. You can leverage emotional motivators such as guilt, fear, outrage, joy, and pride. You can inspire your audience or make it laugh. Polyp man is funny, but the idea of colon cancer is not. Instead of playing upon fear, the designers comfort the readers with advice: stop it before it starts. The text informs but also motivates.

Another strategy is to use logic. Advertisers who choose logic to attract attention often rely on statistics to make their points. Ads may have headlines that begin "two out of three" or "90 percent of all." Appealing to reason or using logic is called *logos* in the lexicon of classical argument.

Information is the focus of PSAs that use an intellectual appeal to get attention. Much of the time, once the logic attracts the attention some kind of emotional appeal contributes to the meaning of the ad. The Feeding Children Better PSAs use bits of information to make an appeal. The ads appeal to the audience's guilt about hunger among children.

The designers of these print PSAs use the visual layout and image to help make the point that these are everyday images we might see in newspapers and magazines. The captions below each picture reinforce the sense that the photos may be from local newspapers, showing them as commonplace occurrences.

Note that the copy—"Elsewhere in America, 12 million children are fighting hunger"—appears in the middle of the page, under the photograph. It clearly announces the topic of hunger in America and presents an arresting statistic. The line also unifies the campaign, appearing in the same box in the same location on all the PSAs in this series.

Body: Provide Reasons

Headlines, as in some of the ads you see in this chapter, are sometimes the only text of ads. But often headlines function like any introduction to catch the audience's attention and draw it into the body of the ad.

Some public service advertisements offer a great deal of information to explain their headlines, and others include little, relying more on the visuals or design. Good copy is clear and logical but does not overwhelm the viewer. After a headline that reads "Colon polyps. Stop them before they go bad" and an illustration of some "bad" polyps, the copy at the bottom of the colon polyp poster creates interest and provides a reason to the audience.

Conclusion: Call for Action

Every public service advertisement, like any proposal, has a clear sense of purpose, an objective. Every designer knows exactly what the audience should take away from the PSA. In product advertising the goal can be specific—buy this brand of toothpaste, for example—or it can be to provide brand identification: an athletic shoe for women might show strong women winning races or tennis matches. In contrast, PSAs raise awareness, motivate people to adopt or change behaviors, or sometimes do both, as the colon polyp PSA does.

The goal of a PSA is the "call to action." This is the final step in the persuasion path. In the colon polyp ad, the call to action tells the reader exactly what the next step is: "Just get a test from your doctor."

Calls to action can take many forms, from asking people to get more information to asking them to do something or stop doing something. Some calls to action ask people to donate money; some ask them for time as a volunteer or mentor. Some calls ask for very specific actions: use a seatbelt, vote, don't drink and drive.

Choosing Your Medium

In thinking about any public service advertisement, consider the form of delivery for your message: how your reader or viewer will encounter the material and what the circumstances of the encounter are. Thinking about how or when your audience will meet your message will help you choose the best form for its function. Your call to action, for example, will vary depending upon the medium you use.

Before you write and design your PSA, think about what form will best deliver your message. Though a few lines of copy that explain a headline are useful to a magazine reader, a driver speeding by a billboard at 60 miles per hour will never be able to read twenty-five words of copy. A billboard might be a good way to deliver a general message—probably just a headline—but not the best method of getting readers to make a phone call or write a letter to a specific address. A billboard can be a good way to get your name and the outline of your idea out to a broad public audience. Since traffic routes are revisited daily, commuters will get the message repeatedly.

In general, talk directly to the audience you imagine. Use short sentences, and don't waste words. Most good copy is informal, brief, and to the point. It can also be playful and clever.

These basic guidelines for some of the major ways to deliver PSAs should help you think about the best medium for your message.

Print Public Service Advertisements Print public service advertisements appear in magazines and newspapers and in the form of posters and billboards. The way the ad looks is as important as what it says. Your call to action can be more specific in a magazine PSA than on a poster or billboard. In a magazine your reader has more time to linger and can jot down a contact number or address. Some elements a print PSA should include are

> ▸ A headline that attracts attention and draws the reader in

> ▸ An image that creates visual interest (pictures, illustrations, the design of the type)

> ▸ Text that presents the message—"pays off," explains, or clarifies the facts or claims of the headline

> ▸ A call to action that states clearly what you want your reader to do: log onto a website, send money, volunteer

> ▸ A logo for the organization that identifies it and provides contact information

Practice 9.7   Analyze Two Ads

1. What might have attracted women to the messages in these ads?

2. What is implied in the text of the ads?

3. How are women portrayed in the ads? Was this an accurate representation of women at the time?

4. With some updating of the look of the women, could the U.S. Employment Service use a similar appeal to women with loved ones in the armed services to work in support of the military today?

These two posters were part of the U.S. government's campaign to recruit women to civil service jobs during World War II.

Television Commercials You have all the benefits of the medium to work with in television: pictures, sound, and text. Even though television is a compelling medium, commercials inspire viewers to tune out. So you have to be immediately engaging through use of an arresting image, language, or music. As you design and write television commercials, you will assemble storyboards, like the ones that follow, indicating what the audience will hear and see in each frame.

Some elements a television commercial should include are

▶ An opening that attracts attention through images, sound, and text (copy or speech)

▶ A middle that explains and clarifies your message

▶ A conclusion that calls for action and may include a phone number or e-mail address

▶ Pictures that can be film, still shots, or text on the screen

▶ Sound that can include music to set the tone or voices of characters speaking directly to the camera, in a dramatic situation, or commenting on the images on the screen in a voiceover

DDB Worldwide in New York created the two television spots shown on the next two pages for the U.S. Department of Transportation National Highway Traffic Safety Administration drunk driving prevention campaign. As you look at the two storyboards, notice how they use pictures, text on screen, voiceover, and sound effects (SFX).

Brochures Brochures are often used in public service advertisements campaigns. A brochure provides more information and more detail about the call to action than a print or television ad. The cover of a brochure invites the reader inside, where more text delivers a longer message than you will find in other media advertising. Some elements a brochure should include are

▶ A cover that attracts attention and announces the topic

▶ Inside panels that give information (usually organized in descending order of importance)

A reader's attention often wanders, so you want to deliver the most important part of your message right away. Some suggestions for the inside panels follow.

▶ Use lists (like this one).

▶ Use parallel construction in your lists.

▶ Be concise, not wordy, and keep your sections brief.

▶ Use headings for new sections.

THE ADVERTISING COUNCIL, INC.

DRUNK DRIVING PREVENTION CAMPAIGN

Public Service Announcements for the U.S. Department of Transportation
National Highway Traffic Safety Administration

"WIGGINS KIDS" :30 CNTD-1330   **(Also available as :20, CNTD-1120)**

(SFX: MOVIE PROJECTOR)

(SFX: OMINOUS RUMBLE FOLLOWED BY SILENCE)

"CARISSA DEASON" :30 CNTD-1430

GIRLS SING: Noooo…(Laughter)…No, I don't wanna give you mine, and no, I don't wanna meet you nowhere…No, want none of your time, and no…

I don't want no scrubs. A scrub is a guy that can't get no love from me. Hangin' out da passenger side of his best friend's ride, tryin' to holla at me. Hangin' out da passenger side of his best friend's ride, tryin' to holla at me…

Volunteer Advertising Agency: DDB Worldwide   C1201

Practice 9.8
Analyze a Commercial

To analyze this ad, answer the following questions.

1. How are the camera angles used?

2. What do you come to know about the story that takes place in the kitchen?

3. This ad is based on the design principle of less is more. What is omitted from the ad?

4. The only sound in the ad is the younger sister's line, "Hey Lina, where's yours?" What is the effect of having silence? Why use type on screen when a voiceover can announce the call to action?

THE ADVERTISING COUNCIL, INC.
CHILD HUNGER CAMPAIGN

"SHARED FOOD" :30 CNCH-1130

YOUNGER SISTER: Hey Lina, where's yours?

1 out of 5 children in the US lives with hunger.

The sooner you believe it, the sooner we can end it.

Call 1-800-FEED KIDS

feedingchildrenbetter.org

Volunteer Advertising Agency: Bartle Bogle & Hegarty   302

▶ Address an individual. One person will be reading this brochure, not a group.

▶ Provide contact information and information about the sponsoring organization on the back cover.

A community group produced the six-panel brochure shown on the next page for a project called Bears on Patrol. (The project is described in Chapter 8.) The group wanted to start a program to supply teddy bears to the local police department so that officers could calm and comfort frightened children. The group wanted to produce one brochure to tell the community about the new program and raise money to keep it going. It wanted the same brochure to help solicit donations from residents and business owners.

Webpages Public service websites combine the characteristics of print, radio, and television PSAs. As is true for all websites, whether they are out to sell you a product or service or have been created in the spirit of public

---

Lists

In the succinct, condensed style of writing text for print and televised public service advertisements, brochures, and websites, you will often find bulleted lists to be a useful way to deliver information. Lists can show steps in a process or give bits of advice.

To protect your child from accidents in the kitchen

- Turn the handles of pots and pans to the back of the stove
- Store all cleaning supplies in a child-proof cabinet
- Keep all knives off countertops
- Discard all plastic grocery bags immediately after use

Lists are a good way to display many examples in a way readers can easily and quickly peruse, choosing the pieces they find most useful.

Many plants in your garden and home are poisonous, if ingested. You probably have at least one from this list:

- Aloe vera
- Chrysanthemum
- Hydrangea
- English ivy
- Poinsettia
- Philodendron
- Rhododendron

In writing lists, always use parallel construction. That is, always use the same structure for the entries. If you begin one item with a verb, all the items on the list should begin with verbs. Make sure the verbs are consistent in tense and person (turn, store, keep, discard). Make sure items have the same level of specificity. For example, in the list of ways to protect your child from accidents, the writer breaks down each activity and focuses on the objects: handles, cleaning supplies, knives, bags.

THE MILTON CARES WITH BEARS MISSION

To provide the professionals who are the first to arrive at scenes of emergency with teddy bears to comfort, console, and calm any young children present. **Bears in action** Emergency response personnel will have Teddy Bears,., each one sealed in a plastic bag, to use in potentially traumatic situations. Some would include:

*TRAFFIC STOPS AND ACCIDENTS.

Accompanied by blaring sirens and flashing lights, police officers can seem very menacing. We hope to stock each patrol car with a Teddy Bear, to help ease the tension at traffic accidents.

panel 5

*DOMESTIC VIOLENCE CALLS.

Unfortunately, these often involve children-sometimes roused out of bed, always deeply disturbed by the turbulence they've been exposed to. Officers can use the Teddy Bear to help children focus on something comforting.

AMBULANCE CALLS.

An injured or anxious child being tended to by paramedics might certainly be calmed by a Teddy Bear.

fold

The **Milton Cares with Bears** program has been initiated by the Pine Tree Brook Neighborhood Association, cosponsored by Pam Dorsey and Dick Russell.

The following organizations have also lent valued support:

Milton Police Department
Fallon Ambulance Service
Milton Kiwanis Club
Bell Atlantic Telephone Pioneers of America
And the generosity of donations by residents of Milton

panel 6

fold

©2004 The Pine Tree Brook Neighborhood Association

MILTON CARES
WITH BEARS

Comfort for
Children in Crisis

front panel

A Pine Tree Brook Neighborhood Association project inspired by the memory of Milton Outreach
Officer Sergeant Jack Moriarty.

Contact:
dickrussell@pinetreebrook.com
11 Gibbons St. Milton, 02186
(617) 696 3751

Tri-fold brochure — double-sided

IMAGINE THIS

It's very dark outside. Flashing lights suddenly appear off in the distance, and in a blink they are all around you, very close. A siren screams, voices shout, a police radio crackles. You can't make out what any of the voices are saying. You search for a familiar face, but in the confusion there isn't one-just strangers, rushing by you, most of them in uniform. Imagine how frightened and alone you feel in the midst of this emergency scene.

Now, imagine that you are 7 years old.

THE BEAR FACTS *panel 2*

It's no secret that police and fire emergencies can be psychologically traumatic to people of all ages-but they can be especially disturbing for children.
The **Milton Cares with Bears** program was introduced, with the cooperation of the Milton Police Department, in Jan. of 2003 under the name of The 911 Bear. Experience has made us realize that we want the child to remember that the Teddy Bear was given to them by a friendly, caring, Police, Fire or EMT personal and not because of a 911 call. COMFORT FOR CHILDREN IN CRISIS. Thus the name change to **Milton Cares with Bears**.

fold

In fact, communities nationwide have started programs to provide their emergency personnel with teddy bears as a new tool. We have established **Milton Cares with Bears** project with the assistance of Milton residents and civic leaders. As one Milton official commented: "My best professional hunch is Teddy Bear can change the atmosphere of domestic violence situations and other emergency events that involve children. "Wouldn't it be great for police officers to pull out a Teddy Bear instead of entering a home with just the usual equipment: gun and handcuffs?"

panel 3

CHILD ABUSE OR NEGLECT REPORTS.

These often bring police to homes where children have experienced trauma and face displacement The Teddy Bear can provide consolation to a child in the midst of turmoil.

COMFORT FOR CHILDREN IN CRISIS Lately,
some disturbing facts have come to light.
Jan. 02 to Nov. 30, 02 there were 146 domestic calls.
Jan. 03 to Nov. 30, 03 there were 180 domestic calls.
A 20% increase. In the first quarter of 04 there have been 64 domestic calls verses 53 for the first quarter of 03.

fold

For 911 calls involving Child/Domestic Abuse, Personal Safety, Vicky McCarthy, Milton Youth Department, put together a list of 9 agencies who can provide help, 24/7, that can be left with the client.Fallon Ambulance Service had the card printed in plastic.

TO DATE

The Pine Tree Brook Neighborhood Association has secured a generous donation of 700 bears. An additional 50 bears have been purchased by The PTBNA.
Milton Kiwanis Club and the Bell Atlantic Pioneers of America have also joined the PTBNA in contributing their teddy bears to the project.

WHAT YOU CAN DO! *panel 4*

We will need financial support to keep the project going. All money received will be applied exclusively to the cost of the teddy bears. Donations may be sent to:

Dick Russell,
11 Gibbons St. Milton, MA. 02185
(617) 696-3751

Checks may be made out to the PTBNA

For more information about the
Milton Cares with Bears project check our web site: www.pinetreebrook.com

---

324

service, the homepage greets the visitor the same way a print ad or brochure cover might—by inviting the reader further into the material. All the benefits of radio and television are available to a webpage designer—pictures, sound, and text—but websites also allow for interactivity, letting visitors respond immediately. On a webpage, you must attract visitors in order to get them to scroll down and use the hot buttons, lists, and menus. One thing webpage designers sometimes forget is that the priority in designing a website is clear writing, not flashy graphics.

Clarity, especially in a website that asks a reader to take some action, comes from uncluttered language and clear organization. Your site must have a single and clear purpose. Navigational tools should link visitors to useful sections that break down that purpose. As in any PSA, you need to think about who your audience is and how you want people to use your website.

A website should include

- A homepage that attracts attention and identifies the purpose of the site through text, graphics, and sound

- Clear navigational tools that link to well-organized sections

- Sections that break down the information and can stand alone

- A section that defines the mission or purpose of the organization and/or website

- A section devoted to the call to action—subscribe, donate, find out more—possibly using interactive buttons

- Contact information: a phone number and address for questions the website doesn't answer, or a "hot" e-mail address

- Links to useful resources that provide more in-depth information about topics related to your issue

- The privacy policy

The Internet is full of models of public service advertisement webpages. A good starting place is the website of the Advertising Council (www.adcouncil .com), which keeps lists of current PSA campaigns and all their materials—for print, radio, television, and the Web.

You will find a more detailed description of what goes into writing and designing websites in Chapter 10.

Iz Yuor Kib Trying to Tel You Sumthing?

COORDINATED CAMPAIGN FOR LEARNING DISABILITIES

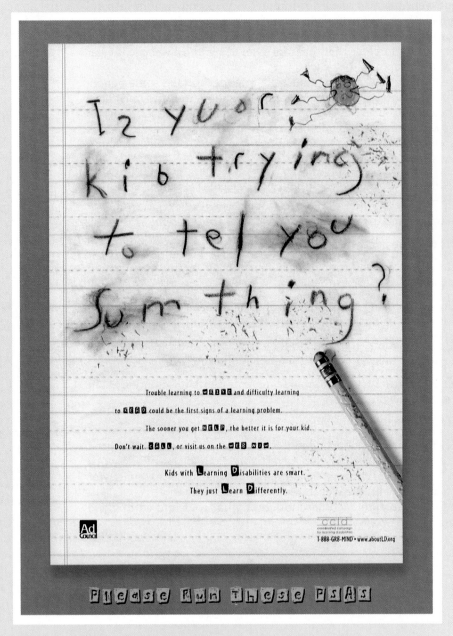

Annotate "Iz Yuor Kib Trying to Tel You Sumthing?"

1. Underline the headline.
2. What do the misspelling and youthful handwriting add to the meaning of the headline?
3. Are the misspelling and youthful handwriting effective techniques?
4. Box in the body of the text.
5. Who is the audience for this text? How do you know?
6. What effect is created by the boxed-in letters? Is this effective?

7. Where does the ad appeal to logic? Where does it appeal to emotion?
8. Put a wavy line under the call to action.
9. How clear is the call to action?
10. Is the call to action well-placed in the body of the ad?
11. Point to design elements that have not yet been noted.
12. Comment on the overall design of the ad, including both text and visuals.

Practice 9.9
Evaluating a Webpage

Read the SPAY/USA homepage. Write a brief review of this homepage, focusing on these questions.

1. What is the focal point of this page?
2. What is the purpose of this page?
3. What questions do you have after reading this page?
4. How do the designers use type? Comment on page organization.
5. Who is the audience for this page?

PRESENTING YOUR WORK: THE PITCH LETTER

Your PSA could be useful to the group or organization whose message you are promoting, so take the time to send a copy, along with a letter, off to them. The letter, sometimes called a pitch letter, piques interest in your concept. No longer than one page, a pitch letter is a quick introduction to your ideas. Always keep in mind that readers are already experts on the material. You will not need to explain insider knowledge. You will, however, need to attract attention to your idea in the first sentence. Giving readers a new way to look at issues they know well will motivate them to read on. Make sure your letter explains how your idea draws on your research and how your insights will bring the message to a new audience or to a traditional audience in a new way.

765 Haneck Road
Yardley, PA 19834

Hanlee Blake, Director
Little Cove Nature Center
Cove Inlet Road
Pocaset, NJ 18762

Dear Ms. Blake:

On a recent school outing, Mrs. Pearson's third grade class was very good about not littering. But, when their field trip was over and their yellow school bus departed, they had no idea that they had transformed the trash receptacles at Dove Pond into a treasure trove of danger for the native wildlife.

Since part of your mission is to educate children and adults about how to keep wildlife safe, we are sending materials we designed as part of our writing class assignment in public service advertising. Our campaign teaches children in a very specific way how to be animal caretakers. Most kids don't know a raccoon could get its nose stuck in a yogurt container and smother, or that animals can get strangled by the plastic rings from six-packs of soda. In researching this project we visited schools and asked children what they know about the dangers we sometimes expose animals to, inadvertently. For example, we asked Mrs. Pearson's class how many of them had released helium balloons up to the sky, and every child raised a hand. When they were asked how many knew that those balloons pop and float back to land or sea and sometimes choke hungry fish and wildlife, not a single child raised a hand.

Our PSA materials are targeted at educating children, grades 1–6, about how their everyday activities can help or hurt wildlife. We would like to offer them to you for your use in help spreading the message about being good friends to wild animals in your backyard and in the wild.

Sincerely,

Amelia Honnecker, Brian Watanabe, Fran Kelly

640 Commonwealth Ave.
Centerville, IL

Second Chance House
110 Main St.
Centerville, IL

Dear Unitarian Universalist Urban Ministry:

Many women who experience domestic abuse are difficult to reach or too scared to get help. It is important that the women of Boston are aware that your ministry provides facilities such as the Second Chance House. We would like to propose two public-service messages that are designed to help people face the facts about domestic violence and not turn away from this problem.

The purpose of the Second Chance House is to provide a safe haven for women and their children and to allow them to escape the horrors of an abusive relationship. Many women in these relationships don't have the courage to leave their partner, and this often leads to death.

We are proposing some ideas that might help your ministry. A print advertisement could be provided at places where women frequently visit—subway cars, health clubs, hair salons, and health clinics. A television advertisement could be aired on the local Centerville stations—4, 5, and 7— during primetime news hours. Both of these public-service announcements could include contact information so that women can quickly and confidentially contact the Second Chance House. We feel that our approach to this serious matter will be effective because it uses statistics to heighten awareness while promoting the resources available at the Second Chance House. These ads will reassure women that they will be safe at the Second Chance House.

Thank you for taking the time to review our ideas. We feel that our advertisements in conjunction with the program at the Second Chance House will assist women in leaving abusive relationships, getting help, and making necessary changes in their lives.

Sincerely yours,

Jeff Carson
Jacqueline Policastro
Katie Ruggeri
Joanna Simone

5,380 times a day

240 times an hour

4 times a minute

Once every 15 seconds

A woman is beaten.

Women don't wait another second . . .

END THE ABUSE

Call Second Chance House for help

Confidential 24-hour hotline:
1.800.123.4567

READINGS

Public service advertising in the United States dates back to 1942. Since then, some causes have remained consistent, some have changed, and new issues have emerged. The first two pairs of selections will give you the opportunity to compare issues, approaches, and design elements in public service advertising then and now. The last group of public service messages are from different student groups in a class that worked with a women's shelter and a homeless shelter. The students created print ads, a webpage, a pitch letter, and a brochure.

Civil Defense: Fallout Shelters and Homeland Security

YOU'VE FLOWN THE FLAG. NOW WHAT?

Since September 11th, 2001, we have all witnessed a powerful resurgence of the American spirit. But patriotism alone is not enough. We must protect ourselves and our families by learning how to be safe and calm in the event of a terrorist attack.

First, make an emergency supply kit. Set aside the supplies you'll need to survive three days at home. You'll need clothes, sleeping bags, nonperishable food and a gallon of water per person, per day. Other items will be helpful too – a flashlight, a battery-powered radio, extra batteries, a first-aid kit and toilet articles.

Second, make a family communications plan. Make sure family members know how to contact each other in an emergency. It may be smart to have everyone call an out-of-state friend or relative. Keep a list of emergency numbers near the phone. Plan how you will evacuate if you are asked to do so.

Third, be informed. In emergencies, planning pays off. If your family knows what to expect, all of you will be calmer in the aftermath of a terrorist event. For details on emergency preparedness, visit our website at www.ready.gov. Or get a free brochure by calling **1-800-BE-READY (1-800-237-3239)**.

Part of a campaign from the U.S. Department of Homeland Security and The Advertising Council. Photo courtesy of Henryk Kaiser/eStock Photo/PictureQuest.

After the September 11, 2001, terrorist attacks, the newly formed Department of Homeland Security sought to prepare the country for more attacks by issuing advisories on how to prepare.

your one
defense
against
FALLOUT
GET FREE BOOKLET
FROM LOCAL CIVIL DEFENSE

In the 1960s the U.S. government tried to prepare people for possible nuclear attack from the Soviet Union by designating, building, and equipping fallout shelters all over the country.

Critical Reading Questions

1. Compare the headlines of these two PSAs. What tone do they create?

2. Read the full text of the Homeland Security PSA. Analyze the language, identifying word choices and literary devices. What is the overall tone of the text?

3. What assumptions about the audience does each PSA make? How do you know?

4. What role do visual images play in each of these PSAs?

5. What are the calls to action of the two PSAs? How easy would it be for the reader to do what each PSA suggests?

6. Compare the persuasiveness of the two PSAs. What appeals does each use? How effective are they?

7. Do you need any historical information to help you make sense of the fallout shelter ads from the 1960s?

Questions for Writing and Discussion

1. Could you reverse time periods for these ads? How would today's American public view the campaign from the 1960s? What, if anything, has changed about the way people view public service advertising?

2. How does the image of the flag play into the message about homeland security?

South Shore Women's Center PSA

Jenna Livingston, Sarah Bomie Chae, Michael Thill, and Alexandria McManus

A student group chose a shelter for women and children as their client. They relied on the combination of typefaces to convey their message.

I burnt my hand on the stove **I fell down the stairs** I slipped on ice He didn't mean to It only happened once He apologized He told me he loves me

South Shore Women's Center provides support and counseling for women and children who are victims of domestic violence. There is a 24 hour hotline (888) 746-2664.

South Shore Women's Center is here to help **stop the excuses.**

Critical Reading Questions

1. How does the variety of typefaces work in this ad?

2. Who is the audience for the ad?

3. What is the purpose of the ad? What is the call to action?

4. Where would you place this ad?

5. How do these writers attempt to break down the obstacles or barriers between their message and their audience?

Questions for Writing and Discussion

6. This ad addresses an audience that might be reluctant to listen. What other audiences might not want to listen? Which other messages would be difficult to deliver? How have these messages been packaged in the past? For example, what kind of antismoking ads do you recall?

7. In an ad directed at women, do you lose all interest of men? Do men need to hear this message as well? Which men?

Tri-City Campaign

Kelly Elterman, Grace Lin, Owen Black, Adam Wescott, and Mariah Freda

A class took on the job of designing PSA campaigns to help Tri-City, a homeless shelter for families in Malden, Massachusetts. The client brought a very specific challenge: raise $250,000 to help finish a housing project. The student groups came up with many ideas ranging from dance marathons to partnerships with hardware stores, shoe stores and day spas. They also developed PSAs that targeted two audiences: (1) the general public, to raise awareness about the existence and mission of Tri-City, and (2) businesses, to solicit partnerships for raising funds.

The group represented here redesigned Tri-City's logo, websites, and print ad. The students use statistics, facts, and logic to appeal to the audience. (The example that follows was designed and written by students. It is not official material of Tri-City Housing.)

RAISE THE ROOF ADVERTISING Box 2023 • 277 Babcock Street • Boston, MA 02215 • (207) 329-70131

April 6, 2005

Ms. Jane Perlman
Tri-City Family Housing
350 Cross Street
Malden, MA 02148

Dear Ms. Perlman,

Tri-City Family Housing has clearly established itself as a small, community-oriented nonprofit organization. Yet as the numbers of homeless and low-income families have increased over the past decade, so has the need for housing. The housing and programs that you provide to homeless and low-income families are needed more than ever, and it is time for Tri-City to look beyond current supporters and expand fundraising efforts.

We plan to approach Boston corporations with the concept of cause marketing. Cause marketing is an up-and-coming concept within the advertising world where a corporation is linked with a charity or nonprofit organization. The corporation donates money to Tri-City and is upheld in return as a contributor to the Boston community. Both Tri-City and the corporation would benefit from such a relationship.

To advertise Tri-City Family Housing to local corporations, we plan to use business magazines and journals as the outlet for raising awareness and acquiring donations. These advertisements will lead corporations to the campaign website, where they will learn more about cause marketing and why Tri-City is a worthy cause. The proposed campaign will be successful because it spreads awareness and also seeks donations, large and small, from area corporations.

We hope that our campaign is most beneficial to your needs, and we look forward to speaking with you in the near future.

Sincerely yours,

The Raise the Roof Advertising Team

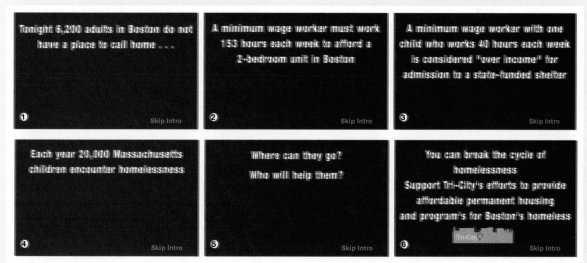

① Tonight 6,200 adults in Boston do not have a place to call home . . . .   Skip Intro

② A minimum wage worker must work 153 hours each week to afford a 2-bedroom unit in Boston   Skip Intro

③ A minimum wage worker with one child who works 40 hours each week is considered "over income" for admission to a state-funded shelter   Skip Intro

④ Each year 20,000 Massachusetts children encounter homelessness   Skip Intro

⑤ Where can they go? Who will help them?   Skip Intro

⑥ You can break the cycle of homelessness Support Tri-City's efforts to provide affordable permanent housing and program's for Boston's homeless   Skip Intro

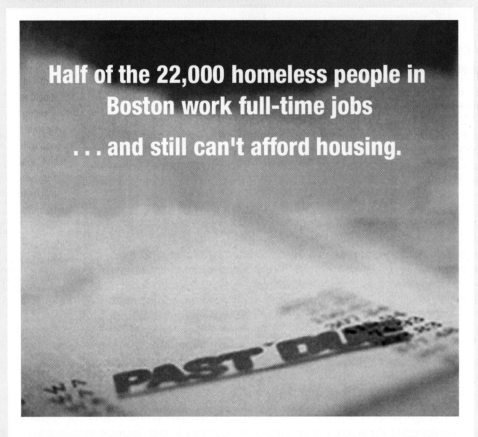

Half of the 22,000 homeless people in Boston work full-time jobs
. . . and still can't afford housing.

Housing is just the beginning. Tri-City understands that homeless families need more than shelter. Tri-City provides support, education and family programming to help get homeless families back on their feet.

Help Tri-City's "Project Hearts & Hands" fundraising campaign and get involved in their mission to break the cycle of homelessness.

Call 781-322-9119 or go to www.wayfibre.com/hearts/ for more information

Critical Reading Questions

1. Who is the audience for the print ads? Why would the target audience pay attention to this ad? How does the headline attract attention?

2. How does the rest of the text of the print ad explain the headline?

3. The print ad mentions family programming. Do you know what family programming is?

4. Do you understand what the Project Hearts & Hands fundraising campaign mentioned in the print ad is?

5. What is the call to action in the print ad?

6. What effect do the statistics have on a visitor to the website?

7. How do you think Tri-City would use the website? Who would visit it?

8. Evaluate the first sentence of the pitch letter. Does it attract attention and help the Raise the Roof Advertising Group gain credibility?

9. How does the use of the term *cause marketing* in the pitch letter help or hurt the appeal to Tri-City?

10. Does the letter offer enough information?

Questions for Writing and Discussion

1. In a large urban area, several nonprofit groups may assist homeless people. Would you want your group to blend in with the others or stand out? Why?

2. In raising awareness about a shelter for homeless people, you also need to raise awareness of the problems of homelessness in general. Where would you go for factual information about the number of people who are homeless in your county, city, or state?

WRITING IN THE WORKS

Interview with Judy Perlman

Judy Perlman is the director of Tri-City Family Housing, a non-profit organization that helps homeless families with shelter and support services, including tutoring for children. Though the group receives some public funding, Tri-City raises funds from private donors and solicits volunteers from the communities that it serves just north of Boston. The group relies heavily on newsletters and direct appeals to private donors to help keep the programs running. Perlman also uses brochures to get donations from businesses.

Judy Perlman

1. How do you use brochures and other PSA materials?

When I first came to Tri-City there was only a newsletter that came out sporadically. I've tried to become more systematic with our material. We produced a brochure, for example, that spelled out what our programs are and included it with grant application packages. When we decided to raise money for the Cross Street project (the project from the student reading in this chapter), we put together a press packet—news clips, our brochure, a copy of the newsletter. Then, we decided we needed something formal, so we chose an annual report. We think of the entire packet as a "leave behind," something potential donors can have to look at after we visit and explain our project.

2. What have you learned about putting together materials that raise awareness about your group?

One thing we discovered is how important presentation is. For example, we wanted our report to have a polished look, an eye-catching design, so we hired a graphic artist to help. We spent money on the visuals, and it was worth it. We also consulted with a freelance grant writer, who helped with the writing of the report as well as some letters of appeal.

3. How important is it that the outside consultants understand your mission?

It's extremely important that anyone who works representing Tri-City understands what we stand for. Some of the students who worked on the Cross Street fundraising project used guilt or fear as a motivator to get people to contribute. They used sad pictures. But after we talked, they realized it was not the tone for us. It's one thing to use pity as a motivator when you are talking about endangered lemurs. It's another thing to do it with homeless families. It's important to focus on the idea that we are working with capable, strong people with positive futures. I told the students to rethink their approach. Our message is that homeless families are just like everybody else; they just need a little help at the right time. Our mission involves respect.

4. How do you use print ads to raise awareness about your organization?

Interestingly enough, we don't use print ads as much as we cultivate relationships with the local newspapers. We send out press releases whenever we have an event and the local daily newspaper, which is starved for news, usually covers it. We get our name out to the public that way. We also try to be a presence in stories about public policy. We try to establish our position on any issue dealing with housing or homelessness in the press. In fact, I've become a resource for local papers (and the

Boston Globe North section) on matters of public policy affecting poor families, the housing market, and other relevant issues. These relationships are mutually advantageous.

5. In writing letters of appeal, which techniques have you found useful?

We used two letters recently. The first one was very effective. It began with a story of a family we helped. It was a story about a mother who got sick and didn't have health insurance and fell into some really hard times. I think using the specific, personal story works well. It's a real story, about real people. We sent this letter out at Thanksgiving and got a good response from donors.

The second letter started with quotes from the children living in Tri-City shelters of families who receive tutoring. We didn't have as much response with this letter. I think it was because the letter took a small piece of what we do—tutor kids, not just shelter them—and focused on that. I think it was too specific about that one service, and may have confused people who didn't know much about us.

The other factor with letters of appeal is timing. Many people gather together all the requests for their money at the end of the year, and decide which groups they will help. So, you're competing with many other groups then, but people are more willing to consider you at that time, too. At other times of the year you might not have as great a response.

Whenever you write a letter of appeal, you have to think about your reader. Some letters will go out to previous supporters, maybe people who donated housewares in the past. They already know about us. We might want to upgrade those donors, ask them to for financial support. We don't need to introduce ourselves to that group, but we can be more specific, treat them as insiders. It's really true that there are different strategies in play with different audiences.

WRITING AND REVISION STRATEGIES

Gathered here are three interactive sections for you to use as you write and revise your public service announcement.

▶ Writer's Notebook Suggestions
▶ Peer-Editing Log
▶ Revision Checklist

Writer's Notebook Suggestions

Use these exercises to do some start-up thinking and writing for your public service message.

Writers and designers say they often get the creative process started by looking at other advertisements, by looking at magazines and photography and art books, and even by reading poetry. Inspiration can come in many ways. Short exercises like the ones that follow can help get your creative process going.

1. Choose one of the images on the following page. Write a headline, text, and a call to action encouraging eighteen- to twenty-two-year-olds to vote.

2. Design a public service advertisement that will appear on the side of a bus. The topic is raising awareness about the dangers of high blood pressure. Research the topic, and define the target audience. Both alert and encourage your audience.

3. Use any news story as the basis for an ad: Use the real-life testimony about the event or some aspect of it as a cautionary tale or as an

example of a behavior or policy that works well.

4. Read the editorial section of a newspaper and develop a PSA (print or television) based on the premise of one editorial or column. Raise awareness or call your audience to a more specific action.

5. Design a storyboard for a television PSA. Your goal is to raise awareness about eating disorders among teens. Your audience is parents.

6. Choose a nonprofit group in your community, and design a calendar for it. The group can either sell the calendar to make money or give it away. The calendar should have a dif-

ferent appeal every month to remind people of the group's activities or mission.

7. Design a new logo for a group in your community.

8. Use an already-existing image for a cause, and rewrite the headline and copy. Use the original call to action.

Peer-Editing Log

As you work with a writing partner or in a peer-editing group, you can use these questions to give helpful responses to a classmate's public service message and as a guide for discussion.

Writer's Name

Date

1. Where did your eyes go first, second, last? Note spots with the numbers 1, 2, 3, etc.

2. Whom does the ad seem to be addressing? Tell the writer to whom the ad would appeal. Tell the writer to whom the ad would not appeal. Who would stop reading or not be attracted at all?

3. Did you stop anywhere because you were confused?

4. Does the ad remind you of any other ads you have seen?

5. Does the design draw you in?

6. Is the language clear?

7. Did you have to start reading from the beginning to understand the point?

8. How did the ad make you feel? Did your feelings change as you progressed through the ad?

9. If you saw this ad again, would you stop to look at it or read it?

10. Tell the writer what you think the audience is called to do, and comment on this goal.

11. Is the call to action realistic?

12. Read over the pitch letter and look for

    a. Any spots that might insult the reader

    b. Any spots that assume the reader is not well-informed

    c. Any places the letter can be condensed

Revision Checklist

As you do the final revision of your public service message, check to make sure that you

❏ Used language appropriate to your target audience,

❏ Created a headline that attracts attention,

❏ Provided compelling reasons in the body of the message,

❏ Included a clear call to action.

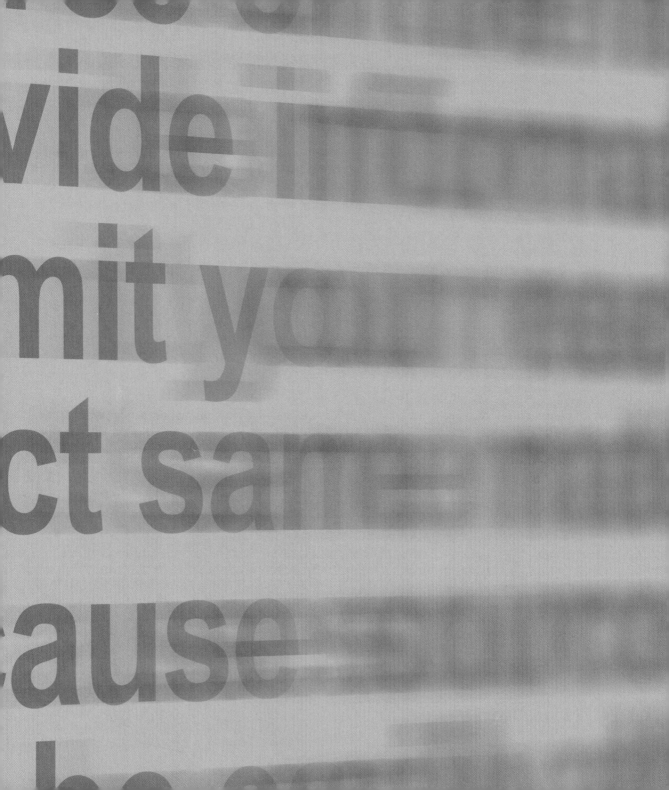

10. WEBSITES

WRITING FOR ELECTRONIC SOURCES

Anyone who has lost track of time when using a computer knows the propensity to dream, the urge to make dreams come true, and the tendency to miss lunch.

— Tim Berners-Lee

ASSIGNMENT

Design and write the text for an informational website (see Chapter 3 for help) or a public service website (see Chapter 9 for help). Create a homepage and three additional pages. Choose one of the following topics (or your own public service issue), and collect and list local resources that people in your community would find useful.

- Food pantries
- Gambling addiction programs
- Learn-to-swim programs
- Places to volunteer your time
- Meals on Wheels programs
- Recycling
- Community gardens
- After-school programs
- Music education

Include links to national sites, but concentrate on resources available in your area. The Writing in the Works website provides information on Web hosting for your webpages.

WEBSITES

Can the ideas of a Greek philosopher from around 300 BC help us write for the most modern medium—the World Wide Web? As it turns out, they can. One of the cornerstones of Aristotle's theory about how to be an effective communicator involved thinking about audience. Aristotle said that you need to think about who your readers are and what they expect from your writing.

Research about how people read on the Web tells us that, in some sense, they do not. For the most part, when people look at webpages they do not read as much as they skim. Think about your own experience on the Net. If you are like most people, you are looking for information when you go to the Web, and you want it quickly and concisely. You might be looking for information for a report for class or to settle a bet, or you might be looking for ratings or reviews of MP3 players or laptop computers, or you might want to look at photos that accompany a news story you heard on the radio.

Even if you are one of the relatively few Internet users who actually spends a lot of time reading e-zines or online newspapers or magazines, you still appreciate economy of language while navigating sites. Once you find what you are looking for, you probably value conciseness, because reading on the Web is slower and more cumbersome than reading on paper. Research shows that people read about 25 percent more slowly on computers, largely because text is not that easy to read on screens. Besides that, the size of the screen limits the number of words, and scrolling up and down and clicking from page to page can be a hassle. Most readers who need to read anything of any real length find that it works best to print out hard copy.

The bottom line is that, to communicate effectively on the Internet, you have to think about what your audience wants or you will not have an audience. The Internet is, by its nature, hot and fast. Users who do not find what they need or want quickly click and zoom off to another site.

Good, tight writing is key. But while brevity is crucial, other factors also determine how well you communicate on the Web. You have to pay some attention to page design. If a page is difficult to read or the navigation is cumbersome or confusing, it will not matter how good your writing is. To make a visit to your site useful and efficient, you need clear content and excellent organization.

Applications: School, Community, Work

Though you might be asked to write an online research paper at school, most of your writing for the Web will take place at work or at home. The Web has become a worldwide community bulletin board, where, among other things, people can post informational websites to make their knowledge available to others. If you are passionate about a subject, posting your informational website and sharing your interest can be satisfying. In a way, publicly expressing your knowledge, research, experience, and expertise on a website is like publishing a book. Knowing how to do it well can make your pursuit even more effective.

In the workplace or in a community group, you could write a website to provide information, to offer services or products for profit, or to persuade people about an issue or a candidate. People with access to the Web often turn to a search engine as a first step in getting information, much as they used a telephone directory in years gone by. A website can supply a list of sources for further investigation—links to related websites and even phone numbers—and much more. The information you provide can have your own imprint. Your pages can give people so much good information they will not have to go anywhere else. Understanding how to make your writing clear, concise, and useful will help you write websites at work and at home that attract visitors and keep them reading.

CHAPTER OBJECTIVES

This chapter is different from other assignment chapters in that it does not supply information about how to develop a topic. In this chapter you will learn how to edit, lay out, and format your writing for Web readers. The chapter will show you how to write clearly for all kinds of websites.

In this chapter you will learn to

▶ write succinctly and concisely, considering how and why readers use Web sources

▶ organize material to use electronic media to your advantage

▶ consider the importance of layout and design in writing for the Web

**Warm-Up Practice 10.1
Collaborative Activity**

1. Make a list of the websites you visit most often. Do they sell products, give news or information, or express a particular perspective or view on subjects?

2. Make a chart dividing the websites you listed into categories.

3. How do your favorite sites compare to your classmates' favorites?

4. Can you think of any website you have visited that you will not go back to? Why?

V I S U A L
L I T E R A C Y

Analyzing Design and Layout of Webpages

Visit two websites: www.graphics.com and www.salon.com. Explore the sites, and then comment on their design:

1. Do the fonts and colors attract your attention? Do the designers include other visual elements that attract attention?

2. Is the layout—that is, the visual organization of the elements—clear and easy to follow?

3. Can you tell what the website is about?

4. How would you improve the look—the font choices, color, other visual elements, and layout—of either of these sites?

UNDERSTANDING WEBSITES

Since the care and feeding of users is your focus, you need to consider how people read pages before you start to write. Researchers tell us that Web users tend to look at pages much as people read newspapers—and this goes for users of all types of websites. First, people scan headlines and subheads for information and to try to find material they want. This means that writing good, meaningful headlines is crucial.

When users decide to spend more time with a section, they find that it is a quicker read if the piece is written in inverted pyramid style, so that they get the main points first. Inverted pyramid style, you may remember from Chapter 6, involves organizing information with a summary and all the main points appearing first and details following in descending order of importance.

Because people use browsers to find information, you cannot assume that visitors to your site will read the pages in a particular sequence. Visitors may begin their tour on a page deep inside a website, rather than at the homepage. A browser search for information on the late rapper Tupac Shakur, for example, might take you to a page within the Death Row Records website, not to the site's first page. Thus each of your pieces should logically follow one another but at the same time must be independent of the others. This practice is called "chunking," because you are doling out your material in related but discrete chunks for the convenience of the reader.

Your piece must be concise—short and to the point. Avoid hyperbole—exaggerated, overstated, adjective-laden language that wastes time and can make the material seem false. Research suggests that Web users, like newspaper readers, have greater trust in material delivered in language that is more neutral, with fewer hyped-up adjectives. In other words, visitors to a site do not like the hard sell, either for a product or an idea.

Pearl Jam

Organization of Websites

When you are planning a site, you will probably find it helpful to sit down and do an outline first. Outlining can help focus your thinking about what you want on your site and how you want to organize and layer information. The longer and wordier the writing, the better your chance of losing readers on the Web.

Research shows that only a relatively small percentage of users will scroll down to look at material that does not initially appear on the screen. There are some exceptions, which we will discuss later, but in general Web users want information quickly. As you think about organizing your material, consider how you can break your topic into smaller, easier-to-scan pieces and post each piece or a small group of related pieces on separate hypertext-linked pages on your site. Hypertext links allow users to click on a single word or phrase and be immediately transferred to another page on your site or a different site.

Write an Outline Writing an outline will help you to see ways to divide your big topic into easily read pieces. Breaking up the material will not only make each portion easier to grasp quickly; it also will help visitors who are looking for specific information. That way, users in search of material on Pearl Jam, for example, will not have to sift through all the material on a website on grunge music to find what they want. Instead they go directly to a page devoted to the band.

I. **Overview: Grunge Music**

  A. History and background

    1. Philosophy

    2. Importance of the movement's roots in Seattle, Washington, and the Northwest

  B. Musical origins

    1. Punk

    2. Alternative rock

  C. Musical characteristics

    1. "Dirty," murky guitar sound

    2. Heavy drumming

II. **The central bands**

  A. Nirvana

    1. History

    2. Members of the band

  B. Pearl Jam

    1. History

    2. Members of the band

  C. Alice in Chains

    1. History

    2. Members of the band

  D. Stone Temple Pilots

    1. History

    2. Members of the band

  E. Soundgarden

    1. History

    2. Members of the band

On the first, or homepage, of this grunge site, you could have one short, concise essay that quickly summarizes this material, giving little detail.

> The grunge movement involved a type of music that sprang up in the late 1980s and early 1990s that embraced defiance but still achieved commercial success.
>
> The genre found its roots in the culture of the <u>Pacific Northwest</u> and embraced a <u>rejection of corporate-dominated popular culture.</u>
>
> Musically, grunge finds its roots in <u>punk</u> and <u>alternative rock</u> and is characterized by a <u>"dirty" or murky guitar sound</u> and <u>heavy drumming.</u>
>
> Influential bands include
>   ❭ Nirvana
>   ❭ Pearl Jam
>   ❭ Alice in Chains
>   ❭ Stone Temple Pilots
>   ❭ Soundgarden

From your quick overview of grunge music, you could link to related pages on your site that offer short essays on all of the subtopics. Each underlined word or phrase represents a link to a subtopic: the link from <u>Pacific Northwest</u> would take you to a page with an essay on how and why grunge sprang up in the region; the link from <u>rejection of corporate-dominated popular culture</u> would go to a piece on the cultural context of the time.

You could set up your links directly in the text, in buttons or a navigation bar on your page, or in both places, allowing users to click on words or phrases in the piece and in a listing on the side or top of the page.

Writing for Websites: Content

These guidelines for writing for the Web might seem familiar to you since concise language and clear organization are important in most writing. Because the Web reader is reading on the screen, rapidly skimming material, and jumping around the site, it is important to pay special attention to several Web-specific aspects of writing.

  ❭ Crafting headlines
  ❭ Writing in inverted pyramid style (the way news stories are arranged)
  ❭ Chunking related material
  ❭ Being concise and careful with language.

Headlines Headlines are very important in writing for the Web. Research tells us that readers scan a site's headlines before they look at any other type.

Practice 10.2
Create an Outline for a Website

Choose a topic you know something about and are interested in, and write an outline for an informational website.

In fact, they often glean much of the information they get from a site from the headlines.

Headlines also break up the type on a page so that reading it does not appear such a daunting undertaking. They alert readers, who are most likely looking for something specific, about where they are in the site. In this way, headlines are a crucial navigating tool. They help users find what they need quickly, the way that road signs might.

As an example, say that you land on a webpage that offers advice on how to get into medical school. The page loads, and there are three headlines over three short essays. The main headline asks, "What's Up, Doc?" The first subhead warns, "The First Cut Is the Deepest," and the last one says, "Talking Cure."

What's Up, Doc?

The First Cut Is the Deepest

Talking Cure

Cute, perhaps, but what is this about? You cannot tell from the headlines. If visitors cannot determine the content of a site from the headlines, many will not waste time sifting through the type but will instead go in search of pages that will likely be more useful. There are, after all, billions of webpages—no shortage of competition for readers' eyes.

What if the headlines were changed so that the main one looks like this?

What It Takes to Get into Med School

The Importance of Grades and Test Scores

Preparing for the All-Important Interview

The headline is now "What It Takes to Get into Med School." The first subhead is "The Importance of Grades and Test Scores." The final one is "Preparing for the All-Important Interview." This is clear. A reader can follow this progression of topics with ease.

The first tip for writing headlines is to avoid trying to be cute or edgy at the expense of meaning. Be direct. Headlines are like road signs. Visitors skimming your page will likely be more annoyed than amused by a road sign that offers them no information or guidance. And, since headlines do function as road signs, keep them short. Limit yourself to about six to eight words. Use action verbs wherever possible, and do not be afraid to drop articles like *the, a,* and *an* or the conjunction *and* if your headline is getting too long.

Inverted Pyramid Like news writers, Web writers organize their material on the basis of the inverted (upside-down) pyramid (see Chapter 6). The main point is reported in the first several sentences; you begin with the conclusion so that what the piece is about is immediately clear. In news stories, *who, what, when,* and *where* are quickly stated. What follows are the details, the explanation of *how* and *why.* This organization makes sense if we go back to Aristotle's directive: think about your reader and what your reader expects. Web users want information quickly. They want to scan, to get to their desired destination as quickly as possible. They are not "pleasure" readers.

Chunking Chunking material on webpages is necessary because of the way browsers produce results for searches and because it helps users find what they are looking for as quickly as possible.

Individual sites tend to be organized in linear fashion, not unlike a publication on paper. The first, or homepage, tells the reader what the site is about. Sometimes that means that a short essay gives an overview of a topic. Most retail sites are organized like catalogs with no real overview, and the homepage instead serves as a product index. Newspaper and magazine sites, like retail sites, tend to feature summaries of stories, called teasers, that link to pieces inside the site.

After that, a series of linked pages usually follows. These pages offer additional or more in-depth information or listings. Often material on these pages will also link to related material on other sites.

While individual sites might be organized like separate publications, browsers don't see sites but rather billions of individual electronic pages containing trillions of words. Browsers search cyberspace for the best match of keywords on pages to help users find specific information quickly.

A browser search might take a visitor to the homepage of a website, but more often search results tend to send users to discrete pages and multiple sites. Once on a page, many users follow links to related material on other sites. A visitor to a site on breast cancer awareness might follow links to pages on the American Cancer Society or the Susan G. Komen Breast Cancer Foundation site.

In other words, you cannot assume that visitors will move through your site sequentially. While material on your site may relate in a logical, sequential fashion, the material on each page must be able to stand independently.

When you are writing the chunk for each page, you will probably be repeating yourself at times to make sure that each self-contained piece is complete and makes sense. Do not worry about it. Some redundancy from page to page is necessary.

When deciding what and how much material to chunk on a page, you need to find a happy medium. Research tells us that users prefer shorter pages. Most Web authorities suggest trying to keep pages to no more than 150 words.

However, research also tells us that visitors want to be able to read deeply about subjects about which they are most interested. Users tend to be willing to stay with longer pages to the extent that they think they will find what they want or need.

Generally, Web designers try to resolve the conflicting goals of the need for speed and the desire for more detail by carefully breaking subjects into subtopics, each placed on a separate linked page.

Sometimes it can be difficult to break up material in a reasonable or sensible way. If you fall into the trap of arbitrarily breaking material into chunks

Practice 10.3   Finding the Most Efficient Organization

Read the following examples about African American inventors, and explain which is the easiest to understand quickly:

1. According to U.S. laws in the early nineteenth century, both slaves and freedmen could patent their inventions.

   Then in 1857, a slave owner named Oscar Stuart patented the "double cotton scraper," which had been invented by one of his slaves.

   A civil suit arose over whether Stuart or his slave had the right to claim the patent. Stuart argued that whatever a slave produced belonged to the master. In response to the suit the patent laws were changed in 1858 so that only freedmen could be granted patents. Thomas Jennings was born in 1791. Jennings, an African-American, was a free tradesman and ran a dry cleaning business in New York.

   On March 3, 1821, Thomas Jennings became the first African-American to receive a patent for a dry cleaning process called "dry scouring." Jennings used the money he earned from his patent to buy his family out of slavery.

2. Thomas Jennings became the first African-American to be granted a patent on March 3, 1821, for a dry-cleaning process called "dry scouring."

   Jennings, who was a freedman in New York and owned a dry cleaning business, used the money he earned from the patent to buy his family out of slavery.

   In the early nineteenth century, when Jennings received his patent, both slaves and freedmen could receive patents, but that changed in 1858 because of a lawsuit. In 1857 a slave owner named Oscar Stuart patented a "double cotton scraper" based on an invention by his slave. A civil suit was pressed over whether Stuart or the slave should have been granted the patent.

   Stuart argued that whatever the slave produced belonged to the master. The U.S. Patent Office subsequently changed the law so that slaves could no longer receive patents.

or fragmenting the material too much, visitors to your site will become frustrated and leave.

Return to the grunge website outline: Your plan calls for placing the history of each band and biographies of its members on a single page. It is not hard to foresee the possibility of exceeding the 150-word-per-page limit here. At this point you might need to use some judgment about how to chunk the material. You could put just the history of a band on one page and link to another page containing the biographies of its members. It would also be possible to give each musician his own page.

Your central criterion for deciding how to chunk should be usefulness. If you have a significant amount of material about each band member and you think users will largely be interested in specific individuals, you might decide to post biographies separately. If, however, you think visitors would be interested in all the band members, you might decide to post all the biographies on a single page and trust that visitors will not find a longer page too daunting.

The 150-word rule is a good guideline, but if visitors find information useful and compelling enough, they will probably print out a longer page and read the whole thing. Again, trying to anticipate the wants and needs of your audience should be the ultimate governing factor.

Conciseness and Language   No matter how you decide to chunk your material, being concise is crucial if you want to keep readers' interest.

Being concise means being as economical with language as possible. Try to write simple, declarative sentences in active voice, and use action verbs as much as possible. Many Web editors suggest drafting what you think you want to say and then trying to cut the number of words by 50 percent or more.

Do not be afraid to use bulleted lists and meaningful sentence fragments. Such devices make material much easier for Web robots (also called spiders, among other names) to scan. If a search engine's Web robot easily scans your site, the site will show up on more searches and thus will have more readers.

Most Web experts suggest limiting each paragraph to a single idea. Typically, this will mean that each paragraph will only include a sentence or two, making things easier for the reader. Shorter, snappier paragraphs, sentences, phrases, and lists are easier to skim.

Long-winded, flabby language slows Web users down and turns them off. Research tells us that language that reads like advertising or marketing is another big turnoff. Web users tend to be media-savvy, and credibility is important to them. They know that it is often difficult to tell who is behind a website and how trustworthy its information is. Obviously, official government sites or those of well-known and respected institutions, like colleges and universities, instantly have more credibility. But many Internet sources do not provide definitive clues about their credibility.

Practice 10.4
Identifying Concise
Language

Look at the two examples,
and decide which is the
quicker read.

1. It was not immediately
    apparent to members of
    the recording industry
    that Napster would some
    day pose a competitive
    threat of the magnitude
    that the Internet-based
    music-sharing service
    would eventually become.
    The companies just didn't
    believe that Napster
    would catch on so quickly
    or broadly. It was also a
    miscalculation on their
    part regarding how much
    users would come to favor
    downloading as a form of
    distribution for music.

2. The recording industry
    failed to see how serious
    a threat Napster would
    become. They failed to
    anticipate

    • How fast Napster would
       grow in popularity
    • How much users would
       like downloading music
       directly

Because they are media-savvy, users expect to find "marketese" on retail sites. They are not surprised to discover cars or portable DVD players being touted with puffed-up adjectives or unsubstantiated, subjective claims. When they are looking for solid information, however, such language serves as a red flag.

Two of the most prominent experts on Web use, Jakob Nielsen and John Morkes, have learned through experiments that using more neutral language in place of exaggerated advertising language increases usability by about 26 percent. Here are the writing samples they used in an experiment. The first is laden with "marketese," and the second uses more neutral language.

1. Nebraska is filled with internationally recognized attractions that draw large crowds of people every year without fail. In 1996, some of the most popular places were Fort Robinson State Park (355,000), Scotts Bluff National Monument (132,166), Arbor Lodge State Historical Park & Museum (100,000), Carhenge (86,598), Stuhr Museum of the Prairie Pioneer (60,002), and Buffalo Bill Ranch State Historical Park (28,446).

2. Nebraska has several attractions. In 1996, some of the most visited places were Fort Robinson State Park (355,000), Scotts Bluff National Monument (132,166), Arbor Lodge State Historical Park & Museum (100,000), Carhenge (86,598), Stuhr Museum of the Prairie Pioneer (60,002), and Buffalo Bill Ranch State Historical Park (28,446).

—Jakob Nielsen, *Designing Web Usability: The Practice of Simplicity*

Nielsen and Morkes assumed that more neutral language would improve the credibility of the piece, but they were surprised to discover an added bonus. More objective language actually made the material quicker and easier to assimilate because readers didn't have to sift through the hyperbole to get to the information. They didn't have to stop to evaluate claims such as whether Nebraska really is "filled with internationally recognized attractions."

The lesson here is obvious. Being clear, concise, and straight with readers will help you reach a wider audience and inform them more effectively.

Designing Websites

Now that you know something about writing for the Web, it is time to start thinking about how to design webpages. As with writing, your key consideration is audience. You now have to figure out how to design pages that help make a user's search easier and faster. As a general rule, good webpage design is about simplicity and usability.

The two major aspects to consider are layout and design elements. Layout involves the general organization or architecture of a page. You want to make sure that the layout of your pages helps visitors find what they need quickly and efficiently. Design elements involve typefaces, type sizes, colors, and graphics, photographs, and other art elements. Besides making pages more attractive, design elements can help add to or detract from the usability of your site.

HTML The building blocks of webpage design are HTML codes. HTML stands for hypertext markup language—the computer codes that dictate what a page will look like. HTML codes determine where type begins and ends, what typeface is used and how big it is, and where pictures should go. You can see the HTML coding behind any webpage by going to the View pull-down menu at the top of your browser window and clicking on Source.

In the early days of the Web, all pages had to be coded by hand. Today easy-to-use WYSIWYG (pronounced wizzy-wig, it stands for "what you see is what you get") software will help you build webpages without having to use HTML. Besides handling all HTML coding chores, Web design software provides templates, or designs, for pages, along with a menu of design elements that you can select.

Many of the larger Internet service providers, like America Online, offer free, easy-to-use webpage software or page templates. In fact, if you wanted to build a page mostly made up of type, even Microsoft Word, the ubiquitous word-processing program, will let you save your documents as webpages.

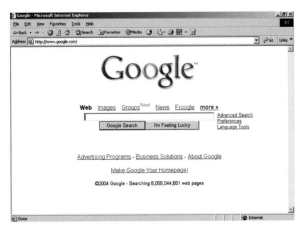

This is the page that you see.

This is the HTML code for the page that you see.

Courtesy of Google.

Layout While webpage software can make creating a page much simpler by offering you a palette of design choices, it will not make design decisions for you, and it will not tell you what makes for good, useful design. Take a look at the Google webpage as it might appear in your browser (see page 353). Now look at the HTML code for this particular page.

While there are billions of webpages, the vast majority use one of two basic types of layout style: simple, which is also called runoff, and grid. The key to deciding which style to use is appropriateness. You need to consider what kind of site you are designing, who will use it, and how they will use it. Will visitors come to your site in search of a quick hit of information, or are they likely to print out pages?

Runoff, a term coined by webpage designer Tim Slavin, is the simplest and most basic type of layout. Most of the earliest webpages are designed in this style. Runoff looks pretty much the way it sounds: type and headlines run from the top of the page to the bottom in a straight line, much like a typewritten page.

Runoff pages are becoming less and less common. Because the style produces pages that typically look like big, daunting masses of gray type and tend to be visually uninviting, runoff is used primarily for medical, technical, academic, or government pages where users are assumed to have a strong interest in the subject matter, want as much information as possible with the fewest distractions, and will most likely print out large portions or all of the material on the site.

The other, and most common, type of layout is the grid style. In this style, material is laid out in square or rectangular blocks. The most common grid layouts consist of three, four, or five sections.

Grid-style layouts offer visitors a tremendous amount of easy-to-scan information. They offer designers a lot of flexibility, letting them guide visitors through a page by placing important information prominently and downplaying less important material.

Typically, a top block runs horizontally across the top of the page. It usually displays the page and/or site title. Researchers tell us that users tend to read pages from the top down. Placing the title of the site at the top of page gives readers the first and most important information about the site: what it is about.

Often, either a second horizontal block or a vertical block down the left side of the page is reserved for buttons or a navigation bar that links to other material on the site. Having this kind of index on each page is vital. It allows users to hop from page to page, and it tells visitors what else on the site may be of interest to them. It is a good way to pull users into your site and keep them longer.

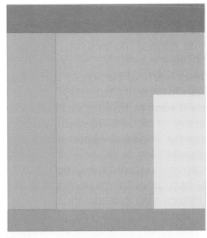

Grid design for a webpage

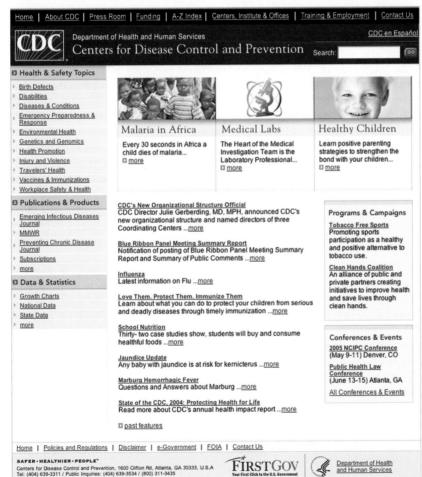

Home | About CDC | Press Room | Funding | A-Z Index | Centers, Institute & Offices | Training & Employment | Contact Us

CDC Department of Health and Human Services
CDC en Español
Centers for Disease Control and Prevention Search: [ ] GO

▣ Health & Safety Topics

> Birth Defects
> Disabilities
> Diseases & Conditions
> Emergency Preparedness & Response
> Environmental Health
> Genetics and Genomics
> Health Promotion
> Injury and Violence
> Travelers' Health
> Vaccines & Immunizations
> Workplace Safety & Health

▣ Publications & Products

> Emerging Infectious Diseases Journal
> MMWR
> Preventing Chronic Disease Journal
> Subscriptions
> more

▣ Data & Statistics

> Growth Charts
> National Data
> State Data
> more

Malaria in Africa
Every 30 seconds in Africa a child dies of malaria...
▣ more

Medical Labs
The Heart of the Medical Investigation Team is the Laboratory Professional...
▣ more

Healthy Children
Learn positive parenting strategies to strengthen the bond with your children...
▣ more

CDC's New Organizational Structure Official
CDC Director Julie Gerberding, MD, MPH, announced CDC's new organizational structure and named directors of three Coordinating Centers ...more

Blue Ribbon Panel Meeting Summary Report
Notification of posting of Blue Ribbon Panel Meeting Summary Report and Summary of Public Comments ...more

Influenza
Latest information on Flu ...more

Love Them. Protect Them. Immunize Them
Learn about what you can do to protect your children from serious and deadly diseases through timely immunization ...more

School Nutrition
Thirty- two case studies show, students will buy and consume healthful foods ...more

Jaundice Update
Any baby with jaundice is at risk for kernicterus ...more

Marburg Hemorrhagic Fever
Questions and Answers about Marburg ...more

State of the CDC, 2004: Protecting Health for Life
Read more about CDC's annual health impact report ...more

▣ past features

Programs & Campaigns

Tobacco Free Sports
Promoting sports participation as a healthy and positive alternative to tobacco use.

Clean Hands Coalition
An alliance of public and private partners creating initiatives to improve health and save lives through clean hands.

Conferences & Events

2005 NCIPC Conference
(May 9-11) Denver, CO

Public Health Law Conference
(June 13-15) Atlanta, GA

All Conferences & Events

SAFER·HEALTHIER·PEOPLE™
Centers for Disease Control and Prevention, 1600 Clifton Rd, Atlanta, GA 30333, U.S.A
Tel: (404) 639-3311 / Public Inquiries: (404) 639-3534 / (800) 311-3435

FIRSTGOV
Your First Click to the U.S. Government

Department of Health and Human Services

The biggest block, in the center of the page, is for the main content. Sometimes, depending on the content, the main block is divided into two columns (vertical blocks) or some number of columns and rows (horizontal blocks). Placing the main content in the center of the page not only makes it easy to find but also is a visual clue that visitors have arrived at the main attraction. On some sites, such as news sites, the content block contains a series of short summaries that link to full-length pieces on other pages.

Various material may appear in the fourth block, which may be placed at the bottom of the page or along the right side. A horizontal block across the bottom may contain links, disclaimers, or a copyright note. A vertical block along the right side of the page may contain more links, photos, graphics, or advertisements. Deciding where to place this fourth block depends on the relative importance of the material. Since readers tend to read pages from top to bottom, placing it at the bottom gives it less visibility than does running it along the right side of the page.

Designers sometimes separate blocks with horizontal and vertical rules. Be judicious in using such rules. They can give a page a cramped, cluttered look. Consider using extra white space to separate material instead. It will make for a much cleaner design.

The keys to making grid layouts useful are consistency and predictability. Once you decide what size to make each block and what kind of material to put in each one, keep your design consistent on every page in your site. This will make the organization of your site predictable for users. As they move from page to page, visitors will know where to look to find the information they need.

A final consideration on grid pages is the length of the page itself. As a general rule, shorter is better. Fitting your material on one screen is best. A longer page increases the risk of losing all but the faithful few visitors.

Design Elements Effective use of design elements requires a certain amount of discipline. Many people are tempted to select overly elaborate or ornate typefaces and graphic elements. Resist the impulse. In webpage design, less really is more. Design with your user in mind, and keep it simple.

Typefaces and Backgrounds The most fundamental design element choices involve type (also called *font*) and backgrounds. First, you need to select typefaces for headlines and body type. The most important consideration is readability. Limit yourself to one typeface for body type and no more than two others—one for main headlines and the other for subheads. If you use too many different typefaces, your page will look like a ransom note and will be more distracting than useful.

The two main typeface families are serif and sans serif. Serif typefaces have little extra strokes at the ends of the main horizontal and vertical strokes. Sans serif faces do not have the little flourishes. Most print publications use serif typefaces for the main body type because serif is believed to be more readable than sans serif when used in a smaller size. On the other hand, Web design gurus say that sans serif type is more readable on computer screens.

You could use the body typeface for the headlines, but contrast tends to create more visual interest, so you might consider using different typefaces for headlines. For example, if you use sans serif type for the body, you might want to use a serif face for the headlines. You might also consider using a heavier or darker type for headlines. Avoid italic and type that looks like handwriting because both tend to be difficult to scan quickly.

You will be able to choose colors for the type and background. To make your page easier to read, ensure that there is a lot of contrast between the type and the background. Black type against a white background may seem dull, but it is the easiest combination to read. Most webpages are black on white, sometimes with some type in another color for accent. Very small white type on a black background can be difficult to read. Be aware of type size when you use highly contrasting background.

Other color combinations do offer enough contrast to be readable, but stay away from type over patterned backgrounds and type over photographs or illustrations. Placing type over a busy background makes the words difficult to read.

Deciding on type size is relatively straightforward. The relative size and darkness of type should help guide a visitor through a page. Visitors' eyes will be drawn to the biggest type on the page first, so the largest and darkest type should be reserved for main headlines. Use a smaller, lighter type for subheads, and the smallest type for your body type.

As a general rule, you want the size of your main headlines to be two to three times as big as your body type. Most body type is 10 to 14 points, so most main headlines should be about 20 to 42 points. You will need to experiment, especially if you use different typefaces for body type and headlines.

As with the layout of your page and choice of typefaces, consistency is important. Once you pick a typeface and size for headlines and body type, remain consistent throughout your pages. If you keep changing them, visitors will find it distracting. It bears repeating that the key to useful webpage design is simplicity and consistency, so users will be able to scan your pages without jarring distractions and navigate your pages quickly and nearly intuitively.

The Children's Literature Web Guide is an example of a personal page. The site designer combines many different typefaces.

1. Count the number of typefaces you see.

2. Does the designer use the different typefaces to emphasize something about the content?

The Children's Literature Web Guide

Internet Resources Related to Books for Children and Young Adults

Features
› What's New!
› What We're Reading: Commentary on Children's Books
› Web-Traveller's Toolkit: Essential Kid Lit Websites

Discussion Boards
› Readers Helping Readers
› Conference Bulletin Board

Quick Reference
› Children's Book Awards
› The Year's Best Books
› Children's Bestsellers

More Links
› Authors on the Web
› Stories on the Web
› Readers' Theatre
› Lots of Lists: Recommended Books

About this Website
› Introduction
› Search this Site

Reprinted by permission of David K. Brown.

Illustrations, Art, and Photos The last major design elements are graphics: photos, art, and illustrations. Try to limit their use for two reasons.

First, either poor choices or overuse of graphics can prove distracting. Research tells us that users' eyes tend to be immediately drawn to big, colorful graphics. Having them on your pages can enhance the presentation of your material if they illustrate a point or add significant information. But if they are not clearly germane or are used merely to create visual interest, or if there are too many, they can distract and annoy users who are trying to find information quickly.

Imagine going to a page to look for statistical data for a report on world hunger and finding a photograph of the Himalayas or a graph tracking the gross domestic product of European and Asian nations in the middle of the page. First you would wonder whether you were in the right place; after that you would probably be a little annoyed. Either way, the likelihood of remaining on the site would fall dramatically. Similarly, if you found a dozen pictures of starving children, the photographs might be deeply affecting, but having to wade through so many would grow tiresome.

That leads to the second reason to limit the amount of artwork on your pages. More art causes the pages to take longer to download. Perhaps when more users have high-speed Internet connections, this problem will become less important, but most users do not have fast hook-ups right now. According to researchers, few people will wait longer than fifteen to twenty seconds for a page to download before losing patience.

Don't Steal Art Many people mistakenly assume that material they find on the Web is free for the taking. That is wrong. Technically, once any material is committed to a tangible medium, it is subject to copyright protection, and it cannot be used without permission from the copyright holder. You can assume that pretty much everything you find on the Internet is protected unless it is clearly marked as being within the public domain.

The law does allow for "fair use" of material protected by copyright. Essentially, it is probably acceptable to download and use a piece of art from the Web for an assignment for class. But before you make numerous copies for distribution, use it on a publicly available site, or try to make money with it in any way, you need to secure the right to do so. Whenever you do use any art created by another person, indicate the source nearby, so that the authorship is clear.

Using art can make for more powerful, effective communication, but as with all aspects of creating a webpage, never forget that you are creating it for a user, not for yourself.

Anatomy of a Webpage

The website shown here in three layers of screen captures illustrates some of the points about the writing and layout of webpages. This website is especially easy to navigate and has many layers, leading from the general to the more specific.

The Densho Website: Homepage

The homepage of the Densho website illustrates the grid layout with multimedia links and five main sections. Each section has multiple branches that lead a visitor through layers of specificity. The site has pop-up footnotes as well.

Homepage for the Densho website

1. First layer is the homepage

2. Simple colors

3. Concise overview of organization and website

4. Easy to see at a glance what might be of interest

5. Headline

6. Chunking

7. Grid layout organization

8. One main typeface (sans serif) in varying sizes and colors

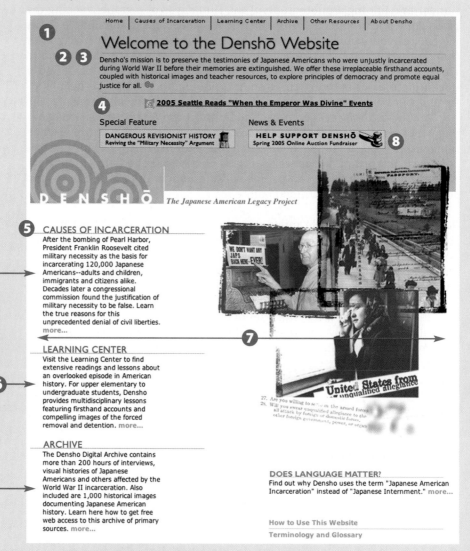

The Densho Website: Second Layer

When we clicked on the headline "Causes of Incarceration" on the homepage, we were linked to a page titled "What does an American look like?" On the right side of this four-paragraph section are links to four subsections that provide background explanation elaborating on the causes.

- History of Racism
- Failure of Leadership
- Wartime Hysteria
- Economic Motives

Notice that the paragraphs and sentences are short and concise.

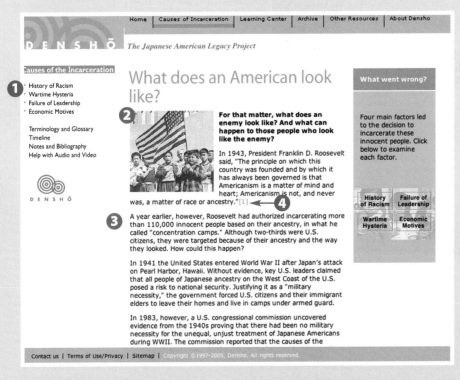

Second layer of the Densho website

1. Outline of ideas with subtopics chunked

2. Limited artwork (makes page load faster)

3. Short paragraphs

4. Pop-up footnotes.

The Densho Website: Third Layer

In the second layer, we clicked on "Wartime Hysteria." This subsection has hyperlinks. Colored type reveals further information is available in yet another layer.

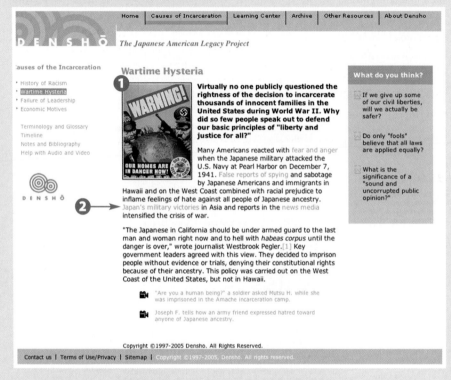

Third layer of the Densho website

1. Photos help explain the topic.

2. Hyperlinks explain ideas, keep chunks short, and provide more depth with another click.

Reading and Analyzing Websites

Because webpages are multidimensional, with hyperlinks and buttons, they are difficult to reduce to a printed page for analysis. In order to analyze a webpage, you must see it on a computer screen. Choose a website you find interesting. Spend some time reading the site and using the buttons and hyperlinks. (You can link to some sites for analysis through the Writing in the Works website.)

Assume the identity of a consultant hired by the group or company responsible for the website you have chosen. Use the scorecard below to help you generate ideas. Then write a two-page memo addressed to the company or group, with the following information.

1. A one-sentence overview of your opinion

2. A detailed evaluation of all aspects, with examples and illustrations to help make your points clear

3. Recommendations for ways to improve the site

SCORE CARD

	1 (weak)	2	3	4	5 (strong)
Headlines					
Organization					
Chunking					
Conciseness					
Design layout					
Typeface					
Graphics					

COMMUNICATING ON THE WEB

The major Internet service providers, like Earthlink and America Online, have made creating personal webpages relatively simple and inexpensive. They offer subscribers easy-to-use software to design pages and provide instructions on how to upload, or send, pages to servers so that they can be accessed on the Internet. The providers let users store pages on their servers at no additional cost. However, most people do not create webpages. Many find the process of planning and writing pages too time-consuming or technically daunting.

This does not mean, however, that legions of users have been shut out of the Web as a medium for communicating and disseminating their ideas. Millions of people communicate on the Web all the time. The Internet is wide open and empowering, and it potentially puts the world's biggest printing press in the hands of anyone and everyone who can get online at home, at work, at school, or at the public library.

Types of Writing for the Web

The elements of good writing are not confined only to the creation of websites. These guidelines can be applied to various other opportunities for writing on the Web.

E-mail and Instant Messages The bulk of the writing that the majority of people do on the Internet takes the form of e-mail and instant messaging. People use e-mail for personal messages, and more and more business is transacted via e-mail as well. You can send an e-mail message to apply for a job. You can also use e-mail to communicate with an elected official about public policy, to express a complaint or a problem with a service or product, or to express your satisfaction with a service or product. E-mail inquiries are a fast and efficient way to get answers to questions about a business or public service.

Getting access to e-mail has never been easier. All Internet service providers offer their users e-mail addresses. Many companies give employees access, and most colleges and universities provide students with accounts. Some major Internet and technology companies offer free e-mail; Microsoft's Hotmail service and Yahoo Mail are two big ones.

Instant messaging (IM) has grown in popularity, particularly among teens. The first and still the biggest IM service is America Online. Instant messaging comes as part of the standard AOL package, and the company also makes free software available on the Web to anyone who wants to use it.

As with all writing on the Web, when composing e-mail or instant messages the key is brevity. E-mail and IM readers expect communication on the Web to be fast. They want the main points right away, and they like short, succinct sentences in active voice. In fact, because instant messaging is even faster than e-mail, many users use phrases instead of sentences and try to abbreviate whenever possible: "how r u?" "am OK."

The tone of e-mail and instant messages is dictated by the situation. Appropriateness is key. A quick message to a friend to verify Friday night plans will likely be much more colloquial and informal than a request to meet with a professor or a supervisor at work. When you write formal e-mail messages, keep them just that—formal—and use correct spelling, grammar, and punctuation.

Messages for a Public Audience Beyond e-mail, the Internet offers many opportunities to publish your thoughts and ideas to communities of users with whom you share a common interest. Millions of people post messages and questions to bulletin boards. Others post product or book reviews to consumer sites like Amazon.com and film reviews to sites like rottentomatoes.com. Still others submit material to e-zines (Internet magazines) or send e-mail to online "blogs" (Web logs), which are pages that serve as a kind of combination of online diary and annotated guide to interesting pages or ideas on the Internet.

Some of these online publications are mediated, or edited, and others are not. This is important for two reasons. First, it tends to affect how you submit material. Unmediated publications, like most bulletin boards and review pages of consumer sites, allow you to post directly onto the site without human intervention. You type your message or review into a dialogue box right on the site. Websites that are edited, like blogs and e-zines, usually require submission by e-mail.

Material on a mediated site tends to be more consistent in quality because it has been screened and selected by an editor. This is not to say that material on bulletin boards and other unmediated sites is not accurate or useful: often it is—and sometimes it is not.

Bulletin Boards Bulletin boards usually are found on websites catering to users with specific shared interests, like Windows or Apple or Linux users, Eminem fans, trail hikers, or vintage Saab drivers. Bulletin boards are places where devotees can post questions and share tips, insights, and information.

Posting material to a bulletin board is simple. Users are required to register on the site and select a user name. To post, you simply click on a button. A dialogue box pops up, and you type your question or comment in the box. Bulletin boards are a great resource if you are looking for kindred spirits or a group of amateur experts with wide-ranging experiences to act as consultants.

Blogs Though most blogs are run by individuals, some are maintained by organizations. Blogs are growing in popularity, and more and more users are either setting up their own sites or are running blogs hosted by larger sites. For

The *Drudge Report* is one of many blogs that offer news from a distinct point of view.

example, rottentomatoes.com, the film review site essentially allows people to set up blogs on the site and post reviews to them.

Because most blogs are run by individuals, they are only as good as the bloggers who run them. They tend to be made up of short essays, along with links to material on sites that influenced the thinking of the bloggers. Sometimes they are just annotated listings of material on sites, for instance, political blogger Matt Drudge's "Drudge Report" site.

There are essentially two types of blogs.

1. Blogs that act as a kind of public, personal journal to reveal the feelings and thoughts of a single individual

2. Blogs that focus on issues or ideas shared by a community, such as blogs that focus more narrowly on politics, car racing, child-rearing, or naturopathic medicine

For perhaps obvious reasons, the more intimately personal blogs tend to draw fewer eyes.

While increasing numbers of people are blogging, most people do not write blogs. But many blogs offer yet another forum for writers who do not want to have to make the commitment to maintaining a website. Besides offering the opinions of the blogger, these sites often solicit and publish e-mail from visitors. Blogs, like bulletin boards, help form and shape Web communities.

Online Review Sites and E-zines A number of consumer and opinion sites on the Web, like Amazon.com and e-opinions, solicit product or other reviews from users, and thousands of people submit to them. These sites make submission simple and nonthreatening—you don't even usually have to sign your review. As with bulletin boards, you will be required to register, and then you will click to get a dialogue box. E-zines are a good place to publish your work. You can find places to publish poetry, fiction, and nonfiction. Submitting material to the biggest, best-known e-zines, like *Slate,* is a formal process, requiring you first to send e-mail to query the editors on their interest in your idea for a piece.

But there are thousands of smaller e-zines out there. Most of them accept direct submissions via e-mail. The best way to find the appropriate e-zine is to look through one of the many e-zine directories. The E-zine Directory at www.ezine-dir.com is a good place to start.

Tips for Communicating on the Web Whether you are posting to a bulletin board or submitting an online review of a DVD burner or a piece about the cultural significance of Radiohead to an e-zine, be aware of what has been written about your subject on the site before. As in any kind of publishing, you do not want to repeat a question or rehash a subject that has recently been comprehensively covered. This advice is especially true when writing for blogs or bulletin boards, which tend to have smaller audiences who keep in touch with the site and know the content well. You should too, before contributing.

- Be aware of what has been posted on the site before (at least in the past few months).

- Be organized. Write with your most important information first, in inverted pyramid style. These are Web readers; they expect to get what they want quickly.

- Be concise. Get to the point. Write short and tight. For bulletin boards, try to confine yourself to no more than two hundred words. While many online review sites will accept up to a thousand words, shorter is better.

Remember, the key to successful writing on the Web is consideration of your audience. As a general rule, people want information as quickly as possible, but they will also be willing to give more time to subjects in which they have a deep interest. It is your call.

WRITING AND REVISION STRATEGIES

Gathered here are three interactive sections for you to use as you write and revise your website.

▶ Writer's Notebook Suggestions

▶ Peer-Editing Log

▶ Revision Checklist

Writer's Notebook Suggestions

You can use these exercises to do some start-up thinking and writing for the Web.

1. Visit rottentomatoes.com and read some film reviews. Then post your own film review.

2. Write an e-mail message to a leader in local government on an issue about which you feel strongly.

3. Post a review of a book on Amazon.com.

4. Enter an online poetry contest. For ideas, refer to the Writing in the Works website.

5. Post a message or comment on one of the blog sites you can link to from the Writing in the Works website.

6. Design your resume page. Keep the resume to one screen. Hyperlinks are optional.

7. Write an e-mail applying for a job or inquiring about the availability of a job.

8. Write an e-mail to your local newspaper or radio or television station responding to an editorial or a story. Clearly express your opinion about the issue or coverage.

9. Write a survey that you could post on a website that asks for responses to questions. Make the questions multiple choice. Alternatively, have visitors rate something—local restaurants, satisfaction with student services at your school, music, or movies.

10. Write a page for elementary schoolchildren. Explain a technical process that you understand well in language that the children can understand. Examples: how a tornado forms, how a tattoo is removed, how to take a patient's blood pressure.

11. Write a page with concise directions on how to do a physical activity: how to salsa, how to throw a good curve ball, how to do a particular group of yoga poses. Consider how diagrams or film clips might help you, but do not rely upon them.

12. Write copy that describes the place you live as if your residence were for sale or rent.

Peer-Editing Log

Giving your audience what they need and want quickly and efficiently are your top goals in writing a website. Ask a friend to look over your site and answer the following questions.

Writer's Name _____

Date _____

1. Are the headlines clear and specific?

2. Is the information written concisely, or did you lose attention or get distracted in the visuals?

3. Is the topic one you are interested in? Does the website create interest, or do you feel that you must have knowledge about the subject to motivate you to read?

4. How many clicks or screens did you have to move through before you found material you thought was useful?

5. Is the language easy to read and scan?

6. Did you get bored or restless when reading the material?

7. How efficient was your search? Was the site clearly organized, or did you have to return to

the homepage several times and restart your search for information?

Revision Checklist

Use the following checklist to anticipate your reader's questions about your trustworthiness.

❏ Do you clearly state who you are in your website and/or who the group you represent is?

❏ Do you make your purpose clear on your website, particularly if you are trying to provide a public service?

❏ Does your site include sources that document claims?

❏ Have you carefully checked out links to your site, making sure they are good, credible, and recently updated sources?

❏ Have you checked carefully for errors in grammar or spelling that may indicate faulty information?

11. FILM REVIEWS

WRITING EVALUATIONS

**I learn more from critics who honestly criticize
my pictures than from those who are devout.**

— Ingmar Bergman

ASSIGNMENT

Write a film review of a movie in current release or on videotape or DVD. Choose a movie that has some artistic merit and aims to provide more than light, mindless entertainment.

Choose the specific publication in which you would publish this review: a newspaper, a magazine, or an online site. Keep this audience in mind as you write the review.

Your research should include

- Reading reviews in your chosen publication

- Finding out what you can about the context and any sources of the film you are reviewing.

People dressed as characters from *Lord of the Rings* in line to see the film in Santiago, Chile, in January 2002.

FILM REVIEWS

When filmmaker Quentin Tarantino's fourth film, *Kill Bill*, was released in the fall of 2003, reviews ranged from raves to pans. One reviewer wrote the following in the *Washington Post*.

> Outrageous, ingenious, inventive and very bloody (to the point of Monty Python-style satire), this movie reconfirms [Tarantino's] status as the master of pop cinema and puts a sense of excitement into the year.
>
> —Desson Howe, *"Kill Bill, Vol. I"*

A reviewer from the *New Yorker* wrote this.

> The movie is what's formally known as decadence and commonly known as crap. Saying that it's an homage to long-established genres in Hong Kong doesn't reduce its pop-nihilistic stupidity.
>
> —David Denby, Capsule Review of *Kill Bill*

Did these two reviewers watch the same film? They did, but they responded from vastly different sensibilities and perspectives. Part of the fun of reading film reviews is seeing how different writers admire and ridicule different aspects of a film. No matter which way they go, though, good reviewers—the ones you can trust—support their opinions with clear and specific evidence.

When you write your film review, you, like a professional reviewer, will have two responsibilities. The first is to evaluate the film by stating your overall opinion—positive, negative, or mixed—and to analyze the film, supporting your opinion with evidence. In a film review your evidence will come from an analysis of the film elements: the story, acting, writing, cinematography, soundtrack, or special effects.

Your second responsibility is to entertain your readers. A good reviewer writes in a lively, engaging voice. People read a film review primarily to find out a reviewer's evaluation of a film, but they also want to be amused by a clever insight or turn of phrase, or diverted into thinking about something in a new way. Part of your job as a reviewer is to convince the reader through your language, voice, and style that you are a person who is smart and perceptive about film, somebody who might even be fun to take to the movies.

Applications: School, Community, Work

Learning how to write an evaluation of a film will serve as a good model for writing you will do in other classes. Book reviews are the staple writing assignments in many subjects. Whether the field is history, psychology, education, or literature, the basic review form is the same: evaluation supported by evidence. You might also be asked to evaluate a work of art for an art history class, a play for a class in modern drama, a speech for oral communication, or a debate for a political science class. In your community, writing evaluations might take the form of reviewing a new restaurant or a new music CD for the town newspaper. Or you may write an evaluation of a project rather than a work of art or a restaurant. A committee member on a town board might review a fundraiser held by a local charity or a town clean-up day and point out the successful or unsuccessful aspects of those efforts.

In the workplace, writing evaluations is part of many jobs: workers write self-evaluations, supervisors evaluate their staffs, managers evaluate projects, teachers evaluate students, and students evaluate their courses and professors. Critics are professional evaluators of plays, films, works of art, books, or music.

CHAPTER OBJECTIVES

In this chapter you will learn to

▶ evaluate the work of others

▶ use analysis to form your opinion

▶ use evidence to defend your opinion

▶ engage a reader with a lively voice

UNDERSTANDING FILM REVIEWS

Your opinion in a review should be informed by your taste as well as by your basic understanding of the elements of filmmaking. When you understand some of the elements that go into a movie's making, you can write with authority and select specific evidence to support your opinions. "I loved the movie" does not give your reader much information, nor does "It was the worst movie I ever saw." But if you can write "The acting was strong but the pace far too slow," you will have been specific and will have identified two elements that support your opinion: acting and pace.

To write a good review, you should also consider the film's genre and your audience, and you will want to write in a lively, intelligent voice. This section will help you understand the following three aspects of film reviews.

◗ Analyzing film elements

◗ Considering a film's genre

◗ Considering voice and audience

**Warm-Up Practice 11.1
Collaborative Activity**

1. List the five best films you have ever seen and the five worst. Next to the title of the film, write the outstanding characteristics of each.

2. Exchange your lists with other students in your group. See if any of your "best" films show up on anyone's "worst" films. Come to a consensus about the five best and worst films.

VISUAL
LITERACY

Interpreting Images

Examine the photographs from *The Last Samurai*, *Lost in Translation*, and *Kill Bill Vol. I*. These shots are narrative in nature, giving the viewer a certain perspective and insight into some element of the respective films.

1. In each of the photos, where is your eye first drawn? What elements in the photograph draw your eye to that point? What significance does this focal point have in each photograph as a whole?

2. Look at the background or setting of each photograph. What information do the backgrounds provide? What tone or mood do they set?

3. Consider the characters in each photograph. What do their expressions reveal about them?

4. Pay attention to the color palettes of each photograph. How do the colors complement or contradict the scenes?

5. What are the narrative elements in each photograph? Whether you have seen the movies or not, what can you infer about each story line from each photograph?

6. Point out any puzzling or unusual elements in each photograph. What function do they serve?

7. How much influence do visual images of films in their ads have on you? Do you ever decide to see a film because of the photograph or illustration in an ad?

Koyuki and Ken Watanabe in *The Last Samurai*

Bill Murray in *Lost in Translation*

Lucy Liu and Uma Thurman in *Kill Bill Vol. 1*.

Analyzing Film Elements

A reviewer judges a film in much the same way a book reviewer judges a story, by evaluating the characters, plot, conflict, and theme. (See Chapter 5 for more discussion of these terms.) But films tell stories through images as well as words. To do justice to a film, you also have to respond to the visual elements: the cinematography, editing, acting, production design, music, and special effects.

When you write your review, avoid the temptation to go through a laundry list of these film elements; rather, choose the ones that are important to the film. For a film full of innovative effects like *The Matrix*, for example, you would probably discuss the computer-generated graphics and cinematography, while for a serious drama like *Schindler's List,* you would likely discuss the writing and the acting. A general understanding of the criteria for evaluating a film will help you understand your choices.

Story Elements The story elements to consider in a film review are characters, plot, and theme.

Characters The characters are the people who inhabit a film. They can be divided into major characters and minor or supporting characters. The main character will go through some sort of change or character development, often called a character arc. As with any kind of narrative, expect this change to grow out of clear motivation and to be believable and incremental. A film that has character, rather than plot, at its center is said to be character-driven.

A screenwriter creates a character on the page, in large part, through what the character says, and the actor creates this character, in part, through the way the dialogue is delivered. Good dialogue is original, believable, and idiosyncratic. Well-drawn characters speak differently from one another and can be judged by their unique use of language or phrasing.

Plot The plot is the story line—what happens to the characters in the film. As in most narratives, the plot usually revolves around a conflict—a clash of ideas or forces, or internal tension of some kind. A good screenplay should not be boring or have puzzling plot twists or meaningless scenes.

A reviewer might hold the screenwriter responsible for a problematic story line or the director for cutting between scenes too quickly and not allowing enough on-screen time to develop parts of the story.

Theme The theme is the idea behind the film, the truth that the filmmakers are exploring or showing. In a drama, the theme might be a social message about the effects of oppression, a demonstration of the wisdom of remaining open to new experiences, or an insight into a life well lived or wasted. An effective theme is subtle and organically integrated into the story, rather than heavy-handed, obvious, or clumsily tacked on.

Some movies are made for pure entertainment, to thrill you or make you laugh, and it might be fruitless to search for a theme in such films. Well-made movies, though, like well-made books, explore important themes and allow for insight along with entertainment.

Visual Elements Visual elements include actors, cinematography, editing, production design, soundtrack, and special effects.

Actors Actors get credit for portraying the basic role and dialogue with imagination. Although actors deliver the lines, screenwriters write them, so be careful in a review to separate the acting (the way the lines are delivered) and the writing (the lines themselves). Humphrey Bogart may have delivered one of the classic film lines in *Casablanca*, "Of all the gin joints in all the towns in all the world, she walks into mine," but the screenwriters, the Epstein brothers, penned it.

When you consider the acting, think about the actor's believability. Actors should be believable in the context of the universe created in the film. It is fine for an actor playing an alien to be wooden or otherworldly, for example, but not so good for a romantic hero. Actors add nuance through facial expression, vocal techniques, gesture, and movement. You can focus on any of these elements in a review to judge the way an actor brings the character to life.

Cinematography The cinematography is the way a movie is filmed: the shots, camera angles, and lighting. Camera angle and lighting can be used to create particular effects; for example, a camera might be pointed down on a dimly lit character to show the character's fright or confusion. To judge the cinematography, you do not necessarily have to know a great deal about the technical aspects of filming. You can evaluate the results. Consider whether the movie is full of "talking heads" (still, close-up shots of people conversing) or of unrelenting, dizzying motion. You can judge whether shots are purposeful and help create a mood or add a layer of meaning. A still camera can be used to create drama and explore characters' actions and reactions. Camera movement—whether it is smooth, jerky, or dizzying—creates its own emotional impact, often paralleling characters' states of mind.

Editing Film editing is the art of juxtaposing the individual camera shots into a coherent final product. Editing creates the sequences of images and the transitions from one scene to the next that tell and advance the story. Editors may splice shots together to create a jumpy mood or to show what is happening simultaneously in two places. Alternately, they may use a lengthy shot to create a naturalistic feel as the camera follows a character through a day's events.

Good editing allows the pace of the film to reflect the dramatic movement of the story. You might note in your review whether quick cuts from scene to scene create an artful effect, create tension, or call unnecessary attention to the editing techniques.

Production Design Production design includes the sets, costumes, locations, and props. For example, lavish period films may be filled with furniture, knick-knacks, and clothing that have to be thoroughly researched in order to give an authentic "feel" to the sets. Sometimes the physical world of the film is so elaborately imagined and created that it is worth a reviewer's commentary.

Soundtrack The soundtrack is the musical score of the film (not the popular songs that often accompany film sequences such as love scenes). It should enhance the mood of the film and place the viewer within the world of the story on an aural level. If the music is inappropriate or distracting, it can achieve the opposite of its intentions, and catapult the viewer out of that world.

Special Effects The special effects are the animation, digital design elements, or stunts in the film. All effects, whether they are high-tech or low-tech, should be meaningful within the world of the film. Innovative animation as in *Toy Story* or the computer-generated effects in *Crouching Tiger, Hidden Dragon* enhance those films and are well worth mentioning in a review. When effects call undue attention to themselves and bring the viewer out of the story, they are probably failing to achieve their purpose.

The Players Film is a highly collaborative medium. If you stay to watch the credits roll at the end of a film, you know that hundreds of people contribute to its creation. Following are brief descriptions of the roles of some of the main players.

Producer The producer pitches the project to potential funders, arranges the financing, monitors the budget, and advises on locations.

Director The film's director interprets the script, oversees the shooting and the actors, and determines the film's style.

Writer(s) One or more writers create the screenplay—that is, they create an original plot and characters, or they adapt already-created ones.

Actors Actors translate the characters from the screenplay onto the screen. When the movie is being filmed, actors typically follow the director's instructions. Afterwards, they help promote the finished movie.

Cinematographer Also known as director of photography, a cinematographer makes decisions about lighting, camera angles, and camera movement, creating the visual style of the film.

Editor A film editor cuts the footage that has been shot to make a finished product. The editor's work is responsible for creating mood through the juxtaposition of shots and for establishing the pace of the film.

Considering the Film's Genre

A film's genre is the category in which it belongs. Each time you review a film, you have to take into account its genre. On the shelves of a video store, the films are arranged according to type: science fiction, horror, suspense, comedy, drama, action, and so on. For the purpose of reviewing, you can further refine these categories into subgenres such as romantic comedy and historical drama.

Though all films need to be entertaining, the genre of a film determines what the audience will expect and how the film will be judged. For example, special effects are more significant in a horror or science fiction film than in a romantic comedy. As you write your review, think of the film you are evaluating as existing within a genre, and use criteria appropriate to the genre.

Once you recognize the genre or subgenre of your film, you can think about the conventions of that genre. Conventions are devices, techniques, or aspects of character or plot that are widely used within a particular genre. In the typical western, for example, when a guy in a black hat rides into town, trouble is brewing. In a horror film, ominous, high-pitched music or a shot of a darkened stairway or closed door foreshadows a terrifying scene.

Sometimes single images from films are so powerful and vivid that they become conventions. In the shower murder scene in Alfred Hitchcock's *Psycho*, the audience sees the shadow of the hand holding a knife, with the shower curtain acting as a scrim (a transparent fabric used to create a special effect). Images like this can become clichés and can be referred to satirically or reverently in other films. A reviewer may sometimes mention these references to previous films if they add to the meaning and interest of the film being reviewed.

Once genre-related expectations are established through repetition and wide use over time, filmmakers can play with them. They can adhere to a genre's conventions or subvert them. Quentin Tarantino subverted gangster film conventions in his 1994 film *Pulp Fiction*, including, for example, a sequence with happy music playing over a horrific scene of mutilation and murder.

Practice 11.2
Identifying Film Elements

1. On television, videotape, or DVD, watch a film with the sound turned off for five minutes. As you watch, take notes on the visual elements of the film. Pay attention to the acting, cinematography, editing, production design, and any special effects. Make a guess about what is happening in the film and what kind of mood is set.

2. Listen to another five minutes of the same video with the picture hidden. As you listen, take notes on the aural aspects of the film: the dialogue, soundtrack, and sound effects. Note what kind of mood the sound elements create.

Practice 11.3
Identifying Film Genres

List five or six film genres or subgenres. Next to each genre write a list of the conventions associated with it.

The details in these two movie posters suggest the movies' genres. *The Silence of the Lambs* (1991) is a horror film, and *Big* (1988) is a comedy.

Thinking about genre and about the audience's expectations concerning genre will help you put the film you are reviewing in a context and generate good reasons to back up your evaluation.

Considering Voice and Audience

Entertaining your reader while offering your opinion of a film requires a lively voice and a clear sense of the audience. *Lively* does not mean "light." An engaging voice captures the reader's attention, but it also must reveal the intelligence and insight you bring to your analysis.

Pauline Kael, who spent twenty-five years reviewing films for the *New Yorker* magazine, was famous for her strong opinions and equally strong voice. In the introduction to her book *For Keeps* she explains the evolution of her voice this way.

> I had written about movies for almost fifteen years, trying to be true to the spirit of what I loved about movies, trying to develop a voice that would avoid saphead objectivity and let the reader in on what sort of person was responding to the world in this particular way.
>
> —Pauline Kael, *For Keeps*

Kael's aim, she says, was to write in a way that sounded like spoken language and avoided sounding like "a genteel, fuddy-duddy stylist who says, 'One assumes that. . . .'"

While trying to connect with your reader and reveal what sort of person you are, you can still tailor your voice to the kind of film you are reviewing. A serious drama requires serious treatment, perhaps a more formal and philosophical voice than a comedy that would best be reviewed in a voice filled with wit and humor.

Finding the right voice for a review can be tricky. Though it is fun to be irreverent, to skewer a bad film with wit and irony, you also have to be careful not to go overboard, sound silly, or sound mean-spirited. Similarly, it is often easiest to write in a serious, even reverent voice about a film you love, but if your voice is overly earnest, your reader may find the review dull or believe that your ability to see the film's flaws has been compromised.

Knowing your audience also helps you find your voice. If you are writing for a local newspaper, you have to assume that readers may not know or care about film terminology. They want to read a clear review that is star-oriented, specific, and well written; they do not expect a comprehensive analysis of film technique. Readers of film magazines such as *Premiere*, *Cineaste*, and *Film Quarterly* probably do want the technique analyzed. These film journals are often written in a serious, academic voice.

Most of the reviews included in this chapter fall in the middle. Newspapers and magazines like the *New York Times*, *Time* magazine, the *San Francisco Chronicle*, the *Washington Post*, and the *Chicago Sun-Times* are considered cultural outlets in which readers can expect to find reviews written with a lively voice, wit, and intelligence.

Online movie reviews are fun to read and fun to write. Many online critics are movie fans who log on to hype a film they love or pan one they hate. Their voices may be less formal or less polished than reviewers who write for print publications, but online reviewers often have interesting insights to offer their readers.

Practice 11.4   Voice and Audience

Below are three excerpts of reviews of the Coen brothers' 1996 film *Fargo*. As you read them, pay attention to the writers' voices. Consider how the voices differ from one another and how the audience for each publication helped shape the voice.

White-out conditions bracket the outskirts of *Fargo*, a warm-hearted tale of cold-blooded murder from the brothers Coen, director Joel and producer Ethan. The opening shot sketches the color scheme: barely discernible through overcast skies and blowing snow, a lone vehicle tows a tan Cutlass Ciera along a God-forsaken strip of highway, a tableau echoed at the end of the film when another car carries its cargo, a sullen murderer, to justice. Front, back, and in between, snow is the dominant visual motif, subzero temperatures the environmental wraparound, a blizzard of white stuff that layers the landscape and fills the frames of pre-cable television screens. *Fargo* mixes a film noir ethos with film blanc visuals.

Set in rural Minnesota in the dead of winter (the place name "Fargo" is the least of the calculated misdirections), when the Siberian express comes sweeping down from Canada, gathering velocity and ferocity, to settle in with bone-numbing, mind-twisting cold, the film luxuriates in seasonal and regional atmosphere. Though a goodly chunk of the nation regularly withstands such polar conditions, the culture of life-threatening winter is seldom glimpsed in American films, perhaps because the rituals of scraping ice off the windshield, praying for the ignition to turn over, wearing headgear for protection (not style) and fur as a survival (not fashion) statement are alien to sun-drenched Hollywood honchos who can wait all day for the light but run like rabbits from frozen precipitation. Given the oppressive force of the elements and the blank existential horizon, it's no surprise that the harsh, protracted weather engenders murderous impulses in borderline personality types, or that monochromatic vistas and cabin fever push rugged individuals over the edge into dementia with alarming regularity. It's the terrain of Wisconsin death trips and home turf to Ed Gein, the original serial killer, and father to screen psychos from Norman Bates to Hannibal Lecter.

—Thomas Doherty, Review of *Fargo* in *Cineaste*

A few years back, Howard Mohr of *A Prairie Home Companion* wrote a book called *How to Talk Minnesotan*. Was it funny? Hey, you betcha. So are the twistings of that frosty, flabbergastingly flat accent as heard on the Minnesota-based *Mystery Science Theater 3000*. Two other gifted natives, the filmmakers Joel and Ethan Coen, have appar-

ently never got over the giggle value of their regional dialect. *Fargo,* their derisive new true-crime comedy, could be subtitled *How to Laugh at People Who Talk Minnesotan.*

The film—which has not much at all to do with Fargo, North Dakota—is about the difficulty real folks have pulling off crimes that always go smoothly in fiction. Jerry Lundegaard (William H. Macy) needs a lot of cash, so he hires two thugs (Steve Buscemi and Peter Stormare) to kidnap his wife for the ransom money. But these guys aren't smooth criminals; they go nuts trying to put on a galosh or scrape the ice off their windshield. Two incompetent murders later, police chief Marge Gunderson (Frances McDormand) commences her investigation. And the bad guys get the frozen sweats.

Macy is an ace at doing hysteria in a narrow range, and Buscemi scores as a sick goofus whom one witness IDs as "funny-lookin'—more than most people even." There's enough gore to make this a *Mystery Violence Theater*. After some superb mannerist films, the Coens are back in the deadpan realist territory of *Blood Simple,* but without the cinematic élan. Fargo is all attitude and low aptitude. Its function is to italicize the Coens' giddy contempt toward people who talk and think Minnesotan. Which is, y'know, kind of a bad deal.

—Richard Corliss, Review of *Fargo* in *Time*,
©Time Inc., reprinted by permission

SPOILERS! This modern classic brought to us by the creative Coen brothers is great for the following reasons:

1. The actors are brilliant, reveling in roles that are interesting to play. Particularly notable are Macy as the feckless Jerry Lundergard, McDormand as the affable, partly pixilated, Chief of Police and of course Buchemi in his element in a role of delicious degeneracy.

2. Dialogue. Or perhaps it is better just to call it quirky conversation, because that's what it is really. You just have to keep smiling at the accents and nonchalant banter, intertwined with telling character development and smart irony. From the cavalier 'Ja' interview between McDormand and the two young women who showed the inept criminals a good time, to the priceless parking lot attendant/authority discourse we are treated to a stream of palaver that is amusing and at the same time insightful. We are so entertained that we don't even find it strange that Buchemi's character uses phrases like *force majeure.*

3. The bizarre circumstances that intersperse the story that are resolved through violence. From the slapstick-like kidnapping scene to the fortuitous highway massacre to the disgusting wood chipper

Poster for *Fargo* (1996)

finale, the violence that underlies the generally flat exterior of the characters, is seemingly incongruous. It is however, a reminder that even though the people in this world are somewhat stolid, tumult and depravity pervades beneath the persona. This is driven home in McDormand's expostulation to the surviving criminal near the end.

4. Jerry Lundergard. There are numerous nuances to the film but the most interesting surround Macy. A cashier gives him an egregious simper in a diner, his inept dealings with his oppressive father-in-law lend him our sympathy and his reply to his son, "Just ask Stan Grossman, he'll tell ya!" makes us cringe. Two scenes with him are very piquant and tell us much about him: the true-coat scam, and the part where he enters his father-in-law's office to discuss a business deal and there is nowhere for him to sit. Simply brilliant! A great movie.

—Randandjanell@jobe.net, Internet Movie Database User Comments on *Fargo*

1. For each review, describe the voice and explain what decisions the writer made about sentence length, sentence structure, word choice, and grammar that helped to create that voice.

2. Write the first few lines of the movie review you are writing for this assignment, or choose another movie you know well. Rewrite those lines for

   a. A scholarly film journal like *Cineaste*

   b. A general circulation magazine like *Time*

   c. An online movie review site

RESEARCH PATHS

Film reviewers may seem to have a cushy job, watching movies and eating popcorn all day, but watching the movie is a small part of the process. Taking notes, researching the film, and putting it in context for a reader require strong research, analytic, and organizational skills.

Watching a Film: Big Screen or Small?

Some reviewers feel that it is far better to watch a film in a theater than on a television set, even one with a big screen. They argue that going to the cinema provides a richer experience than watching a film alone or with a few friends. In a theater, you share the audience's collective response to the movie. One person could laugh inappropriately, setting off others, or someone else could gasp in horror, intensifying your own chills. The audience as a whole could break out in contagious laughter, cheers, or applause. Many in the film business also argue that seeing a film on its intended scale, with the imagery and sound in their full glory, has a much greater impact than watching a film reduced on a television screen.

On the other hand, reviewers often have access to advance videos and DVDs. You may find that watching movies on your own schedule, free from distraction, allows you to be more alert and watch more attentively.

The main advantage of watching a film on your television is that you control the clicker. You can stop, rewind, and watch the whole film or selected scenes many times. You can also more easily extract snippets of dialogue to use as supporting evidence. DVDs give you access to outtakes, director's comments, and other contextual information to include in your analysis. This more leisurely viewing allows for a more meditative, if less spontaneous, response to a film.

Taking Notes

If you decide to go out to a movie, taking notes in a darkened theater requires skill. Even a small flashlight distracts other viewers, and you might get pelted with popcorn if you try to use one. Take a notebook, and write brief notes to yourself in large, legible handwriting. Immediately after you have viewed the film, sit down to fill in the blanks. Write down the plot's basic sequence of events if it is complicated and might be hard to reconstruct later from memory.

Take notes on your responses and your insights about the film elements. Write down memorable pieces of dialogue. Note your emotional responses, such as whether the music moves you to tears or to distraction. Use the notepad to remind yourself of the experience of viewing the film and to prompt deeper analysis, but not to write down facts that you can find later.

You can always get the names of the actors and filmmakers from the ads or from the movie's website.

Some reviewers like to watch a movie twice, the first time to respond purely to the film experience, and the second time to take notes and be more analytical. Watching a movie at home, of course, makes this an easier and less-expensive process. In any case, take good notes during the movie and write or type them up immediately afterwards, adding details and examples.

Researching Background and Context

You can find information about a film's director, writer, actors, and original source in a number of places. The movie's website is an easy place to start, but be aware that it is a biased source of information. The film's promotion department builds the website, and its focus is to sell the movie. Nonetheless, you can get good information about the cast and details about the production, even the correct spelling of the characters' names, on the site.

Of all the movie databases on the Internet, perhaps the most comprehensive and most objective is the Internet Movie Database at http://www.IMDb.com. It catalogues a great deal of information about current movies, including biographies of filmmakers and casts, movie trivia, information about the locations, and relevant anecdotes about making the movies. Finding this information before you write your review can be fun and useful, even if not all of it will make its way into the review.

More serious and scholarly sources are film encyclopedias and general histories that you can find in a good college library. One of the best is David Cook's *History of Narrative Film*, which also has a detailed glossary of film terms for those who want to explore this field in more depth. Another excellent resource is Gerald Mast and Bruce Kawin's *A Short History of the Movies*.

Use context and background information sparingly in your review, however. You do not want or need to sound as though you know every single detail about the film. The review is about your evaluation of the movie, not your comprehensive knowledge about it. Sometimes it is more important to have the information to add to your own understanding of the movie than to include it in the review itself.

Yet if you discover something important or interesting about the making or distribution of a film, by all means include it if it works with the points you wish to make. For example, the movie *O* released in 2001 updates Shakespeare's classic tragedy *Othello* by setting the story in a modern high school. That background information needs to be briefly mentioned in a review. Even more interesting is the fact that the movie was set for release in 1999 but was held up for two years because of real violence that beset American high schools at that time. This is how Mark Caro of the *Chicago Tribune* begins his review of *O*.

**Practice 11.5
Exploring a Website**

Go to the Internet Movie Database at **http://us.IMDb.com.** Spend some time exploring this site. Write a list of the kind of information you can find at the site that would provide a reviewer with background and context information for a particular film.

Setting a Shakespearean tragedy in an American high school doesn't seem like too much of a stretch given the very real tragedies that had occurred at schools in West Paducah, Ky.; Jonesboro, Ark.; and Springfield, Ore., before Tim Blake Nelson even began to film *O*, a loose reworking of *Othello*.

Yet the April 1999 massacre at Columbine High School in Littleton, Colo., and the ensuing presidential-campaign uproar over violence in entertainment led a squeamish Miramax to shelve the finished movie for almost two years; the distributor sold it to Lions Gate Films this spring after the producers filed a breach-of-contract lawsuit.

Caro found this information important enough to lead with it, in part, one would think, because he uses it in the next paragraph to set up his evaluation.

Now *O* finally has arrived . . . the story has lost none of its potency. And that's how it should be. Shakespeare's works, after all, have endured for four centuries, so if a movie like *O* didn't have a shelf life of more than two years, it couldn't be a very serious work. And Nelson is deadly serious.

Background information, often interesting in and of itself, adds even more value to a review if it leads the reader to your main point. Caro uses the story of *O*'s delayed distribution to make the point that the timeless nature of the story contributes to the film's success. Any background and contextual information you use should be done not in isolation but in service to your evaluation of the film.

ANATOMY OF A FILM REVIEW

Although film reviews have flexible structures, most reviewers cover the same basic elements.

- ▶ An introduction, which could include background and contextual information

- ▶ A thesis that presents the reviewer's argument

- ▶ A brief plot summary

- ▶ An analysis of the most significant criteria, with specific evidence to support the analysis

- ▶ A conclusion that often answers the bottom-line question: is it worth my money to see this film?

Read the following review of Clint Eastwood's *Mystic River* (2003) written by Jeffrey M. Anderson of the *San Francisco Examiner*. The annotations on the review and the following discussion will help you identify and understand these elements.

Clint's Wild "River"

JEFFREY M. ANDERSON

Starring Sean Penn, Kevin Bacon, Tim Robbins, Laura Linney. Directed by Clint
Eastwood; written by Brian Helgeland, based on the novel by Dennis Lehane.
Rated R for language and violence. Opens today in San Francisco theaters.

Introduction

Evaluation

Context

After three very good pulpy potboilers, *True Crime*, *Space Cowboys*, and *Blood
Work*, Clint Eastwood has taken off the kid gloves and hunkered down to
work. The result, *Mystic River*, is yet another great film from one of the half-
dozen greatest American filmmakers working today.

Taken from the novel by Dennis Lehane and adapted by Brian Helgeland
(*L.A. Confidential*, *Blood Work*), *Mystic River* details a Boston murder case that
brings three childhood friends back together.

Body

Plot Summary

As children, Jimmy, Sean, and Dave are playing hockey in the street when a
grown man pretending to be a cop whisks Dave away in the back of his car. The
resulting traumatic experience, four days locked in a basement, leaves the grown
Dave (Tim Robbins) shaken—a "basket case" as one character calls him.

Plot Summary

The grown Sean (Kevin Bacon) is now a cop, working with a wisecracking
partner called Whitey (Laurence Fishburne). And Jimmy (Sean Penn) runs a
corner store, has several daughters including a precocious nineteen-year-old,
and seems to enjoy several Godfather-like ties to the underworld. His wife
(Laura Linney) encourages him in slightly frightening ways.

Plot Summary

When Jimmy's eldest daughter turns up murdered, Sean takes the case and
Dave—who came home that night with blood on his hands—is one of the suspects.

Thesis

Actually, the murder case only serves as a means to an end. *Mystic River* more
or less guides its characters toward some inexorable fate, predetermined at the
moment young Dave gets in the car. In this way, *Mystic River* takes on a Sergio
Leone-like epic nature, with a cruel God its major player. (A smaller tribute to
Leone comes with a nifty walk-on by Eli Wallach, Eastwood's *The Good, the Bad
and the Ugly* co-star.)

Context Story

Along with John Carpenter, Eastwood remains one of the last of a dying breed
of meat-and-potatoes filmmakers, descended from Howard Hawks and Raoul
Walsh. Falling somewhere between arty show-offs and hacks-for-hire, Eastwood
believes in storytelling above all, followed by providing any and all details to
make that storytelling a rich experience. In short, he cares.

Looking back over just about any scene in the film, one can take away fruitful little moments of truth. As Dave's hapless, slightly dim wife, Marcia Gay Harden gets away with most of them. She continues to check the papers for some mention of Dave's cover story—that blood on his hands came from a mugger—and we can constantly see the frustrated indecision in her eyes.

Robbins also demonstrates how to show a character constantly thinking. His haggard face reveals signs of having been worn down by constant nightmares, and constant re-thinking of his fate. At one point Dave sits and watches Carpenter's *Vampires* on TV and compares his life (unfavorably) to one of the bloodsucker's, the bottle of an untouched beer poking up from between his knees.

Penn, in addition, delivers one showstopping scene after another, unleashing his anger, grief and frustration, oftentimes crumpled up on a stoop or in a deck chair, staring at nothing.

But it would be wrong to single out any one of these performances. Eastwood has assembled a bonanza cast here and each comes out shining.

Above all, *Mystic River* shows Eastwood unafraid of the dark. Rather, he's drawn again and again to pessimistic stories about man waffling between ego and id and eventually losing to the latter. In films as varied as *Tightrope*, *Bird*, and *Unforgiven* he simultaneously explores the unholy lure of violence while exposing its nauseating underbelly.

Admittedly, Eastwood has picked up a few bad habits previously belonging to John Ford, an overuse of music, oddly placed bits of comedy business, and a penchant for closing speeches. But those foibles made Ford no less of an artist, and the same goes for Eastwood.

Eastwood leaves *Mystic River* with a wordless exchange, characters eyeballing each other across the street while a noisy parade trumpets past. It's a devastating, perplexing ending, leaving us with a kind of "What do we do now?" feel. But we know in our heart of hearts that the answer won't be anything nice. Fate's heavy hand has still not relaxed its grip.

Margin annotations:
- **Body**
- **Conclusion**
- Topic Sentence (positive aspects) Acting
- Acting
- Acting
- Film's Theme
- Topic Sentence (negative aspects)
- Focus on Thesis

Introduction

Your review's opening should hook the reader and establish your credibility as a writer who has something interesting and important to say. By the end of the introduction, which can extend over a few paragraphs, your reader should know your overall opinion of the film and be eager to find out what helped you form that opinion.

One good way to begin is to provide some of the context you have uncovered in your research that would get your reader into the world of the film. Some options you have for providing context are these.

▶ Comparing a film to others by the same director

▶ Comparing a film to others by the same writer

▶ Comparing the film to others starring the same actor(s)

▶ Comparing an adapted film to its original source

▶ Comparing a film to other films with similar themes

Practice 11.6   Assessing Introductions

Playwriter-turned-screenwriter David Mamet wrote and directed *Heist*, a crime caper starring Gene Hackman, Danny DeVito, Rebecca Pidgeon, and Delroy Lindo. *Heist* was released in 2001 to generally good reviews. Read the following introductory paragraphs of four reviews of the film.

> Even a mediocre David Mamet movie is still a David Mamet movie. That means there are lines to savor, partly because the lines are so good, partly because they are so Mamet. Take this one from *Heist*, spoken by Danny DeVito in full DeVito-like exasperation: "Everybody needs money! That's why they call it money!"
>
> —Mick LaSalle, Review of *Heist* in *San Francisco Chronicle*

You know that thing he does? You know. The thing. He does a thing where, what I'm saying is it's a thing, a thing. Everybody talks in such a rhythm it's so real but then it's also not real, it sort of sings and dances and you're thinking, what the hell. . . . That's what he does. And what I'm saying is He's done that thing again. That thing. This time the thing that David Mamet has done is called *Heist*. A typical product that will excite those who love his dialogue-dense, vernacular-vivid style, and irritate those who hate it. For the believers at least, it's quite a thing: games within games, stratagems within stratagems, gambits within gambits, twists within twists, words within words. Imagine a pretzel baked jointly by Samuel Beckett and George V. Higgins, really salty and twisty.

> —Stephen Hunter, Review of *Heist* in *Washington Post*

In *Heist* David Mamet applies himself to a creaky subgenre: the last-big-score picture, in which an aging master thief is paired with a cocky, not entirely reliable youngster. The formula has been worked over so many times in the past—so many times this year,

for that matter—that even as shrewd an operator as Mr. Mamet may not have much to add. This director, whose film-making career has been a series of self-subverting genre exercises, plays it straight this time, and what *Heist* lacks in novelty it makes up for in solid entertainment.

> —A. O. Scott, Review of *Heist* in *New York Times*

David Mamet's *Heist* is about a caper and a con, involving professional criminals who want to retire but can't. It's not that they actually require more money. It's more that it would be a sin to leave it in civilian hands. Gene Hackman plays a jewel thief who dreams of taking his last haul and sailing into the sunset with his young wife (Rebecca Pidgeon). Danny DeVito is the low-rent mastermind who forces him into pulling one last job. Hackman complains he doesn't need any more money. DeVito's wounded reply is one of the funniest lines Mamet has ever written: "Everybody needs money! That's why they call it money!"

> —Roger Ebert, Review of *Heist* in *Chicago Sun Times*

1. Identify the technique(s) each writer uses to begin his review.

2. What information is included in all the introductory paragraphs?

3. Identify each reviewer's opinion. Do any paragraphs neither imply nor state the reviewer's opinion?

4. In *your* opinion, which review does the best job of hooking the reader? Why?

5. Choose a movie you have recently seen. Use the same technique as any one of the four reviewers to write an introduction for a review.

Practice 11.7
Identifying Thesis Statements

Read two film reviews (from newspapers, magazines, or websites) of a film you have recently seen. Identify and copy out the reviewer's thesis in each review.

1. How are the reviewers' theses different?

2. How are they similar?

3. Write a thesis for a review you might write for this film.

Providing some context or background information helps the reader make connections between the film being reviewed and other, more familiar films. *San Francisco Examiner* reviewer Jeffrey M. Anderson opens his review of *Mystic River*, for example, by comparing it to three previous movies that Clint Eastwood directed and finding *Mystic River* the best of the lot. Anderson gives his general evaluation in the very first paragraph, calling *Mystic River* "yet another great film," and he also acknowledges Dennis Lehane, the writer of the novel from which the film was adapted, and Brian Helgeland, the screenwriter.

Anderson's introduction ends with a clear segue to the plot summary. Some reviews begin with the brief plot summary; others start by recreating a scene from the film or quoting interesting dialogue. No matter how you choose to introduce your review, however, be sure to include your general evaluation. Your reader should know what you think of the film by the end of your introduction.

Thesis

Your thesis in your film review is the point you are prepared to argue and support through your analysis, and it stems from your assessment of how well the film succeeds in fulfilling its intentions and your expectations. You may not expect a mainstream action film to uncover universal truths or use experimental cinematic techniques, but if it does, it may surprise and please you. On the other hand, you might find such a film pretentious if it fails to deliver the action-filled entertainment it promised.

In a way, the thesis explains why you feel the way you do about the film. Although Anderson sets up his thesis in the first paragraph—the reader knows he thinks that *Mystic River* is a "great film"—he waits until the sixth paragraph, after he has explained the plot, to be specific. When he writes that the characters are guided to "some inexorable fate, predetermined at the moment young Dave gets in the car" and then asserts that the film "takes on a Sergio Leone-like epic nature, with a cruel God its major player" he has presented his thesis.

Some reviewers wait until they have built a case, leading readers through their analysis to their thesis, which can appear toward the end of the review. Most reviewers, however, present the thesis quickly—if not in the first paragraph, then soon after. A. O. Scott states his thesis at the end of his introduction to his review of *Heist*. The last line reads, "This director, whose film-making career has been a series of self-subverting genre exercises, plays it straight this time, and what "Heist" lacks in novelty it makes up for in solid entertainment." Scott's evaluation is mixed; he likes some aspects of the film but not others. His thesis tells the reader that he will support his evaluation by proving that the film lacks originality but delivers "solid entertainment." A good thesis does not just state whether you like a film, but also sets forth a more specific argument that analyzes the important, underlying strengths or weaknesses.

Brief Plot Summary

Somewhere in your review, usually near the beginning, include a brief overview of the film's plot. A plot summary, like a summary on a book jacket or the first page of your phone bill, hits the highlights but leaves out the details. A summary should be both specific and concise.

Think of your reader when you write your plot summary. A reader turns to a review to find out what the movie is about and whether to spend time and money to see it. Most readers do not want to know every detail of the story and every twist of the plot. Be careful not to give away any surprises; do not ruin the reader's pleasure of watching the story unfold in the film.

Anderson's quick three-paragraph plot summary gives an overall sense of the plot of *Mystic River* without giving away a thing about the surprises or twists in the story. He does tell the reader that Dave is one of the suspects, but he does not explain too much. Nor does he give away the surprise ending (neither will we). Those details are best left for viewers to discover while watching the film.

Remember that a review is not a retelling of the story, but an analysis of a film as a whole. Plot, or story, is only one element in the analysis and one small part of the review. Your aim should be to give the reader a sense of what the story is about, adding as many plot details as necessary to give context to your points about other elements—the acting or the cinematography, for example.

Analysis

An analysis examines the elements that go into the creation of a work. In the analytical section of a film review, which usually comprises most of the main middle section, you prove your thesis by selecting and discussing those elements—the story, characters, direction, music, editing, cinematography, acting, costumes, special effects—that support your overall evaluation of the film's strengths and weaknesses.

You do not have to examine all the elements, of course. That kind of exhaustive analysis would tire both you and your reader

Practice 11.8
Writing Summaries

Surprisingly good plot summaries often appear on the backs of video boxes or in capsule reviews. For example, here is the summary of *Mystic River* from the Internet Movie Database website.

> Childhood friends Jimmy Marcus (Penn), Sean Devine (Bacon) and Dave Boyle (Robbins) reunite following the death of Jimmy's oldest daughter, Katie (Rossum). Sean's a police detective on the case, gathering difficult and disturbing evidence; he's also tasked with handling Jimmy's rage and need for retribution.
>
> —Internet Movie Database, Plot Summary of *Mystic River*

The summary for *Lord of the Rings* released in the winter of 2001 reads like this.

> In a small village in the Shire a young Hobbit named Frodo has been entrusted with an ancient Ring. Now he must embark on an Epic quest to the Cracks of Doom in order to destroy it.
>
> —Internet Movie Database, Plot Summary of *Lord of the Rings: The Fellowship of the Ring*

Choose a movie you know well—one you are reviewing for this assignment or have seen many times—and write a one- or two-sentence summary. Provide a reasonable overview of the story.

and is outside the scope of a film review. Your task is to be selective, choosing the elements that provide the best evidence to support your thesis. Because Anderson is interested in the epic nature of the film and its preoccupation with "inexorable fate," he chooses to focus on the story elements, the acting, and the themes in his review of *Mystic River*. Other reviewers of *Mystic River* have looked more closely at the dark and rain-drenched setting, the operatic score also written by Eastwood, and the camera work that examines minute details such as the lips of a phone caller as well as the expansive view of a Boston neighborhood from above.

Examine some elements that can be praised and some that can be criticized. You enhance your credibility and show your critical skills if you can discern what works well and what does not. If you can point out an excellent actor in an otherwise lackluster cast or a dud of a speech in an otherwise brilliantly written script, your reader will more likely trust that your judgment is thoughtful and not necessarily swayed by your overall opinion of the film. Anderson, in his next-to-last paragraph, does just that and shows that his assessment of Eastwood as a great artist does not make him overlook a few "bad habits" reflected in the film.

The following excerpts show how a wide range of film reviewers have analyzed selected film elements. Pay attention to how the reviewers' opinions of the films' overall worth are telegraphed in many of their comments.

Acting

There has probably been no piece of casting this year more ineffably Hollywood than Cher as a busy, weary public defender in Peter Yates's *Suspect*—Cher as a dedicated drudge. Cher being Cher, when she represents a man accused of murder, in a Washington, D.C., courtroom, before a rigid, cold-eyed judge, she wears a black leather jacket, and her long thick hair is loose on her shoulders. She's all wrong for this public defender: her hooded, introspective face doesn't give you enough— she needs a role that lets her use her body. With the camera on her steadily here, you might be watching a still picture.

—Pauline Kael, Review of *Suspect* in the *New Yorker*

Cher is right at home in the screwball ethnic comedy *Moonstruck*. She doesn't stare at the camera and act the goddess. She moves around, she shouts, and when she lets her hair down a huge dark mass of crinkly tendrils floats about her tiny face. (What a prop!) Cher isn't afraid to be a little crazy here, and she's devastatingly funny and sinuous and beautiful.

—Pauline Kael, Review of *Moonstruck* in the *New Yorker*

Writing

Mamet demands that actors recite his words with distancing rhythms and cadences that make the conversations sound as if they took place on an alternative universe that parallels but does not connect to our own. This alienating verbal style puts peculiar emphasis on phrases like "You're a real gent" and "I'm loyal and true and I'm not hard to look at," emphasizing the artificiality of the situations and making any kind of involvement with the characters hard to imagine.

—Kenneth Turan, Review of *The Spanish Prisoner* in the *Los Angeles Times*

Theme

The point of this 157-minute picture seems clear. Every married person has within himself or herself a secret cosmos of sexual imaginings, longings, fantasies and perhaps extramarital actions. The actual marital life of a husband and wife involves only a portion of the sexual cosmos of each.

—Stanley Kaufmann, Review of *Eyes Wide Shut* in *New Republic*

Cinematography

Steven Soderbergh's great, despairing squall of a film, *Traffic*, may be the first Hollywood movie since Robert Altman's *Nashville* to infuse epic cinematic form with jittery new rhythms and a fresh, acid-washed palette. The agitated pulse of the hand-held camerawork (by the director working under a pseudonym) that roughly elbows its way into the center of the action is perfectly suited to the film's hard-boiled subject, America's losing war on drugs. The color scheme sandwiches a few lush patches between sequences filmed in two hues—an icy blue and sun-baked yellow-orange—that are as visually discordant as the forces doing battle.

—Stephen Holden, Review of *Traffic* in the *New York Times*

Editing

[The drug] sequences are done in fast-motion, to show how quickly the drugs take effect—and how disappointingly soon they fade. The in-between times edge toward desperation. [Director Darren] Aranofsky cuts between the mother, a prisoner of her apartment and diet pills, and the other three [characters]. Early in the film . . . he uses a split screen in which the space on both sides is available to the other (Sara and Harry each have half the screen, but their movements enter into each other's halves). This is an effective way of showing them alone together. Later, in a virtuoso closing sequence, he cuts between all four major characters as they careen toward their final destinations.

—Roger Ebert, Review of *Requiem for a Dream* in the *Chicago Sun-Times*

Production Design

The genuine magic in *Episode I* is all in its design. Conceptual artist Doug Chiang and production designer Gavin Bocquet give us breathtaking vistas, fabulous imaginary cities that range from the Florentine splendor of Queen Amidala's domain to the teeming metropolis of Coruscan. The vaultlike Galactic Senate, whose box seats float through the air, is a triumph of baroque futurism. The sunset-drenched, open-air Jedi council chambers (shades of *Blade Runner*) glow like a remembered childhood picture book. (The art nouveau, glass-bubble undersea city, however, looks like a floating Lamps Plus showroom to me.) The massive, tree-crunching tanks of the droid armies have a brutal beauty; there's visual wit in the insectlike robot soldiers who do the Trade Federation's dirty work. Indeed, there's often so much to take in you wish Lucas would hold his shots longer, and let us feast on the details.

—David Ansen, Review of *Star Wars: Episode I, The Phantom Menace* in *Newsweek*

Soundtrack

Slowly, however, the communal oddity of the new picture began to hit home. For some reason, I caught it first in the soundtrack, notably in the sharp sprinkling of Ravel that Anderson throws over his chosen people—a pizzicato passage from the String Quartet which tightens our sense of the Tenenbaums as unpredictable toys, either running down or whizzing out of control.

—Anthony Lane, Review of *The Royal Tenenbaums* in the *New Yorker*

Sound Effects

From the first, rhythmic, exquisitely separated sound of a chopper going *chtt-chtt-chtt*, which suggests both an eerily dry laugh and hoarse admonition, to the heartbeat-thumping of a single bass that marks the film's arrival at the mysterious locus of pure, horrifying evil, you know you are in the presence of a master—and a masterpiece—with *Apocalypse Now Redux*.

—Susan Stark, Review of *Apocalypse Now Redux* in *Detroit News*

Special Effects

It's a heady and delirious brew, too. The action is dexterously produced, thanks to the martial choreography of Mr. Yuen, best known to American audiences for the high-flying flights of *The Matrix*. The action in *The Matrix* was put together with a process called Bullettime, and here it should be termed Ballettime, as the performers soar gracefully over rooftops and up the sides of buildings as softly as leaves dancing in the air on an autumn day. Mr. Lee has found a way to make even the action feel poetic and spiritual, while sparked by a high adrenaline content.

—Elvis Mitchell, Review of *Crouching Tiger, Hidden Dragon* in the *New York Times*

Conclusion

Wrap up your film review with a brisk conclusion. A review is too short and too compact to need a detailed summary or recapitulation. Conclusions are as individualistic as introductions. You can be as creative as you wish, as long as you leave your reader with a clear sense of your opinion of the film.

Many reviewers end with a clever or witty line or two that reprise the main point(s) in the analysis and give the bottom-line evaluation of the film. For example, Mitchell ends his review of *Crouching Tiger, Hidden Dragon* (excerpted above) by referring to the special effects and reiterating his praise for the film: "*Crouching Tiger, Hidden Dragon* glides through the trees like its characters; it's an epic that breaks the laws of gravity."

Anderson's conclusion about *Mystic River* is more straightforward. Although he gives some details of the movie's ending, he does not give away any surprises. He shows the ambiguity and perplexing nature of the movie's conclusion. His final sentence, "Fate's heavy hand has still not relaxed its grip," refocuses the reader's attention on the film's serious themes and the reviewer's thesis about the inexorable and cruel nature of fate.

Whale Rider: This Girl, She Goes!

ANN HORNADAY

Read the following film review of *Whale Rider,* an independent film released in the spring of 2003. Pay close attention to how critic Ann Hornaday organized her review: the introduction, thesis, brief plot summary, analysis, and conclusion.

Between the violin prodigy in *Together*, the kids of *Spellbound*, and now the young heroine of *Whale Rider*, summer 2003 is shaping up to be the Season of the Kids. At a moment when theaters are sagging under the weight of bloated greenies, trench-coated cyber-dudes and characters that seem more confected than created, live-action rugrats are quietly proving to be the most compelling and inspiring characters on-screen.

The girl at the heart of *Whale Rider* is no exception; in fact, she might be the most awesome hero—fictional or otherwise—so far. In a movie that unfolds like an ancient fable, yet one grounded in the social and political realities of the present, thirteen-year-old actress Keisha Castle-Hughes takes instant command and

Poster for *Whale Rider,* 2003

never lets go. With uncommon assurance and focus, she leads viewers on a fantastic journey through the natural, cultural and imaginative world of the Maori culture in her native New Zealand, and in so doing she delivers one of the best performances—and movies—of the year so far. Remember Lou Grant snarling to Mary Richards, "I hate spunk!" In Castle-Hughes's case, even he would be forced to make an exception.

Whale Rider opens with the birth of twins, a brother and a sister, whose grandfather Koro (Rawiri Paratene) is chief of the Ngati Konohi tribe in the seaside village of Whangara, on the North Island of New Zealand. According to Maori lore, the Ngati Konohi came to New Zealand when the legendary ancestral figure Paikea led them to the island while riding on the back of a whale. Ever since, tribal leadership has passed as a patrimony from firstborn son to firstborn son. When Koro's grandson dies, that chain is broken. What's more, the twins' heartbroken father (Cliff Curtis), whose wife died in childbirth, flees his overbearing father for Europe, leaving the crusty old chief and his quietly indomitable wife, Flowers (Vicky Haughton), to care for the little girl, whose father has defiantly named her Paikea.

Young Pai (Castle-Hughes) has grown up as something of a tomboy in her family's seaside village. She's clearly tough enough to go barefoot most of the year and give as good as she gets with the macho boys in her class at school. But although she shows all the qualities of leadership and integrity that her grandfather is looking for in the next tribal chief, he refuses to see her as anything but an inferior female—even as he tenderly carries her to and from school each day on his bicycle. When Koro finally decides to gather all the firstborn boys in the village to decide on a future leader, he cruelly excludes Pai from the ritual education in chanting, tribal history, and jousting with a weapon called a *taiaha*.

Partly out of will but mostly due to a deep mystical calling, Pai educates herself in the ancient ways, proving herself both spiritually and physically to be the clear chosen leader of her people. Blinded by sexism and bitterness, her grandfather still can't see what's before his eyes until *Whale Rider*'s breathtaking climax, a beautiful, emotionally affecting passage in which the movie's story, scenery and aura of magic realism come together with spellbinding force.

New Zealand writer-director Niki Caro, whose first movie, *Memory & Desire*, wasn't released in the United States, has adapted Witi Ihimaera's best-selling novel with swiftness, grace and an unerring sense of place. Filmed in the actual village of Whangara, *Whale Rider* is redolent of surf and salt; using plenty of landscape to place her characters in context, Caro immerses viewers in the austere beauty of coastal New Zealand and in the turquoise depths just beyond. But in addition to opening up a magnificent outer world to viewers, Caro limns its inner subtleties. Using relatively few words, she skillfully portrays the poverty, frustration and dislocation of contemporary Maori life. Pai's uncle Rawiri (Grant Roa), for example, was a taiaha champion; these days he mostly drinks beer and smokes marijuana with his equally lazy friends.

Most of the tension in *Whale Rider* is generated by Pai and her obstinate grandfather, who clearly loves the little girl but can't see past his own rigid notions of gender and tradition. Although Pai calmly fulfills every test of an anointed leader, the most difficult one seems to come the most easily to her. In the face of almost unspeakable rejection by her grandfather, she responds only with understanding, forgiveness and quiet perseverance. Although *Whale Rider* is sure to strike viewers as a magnificent portrait of New Zealand as well as a fable, it's even more admirable—and enduring—as a thoughtful, vivid spiritual coming-of-age story that transcends its particular cultural context.

Audiences will be relieved to know that Paratene, who plays Koro, is in real life the warm, genial former host of a children's television program in New Zealand; as for Castle-Hughes, she was plucked as an eleven-year-old out of 10,000 girls who had tried out for the part. Clearly, the director has a shrewd eye for talent. Castle-Hughes never misses a step as a brave, charismatic protagonist who uses the wisdom of her ancestors to teach her parents well. Pai is an unforgettable character, Castle-Hughes is a revelation in a part she was born for, and in Whale Rider Caro has given both of them—and audiences—a movie they richly deserve.

Annotate *"Whale Rider: This Girl, She Goes!"*

1. Underline all passages that give some context or background information. Where do they appear in the review?

2. Note where the introduction ends and the body of the review begins. Underline the thesis of this review.

3. Star the paragraphs that present the plot summary. How much of the review do they encompass?

4. Underline and identify the film elements Hornaday discusses in this review.

5. Bracket the concluding paragraph. Comment in the margin on how Hornaday ends her review.

📺 READINGS

Janet Maslin, reviewing for the *New York Times,* and Roger Ebert, reviewing for the *Chicago Sun Times,* take different views of the 1999 film *Fight Club,* a film that some call a modern classic. Student Trish DeWolfe writes a rave review of *Chicago* (2003), and *New Yorker* film critic David Denby gives *Seabiscuit* (2003) a mixed review.

Such a Very Long Way from Duvets to Danger

Janet Maslin

Janet Maslin began her career in 1972 at *Rolling Stone,* writing about rock and roll. She had brief stints at the *Boston Phoenix* and *Newsweek* and began reviewing films for the *New York Times* in 1977. She was chief film critic for the *Times* from 1993 until she resigned in 1999.

Of the two current films in which buttoned-down businessmen rebel against middle-class notions of masculinity, David Fincher's savage *Fight Club* is by far the more visionary and disturbing. Where *American Beauty* hinges on the subversive allure of a rose-covered blond cheerleader, Mr. Fincher has something a good deal tougher in mind. The director of *Seven* and *The Game* for the first time finds subject matter audacious enough to suit his lightning-fast visual sophistication, and puts that style to stunningly effective use. Lurid sensationalism and computer gamesmanship left this filmmaker's earlier work looking hollow and manipulative. But the sardonic, testosterone-fueled science fiction of *Fight Club* touches a raw nerve.

In a film as strange and single-mindedly conceived as *Eyes Wide Shut,* Mr. Fincher's angry, diffidently witty ideas about contemporary manhood unfold. As based on a novel by Chuck Palahniuk (and deftly written by Jim Uhls), it builds a huge, phantasmagorical structure around the search for lost masculine authority, and attempts to psychoanalyze an entire society in the process. Complete with an even bigger narrative whammy than the one that ends *The Sixth Sense,* this film twists and turns in ways that only add up fully on the way out of the theater and might just require another viewing. Mr. Fincher uses his huge arsenal of tricks to bury little hints at what this story is really about.

Fight Club has two central figures, the milquetoast narrator played by Edward Norton and his charismatic, raging crony played by Brad Pitt. The narrator has been driven to the edge of his sanity by a dull white-collar job, an empty fondness for material things ("I'd flip through catalogues and wonder what kind of dining set defined me as a person") and the utter absence of anything to make him feel alive. Tormented by insomnia, he finds his only relief in going to meetings of twelve-step support groups, where he can at least cry. The film hurtles along so smoothly that its meaningfully bizarre touches, like Meat Loaf Aday as a testicular cancer patient with very large breasts, aren't jarring at all.

Poster for *Fight Club* (1999)

The narrator finds a fellow twelve-step addict in Marla, played with witchy sensuality by Helena Bonham Carter and described by the script as "the little scratch on the roof of your mouth that would heal if only you could stop tonguing it—but you can't." As that suggests, Marla's grunge recklessness makes a big impression on the film's narrator, and can mostly be blamed for setting the story in motion. Soon after meeting her he is on an airplane, craving any sensation but antiseptic boredom, and he meets Mr. Pitt's Tyler Durden in the next seat. Surveying the bourgeois wimp he nicknames Ikea Boy, Tyler asks all the hard questions. Like: "Why do guys like you and I know what a duvet is?"

5   Mr. Norton, drawn into Tyler's spell, soon forsakes his tidy ways and moves into the abandoned wreck that is ground central for Tyler. Then Tyler teaches his new roommate to fight in a nearby parking lot. The tacitly homoerotic bouts between these two men become addictive (as does sex with Marla), and their fight group expands into a secret society, all of which the film presents with the curious matter-of-factness of a dream. Somehow nobody gets hurt badly, but the fights leave frustrated, otherwise emasculated men with secret badges of not-quite-honor.

Fight Club watches this form of escapism morph into something much more dangerous. Tyler somehow builds a bridge from the anti-materialist rhetoric of the 1960s ("It's only after we've lost everything that we're free to do anything") into the kind of paramilitary dream project that Ayn Rand might have admired. The group's rigorous training and subversive agenda are as deeply disturbing to Mr. Norton's mild-mannered character as Tyler's original wild streak was thrilling. But even when acts of terrorism are in the offing, he can't seem to tear himself away.

Like Kevin Smith's *Dogma*, *Fight Club* sounds offensive from afar. If watched sufficiently mindlessly, it might be mistaken for a dangerous endorsement of totalitarian tactics and super-violent nihilism in an all-out assault on society. But this is a much less gruesome film than *Seven* and a notably more serious one. It means to explore the lure of violence in an even more dangerously regimented, dehumanized culture. That's a hard thing to illustrate this powerfully without, so to speak, stepping on a few toes.

In an expertly shot and edited film spiked with clever computer-generated surprises, Mr. Fincher also benefits, of course, from marquee appeal. The teamwork of Mr. Norton and Mr. Pitt is as provocative and complex as it's meant to be. Mr. Norton, an ingenious actor, is once again trickier than he looks. Mr. Pitt struts through the film with rekindled brio and a visceral sense of purpose. He's right at home in a movie that warns against worshiping false idols.

Fight Club is rated R (under seventeen requires accompanying parent or adult guardian). It includes bloody fights, grisly touches, sexual situations and nudity, profanity and assorted intentional gross-out shocks, including the rendering of human fat into soap.

Critical Reading Questions

1. What contextual and background information does Maslin include in her review? Would you like more? Less? Why?

2. What does Maslin think are director David Fincher's intentions in this film? Does she think he fulfilled them? Cite a line from the review to support your answer.

3. How much of the plot does Maslin reveal? Where? Do you think she gives away too much? Just enough? Why?

4. What film elements does Maslin discuss to support her thesis that *Fight Club* "touches a raw nerve"? Do you think she makes a convincing argument? Why?

5. Maslin asserts that *Fight Club* "sounds offensive from afar." What argument does she put forth to explain the

importance of the violence it portrays? Do you agree or disagree? Explain your answer.

6. Define Maslin's voice in this review. Choose a few specific lines from the review, and explain how they helped you form your opinion of her voice.

7. Does Maslin end the review effectively? Why?

Questions for Writing and Discussion

1. How explicit do you think filmmakers should be in depicting violence on the screen? When is it appropriate, and when is it gratuitous? If you have seen *Fight Club*, comment on the violence in this film.

2. Maslin names a number of films that explore contemporary manhood. Some films, she says, are built around "the search for lost masculine authority." What do you think defines masculinity in contemporary society?

Fight Club

Roger Ebert

Roger Ebert is arguably the best-known film critic in the country. On his long-running television show *Siskel and Ebert at the Movies* (now *Ebert and Roeper*) he popularized the "thumbs-up, thumbs down" motif. He is the film critic for the *Chicago Sun Times*, has won a Pulitzer Prize for film commentary, and has published fifteen books on film.

Fight Club is the most frankly and cheerfully fascist big-star movie since *Death Wish*, a celebration of violence in which the heroes write themselves a license to drink, smoke, screw and beat one another up.

Sometimes, for variety, they beat up themselves. It's macho porn—the sex movie Hollywood has been moving toward for years, in which eroticism between the sexes is replaced by all-guy locker-room fights. Women, who have had a lifetime of practice at dealing with little-boy posturing, will instinctively see through it; men may get off on the testosterone rush. The fact that it is very well made and has a great first act certainly clouds the issue.

Edward Norton stars as a depressed urban loner filled up to here with angst. He describes his world in dialogue of sardonic social satire. His life and job are driving him crazy. As a means of dealing with his pain, he seeks out twelve-step meetings, where he can hug those less fortunate

than himself and find catharsis in their suffering. It is not without irony that the first meeting he attends is for post-surgical victims of testicular cancer, since the whole movie is about guys afraid of losing their *cojones*.

These early scenes have a nice sly tone; they're narrated by the Norton character in the kind of voice Nathanael West used in *Miss Lonelyhearts*. He's known only as the Narrator, for reasons later made clear. The meetings are working as a sedative, and his life is marginally manageable when tragedy strikes: He begins to notice Marla (Helena Bonham Carter) at meetings. She's a "tourist" like himself—someone not addicted to anything but meetings. She spoils it for him. He knows he's a faker, but wants to believe everyone else's pain is real.

On an airplane, he has another key encounter, with Tyler Durden (Brad Pitt), a man whose manner cuts through the fog. He seems able to see right into the Narrator's soul, and shortly after, when the Narrator's high-rise apartment turns into a fireball, he turns to Tyler for shelter. He gets more than that. He gets in on the ground floor of Fight Club, a secret society of men who meet in order to find freedom and self-realization through beating one another into pulp.

It's at about this point that the movie stops being smart and savage and witty, and turns to some of the most brutal, unremitting, nonstop violence ever filmed. Although sensible people know that if you hit someone with an ungloved hand hard enough, you're going to end up with broken bones, the guys in *Fight Club* have fists of steel, and hammer one another while the sound effects guys beat the hell out of Naugahyde sofas with Ping-Pong paddles. Later, the movie takes still another turn. A lot of recent films seem unsatisfied unless they can add final scenes that redefine the reality of everything that has gone before; call it the Keyser Soze syndrome.

What is all this about? According to Durden, it is about freeing yourself from the shackles of modern life, which imprisons and emasculates men. By being willing to give and receive pain and risk death, Fight Club members find freedom. Movies like *Crash* must play like cartoons for Durden. He's a shadowy, charismatic figure, able to inspire a legion of men in big cities to descend into the secret cellars of a Fight Club and beat one another up.

Only gradually are the final outlines of his master plan revealed. Is Tyler Durden in fact a leader of men with a useful philosophy? "It's only after we've lost everything that we're free to do anything," he says, sounding like a man who tripped over the Nietzsche display on his way to the coffee bar in Borders. In my opinion, he has no useful truths. He's a bully—Werner Erhard plus S & M, a leather club operator without the decor. None of the Fight Club members grows stronger

or freer because of their membership; they're reduced to pathetic cultists. Issue them black shirts and sign them up as skinheads. Whether Durden represents hidden aspects of the male psyche is a question the movie uses as a loophole—but is not able to escape through, because *Fight Club* is not about its ending but about its action.

Of course, *Fight Club* itself does not advocate Durden's philosophy. It is a warning against it, I guess; one critic I like says it makes "a telling point about the bestial nature of man and what can happen when the numbing effects of day-to-day drudgery cause people to go a little crazy." I think it's the numbing effects of movies like this that cause people go to a little crazy. Although sophisticates will be able to rationalize the movie as an argument against the behavior it shows, my guess is that audience will like the behavior but not the argument. Certainly they'll buy tickets because they can see Pitt and Norton pounding on each other; a lot more people will leave this movie and get in fights than will leave it discussing Tyler Durden's moral philosophy. The images in movies like this argue for themselves, and it takes a lot of narration (or Narration) to argue against them.

Lord knows the actors work hard enough. Norton and Pitt go through almost as much physical suffering in this movie as Demi Moore endured in *G.I. Jane*, and Helena Bonham Carter creates a feisty chain-smoking hellcat who is probably so angry because none of the guys thinks having sex with her is as much fun as a broken nose. When you see good actors in a project like this, you wonder if they signed up as an alternative to canyoneering.

The movie was directed by David Fincher and written by Jim Uhls, who adapted the novel by Chuck Palahniuk. In many ways, it's like Fincher's movie *The Game* (1997), with the violence cranked up for teenage boys of all ages. That film was also about a testing process in which a man drowning in capitalism (Michael Douglas) has the rug of his life pulled out from under him and has to learn to fight for survival. I admired *The Game* much more than *Fight Club* because it was really about its theme, while the message in *Fight Club* is like bleeding scraps of Socially Redeeming Content thrown to the howling mob.

Fincher is a good director (his work includes *Alien 3*, one of the best-looking bad movies I have ever seen, and *Seven*, the grisly and intelligent thriller). With *Fight Club* he seems to be set-ting himself some kind of a test—how far over the top can he go? The movie is visceral and hard-edged, with levels of irony and commentary above and below the action. If it had all continued in the vein explored in the first act, it might have become a great film. But the second act is pandering and the third is trickery, and whatever Fincher thinks the message is, that's not what most audience members will get. *Fight Club* is a thrill ride masquerading as philosophy—the kind of ride where some people puke and others can't wait to get on again.

Reprinted by permission of Universal Press Syndicate.

Critical Reading Questions

1. What is Ebert's opinion of *Fight Club*? Where do you first know this opinion?

2. Identify the positive and negative qualities Ebert writes about in his review.

3. How much of the plot does Ebert reveal? Where? Do you think he gives away too much? Just enough? Why?

4. Where in the review does Ebert give contextual and background information? Compare the amount and placement of this information with Maslin's review above.

5. Define Ebert's voice in this review. Choose a few specific lines from the review, and explain how they help you form your opinion of his voice.

6. What are the points on which Ebert disagrees with Maslin? Who do you think makes a more convincing case?

Questions for Writing and Discussion

1. Ebert asserts that people will like *Fight Club* because of the violent behavior it shows and will ignore the film's argument against this behavior. He writes that "a lot more people will leave this movie and get in fights than will leave it discussing Tyler Durden's moral philosophy. The images in movies like this argue for themselves." Do you agree or disagree with Ebert?

2. Do you think violent movies promote violent behavior?

With a Little Dazzle, *Chicago* Jazzes Up the Silver Screen

Trish DeWolfe

Trish DeWolfe wrote this film review for her writing class in 2003.

Is it possible to get away with murder? What if you fire a gun with plenty of witnesses around? Sure. As long as you have the money to hire a top-notch, smooth-talking lawyer, anything is possible. Being a celebrity doesn't hurt your chances either. Even if you aren't famous, don't fret because chances are the media will sweep you up in their frenzy and make you a star.

No, no, I'm not referring to O. J. Simpson or the club shootings involving P. Diddy. I was talking about the recent Oscar winner for Best Picture, *Chicago*. Under careful direction, this star-studded cast produces one of 2002's most entertaining films. Based in the 1920s prohibition era, *Chicago* carries many themes still very alive today—sex, jealousy, and plenty of scandal.

First-time film director Rob Marshall deserves the Rookie of the Year Award for his big screen adaptation of the Broadway hit. *Chicago* led the Oscar race this year with thirteen nominations, winning six awards. And to think this picture almost didn't get made! Miramax struggled to find a concept that would bring the stage production to the silver screen in a credible and enticing manner. When Marshall suggested the musical numbers be staged in the mind of Roxie Hart, the studio realized he was on to something.

The film dives into action when wanna-be showgirl Roxie Hart (Renee Zellweger) shoots her lover after he goes bad on his promise to make her a star. From there, she is sent to prison, joining murderess row along with her idol, Vaudeville star Velma Kelly (Catherine Zeta-Jones). Notorious for his courtroom murder wins, attorney Billy Flynn (Richard Gere) is hired to defend both women. With some public relations help from Flynn, Roxie becomes Chicago's newest sweetheart and manages to rally the entire city behind her. Sensationalized by the press, scandalous-nobody Roxie Hart becomes a household name. (Can you say Monica Lewinsky?) Roxie's newfound popularity leads to competition with Velma Kelly, former "It girl" and fellow killer. The entire trial becomes more of a circus than a legal proceeding and is merely another form of entertainment. Who ever said Chicago and Hollywood are all that different?

While Zellweger's performance as the delusional Roxie Hart appears forced at times, she has an adorable charm that makes you root for her obviously guilty character, which could not have been pulled off by many other actresses. With some studio assistance, Zellweger sells her cutesy voice but don't expect to ever hear her perform live.

Gere is surprisingly good in this uncharacteristic role. His ventriloquist number with Zellweger, "We Both Reached for the Gun," is an impressive showcase for both actors and one of the film's highlights. Gere's portrayal of a greedy, tap-dancing lawyer earned him a Golden Globe, but his performance did not match the likes of Adrien Brody and Jack Nicholson, justly omitting him from the Oscar race.

Packed with plenty of star power, *Chicago* has appearances by John C. Reilly, Taye Diggs, Lucy

Liu, and Mya. Each adds his/her own little touch to the film, particularly Reilly as Roxie's pathetic, heart-broken husband. The only detraction is Christine Baranski as reporter Mary Sunshine. Baranski appears to fall victim to a bad case of overacting. However, as the film progresses it becomes clear that her excessive dramatization is simply an attempt to steal scenes. Undoubtedly, the real standout performances are delivered by Best Supporting Actress nominees Queen Latifah and Catherine Zeta-Jones.

Queen Latifah plays Mama Morton, the sometimes helpful but always self-interested prison guard. Her performance of "When You're Good to Mama" is a booming, confident number that shows her musical talent isn't limited to rapping. She may not have a huge role, but Queen Latifah has a potent presence whenever on screen.

Oscar winner Catherine Zeta-Jones is perfect as the self-absorbed, conniving, washed-up star. Her powerful voice sets the precedent for the later acts in opening number, "All That Jazz" where she performs after murdering her cheating husband and sister. As a former dancer, she turns in the impressive solo number "Can't Do it Alone" which she adeptly carries. Her screen presence is more than intriguing, making it nearly impossible to keep your eyes off her.

Fortunately, Marshall knows how much "Razzle Dazzle" is enough unlike 1999's *Moulin Rouge*. He doesn't cross the line with over the top cinematography and excessive editing that will leave you with a headache. Staging the musical numbers in Roxie's mind could have turned into a confusing disaster but each song follows the film's plot and helps it progress. While *Moulin Rouge* used modern songs like *Material Girl* to appeal to the younger audience, *Chicago* doesn't need to make such futile attempts. You don't even need to be a fan of musicals to enjoy this film; all you have to do is watch and you'll be pulled right in.

Greed, murder, sensationalism of the press . . . are we really watching a film set in the flapper era? If *Chicago* is any indication of how people's characters have changed, then the costumes are one of the few differences between then and now. Marshall undoubtedly hit big with this picture and hey, if he ever decides to make a modern-day version of *Chicago*, maybe he can teach Johnnie Cochran how to dance.

Critical Reading Questions

1. How important or interesting is the background information that DeWolfe includes in her review? How well does she integrate it into the review?

2. What is DeWolfe's opinion of *Chicago*? Where does she first let the reader know her opinion?

3. Does the introduction succeed in capturing your attention? Is it an effective way to begin the review?

4. How successful is DeWolfe in giving a brief plot summary without going into too much detail?

5. What is the review's thesis?

6. What film elements does DeWolfe discuss? Does she support her thesis convincingly?

7. How does DeWolfe conclude this review? Is the conclusion satisfying?

Questions for Writing and Discussion

1. Do you agree with DeWolfe that "sex, jealousy, and plenty of scandal" are very contemporary themes?

2. How much power does the press have today in swaying public opinion?

WRITING IN THE WORKS

Roger Ebert

Interview with Roger Ebert

Film critic Steven Snyder interviewed Roger Ebert and published this interview on the website **http://www.movies.zertinet.com** right before the Oscars were awarded for the 2002 movies.

When Roger Ebert talks about movies, the world listens.

He is the only critic to ever win the Pulitzer Prize, is host of the country's most popular movie review television show, and is perhaps the most widely referenced printed critic in the nation. His columns, which appear in the *Chicago Sun-Times*, are regularly quoted by movie studios themselves.

His story is a fascinating one, and I recently had the opportunity to have a discussion with Ebert about his life, his goals, and his philosophy as a critic. I also asked him about his upcoming Overlooked Film Festival, which I will be attending and covering in late April, and about next week's Oscar competition, which he clearly has opinions about.

In the coming weeks, both at his film festival in Champaign, IL and at the Wisconsin Film Festival in Madison, you will have a chance to meet the most respected critic in America. For now, here's an inside look at this most amazing man.

About Life

You are the only film critic to receive the Pulitzer Prize. What do you think sets you apart from the hundreds of other critics that write about a given film?

Every critic worth reading is set aside from all the others, because he or she is writing from a highly personal perspective, in a style that has evolved in response to the job. It is not for me to describe my own writing, but I will say that I happily go into various modes for different kinds of movies, that I try to be conversational and even use direct address, and that I do not have any rules for what a review is.

How did you make the move from working exclusively with printed reviews into the realm of your television show? Was it your idea, or were you approached to do it? Which do you enjoy more?

I am basically a creature of print. Gene (Siskel) and I were recruited by the local PBS station, never gave up our day jobs, and the rest is history. (Co-host Richard) Roeper follows in the tradition.

How do you remain motivated to write reviews when there are so many films to view on a weekly basis—often films that you do not particularly like? Do you ever get burnt out?

I try to review most every film of any relevance that opens here. I'm motivated by the fairly enormous audience for the web site (www.suntimes.com/ ebert), my syndication, and my *Movie Yearbook*, who all expect not just the big films but as many reviewable films as possible.

I noticed that your review of *The Shawshank Redemption* originally assigned the film 3.5 stars, but later the film was included in your book *The Great Movies* as one of the best works of all time. That is quite a change in opinion. What caused you to change your mind, and what recent films besides *Shawshank* do you now wish you could go back and change your rating on?

Stars are relative, not absolute. They are also very silly. I refuse to get into discussions about them.

What is the purpose of a film critic? Do you believe it is a critic's place to tell moviegoers what they "should" like? For instance, a film like Adam Sandler's *Mr. Deeds* sets its sights low. So, when you go in to a film like that, do you believe it should be graded on how well it accomplishes what it sets out to do, or do you think, as a critic, you should be trying to direct moviegoers to more substantive work?

The critic speaks entirely from a personal point of view. His purpose is (1) to write in such a way that the reader will be able to decide if a given movie is worth seeing, (2) always to entertain or absorb, and (3) sometimes even to educate or inspire.

You attended the University of Illinois Champaign–Urbana for both undergraduate and graduate studies. At what point did you decide to be a film critic, and how did you go about securing your first and only position with the *Chicago Sun-Times*?

I never sought this job. I was a Ph.D. candidate in English at the U of Chicago while working at the *Sun-Times.* The position opened up, and I was offered it. One of the best days of my life.

How has your life changed since the death of Gene Siskel?

I miss him all the time. He was a great friend and a treasured sparring partner.

What films would count as your "guilty pleasures?"

Recently: *Anaconda* and *Lara Croft, Tomb Raider.*

About the Oscars

None of the films nominated for best picture this year made your top 10 list for 2002. Do you feel the Oscars are an accurate representation of the best the year had to offer?

Why should this year be any different than any other year? Only a certain kind of film can hope to be nominated.

Who do you believe should and will win best picture this year, out of the chosen nominees?

Will win: *Chicago.* Should win: *Gangs of New York.*

As a film critic, I watch the Oscars closely and attempt to voice my opinion about them because I believe it is the most popular indicator the future will have about the best films from a given year. Do you agree with this philosophy, or do you find yourself paying little attention to what happens on Oscar night?

Yes (I pay attention), but in terms of current marketing and publicity more than in terms of future indicators.

Last year, you came out strongly in favor of Robert Altman receiving the best director statue for, more or less, a career's worth of work that went previously unrecognized by the Academy. Do you feel the same this year about Martin Scorsese, who directed a film that you gave only 3.5 stars?

Scorsese deserves that Oscar, period.

Are there any smaller categories, aside from best picture, director, acting and screenplay, that you watch closely?

Documentaries and animation are fascinating fields for me.

What, in recent memory, do you believe is the biggest mistake the Academy has made?

Giving the best picture award to *Gladiator.*

About Ebertfest

How did your "Overlooked Film Festival" come about? Where did the idea originate and why is it something you have continued to work on for five years running?

My alma mater asked me to do a film festival. As a critic I could not accept favors from studios by inviting premieres and stars to town, but as a critic I could offer exposure to overlooked films, genres, styles and formats.

What do you consider to be the greatest success of your film festival? What film are you most proud to have brought to your fan's attention that would have otherwise gone unnoticed?

A wise parent does not have a favorite child. But the premiere of *Dance Me to My Song* and the onstage appearance of the courageous Heather Rose will always have a special place in my heart.

Has there been a film that you are passionate about, but have been unable to work into your festival? How hard is it to find the copies of these "overlooked" films?

This year, I wanted *Wit*, but (director) Mike Nichols said it was "not overlooked." I argued that the very fact that it was made for cable (HBO) indicates that the mainstream shies away from such serious material.

Tell me a bit about your decision process for this year's films.

There's no process. It just sort of happens as a dance involving my taste, my whims, what I see, and what is available.

During the five-day festival, you introduce every film, facilitate every postfilm discussion, and seem to run nonstop during each day's festivities. Do you find you have time to actually enjoy the festival you have helped create? Or does it pass by too quickly to notice?

I enjoy every movie. I like doing stuff like that.

If you could put on a festival of your ten favorite films for the entire world to see, what would they be?

Well, in the most recent *Sight and Sound* poll, I voted for *Aguirre, Wrath of God* (Herzog); *Apocalypse Now* (Coppola); *Citizen Kane* (Welles); *Dekalog* (Kieslowski); *La Dolce Vita* (Fellini); *The General* (Keaton); *Raging Bull* (Scorsese); *2001: A Space Odyssey* (Kubrick); *Tokyo Story* (Ozu); *Vertigo* (Hitchcock) as the top films of all time.

A highlight of this year's fest, by the way, will be the showing of Ozu's silent film "*I Was Born, But . . .*" with a live performance by a benshi, or simultaneous performer/commentator, from Tokyo.

WRITING AND REVISION STRATEGIES

Gathered here are three interactive sections for you to use as you write and revise your film review and as you apply what you have learned to writing in other classes.

▶ Writer's Notebook Suggestions

▶ Peer-Editing Log

▶ Revision Checklist

Writer's Notebook Suggestions

These short exercises are intended to jump-start your thinking as you begin to write your film review.

1. Write an e-mail message to a friend telling him or her about the most recent movie you have seen. Write the message in your own voice.

2. You have just been hired to write blurbs for the backs of the boxes of new video releases. You are limited to one paragraph per film. Write blurbs for two movies you have seen recently, one you liked and one you did not. Remember that you have been hired to sell the films, not review them.

3. Decide on a movie, perhaps one that you've seen recently, perhaps the one you intend to review. Write its name in the middle of a blank sheet of paper and circle it. Create a cluster of words and phrases that express your varied responses to the film. (You may want to reread the section on clustering on page 11 in Chapter 1 before you do this exercise.)

4. Make a list of the most clichéd movie review phrases you can find in ads or reviews in your local newspaper.

5. On a piece of paper, write the words *cinematography*, *soundtrack*, and *special effects*. Under each heading, write a list of excellent examples of that element from movies you have seen.

6. On a piece of paper, write the words *acting*, *production design*, and *screenplay*. Under each heading, write a list of terrible examples of that element from movies you have seen.

7. Write an advertisement for your favorite movie. It can be an ad for a newspaper, a radio spot, a poster, or a website.

8. Write a trailer for a movie you have seen recently. Include descriptions of the visual elements in your script.

Peer-Editing Log

As you work with a writing partner or in a peer-editing group, you can use these questions to give helpful responses to a classmate's film review and as a guide for discussion.

Writer's Name

Date

1. Bracket the introduction. Does it grab your attention? Why? Suggest one way to strengthen the introduction.

2. Can you tell by the end of the introduction what the reviewer's opinion of the film is? State it in a sentence.

3. Underline all the sentences that provide background or contextual information. Is the information interesting? Could any be cut? What other information would you like?

4. Underline the thesis when it is first stated. Also underline any times the thesis is restated in the review. Does the writer prove this thesis? Can you suggest a way to state the thesis more clearly?

5. Identify the paragraphs that give the plot summary. Does any information give away surprises or twists? Is there too much detail, and could some of it be cut? Do you need more information to make sense of the film's story?

6. Identify the film elements the writer uses to prove the thesis. Does the writer use visual elements like cinematography, acting, and production design? Has the writer clearly tied the film elements to the thesis? If not, how might this be done?

7. Do any of the points need more support? Where could the writer use a quotation or a specific example from the film to pin down an idea?

8. Mark any places where the voice sounds lively and engaging. Mark places where it could be improved.

9. Is the conclusion satisfying? Make a suggestion to strengthen the ending.

Revision Checklist

As you do your final revision, check to make sure that you

❑ Wrote an introduction that brings your reader quickly into the film

❑ Stated your opinion of the film in a clear thesis statement

❑ Provided background or contextual information

❑ Wrote a plot summary that contains only essential information and at the same time does not give away any surprises or plot twists

❏ Selected the criteria that best support your opinion of the film

❏ Included some discussion of the visual aspects of the film

❏ Provided specific evidence to support your opinion of the film

❏ Wrote in a professional and lively voice

❏ Avoided clichéd language

❏ Wrote for the specific audience you have selected

❏ Included a clear bottom-line evaluation of the film

❏ Concluded strongly, perhaps refocusing on your thesis

12. PROFILES

WRITING ABOUT OTHERS

**An ordinary life examined closely reveals
itself to be exquisite and complicated,
somehow managing to be both heroic
and plain.**

—Susan Orlean

ASSIGNMENT

Write a five- to seven-page profile. Choose an interesting person or group of people to whom you have access and whom you can interview in person. Paint a word portrait, complete with interpretation and analysis. Be sure that your profile has a clear focal point and an interpretive thesis, or "nut graf" as it is sometimes called.

Daphne Confar's portrait of her mother, entitled *Judy Remains Resilient.*

PROFILES

In painting a portrait, an artist sets out to create a likeness of a person, a recognizable image. The artist's aim, however, is only in small part to record the details of the subject: color of hair, slope of nose, or smile. The real art of portrait painting lies in the way the artist interprets and reveals the subject. In a good portrait, through some combination of light and shadow, expression, and detail, the essence of the subject emerges, not just the likeness but also the character.

A profile is a portrait in words. It provides an in-depth look at a person or sometimes a group of people from a specific perspective or angle. This angle makes the portrait very different from a general picture of a person, what might amount to a simple "driver's license" description: height, weight, and date of birth, for example. Here, for example, are facts about a writer whose books you may know. Even if you are familiar with this man's books, you may not recognize him from the general view that follows.

> He was born in Springfield, Massachusetts, on March 2, 1904, and graduated from Dartmouth College in 1925. At Oxford University, he studied towards a doctorate in literature. There he met Helen Palmer, the woman he eventually married. After returning to the United States, he worked for a humor magazine. Later, he joined the army during World War II and was sent to Hollywood where he won several Oscars for his documentaries about Adolph Hitler, and one for a cartoon called "Gerald McBoing-Boing."

These dryly listed facts about the writer's life do not give a clue about who he really is. Instead of a portrait, which reveals some basic element of character, we get a snapshot: information without interpretation.

The following paragraph, which interprets this person's character, provides a perspective, and it helps reveal the writer, whom you will now most likely recognize.

> He used to doodle in school, strange little drawings. His high school art teacher told him never to plan a career in art. Likewise, his writing teacher at Dartmouth College discouraged him from becoming a writer. Even his fraternity brothers voted him least likely to succeed. Being misunderstood, though, would not get in his way. This writer's first children's book was rejected 43 times. Then a friend agreed to publish it. The writer went on to win an Oscar for a cartoon, but even more importantly, he kept trying new things. At the encouragement of his publisher, he set out on a campaign

against boring children's books, hoping to make learning to read more interesting than Dick and Jane had. And, in 1954, using a list of 220 words he thought a first grader could learn, he wrote an instantly successful book. It was called *The Cat in the Hat*.

—Adapted from *Outpost 10F*, *Poetry Guild*, and *Stories for a Teen's Heart*

The writer, of course, is Theodore Geisel, known all over the world as Dr. Seuss, author of *How the Grinch Stole Christmas*, *Green Eggs and Ham*, and forty-two other children's books. The second paragraph, rather than just listing biographical facts, creates a portrait of this unique artist, focusing on his quirky sensibilities, his "misunderstood" character, and his early conflicts.

Your goal in writing a profile is to bring this kind of character interpretation to your description of one or more people. Author Megan Easton compares writing a profile to going through somebody's house and closets in search of a few items that define the identity of their owner. Writing the profile is like arranging just those items on the sidewalk in front of the house and saying, "This is who lives here." By choosing the parts of a life to highlight, you create a clear, focused impression of the person—a portrait.

Readers are always interested in looking at the items on the sidewalk, which is why profiles in magazines and newspapers are always popular. Offering a glimpse into the lives of others appeals to people's voyeuristic and philosophical sides. By looking closely at the struggles, commitments, and decisions of others, we may recognize ourselves. Along the way, we also learn about the professions, passions, and lifestyles of famous, infamous, and even ordinary people, and perhaps extend the boundaries of our own lives.

Applications: School, Community, Work

The interviewing, observation, electronic, and print research skills you use in writing a profile will prove useful in writing many types of research papers in your college classes. You might write a historical biography in a history, science, psychology, or literature class, for example. Equally likely, you might be asked to write about a person who influenced you or whose experiences inspired you or others for a course in philosophy, education, or communication. In all these cases, you will want to find a narrow angle or perspective and focus on a specific aspect of the person's life, rather than write a comprehensive biography of an entire life.

Published profiles appear just about everywhere in community, workplace, and professional settings. You can read about people not just in *People* magazine, but also in community and business newsletters, quarterly reports,

Warm-Up Practice 12.1
Collaborative Activity

1. Go out to a public place: a restaurant, park, or a lobby, for example. Choose one person to observe for as long as ten minutes. Make note of the person's gestures, body language, clothing, and hairstyle. If you can catch a few words of dialogue, write them down.

2. Decide what impression that person made on you.

3. Without telling your reader what you think about the person, describe, in one paragraph, what you observed. Select and arrange details and choose words that will help shape your reader's impression.

4. When you return to the classroom, read your paragraphs out loud. Have classmates tell you what impression they get from your writing.

and publicity material. College and university alumni magazines publish profiles about employees and graduates. Many community and special-interest groups produce specialty publications profiling members or groups of people who might be of interest to members. Whether the person is a town engineer, a drummer, an orchid fancier, or a skateboarder, undoubtedly some newsletter, website, or magazine highlights that specialty and publishes profiles. Newspapers also often profile ordinary people who have faced extraordinary circumstances.

CHAPTER OBJECTIVES

In this chapter, you will learn to

▶ Find a focal point or interpretive thesis for a profile

▶ Combine narrative and expository writing

▶ Integrate multiple research sources, including interviewing, direct observation, print publications, and online sources

UNDERSTANDING PROFILES

Writing a profile allows you to combine many of the skills of writing exposition, narration, argumentation, and analysis. You can begin to understand the profile form by considering some of its typical elements and by thinking about who would make a good subject for a profile.

Profile Elements

Typically, in a profile you will try to include the following elements.

▶ Physical description

▶ Quotations from the subject

▶ Quotations about the subject

▶ Examples

▶ Anecdotes

▶ Factual information (exposition)

Physical Description Physical description should be brief and relevant. You do not have to create a feature-by-feature portrait as much as a glimpse of some defining characteristics that reflect the points you wish to make about your subject. You can enhance the physical description by putting the character in a setting, especially a setting that helps emphasize a character trait.

In the following excerpts , the writer J. R. Moehringer describes his subject, Marion Pritchard, an eighty-one-year-old psychoanalyst from Vermont

Analyzing Portraits

Choose one of the portraits in this chapter.

1. What impression do you get about the character in the painting or photograph? What specific details contribute to your interpretation?

2. Think about the photographer's intentions in taking the photograph or the painter's intentions in painting the portrait. What decisions did the photographer or painter make that influence your interpretation of the subject?

3. What can a painter do that a photographer cannot in creating a portrait? What can a photographer do that a painter cannot?

4. Think about a painter's intentions in painting a portrait. What decisions does a painter make that can influence the viewer's interpretation of the subject?

who "rescued scores of children from the Holocaust, survived seven months in a Nazi prison, and killed one Nazi who got in her way." (You can read the full profile to see how Moehringer integrated these elements into the piece.)

> Standing in her garden, not much taller than her sweet peas and daylilies, Pritchard doesn't look like the intrepid rescuer who defied the Third Reich. Sitting in her book-lined living room, speaking in a thin voice that crackles like a fire, she gives no hint of the cunning rebel who risked her life for strangers.
>
> —J. R. Moehringer, "A Hidden and Solitary Soldier"

By situating her in her garden and comparing her height to the height of her garden plants, Moehringer neatly contrasts Pritchard's physical smallness with her heroic stature. Her "book-lined living room" suggests her educated mind, and her "voice that crackles like a fire" allows the reader to see how vibrant she is at age eighty-one.

Quotations from the Subject Quotations are the lifeblood of a profile. They allow the reader to hear voices other than yours, and they bring characters directly to the reader through what they say and the language they use. Sometimes how a character says something—the words she chooses, the way her voice lowers—can be as significant as what she says. Likewise, a gesture can be as telling as a quotation and can imply information about character.

> Pritchard coughs and covers her mouth. She looks away and her eyes fill with tears. "It's funny," she says. "You can tell a tale a lot of times and then, suddenly, for some reason, it gets harder."
>
> — J. R. Moehringer, "A Hidden and Solitary Soldier"

In this quotation and description, instead of plowing through a lot of biographical facts, we get to see how Pritchard's past still bears down on her, even after so many years.

Quotations about the Subject Like quotations from your subject, quotations about the person give meaning that goes beyond simple information. Such quotations are powerful because they are the firsthand testimony of people who know the subject or who know about the issues raised in your profile.

Quotations from others allow for multiple perspectives on your subject. You and your reader get to view the subject from the points of view of people who know the subject in different ways, as a colleague, for example, or a spouse, a rival, or a best friend. These different perspectives are important in showing different sides of your subject; they allow you to draw a complex character who, like all of us, has many layers. Erika Polak's family had been sheltered by Pritchard during the war. Though Polak was quite young when Pritchard helped her family, she makes an excellent firsthand source. Though some of what she has to say about Pritchard is paraphrased, notice that the quotation has the sound of conversation.

> Meeting Pritchard many years after the war, Erika Polak had trouble believing this small, dignified grandmother was once all that stood between her and the camps. "She's such a tiny woman," Erika says by phone from her home in Holland. "She came from a very sophisticated family. And then, to go underground, to do such brave things? It's unbelievable."
>
> — J. R. Moehringer, "A Hidden and Solitary Soldier"

Polak's testimony about Pritchard reveals her awe at Pritchard's bravery during the Holocaust. That Polak's family was sheltered by Pritchard, of course, means that her admiration is based on firsthand knowledge. Her expertise is unquestionable. An expert who knows about the issues in the profile also makes a good source for quotations.

> People who make such decisions [to help others at risk to themselves] are the products of extraordinary parents, says Eva Fogelman, who has studied Holocaust rescuers, including Pritchard, for years. Most rescuers, Fogelman has found, were given an exquisite sense of justice as children, along with an unwavering self-confidence, "so they could withstand fears."
>
> — J. R. Moehringer, "A Hidden and Solitary Soldier"

As someone who has studied Holocaust rescuers, Fogelman speaks as an expert. Her views provide a wider context for the story, viewing Pritchard as part of a group with similar characteristics.

Portrait of Andy Warhol by Jamie Wyeth (1976).

Examples Your profile needs proof, examples that back up your generalizations and theories about your subject. These examples can illustrate how or when your subject did something noteworthy or revealing of character. To illustrate the concept of Pritchard's lasting emotional scars, Moehringer begins with a basic topic sentence making a generalization, and then cites two examples to prove the generalization.

> Memories of prison return to her, unbidden, at odd moments. In an elevator or a strange bathroom, if the door doesn't open right away, she feels trapped. Having a manicure, she recalls the way she filed her nails in prison, by rubbing them against her cell walls.
>
> — J. R. Moehringer, "A Hidden and Solitary Soldier"

Anecdotes Some of the best examples come in the form of anecdotes, or small stories. Your source can be your subject or people who know your subject well. The following anecdote, told by Pritchard, combines paraphrase and direct quotation.

> Then there was the Nazi she killed, a sadistic Dutch policeman she'd known all her life. He surprised her one night at the farmhouse, no sound of a motor to warn her, no time to hide the Polaks in the pit. Acting on a tip, the policeman crept up to the farmhouse on foot and burst in the door. "Somebody must have betrayed us," Pritchard says.
>
> In that terrible moment, Pritchard says, there was no choice. Behind some books on a shelf was a gun given to her by a friend. She grabbed the gun and fired. "One shot," she says. "Dead as a doornail."
>
> She doesn't remember pulling the trigger.
>
> — J. R. Moehringer, "A Hidden and Solitary Soldier"

Notice the way the writer selects certain details—the gun that was given to Pritchard by a friend was behind some books—and the way the writer selects the quotations to enhance the anecdote.

Factual Information Embedded in your profile should be factual information that deepens your reader's understanding of the subject. Explanatory, or expository, passages explain everything from background information on the subject's life to concepts needed to understand the world in which the subject lives.

Print and electronic sources will provide many different kinds of information that will help you develop your profile. Statistics might help clarify context and give a fuller understanding of how unique or typical your subject is. Research studies, like the one on Holocaust rescuers, might provide a context for social or political issues raised in the profile. The following paragraph explains Pritchard's worldwide fame.

In 1981, Pritchard was honored by Yad Vashem, Israel's official Holocaust authority, as one of the "Righteous Among the Nations." Her name was placed in the pantheon of Israel's national heroes, alongside Holocaust rescuers such as Oskar Schindler.

— J. R. Moehringer, "A Hidden and Solitary Soldier"

Knowing that Pritchard is listed alongside the more famous Holocaust rescuer Oskar Schindler helps us gauge the significance of her contribution. The fact gives a context for understanding how important Pritchard's work was.

Choosing a Good Profile Subject

A good profile subject is noteworthy, a person or group of people whose story might be interesting to your readers. You do not have to admire the people you write about, but you should find their accomplishments, lifestyles, or philosophies interesting and maybe even fascinating.

Although many published profiles are written about famous people, do not be discouraged if you lack access to celebrities. Not all profiles published in newspapers and magazines are about the rich and the famous. The media are starting to heed the old axiom that everybody has a story.

The ordinary-person genre has become a professional crusade for one reporter. David Johnson, at the Lewiston, Idaho, *Morning Tribune*, selects a name randomly out of the phone book for his features about people not normally considered newsmakers. Johnson has been writing his column "Everyone Has a Story" for twenty years and has written over a thousand pieces about ordinary people. If asked the right questions, most people have interesting stories to tell. By making random calls, Johnson often stumbles across great subjects. He has phoned and written about a professional wrestler, a hairstylist for corpses, the most productive marijuana producer in Idaho, and "a little girl who just turned nine on the day her phone happened to ring."

Profile Topics from Student Papers This brief list of profile topics demonstrates the range of subjects students have written about. Student writers discovered these subjects at their colleges, in their neighborhoods, in their family's circle of acquaintances, and by word of mouth.

▸ A registered dietician who teaches nutrition and has a sensible, workable recipe for healthful living

▸ An eighty-one-year-old Russian immigrant who has lived through "World War II, Communism, Stalin, Brezhnev, Gorbachev, and the break-up of the Soviet Union"

▸ High school chess players who challenge the "chess nerd" stereotype as well as one another

▸ A local band that combines punk rock with Irish sentimentality

---

Practice 12.2
Identifying Profile Elements

1. Find a published profile you like (from a recent publication or from the readings in this chapter), and get a handful of highlighters. As you read the profile, use different colors to highlight all the following elements that you can find.
   • Physical description
   • Quotations from the subject
   • Quotations about the subject
   • Examples
   • Anecdotes
   • Factual information

2. By looking at the color patterns, make an assessment of the kinds of elements the writer used. Which elements did the writer rely on most?

Head of a Girl (Girl with the Pearl Earring) by Jan Vermeer (1632–1675).

❯ A college woman who wears the college mascot suit and views college sports from this unique perspective

❯ An international student from Romania who brings a more global perspective to American popular culture

❯ A fifty-five-year-old college student who is taking her turn to get an education after raising a family of four

❯ A middle-aged Cambodian x-ray technician who escaped the killing fields under the Pot Pol regime in the 1970s

❯ A college athlete who has found a way to balance the stresses of athletics and academics, but not without some wear and tear

❯ A director of a summer arts camp for inner-city kids who believes that the arts teach essential cognitive skills

Using *I* in a Profile

Sometimes profile writers are characters in their stories, but it is a good idea not to invite yourself into somebody else's story unless you have a good reason to be there. Most of the time, the writer should be in the background and the subject in the foreground. In other words, you do not have to appear as a character in the profile simply to ask the questions. If you are using yourself as a transitional device, a link between chunks of information or anecdotes, you can easily cut yourself out. In a profile of a businessman who dropped out of the corporate world to become a teacher, you might have written the following.

> "Why did you leave your successful career in business to become a teacher?" I asked him next. He told me he left to "follow a voice I heard every morning just as I was waking up."

You can use the same material without reference to yourself and without quoting your questions.

> Monroe left his successful career in business to "follow a voice I heard every morning just as I was waking up," he says.

Sometimes writers have good reasons to be in the story. The profile of the toughest professor on campus, "The Top Drill Instructor in Boot Camp 101" (pages 443–447), was written by the professor's former student. In this case, the writer was a good eyewitness. He saw the subject over time and gathered many anecdotes from personal observation that he could not have gathered any other way. By including himself in the story, he becomes a credible source of information and insight.

Another profile writer, Darcy Frey, traveled to the North Pole to spend time with a scientist who tracks bird populations. She includes herself in her narrative about building a fence so that polar bears could not eat the two of them "down to the toenail." The writer would have misled her readers if she had not included herself, since most of the time the scientist spends his three months at the North Pole alone. Also, since the scientist is so used to arctic conditions, Frey can better explain the experience of the cold, harsh climate from her own point of view. She made a well-reasoned choice to include herself in this profile.

You should assume that you will not be in the story unless the circumstances of the reporting—your intimate knowledge of the details of the story, for example—need some clarification. Always remember that the spotlight should be on your subject, not on you.

SIDEBAR

**Practice 12.3
Choosing a Good
Profile Subject**

1. List five possible profile subjects. Think of people you know or people you have heard about who have had interesting experiences, do interesting work (perhaps in a field you might want to enter), have interesting interests, or espouse interesting philosophies.

2. Choose one subject from your list and freewrite for five minutes about that person. What are possible points of tension or conflict in the person's story? What would you want to find out about him or her? What questions would you ask?

Finding the Story As important as choosing a good profile subject is finding the story in your subject's life that resonates and will have meaning for your reader. You can often locate this meaning in a point of tension or conflict. If you were writing a profile of a wrestler, for example, a point of conflict might be whether professional wrestling is above-board and how this particular wrestler deals with the perception of fakery in the sport. A profile about a student athlete might explore the tension between the demands of academic work and athletic training.

As you think about how to focus your profile, consider these questions.

1. Is your subject in some way related to a news story or a current trend or idea?

2. Is your subject in some way unusual, odd, or offbeat?

3. Can you link your subject to a noteworthy achievement, an innovation, a contribution, or a discovery?

4. If your subject is not unique, how does he or she fit in? Does your subject represent what is typical about a profession, interest, lifestyle, or conflict? Can your subject reveal something found in others with the same profession, interest, lifestyle, or conflict?

5. Why would readers be interested in this person? What is the payoff for readers?

RESEARCH PATHS

How interesting your reader finds your story hinges on what you discover and uncover in your research. The more you learn, the stronger and more credible your voice becomes and the more you will liven and focus your writing. A well-researched profile includes

▶ Print and electronic sources

▶ Interviews with many people (multiple sources)

▶ Direct observation of the person in a place that has relevance to him or her

Print and Electronic Sources

Start your research at the library, where you can educate yourself about your subject's field. Background information gives you insight into the world you are revealing in your profile as well as contextual information—facts and statistics you may need to integrate into your profile.

If you are researching a female firefighter, for example, read about the history of women as firefighters. Begin with a LexisNexis online search,

Civil War Private Emory Eugene Kingin, Fourth Michigan Infantry, U.S. Army

Practice 12.4
Search for Sources

Possible profile subjects include:

- A high school teacher who has just been named Math Teacher of the Year

- A college student who is a professional figure skater

- An inventor who is working on creating a nonpolluting combustion engine

- A marathon runner

Choose one of these subjects or one from the "Profile Topics from Student Papers" section on pages 421 and 423, and do a search for print and electronic sources that you could read for background information. List at least three sources. Use correct bibliographical citation, as shown in Chapter 15.

which you can do at most libraries. Find magazine articles, trade journals, and books about firefighting. Read personal accounts; find out what percentage of the country's firefighters are women; become thoroughly familiar with the conflicts and controversies surrounding women who are breaking into traditionally male fields. Find out if the physical qualifications for women are the same as for men. This kind of information adds depth and interest to a profile.

Background research also helps you prepare for interviews and gives you an insider's view. You can usually write better questions after you have done some initial background reading. If your subject has any publications, be sure to read those as well. Not only will you gain insight into your subject's ideas, but you will also be able to establish a better rapport when you can open an interview, or a request for an interview, with a statement like, "In your book [article, interview], you said . . . ."

Keep detailed and accurate notes as you do your research. Be sure to copy direct quotations word-for-word, and put quotation marks around any words you take from a source. As with all quoted material, note the following.

▶ Author(s) or editor(s)

▶ Title of book, magazine, or website

▶ Publisher

▶ Date of publication

▶ Page numbers of the quotation

In a published profile, the convention is to cite the sources in the text of the profile rather than on a separate Works Cited page, though many writing instructors require both in-text citations and a Works Cited page at the end of the article. In either case, you need to record all the pertinent information for your attribution. (See Chapter 15.)

Interviews

Interviews are the mainstay of field research. Through interviewing sources, you gather firsthand information from experts as well as opinions, responses, and thoughts from anyone familiar with the subject. If you have never conducted an interview before, you might find it daunting. To reduce your stress level as you prepare for an interview, read the following tips. Once you begin using interviewing as a research method, you may discover that it is a fascinating way to gather information.

Tips for Good Interviews   Though conducting an interview might seem as simple as having a conversation, planning ahead and good preparation will help you get the best material possible. Here are some ways to get ready for an interview.

Start Early Often it takes more time than you expect just to set up a time to talk. Allow lots of time for phone tag. Make the initial contact by phone or e-mail, and be clear about how much of the person's time you wish to use. Sometimes the person may have only an hour to spare; other times, you may be able to shadow him or her for a day or an afternoon. Leave your telephone number, e-mail address, and a good time to reach you, in case your source needs to change plans.

Set Up the Interview Try to interview your profile subject in person so that you can gather much more information about the person than just quotations. If you can hold the interview in the subject's workplace or home, pay attention to the setting. Small details—a community service award on the wall, a cluttered desk, or a neatly alphabetized jazz collection—provide telling details about the person's interests and style. Pay attention to the physical details of your subject as well. A small detail of dress or an idiosyncratic gesture can bring your subject to life for your reader. Though it is best to interview in person so that you can observe these details, telephone or e-mail interviews can also provide good information and good quotations.

Make a Contact List Make a list of people who know your subject and people who know the issues discussed in the profile. As you interview your subject and even the secondary sources, ask for names of other people knowledgeable about the subject or the subject's field. Be sure to record the contact information accurately.

Read about Your Subject (if Possible) and Your Subject's Field before the Interview Go into the interview informed. If your source is an expert, he or she may have written books or articles on a topic. Read these publications for background information. If your source works in an organization or company, contact the publicity department to get biographical information. You might want to enter your source's name into an Internet search engine and check out the results before you sit down to talk. Any reading you can do ahead of time will make your interviews more focused and more productive.

Prepare for the Interview Figure out generally what you want to know, and write a list of questions. Preparing at least ten questions ahead of time will help you focus on important aspects of the subject's life and work. Ten questions also provide enough variety so that if one topic does not generate much conversation, you can move on to another.

Try to frame open-ended questions, not ones that can be answered by yes or no. Ask "How do you think the Internet will be used in the future?" rather than "Do you think the Internet will only be used for shopping?" Of course, there is no need to stick to the script if the conversation takes an interesting turn.

Allison Roberts was a junior at Berkeley High School in California when she won first place in a *New York Times* photography contest for this portrait of Rachel Seban.

Have your tools ready: paper, pens, a tape recorder if you have permission to tape the interview. If you are using a tape recorder, make sure that it is working, and always make backup notes in case it fails.

Conduct the Interview Introduce yourself, and begin the interview. If you find it hard to start, you can always ask general, resume-type questions about where your subject grew up and went to school, what kind of family he came from, and how she got involved in a particular occupation, interest, or lifestyle. "What are you doing when you are not working (in school)?" often opens up an interesting path of inquiry.

Listen especially for brief stories, known as anecdotes. Anecdotes can reveal a great deal about your subject and can illustrate a point about your subject by showing rather than telling. Reporters often used "evergreen" questions: simple questions that help solicit anecdotes. Writing coach John Rains suggests these evergreen questions.

1. Who influenced you most in your life?

2. How would you describe yourself as a (fill in the blank—boss, student, mother, actress, doctor)?

3. What was the best (or worst) thing that ever happened to you?

4. What has surprised you about your (job, interest, lifestyle)?

Aim for an informal and easy tone. The most productive interviews are conversations, not question-and-answer sessions. Make eye contact. Follow up on brief yes-no–type answers. Ask your source to explain or elaborate. Take good notes. Jot down observations and descriptive details that might help set a scene or show character. Ask your subject about other sources: other people to interview, something you might read, a place you might visit. Be sure you have the proper spelling of your subject's name and title. Thank him or her, and ask if you can call with follow-up questions. Do not agree to an interview based on approval of your completed article. Getting a source's approval will tie your hands and bias your story. Most sources do not get to see a story until it is published.

Transcribe Your Notes As soon as possible after the interview, transcribe or rewrite your notes. Add any details of physical appearance or setting that might be useful to remember later. This is a time-consuming process, but do not put it off. The sooner you rewrite your notes, the more you will remember.

Read Your Notes Critically Annotate your notes as you read through them. Underline important information. Make stars next to or highlight good quotations that are particularly well stated or pertinent to your focus. Cross out irrelevant information so that you will not have to reread it, but do not delete it totally in case your focus changes.

Interviewing Secondary Sources If you just tell a story from your subject's perspective, you have not written a profile as much as an as-told-to story—a story told from only your subject's point of view as he or she tells it to you. Your reader gets only your subject's point of view. To develop a more balanced and more complex perspective (even a contradictory or negative one), provide your reader with multiple points of view about your subject. Interview as many people as possible who can provide insight into your subject or into the subject's field of interest.

These secondary sources can be coworkers, relatives, neighbors, or competitors, to name a few. If you are writing about the owner of the first Vietnamese noodle shop in town, for example, interviewing nearby restaurant owners might give you an interesting perspective on the business. Interviewing the owner's spouse, children, chef, and servers adds other, more personal layers to the story. Phoning the restaurant reviewer who gave the new restaurant four stars might tell you even more about the owner's abilities.

The commentary of these "supporting characters" provides the multiple perspectives that make for an interesting and credible story. Including the various ways people see your subject helps give balance to your profile. But you must be careful to consider the sources. Some may be biased either for or against your subject. The rival restaurant owner has a lot at stake, as does the owner's award-winning chef. Make sure to evaluate sources and reveal their relationships to the subject, so that your readers have full knowledge of their biases and can make their own judgments.

Choosing Good Quotations Good quotations can be irreverent, eccentric, funny, witty, wry, angry, or emotional. What they should not be is boring, self-evident, or confusing. Quotations can reveal character, sum up a point, create an image, or provide irony, insight, or tension for the piece. Quotations should be articulate, clear, and accessible, unless what they are intended to reveal is a person's nervousness or perhaps evasiveness.

As an interviewer, you try to get good quotations and to record them accurately. As a writer, you try to select the best quotations and use them to their best advantage. Avoid quotations that state the obvious or add no new information. You can integrate quotations into your profile by using partial quotations, by using full quotations, and by paraphrasing.

> ▶ A full quotation is a full sentence or two, transcribed exactly as spoken, and reproduced inside quotation marks and with attribution to the speaker.

"We like to be called cooks," DiPaola says. "A chef is a person who carries a clipboard and pen and runs around the dining room taking credit for everything."

▶ A partial quotation uses selected words or phrases, in quotation marks, with attribution.

DiPaola says that they prefer "to be called cooks."

▶ A paraphrase is someone else's idea in your language. It is not enclosed in quotation marks, but it is clearly attributed to the speaker.

DiPaola says he does not like the snob-appeal of being called a chef.

Use full or partial quotations when the language is clear and powerful and the words provide insight into a character. Paraphrase long or wordy statements or statements in fuzzy, vague, grammatically incorrect, or confusing language.

Practice 12.5   *Choosing Good Quotations*

Below is a list of quotations gathered for a profile written about Damian DiPaola, the owner and chef (or as he prefers it, "cook") at an Italian restaurant. Journalist David Maloof gathered these quotations from interviews with DiPaola and from observing DiPaola in conversation with coworkers. Decide which quotations you would (a) quote fully, (b) quote partially, (c) paraphrase, or (d) omit. Explain why you made those decisions.

1. "I've been making cappuccinos since I was four years old in my Dad's café."

2. "My sister taught me English and Italian when I first came to this country."

3. "My mother had a knack for making the greatest dinners with the least ingredients. She used lots of vegetables and fish and pasta. My father would make the elaborate meals, such as lobster *fra diavlo* and rack of lamb."

4. "A chef is someone who runs around with a clipboard and a pen and then goes out in the dining room and takes credit for everything."

5. "Growing up as a kid, I was very irresponsible."

6. "When I was 13, I was the same size I am now, and I used to go out to nightclubs with older workers from my father's café."

7. "I was 28 when I got married."

8. "I did have a house, but when I bought my [business] partner out I had to sell the house."

9. "About a year ago, I weighed 205. I lost 35 pounds. I ate a lot of angel hair pasta with escarole in chicken broth."

10. "When I bartend, no one wants to sit at the bar."

11. [to a waitress] "You don't like Frank Sinatra, it doesn't make you a bad person. It just means you have lousy taste in music." [waitress] "You ever hear of the group 'Phish'?" [him] "You ever hear of the group 'Calamari'?"

12. "You have to be very disciplined to run a good restaurant."

13. "We're not 'chefs' here. We prefer to be called 'cooks.' 'Chef' is a French word. It means 'chief' or 'commander' of the kitchen."

14. "[Scuba] diving is very effortless. It's timeless. It's almost like flying—not a plane, but like a bird. You can do cartwheels, somersaults. It's like dancing. It's very relaxing. It's another world."

—David Maloof, Notes for "Pan Music"

How to Punctuate Quotations

1. To punctuate a quotation that is a statement,

- Separate the attribution from the quotation with a comma:

   "Students genuinely fear him," said Graveline.

- Put periods inside quotation marks:

   He said, "I have the other one at home."

2. When the quotation is a question, put the question mark inside the quotation marks:

   "So why do you keep teaching?" I ask.

3. When a quotation is part of a question, put the question mark outside the quotation marks:

   What did he mean by "Marcus had eight assists"?

4. When the quotation is interrupted by the attribution, use a comma before the attribution inside the first quotation marks, and after the attribution:

   "Nice lead," he said, then commented, "if we don't count its being dull, pointless, and triply redundant."

5. When you are quoting somebody speaking about a quotation,

- Use single quotation marks to set off the words that the speaker is quoting.

- Use double quotation marks around the speaker's full statement.

   "Students would come in crying 'mental abuse' or 'I can't take it in there,'" says BU grad Maryellen Kennedy.

Direct Observation

Novelist Eudora Welty said, "Stories don't happen nowhere." She was talking about the significance of setting in creating an impression. Characters in profiles, as in fiction, inhabit places, and the places they inhabit reveal something about who they are.

Whether you do your interview in your subject's native habitat or elsewhere, you can observe the setting and watch your subject in action. One student, writing a profile of a nutritionist, visited her office. The student begins her profile this way.

> Bright red Coca-Cola bottles intermix with Special K cereal boxes on the top of her food pyramid shelf. Tiny sugar cubes, used to illustrate how much sugar is in different sizes of soda, form geometric shapes from the size of a three-ounce piece of steak to an extra-large pancake. On the shelf below, vitamin C-dense Tropicana orange juice box mingles with the fiber-rich Quaker Oats box, decked out in its reds, whites, and blues. Every flavored water drink out on the market from pineapple to strawberry line the third shelf like a row of soldiers.
>
> —Yoonie Park, "Hold the Line in Body Fat"

The description of the office shelves brings the reader into the subject's nutrition-savvy world and leads to the writer's assessment that the subject "doesn't offer the quick fix; instead, she brings us a pinch of fun and enjoyment with eating healthfully."

Portrait of a man with a cigar, Lubbock, Texas, by Pam Berry.

Practice 12.6   Observing Characters in Action

A profile of Kara Walker, who has been called one of the "hottest and most controversial Black artists in America" begins with a scene showing her creating a silhouette. Her silhouettes of nineteenth-century plantation life have garnered her much public attention and many honors, including a $190,000 MacArthur Foundation genius award when she was twenty-seven. As you read, mark the observed details the writer includes.

Kara Walker, a tall, slender young woman dressed in blue jeans, white T-shirt, and a gray hooded sweatshirt, stands before a studio wall covered with black paper. A Radiohead CD plays in the background as she contemplates the empty blackness. Suddenly, as though something has just occurred to her, she starts to draw quick, light, sure lines with a white wax pencil held in the long, elegant fingers of her right hand. In a matter of minutes, she has laid down an arresting image of a hoop-skirted and frilly-bonneted black woman expressing milk from her breast directly into the mouth of a small child.

As soon as she finishes the drawing, she picks up an Exacto knife and begins deftly cutting along the white lines, occasionally editing with the knife, adding details as she excises the woman from the paper. As quickly as she has drawn the figure, she cuts it out, flips it over, and pins it onto a white wall. It is a startling performance, as though she has conjured a shadow from the past.

—Edgar Allen Beem, "Cutting Edge or Over the Line?"

1. What is the overall impression of Kara Walker that you get from this passage? Which details lead you to that conclusion?

2. Choose someone you know well— a parent, sibling, partner, or friend— and describe that person in action, doing something that reveals some aspect of his or her character. Choose your details deliberately.

If you can shadow your profile subject for a day or an afternoon and observe him or her in daily life—teaching nutrition, racing dirt bikes, or painting a picture—you will find revealing details and establish a solid narrative base for your profile.

Take notes as you observe your subject during the interview or in action. Observe the gestures, pauses in conversation, and mannerisms that reveal some quirk or characteristic. Observe the setting: the earth tones of the organic farmer's kitchen or the original art over the mantelpiece in the dining room. All these details may come in handy when you are creating a scene in your profile.

ANATOMY OF A PROFILE

Writing teacher and journalist Don Murray writes, "Readers should be drawn into a piece of writing so they will follow a trail that leads to meaning. The writer must create a path of continual seduction that keeps readers interested and eventually satisfy them." In considering how to structure your profile, think of your reader and the questions your reader will have about the topic. Murray suggests that most writing can be conceived of as a conversation with a reader who interrupts to say

How come?

How do you know that?

Says who?

I don't get it.

What do you mean?

I'd like to know more about that . . .

Why'd she do that?

Tell me more.

Stop. Enough already

Get to the point

Whoa. Back up, I don't understand . . .

With your reader firmly in mind, consider the overall structure of a profile: the lead, the nut graf, the body, and the conclusion. Read the following profile of Heidi Heitkamp, a gubernatorial candidate in Bismarck, North Dakota, who was recovering from cancer as she was running for office. Notice the annotated elements of structure, which are then discussed in more detail.

Running for Office, Running for Life

JUDITH NEWMAN

Deck

She was in a dead heat in the North Dakota governor's race. As it turned out, the election was only half her battle.

Lead

Direct Observation
Character
In Action

Part I:
Lead and
Nut Graf

November 7, 2000: At the Holiday Inn in Bismarck, N.D., Heidi Heitkamp, the Democratic candidate for governor, charges to the podium, her trademark mane of red hair moussed into submission. Heitkamp, 45, is big, beautiful and lit up from the inside. The election results aren't all in, but she appears jubilant.

Quotation from Subject

"Isn't this a wild ride?" she shouts to the cheering crowd. As she speaks, she pummels the air with her right fist—the one sign that something about this campaign is different.

Nut Graf

The fist is grotesquely swollen, each finger a sausage, with no break between wrist and forearm. It's the telltale sign of lymphedema, the fluid retention that may occur after losing lymph nodes. And it is the only evidence that six weeks earlier, Heitkamp had her right breast and 18 cancerous nodes removed—the only hint that she is fighting not just for her career, but for her life.

Thesis

> The word was out: The woman who would be governor might **not be alive** to serve for a second term.

All that summer Heitkamp, the state's popular attorney general, and Republican John Hoeven had been in a statistical dead heat in the race for governor. Then Heitkamp saw her doctor about a lump under her arm. On September 15 she and her husband, family practitioner Darwin Lange, learned it was malignant.

Heitkamp didn't dwell on the negative. "I know this sounds corny, but when you come from a big family, you always worry about how something that happens to you will affect them," says Heitkamp, who has six siblings and two children (ages 15 and 11). "I felt this would be rougher for them to hear than it was for me. My personality type is, okay, you get three minutes to feel sorry for yourself, then you start dealing with it.

The word was out: The woman who would be governor might **not be alive** to serve for a second term.

"Well," Heitkamp adds with a laugh, "maybe I would give myself a few more minutes."

But Heitkamp had something else to contemplate: 474,000 voters. She never considered keeping her cancer a secret. "People have a right to know about the health of elected officials," she says. But she wanted to wait— first, to find out the kind of cancer and second, to tell her family.

She didn't have that luxury: Someone leaked the news. Heitkamp gathered her family, who took it hard—"very hard," says her sister Holly. Then on September 20 at a press conference, she didn't hold back. "I mean, this is as much a surprise to me as it is to you guys," she said, her eyes filling up.

About a week later, after Heitkamp's surgery, she learned the cancer was Stage IIIA—it was advanced and had spread to her lymph nodes. Yes, she would need chemotherapy and radiation, but she could stick with the campaign. Besides, her family wouldn't let her do otherwise. Her 15-year-old daughter, a swimmer, was direct: "Well, you're not going to get out now are you? It's like quitting in the last leg of the 100 meter."

The press focused on her health. A candidate with breast cancer is news; one with advanced cancer—stop the presses!

North Dakota's *Forum* and *Tribune* ran stories putting the five-year survival rate for a Stage IIIA cancer at 56 percent. Although they quoted experts saying Heitkamp's prospects were better, word was out. The woman who would be governor could have as little as a 56-percent chance of being alive a second term.

After reading what she took to be her death sentence, Heitkamp rushed to reassure her family: "My daughter's at a swim meet—how can I control what she's listening to? And I'm worried about my mother."

Her mother's reaction surprised her. "She said, 'How are you?'—not all grim and serious, but like, 'Hi! How the heck are ya?' And I said, 'Not bad for someone who's half-dead!' We couldn't stop laughing."

As it turned out, the outlook was not so grim. "I've received some good news," she told the public. "Doctors expect me to make a full recovery."

At any point, Heitkamp could have shaken fewer hands, cuddled fewer babies, stopped those 200-mile treks between Bismarck and Fargo. After her first chemo treatment, she needed her white-blood-cell count checked. If low, it meant she was susceptible to infection. Retreating into a back room of a Fargo clinic to have blood drawn, she looked pale and forlorn.

But when the results came, Heitkamp waved the paper at a campaign worker. "Look!" she said. "A normal count is about 4.5 to 11; I'm 4.9. The doctor told us if the count went to one, I'd have to avoid crowds and take precautions. But my white blood cells are reading favorably. We're ready to fight the rest of the campaign!"

Fight, as it turned out, was the operative word. During a radio show, outgoing Republican governor Ed Schafer described his initial 18-hour days, then added, "I hope Heidi isn't going to get herself in a situation where physically it would be to her detriment to continue on in this job."

Then things got weird. A Bismarck man contacted the Heitkamp campaign to tell this story: A man identifying himself as a pollster had asked whom he was voting for. When he said Heitkamp, the pollster pressed on, "You know she's very sick, right?" Then the pollster cited possible side effects of cancer treatment—"hair falling out, lack of strength and so forth"—and concluded, "And you're still going to support Heidi Heitkamp?"

Hoeven's campaign denied involvement. Still, said his campaign manager, Carol Olson, there was no way to control thousands of supporters. And by November, Hoeven was leading by three percentage points, according to a poll. Even more significant, Heitkamp had dropped among women.

[Margin annotations:]

Part III: Reaction Quotation from subject.

Anecdote

Body

Quotation about subject (from radio show)

Part IV: Fight

Anecdote (unnamed source)

Facts from Poll

Quotation (paraphrased from campaign manager)

Direct Observation

Conclusion

Part V: Conclusion

Quotation from subject

Election night, 11 P.M. Heitkamp can't ignore Hoeven's ten-point lead. Tearfully, the woman who would have been North Dakota's first female governor concedes, saying, "This is the proudest moment of my life."

Now spending time with her kids and volunteering, Heitkamp has a message for anyone who has a loved one with cancer: "I hope everyone gives her the ability to do her job and live her life. Because if the message is 'Go home, quit and *if* you can prove you're cancer-free, we'll let you back in the land of the living'—well, you start to believe it yourself."

Pausing, Heitkamp beams. "Every day is a contest," she says simply. "Gotta keep your eye on the prize."

Quotation from subject

The Lead

Profiles have to hook a reader's attention immediately. The introductory section of a profile, the lead, can be the opening paragraph, or it can consist of several paragraphs that set the opening scenes. These opening paragraphs do not have to churn out the hard news and tell the who-what-when-where information but can spend some time piquing the reader's curiosity.

In "Running for Office, Running for Life," Newman uses a classic scene-setting lead. It is election night in Bismarck, North Dakota, and the reader's first glimpse of Heitkamp is the gubernatorial candidate in action as she "charges to the podium." Newman describes Heitkamp's appearance and draws the reader's attention first to her hair "moussed into submission," then her size, her voice, and finally her fist, the swollen state of which reveals the focus of the profile: a woman fighting not only for her career but also for her life.

Two other often-used and effective ways to begin profiles are by using anecdotal leads and by using generalization leads. An anecdotal lead hooks a reader by telling a brief but complete story. To work well, the story must shed some light on the profile subject and give the reader some insight into the person's character. A generalization lead begins with a broad, umbrella statement, then narrows down to the specific point, or person, of the profile.

You can experiment with different kinds of leads for different kinds of writing. Just keep in mind that the purpose of the lead is to pull the reader into the story both through artful writing and by moving to the main ideas of the story.

The Nut Graf or Interpretive Thesis

A profile often explicitly states its thesis directly after the lead. Journalists call this thesis paragraph the *nut graf. Nut* means the kernel of the idea; *graf* is journalistic shorthand for "paragraph." Some call this paragraph the

Practice 12.7 Identifying and Analyzing Types of Leads

Identify whether the writer uses a scene, an anecdote, or a generalization in the three leads below. Analyze each lead briefly, explaining what the writer accomplishes by using that particular technique.

1. China's Cultural Revolution was in full force in 1968, when Shen Tong was born. His grandparents had been among its first victims; when his grandfather openly criticized the village mayor, he and his wife became targets for the Red Guards.

   The day before they were to be paraded through their village in dunce caps, they hanged themselves from their bamboo bed frame.

   Shen's father, a poet and intellectual, was forced to work in a paint factory. His mother was a nurse, but worked as a "doctor" in a clinic, along with other doctors without proper training. Housing was assigned, and Shen, his parents, his sister, and his maternal grandmother moved to a crumbling two-room mud-and-brick house in an alley off Changan Avenue in Beijing, about fifteen minutes from Tiananmen Square. Shen experienced early the harshness of China's government.

   —Midge Raymond, "The Long Journey Home"

2. Tonight, an artist in Allston will eat tripe. On Newbury Street, a weary shopper will eat beef tendon. And in Harvard Square, students and parents and the odd out-of-towner will slurp their way through a selection of intensely flavored and very inexpensive noodle soups they'd probably never heard of just two years ago.

   These parallel dining adventures come courtesy of Duyen Le, the accidental noodlemonger from Vietnam whose Pho Pasteur restaurants have taken pho, the steaming soul food of northern Vietnam, from Formica tabletops in Chinatown and Dorchester to higher-rent neighborhoods where, not so long ago, the prevailing notion of ethnic food featured spaghetti carbonara.

   Le may be the quietest titan of the Boston food scene.

   —Kelly Horan, "The Quietist Mogul"

3. "Thank you. Have a nice day." These words find their way through his dark tangled beard, and reach the ears of every customer Mohammad "Hammad" Eldin helps in a convenience store in Brooklyn, New York. Hammad—as he likes to be referred to by his friends, and therefore his customers—stands no taller than 5'9", even with the hand-woven praying cap sitting firmly atop his head. A Palestinian native, Hammad dresses in the traditional Arabic white robe or *galabiya,* and wears a beard extending down to his chest.

   He picks up a newspaper from the stack that he has for sale. This one is a paper in his native language. On the cover: a picture of a woman crying over a make-shift tombstone for her son, who was killed in the war in the Middle East. "Stuff like this happens every day in my country," he says, nodding his head with grief.

   Things like this did not happen to him in his own country however; they didn't happen until he came to the United States.

   —Noanna Tzinakos, "United We Stand"

"bridge," and another way to understand its function is that it bridges the lead and the body of the paper.

The nut graf announces your focus—that is, your interpretation of your subject—and it stems from your analysis of your subject. In the lead above about Heidi Heitkamp, for example, the nut is included in the phrase "the only hint that she is fighting not just for her career, but for her life." Heitkamp's story flows from that point; it is one of overcoming physical obstacles, her illness and its complications, on her way to political office. The dominant impression set in this lead is that Heitkamp is a fighter and a survivor, and this image is woven through the entire profile.

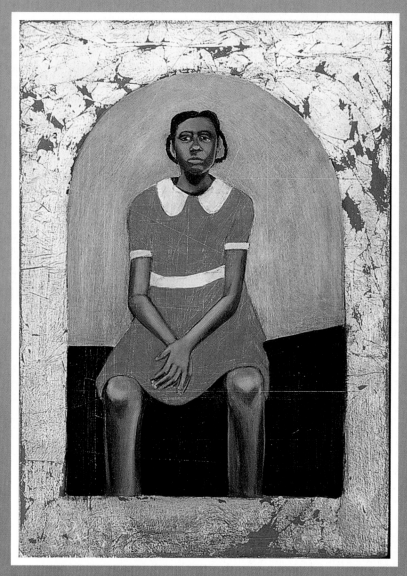

One Girl Child by Daphne Confar

When you write your profile, you might not find your focus until you have completed your research. Research often uncovers a new insight into your subject, one that you might not even have been seeking. Research may help you unearth a compelling, previously untold story. Peter Scanlan, in *The Quill*, a publication of the Society of Professional Journalists, gives this advice for finding or developing a profile focus: look for conflicts, questions, obstacles, or "pivotal moments" in someone's story.

These can be

▶ When things have changed

▶ When things will never be the same

▶ When things have fallen apart

▶ When you don't know how things will turn out

Although a profile writer typically crafts a clear nut graf while developing a piece, sometimes the editor cuts the thesis statement from the body of the piece and pastes it in the "deck," the explanatory sentence or two set apart from the story, usually directly under the headline. For example, the thesis in Shen Tong's story in Practice 12.7 does not appear explicitly in the excerpted lead. Rather, it appears in the deck and reads, "A leader of the 1989 student movement in China that culminated in Tiananmen Square, Shen Tong . . . fled Beijing in the aftermath of the massacre. Still in exile ten years later, he continues the struggle for democracy in a China he hopes will one day welcome him back."

In "The Quietest Mogul," also in Practice 12.7, the nut graf is the third paragraph, which begins "Le may be the quietest titan of the Boston food scene," but the story's thesis also appears in the deck, which reads "Meet Duyen Le, the low-key restaurateur who built a tiny noodle stand into the Starbucks of Vietnamese food." If you are looking for the focus of a published profile, you can sometimes find it in the nut graf, sometimes in the deck, and sometimes, with slightly different wording, in both places. If you are having trouble finding your own focus for a profile, write a deck for your piece. In a sentence, introduce your profile subject and tell your reader what point you are going to make.

The opening of a profile provides the map for the rest of story. In the opening section—the lead and nut—you give the reader a good sense of where your profile is headed. That destination is the interpretation of your subject. You will spend the rest of the article leading your reader through that interpretation, showing why and how it works.

Practice 12.8

Identifying the Nut Graf or Interpretive Thesis

Find three profiles published in newspapers, magazines, or websites. For each, identify and underline the nut graf. If you do not find a nut graf directly after the lead paragraph(s), see if it has been pulled out and put in a deck. For each nut graf you identify, comment on how well you think it presents the profile's focus. Explain your reasoning.

The Body of the Profile

When you are ready to write the middle section of your paper, you should have a sheaf of notes filled with quotations, observations, and information from print and electronic sources and interviews. How do you organize this material? As with all your writing, the organization stems from the focus of the piece. Once you have clarified your thesis, you can start making decisions about structure.

Your first step is to figure out a logical pattern of development that stems from your nut graf. Generate a list of main topics: major points you plan to address in the profile. An outline, list, or any other organizational scheme is key at this stage to help you put your main points into a coherent order. Some writers use elaborate color schemes or put sequential numbers on their notes that correspond to the topic number in the outline. Others, for long projects, create folders for each main topic and sort their research into them. Do whatever works best for you to organize your material into topics and put the supporting evidence with the appropriate topic.

In general, put your strongest arguments toward the end of your piece. Remember that an outline is an organizational guide, not an inflexible one. As you come up with new ideas or decide that some ideas have to be put in the trash, revise your thinking and your outline.

If you have done your research well, you will have more material than you can use in your profile. Though it is good to have a lot of material to choose from, do not force material into your profile unless it fits. Think of the extra material as adding to your knowledge and authority on the topic. Even if it does not appear in the piece, the material will inform your voice and enhance your credibility.

Notice that Judith Newman divides her profile of Heitkamp into five sections, separated visually by white space and structurally into an introduction, three middle sections, and a conclusion. The middle section, begins with a flashback from election night to the previous summer when Heitkamp, while running her campaign for governor, discovers that she has cancer. Newman develops this first middle section, Part II, by narrating the story of Heitkamp's discovery of the disease and her revelation of it to her family and her constituents. Into this narrative, Newman weaves exposition—information about the disease and about the local press coverage.

Part III moves the story forward and reveals the strong, positive reaction of family and of Heitkamp herself. Set against this optimism, Part IV dramatically renders the fight that Heitkamp waged against her cancer and against the negative publicity her illness garnered. Throughout the story, the reader learns about her particular illness, about the smear campaign waged against her, and a great deal about Heitkamp's fighting spirit. Newman's well-integrated research—her direct observation of Heitkamp on election eve; her interviews with Heitkamp, her sister, her daughter, and her rival's campaign manager; and her consultation of media sources, local newspapers, a radio show, a poll—adds color, drama, and information to this profile. By the end of the body of the profile, Newman has justified her interpretation and filled in the details of her thesis: here is a woman "fighting not just for her career, but for her life."

Conclusion

A successful conclusion in a profile can present an image or quotation that leaves a final impression on readers, reminding them of your focus. The Heidi Heitkamp profile ends by returning to the introductory scene later on election night. Heitkamp concedes defeat in the election but asserts her victory in life. "'Every day is a contest,' she says simply. 'Gotta keep your eye on the prize.'" Newman's framing technique leaves the reader with a picture and a final impression of Heitkamp.

The Top Drill Instructor in Boot Camp 101

JACK FALLA

This piece is slightly adapted, with the author's permission, from a version with the same title published in August/September 1984 in *Campus Voice*.

The bullwhip lay on the bookcase, coiled around its wooden handle like a snake around its rattle.

I was in the second-floor office of associate professor Gerald Powers at Boston University's College of Communication. A student carrying a sheaf of papers had slunk away from Powers's desk as I entered, "REWRITE" scrawled across the top paper in red pencil. The whip had struck again.

"Not my day to be popular," said Powers, rising from his chair to shake hands. He is a slight man, perhaps 5 feet 9, with close-cropped graying hair, and a reserved, somewhat bemused manner.

"At least you spared him the stamp," I said, nodding toward the open door. We could hear the retreating student's footsteps in the hall.

"Oh, I still have it," said Powers, smiling for the first time and opening his desk drawer to take out a rubber stamp that says REWRITE in block letters. "And I have the other one at home."

The other stamp is even more succinct; it simply reads BULLSHIT.

The stamps and Powers's willingness to use them on students' papers are two of the reasons he carries the reputation that inevitably falls upon one faculty member at every college in the world: toughest sumbitch on campus. Powers is one of those professors from whom hordes of students recoil at preregistration, choosing instead to slink over to the "twinkies" courses. Yet, somehow the sumbitches manage to endure.

For 20 years, Powers has taught various writing courses within BU's Public Relations Department. And for 20 years he has ritualistically slain compromise in the first minute of the first class. His usual greeting:

"Deadlines are immovable. Meet them if it kills you. The only excuse for failing to turn in a paper on time is a death in the family. In which case," he adds, "I prefer that the death be yours."

Neal Boudette, a recent survivor of a Powers class, recalls another intimidating tactic: "One day Powers opened his briefcase in class and took out that whip. He said, 'This is a gift from former students. They thought it symbolized the way I work.' I said to myself, 'This man is a lunatic. He uses terror to teach.'"

"I try to set the tone early, says Powers, describing his First-Day-of-Class Grand-Entrance Fantasy. "I think I should enter the class ahead of a train of graduate assistants carrying my briefcase and books, backed up by an orchestra playing the march from Verdi's *Aida*."

That would certainly get the class's attention, I agreed.

It is also a day-one ritual for Powers to tell his students that almost every assignment will have to be rewritten—twice. At which point some unfortunate will inevitably raise his hand and ask, "What if you do it right the first time?"

"Humor me," he will say.

"I think students take his classes as some kind of self-flagellation," says BU grad Denise Graveline. "They know Powers's reputation, and they want to see if they can meet the challenge."

Meeting the challenge takes a strong self-image on the students' part, because Powers, like many professors of the hard-line persuasion, can be brutal in class.

For example, one student began an editorial with, "In this modern world of ours today. . . ." Powers read it aloud. "Nice lead," he said, then commented, "if we don't count its being dull, pointless, and triply redundant."

Then there was the now-famous classroom argument between Powers and a student who tried playing hardball in defense of his use of the alleged word "irregardless."

"Not a proper word," said Powers.

"It's in the dictionary," yelled the student, who then had the temerity and monumental bad judgment to charge to the front of the room and bang his *Webster's* down on the table.

"My dear boy," said Powers, picking up the dictionary and sliding into what he calls his full William F. Buckley, "let us read the definition. 'Irregardless: illiterate use of the word regardless.'"

Powers's students routinely receive graded papers bearing so much red penciling that it looks as though Powers has bled on them.

"Nice typing. Horrible writing," is a frequent comment in the river of red. And to a student who once argued that good layout photos would help "carry his story," Powers replied, "Illustrating that story would be like perfuming a pig."

"He demeaned us," says former Powers student Bob Hughes, "until most of us rose above ourselves in the effort to prove we were better than he gave us credit for being." No one escapes Powers's sarcasm. A graduate assistant once gave a lecture while Powers observed from the back of the room. The students were less than animated, prompting the grad assistant to say with forced good humor, "Professor Powers, is there something you can do to wake up the class?"

"Begging your pardon," replied Powers, "I wasn't the one who put them to sleep."

And to a student who was considering a freelance writing career, Powers advised, "An excellent idea, particularly if you had the foresight to be born the daughter of a railway magnate."

Three or four weeks into each term, the school's advising center begins to resemble a refugee processing station with students in dazed or indignant retreat from Powers's thermonuclear teaching.

"Students would come in crying 'mental abuse' or 'I can't take it in there,'" says BU grad Maryellen Kennedy, who observed these semiannual crises during four years of working in the advising center. "A lot of people transfer to other courses, but all that does is add to the Powers mystique."

"Students genuinely fear him," adds Graveline.

But, like other sumbitches from the football field to the physics lab, Powers claims he doesn't care.

"I'm an elitist," he says, pointing out that his teaching methods derive from the classical private-school tradition as he experienced it at Boston Latin, St. Sebastian's, and Harvard.

"I divide student into four categories," he says. "First are those I actively detest. The brownnosers, grade grubbers, and B.S. artists. Then there are what I call the Rimless Ciphers. They're neuter. They occupy space. I'm neither for them nor against them. The largest group is made up of pleasant, nice people. I have great empathy for students in this group who try hard. Finally, there is a small group—the select and gifted few—the ones you never forget."

Powers may be harder on his protégés, however, than on any of his other students. I recall one of the chosen, a senior who had done well in two of Powers's courses and who was suddenly doing poorly after going through that most painful of undergraduate crises: Breaking Up with the Girlfriend. There were some of us who feared for the young man's emotional stability. Powers was not among us.

"Do you know what Robert Frost once said was all he knew about life?" Powers said to the student. "'It goes on.' When you come into this class you leave your personal problems outside."

Yet Powers has a single overwhelmingly redeeming feature that he probably shares with a good many other campus SOBs. He will go the mat for his students.

Kennedy describes a typical scene at the student advising center: "The reception room would be crowded with students waiting to see advisers, and suddenly Powers would burst in with a student in tow. Immediately, Powers's student would become the best kid with the most pressing problem in the entire university. Powers would have to get him into this course or out of that course, and it would have to be done that minute. Sometimes Powers would just bypass everyone and go charging into a dean's office."

"When alumni return to school, the one name you hear most often is Powers," says Graveline. "The message is usually 'If you can get through Powers's courses—and put up with him telling you to straighten your tie and shine the back of your shoes—you can probably survive the transition from campus to the world of work.'"

Powers readily admits that he is more concerned with his students' job search than with their paper chase. Each year he places dozens of students in high-paying internships with such corporate giants as Ford, Alcoa, and General

Electric. He sends these former waitresses and lifeguards away in May with the admonition, "Screw up and you'll answer to your boss this summer and to me next fall."

But Powers's students—those who survive, that is—don't often screw up. And as much as they may curse his name as they're plowing through yet another endless rewrite, a large percentage will someday look back and realize that he was the one professor who made a difference in their lives.

I lifted the bullwhip off the bookcase and let it uncoil on the floor.

"So why do you keep teaching?" I asked.

"Same reason most of the other SOBs in this profession do it," he said, leaning back in his chair. "I do it for the money."

I put the bullwhip back on the shelf. We went to lunch. I bought.

Annotate "Top Drill Instructor in Boot Camp 101"

1. Bracket and identify the type of lead in the profile. Find examples of narrative and exposition

2. Underline the nut graf.

3. Circle places the writer refers back to the nut graf, repeating or slightly varying the language in the nut graf.

4. Look carefully at the way the pieces of this profile are linked together. Box any transitions or note any transitional devices used in this profile.

5. Circle the sources the first time the writer uses them in this profile. Whom has he interviewed? What has he observed? What research has he done?

6. The writer has used white space as an indication that the profile is divided into two main sections. Bracket the two sections, and note the main point in each.

▶READINGS

Two profiles in this section highlight the extraordinary lives of ordinary people: a Hmong high school student in Stephen Magagnini's "Hmong Teen Builds Future in Two Conflicting Worlds," and a Palestinian-American newspaper dealer in student Noanna Tzinakos' "United We Stand." Susan Orlean's "Show Dog" profiles an extraordinary dog, Biff Truesdale, champion boxer.

Hmong Teen Builds Future in Two Conflicting Worlds

Stephen Magagnini

Stephen Magagnini won the American Society of Newspaper Editor's contest in the diversity writing category for his series on the Hmong people, Laotian refugees who "were driven from the mountains of Laos by the Vietnamese and Lao communists in 1975." Many Hmong fled to camps in Thailand and from there to America, creating large Hmong communities in California, notably in Sacramento, where Magagnini writes for the *Sacramento Bee*. Magagnini's writing has won numerous awards; the Columbia School of Journalism has honored him twice. Part of his award-winning series on the Hmong was this profile on Julie Chang, a teenager who "straddle[s] two worlds often at odds."

Julie Chang showed off her moves at her first-ever teen dance, causing her first-ever breakup—all on the same wild night.

"This was the first time I went to a party in my whole life," says Chang, 16, her fingers combing raven locks that flow past her waist. "It was so fun."

She boogied to "Larger Than Life" by the Backstreet Boys that fateful May night, then was confronted by her jealous boyfriend, who didn't know how to fast dance.

"He said it's over. His friend was saying that I was dancing with other guys—those were my girlfriends! I was so mad, too. I didn't cry—I'm not the one who broke up. I didn't do anything wrong . . . I was saying forget it, he's too old anyway. He's 21."

5   Her words pour out like a mountain stream in May. It's all part of Julie Chang's grand American adventure. She's 4-foot-11 without her high-heeled Soda shoes, but larger than life—a diminu-tive dynamo who honors her ancient culture while embracing the raft of opportunities that have come her way in Sacramento.

Things other American teens take for granted are landmarks in Julie's life: She recently saw her first movie and dined at her first all-you-can-eat buffet.

The future of the Hmong will fall on the shoulders of hundreds of young people like her who straddle two worlds often at odds.

Balancing those worlds will challenge Julie in ways she can't imagine.

It's 5:30 A.M. in her family's mildewed Meadowview apartment. The aroma of fried hot dogs, green beans and fresh-steamed rice wafts from the kitchen. Even her father's prize fighting cock is asleep, but Julie has already showered, dressed and made breakfast for her family—14 in all, including nine younger brothers and a baby sister.

10   For her grandmother, afflicted with dizzy spells and high blood pressure, she has prepared a medicinal chicken soup. "It's part of my job," she says. "I'm proud of it."

She was up past midnight studying for a history test, but there's not a crease on her eager face, not a shadow under her mahogany eyes. She hems her black bell bottoms while a parade of bleary-eyed brothers emerges from the bedroom.

One by one, they hop onto giant 50-gallon water jars—left over from Y2K, when many Hmong thought the world would end—surrounding a small oval kitchen table, and devour breakfast.

Also in the kitchen are two 40-pound bags of rice, a neatly stacked pile of clean dishes Julie washed the night before, and a list of 50 phone numbers—all for members of the Chang clan.

Soon, the three-bedroom house returns to its normal chaos: children bouncing on the sofa and chasing one another around the living room, babies bawling, the phone ringing.

15   Gliding through this kinetic sea is Julie Chang. Burbank High sophomore, big sister, chief cook and wok washer, laundress, textile artist, tutor, interpreter and the shining hope of the Chang family.

"Sometimes I have so much to do, I don't have time to go to sleep," says Julie, who shares a bedroom with her five oldest brothers. "Last night, I slept on the sofa."

At 7:20 A.M., Julie's mom begins ferrying children to school in her red pickup. She drops Julie and her brother Meng, 15, at Luther Burbank High School.

More than 500 Hmong attend Burbank, making them the school's largest ethnic group. They shine on the chess team, the volleyball team, in student government and the math/science engineering academy. Burbank has its share of ethnic tension, but most Hmong mix easily with other kids.

Miraculously, Julie is managing a 3.5 GPA. She's also president of an Asian-American girls club, a regular at the Friday afternoon Hmong forum and the star of Xavier Young's "All Hmong, All The Time" language class.

20   A few months ago her father, who earns $900 a month washing rental cars at Sacramento International Airport, paid her the ultimate compliment: He bought her a computer.

The computer, now squeezed into her bedroom, "is helping a lot," Julie says. But she still has to wait for her brothers to fall asleep before she can concentrate. "They're so annoying, talking talking talking . . .

"I love my life and I'm very happy, but I wish I was a boy," she confides. "Girls do so much more work. I've been cooking since I was a little girl in the refugee camp."

Culture Shock

Until she came to Sacramento six years ago, Julie had never been beyond the barbed wire of the Thai refugee camp where she was born.

From the time she was 6, she and her mom embroidered Hmong story cloths known as *pa ndao* that tell the Hmong odyssey through pictures. Julie stitched stories of a war she'd never seen in a country she'd never visited, then sold them in the camp.

25   Her family was among the last wave of Hmong refugees to leave the camps. Her grandparents held out hope of returning to Laos to the last.

In 1994, armed only with her ABCs and 1-2-3s, she was thrust into the fifth grade at Freeport Elementary School. Her initial excitement turned to sorrow when the other Hmong girls in her class tired of translating for her. "I understood what they were talking about, but I couldn't say it back."

Her parents were struggling, too. They felt abandoned by her aunt, who had sponsored them in Sacramento, then moved to Minnesota. "My parents said, 'Why is she going over there? We came over here because of her.'"

Julie's a fast learner. She taught herself to read and write Hmong in two months, and she's steadily mastering English. When her grandmother had surgery to remove a fist-sized growth on her back, Julie went to the hospital—a place she'd never been before—to translate.

"I cannot really translate from English to Hmong," she says. "There's no word for 'complicated' in Hmong."

30 And that, in a word, describes the Hmong predicament: America is a land of many belief systems, cultures and lifestyles, confusing newcomers who have lived by the same rules for centuries.

As the eldest daughter in a Hmong family, Julie rarely has time for fun.

"Fun?" she does a double take. "I never have time to go play my sport, volleyball." In six years here, she has seen one movie, *Godzilla*, and then only on a field trip. She does watch Hmong videos and catches snatches of *Friends* on TV.

The other night, she awoke at 4 A.M. to finish *Sweet Valley High*, the latest in her diet of teen romance novels.

Even then, the house isn't always peaceful. Sometimes Julie can hear her 75-year-old grandmother, recently widowed, crying in the next room or listening to sad Hmong songs. Sometimes Julie reads while brushing her teeth.

35 Julie's brains, looks and work ethic have already generated several marriage proposals, including one from the guy who broke up with her at the dance.

"He still calls me every day," she says. "He says he's sorry, he wants another chance because it's hard to find a girl like me."

He comes over Saturday nights and talks of love, "but I'm not taking it seriously," she says. "I don't have time to date. Education is more important."

Her mother, Cheng Thao, begs Julie, "Don't get married early. You're the only one who can help me." It's Julie who helps her mom shop, Julie who helps her grandmother cash her SSI (Supplemental Security Income) check. Julie who explains the notes from school, Julie who plans her siblings' birthday parties.

But Julie and her mom both know that when a traditional Hmong girl marries is often beyond her control.

Orphans Reborn

Cheng Thao, 33, met her husband in the refugee 40 camp in 1983. She was brushing her teeth when he claimed her. He softened her up with love talk, and three weeks later, they married.

She still waits for him to come home at 11:30 P.M. after eight hours of washing cars.

At 34, Chang Lor is a handsome, practical man in a black Nike cap. His family adores him. "My dad caught a sturgeon in the river," brags son Meng. "He can wash 30 cars in an hour."

Chang's a firm believer in shamanism, but he allows his sons to hedge their spiritual bets: They go to Christian Sunday school.

Still, he values his Hmong heritage enough to set aside $15 a week for flute lessons for his eldest sons, Meng and Tou.

Meng finds it boring, but Tou, 13, enjoys feel- 45 ing the music vibrate through him. He takes his flute off the wall and plays one of the 11 tunes he's mastered, a song about orphans being reborn. It's a fitting metaphor for the Hmong, orphans of history being reborn in America.

Chang also has enrolled Meng and Tou in Hmong 2000, a paramilitary youth group that meets Tuesday and Thursday nights. He sent Julie, too, but she quit to concentrate on school.

Chang's father, Choua Neng Chang, was a soldier for 20 years and mayor of a mountaintop county of 20,000. He was renowned as a mediator, investigator and judge.

After Laos fell to the communists in 1975, Choua Neng Chang moved his family into the highlands and fought with the Hmong guerrillas.

In April 1981, the Changs and about 1,000 other Hmong lashed bamboo trees into rafts and fled across the Mekong River into Thailand. About half drowned in the crossing.

50 Julie's dad studied English for two years in Sacramento but still finds the language frustrating. He dreams of buying a home and seeing his children through college. He expects Julie to lead the way.

Hmong Girls Doing Well

Like Julie, half of the Hmong girls at Burbank have B averages or better, compared with 40 percent of the boys, says principal Kathleen Whelan. Only 25 girls—10 percent—have less than C averages, compared with 23 percent of the boys.

The disparity can be traced to the culture—while boys are often allowed to go out and play with their friends and roam the streets, Hmong parents keep a much tighter rein on their daughters, says Mai Xi Lee, a Hmong counselor at Burbank. "For a lot of girls, school is their only outlet."

Still, the girls' success is remarkable given their responsibilities at home, Lee says.

Julie's brother Meng, who also maintains a B-plus average, does vacuum, wash some dishes and make a few meals. But little is expected of their younger brothers.

55 Lee calls Julie "your typical Hmong girl but more so. Not only is she an obedient daughter who knows her duties quite well, she also knows American culture well enough to do well in school so she can be successful at whatever she wants to do."

Julie handles her many roles with grace and pride, partly because she was raised in an all-Hmong environment that offered no choice, and because her parents are wise enough to nourish her dreams.

But some of Julie's Hmong peers at Burbank, especially those born in America, find it harder to balance both worlds.

"I'm going through the struggle right now," says Mary Xiong, a freckle-faced senior who won a scholarship to St. Mary's College in Moraga. She says that when she becomes the Hmong Oprah, her first talk show topic will be "Double Lives of Hmong Youth."

Sometimes her parents support her desire to pursue a career. "Then, they'll give me lectures: 'You're getting old. You'll be 18 soon. When are you going to marry your boyfriend?'"

60 Traditional Hmong girls aren't allowed to date, partly because some Hmong parents believe their daughters will be kidnapped into marriage or their suitors will spike their drinks with a magic potion to turn them into love slaves.

If a Hmong boy breaks up with a Hmong girl after several months, he may have to pay her parents a fine, even if there was no physical contact.

Mary, yearbook editor and president of the Hmong club, says at 13 she was ready to marry her first crush, but thankfully he backed off. She says her aunt wasn't so lucky: "She got married last summer at 18 . . . Now she's pregnant and divorced."

Mary swears she won't get married until she's 30 or 40. Julie says she wants to wait at least until she has finished college. But despite the pitfalls of early marriage, counselor Lee estimates as many as 60 Hmong girls at Burbank—more than one in five—are already married. Some became wives at 14.

Julie's Dreams

At the Friday afternoon Hmong Forum led by Hmong teacher Xavier Young, Julie and other students open up about how hard it is to reconcile their modern American dreams with the expectations of their old world parents.

65 "The only time I can talk to my dad is when we're eating dinner," says one girl. "I'd like to talk to him about education, but I'm just embarrassed."

Yee Xiong, 17, lost two older brothers in the secret war in Laos. But when he asks about the war, "My dad just walks away or turns the TV louder . . . it's just too painful to talk about."

Young, one of nearly 40 Hmong teachers who have been hired by the Sacramento City Unified

School District in recent years, appreciates how hard it is for Hmong kids and parents to know one another.

"A lot of our students are hitting the same wall over and over again," he says, "but at the same time, a lot of these students are going to come back and lead us whether they like it or not."

He's counting on Julie to become one of those leaders.

70   After a long day of French adjectives, Bolshevik history, probability, anatomy and Hmong language, Julie presides over a meeting of the all-girl She Club.

Today the club, which deals with everything from leadership skills to breast cancer, is preparing a dance performance.

Julie shows a sextet of Asian-American girls how to gracefully twirl their hands and move their feet to a haunting Hmong love song. The song is about the first stages of a breakup (moral: You'll feel the heartache later).

At 5 P.M. her mother drives her home, where anarchy reigns. Meng has pulled out a hunk of frozen mystery meat from the freezer. He's hacking it up for dinner, stopping now and then to attend to a crying baby. The other kids draw with colored markers, watch TV or chase one another around the house.

Julie takes over, cooking a dinner that's not unlike the breakfast she made 14 hours earlier.

75   It's not until Saturday afternoon that she's able to steal a few moments for herself in the cool confines of the library a few blocks from her home. She asks the librarians to help her research how to become a registered nurse, a teacher, a scientist.

Tears shine in Julie's eyes when she thinks of Laos, the country that has shaped so much of her life, even though she has never even been there. "We don't have a country of our own," she laments.

But she's making America her own and says she's impatient to join the new wave of Hmong leaders.

"I feel like I want to be in college, right there, right now," she says. "It seems so incredible to make my dreams come true."

But Julie's blueprint for life in America was about to change dramatically.

"It's Too Late"

After Julie came home from summer school at the end of July, her cousin showed up to fix her computer. He brought with him Kou Vue, a 17-year-old boy Julie met about a year ago at a meeting of Hmong 2000, the paramilitary youth group.

The computer fixed, the three of them got into   80 Kou's car. But Kou dropped off Julie's cousin first, then told Julie he planned to marry her.

She was shocked: "We never went out: he just came to visit me. We never actually talked about love."

What happened next was even more of a shock.

Kou, a junior at Florin High, took Julie to his home, where all his relatives were waiting for her. As they walked through the front door, a shaman swirled a live chicken over their heads—a traditional Hmong ceremony marking the start of the marriage.

The next day, Julie's mother called and offered to take her home.

"No," said Julie. "It's too late." In Hmong culture, she knows, leaving once you've been claimed   85 by a boy can ruin your reputation for life.

"He's a nice guy; you'll have a nice future," her mother responded.

Julie felt scared, confused and excited all at once. She likes Kou, and says she went with him of her own free will. Yet she knows little about him except that he gets good grades and everybody thinks he's nice. And, she says, he has promised to support her dream of going to college.

A bride price was set—$6,400—and the wedding took place Aug. 4 at her parents' home.

"I feel so bad for myself," Julie said during her third day in Kou's house—the day the Hmong believe a bride's fate is sealed. "I shouldn't have come with him that day. Before this, I told the whole world I didn't want to get married."

But, like a million Hmong girls before her, she's resigned to her fate. "Everyone regrets it after we get married," she says. "But I think he loves me, so I will stay with him."

Critical Reading Questions

1. Identify the lead. What technique does Magagnini use in the lead? How successful is the lead in drawing you into this profile?

2. What is the main point of this profile? Does the nut graf announce this point? Where else does Magagnini seed this thesis into the piece?

3. Find an example of the following elements: physical description, quotation from Julie Chang, quotation from another source about her, anecdote, factual information. What does the writer reveal through each of these elements?

4. What kind of research did Magagnini do for this piece? List specific examples of his research under these categories: print and electronic sources, interviews, and direct observation.

5. Magagnini's writing is filled with metaphorical language. For example, in the lead he writes that Julie Chang's "words pour out like a mountain stream."

Later he writes, "Gliding through this kinetic sea is Julie Chang ..." Find some other examples, and evaluate their freshness and effectiveness.

6. How effective is the quotation that ends the profile? What impression does it leave on the reader?

Questions for Writing and Discussion

1. In an interview with Keith Woods, editor of *2001 Best Newspaper Writing*, Magagnini talked about his shock when he discovered that Julie Chang had gotten married. Were you similarly shocked? How does her marriage affect your understanding of the "balance" Chang achieves between Hmong and American culture?

2. Commenting on this series, Woods wrote, "The result is a series that at once reveals and explains the things that make the Hmong different while grounding the stories in the struggles and triumphs of our common humanity." Explain why you agree or disagree with this statement in relation to this profile.

United We Stand

Noanna Tzinakos

Noanna Tzinakos wrote this profile of a Palestinian-American newspaper dealer for her writing class. She shows Hammad Eldin's life before and after the 2001 bombing of the World Trade Towers in New York City and reveals how the tragic event touched him and his family.

"Thank you. Have a nice day."

These words find their way through his dark tangled beard and reach the ears of every customer Mohammad "Hammad" Eldin helps in a convenience store in Brooklyn, New York. "Hammad"—as he likes to be referred to by his friends, and therefore his customers—stands no taller than 5'9", even with the hand-woven praying cap sitting firmly atop his head. A Palestinian native, Hammad dresses in the traditional Arabic white robe or *galabiya* and wears a beard extending down to his chest.

He picks up a newspaper from the stack that he has for sale. This one is a paper in his native language. On the cover: a picture of a woman crying over a make-shift tombstone for her son, who was killed in the war in the Middle East. "Stuff like this happens everyday in my country," he says, bending his head with grief.

Things like this did not happen to him in his own country, however; they didn't happen until he came to the United States. For thirteen years Eldin worked in and owned a thriving newspaper stand between 26th and 27th Streets on 8th Avenue in Midtown Manhattan. People's daily routines wouldn't start and often their first words of the day weren't uttered until they turned the corner and stepped under the awning of Hammad's stand. What would be there to greet them: a hot, fresh pot of coffee, any newspaper or magazine in the country, a greeting, and a warm smile. He would not even need to ask his regulars what they were having; whatever it was would just be ready for them when they arrived. Hammad knew his customers. Hammad loved his customers.

"He was, honestly, the first person I would speak to when I would get out of the subway in the morning. He'd be there every day with my light-and-sweet coffee waiting for me. I would go to class smiling, even after such a gritty commute," reminisces Eleni Tzinakos, a student at the Fashion Institute of Technology, and customer of Hammad's.

Daniel Gold, a stockbroker at a firm down the street from the stand, or "dark coffee one sugar" as Hammad would call him, was a regular: "I remember it being the dead of winter—around the holiday season—and there he'd be, in his stand, exposed to the cold, with his ethnic music in the background, doing his job as if it were a perfect spring day. He never complained or had a bad thing to say. It kind of baffled me how someone in the middle of this hustle and bustle could always be so pleasant."

There he was, in the middle of the "hustle and bustle," when New York City saw its two towers, which stood as a landmark, crumble like a deck of cards on September 11th. Hammad ran alongside the rest of those who tried to escape falling debris, in disbelief of what had happened.

As he stares at the "United We Stand" sticker on the front door of the convenience store, he recalls that day: "As we walked over the [Brooklyn] Bridge, I listened to what everyone was saying.

They were talking about how some planes crashed into the towers, and they thought it could be terrorism. All I could think about was, 'Who could do this bad thing?'"

When New York City tried to get back to normal the following Monday, Hammad too, tried to go back to the routine, as much as possible. When he opened up his shop for the first time post-9/11, he knew it would not be the same—that it could not be the same as before. He went through the usual routine, pushed up the gates, laid out the newspapers, and brewed the coffee. As he suspected, it was different. The regulars came less frequently. Fewer people came. Passersby would cross the street, making sure to avoid eye-contact with Hammad.

10 "'No one comes any more.' [Hammad] told me one morning that I went for coffee. It was a few weeks after September 11th. He wasn't that smiling, cheerful guy that stood there a few weeks earlier," said Eleni.

The same trend would continue for a few weeks, with "good days and bad," as Hammad puts it. Then, Hammad recalls, one morning in November: "I was sleeping, and I hear the phone ring. I thought I was dreaming, but it wouldn't stop ringing." On the other end of that phone call—someone from the NYPD asking for a Mr. Mohammad Eldin to come to a location he was very familiar with—between 26th and 27th Street, on 8th Avenue in Manhattan.

Indeed, the location was familiar; the sight however could not have been more foreign. All that stood in the spot where he would brew coffee, and lay out the newspapers, was a pile of burned, unrecognizable rubble. "I looked, and I couldn't believe it, you know. What did I do to deserve this?" he asked. Hammad knew what he had done wrong—nothing, except look like, and be a man from the Middle East after September 11th. Hammad struggled without the stability of his stand, and looked for job-after-job, to no avail. Nobody would hire him with his beard, robe and dark skin. "After this happened, and I couldn't find [a] job, I start to think 'Maybe I should cut my beard, or wear blue jeans or something, so they won't think I'm one of the bad guys.'"

Hammad did not do that though. He remembers going home to his wife Luma one night after a long day of job-hunting, and crying. He cried for his life savings, which were lost; for the lives that were lost in September 11th; because he felt lost.

"Hammad, you can't just let them believe we are the same as those people that did this horrible thing," are the words that Hammad remembers his wife telling him that night. "'You cannot and should not change who you are, but you can make people see you, and love you—by being Hammad,' she told me. I thank her for everything," he says. Two years, and some time has passed since Mohammad Eldin became one of many Arabic people to be persecuted, harassed, or mistreated since September 11th. He's moved on with his life, and his business. He managed to save and gather up enough money to lease a convenience store, and is, once again, doing what he once loved. As a few Middle Eastern teens from the neighborhood exit the convenience store, Hammad wishes them a nice day as usual, and gleams with contentment. The girls were wearing the traditional wrap around their heads, and the boys spoke to him in Palestinian. "I wasn't the only Arabic person who something bad happened to. Those kids that just left, the boy has told me they get called bad names everyday at school. But, look, they still show pride in their culture. They still live life."

Recently gaining his American citizenship, 15 Hammad says, that despite what happened, he counts his blessings for being in this country. He also notes that he feels as though he gets the "best of both worlds" between his native Palestinian background, and his new-found American lifestyle. He speaks of going to Palestine in the summer for vacation. " I feel like, here, I'm looked at as Palestinian, and I know when I go back, they'll call me 'American.' I like it, because I feel like I am both."

Hammad, with his beard longer now than it had been in pictures he showed taken just before September 11th, and without any jeans in sight, is smiling once again. He's once again in a familiar spot—behind a counter helping to start off and be part of people's days. Although he confesses in the back of his mind he still yearns to find those who set his stand ablaze, it seems as though Hammad has once again found comfort and security. He's found his niche. He's found new "regulars," and they've found him.

Critical Reading Questions

1. What impression do you have of Hammad Eldin as Noanna Tzinakos introduces him in the first section of the profile? What details contribute to your impression?

2. In the nut graf, Tzinakos hints at the events she will recount when she says, "Things like this did not happen to him in his own country, however; they didn't happen until he came to the United States," but she withholds the details. Is this an effective technique? Why?

3. How does Tzinakos develop her profile? What elements—physical description, quotations from and about the subject, examples, anecdotes, factual information—does she weave into the portrait? Which are most memorable?

4. What research has Tzinakos done for this profile? Are there places where you think the profile needs more information?

5. The last four paragraphs create a concluding scene, bringing the reader two years past September 11 and its effect on Eldin. What details in the conclusion reveal Eldin's character and the quality of his life? In what ways has your impression of him changed or deepened from the opening scene?

6. How effective is the title of this profile in summing up its central points?

Questions for Writing and Discussion

1. Many stories have emerged from the events of September 11, 2001—stories full of tragedy, heroism, patriotism, division, and unity. How does Hammad Eldin's story extend your understanding of that event?

2. Explain why you think Hammad Eldin's story is, or is not, important to tell. What stories define September 11 for you?

Show Dog

Susan Orlean

One of the most celebrated practitioners of "literary journalism," a nonfiction genre that uses many of the literary techniques of fiction, Susan Orlean is probably best known for her book *The Orchid Thief,* which was made into the movie *Adaptation* in 2002. She also writes for *Rolling Stone, Vogue, Esquire,* and the *New Yorker.*

Orlean's profiles have garnered much praise for their insight and their craft. David Remnick, editor of the *New Yorker* and of a collection of profiles from the *New Yorker,* wrote: "But whether it is in *The New Yorker* or elsewhere, the Profile is a terribly hard form to get right. Susan Orlean manages it with a subject who can only bark."

In an interview at the University of Oregon, which follows the profile, Orlean talks about her interest in "ordinary-people stories." "After doing celebrity journalism, I realized

I was more interested in the things I walked past every day, the stuff people usually miss. I'm primarily interested in the tiny master—a person with a tiny domain over which they are the master." In "Show Dog," Orlean carefully observes Biff Truesdale, a champion boxer who is the master of the show dog domain.

If I were a bitch, I'd be in love with Biff Truesdale. Biff is perfect. He's friendly, good looking, rich, famous, and in excellent physical condition. He almost never drools. He's not afraid of commitment. He wants children—actually, he already has children and wants a lot more. He works hard and is a consummate professional, but he also knows how to have fun.

What Biff likes most is food and sex. This makes him sound boorish, which he is not—he's just elemental. Food he likes even better than sex. His favorite things to eat are cookies, mints, and hotel soap, but he will eat just about anything. Richard Krieger, a friend of Biff's who occasionally drives him to appointments, said not long ago, "When we're driving on I-95, we'll usually pull over at McDonald's. Even if Biff is napping, he always wakes up when we're getting close. I get him a few plain hamburgers with buns—no ketchup, no mustard, and no pickles. He loves hamburgers. I don't get him his own French fries, but if I get myself fries I always flip a few for him into the back."

If you're ever around Biff while you're eating something he wants to taste—cold roast beef, a Wheatables cracker, chocolate, pasta, aspirin, whatever—he will stare at you across the pleated bridge of his nose and let his eyes sag and his lips tremble and allow a little bead of drool to percolate at the edge of his mouth until you feel so crummy that you give him some. This routine puts the people who know him in a quandary, because Biff has to watch his weight. Usually, he is as skinny as Kate Moss, but he can put on three pounds in an instant. The holidays can be tough. He takes time off at Christmas and spends it at home, in Attleboro, Massachusetts, where there's

a lot of food around and no pressure and no schedule and it's easy to eat all day. The extra weight goes to his neck. Luckily, Biff likes working out. He runs for fifteen or twenty minutes twice a day, either outside or on his Jog-Master. When he's feeling heavy, he runs longer, and skips snacks, until he's back down to his ideal weight of seventy-five pounds.

Biff is a boxer. He is a show dog—he performs under the name Champion Hi-Tech's Arbitrage—and so looking good is not mere vanity: it's business. A show dog's career is short, and judges are unforgiving. Each breed is judged by an explicit standard for appearance and temperament, and then there's the incalculable element of charisma in the ring. When a show dog is fat or lazy or sullen, he doesn't win: when he doesn't win, he doesn't enjoy the ancillary benefits of being a winner, like appearing as the celebrity spokesmodel on packages of Pedigree Mealtime with Lamb and Rice, which Biff will be doing soon, or picking the best-looking bitches and charging them six hundred dollars or so for his sexual favors, which Biff does three or four times a month. Another ancillary benefit of being a winner is that almost every single weekend of the year, as he travels to shows around the country, he gets to hear people applaud for him and yell his name and tell him what a good boy he is, which is something he seems to enjoy at least as much as eating a bar of soap.

· · ·

Pretty soon, Biff won't have to be so vigilant 5 about his diet. After he appears at the Westminster Kennel Club's show, this week, he will retire from active show life and work full time as a stud. It's a good moment for him to retire. Last year,

Lord Augustus of Sandwich (Augie), a white boxer. Photograph by John Shane

he won more shows than any other boxer, and also more than any other dog in the purebred category known as Working Dogs, which also includes Akitas, Alaskan malamutes, Bernese mountain dogs, bullmastiffs, Doberman pinschers, giant schnauzers, Great Danes, Great Pyrenees, komondors, kuvaszok, mastiffs, Newfoundlands, Portuguese water dogs, Rottweilers, Saint Bernards, Samoyeds, Siberian huskies, and standard schnauzers. Boxers were named for their habit of standing on their hind legs and punching with their front paws when they fight. They were originally bred to be chaperons—to look forbidding while being pleasant to spend time with. Except for show dogs like Biff, most boxers lead a life of relative leisure. Last year at Westminster, Biff was named Best Boxer and Best Working Dog, and he was a serious contender for Best in Show, the highest honor any show dog can hope for. He is a contender to win his breed and group again this year, and is a serious contender once again for Best in Show, although the odds are against him, because this year's judge is known as a poodle person.

Biff is four years old. He's in his prime. He could stay on the circuit for a few more years, but by stepping aside now he is making room for his sons Trent and Rex, who are just getting into the business, and he's leaving while he's still on top. He'll also spend less time in airplanes, which is the one part of show life he doesn't like, and more time with his owners, William and Tina Truesdale, who might be persuaded to waive his snacking rules.

Biff has a short, tight coat of fox-colored fur, white feet and ankles, and a patch of white on his chest roughly the shape of Maine. His muscles are plainly sketched under his skin, but he isn't bulgy. His face is turned up and pushed in, and has a dark mask, spongy lips, a wishbone-shaped white blaze, and the earnest and slightly careworn expression of a small-town mayor. Someone once told me that he thought Biff looked a little bit like President Clinton. Biff's face is his fortune. There are plenty of people who like boxers with bigger bones and a stockier body and taller shoulders—boxers who look less like marathon runners and more like weight lifters—but almost everyone agrees that Biff has a nearly perfect head.

"Biff's head is his father's," William Truesdale, a veterinarian, explained to me one day. We were in the Truesdales' living room in Attleboro, which overlooks acres of hilly fenced-in fields. Their house is a big, sunny ranch with a stylish pastel kitchen and boxerabilia on every wall. The Truesdales don't have children, but at any given moment they share their quarters with at least a half dozen dogs. If you watch a lot of dog food commercials, you may have seen William—he's the young, handsome, dark-haired veterinarian declaring his enthusiasm for Pedigree Mealtime while his boxers gallop about.

"Biff has a masculine but elegant head," William went on. "It's not too wet around the muzzle. It's just about ideal. Of course, his forte is right here." He pointed to Biff's withers, and explained that Biff's shoulder-humerus articulation was optimally angled, and bracketed his superb brisket and forelegs, or something like that. While William was talking, Biff climbed onto the couch and sat on top of Brian, his companion, who was hiding under a pillow. Brian is an English toy Prince Charles spaniel who is about the size of a teakettle and has the composure of a hummingbird. As a young competitor, he once bit a judge—a mistake Tina Truesdale says he made because at the time he had been going through a little mind problem about being touched. Brian, whose show name is Champion Cragmor's Hi-Tech Man, will soon go back on the circuit, but now he mostly serves as Biff's regular escort. When Biff sat on him, he started to quiver. Biff batted at him with his front leg. Brian gave him an adoring look.

10   "Biff's body is from his mother," Tina was saying. "She had a lot of substance."

"She was even a little extreme for a bitch," William said. "She was rather buxom. I would call her zaftig."

"Biff's father needed that, though," Tina said. "His name was Tailo, and he was fabulous. Tailo had a very beautiful head, but he was a bit fine, I think. A bit slender."

"Even a little feminine," William said, with feeling. "Actually, he would have been a really awesome bitch."

. . .

The first time I met Biff, he sniffed my pants, stood up on his hind legs and stared into my face, and then trotted off to the kitchen, where someone was cooking macaroni. We were in Westbury, Long Island, where Biff lives with Kimberly Pastella, a twenty-nine-year-old professional handler, when he's working. Last year, Kim and Biff went to at least one show every weekend. If they drove, they took Kim's van. If they flew, she went coach and he went cargo. They always shared a hotel room.

15   While Kim was telling me all this, I could hear Biff rummaging around in the kitchen. "Biffers!" Kim called out. Biff jogged back into the room with a phony look of surprise on his face. His tail was ticking back and forth. It is cropped so that it is about the size and shape of a half-smoked stogie. Kim said that there was a bitch downstairs who had been sent from Pennsylvania to be bred to one of Kim's other clients, and that Biff could smell her and was a little out of sorts. "Let's go," she said to him. "Biff, let's power switch," he started to jog. His nails clicked a light tattoo on the rubber belt.

Except for a son of his named Biffle, Biff gets along with everybody. Matt Stander, one of the founders of *Dog News*, said recently, "Biff is just

very, very personable. He has a *je ne sais quoi* that's really special. He gives of himself all the time." One afternoon, the Truesdales were telling me about the psychology that went into making Biff who he is. "Boxers are real communicators," William was saying. "We had to really take that into consideration in his upbringing. He seems tough, but there's a fragile ego inside there. The profound reaction and hurt when you would raise your voice at him was really something."

"I *made* him," Tina said. "I made Biff who he is. He had an overbearing personality when he was small, but I consider that a prerequisite for a great performer. He had such an *attitude*! He was like this miniature *man*!" She shimmied her shoulders back and forth and thrust out her chin. She is a dainty, chic woman with wide-set eyes and the neck of a ballerina. She grew up on a farm in Costa Rica, where dogs were considered just another form of livestock. In 1987, William got her a Rottweiler for a watchdog, and a boxer, because he had always loved boxers, and Tina decided to dabble with them in shows. Now she makes a monogrammed Christmas stocking for each animal in their house, and she watches the tape of Biff winning at Westminster approximately once a week. "Right from the beginning, I made Biff think he was the most fabulous dog in the world," Tina said.

"He doesn't take after me very much," William said. "I'm more of a golden retriever."

"Oh, he has my nature," Tina said. "I'm very strong-willed. I'm brassy. And Biff is an egotistical, self-centered, selfish person. He thinks he's very important and special, and he doesn't like to share."

. . .

20   Biff is priceless. If you beg the Truesdales to name a figure, they might say that Biff is worth around a hundred thousand dollars, but they will also point out that a Japanese dog fancier re-

cently handed Tina a blank check for Biff. (She immediately threw it away.) That check notwithstanding, campaigning a show dog is a money-losing proposition for the owner. A good handler gets three or four hundred dollars a day, plus travel expenses, to show a dog, and any dog aiming for the top will have to be on the road at least a hundred days a year. A dog photographer charges hundreds of dollars for a portrait, and a portrait is something that every serious owner commissions, and then runs as a full-page ad in several dog show magazines. Advertising a show dog is standard procedure if you want your dog or your presence on the show circuit to get well known. There are also such ongoing show dog expenses as entry fees, hair-care products, food, health care, and toys. Biff's stud fee is six hundred dollars. Now that he will not be at shows, he can be bred several times a month. Breeding him would have been a good way for him to make money in the past, except that whenever the Truesdales were enthusiastic about a mating they bartered Biff's service for the pick of the litter. As a result, they now have more Biff puppies than Biff earnings. "We're doing this for posterity," Tina says. "We're doing it for the good of all boxers. You simply can't think about the cost."

On a recent Sunday, I went to watch Biff work at one of the last shows he would attend before his retirement. The show was sponsored by the Lehigh Valley Kennel Club and was held in a big, windy field house on the campus of Lehigh University, in Bethlehem, Pennsylvania. The parking lot was filled with motor homes pasted with life-size decals of dogs. On my way to the field house, I passed someone walking an Afghan hound wearing a snood, and someone else wiping down a Saluki with a Flintstones beach towel. Biff was napping in his crate—a fancy-looking brass box with bright silver hardware and with luggage tags from Delta, USAir, and Conti-

nental hanging on the door. Dogs in crates can look woeful, but Biff actually likes spending time in his. When he was growing up, the Truesdales decided they would never reprimand him, because of his delicate ego. Whenever he got rambunctious, Tina wouldn't scold him—she would just invite him to sit in his crate and have a time-out.

On this particular day, Biff was in the crate with a bowl of water and a gourmet Oinkeroll. The boxer judging was already over. There had been thirty-three in competition, and Biff had won Best in Breed. Now he had to wait for several hours while the rest of the working breeds had their competitions. Later, the breed winners would square off for Best in Working Group. Then, around dinnertime, the winner of the Working Group and the winners of the other groups—sporting dogs, hounds, terriers, toys, non-sporting dogs, and herding dogs—would compete for Best in Show. Biff was stretched out in the crate with his head resting on his forelegs, so that his lips draped over his ankle like a café curtain. He looked bored. Next to his crate, several wire-haired fox terriers were standing on tables getting their faces shampooed, and beyond them a Chihuahua in a pink crate was gnawing on its door latch. Two men in white shirts and dark pants walked by eating hot dogs. One of them was gesturing and exclaiming, "I thought I had good dachshunds! I thought I had *great* dachshunds!"

Biff sighed and closed his eyes.

While he was napping, I pawed through his suitcase. In it was some dog food; towels; an electric nail grinder; a whisker trimmer; a wool jacket in a lively pattern that looked sort of Southwestern; an apron; some antibiotics; baby oil; coconut-oil coat polish; boxer chalk powder; a copy of *Dog News*; an issue of *ShowSight* magazine, featuring an article subtitled "Frozen Semen—Boon or Bain?" and a two-page ad for Biff, with a full-page, full-color photograph of him and Kim posed in front of a human-size toy soldier; a spray bottle of fur cleanser; another Oinkeroll; a rope ball; and something called a Booda Bone. The apron was for Kim. The baby oil was to make Biff's nose and feet glossy when he went into the ring. Boxer chalk powder—as distinct from, say, West Highland–white-terrier chalk powder—is formulated to cling to short, sleek boxer hair and whiten boxers' white markings. Unlike some of the other dogs, Biff did not need to travel with a blow dryer, curlers, nail polish, or detangling combs, but, unlike some less sought-after dogs, he did need a schedule. He was registered for a show in Chicago the next day, and had an appointment at a clinic in Connecticut the next week to make a semen deposit, which had been ordered by a breeder in Australia. Also, he had a date that same week with a bitch named Diana who was about to go into heat. Biff has to book his stud work after shows, so that it doesn't interfere with his performance. Tina Truesdale told me that this was typical of all athletes, but everyone who knows Biff is quick to comment on how professional he is as a stud. Richard Krieger, who was going to be driving Biff to his appointment at the clinic in Connecticut, once told me that some studs want to goof around and take forever but Biff is very businesslike. "Bing, bang, boom," Krieger said. "He's in, he's out."

25   "No wasting of time," said Nancy Krieger, Richard's wife. "Bing, bang, boom. He gets the job done."

After a while, Kim showed up and asked Biff if he needed to go outside. Then a handler who is a friend of Kim's came by. He was wearing a black-and-white houndstooth suit and was brandishing a comb and a can of hair spray. While they were talking, I leafed through the show catalog and read some of the dogs' names to Biff, just for fun—names like Aleph Godol's Umbra Von Carousel and Champion Spanktown Little Lu Lu and Ranchlake's Energizer O'Motown and Champion Beaverbrook Buster V Broadhead. Biff decided that he did want to go out, so Kim opened the crate. He stepped out and stretched and yawned like a cat, and then he suddenly stood up and punched me in the chest. An announcement calling for all toys to report to their ring came over the loudspeaker. Kim's friend waved the can of hair spray in the direction of a little white poodle shivering on a table a few yards away and exclaimed, "Oh, no! I lost track of time! I have to go! I have to spray up my miniature!"

. . .

Typically, dog contestants first circle the ring together; then each contestant poses individually for the judge, trying to look perfect as the judge lifts its lips for a dental exam, rocks its hindquarters, and strokes its back and thighs. The judge at Lehigh was a chesty, mustached man with watery eyes and a solemn expression. He directed the group with hand signals that made him appear to be roping cattle. The Rottweiler looked good, and so did the giant schnauzer. I started to worry. Biff had a distracted look on his face, as if he'd forgotten something back at the house. Finally, it was his turn. He pranced to the center of the ring. The judge stroked him and then waved his hand in a circle and stepped out of the way. Several people near me began clapping. A flashbulb flared. Biff held his position for a moment, and then he and Kim bounded across the ring, his feet moving so fast that they blurred into an oily sparkle, even though he really didn't have very far to go. He got a cookie when he finished the performance, and another a few minutes later, when the judge wagged his finger at him, indicating that Biff had won again.

You can't help wondering whether Biff will experience the depressing letdown that retired competitors face. At least he has a lot of stud work to look forward to, although William Truesdale complained to me once that the Truesdales' standards for a mate are so high—they require a clean bill of health and a substantial pedigree—that "there just aren't that many right bitches out there." Nonetheless, he and Tina are optimistic that Biff will find enough suitable mates to become one of the most influential boxer sires of all time. "We'd like to be remembered as the boxer people of the nineties," Tina said. "Anyway, we can't wait to have him home."

"We're starting to campaign Biff's son Rex," William said. "He's been living in Mexico, and he's a Mexican champion, and now he's ready to take on the American shows. He's very promising. He has a fabulous rear."

Just then, Biff, who had been on the couch, jumped down and began pacing. "Going somewhere, honey?" Tina asked.

He wanted to go out, so Tina opened the back door, and Biff ran into the backyard. After a few minutes, he noticed a ball on the lawn. The ball was slippery and a little too big to fit in his mouth, but he kept scrambling and trying to grab it. In the meantime, the Truesdales and I sat, stayed for a moment, fetched ourselves turkey sandwiches, and then curled up on the couch. Half an hour passed, and Biff was still happily pursuing the ball. He probably has a very short memory, but he acted as if it was the most fun he'd ever had.

Critical Reading Questions

1. Which details in the lead paragraphs reveal Orlean's point of view about Biff Truesdale? What tone do these paragraphs set for the rest of the profile?

2. Although a dog is a nontraditional profile subject, Orlean uses many of the traditional profile elements in this piece. Find examples of physical description, quotations, examples, anecdotes, and factual information, and explain their function in the profile.

3. Orlean organizes this profile in a number of scenes: at Biff's owners' home in Massachusetts, at his trainer's home in Long Island, at the Lehigh Valley Kennel Club in Pennsylvania. What does each of these settings reveal about Biff? Do they reveal different facets of his world?

4. Aside from direct observation, what other kinds of research does Orlean do for this profile?

5. Often magazine profiles are designed with "pull-out quotes," a line or two that is pulled out from the piece and emphasized by being boxed or written in bold print. What sentences would you choose as pull-out quotes to help the reader focus on Orlean's main ideas in this profile?

6. What are some notable aspects of Orlean's writing style? Support your ideas with specific examples from the profile.

7. Note the verbs Orlean uses to describe the Truesdales and herself in the final paragraph. What point might Orlean be making?

8. From time to time, Orlean enters this profile as a character, using the first-person I and recording her role as observer and participant in the scenes. Find a few places where she uses first person, and explain whether you find this technique effective.

Questions for Writing and Discussion

1. What do you think about using a dog—or another unusual subject—as the subject of a profile? In what way would the piece have changed, and would the change be for the better or for the worse, if Orlean had profiled the Truesdales, for example?

2. What has Orlean revealed about the world of people who inhabit the show dog circuit?

WRITING IN THE WORKS
Interview with Susan Orlean

Susan Orlean

What is it about so-called ordinary people that attracts you as a writer?

Writing about "ordinary" people is about following my own curiosity. After doing celebrity journalism, I realized I was more interested in the things I walked past every day, the stuff people usually miss. I'm primarily interested in the tiny master—a person with a tiny domain over which they are the master. I wrote a piece about a New York City cabdriver who is also the king of the Ashanti tribe in America. After that experience, I realized—you never know. Any other cab driver I meet, any ordinary person, could be a king. It made me step lightly.

What are some of the challenges of writing about people who aren't well known?

One obstacle you face when writing about ordinary life is that you can't possibly know what the story is in advance of writing it. Finding what the story is—reporting the story—is the journey you take as the writer. And that means, of course, that I can't go into the process already knowing what it is I'm going to write—which often makes it hard to pitch the idea to an editor! Beyond that, it's never easy to convince an editor to run a story about "nothing."

Another challenge is that it simply isn't easy to write about people who aren't used to being written about. The subjects themselves offer some resistance, at first. "Why would you want to talk to me?" is a pretty standard reaction. I have to convince them that it is interesting for me to talk to

them, and to see them doing just what they would normally do.

Obviously, though, people love reading your profiles. Are there barriers you need to get your readers past?

Yes. Readers are initially resistant to a story about an "ordinary" person. Persuading someone to read a piece about a 10-year-old boy who's not a "star" is quite a challenge. All you can bring to it is your passion. There's got to be something you're trying to say. And there had to be a reason that a reader will what you're writing. There's nothing that's obviously sexy about these stories. So, among other things, you need to write a good lead.

Your leads are often called the best in the business. What can you tell us about them?

Good leads are crucial, especially when you're writing unconventional ordinary-life stories. They're the point at which you gain—or lose—the reader's attention. I like a lead that makes you stop, that catches or captures you for a second. Dissonant leads, jangly leads, slightly troubling leads all make you want to read a little bit more. They leave you puzzled in a good way.

What would you advise beginning writers on developing leads?

Think of the opening of a piece as a bit of acting. You don't have to maintain the lead's tone throughout the entire story. It's a chance to be a little daring and get the reader engaged. I sometimes like having a first section that's maybe a bit exaggerated. Another thing to remember is that you don't have to make the lead do all the work of telling what the story is about. It's not a suitcase jam-packed with the entire piece. An overloaded lead is quite off-putting. A lead does not have to be a topic sentence.

You've described the stages of putting together a story as reporting, thinking, and writing. How do you approach the reporting stage?

I believe in being unprepared in certain ways. You're going into another world; doing extensive background research first can close you off to observing it. It's good to be uncomfortable, to use your instincts and intelligence and curiosity to look at this strange new world you're exploring. You have to use your wits. Anything factual you can check on later.

Overresearching also tips the psychological balance between you and your subject: I'm the reporter, I have knowledge and power. You're only the ordinary person. That intimidates the people you're observing and writing about.

In a way, the ignorance or freshness you bring to a new subject is the greatest asset a writer can have. The writer is there to learn, after all, and it's best to learn from the people you're writing about, in their words. And afterward, if you need to go back or go to the library for factual information, that's not hard.

What's critical in getting the people you're writing about to open up to you?

You have to develop emotional strategies about how to get into people's lives. What works for me might not work for everybody. What is critical, though, is the ability to cultivate in yourself a genuine empathy, to be as open as you possibly can. The more authentic ingenuousness you can bring to a reporting situation the better. Think of yourself as a privileged visitor.

You've talked about your preference for "hanging out" with your subjects rather than interviewing them. Why is that?

I like having as much unstructured time with the people I'm writing about as possible. It's important for me to be with people while they're doing something, ideally, while they're doing just what they would normally be doing if I weren't there. That's much more valuable than having them just sitting there talking at me. So I rarely ask questions in the form of an interview.

What sort of stylistic guidelines do you keep in mind when writing?

I'm a great believer in simple, very strong language. There are two things that are critical to avoid. The first is what the *New Yorker* calls "elegant variation," fancying up your writing unnecessarily. The other is indirection. Be clear about time and place: When and where is the story unfolding? What are you talking about?

You also shouldn't raise questions without answering them or create images or metaphors that don't ultimately deliver what they promise. It's sometimes OK to bring something in that doesn't explicitly advance the plot but merely adds atmosphere. That's a purposeful aside. You can take the reader down a little cul-de-sac, but then you have to bring him back to the main road.

Something else to keep in mind: facts are poetry. People like scenes and anecdotes, and they'll happily read them if they're short enough, but they also need facts and exposition to break up the scenes. You have to deliver the factual information in an elegant, interesting way, of course.

But even with all these "guidelines," much of the process is magical. So the question is, how do you encourage in yourself those more creative, lyrical, magical moments of your writing?

Portrait of Shantay, a male performer.

WRITING AND REVISING STRATEGIES

Gathered here are three interactive sections for you to use as you write and revise your profile.

▶ Writer's Notebook Suggestions

▶ Peer-Editing Log

▶ Revision Checklist

Writer's Notebook Suggestions

These short exercises are intended to jump-start your thinking as you begin to write your profile. They also might provide some useful topic suggestions.

1. Choose a person to describe, perhaps a classmate. Describe the subject's clothing in three sentences that also give your reader a strong impression of character. Here is an example.

   He's clad in wrinkled khakis and a long-sleeved shirt adorned with a fine patina of fuzz, and his steel wool-colored hair hasn't recently encountered a comb. If Fay looks like hell, he feels even worse. While on the trip, he contracted filaria, a blood-borne infestation of tiny, threadlike worms that, if left untreated, can block the flow of lymph inside a victim's body and cause the extremities to swell to a grotesque size. . . . Fay grimaces and peers through Coke-bottle glasses—he's had trouble with his eyesight since childhood—into a forest of Brooks Brothers suits and elegant dresses.

   —Patrick J. Kiger,
   "Grand March of an American Misfit"

2. Listen in on a conversation—in a café, in a bookstore, or on public transportation. Take notes, and then write up a page of your overheard conversation. Use spoken and unspoken communication: include all gestures, facial expressions, pauses, and inflections (when voices rise or fall, become whispers, and so on.).

3. Look through the business section of the phone book for interesting occupations. Make a list of businesses you want to know more about.

4. Write a brief portrait introducing your best friend. Focus on a single aspect of his or her life or a single character trait.

5. Watch a profile documentary film. Make notes of how many quotations from the subject you hear. What sources are quoted, and what do they have to say? How many anecdotes do you hear? How does the filmmaker move the story from one time period to another?

6. Attend a sporting event and observe one player during play, on the bench, and after the game. Record all gestures, signs of emotion, and actions. Afterwards, write a descriptive lead for a profile on the player.

7. Observe someone with a technical skill, such as a bread-baker, an interpreter for the deaf, a dentist, or a plumber. Write a one-paragraph description of the process you observed, making it easy to understand.

8. The following description is from a profile of Lieutenant Colonel Robert O. Sinclair, commander of the Thirteenth Marine Expeditionary Unit of Camp Pendleton, California. Look carefully at the way the writer, Mike Sager, uses the present tense to pull the reader into the scene. Note the way he uses repetitive sentence structure, verb choice, and sensory detail and the way he emphasizes the details of the description with explanation.

His pale-blue eyes are bloodshot from lack of sleep. His face is camouflaged with stripes and splotches of greasepaint—green, brown, and black to match his woodland-style utilities, fifty-six dollars a set, worn in the field without skivvies underneath, a personal wardrobe preference known as going commando. Atop his Kevlar helmet rides a pair of goggles sheathed in an old sock. Around his neck hangs a heavy pair of rubberized binoculars. From his left hip dangles an olive-drab pouch. With every step, the pouch swings and hits his thigh, adding another faint, percussive thunk to the quiet symphony of his gear, the total weight of which is not taught and seldom discussed. Inside the pouch is a gas mask for NBC attacks—nuclear, biological, or chemical weapons. Following an attack, when field gauges show the air to be safe once again for breathing, regulations call for the senior Marine to choose one man to remove his mask and hood. After ten minutes, if the man shows no ill effects, the rest of the Marines can begin removing theirs.

—Mike Sager, "The Marine"

Choose someone to describe. Write a one-paragraph description, imitating Sager's style. Use similar sentence structures, details, and combination of description with explanation.

9. Choose one of the paintings or photographs that create visual profiles in this chapter, and write a paragraph translating what you see into descriptive language.

Peer-Editing Log

As you work with a writing partner or in a peer-editing group, you can use these questions to give helpful responses to a classmate's profile and as a guide for discussion.

Writer's Name _____

Date _____

1. Bracket the lead of this profile. What kind of lead is it? Could the profile start with a more interesting scene, anecdote, or generalization, perhaps one found later in the piece?

2. Underline the nut graf. Does the nut come too early or late in the profile? Judge this by asking whether the lead has set up the nut sufficiently. Does the focus seem like a natural extension of the opening? Does it seem artificially tacked on? Can the wording be more specific?

3. Is the nut graf a good overview of the story? Does it deliver everything it promises? Point out places where the writer refers to the idea in the nut, reinforcing and developing the thesis as the profile progresses. Locate any missed opportunities to remind the reader of the focus of the profile.

4. Look at the way the profile is organized. Make a quick outline of the profile's structure. What might strengthen the organization?

5. Circle major transitions between sections. Do the sections have good transitions? Do the narrative sections tie in with the factual, expository ones?

6. Does the story show and tell? Identify places where the writer uses description, anecdotes, examples, and facts. Does the profile need more of these elements to illustrate the generalizations made in the paragraphs?

7. What is the major impression you get of the profile subject? What details lead you to this impression? Could the writer insert more description, anecdotes, or character-in-action scenes to reveal character?

8. Annotate the sources the writer integrates into the profile by marking the places the writer uses direct observation (DO), interviews from the subject and about the subject (I), and print or electronic sources (PS or ES). Could the profile use another source or two? Are there good quotations from reliable sources? Is the attribution clear?

9. Does the profile achieve a sense of balance? Does it have quotations from enough sources to create multiple perspectives of the subject? If the subject is being praised, are there enough illustrations, quotations, and evidence to support this praise?

10. Bracket the conclusion. Does the profile end with a memorable image? Is there a way to strengthen the conclusion?

Revision Checklist

As you do your final revision, check to make sure that you

❑ Wrote an engaging lead

❑ Announced your thesis in a clear nut graf or in the deck

❑ Created a major impression of your profile subject

❑ Used some or all of the typical profile elements to add color, interest, and depth
  • Physical description
  • Quotations from the subject
  • Quotations about the subject
  • Examples
  • Anecdotes
  • Factual information

❑ Created a multifaceted portrait by using different perspectives from your sources

❑ Clearly attributed research from direct observation, interviews, and print and electronic sources

❑ Limited or eliminated the use of the first-person (I)

❑ Provided clear transitions for your reader

❑ Concluded memorably, perhaps with a lingering image of your subject

13. RESEARCH ARTICLES

ANALYZING TRENDS

It is a capital mistake to theorize before one has data.

—Sir Arthur Conan Doyle

Some trends are more visible and long-lasting than others.

RESEARCH ARTICLES

In 1995 a Harvard researcher named Robert Putnam became famous for asking this question: why do people bowl alone? The question, based on Putnam's research into the decline of bowling leagues—down 40 percent between 1980 and 1993—led to his overnight fame. He was invited to Camp David to consult with then-president Bill Clinton; senators quoted him in speeches; his picture appeared in *People* magazine. Putnam's statistics about how people are less likely to bowl in leagues, go to PTA meetings, and go on picnics reveal trends in a changing society that, he says, show how people have become disconnected from family and community. For Putnam, bowling leagues are a metaphor for communities in decline. As Putnam said in an interview with National Public Radio, "People watch *Friends* on TV—they don't have them." What brought overnight acclaim was Putnam's use of statistics to prove what some had already suspected: during the second half of the twentieth century, people in the United States have become increasingly alienated from one another.

Putnam's book, *Bowling Alone: The Collapse and Revival of American Community*, became a best-seller as thousands of readers were drawn to his explanations of causes and effects of social trends in America. His inquiry started with a hunch he had about membership in clubs. A conversation with a friend who owned a bowling alley confirmed Putnam's suspicion: membership in bowling leagues was down by nearly half, jeopardizing the bowling industry. League members, his friend said, eat three times more pizza and drink three times more beer than do solo bowlers, and the money is "in the pizza and beer, not in the shoes and balls."

Putnam's use of statistics to document trends in civic life in the United States is at the heart of what appeals to readers about his book. People like thinking and talking about trends—where patterns of behavior originate and what they imply about the future. The use of statistics gives us concrete evidence on which to base our thinking about trends. Economists, biologists, sociologists, teachers, and writers in diverse fields explore patterns in behavior and interpret the meaning of trends. Each discipline finds a different line of inquiry. Given a common starting point, such as "More girls than ever are playing competitive sports," writers from different fields will arrive at many different theories. A social scientist might focus on the connection between playing sports and higher self-esteem. A medical reporter might trace the increase of injuries to women or the benefits to their overall health. A sports writer might look at how competitive sports have been changed by the wave of female competitors. Each of these writers will take a different path into the subject and arrive at a theory connected to the trend. Each will gather research from many sources to back up the theory.

Applications: School, Community, Workplace

You research, analyze, and write about trends for a wide range of classes. In examining and analyzing social, scientific, and psychological trends, your research allows you to see academic theories in action in the world, both currently and historically. By looking at consumer patterns, for example, you will be able to see business and marketing principles in action. Studying statistics about housing could help you form your own theory about social change in a region. Students often propose such papers as senior theses in history, sociology, psychology, education, and literature. Because identifying trends helps explain and predict patterns, you will find many ways to use the skills involved in explaining patterns of behavior outside of school. Close to home, community activism begins with gathering good data to support an argument. A neighborhood group would be interested in crime statistics, for example, and in determining whether their increase or decrease is related to a change in the community.

Knowing how to use data to speculate about causes and effects will help you frame arguments on behalf of an advocacy group to an audience of policymakers. Whether you are lobbying for more school art programs, less pesticide use, or increased spending for health care, your argument will be based on explaining causes and effects of trends. On the job, you will try to understand patterns in behavior in many fields. A demographer or statistical analyst might make a whole career out of researching trends to help explain behavior. If you work in marketing or sales, you will measure trends and use them to measure progress or predict growth. Politicians use surveys and polls to measure trends in public opinion. Educators look for the causes and effects of trends among students. Medical practitioners and insurance underwriters assess risk by looking at causes and effects. In fact, most fields involve thinking about what lies beneath patterns and trying to make them more predictable and useful.

CHAPTER OBJECTIVES

In this chapter you will learn to
▶ write a thesis that presents a trend
▶ analyze and explain the causes and effects of the trend
▶ research a trend by using statistics, facts, and expert opinion

UNDERSTANDING TRENDS

To identify a trend, look for a pattern in culture or in nature, and note any change in the usual pattern. For example, you may have read that the flu hit one town particularly hard, with more cases occurring there than anywhere else. Or, perhaps, more people than ever report incomes under the poverty line in rural areas of your state. Or, young men no longer make up the majority of identified compulsive gamblers; elderly women problem gamblers are suddenly most numerous. Each of these represents a trend, or a change in an expected pattern.

Some trends involve patterns of behavior that have been documented for hundreds or even thousands of years. People throughout time and in many cultures have exhibited eating disorders, for example. If you want to see whether anorexia is a trend, ask some questions and do some research to find out whether more people—or fewer people—are considered anorexic now than at another time. Is a different category of people involved now? Does society or science view anorexia in a new or different way; if so, how? You might be able to pinpoint a trend if you discover a significant increase in the number of people or a difference in the type of person treated for this disorder, or you might find a new trend in the way anorexia is being treated.

You can also begin to identify trends by reading news stories, talking to people, watching television, and listening to the radio. Your town's recent decision to make one night of the week a family night could be the beginning of a trend: life has gotten so stressful and fast-paced that family members do not spend time together. You can ask: Is this true only in my town, or is it part of a larger pattern? Perhaps it is just a fad, and not worth lengthy analysis. To figure out whether something is a trend, you can ask some questions.

▶ Is this one isolated case, or does it fit into a pattern?

▶ Are there noteworthy increases or decreases in its occurrence?

▶ Are significant causes driving this change?

▶ Are there significant effects of this change?

Identifying Causes and Effects

To develop your trend analysis, you need to look at the causes and effects of the trend. Readers want to understand what caused the trend and whether the effects on daily life, society, or the world will be negative or positive. With this kind of analysis, readers can both understand the trend and also be prepared for its fallout or its beneficial effects.

Is there an upswing in hard-core gambling among young men? Why? Bella English, whose article "Old Game, New Players" explores hard-core gambling among young people, says that one major cause is the "prevalence of legalized gambling in society." She gives examples: "Pass any grocery store or gas station and you will see lottery tickets on sale. . . . Television brings you the lucky numbers. It's not unusual for parents and grandparents to buy even the youngest children scratch tickets for their birthdays or Christmas." English cites bingo nights, the publication of point spreads in the sports' sections of daily newspapers, casinos, and track and Internet betting as examples of how widespread gambling is. She speculates that these causes have resulted in a "gambling culture."

In some cases, the effects of a trend are not yet known. The fact that fewer new doctors are choosing to become surgeons might lend itself to looking for causes. The effects, other than the obvious effect of having fewer surgeons, are still unclear. Will this trend eventually lead to less selectivity in the field and therefore surgeons who are less qualified? Will the cost of surgery increase? Will illnesses have to be more severe before surgery becomes an option? Though these implications are logical, they are also highly speculative. No proof exists for them yet. The trend is well documented, but it is still too recent to have clear-cut effects. It might be more worthwhile and more feasible to explore the reasons why young doctors are not going into surgery.

The decision to focus on cause, on effect, or on both is usually driven by the type of trend you are writing about and the kind of information you unearth in your research.

RESEARCH PATHS

To prove a trend exists and to be able to speculate about causes, you will be collecting materials online, in the library, and in interviews. Here are some suggestions on how to go about researching this assignment.

Keeping Track of Your Research

Researching trends will involve many sources. While taking notes, always keep track of your research path. Do not wait to see whether you will use the source in your writing. Instead, while you are in the early steps of reading and note taking, make photocopies of your sources, and print anything you discover on the Web. This kind of attention will make your work easier if you need to retrace your steps to get more information.

For each source you examine, make note of the following information:

❯ Author
❯ Article or chapter title
❯ Full journal name or book title
❯ Date and place of publication
❯ Page number(s)
❯ For websites, full URL and date

Practice 13.2
Causes or Effects?

For two or three of the following trends, make a list of causes and effects you might explore. Decide whether you would choose to write an article about causes, effects, or both. Explain your reasoning.

• Single mothers
• Women clergy
• Internet dating
• Extreme sports
• Stay-at-home fathers
• Teen cell-phone and pager use

How Graphs Explain

Step 1: Analyze one of the graphs or charts on pages 482–484 in this chapter, and write a three-sentence critique, answering the following questions.

1. What is the main point of the graph?

2. How clear is the information?

3. Do the illustration and design help you understand the information, or do they get in your way? How? Explain.

Step 2: Create a poll or survey, and administer it to classmates and friends. Report your findings in the form of an informational graph or chart. Use color and illustration to make it as visually appealing as possible.

Step 3: Critique each other's graphs or charts using the three questions in step 1.

Brainstorming

Your work for this assignment might begin with a hunch. In talking about *Bowling Alone*, Robert Putnam says his idea about the disintegration of community blossomed during a conversation at a fundraising event. He knew that membership in the Boy Scouts, the Red Cross, and even the PTA was down, but the owner of a chain of bowling alleys brought the bigger picture into perspective. People weren't only dropping out of public service; they were also not showing up for league bowling, which was cutting deeply into the bottom line at bowling alleys. It wasn't just a problem for "do-gooder organizations," as Putnam puts it.

Once you have a hunch about a trend—more of your friends and acquaintances seem to be avoiding meat or are buying lottery tickets—you can explore the general topics of vegetarianism or gambling, in these cases. Browse through books or articles, or search the Internet to find recent studies or new thinking on the topic. Like Putnam, you might explore topics through conversations. Have your friends noted these changes? What do they think might be the causes and effects?

Large libraries have many versions of searchable databases, like Info-Trac, that list books, periodicals, and newspaper articles in one central place. Your library may also have search tools on CD-ROM. Doing subject searches to browse through these databases can help you find many different aspects of your topic. Though some databases include the full text, you will also find many citations that will send you to the periodicals themselves or to microfilm or microfiche to find the full articles. Even though this kind of research may require extra steps, it can provide sources you might not have access to any other way. For more information on research see Chapter 14.

Your reading and thinking about gambling, for example, might lead you to topics that are related to gambling but branch off from it. You might be-

A change in the number of elderly women who are compulsive gamblers may represent a trend—a change in an expected pattern.

come interested in the effects of legalized gambling on a certain place: Do casinos help or hurt a particular region? You can consider the economy, and how workers have been affected. You could consult people employed by the casinos. You also might want to think about how the crime rate has changed and ask the police about how the area was before and after the casino opened. As you talk to people employed by casinos, you might find that although they have better-paying jobs, their property values have gone down. You might discover that people do not want to buy houses in a town with a casino. Chances are that you would not have made this connection before you did some research. As you investigate your topic, the focus of your article will begin to take shape.

Cause and Effect and Logical Thinking

Confusing Cause and Effect: The Post Hoc Fallacy

Walking under a ladder causes bad luck. So does letting a black cat cross your path, breaking a mirror, and spilling salt. Dropping a glass means that company is coming. Finding a four-leaf clover brings good luck. These superstitions are all based on the faulty assumption that because two events happen sequentially, the first has caused the second. You can see how the superstitions may have arisen: people walk under ladders at a building site and perhaps occasionally bricks fall on their heads, or company seems to arrive just when you've dropped the crystal. One coincidence leads to a generalization, but in fact one event does not necessarily mean that the second will follow. Statisticians phrase it this way: correlation does not prove causation. Logicians use the Latin phrase *post hoc, ergo propter hoc,* meaning "after this, therefore because of this," to describe this error in reasoning. When you write about causes and effects, be careful to avoid this fallacy.

Assigning Singular Cause

If you have determined a cause-and-effect relationship between two events, do not assume that any one cause is the only cause. Sometimes a cause can be one of many; and other causes may be hidden or more significant. For example, if you are looking at the growing problem of obesity among children, you might assume that the cause is the decrease in physical activity among children. You know that one reason for weight gain is burning fewer calories, so inactivity could certainly be a cause of obesity. However, there are enough skinny couch potatoes around to make you look for other causes as well. A slow or malfunctioning metabolism might cause weight gain; calorie-laden fast-food can cause weight gain; genetics may play a part. The causes of obesity are multiple and complex.

Gathering Material That Proves the Trend Exists

You must prove to your readers not only that the trend exists, but also that its scope, scale, or implications are significant. You do this by finding the research and the most recent studies on the topic. Then you draw your conclusions. Focusing on the trend of teen gambling, writer Bella English cites studies, for example, by Harvard University psychologist Howard Shaffer.

> What is new and troubling is the number of young people like Christopher who have become hard-core gamblers. A recent analysis by Shaffer shows that the rate of problem gambling among youths nationwide is more than double that of adults. Of the teenagers who gamble, nearly 10 percent will have a serious problem with it, compared with about 4 percent of adults.
>
> In Massachusetts—with its popular lotteries and tracks and with casinos in nearby states—5 percent of the adult population or about 250,000 people have gambling problems, although only about 2 percent are defined as "compulsive gamblers." Men are more likely to have trouble than women, but with the advent of readily accessible games like the lottery and Powerball, the gender gap is closing. Among the state's adolescents, 12 to 15 percent suffer from problem gambling,

according to the Massachusetts Council on Compulsive Gambling.

—Bella English, "Old Game, New Players"

The writer makes a clear and compelling case for the existence of the trend by using statistics from the Massachusetts agency on compulsive gambling. Her use of statistics and the comparison to the number of adult gamblers show the scale and scope of the problem among young people. The conclusion she draws from this research seems well supported: young people make up a new group of hard-core gamblers.

Where to Research

Researching a trend involves all research paths and both primary and secondary sources. Chapter 14 details many aspects of the research process and includes tips on how to take notes and evaluate sources.

Library Research   Books can be sources of background material, but to be helpful with trends, they need to have recent publication dates. Other resources in the library are indexes; full texts of journal, magazine, and newspaper articles on microfilm or microfiche; and census information.

Internet Search Engines and Directories   You will find much current information by using directories and search engines on the World

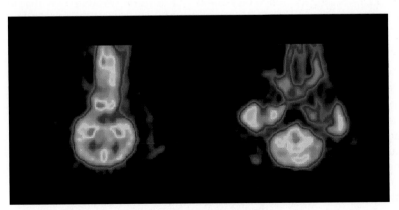

An image of a baboon brain scan shows the effect (red area) of an inhaled substance, toluene. Inhalant abuse is a rapidly growing trend among young people.

Practice 13.3
Working with Statistics

1. The following data from the National Center for Health Statistics suggest several trends. If you encountered these statistics, what conclusions could you draw? What is the implied pattern? Write a sentence stating each trend you identify.

- The average number of children born to women over a lifetime in 2000: 2.1. (2.1 is considered the replacement level for the population.)
- The average number of children born to women over a lifetime during most of the 1970s and 1980s: fewer than 2.
- Birthrate for teenagers age fifteen to nineteen in 2000: 48.5 births per 1,000 females.
- Birthrate for teenagers age fifteen to nineteen in 1991: 62.1 per 1,000 females.

—National Center for Health Statistics, News Release

2. Next, work with one of the trend you have identified.

 a. Make a list of causes you suspect might be behind this trend.

 b. What might be the results? List your speculations about the effects.

 c. How would you check out your theories about causes and effects?

Wide Web, which makes them good choices for researching current trends. Not all Web material is equally useful or accurate, so carefully evaluate Web sources. Use the checklist on pages 555–557 to evaluate webpages for authority, currency, and bias.

The U.S. government's official website at http://www.FirstGov.gov is a portal that leads you to census data, studies, and other sources of statistical information that can be useful in writing about trends. Any state's depart-

SIDEBAR

Reading Statistics with a Critical Eye

Statistics can be used or misused, depending on how ethical a writer is. Statistics might be distorted to understate or overstate a trend. For example, you might read that 50 percent of the police officers in a small town in Ohio were killed on the job last year. That rate is up 100 percent from the year before. The implication is that this is a dangerous town with a steeply climbing crime rate. The fact of the matter is that the town had two officers, and one was killed while helping a motorist change a tire. While it is true and unfortunate that one of the two officers was killed last year, it is misleading to say that 50 percent of the force was killed on the job last year.

Statistics, even those that are factual, are not always accurate without a clear context. You must be careful not to use every statistic you find without evaluating it and its source. You must also be careful to use statistics responsibly.

Here is an example of a statistic that needs a full explanation.

The United States Fire Administration (USFA) announced today that 441 firefighters died while on-duty in the United States in 2001. This total, which is more than four and one-half times the average annual number of firefighter deaths for the last decade, includes 343 firefighters lost at the World Trade Center on September 11. The loss represents the worst total since the USFA began tracking firefighter fatalities in 1977. USFA is a part of the Federal Emergency Management Agency. "2001 was a tragic year for America's fire service," R. David Paulson, United States Fire Administrator, said.

"In addition to the many local heroes who died serving their communities nationwide, the eyes of the world turned to New York City on September 11."

—United States Fire Administration, Press Release

Numbers can also underplay a trend. It does not seem noteworthy to report that twenty students from the University of Cincinnati will spend spring break building houses with Habitat for Humanity. But if you find out that six hundred students from all over Ohio are building houses for the poor, as compared with two hundred last year, the numbers start to build a full and reliable picture of a trend.

Numbers can be translated to obscure information or to be more useful to readers. You can say that in 1999 there were 47,895 accounting majors at colleges nationwide. This seems like a lot of prospective accountants. Still, there were 13,325 fewer accounting majors in 1999 than there were in 1995. In context, this statistic can be even more accessible to readers.

Some industry specialists say interest in accounting careers has waned on campuses even though demand remains relatively strong. According to a 2001 study commissioned by the American Institute of Certified Public Accountants, the number of college students choosing an accounting major dropped more than 21 percent from a high of 61,220 in the 1994–95 school year to 47,895 for 1998–99, the most recent year for which figures are available.

—Barbara Claire Kasselmann, "More Than Debits, Credits"

ment of public health can offer reliable information as well. In general, the most reliable, unbiased sources of statistical information are .gov and .edu sites.

Internet Databases Databases that are available on a subscription basis provide excellent material not usually available on the free Web. Databases like LexisNexis, Proquest, and InfoTrac, which are described in more detail in Chapter 14, may be available to you because your library has paid a fee. You gain entry by logging on through your library or by using a password.

Practice 13.4   Using Statistics

Write two generalizations based on statistics—using data from Figure 13.1, Figure 13.2, Figure 13.3, and Figure 13.4.

FIGURE 13.1

Map showing adults and children living with HIV/AIDS and showing three main modes of transmission, 2002

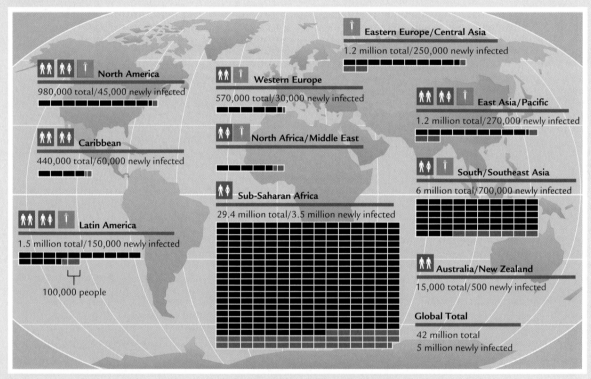

Source: Bryan Strong, Christine DeVault, Barbara W. Sayad, and William L. Yarber, *Human Sexuality: Diversity in Contemporary America* (5th ed.) (New York: McGraw-Hill, 2005, p. 577) (based on data from Joint United Nations Programme on HIV/AIDS [UNAIDS] and World Health Organization, 2002).

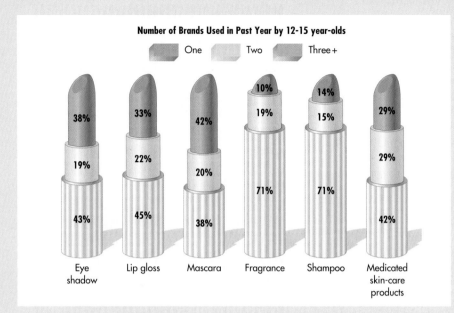

FIGURE 13.2
Pictograph showing teen product loyalty, United States, 1992

Source: Data from "Those Precious Thirteen-Year-Olds," *Brandweek*, January 25, 1993, p. 13, as presented in Wayne D. Hoyer and Deborah J. MacInnis, *Consumer Behavior*, 3rd ed. (Boston: Houghton Mifflin, 2006), p. 361.

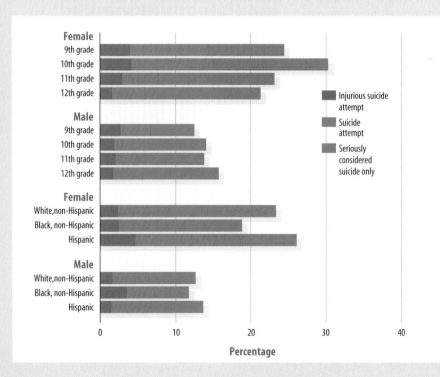

FIGURE 13.3
Bar graph showing suicide rates in grades 9 through 12, United States, 1999

Note: Response is for the twelve months preceding the survey. Among students who attempted suicide, 6 percent did not report seriously considering suicide.

Source: Data from Centers for Disease Control and Prevention, National Center for Chronic Disease Prevention and Health Promotion, National Youth Risk Behavior Survey (YRBS).

FIGURE 13.4 Graphic and copy memorializing American casualties in Iraq

A Thousand Lives by Thomas Starr

Each time a milestone of America's war dead is reached in Iraq, the appropriate number of photographic portraits is published to illustrate the cumulative loss of life.

While it is a fitting memorial to see these Americans as they were, the portraits contradict the concept of death. Viewers are reminded more of a page from a yearbook than the documentation of a tragedy.

In colonial Massachusetts, photographic portraits were not an option, but war deaths were still reported visually: with the simple silhouette of a coffin for each casualty.

Captions identified the otherwise identical images. Visually, it was less personal, but in content it was more to the point. This tradition continued into the twentieth century with photographs of flag-draped coffins returning to American soil. In the war in Iraq, however, such images have been censored.

Today, when confronted with photographs of 1,000 casualties in Iraq, we don't question why we are shown vitality when the words indicate the opposite. We understand—on an intellectual level. But on an emotional level—the level on which images operate—the pictures cancel out the words.

Perhaps this is why photojournalists are no longer allowed to depict the coffins of our returning war dead. Faces belie coffins.

Source: Boston Globe, September 14, 2004.

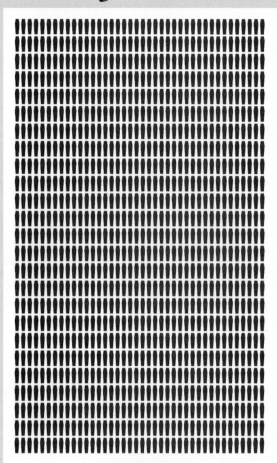

Interviews

Interviewing is an important part of making your trend research original. Through interviews, you gather quotations that help ground your research and give it context. Quotations can help enliven facts and statistics.

Consulting Experts Experts are people who work in relevant fields and have a deep knowledge of the subject of your trend analysis. Doctors, researchers, and authors of books make good sources and can provide excellent primary source material, making your paper more original than if you relied only on published sources.

Consulting Practitioners Practitioners—people who have experienced or observed the trend or who personify it—are also experts. They help make the trend relevant and give it a human side. For some tips on interviewing, refer to pages 426–429 in Chapter 12 and pages 550–553 in Chapter 14.

ANATOMY OF A TREND ANALYSIS

Weaving together multiple sources for a research paper involves making sure you have a strong focus and that you use transitions to connect all the pieces. Your pieces must flow logically as you build your analysis. The four basic elements of a trend analysis are

- Thesis
- Introduction
- Body
- Conclusion

Male Call on Campus:
Enrollment Trends Widen Gender Gap, Upset Social Scene

DAVID ABEL

There were more men on the dance floor than usual. But not enough. As Sheila Erimez slipped on her high heels, the beat of salsa beckoning her, she watched as some women in Boston University's ballroom dance club reluctantly decided to dance the sensuous samba with one another. Others resorted to taking turns with the available men.

Narrative introduction that captures interest and puts the reader into a scene

"There just aren't enough guys to go around," said Erimez, a slender blond junior majoring in English. "They're dropping off like flies. Wherever you go on campus, there are more girls than guys."

The 20-year-old and her friends were griping about an increasingly depressing fact of life for many women at colleges throughout the country: Today less than 45 percent of US undergraduates are men, down from 55 percent in 1970, according to national surveys. Utah is now the only state with more men than women in college. Last year, women accounted for 56 percent of all students at colleges in Massachusetts.

Thesis
Statement of the trend
Statistical proof that the trend exists

The gender gap is particularly pronounced at Boston University, where women now account for 61 percent of the total undergraduate student body. Women dominate classes and student government. Theater troupes are des-

Introduction

perate for male actors, and men are so scarce that women often outnumber them at that once all-male bastion, the gym.

Thesis with statistics

The increasing dominance of female students in American higher education is particularly striking because they represent just 49 percent of the population between ages 18 and 24.

Transition

Possible causes

To explain the trend, some argue that boys have fewer role models and are falling behind as girls are given more attention in school. Others believe that the changing ratio is more a reflection of greater numbers of older women returning to college.

Possible causes

Transition

At BU, the theories include the school's abandonment of its varsity football and baseball teams, the university marketing itself as a "safe, urban school," and the popularity of its many study-abroad programs with women.

Quote from an expert in the field

"We really don't know why this is happening," said Kelly Walter, director of admissions at BU. "It concerns us in that ideally it should be 50 percent men and 50 percent women. But we're not planning on making it easier for men to get in. That would be illegal. We're most concerned with enrolling those students who are most academically qualified."

Transition

Whatever the cause, women have been extending their majority over men at BU since the late 1980s. This year, women account for 62 percent of the freshman class, and school officials expect the gap may widen over the next few years.

The disparity is even greater at some of the university's undergraduate schools. In the College of Arts and Sciences, BU's largest school, 67 percent of freshmen are women; in the College of Communication, 69 percent of freshmen are women, and in Sargent College of Health and Rehabilitation Sciences, 83 percent of freshmen are women.

Body

The imbalance has long piqued women at BU, but, each fall, freshman women who expected a more balanced social scene are particularly bitter.

Quotation from a "practitioner"—someone who is involved in the trend

"It pains me; it's very hard to meet guys," said Amy Horowitz, 18, a freshman, while dining in a female-dominated dinner crowd at the university's student union. "If I knew this before coming here, it definitely would have factored into my decision. I guess I feel a little gypped."

Secondary source—a report

Comment on the seriousness of the trend

A recent study by the American Council on Education suggests that talk of a male crisis in higher education is overblown. Men still predominate in doctoral, professional, and master's programs such as business and engineering. They also continue to maintain a majority, if slimmer than ever before, at top schools such as Harvard and the Massachusetts Institute of Technology.

One of the main (reasons) for the uptick, the report says, is that more minority women than men are going to college.

Cause

"We can't get distracted by talk of broad problems," said Jacqueline King,
the report's author and director of ACE's Center for Policy Analysis. "We do
have pockets of real concern. The gaps are biggest between the racial gaps.
For African-American men, for example, it's not cool to look smart, and so
many have little interest in college."

Quotation from an expert

Tom Mortenson, a senior scholar at the Center of the Study of Opportunity in Higher Education, disagrees.

Another expert

ansition (While he acknowledges concern over minorities,) he said he believes there's
a larger problem for all men—and that it's only getting worse. His evidence: 54
percent of all bachelor's degrees went to white men in 1977; 20 years later,
men are getting less than 45 percent. By the end of this decade, he believes,
the number will drop to 40 percent.

"What this reflects is that schools and family circumstances are not helping
boys enough," he said. "The problem is boys don't have enough adult male
role models, and that our increasingly urbanized world caters less to men than
it used to."

Discussing causes

The problem of declining male enrollments has even sparked talk of affirmative action for men. At a recent meeting of the National Association for
College Admission Counseling, the issue was front and center. At one panel
meeting, academics explored the topic "Are Our Boys at Risk?" while another
session was called "Where Have All the Men Gone?"

An effect

ody Although male affirmative action is still little more than a hypothetical for
academics to mull at conferences, it's a concept some students at BU find appealing.

It's not rare there for large introductory classes in psychology or political
science to be two-thirds women. Men are outnumbered by nearly 2 to 1 on
the main student governing body, the executive board, and both the president
and vice president are women. And to fill the gap on the social scene, parties
often include students from other schools.

Effects

Of course, not everyone considers the unequal ratio a problem. On a recent night at the Sargent gym, Chris Szczerban was sweating on a stationary
bicycle, the only guy in a room filled with women trudging along on other exercise equipment.

"I went to an all-guys high school," the 19-year-old sophomore said. "I
would say this is definitely a good thing."

*Effects as seen by a
practitioner*

Effects as seen by a practitioner

Body

Effects

Speculation by an expert about possible effects

Effects

Back to narrative scene—a narrative frame

Conclusion

Ends with quotation

And while straight women may complain, the lesbian culture is thriving, said Emily Lyman, 20, a junior who is president of Spectrum, BU's gay and lesbian group. "It's not hard for a lesbian to get a date here," she said.

Many professors also see the influx of women as a benefit. For Richard Ely, who teaches Introduction to Psychology, a large class where it is easy to count the men, women play "a civilizing role."

"There is certainly far less of a macho, testosterone atmosphere," he said. "For teaching, it's particularly good and allows you to try new things and raise controversial views. I might feel less comfortable doing that in a class 75 percent men."

The lack of machismo has other perks, too. According to Herb Ross, BU's associate dean of students, the incidence of violence and other disturbances in student dorms has decreased as the ratio of women has increased.

Still, for most, the problems of the gender gap outweigh the benefits.

For instance, film major Pierluigi Cothran last week posted fliers in the theater school, desperately beseeching: "Male Actor Needed for Student Film." As much as the 20-year-old junior has looked, he hasn't had any luck.

"No one has responded at all," he said. "It's just really hard to find guys at this school."

As the salsa music throbbed earlier this week below the student union, Erimez and a group of other well-dressed women watched forlornly as more women filed into the dance hall. One told a story of having to compete with another woman in a ballroom dancing competition last year. Another complained about how many of the men on campus are homosexuals, or jocks uninterested in dancing with women.

"I just wish I had a partner," she said. "I don't want to look ridiculous dancing with another woman again."

Thesis

Your research will help you formulate your thesis, which is your answer to the question: What is your point? In a feature, as in a profile, your thesis often appears early, after the introductory paragraph(s), and it is rarely the first sentence. The thesis, which is usually a sentence or two, is important because the focus of your whole trend analysis is located there. Readers expect a clear, direct statement of the main point that they can easily follow. In "Male Call on Campus," the thesis statement extends over several sentences and provides proof the trend exists.

Today less than 45 percent of US undergraduates are men, down from 55 percent in 1970, according to national surveys. . . . The increasing dominance of female students in American higher education is particularly striking because they represent just 49 percent of the population between ages 18 and 24.

The thesis discloses the trend and its context, proving its noteworthiness. If the population had more women than men, the trend of more women attending college would not be as significant. But since men outnumber women in the college-age bracket, why the men aren't attending college in the same numbers as women is a mystery that requires explanation.

Your thesis might give an overview of the trend before you prove it exists, as does this one from an article about young Republicans.

At campuses across the country, undergraduates like Charles Mitchell have organized for an assault against the university establishment not seen since the 1980s when Reagan's popularity triggered a youthquake of conservative campus activism. Today's surge reflects a renewed shift pronouncedly to the right on many defining issues, after several years during the Clinton presidency when students gravitated toward more liberal political labels.

—John Colapinto, "The Young Republicans"

Introduction

Though the thesis is the main point of the article, writers do not start with it. A good introduction attracts your reader into the story and to the thesis. Most trend feature introductions fall into one of two categories: exposition (an explanation of the topic) or narration (a story that creates a scene introducing the topic).

Expository Introduction

An expository beginning can use any one of a number of techniques to explain the topic in a way that engages the reader. You can define the terms, begin with a compelling analogy or metaphor, or offer a fact or statistic.

Perhaps the most ironic aspect of the struggle for survival is how easily organisms can be harmed by that which they desire. The trout is caught by the fisherman's lure, the mouse by cheese. But at least those creatures have the excuse that bait and cheese look like sustenance. Humans seldom have that consolation. The temptations that can disrupt their lives are often pure indulgences. No one has to drink alcohol, for example. Realizing when a diversion has gotten out of control is one of the great challenges of life.

—Robert Kubey and Mihaly Csikszentmihalyi, "Television Addiction Is No Mere Metaphor"

Practice 13.5
Write an Outline

Outline "Male Call on Campus."

Narrative Introduction

Narrative beginnings ease the reader into the topic, often by describing a setting, quoting a character in the story, or telling a short anecdote. "Male Call on Campus" begins with a narrative about a ballroom dance class. The writer steps away from the narrative and into exposition in paragraph 4.

Body

After attracting the reader's attention with an introduction and a thesis that reveals that the trend is worthy of examination, your article can take one of several directions. In considering the trend you choose to write about, you will decide to analyze the causes, the effects, or both. By the time you begin writing the body of your article, you should have made a decision about where your emphasis lies.

Once you decide on the emphasis, you can find a structure that best showcases your approach. Here is one organization for an analysis that focuses on causes and effects.

Part 1: Define the trend and prove it exists.
Part 2: Discuss causes.
Part 3: Discuss effects.

You might decide to explore only causes or only effects of a trend. You might organize your analysis chronologically, listing causes or effects in the time sequence they occurred, starting with the earliest and ending with the most recent. Or you might organize it in order of importance, with the most important causes or effects first, followed by the next most important, and so on. Here, for example, is an outline of causes for the decline in the worldwide frog population. The writer organizes the trend analysis around the causes listed in order of significance.

I.   Introduction to the trend: Frogs are dying off worldwide
     A. Cause: Destruction of habitats
II. Habitats necessary for reproduction and protection
     A. Cause: Climate change and pollution
     B. Cause: Decreasing air moisture
III. Pollutants easily absorbed by the skin of frog
     A. Cause: Disease
IV. Conclusion: Why is the trend significant? Frogs are seen as an
     "indicator species," reflecting the health of the planet in general.

In "Male Call on Campus," the writer shifts from narrative into talking about effects and causes. He begins the body by stating, "To explain the trend . . . ." He speculates about causes, including lack of role models and racial gaps, but spends much of the article discussing effects, which are both positive and negative. The writer explains a new point, uses quotations to comment on it, and moves on to the next new point. Alternating between points and quotations provides a sense of perspective. Sources include students involved in the trend and experts who have studied or observed it. What binds the points and quotations—and any shifts from explaining causes to explaining effects—are good transitions that show movement from one idea to another. (See the Sidebar for more on transitions.)

Conclusion

You want to leave your reader with a sense of conclusion as well as a sense of continuation. In other words, you want to bring home your main point, and you want your reader to continue to ponder your ideas. End with an image or quotation that leaves the reader with something to think about.

One technique writers often use is returning to an image or narrative from the opening. "Male Call on Campus" ends with the same ballroom dance class it begins with, plus a quotation that makes memorable the trend of decreasing numbers of males on college campuses.

Transitions

SIDEBAR

Feature articles that explore the causes and effects of trends are complicated pieces of writing. You have to be especially careful not to confuse your reader as you navigate from section to section—from identifying the trend, to proving it exists, to looking at causes and/or effects. You also have to chart a clear course within the sections as you integrate your research, moving between a generalization and its supporting facts, statistics, and quotations.

Stated Transitions

Transitions alert your reader to a change in topic. Stated transitions have specific functions. Here are some of the most common ones.

- Showing chronology (*first, before, later, after*)
- Showing comparisons (*likewise, in this case*)
- Showing contrast (*on the other hand, however, but, although*)
- Showing cause and effect (*because, therefore, as a result*)
- Showing additional thoughts (*also, moreover, and*)
- Showing illustrations (*for example, so you see*)

A more subtle way to link ideas together as you move from paragraph to paragraph or section to section of your article is to echo key words or phrases. You would expect, for example, in a discussion of causes and effects, to use those words often, so as to keep your reader aware of when you are discussing causes and when effects. Although repeated use of a word often sends writers scurrying to their thesauruses, it is sometimes better to repeat the word itself than to risk confusion on the part of the reader.

Another way to provide clear transition is to restate the thesis. If you are looking at the trend of increased binge drinking on college campuses, keep your reader focused on that thesis. You can repeat the phrase "increased binge drinking on college campuses" or find a slight variation like "irresponsible drinking" that reminds the reader of your main point and helps create cohesion within the piece.

Implied Transitions

Transitions can be suggested or implied by the way you order your ideas within a paragraph or section. For example, if you order a section chronologically, spatially, or in order of importance, you set up a pattern in readers' minds; the transitions are, in effect, embedded in the structure.

Fraternities of the Future: Dry or Wet?

CAITLIN AUSTIN

(The names of all brothers have been changed to protect their identity.)

My feet stuck slightly to the hardwood floor as I entered the musty 6-story brownstone of fraternity Lambda Chi Alpha. The beer leftovers from a Friday night bash were strewn across the front hall, broken glass and railings dangling precariously from their original place. "Sorry about the mess," said Matt, my high school sweetheart, smiling as I entered tiptoeing over the debris. "We had a little party last night."

We cautiously made our way through the front hall, entering "Phirst Phront," the title displayed boldly above the door's entrance in different colored beer caps. We entered the dark room where I would be conducting my interviews. Empty six-packs draped the pipes above my head, and a small cat the brothers called "kitty" welcomed me with her dusty paws. Looking at the mess again, I questioned why anyone would want to live here. Matt laughed. "The parties here are worth the cleanup."

It was these notorious parties that had brought me to LCA's door. Reputed as the fraternity that drank the most on campus, this home had come to be known as "party central" to a large majority of University students, as well as a home to Matt, who now was a sophomore and brother within the house walls. Lambda Chi, home to 39 brothers, sits overlooking the water, a brownstone that 10 years ago was estimated as being worth over $12 million. I could still glimpse its paneled walls and historic mementos through the party ruin. "The house itself was enough to get me to join," Matt joked.

Beyond the architectural beauty of the Lambda Chi house, my own experiences there have lead me to believe that the party atmosphere plays a significant role in encouraging students to join, but it has also created a major problem for fraternities as well as for the brothers themselves.

Researchers investigating the use of alcohol among college students have concluded that fraternities help to foster a drinking atmosphere. For example, Harvard researcher Henry Wechsler found that students living in the Greek system were more likely than other students to say that drinking and partying are important college activities. Wechsler's research, which he details in *Dying to Drink: Confronting Binge Drinking on College Campuses*," includes facts, figures, and many personal stories about alcohol use on college campuses.

Wechsler found that brothers were twice as likely as other students to become binge drinkers in college.

"If you just want to hang out," says sophomore Eric, echoing Wechsler's findings, "drinking will play a role. The fraternity increases the amount you drink. It makes drinking what you do for fun."

In the case of LCA, alcohol has become a necessity for fun, making the purchase of up to ninety 30-packs of beer for just one party the norm. Many brothers, including Matt, will consume as many as 15 to 25 beers a night, two to three times a week.

But the hard partying has hurt the Greek system. A series of well-publicized deaths due to binge drinking at fraternities has created a public-relations problem for the groups. And the organizations also have faced a liability problem. In the 1980s, the National Association of Insurance Commissioners ranked fraternities and sororities as the sixth worst risk for insurers because of the rising number of lawsuits and insurance claims resulting from binge drinking and hazing. In response to the problem, eleven national and international fraternities now require most of their houses to be alcohol-free, or "dry," and discussions elsewhere are ongoing, according to an article in the *New York Times* magzine, "Ban of Brothers" (January 9, 2005).

But there is resistance on a lot of fronts. The brothers view their drinking as a necessary "stress release." Adam, a senior, downplays the problem and says, "It's just a regular thing to drink a lot in college."

Jeremy, the president of the LCA, theorizes that the more you drink in college the less you will when you leave. But Eric voices the justification you hear most often: "Everybody knows that too much alcohol is going to kill you or make you drunk. People know that. It's really about being responsible."

I was standing above Matt's shaking body when I realized LCA's concept of responsible drinking was flawed. He lay sprawled next to me, his body lifeless and cold, the whites of his eyes visible when his figure shook with seizures, pausing every few moments to vomit in the trashcan at his side. I was sure of it this time. He had drunk himself to death. Tightly grasping the phone in my hand, ready to dial 911, I waited throughout the night, watching my "responsible" and "in control" boyfriend struggle for his life. "Matt never drank a lot in high school," commented friend Joe. "He was not even close to being an excessive drinker." Things had changed.

In 1993, 337 people drank themselves to death, according to The National Institute on Alcohol Abuse and Alcoholism; Scott Kreuger, a freshman at

MIT, became a part of this trend in 1997, dying from alcohol poisoning, after losing consciousness at a fraternity party. Several hundreds of college students have died of alcohol poisoning since Kreuger's death. Louisiana State University student Benjamin Wayne consumed approximately 25 drinks and was found to have a blood alcohol level of 0.588, six times the legal limit. Since the deaths, charges have been filed holding both fraternities "responsible."

In response to the extensive liability risks that come with "wet" fraternities, many on-campus frats have chosen to turn in their drinking permits. In exchange they receive a new title and lifestyle, one that is commonly referred to as "dry." "Dry" fraternity brothers, unlike LCA, are not permitted to drink in their homes or on their property at all, or their charters will be revoked. Fraternities such as Phi Delta Theta provide alternatives to drinking that don't associate parties with alcohol, such as baseball games and non-alcoholic cookouts. Brothers within the fraternity say they feel no need to drink at all; in fact, 10 to 12 brothers, one-third of the house, abstain totally from alcohol. "There is more pressure to drink in a frat like LCA. Those frats have alcohol as their center. Here there is no pressure," commented sophomore Alex.

Although seemingly ideal, dry fraternities do have problems, and unsurprisingly the root cause behind them is alcohol, or rather the lack of it. Many of the brothers within Phi Delta Theta worry about the social scene. "There have been discussions of people wanting to leave. The fact that we cannot drink here scatters people on the weekends. It hurts the cohesion of the house," said freshman Brian. "Drinking, after all, is a big part of the social life in college."

Along with the social dilemmas, the very membership of dry fraternities is also affected by the lack of alcohol. Phi Delta Theta was able to entice only 9 freshman to join this fall, as opposed to the 16 who rushed LCA, a considerable difference. Pledges mentioned the social benefits that come from a drinking lifestyle. Dry fraternities just cannot compete socially with frats like LCA.

"As long as there are 10 other frats serving alcohol," Matt states, "people will just wait in line for those parties."

Thus, it becomes easy to determine socially why LCA is an attractive choice for many freshmen. Oozing party allure, it offers a social experience filled with parties—and of course alcohol. Upperclassmen admit there is just no fair comparison between the social life at a wet fraternity and the social life at a dry frat. Even I prefer the typical party at LCA to those at Phi Delta.

So one is left to question the future of these "dry" fraternities. Praised by colleges and Universities as the "Greek societies of the next generation," frats such as Phi Delta Theta are encouraged and congratulated by their national chapters. Lacking the incredible liability concerns and damage costs that come with wet fraternities, they would appear to be flourishing homes proving once again that Greek life is not about alcohol, but friendship, loyalty and support.

Still, fraternities such as LCA, with their "Animal House" image, are not dying out. On the contrary, despite the pressure to become dry due to liability concerns, fraternities such as LCA refuse to give up their privilege, demanding their right to drink "responsibly," and new pledges line up.

"Alcohol isn't everything fraternities are about," says Ric, a freshman pledge at LCA, "but it's a part of social life that can't be replaced by ping-pong tournaments and movie nights."

Annotate "Fraternities of the Future: Dry or Wet?"

1. Underline Austin's thesis.

2. Note in the margin whether Austin uses a narrative or expository introduction.

3. Circle any statistical information.

4. Put check marks next to Austin's sources.

5. Identity the causes Austin cites with a star.

6. Identify the effects Austin cites with a plus (+) sign.

7. Put a wavy line under transitions, either implied or directly stated.

8. Write question marks next to any spots where the information was surprising or unclear.

9. Underline Austin's ending.

READINGS

The readings that follow explore issues that have been around forever (such as gambling addiction) and trends that came about because of new technology (like blogging). All attempt to explain human behaviors—the causes and effects of what people choose to do.

Giving Girls a Sporting Chance

Anne Driscoll

In "Giving Girls a Sporting Chance," journalist Anne Driscoll focuses primarily on the effects of girls' increased access to athletics since the passage of the 1972 law known as Title IX.

Dan Cullen was a fifth-grader at Rupert Nock Middle School in Newburyport when, two years ago, he invited the girls to play kickball with the boys. Dan, who is freckle-faced, not particularly tall for his age, but self-assured, says he didn't think twice about the invitation: It was, after all, Dan's black kickball the boys had been using at recess ever since somebody kicked the school kickball so hard it burst.

"Yeah, we didn't have enough players, and nobody else wanted to play," says Dan, now 13, matter-of-factly.

"Dan invited Emily to play, and we just followed," says Jamie Connor, a 12-year-old girl who, at 5 feet 4 or so, towers over Dan.

By sixth grade, the game was part of the daily routine. At recess one day, about 20 boys and girls were playing kickball in mixed teams on the sloping land near the school's side entrance. As one girl walloped the ball, sending it sailing through the air, several of her teammates—boys and girls—screamed in the excitement of the moment. No one kept score, yet they all seemed keen on the play and the game.

Recess a generation ago, when Chinese jump rope was as common as chalk, was that short period when girls played their games together, away from the boys, while the boys did whatever it was boys would do—wrestle in the mud, race one another, or hurl a football down the field. But for these teams of sixth-graders in Newburyport, sex-segregated recess would seem totally weird. Stupid, even. Playing together, competing against one another, and even being friends with one another are normal for most of them, regardless of gender.

"I think the boys have gotten good about our playing with them, because we can beat them at stuff and they can beat us at stuff—it goes both ways," says Taylor Nelson, 12, a competitive swimmer and soccer, basketball, and lacrosse player who is nearly as tall as her friend Jamie.

"The girls look at us in a different perspective, and we also look at them in a different perspective," says Dan, now in seventh grade. "They know what happens to us and why we get so competitive, and we know how they can get competitive, too. I kind of think that's broken down the walls, so to speak, between the boys and the girls. Although you don't exactly think of that when you go over to say hi to them."

Dan and his best friend, David Moreno, as well as the group of girls Dan and David count as friends—Jamie, Taylor, and Hilary Walentuk—are among some 44.7 million American youths between 7 and 17 who participate in organized team sports, according to the National Sporting Goods Association in Mt. Prospect, Illinois. And 43 percent of those players are girls, so the experience of athletic competition is increasingly a common denominator between the sexes, helping prepare both boys and girls for the future.

Why do girls today feel they can compete athletically with boys? Why do boys feel more comfortable relating to girls as equals and as friends? What has changed in the culture that has leveled the playing field? Some researchers believe it is the trickle-down effect of Title IX, an act carried on the muscular back of the feminist movement that has changed girls' lives more than any law since the one that gave women the right to vote.

The 1972 law known as Title IX decreed that any school receiving federal funds—kindergarten through college—had to provide girls the same access to programs that boys had, including sports. Title IX has not only made playing sports normal for girls of every age and ability, it has changed the culture. The lessons learned through athletics give girls a stronger, more confident, more disciplined outlook on their futures—an advantage boys have always had. And with girls gaining ground on boys' athletic turf, both have a new common experience and a new way to interact.

Title IX did more than just level the playing field; it put boys and girls literally on the same playing field. And researchers are still exploring what that will mean for both sexes.

When Sumru Erkut, associate director of the Center for Research on Women at Wellesley College, and three colleagues embarked on their 1996 investigation of girls and self-esteem, they expected to find that girls gain their sense of worth from taking care of others. But in their nationwide survey of 362 girls between the ages of 6 and 18, nearly half said the activity that made them feel

Tennis player, c. 1900. Looking at women's tennis fashions reveals more than just information about clothing of the time. Notice how the image of women as athletes also evolves.

good about themselves was athletics. The next most common choice—at 19 percent—was an arts-related activity such as music or dance. When the girls were asked why sports made them feel good about themselves, a significant number said it was because of the sense of mastery that playing sports provided.

A 1997 study, done for the President's Council on Physical Fitness and Sports, found that participating in exercise and sports enhanced both the physical and mental health of adolescents, improving self-esteem, self-confidence, competence, en-

Lili de Alvarez at Wimbledon, 1926

an affirmative way. . . . It's an avenue for you to feel good about yourself because you can do it well—the competence motivation. So many girls say, 'I love it because I feel good about it.' Now they're discovering they also get the attention of the coaches and several other adults, including their parents."

The Women's Sports Foundation has been collecting data on women and athletics since Billie Jean King helped found it in 1974, two years after Title IX was passed. One of its most surprising and illuminating studies—an examination of the relationship between girls playing sports and teenage pregnancy—was released in May 1998. The researchers found that female teenage athletes are more likely than nonathletes to be virgins and more likely to delay sex; they have sex less often and have fewer sex partners; and they are more likely to use birth control and less likely to get pregnant as teenagers.

The researchers believe that athletic girls tend to avoid risky sexual behavior because team sports provide girls with a powerful social network, one removed from the pressures of the dating scene. Athletics also provides girls with an alternative way to establish self-worth, one based on a practical ponytail and low-maintenance makeup rather than elaborate hairstyles and heavy eye shadow. Girls who achieve success and status on the field, the authors say, may be less eager to trade sex for social approval.

And, as Erkut believes, sports give girls a new way to appreciate the power of their own bodies. Girls of every generation have grown up knowing that their bodies are supposed to be attractive to boys and acceptable to other girls, yet more than ever, girls are coming to understand that their bodies don't just have to stand around looking nice. They can shoot layups, block goals, hit home runs, and clear hurdles.

After school, it's usually a tossup. Should Jamie Connor and her best friends hang out,

vironmental health, and body image. Other independent studies have confirmed that girls who play sports score better on achievement tests; they are also more likely to graduate from high school, to continue their education, and thus to have greater earning potential. Girls who are physically, mentally, and emotionally stronger have a better chance of competing in the classroom—or in the boardroom.

"The world has not caught up with the fact that sports is part of the everyday world of girls," says Erkut. "It gives girls many different things to feel good about. It gets them to use their body in

maybe dressing up in Jamie's mom's bridesmaid dresses, or play sports outside? Often, they make time for both.

Jamie's is the only bedroom on the second floor of her home, so after school lets out, she, Taylor Nelson, and Hilary Walentuk often congregate in the white room with pink ribbon stencils and posters of the Backstreet Boys, then drag out a collection of taffeta, chiffon, and lycra dresses. They take turns making one another up with eye shadow and blush, then model before a big mirror in the hall and pose for photographs with a camera that belongs to Jamie's mom, Ann Marie Connor.

Then the three girls will strip off their dress-up clothes, jump back into their cargo pants or jeans and T-shirts, and head out to the backyard. "We play sports about half the time," says Jamie, "although most of the time, we dress up, put on makeup, and stuff like that." "You can be a girl and do girl stuff and also be competitive and have fun at that, too," adds Taylor.

Jamie's mother couldn't agree more. "I am an avid cyclist, and I can go 27 miles and she's right behind me," says Connor. "She's competitive, and she likes to keep up with Mommy. That's why I named her Jamie—because when she fills out a job application they won't know whether she is a boy or girl. I want her to succeed. I want her to be self-supporting and not rely on anyone. It's a very hard world out there," says Connor, who was a member of her high school track team in Peabody.

"Girls are getting more competitive," she says. "They're skateboarding, rollerblading. Before, only the jocks did sports, the tomboys. But now it's a way of life for everyone. I was definitely a tomboy. My hair was in a ponytail every single day, and I never wore makeup until I graduated. But Jamie is a girl who can be girly with her friends, who likes to paint her nails, who likes to put glitter on her eyes, and who is thoroughly enjoying life as a girl."

Connor believes that the rules she learned playing sports helped her compete in the work force—

Althea Gibson at Wimbledon, 1957

when, for example, she became the only woman in the sales department of a technology firm. She thinks that sports provide a milieu for more common experiences and, she hopes, greater acceptance between the sexes.

Jamie thinks that's already happening. "What do boys like in a girl? I really don't know," she says. "They want them to be athletic, they want them to be in sports, but they want them to be pretty, too. I guess there's room for everybody."

In 1971, the year before Title IX was passed, only one in 27 American girls played high school sports. Now, one in three does, compared with

Billie Jean King at Wimbledon, 1982

effect so that in increasing numbers, girls—beginning as young as age 5—are playing competitive sports. The Title IX law may apply strictly to federally funded schools, but it has set a precedent and prompted an ever-growing number of girls to join intramural, club, school, church, and town-organized sports programs.

More than 4 out of 10 of the 44.7 million youngsters playing baseball, basketball, soccer, softball, and volleyball are girls. More than 14 million girls age 6 and older played basketball in 1996, a 28 percent increase from the previous decade. And even sports that have been slow to attract female athletes have seen tremendous growth. In 1990, there were about 5,500 female ice hockey players; today, more than 24,000 girls play, three-quarters of them under the age 16.

Sixth-grade teacher Dan Sullivan has been watching girls overcome hurdles ever since he began teaching science at the Nock Middle School in 1972. In addition to his classroom teaching, he coached boys' football in middle school and high school for 20 years and girls' high school track for 10. During one four-year period, his track team grew from 32 girls to nearly 60, and he saw the girls working just as hard, competing just as fiercely, and achieving just as much as the boys did.

"Now you can go up and see a girls' field hockey game on Friday night under the lights," says Sullivan. "There's no difference [between boys and girls] in the significance of the sport being played. Girls play in the stadium, they play under the lights, they play in front of crowds. All of this has enhanced girls' participation in the sports." By age 11 or 12, many of the girls in Sullivan's class have already had five or six years of experience playing sports in school intramural programs, club teams, youth leagues, or Catholic Youth Organization programs.

What has all that sweat, hard work, muscle soreness, and joint pain gotten the girls? Sullivan says even the merely average athletes have been

one in two boys. And the increase in girls' participation rates continues to exceed that of boys. In the school year ending in 1997, high school girls' participation grew to a record 2.5 million, 4 percent higher than the previous year—and double the growth in boys' participation, according to the National Sporting Goods Association figures.

This means schools are providing girls widespread access to a domain that previously belonged primarily to boys: the experience of competing, being a teammate, and asserting their physical power and mastery.

And it's not just high school athletes who are playing more: Title IX has had a mainstreaming

able to translate their experience as members of a team, as competitors, as disciplined and serious sportswomen, into a blueprint for success in the classroom or later in careers—an advantage boys have always enjoyed. And Sullivan's observations seem to be supported by research. One study found that 80 percent of female leaders at Fortune 500 companies said they had been athletes or tomboys when they were girls.

Sullivan's colleague Carol Snow, a sixth-grade social studies teacher, has seen enormous cultural changes at Newburyport High School since the '70s, when she played field hockey there in a shoddy uniform, with no shin pads. She believes that growing parity between boys' and girls' sports provided for by Title IX has affected girls on and off the field, in every area of life. "Girls seem to have more of a sense of confidence," Snow says. "Whether it be in a discussion or whatever, they realize they are just as valuable." The girls Snow teaches in 1999 are markedly different from those she remembers from 1979. These days, she says, girls are more willing to speak up. They are more confident, more willing to express ideas, and more comfortable with themselves. They move more freely in the world.

"At the beginning of the year, when [the class] first came in," Snow says, she "had the desks set up facing each other, so there were two rows. This was just the first day. Now, we know these kids and they know each other, yet all the boys sat on one side of the room, all the girls on one side. And I thought, 'This is unreal.' I didn't say anything to them, I was still watching. And I went into [Sullivan's classroom], and it was the same thing. But I would say within a week, it was mixed. It was a girl that made the first move. She said, 'I'm going to sit on that side.' Then they all mixed together."

When Elizabeth Suda was 3, she pulled on a pair of pink tights and a leotard and began 10 years of studying ballet. "I always thought of myself as a ballet dancer," she says. It wasn't until she tried T-

Serena Williams at the U.S. Open, 2004

ball in the fourth grade that she experienced a team sport. "I didn't really like it," she recalls. "The only thing I liked was when I hit the ball and ran the bases."

Elizabeth, now 18, liked running so much that she joined the track team during her freshman year at Newburyport High. She was hobbled by injuries her first two years, but in her senior year she won all 10 track races she competed in—and she ran cross-country all four years of high school, too. When she graduated in June, she was the first female in 76 years to win the Ryan Cup, the alumni association's annual award to an outstanding high school athlete and scholar.

Elizabeth says that training, practicing, and competing on the track team, alongside the boys' team and with the same coaches, helped strengthen her in ways beyond the physical. For one thing, she made friends with both female and male teammates. "There really wasn't much difference between us," she says. "We were all runners. Of course, the fast boys can run faster than the girls, but a lot of us were the same as the boys. I guess the boys just think of us as regular people. They'd cheer us on just like they'd cheer each other on."

Elizabeth's former teammate Ryan Spinney, a senior at Newburyport High and captain of the boys' cross-country, indoor track, and outdoor track teams, agrees. "All the girls have determination; I admire that. They're not different than the guys—anybody who is an athlete is an athlete. . . . I don't really understand the concept of girls being inferior to men," Ryan says. "It's just dumb. That whole concept is just ridiculous. Most of my friends are with me on that."

If she hadn't been competing, Elizabeth says, she might have had more time to play the violin and cello, pursue art, and sew dresses with her mother, but she wouldn't have become the person she is now. Sports, she says, "gives you self-esteem and confidence and humbles you at the same time. . . . It helps you take risks. When you're running a race, you are real vulnerable. Being injured was a blessing in disguise—it taught me things in life don't come easily, you have to work through a lot of pain. It's also helped me work hard, to push myself."

Sumru Erkut says the impact sports have on girls' lives is complex. "It doesn't work for all girls," she says. "Some girls may enjoy playing sports because it's a way to spend time with friends; others like it because it's a way to take control of their bodies. Still others find it a diversion from a difficult home life, and for others, they learn to make good decisions because they have to be good at making decisions on the field. For others it helps them make plans, weigh long-term planning. Sports offer all-around positive effects, but we don't really know how it works and why. I am searching to identify the reasons."

In the meantime, Taylor Nelson speaks for herself, her friends, and many of the 19 million US girls playing team sports when she says simply, "It's important for me to feel strong."

Critical Reading Questions

1. Driscoll's long introduction sets up the contrast between recess activities today and "recess a generation ago." What are the points of contrast? Do you find this an effective introduction? Why?

2. Locate Driscoll's thesis. What expectations are set up in the thesis for the rest of the article?

3. How does Driscoll convince you that the trend exists of more girls participating in athletics? Do you find her proof effective? Explain.

4. What kind of research did Driscoll do for this article? Make a list of print and electronic sources she consulted and practitioners and experts she interviewed.

5. What do you think is the best quotation in the article?

Questions for Writing and Discussion

1. Does your experience growing up support Driscoll's thesis? Cite an anecdote or example with which you have personal experience.

2. Can you imagine a change in this trend? Might the numbers of females participating in sports level off or fall?

My So-Called Blog

Emily Nussbaum

Web logs, or blogs, that run commentary posted by individuals on the Internet are a new trend in electronic communication. Special-interest blogs can keep you in touch with perspectives and points of view you might share, and they can help you find material that you and "like-minded" people might want to read. One type of blog, the online diary, is becoming a popular form of self-expression among young people. In the article that follows, Emily Nussbaum says that the attraction of an online journal is that it is like "a hyperflexible adolescent body" that you can change easily and at will. But these very personal blogs are posted in a very public arena, inviting comments. Are blogs an online "Breakfast Club" breaking down barriers, or are they a way to extend cliques to the Internet? Nussbaum discusses some of what draws young people to posting personal insights and speculates on some of the effects of a trend that is still too new to evaluate.

When M. gets home from school, he immediately logs on to his computer. Then he stays there, touching base with the people he has seen all day long, floating in a kind of multitasking heaven of communication. First, he clicks on his Web log, or blog—an online diary he keeps on a Web site called LiveJournal—and checks for responses from his readers. Next he reads his friends' journals, contributing his distinctive brand of wry, supportive commentary to their observations. Then he returns to his own journal to compose his entries: sometimes confessional, more often dry private jokes or koanlike observations on life.

Finally, he spends a long time—sometimes hours—exchanging instant messages, a form of communication far more common among teenagers than phone calls. In multiple dialogue boxes on his computer screen, he'll type realtime conversations with several friends at once; if he leaves the house to hang out in the real world, he'll come back and instant-message some more, and sometimes cut and paste transcripts of these conversations into his online journal. All this upkeep can get in the way of homework, he admitted. "You keep telling yourself, 'Don't look, don't look!' And you keep on checking your e-mail." M. is an unusually Zen teenage boy—dreamy and ruminative

about his personal relationships. But his obsessive online habits are hardly exceptional; he is one of a generation of compulsive self-chroniclers, a fleet of juvenile Marcel Prousts gone wild. When he meets new friends in real life, M. offers them access to his online world. "That's how you introduce yourself," he said. "It's like, here's my cellphone number, my e-mail, my screen name, oh, and—here's my LiveJournal. Personally, I'd go to that person's LJ before I'd call them or e-mail them or contact them on AIM"—AOL Instant Messenger—"because I would know them better that way."

Only five years ago, mounting an online journal or its close cousin, the blog, required at least a modicum of technical know-how. But today, using sites like LiveJournal or Blogger or Xanga, users can sign up for a free account, and with little computer knowledge design a site within minutes. According to figures released last October by Perseus Development Corporation, a company that designs software for online surveys, there are expected to be 10 million blogs by the end of 2004. In the news media, the blog explosion has been portrayed as a transformation of the industry, a thousand minipundits blooming. But the vast majority of bloggers are teens and young adults. Ninety percent of those with blogs are between 13 and 29 years old; a full 51 percent are between 13 and 19, according to Perseus. Many teen blogs are short-lived experiments. But for a significant number, they become a way of life, a daily record of a community's private thoughts—a kind of invisible high school that floats above the daily life of teenagers.

Back in the 1980's, when I attended high school, reading someone's diary would have been the ultimate intrusion. But communication was rudimentary back then. There were no cellphones, or answering machines; there was no "texting," no MP3's or JPEG's, no digital cameras or file-sharing software; there was no World Wide Web—none of the private-ish, public-ish, superimmediate forums kids today take for granted. If this new technology has provided a million ways to stay in touch, it has also acted as both an amplifier and a distortion device for human intimacy. The new forms of communication are madly contradictory: anonymous, but traceable; instantaneous, then saved forever (unless deleted in a snit). In such an unstable environment, it's no wonder that distinctions between healthy candor and "too much information" are in flux and that so many find themselves helplessly confessing, as if a generation were given a massive technological truth serum.

A result of this self-chronicling is that the private experience of adolescence—a period traditionally marked by seizures of self-consciousness and personal confessions wrapped in layers and hidden in a sock drawer—has been made public. Peer into an online journal, and you find the operatic texture of teenage life with its fits of romantic misery, quick-change moods and sardonic inside jokes. Gossip spreads like poison. Diary writers compete for attention, then fret when they get it. And everything parents fear is true. (For one thing, their children view them as stupid and insane, with terrible musical taste.) But the linked journals also form a community, an intriguing, unchecked experiment in silent group therapy—a hive mind in

which everyone commiserates about how it feels to be an outsider, in perfect choral unison.

For many in the generation that has grown up online, the solution is not to fight this technological loss of privacy, but to give in and embrace it: to stop worrying and learn to love the Web. It's a generational shift that has multiple roots, from Ricki Lake to the memoir boom to the A.A. confessional, not to mention 13 seasons of "The Real World." The teenagers who post journals have (depending on your perspective) a degraded or a relaxed sense of privacy; their experiences may be personal, but there's no shame in sharing. As the reality-television stars put it, exposure may be painful at times, but it's all part of the process of "putting it out there," risking judgment and letting people in. If teen bloggers give something up by sloughing off a self-protective layer, they get something back too—a new kind of intimacy, a sense that they are known and listened to. This is their life, for anyone to read. As long as their parents don't find out.

.   .   .

It was early September, the start of the school year in an affluent high school in Westchester County, just north of New York City, where I was focusing my teen-blogging expedition. The halls were filled with students and the walls were covered with posters urging extracurricular activities. ("Instant popularity, minus the hazing," read one.) I had come looking for J., a boy I'd never seen, though I knew many of the details of his life. (J., like most of the teenage bloggers I interviewed, insisted he not be identified, in part because his parents didn't know about his blog.) On a Web site called Blurty, he kept an online journal, titled "Laugh at Me." In his user profile he described himself this way: "I have depression, bad skin, weight problems, low self-esteem, few friends and many more reasons why I am angry." In his online outpourings, J. inveighed hilariously against his parents, his teachers and friends who had let him down. "Hey everyone ever," he wrote in one entry. "Stop making fun of people. It really is a sucky thing to do, especially if you hate being made fun of yourself. . . . This has been a public service announcement. You may now resume your stupid hypocritical, lying lives."

I was half-expecting a pimply nightmare boy, all monosyllables and misery. Instead, J. turned out to be a cute 15-year-old with a shy smile. A little bit jittery, he sat with his knees apart, admiring his own Converse sneakers. He had chosen an unfortunately public place for this interview—a stairwell near the cafeteria and directly across from the teacher's lounge—although he insisted that we were in an obscure location.

J. had had his Blurty journal for about a year. He called it "better than therapy," a way to get out his true feelings—all the emotions he thought might get him in trouble if he expressed them in school or at home. Online, he could blurt out confessions of loneliness and insecurity, worrying aloud about slights from friends. Yet despite the fact that he knew that anyone who wanted to could read his journal—and that a few friends did, leaving comments at the ends of his posts—he also maintained the notion that what he was doing was private. He didn't write for an audience, he said; he just wrote what he was feeling.

Writing in his online journal was cathartic for him, he said, but it was hardly stress-free. A week earlier, he left a post about an unrequited crush, and an anonymous someone appended negative comments, remarks J. wouldn't detail (he deleted them), but which he described with distress as "disgusting language, vulgarities." J. panicked, worried that the girl he liked might learn about the vulgar comments and, by extension, his attraction to her. It was a somewhat mysterious concern. Couldn't the girl have read his original post, I asked? And anyway, didn't he secretly want her to read his journal? "Of course," he moaned, leaning against the banister. "For all I know she does. For all I know, she doesn't."

J.'s sense of private and public was filled with these kinds of contradictions: he wanted his posts to be read, and feared that people would read them, and hoped that people would read them, and didn't care if people read them. He wanted to be included while priding himself on his outsider status. And while he sometimes wrote messages that were explicitly public—announcing a band practice, for instance—he also had his own stringent notions of etiquette. His crush had an online journal, but J. had never read it; that would be too intrusive, he explained.

In any case, today he was in a strikingly good mood. After a year of posting his journal on Blurty, which few of his fellow students used, he was switching to a different Web site: LiveJournal, the enclave of many kids in his school's punk set. He'd spent the last day or two transferring all his old posts, setting up a friends list and concocting a new "icon," the tiny symbol that would represent him when he posted: a blurry shot of his face in profile. Unlike Blurty, where accounts are free for anyone who signs up, LiveJournal was restricted. (That policy has since changed.) You either had to pay to join (which J. couldn't afford) or be offered a coveted membership—a private "code"—by someone who already belonged. The policy was intended to make members accountable to one another, but it also had the effect of creating an invisible clique. For J., it was a sign that he might belong at last.

While the sites that are hosts to online journals may attract different crowds, their formats vary only slightly: a LiveJournal is a Blurty is a Xanga is a DeadJournal is a DiaryLand. A typical page shows a dated list of entries, beginning with the most recent. Many posts are short, surrealistic one-liners: "I just peeled a freckle off my neck. Does that mean it's not a freckle?" Others are more like visual poems, featuring a quirky series of scanned pictures (monkeys and robots are popular), a quote from a favorite song or a link to a strange news story. Some posts consist of transcripts of instant-message conversations, posted with or without permission (a tradition I discovered when a boy copied one of our initial online conversations under the heading "i like how older people have grammar online").

But a significant number of writers treat their journals as actual diaries, toting up detailed accounts of their day. "I watched the miracle of life today in bio, and it was such a huge letdown," read one post. "I was expecting it to be funny and sexual but it was way too scientific for my liking, and a bit yucky too, but not as bad as people made it out to be. Although, my not being able to laugh made me feel a bit too old. Current mood: disappointed."

Then there are the kinds of posts that fulfill a parent's worst paranoia. "It was just a nite of lying to my dad," reads one entry posted last fall. "At like 7ish we started drinking, but i didn't have THAT much. And i figured out y i drink so much. Cuz i really really don't like being sober with drunk people. . . . i have more homework to do than imaginable. And to make it better, im hungover and feel sick. Great . . . great. DRINKING IS BAD!!"

Other entries are just plain poignant. "My father is suing my mom on no real grounds. He just wants to 'destroy her' and I am trying my best to stay 'neutral.' Things seem real foggy, but I am told that they should turn out for the best. I just don't know. Affection needed. Current mood: indescribable."

. . .

If a journal may look at first like a simple recitation of events, the fact that readers can comment renders it deeply interactive. (On some sites, like Xanga, you can give "eProps" for particularly good posts—the equivalent of gold stars.) Most com-ments are wisecracks or sympathetic one-liners. Occasionally people respond with hostility. The threads of comments can amount to a public mini-conversation, in which a group of friends debates a subject or plans an event or offers advice. "I need your help," one poster wrote. "Yes, your help. You, the one reading this . . . what am i supposed to do when the dynamic of a once-romantic relationship sort of changes but sort of doesn't, and the next week i continually try to get in touch with the girl but she is either not there or can't talk very long, and before this change in the dynamic she was always available?" A string of friends offered suggestions, from "don't call her so much" to "confront her . . . what she's doing isn't fair to you."

In daily life, most bloggers don't talk about what they say online. One boy engaged in vociferous debates on Mideast policy with another blogger, a senior a year ahead of him. Yet the two never spoke in school, going only so far as to make eye contact in the halls.

Silences like this can create paranoia. It may be that friends just didn't read the post. Or it may mean they thought the post was stupid. There's a temptation to take silence—in real life or online—as a snub. "If I get a really mean comment and I go back and I look at it again, and again, it starts to bother me," M. told me. "But then I think, if I delete it, everyone will know this bothers me. But if I respond, it'll mean I need to fight back. So it turns into a conflict, but it's fun. It's like a soap opera, kind of."

It's a drama heightened by the fact that journals are linked to one another, creating a constant juxtaposition of posts among the students. For example, on LiveJournal, you can click a "friends" link and catch up on your friends' experiences without ever speaking, with everyone's accounts posted next to one another in a kind of word collage. For many, this transforms daily life. Teen bloggers are constantly considering how they'll turn a noteworthy moment into an online post. After a party or a concert, these accounts can amount to a prismatic portrait of the evening.

But even this endless linking only begins to touch on the complex ways these blogs are obsessively interconnected and personalized. L. has had an online journal for two and a half years, and it has morphed along with her. At first, her interest list (part of the user profile) consisted of topics like aromatherapy, yoga and Zen—each of which linked to people with the same interest. She deleted that list and started over. In her next phase, she was obsessed with Freudian psychology. Now she lists fashion trends and belongs to the Flapper, Saucy Dwellings and Sex Tips blog rings.

Over the course of the fall, she changed the title of her Web log more than five times. L. relishes the way subtle choices of design and phrasing lend her posts a winking mysteriousness, hinting at feelings without making them explicit. "I don't think I reveal too much; if I'm upset, I don't say why," she told me. "In the beginning, I was just like, there shouldn't be private posts, this should all be public. But then it makes you very vulnerable." And her attitude goes double for her parents. "I don't talk to them about anything. They'll be like, 'How was school?' And I'll be like, 'Fine.' And that was it."

Many of a journal's markers of personal identity are hilariously telegraphic. There are sometimes slots for a journalizer's mood and current music. (Sample moods: "stoned," "restless," "accomplished," "confused" and "braces off Tuesday.") Journal writers link en masse to sardonic identity questionnaires, like "How Indie Am I?" And every once in a while, someone posts a random list of questions, and everyone's journal fills up with simultaneous answers to queries like "Do you believe in an afterlife?" or "Name Four Things You Wish You Had." ("1. A flat tummy; 2. people that would miss me; 3. my copy of 'perks of being a wallflower' back; 4. talent at ANYTHING.")

It's possible to make posts private—or "friends only"—but many journal keepers don't bother, or do so only for selected posts. The general degree of anonymity varies: some bloggers post their full names, others give quirky, quasi-revelatory handles. No wonder everyone is up till 5 A.M. tweaking their font size and Photoshopping a new icon. At heart, an online journal is like a hyperflexible adolescent body—but better, because in real life, it takes money and physical effort to add a piercing, or to switch from zip-jacketed mod to Abercrombie prepster. A LiveJournal or Blurty offers a creative outlet with a hundred moving parts. And unlike a real journal, with a blog, your friends are all around, invisible voyeurs—at least until they chime in with a comment.

. . .

For many of the suburban students I met, online journals are associated with the "emo" crowd—a sarcastic term for emotional, and a tag for a musical genre mingling thrash-punk with confessionalism. The emo kids tend to be the artsy loners and punks, but as I spent more time lurking in journals and talking to the kids who wrote them, I began to realize that these threads led out much farther into the high school, into pretty much every clique.

On a sunny fall day, M. and his friends were hanging out in front of a local toy store, shooting photos of one another with digital cameras, when a group of three girls sashayed by. They sported tank tops, identical hairbands and identical shiny hair. I walked over to them and asked if they have LiveJournals. "No," one said. "We have Xangas."

They were all 15, around the same age as M. and his friends. But the two groups had never read the other's posts. M.'s crowd was emo (or at least emo-ish; like "politically correct," "emo" is a word people rarely apply to themselves). These girls were part of the athletic crowd. There was little overlap, online or off. But the girls were fully familiar with the online etiquette M. described: they instant-messaged compulsively; they gossiped online.

With so much confessional drama, I began to wonder if interactions ever swung out of control. Does anyone ever post anything that seems like too much information? I asked. They all nodded intently, tossing nervous eye contact back and forth.

"Yeah," one of the girls replied finally, with a deep sigh. "This one girl, she was really upset, and she would write things that had happened to her that were really scary. Private things that didn't really need to be said on the site—"

Her friend interrupted: "But she knew she was putting it out there. She said, 'I don't care.'"

"It was nice that she was comfortable about it," suggested the third girl.

Her friend disagreed. "It was not nice."

What kinds of things did she write about? I asked. Eating disorders? Sex? "All of it," they said in unison. "All of it."

I walked back to M. and his group. "Those girls are just, like, social girls," said M. dismissively. When I told him they had online journals, he seemed astonished. "Really?" He said. "Huh." He watched with amusement as they walked away.

Blogging is a replication of real life: each pool of blogs is its own ecosystem, with only occasional links to other worlds. As I surfed from site to site, it became apparent that as much as journals can break stereotypes, some patterns are crushingly predictable: the cheerleaders post screen grabs of the Fox TV show "The O.C."; kids who identify with "ghetto" culture use hip-hop slang; the geeks gush over Japanese anime. And while there are exceptions, many journal writers exhibit a surprising lack of curiosity about the journals of true strangers. They're too busy writing posts to browse.

But even diaries that seem at first predictable can have the power to startle. Take J.K., whose Xanga titled "No Fat Chicks" features a peculiar mix of introspection and bully-boy bombast. Some of J.K.'s entries this fall brooded on his bench-warmer status on the football team. "Do the coaches want me to quit?" he worried in one post. "I know that some people have to sit out, that's just the way it works, and I accept that. But does it have to be me when we're down 36 points and the clock is winding down?"

In J.K.'s diary, revelations of insecurity alternate with chest-beating bombast, juvenile jokes and self-mocking claims of sexual prowess. From a teen poet, you expect angsty navel-gazing; it's more surprising to find it in a jock like J.K. In one post, he analyzed his history as a bully during "middle school, the time of popularity," when he did "things too heinous to even mention." In response, a reader posted a long, angry comment, doubting J.K.'s sincerity: "I don't think you understand what hatred I used to have for you because of how you made me feel . . . you can't go back in time, but you can try to make up for what you've done in the past."

Occasionally, a particularly scandalous site will gain a wider readership. It's a social phenomenon made possible by technology: the object of gossip using her Web site as a public stage to tell her side of the story, to everyone, all at once. As I asked around the high school, I found that many other students had heard of the girl the "social girls" had described to me—a student whose confessional postings had became something of a must-read the spring before. Over the course of a monthslong breakdown, she posted graphic descriptions of cutting herself, family fights, sex. It was all documented on her Web log, complete with photos and real names. (She has since removed the material from her site.)

The blog turned her into a minor celebrity, at first among the social crowd, then among their friends and siblings as well. "We were addicted—we would track every minute," one student explained. "We would call each other and go, 'Oh, my god, she wrote again!'" With each post, her readers would encourage her to write more. "Wow u should be writing a book," one wrote. "Ur stories are exactly like one of those teen diary books that other teens can relate to. That might sound corny but its so true."

The girls who read the journal were divided on the subject. Some called the Web site an unhealthy bid for attention—not to mention revenge, since she often posted unflattering details about her ex-boyfriend and former friends. Others were more sympathetic. "I think I empathized with her after reading it, because I'd just heard the stories," one girl explained. "But then she was saying, 'I felt so sad, and I was in this really dark place, and my parents were fighting, and I was cutting myself'—so I could understand it more. Before, it was just gossip. It made her seem more like a person than just, like, this character."

These dynamics are invisible to most adults, whether at home or school. Students occasionally show the school psychologist their journals, pulling up posts on her computer or sharing printed transcripts of instant messages. But the psychologist rarely sought them out herself, she told me, and she was surprised to hear that boys kept them. She called the journals a boon for shy students and admired the way they encouraged kids to express themselves in writing. But she also noticed a recent rise in journal-based conflicts, mostly situations where friends attack one another after a falling out. "They think that they're getting close by sharing," she said, "but it allows them to say things they wouldn't otherwise say, to be hurtful at a distance." When I mentioned the material I'd read about the girl who was cutting herself, she went silent. "You know," she said, "I really should read more into these."

The scandalous journal is an extreme variation, but teen bloggers often joke about the pressure to post with angst; controversy gets more commentary, after all. (Entries often apologize for not having anything exciting to say.) But if there's something troubling about the kind of online scandal that breeds a high-school Sylvia Plath—an angstier-than-thou exhibitionism—there's also something almost utopian at the endeavor's heart. So much high-school pain comes from the sense of being alone with one's stupid, self-destructive impulses. With so many teenagers baring their vulnerabilities, there is the potential for breaking down isolation. A kind of online Breakfast Club, perhaps, in which a little surfing turns up the insecurity that lurks in all of us.

. . .

For some journal keepers, the connections made online can be life-altering. In late November, I checked in on J., the author of "Laugh at Me." All fall, his LiveJournal had been hopping, documenting milestones (a learner's permit!), philosophical insights, complaints about parental dorkiness and plans for something called Operation Backfire, in which he mocks another kid he hates—a kid who has filled his own journal on Xanga with right-wing rants. "I felt happy/victorious," wrote J. about taunting his enemy. "And rightly so."

In the new context of LiveJournal, J.'s posts had become increasingly interactive, with frequent remarks about parties and weekend plans; they seemed less purely rantlike, and he was posting comments on other people's journals. When I contacted him via instant message, he told me that he was feeling less friendless than he was when the semester started. "I feel more included and such," he typed just after Thanksgiving, describing the effect of having switched to LiveJournal from his more isolated Blurty. "All community-ish." He was planning to attend a concert of World/Inferno Friendship Society, a band with a LiveJournal following. And he'd become closer friends in real life with some fellow LJ'ers, including L., who had given J. an emo makeover. He'd begun wearing tight, dark jeans and had "forcibly retired" his old sneakers.

Once J. decided to switch to LiveJournal, LiveJournal began changing him in turn. Perhaps he was adjusting himself to reflect the way he is online: assertive and openly emotional, more than a bit bratty. He'd become more comfortable talking to girls. And if he seemed to have forgotten his invocation not to make fun of anyone, at least he was standing up for himself.

J. had also signed up for a new online journal: a Xanga. He got it, he said, to branch out. He wanted to be able to comment on the journals of other students he knows are out there, including that of bully-boy J.K., where I was surprised to find one of J.'s comments in early November. "I made a xanga for myself because i keep hearing that that's whats 'cool' now," he wrote on his LJ with a distinctive mixture of rue and satisfaction, the very flavor of adolescent change. "And yet i always try to pride myself on not following status quo. I'm a hypocrite. O yes i am. Current mood: Hypocritical. Current music: Mogwai."

Critical Reading Questions

1. What type of opening does Nussbaum use? Who are her readers? Can you tell who her readers are from the opening?

2. How does Nussbaum prove that the trend exists?

3. Name a few of the sources consulted in the article.

4. Why do you think Nussbaum includes the scene where she interviews J.?

5. What are some of the effects of blogging?

6. Nussbaum has divided the article into four sections. What is the main point of each section?

Questions for Writing and Discussion

1. One blogger says he would "go to a person's LJ before I'd call them or e-mail them or contact them on AIM—the AOL Instant Messenger—because I would know them better that way." Do you agree with this thinking? Does electronic communication allow people to be more honest?

2. How deep a look inside youth culture can a reporter really get? In this article, for example, do you believe that Nussbaum has gotten close to the reality of this subject?

M.D. Realities:
Medical Schools Take on Decade-Long Applications Slump as Prospective Students Face Doubts

Camille Rodriguez

When writing student Camille Rodriguez started to research her trend, she believed that her mission was to examine the causes for the steady decline in medical school applications. Instead, she found out that the trend had shifted to an upswing in number of applications. Based on her preliminary research, she changed her focus, refined the topic of her trend research paper, and set out to look at why medical school applicants seem more plentiful in some years than in others.

Camille Rodriguez

EN 201

May 23, 2004

Abstract

Between 1997 and 2002 medical school applications fell nearly 22 percent. Some attribute this downward trend to declining social status of doctors, rising malpractice premiums, and the rise of managed care. However, applications to medical schools in the United State rose in 2003. Studies show that more women are applying to medical school, and some previously rejected applicants are reapplying. Experts also see the downward trend as part of a natural cycle with no correlation to financial or social issues.

M.D. Realities

It is the middle of May, and many colleges around the country have already begun their summer vacations, but a number of students are still swarming around the second floor of the 42nd street New York Public Library. Their destination is the Academic Information section. This part of the library isn't where you'll find information on your social studies or biology class. This is where the library keeps test-preparatory materials and guides to professional schools.

The sounds of people shifting in their chairs, flipping through pages, clicking computer keys and the occasional sneezing fit echo in the large room. Every small sound elicits a wave of heads turning. Yet, for the most part, people remain fixated on the piles of the information before them.

It's apparent that the titles of the books these particular library patrons choose include either the acronym MCAT or the words "medical school." One student stares at the question, "Which of the following best accounts for the higher acidity of phenol compared to ethanol (Kaplan, 24)?"

These college students are preparing to embark on one of the most demanding and difficult academic paths: becoming a doctor. And they're getting an early start. "I'm just a freshman, but I know that medical school is extremely competitive. If I want my application to be great, I need to start preparing now," says Daniel Gurdak, a freshman from Lehman College in Bronx, New York, as he skims through a chapter titled, "Getting into the Top Medical Schools." "A lot of people I know are starting to consider medical school" (personal communication, May 18, 2004).

Gurdak and the other students poring over test-preparation material, catalogs, and magazine ratings of medical schools may be part of a new trend toward an upswing in interest among American students in becoming physicians. Some recently released figures on medical school applications showed that after declining for six years, applications to medical schools in the United State rose in 2003. According to the Association of American Medical Colleges, 34,785 people applied to attend medical school in the 2003-2004 school year. That represented a 3.4 percent increase over last year's total of 33,625 (Howell, 2003).

The new figures came in the wake of six years, between 1997 and 2002, in which applications fell nearly 22 percent. A study by the American Medical Association said that applications declined from 43,016 in 1997 to 33,625 in 2002 and that they peaked in 1996 at 46,965 (Smith, 2003).

During the downswing, experts blamed the slump on the declining social status of doctors, rising malpractice premiums, and the rise of managed care, which many physicians felt was tangling them in red tape as well as hurting their ability to deliver high-quality health care.

Michael Preston, executive director of MedChi, the Maryland State Medical Society, explained it this way. "It's not just reimbursement and the income side," he said. "As much as anything it's about the loss of autonomy and personal freedom that has historically been associated with the practice" (Is There a Doctor in the House? 2003, para. 15).

Supporting that view, a study done in 2003 by Merritt, Hawkins & Associates, a physician search and consulting company in Dallas, Texas, found a significant amount of job dissatisfaction in the medical profession. Largely citing the difficulties associated with managed care and malpractice, the survey found that 24 percent of doctors in their final year of medical residency said that if they had it to do all over again, they would select another field instead of medicine. In comparison, only 5 percent of similar medical residents in 2001 said they would pick another field (Survey of Final Year Medical Residents, 2003).

Besides concerns about loss of autonomy from managed care and the rising costs of malpractice insurance, Dr. Barbara Barzanky a member of the American Medical Association's medical education council, also noted that many prospective students were being lured away by the promise of lucrative jobs in new economy fields like high technology (Lusk, 2002).

Dr. Perry Pugno, director of the division of medical education at the American Academy of Family Physicians, agreed. "Forces are drawing [some prospective students] toward other things, rather than away from medicine," he said (Schnieder, 2003, para. 12). While the heads of some students may have been turned by the promise of fat paychecks, the AMA's Barzanky said other students were not so much lured to other vocations as they became wary of the prospect of having to face big medical school debt (Lusk, 2002). According to the Association of American Medical Schools, medical school graduates in 2003 carried more than 4.5 times more debt than graduates did in 1984, when the average debt was $22,000 for public school graduates and $27,000 for private school graduates. By 2003, the average was $100,000 and $135,000 for public school and private school graduates, respectively (AAMC Launches Effort to Reduce Costs of U.S. Medical Education, 2004).

Prospective medical student Daniel Gurdak says that issue of financial support will be one of the most important factors in his decision whether to continue along his pursuit of becoming a doctor. "As nice as it would be to go to medical school, I don't know if I could spend that much money to do it, unless I got good financial aid," he said.

Given that virtually all of the issues cited as reasons for the slump in interest in medical school are still present, why do many doctors and medical school officials now believe that they are beginning to see a turnaround? Many medical school administrators say that the recent rebound is not the start of a new trend, but part of a larger one. Dr. Robert F. Jones, vice president for medical school services and studies of the Association of American Medical Colleges, put it this way: "Generally, medical school applications run in cycles," he said (Schneider, 2003, para. 4).

These officials said that concerns about the six-year downward movement were misplaced and that a more accurate picture of medical school applications could be gained by looking at patterns over a longer period of time. According to a study this year by Dr. Abigail Zuger published in the *New England Journal of Medicine*, changes in the numbers of US medical school applicants over the past 20 years have tended to be cyclical, without any apparent correlation to increased publicity about financial or social problems facing physicians (Zuger, 2004).

As evidence that the 2004 upswing is likely to continue, medical experts pointed out that this year's 5 percent upsurge in first-time applicants suggests that the trend toward increase in applications will continue since first-timers who get rejected often reapply in later years (Fong, 2003). Another segment of potential applicants is also trending up: women. In 2003, 17,672 women applied to medical schools, for the first time outnumbering male applicants (Fong, 2003).

"This isn't a one-time event," said Dr, Jordan Cohen, president of the American Association of American Medical Colleges. The number of female applicants has been steadily growing over the past 20 years and is likely to continue, he said. "We're seeing more women in our medical schools and in out facilities" (Silverman, 2004, para.3).

Medical school authorities said that even during the years of slumping applications, fears of shortages of qualified candidates were overblown. Dr. Jones pointed out that throughout the years of declining applicants there was still a large and qualified pool from which medical schools could choose. He said that even at its lowest point medical schools had about two applicants for every spot (Schneider, 2003).

Dr. Jones said that the bottom line is that despite the problems of slight decline in social status of doctors, the loss of autonomy and other hindrances brought about by managed care, and the rising cost of malpractice coverage, becoming a doctor is still one of the best careers for doing well financially while still doing good. "People worry when the applicant pool declines," he said. "[But] the message is that medicine is consistently an attractive career path" (Schneider, 2003, para.7).

Clearly, the medical establishment thinks that the 6-year downswing is over, and there is strong evidence to support this position, from the study of the cyclical nature of applications over a twenty-year period to the increase in first-time applicants, and the general trend of rising interest among women.

In the final analysis, however, it is impossible based solely on this year's numbers to draw any definitive conclusion about whether we are seeing the continuation of a larger cyclical pattern or possibly a one-year blip in a longer downward spiral. We will need more evidence, more numbers.

Both medical school and governmental officials would do well to continue watching those numbers. If this year's increase proves to be part of a larger cycle, then they will not have to make any immediate adjustments. But if it should turn out that this year was an anomaly in an overall pattern of declining interest among students in careers as physicians, the professional and public policy ramifications could be serious, even dire.

References

AAMC launches effort to address rising costs of U. S. medical education. (2004, April 26). Retrieved July 1, 2004, from http://www.aamc.org/newsroom/pressrel/2004/040426.htm

Fong, T. (Prospective) docs are in: Rise in medical school applications counters trend. (2003, Nov. 10). *Modern Healthcare*, p. 20. Retrieved May 22, 2004, from Lexis-Nexis database.

Howell, W. (2003, December). Medical school applications increase. *AAMC Reporter*. Retrieved May 20, 2004, from http://www.aamc.org/newsroom/ reporter/dec03/medicalapps.htm

Is there a doctor in the house? Maybe not. (2003, June 6). *American City Business Journals, Baltimore Business Journal*. Retrieved May 20, 2004, from Lexis-Nexis database.

Kaplan, Inc. MCAT 45: Advanced prep for advanced students, 2004 edition. (2004) New York: Simon & Schuster.

Lusk, K. (2002, October 14). Medical school applications continue to decline. *Chattanooga Times Free Press*, p. A4. Retrieved May 18, 2004, from Lexis-Nexis database.

Merritt, Hawkins, & Associates. (2003) 2003 Survey of final-year medical residents. (Vol. 21, no. 3). Irving, TX: Author.

Schnieder, M.E. (2003, Oct. 1) Medical school application once again on the rise: Reversal of a six-year decline—Practice Trends. *OB/GYN News*. Retrieved May 18, 2004, from http://articles.findarticles.com/p/articles/mi_m0CYD/is_19_38/ai_109025375

Silverman, J. Women fuel rise in medical school applications. (2004, Jan.1) *Clinical Psychiatric News*, 32: 1. Retrieved on May 18, 2004, from http://global.factiva.com/en/arch/display.asp.

Smith, S. (2003, Sept. 3). Med school applicants fall 22 percent since 1997. *The Boston Globe*. Retrieved May 23, 2003, from http://www.boston.com

Zuger, A,, M. D. (2004, Jan. 1). *NEJM Special Report*, 350(69-75). Retrieved May 18, 2004, from http://www.medical-journals.com/r042.htm

Critical Reading Questions

1. Identify Rodriguez's thesis.

2. Make a list of the causes that Rodriguez identifies. Can you find causes for the slump as well as the subsequent rise?

3. What effects of the trend does Rodriguez include?

4. Rodriguez used many statistics gathered from her research. How do the numbers help convince you about her points?

Questions for Writing and Discussion

1. Would you agree that there has been a "slight decline in the social status of doctors"?

2. Would you identify medicine as an attractive career path? What has shaped your opinion of medicine as a career path?

Old Game, New Players

Bella English

Journalist Bella English relies on storytelling techniques to illustrate the trend of teens becoming addicted to gambling. Her analysis of the trend, primarily its causes, revolves around a central character and his story.

Christopher adored gambling. The video poker, the slots, the dogs, his sports teams—each was as enticing as the next. He knew his way around the track blindfolded and would tear through the handicapping guides as if they were dime mysteries. He had his favorite set of poker machines at his casino of choice, Lincoln Park in Lincoln, Rhode Island.

He had his own bookie, too, who had noticed him one night playing the slots at Lincoln Park and asked if he wanted to make "some real money." His first sports bet with the bookie was like that first hit of heroin. Christopher was hooked. "Say you bet $1,000, and you lose it," he says. "You put $2,000 on the next game."

Like most gamblers—except maybe James Bond—Christopher lost a lot more than he won. Even after he dropped between $30,000 and $40,000 in just six months, he somehow found the money to feed his habit. To cover his debts, he indulged in what he calls "creative financing," in-cluding writing bad checks. He borrowed $400 from a friend and didn't pay it back. He filched relatives' ATM and credit cards. He stole from his sister. But no matter how much he got his hands on, it was never enough.

One night last May, already deeply in debt, he went to the casino and blew another $500. In despair, he drove to a bridge and smoked a pack of cigarettes while pondering a plunge. Finally, a police officer moved him along. Christopher drove away in tears. Burdened by his addiction, he felt world-weary.

He was barely 18 years old.

. . .

Gambling has been with mankind since ancient times. As Howard Shaffer, a psychology professor at Harvard University, likes to point out, Roman guards cast lots over Christ's robes during the Crucifixion. But what is new and troubling is the number of young people like Christopher who have become hard-core gamblers. A recent analysis by Shaffer shows that the rate of problem gambling among youths nationwide is more than double that of adults. Of the teenagers who gamble, nearly 10 percent will have a serious problem with it, compared with about 4 percent of adults.

In Massachusetts—with its popular lotteries and tracks and with casinos in nearby states—5 percent of the adult population, or about 250,000 people, have a gambling problem, although only about 2 percent are defined as "compulsive gamblers." Men are more likely to have trouble than women, but with the advent of readily accessible games like the lottery and Powerball, the gender gap is closing. Among the state's adolescents, 12 to 15 percent suffer from problem gambling, according to the Massachusetts Council on Compulsive Gambling.

For Christopher, it began innocently enough. He and some college buddies were sitting around the dorm drinking beer in the fall of 1997, his freshman year, and someone suggested a drive to the Newport Jai Alai and Casino in Rhode Island. The colorful flashes of the video games and the carnival noises of the slots were like the Pied Piper, beckoning him deeper and deeper into the gambling culture. Worst of all, Christopher got lucky. The hundred bucks he pocketed that night was chump change compared with the thousands he would later lose. His habit was financed in part by a campus job that paid nearly $10 an hour, a job he would eventually lose because of his habit. Gambling would come before everything else, including work.

During Christmas vacation that year, he headed to Lincoln Park Casino every day. The casino wasn't far from his home in a suburb south of Boston, and he loved betting the dogs over simulcast and playing video poker. It was easy money, better than flipping burgers at McDonald's, like other teens. One night, he won $700. The scene was way cool:

the dim lighting, the older crowd, the clinking of mixed drinks, all of it wrapped in a blue veil of smoke.

Last March, Christopher stopped attending classes, though he continued to live in his dormitory. In April, his parents, who had no idea he wasn't in school, received their bank statements and confronted Christopher about large withdrawals. There was a big scene, with the mother crying, the father and son yelling. An ultimatum was delivered: Christopher could either attend Gamblers Anonymous meetings or be cut off from the family. "I didn't feel like being homeless," Christopher says. So he agreed to go to a meeting. Still, he continued to deny he had a problem. "Lots of college kids gamble," Christopher says. "If they don't go to the casino, they play poker or blackjack all night long. The difference is, not a lot of them have money. When I had $500 in my wallet, I felt like a big man on campus. I'd take a new kid to the casino, he'd win 20 bucks and be all jazzed and want to go again."

. . .

What Christopher didn't know was that he had a disease he'd never heard of: pathological gambling. The American Psychiatric Association defines it as a mental disorder with symptoms that include a loss of control over gambling, a progression in frequency of wagering and the amount wagered, a preoccupation with betting, and a continuation of the gambling despite adverse consequences.

Unlike Christopher, most people can gamble without losing control. Even basketball superstar Michael Jordan, whose penchant for betting is well known, can't necessarily be labeled a problem gambler. "If Michael Jordan spends $50,000 on a golf game," says Shaffer, "he can afford that. He makes that money during a catnap, and you can't assume he's got a problem. But if you've got a kid who's spending $200 regularly and can't afford it, that's a problem. It's the consequences that define the problem."

And so it goes with compulsive gamblers like Christopher: They play, they lose, they play some more in an attempt to stay even. They can never get ahead. Much as an alcoholic will awake with a hangover and have a drink to steady his hands, a compulsive gambler will lose and play again and again and again. And much as an alcoholic will build up a tolerance to the bottle, a gambler builds up a tolerance to the loss. Gambling, like alcoholism, is a progressive disease: It's always just one more roll of the dice, spin of the wheel, or bet at the window.

Shaffer and other experts believe the prevalence of legalized gambling in society is the reason kids are getting hooked. Pass any grocery store or gas station, and you will see lottery and scratch tickets on sale; in 1997, the Massachusetts Lottery sold more than $3.2 billion in games of chance, some of it to underage youths. Television brings you the lucky numbers. It's not unusual for parents and grandparents to buy even the youngest children scratch tickets for their birthdays or Christmas. Many churches sponsor weekly bingo nights. Most large newspapers, including *The Boston Globe*, publish point spreads in their sports sections.

Then there are the tracks, open to those 18 and older in Massachusetts, and the casinos in neighboring Rhode Island and Connecticut. And, according to Christopher and other young people, many high schools have their own resident bookie, a classmate with whom students place sports bets. The Internet also offers scores of gambling sites, where all you need is access to a computer and a credit card. Ready cash for the casinos and the track is more accessible these days, too, with an ATM seemingly on every corner.

"Kids today have grown up in this culture," says Kathleen Scanlan, director of the Massachusetts Council on Compulsive Gambling, a state agency that offers information and referral services to problem gamblers. "A lot of them are in a lot of trouble." Shaffer is even more blunt: "For some kids, gambling is the crack of the '90s."

It wasn't always this way. "When I was growing up," Shaffer says, "the nightly news led with the weather report. Now they lead with the winning lottery numbers." By the time teenagers are in their senior year of high school, he says, nationally, 90 percent have gambled. "Young kids gamble over pogs," colorful cardboard disks, with the victor taking the spoils, he says. "You can see the seeds being sown there."

Those seeds may take root in high school and spread in college: Addiction experts in Massachusetts are regularly called onto campuses to consult on gambling issues. In July 1997, the Middlesex district attorney's office ended a nine-month investigation into organized sports gambling at Boston and Bentley colleges by announcing the indictments of six men, some of them students, on 63 charges of illegal bookmaking. Earlier, the office had uncovered student-run bookie operations at both schools. Sports gambling is particularly popular with youths, because bets can be placed with no money up front.

But gambling—both by youths and adults—is often swept under the rug, because it is the "invisible addiction." Even those closest to the gambler usually don't know the extent of the problem. "There aren't the physical signs you see with alcohol or drug abuse: the staggering, the stumbling, the slurring of words," Scanlan says. Nor is there the stigma; instead, there is what she calls the "acceptability and accessibility of it."

. . .

Christopher's parents were shocked when they found out about their son's problem. "We're not gamblers, we're not drinkers, we're not smokers," says Christopher's father, Joseph. "We didn't even know about gambling, quite frankly."

Joseph went to the Gamblers Anonymous meetings with Christopher, to find out what, exactly, his eldest son was up against. Now he is a man with a mission. "It's become almost a ministry for me," says Joseph, who works in the computer industry and describes his large, close-knit family as "middle-class, vanilla-type people."

"For me and my wife," he says, "gambling is like cancer. It's a disease as deadly as cancer. It's one that can be dealt with through therapy and that one can learn to live with. We love our son. We don't want him to die. Every day that he is alive, there's a chance he will get better." Joseph is a big fan of Gamblers Anonymous. "You wouldn't think it," he says, "but from a father's perspective, there's a dozen great role models in that room."

Still, he has no illusions about the enemy his son is up against. Last spring, when Christopher was at his lowest point, he asked his father to bail him out. Joseph agreed to pay the $900 Christopher owed the bookie he'd met at Lincoln Park. If the money wasn't paid, Christopher told his father, he'd be beaten up or killed. Joseph accompanied his son to the appointed place—a convenience store in the town where Christopher attends college—to make sure the money actually got to the bookie. While the father waited in the car, the son went behind the building to pay off his bookie. When he returned to the car, Christopher thanked his dad. "He said, 'Boy, am I glad it's over. I'll never do it again.'"

But the money never reached the bookie. Several days later, Joseph learned that Christopher had pocketed the $900 and gambled it away almost immediately. The memory is still painful. "What was hard," Joseph says, "was that he could look us in the face and lie with such great conviction."

After learning his lesson the hard way, Joseph stopped bailing Christopher out. The men in Gamblers Anonymous reinforced that decision, saying he would just be enabling his son. "Like giving him a loaded gun" is the way one put it.

Should parents help pay their teenagers' gambling debts? The question comes up all the time on the hot line run by the Council on Compulsive Gambling. "It's a very difficult decision," says JoAnn Cailler, the council's program director. "Sometimes, it means having to take a second mortgage on the home. Parents worry that they may be helping their child to gamble. But they may also worry about their child's safety. It's a real difficult place for a parent to be."

. . .

No one really knows why some people are more vulnerable than others to compulsive gambling; why one teenager can bet occasionally on his favorite team while someone like Christopher bets hundreds of dollars a week. Shaffer, who is the director of the division on addictions at Harvard Medical School, says new evidence indicates that compulsive gambling may have genetic origins. "There is evidence of a biogenetic vulnerability," he says. "It does tend to run in the family, but then again, most families tend to grow up in the same house."

A recent study also shows a link between gambling and other high-risk behavior among teenagers. Dr. Elizabeth Goodman of Children's Hospital in Boston surveyed 17,000 teenagers from Vermont. Fifty-three percent said they had gambled; 7 percent reported having a gambling problem. A closer look showed that those with a gambling problem also reported problems with alcohol and drugs. "Youths who had problems due to gambling were more likely to have used cocaine more than three times in the past month," says Goodman, whose study was published last summer in the *Journal of the American Academy of Pediatrics.*

Christopher fits that profile. He has had problems with binge drinking, has smoked marijuana since he was 12 years old, and has experimented with harder drugs.

"Pathological gamblers often are seeking a high through gambling," says Goodman. "The process of gambling is having some sort of physiological effect on the body. We don't know exactly what that effect is."

But gamblers do. It's mind-altering, they say, like cocaine; better than the best sex they ever had. Many gamblers will tell you that they literally shake, like an alcoholic, when placing a bet. Listen to Christopher: "For me, it's the high, the adrenaline, the thrill, the risk. There's nothing like it in the world. Nothing else matters when you're gambling."

Those gamblers who are substance abusers swear that the bottle is easier to beat than the bet. Sam, 52, attends both Alcoholics Anonymous and Gamblers Anonymous meetings. "Gambling is a much more difficult addiction," he says. In his high school yearbook, Sam was named the "first man to take a gamble." That was 35 years ago; his youthful habit became an addiction that he still struggles with today.

"I thought it was really cool at the time," he says of his youthful gambling. "I've lost thousands and thousands and thousands of dollars. If kids get hooked, it will be a lifetime recovery process. It goes right to their heads. They think it's easy money, but there can be lifetime consequences."

Youths, who tend to be more risk-oriented than adults, also have an illusion of control over their gambling. "There's a sense that they have a special skill," says Howard Shaffer, "when there is no skill at all in gambling. That's why it is called gambling."

·   ·   ·

Christopher attended his first Gamblers Anonymous meeting last May. Every night, there is a Gamblers Anonymous meeting somewhere in the Boston area. Modeled after Alcoholics Anonymous, Gamblers Anonymous follows a similar 12-step program, starting with the acknowledgment that the gambler is powerless over gambling, that life has become unmanageable.

One may imagine that gamblers are all seedy-looking guys in polyester pants, with protruding bellies, beard stubble, and bleary eyes. A Gamblers Anonymous meeting will quickly dispel that myth. Many of the people who attend are middle-class; they hold jobs and pay taxes. Others have lost their jobs because of gambling and are attempting to dig their way out of a hole. Most of them are in their 40s, 50s, or 60s, but many describe a problem that started decades earlier.

You won't see many young faces at these meetings. The few who attend swear it has helped, but getting teenagers to go is difficult. They deny they have a problem, or their parents bail them out. Then there are more practical concerns: how to get to the meetings, for instance. Recently, two teenagers arrived at a meeting at Curry College in Milton by bus. They weren't yet old enough to drive, and their parents had no idea they were in trouble. Christopher is a rarity: His father attends the meetings with him.

Whether a gambler is young or old, there isn't much help available for the addiction. Nationally, there are 13,000 programs for substance abusers but fewer than 100 for people with gambling problems. Massachusetts spends a total of $1.1 million each year on problem gambling, of which $270,000 goes toward treatment programs, or a little more than a dollar per gambler. (Ironically, those funds come from unclaimed lottery receipts.) That money is divided among 17 treatment centers, most of them operating out of substance-abuse sites.

The oldest program is The Mount Auburn Hospital Center for Problem Gambling, which was established 10 years ago. The Cambridge center evaluates gamblers and offers individual psychotherapy as well as group and couples therapy. It also consults to Boston-area colleges.

"We're really interested in helping people understand what makes them do what they do," says Dr. Lance Dodes, a psychiatrist who serves as the clinic's director. He is hopeful about teenage gamblers, he says, for the same reason why he is hopeful about teenagers in general: They often grow out of their troubles. "Just as there are a lot of people who overdrink in college but don't go on to become alcoholics," Dodes says, "there are a lot of young people who gamble but don't go on to become compulsive gamblers. The problem is, compulsive gamblers often start early."

Like Gamblers Anonymous meetings, such centers do not see many young gamblers. "There's not a lot at stake at this point in their lives," explains Marilyn Feinberg, a therapist at the Mount Auburn center. "Compulsive gamblers who have families and have gotten into a lot of trouble, they usually have some hope of reconciliation with their wives, and that can be very helpful in getting them into your office and into treatment."

Prevention would naturally be the best "cure." But while teenagers are bombarded with information about the dangers of drinking, drugs, and sex, gambling gets little attention. When it can find a volunteer and a receptive school, the Council on Compulsive Gambling will send a recovering gambler to high schools to speak to students.

There are broader moves afoot to control the pervasiveness of gambling in society. Consumer-rights guru Ralph Nader has launched a campaign to make Las Vegas, which has invested heavily in child-oriented arcades and shows, less family-friendly. Howard Shaffer has been consulting with the gaming industry to help casinos develop guidelines on responsible gambling, which means no underage gamblers. In June, President Clinton's commission on compulsive gambling is expected to release a national report on the extent of gambling, including a section on youths, with recommendations for dealing with the problem.

Shaffer, who counsels compulsive gamblers, says cognitive therapy seems to work the best; that is, changing the way gamblers think about their behavior. More practically, it involves lifestyle changes, such as taking a different route home to avoid the track.

Together, Shaffer and his patients come up with a plan. Reestablishing meaning in their lives, whether it be from religion or relationships, works for some people. Others recover cold turkey, on their own. But for people who can't quit gambling that way, drugs such as those used for obsessive-compulsive disorder are being tested. "They're trying antidepressants and anti-anxiety agents," says Shaffer. "It's almost a shotgun approach to see which one works."

.   .   .

Christopher's journey has been one step forward, two back; two steps forward, one back. He and his parents know the road to recovery is pocked with potholes.

At his first Gamblers Anonymous meeting, in a basement room of Southwood Community Hospital in Norfolk, Christopher listened to the tales of men losing their wives, their homes, their kids, their sanity, their freedom. He still didn't get it. "I thought I was invincible. They're all old guys," he recalls.

Two days after that meeting, Christopher went out and gambled for three days running, losing $500. Shaken, he went to a second meeting, stood up, and announced, "I'm Christopher G., and I'm a compulsive gambler." It was the first time he'd admitted it, and it felt good.

But even after his admission, the grip of gambling proved too powerful. Christopher left that meeting and drove straight to Lincoln Park. In his pocket was $500, money he'd stolen from his sister and borrowed from friends. Within an hour, it was gone. Furious at himself, Christopher peeled out of the casino parking lot and drove to a bridge, where he parked his car and smoked cigarette after cigarette, flicking them into the water below. "I thought a jump might hurt for a second," he says now, "but then the pain will be over."

Christopher probably would not have jumped—"I'm a major chicken," he says. At any rate, the police car pulled up and the officer told him to move on. He drove home, remembering one of the tenets of Gamblers Anonymous: Write down your feelings and the damage your gambling has caused. In his room, Christopher scribbled nonstop. It all come out: the stealing, the lying, the cheating, the pain, the suicidal thoughts. Then, he woke his father and handed him the statement. Both were in tears.

That night, May 21, father and son once again attended a Norfolk meeting together. The summer unfolded nicely for Christopher. Accompanied by his father, he attended meetings faithfully. The older men were touched by Christopher; in him, they saw themselves, 20, 30, or 40 years earlier. Christopher also enrolled in summer courses at his college to make up the credits lost to gambling in the spring.

In September, his parents accompanied him to a Gamblers Anonymous potluck. Christopher, who brought the potato salad and cole slaw, was the youngest one there by decades. "I feel like I'm one of them," he says. "I never lost a wife, a house, or kids to gambling. But I'm a compulsive gambler, and they're compulsive gamblers. I stole, they stole."

Besides absorbing horror stories from the men, he was picking up coping strategies: how to avoid a bet, how to use a buddy list. How, just as an alcoholic can't have even a sip, he couldn't bet even a quarter.

At a mid-September meeting, Christopher gave the group a sunny progress report. "On Friday night, there was a big back-to-school party. After, I went to a store and bought a scratch ticket, but I didn't scratch it; I gave it to my best friend. I took an algebra test, got into honors, and had a terrific job interview. Things are looking up." The men applauded.

At that point, Christopher was 140 days clean. "I told the bookie I moved. I never carry more than $20 in my pocket. I'm the luckiest man on earth to get out of the hell I created for myself," he announced.

. . .

Six weeks later, Christopher is sitting in a folding chair in the basement room of Southwood Community Hospital. His father sits next to him, studying the text intently while the young man fidgets in his seat like a bored child at church.

Tonight, Christopher will not stand up and share his story. There are too many people; he'd be embarrassed. Besides, the news isn't good. If he did stand up, here's what he says he would say: "Life sucks. I've been gambling again and doing drugs. Right now, I don't feel like coming here on Thursday nights. I'm listening, but I'm not absorbing it."

Christopher's road to recovery, which seemed so promising in early September, collapsed shortly after his college classes resumed. During his second week of school, he returned to Lincoln Park and blew $500 on the dogs and video poker. He began popping Ecstasy, a popular amphetamine on college campuses, and now feels he is saddled with two addictions. "I've been gambling to see if I can win money to pay off the drug dealer," he says. At the moment, he figures he owes $3,000 in gambling and drug debts, money his parents will no longer pay. Christopher has begun therapy and has started attending weekly Narcotics Anonymous meetings, too.

"It's a war," his father says. "And we're not about to give up. Do I have the answer today? No. Will we get through this? Yes."

Still, it is, as Gamblers Anonymous has told them, a war to be fought one day at a time. At this particular meeting, it has been 12 days since Christopher last gambled. Still, the urge is there. "The fall is really hard because of all the sports teams," Christopher says. "And Super Bowl Sunday will be terrible."

But a month later, Christopher's parents pull him out of school, because he is failing all of his classes. Christopher is now planning on joining the military to "get away from the drug and gambling culture and to grow up," his father says.

Christopher's advice to other kids in trouble with gambling? "Get help. Talk to people. Don't give up. Even if you slip and mess up again, you can still pull yourself out." He pops his knuckles and jiggles his leg nervously as he speaks. His handsome face is a mask of misery.

"I'm only 18," he says. "I don't want to end up at 58 losing my wife, my home, and my job. I'm 18, and I'm scared."

Critical Reading Questions

1. Outline this article, making note of English's organization.

2. Does Christopher seem like a real person? Does the writer make his story believable? Why?

3. How does the author use quotations in this analysis? Make a list of the sources. Which ones does she rely on most heavily? How do they help explain the trend?

4. What are some of the causes of compulsive gambling that English presents? What are some effects?

Questions for Writing and Discussion

1. Though the trend of teens becoming compulsive gamblers is on the rise, as proven by English's research and statistics, the problem is not all that widespread. Is this a topic worth reading and writing about? Why?

2. In a couple of places, the author compares addiction to drugs and alcohol to a gambling addiction. How are the two alike or different? Why do you think she uses that analogy?

3. Would you say that gambling is a serious problem for society? What are the effects on society of an increase in the rate of teen gamblers?

WRITING IN THE WORKS
Interview with Bella English

Bella English

1. Talk a little about finding topics to write about. Do you come up with the topics yourself, or are you assigned topics?

Figuring that the best defense is a good offense, I generally come up with my own ideas; I keep a running story list. Otherwise, you are at the mercy of assignment editors. Also, since I'm "out there" reporting, I have more access to lots of sources and ideas.

2. How do you find sources for your stories? In "Old Game, New Players," Christopher, who is at the heart of the story, is a compulsive gambler and a teen. Obviously you don't find sources like that in the Yellow Pages. Did you find him after you thought of the topic, or was he there first?

I found Christopher after I had the topic; I found him through a quasi-state agency that was running radio commercials for a help line for compulsive gamblers. (I had heard the blurb on the radio.) I interviewed those folks for their expertise, and also asked for a teenager, and they came up with him.

3. In writing about teen gambling you include a lot of research, first proving Christopher is part of a larger trend, then theorizing about the causes. How much of your time on a project like this article do you spend on the research, and how do you do it? How much can you do online? Do you have to go to certain places to get research?

I didn't do much research on the Web, as it was not as prevalent then as it is now. I did lots of primary-source interviewing, attending Gamblers Anonymous meetings, interviewing addicted gamblers and their families, as well as therapists. I also went to a casino in Rhode Island.

4. Interviewing is probably the part of writing trend features that makes most beginners nervous. How do you prepare for an interview? Do you rely on pre-written, scripted questions or is some of it intuitive? Do you have to visit a person several times to feel an interview is complete?

First of all, I like to interview a person in his or her "native habitat," that is, the home. I can get a better feel for a person through seeing how he/she lives; I can also get good details (what's in their bookcase, their refrigerator? are they clean or messy? are there family photos around?) All of these little details can create a rich tapestry, especially if it's a profile. I would suggest beginners make a list of questions; sometimes, sources can be intimidating and throw off the train of thought. I sometimes make a list, simply to remind myself of questions I might forget! It's important to follow up on a question; that is, if the source says something that needs more explanation, don't just drop it. And his/her answer often leads to another, related question. So, a lot of interviewing is intuitive. If I'm doing a profile, I like to see a person at least twice before writing. And of course, I need to talk to others about that person; it could be parents, or a teacher, friend, colleague, even someone who doesn't care for him/her. (I often ask whom I should call; both pro and con. It's surprising how many people will actually come up with "con" names that truly are "cons.")

5. How difficult is making all the pieces come together? What's your writing process? Do you lay out all your notes on the floor or have some kind of numbering system?

First, I go through all my notes and highlight the most relevant stuff. Usually, before I sit down to write, I'll already have a lead in mind. Sometimes, more than one! I get a rough draft down fairly quickly, and spend more time editing/rewriting than actually writing that first draft.

6. Throughout "Old Game," you artfully weave Christopher's story. Talk about how important narrative is to you in writing about trends, how you learned to write good narrative. What writers have you learned the most from?

I believe narrative writing is important because it's a way to put a human face on an issue, and a way to invite the reader into a person's life. I believe journalism is mostly on-the-job training, so I would say I learned from just doing it, over and over again. Also, from reading other people's writing. I always read the Pulitzer entries, and winners, in the feature writing category. There's such good writing there. I love John McPhee's writing that used to be in the *New Yorker*. He was amazing in his reportorial detail and in his prose.

WRITING AND REVISION STRATEGIES

Gathered here are three interactive sections for you to use as you write and revise your trend research article.

▶ Writer's Notebook Suggestions
▶ Peer-Editing Log
▶ Revision Checklist

Writer's Notebook Suggestions

You can use these exercises to do some start-up thinking and writing for your trend research article.

1. Go to a shopping center and choose a store. Interview sales staff about some new development in the store: a new product or style. Write one paragraph about your findings, incorporating quotations and statistics that you have gathered.

2. Observe a high-traffic area for an hour, noting patterns in behavior. Choose one of the following behaviors, or identify your own.

   ▶ The way people interact with ATM machines
   ▶ The way people behave on public transportation
   ▶ The way people cross a busy intersection

Write a generalization about behavior within the context. What can you say, in general, about people who ride the bus? Or about the way people behave with an ATM?

3. Research the nutritional data from a fast-food restaurant. Write a paragraph for an average reader that clearly explains how much fat, sugar, and salt are in the most popular items. Use analogies to help make the facts clear.

4. Survey a group of college freshmen. Ask how many hours of television they watch each day or during the average week. Follow up by asking what they watch, and why. Survey the same number of seniors, and ask the same questions. Write a paragraph explaining your findings.

5. Do a survey in your writing class. How many people write drafts of assignments in longhand first, and how many type directly on their word processors? Find out whether this behavior has changed since high school. Speculate why.

6. Describe a person who illustrates a trend.

7. Find out the most popular foods at your college dining hall, cafeteria, or coffee shop. Try one,

and describe the taste and texture. Interview people who have eaten the food (or cooked or served it), and collect quotations. Write a description, incorporating the quotations.

8. Identify a trend at your school or in your community. Some examples: Have you found that more (or fewer) of your friends are interested in careers in the military? Do you find more interracial dating than before? Are there more smokers on your campus these days? Do at least three person-on-the-street interviews, finding out what people think are the causes and/or effects of the trend. Be sure to get names, approximate or accurate ages, occupations, and places of residence for all the people you interview. Try to get a mix of gender, age, and ethnicity, if possible. After you complete your interviews, write a page on your findings, integrating the quotations as you discuss possible causes and effects of the trend. Be sure to attribute quotations accurately and completely. For example: "Rebecca Wong, an eighteen-year-old freshman at Central College, says, "Dating a guy on my floor would be like dating my brother.""

Peer-Editing Log

As you work with a writing partner or in a peer-editing group, you can use these questions to give useful responses to a classmate's trend research piece and as a guide for discussion.

Writer's Name _____

Date _____

1. Underline the introduction and note in the margin which type of beginning the writer used—narrative or expository. Did the introduction get your attention? Why? What might make it stronger?

2. Put two lines under the thesis. Does the topic seem noteworthy or interesting to you?

3. Star the area where the writer provides proof that the trend exists.

4. Note causes in the margins. Note effects in the margins.

5. Number the sources you find.

6. Put a wavy line under transitions, and identify any areas that need transitions with a "T."

7. Does the writer explain the causes and/or effects well? Do you see the logic in the argument?

8. Can you think of anything the writer might add? More quotations from observers or experts? More facts or statistics?

9. Is all research well cited within the text? Do you wonder about the source of any facts or statistics? Note any place where research needs a source or attribution.

10. Bracket the conclusion. Does the writer end strongly?

Revision Checklist

As you do your final revision, check to make sure that you

❑ Wrote an engaging introduction

❑ Stated your thesis clearly and accurately

❑ Provided proof that the trend exists

❑ Provided an explanation of causes and/or effects

❑ Cited sources accurately and fully

❑ Used good transitions to show new aspects of your analysis

❑ Included a good ending that leaves the reader with a lasting impression.

RESEARCH and DOCUMENTATION

PART III

14. RESEARCH

Research is formalized curiosity. It is poking and prying with a purpose.

—Zora Neale Hurston

RESEARCH

Are teens more or less likely to smoke cigarettes now than they were ten years ago? Is there a link between where teens live and whether they are likely to smoke? You might be asking these questions as you write an editorial about smoking bans in public buildings or develop an ad campaign against smoking. You might need this information to help you define and explain a trend for a research article. Most writing projects you do will involve some kind of research, and that research will start with questions like these.

Focusing on a question or two, you could find a computer, log onto the Internet, and start searching for webpages with answers. You could also go to a library and talk to a reference librarian. Taking another approach, you could find experts who can send you to good sources for information. Which approach would be the most effective and the most efficient? A good researcher knows how to use a variety of search tools. No single tool can do every research task. As you will see in this chapter, the best research uses a combination of approaches.

More people than ever are incorporating research into their everyday lives, using the Internet for comparison shopping and finding out about medical conditions, and consulting experts through e-mail. The Internet makes it possible to research quickly and well, as long as you know the variety of tools available online.

Still, some inquiries need other approaches. Complex questions like, "What were the effects of the Industrial Revolution on women?" might be best answered in a book or a specialized database available at the library. Research for some projects may even take the form of interviewing experts or hunting through archives and public documents like birth and death records in the county courthouse.

A huge array of research tools—books, websites, directories of experts, and public documents, to name just a few—is available through your Internet connection and at your school or public library. There are so many tools, in fact, that choosing the right ones can be a researcher's most baffling problem. What is a Web directory? How do you find the best books among the stacks at the library? Why use a book if you have an Internet connection? Dealing with the vast array of sources may lead researchers into winding paths that consume lots of time and sometimes yield very few quality results.

In this chapter, you will learn to research more efficiently and effectively, following a research path that ends in high-quality information. You will also learn some ways to make your writing more creative through research.

CHAPTER OBJECTIVES

In this chapter you will learn to

- ▶ brainstorm by browsing online, in bookstores, and in libraries
- ▶ narrow your topic and formulate a research question
- ▶ create a working bibliography
- ▶ read with focus, take useful notes, and avoid plagiarism
- ▶ evaluate bias in your sources
- ▶ use books, periodicals, newspapers, interviews, and the World Wide Web

BRAINSTORMING: RESEARCHING TO DISCOVER TOPICS

Many people in creative professions—such as designers, architects, and film producers—use research to jump-start new projects and get ideas flowing. The Researching in the Real World profiles in this chapter show you how people tailor research to their professions. Some people in technical and scientific fields say that even before they have a topic firmly fixed, they first brainstorm by doing a quick electronic keyword search. Many professionals report browsing through "bricks and mortar" or even electronic bookstores like Amazon.com for inspiration.

Researchers who use this browsing method say they look for unusual twists on familiar subjects by reading through titles and leafing through books, noting chapter titles and authors. And they look at current journals that reflect recent topics and trends in specific fields of study. Browsing through journals and magazines at the library or bookstore might even be easier and more useful than surfing the Internet with keywords. Current professional and scholarly journals and other periodicals reflect the most up-to-date thinking, and it may be easier to evaluate the credibility of sources in the library than online. Later in this chapter you will see how important evaluating credibility is, and why the publications you find in bookstores and libraries, which have been reviewed and selected, might be more reliable than Internet sources.

You can browse the "virtual shelves" at the library by beginning with a hunt through the online subject catalog. Libraries own a great variety of encyclopedias, guides, dictionaries, bibliographies, and other general reference works that can give you an overview of a subject you might not know much

Boston University Libraries

Telnet to Catalog   ## Web Catalog

Search
Author
Title or Journal Title
Word
Author / Title
Subject Headings
Call Numbers
ISBN, OCLC
Gov. Doc. Numbers

Reserve Services
By Course Number
By Professor's Name

Help and Renewal
Library Information
Borrowing Record
Book Renewal
Library Purchase Request

BU Library Web Sites

| Boston University Libraries | ▾ | Go |

Boston Library Consortium
BLC Gateway‖ Virtual Catalog ‖

Library subject online catalog. (Courtesy of Mugar Memorial Library, Boston University)

about. You can find these sources in the catalog at the library or with the help of librarians.

Online encyclopedias such as *Britannica Online* provide broad background information. For example, the following entry shows the result of a keyword search for "carbon dating" in order to research the way archeologists use carbon dating on digs.

Carbon-14 Dating and Other Cosmogenic Methods, from *Dating*

The occurrence of natural radioactive carbon in the atmosphere provides a unique opportunity to date organic materials as old as 50,000 years. Unlike most isotopic dating methods, the conventional . . .

Radiocarbon Dating

Scientists in the fields of geology, climatology, anthropology, and archaeology can answer many questions about the past through a technique called radiocarbon, or carbon-14, dating. One key to understanding how and why something happened is to pinpoint when it happened. (See also Anthropology, . . .

Carbon

Without the element carbon, life as we know it would not exist. Carbon provides the framework for all tissues of plants and animals. These tissues

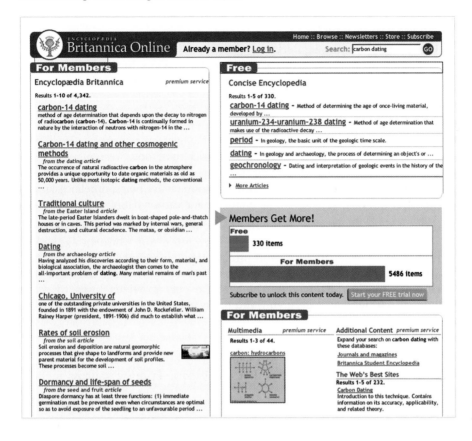

Online search for "carbon dating" from the *Encyclopaedia Britannica*

are built of elements grouped around chains or rings made of carbon atoms. Carbon also provides common fuels—coal, coke, oil, gasoline, and natural . . .

You can also search the *Britannica Elementary Encyclopedia* for articles about carbon dating.

Carbon Dating

Introduction to this technique. Contains information on its accuracy, applicability, and related theory.

Archaeology and Ancient History: Archaeology

British Broadcasting Corporation

Resource on various aspects of this study of the material remains of the past human activities. Includes illustrated articles on marine and virtual archaeology, carbon dating, and the Piltdown man. Also contains reports on the British sites, and game.

Learning from the Fossil Record

University of California, Berkeley

Educational reference on paleontology, for students. Includes classroom activities and projects on plate tectonics, dinosaurs, carbon dating, fossils, and climate change. Provides access to related educational resources.

Prehistory

Teacher Net

Collection of resources on evolution, agriculture, tools, weapons, art, the major civilizations, and archaeology of this period of ancient history. Facilitates access to picture galleries, guided tours, interactive maps, timelines, and online books. Includes sections on dinosaurs and carbon dating techniques.

You can see the usefulness of this site for beginning your research path. Each of the headings provides a snippet of information that you can explore in more depth if it is pertinent to your project. If you were researching a coastal dig, for example, "Learning from the Fossil Record" promises material that deals with marine archeology. The website also provides links to other sources and other websites, giving you many avenues to follow.

Primary and Secondary Sources

Library and Internet research can lead you to primary sources, which are original or firsthand documents that detail data. Primary sources include the following.

R E S E A R C H I N G · I N · T H E · R E A L · W O R L D

Peter Olotka
Game Designer

Peter Olotka designs interactive games for educational settings such as museums and public television and for the NBA. His games have involved topics as far-flung as subatomic particles, wildfires, and aliens. He invented a board game that is now a website, CosmicEncounter.com. His research begins with a thorough interview of his client and then consultations with experts in the fields. Still, he says, "Seventy-five percent of our research is done online."

Olotka often researches technical information that is hard to verify. After getting some facts from Internet sources, particularly .gov sites, he consults experts to check them out.

Olotka always looks for the most up-to-date sources, especially in books about technology, which can easily be outdated. Some problems Olotka has found doing research have been related to not being an expert in the fields he is researching. "The thing that is surprising is how difficult it often is to nail down an elusive bit of information. In part that is because we are laymen in a professional world, so we don't know where to look."

- Interviews (with experts, practitioners, and witnesses)
- Public documents (like tax records, police reports, government studies, census data, minutes from meetings with public officials—anything available through the Freedom of Information Act)
- E-mail
- Diaries, letters, and journals
- Manuscripts, music, films, speeches, and works of art
- Experiments and observations
- Surveys and polls
- Autobiographies
- Journals

Using or consulting primary sources will tend to make your writing more credible and original, and less derivative. Sometimes, however, primary sources may be unavailable or not appropriate for your assignment. In the course of your research, you may also want to read what other people have thought or figured out about a topic. Secondary sources analyze and interpret original sources. They include the following.

- Analytical books
- Commentaries in magazines and journals
- Newspaper articles
- News broadcasts
- Reviews
- Online discussions, bulletin boards, and listservs
- Biographies

Remember always to give credit to the writer responsible for the research and ideas. See Chapter 15 on how to cite and attribute sources.

NARROWING YOUR TOPIC AND FORMULATING A SPECIFIC RESEARCH QUESTION

For each type of writing assignment you research, you will have to do some preliminary reading to help you narrow your topic. For example, you might be assigned a research paper for a sociology class about new trends on college campuses. You know that the topic is far too broad and that you will have to narrow it to one area of college life: academic, extracurricular, sports, social, or community service. You still need to refine your topic more. Let's say you choose to look at new trends in the social life of college students. You do some preliminary reading in current newspapers and magazines to see what trends are in the news. You discover, as Caitlin Austin did when she was writing "Fraternities of the Future: Dry or Wet?" (reprinted in Chapter 13), that drinking in fraternities is a serious problem and that banning alcohol from fraternity houses is a current trend. If this topic interests you, you have found a narrow enough topic to begin your research.

Topics related to college students and drinking
Straight edge
—No drinking at all
Binge drinkers
—Effects on health
—Effects on academic performance
Fake IDs
—How they are acquired
Alcoholism among college students
—How many alcoholics get their start in college
Drinking at fraternities
—Deaths due to drinking at frats
—Other crimes involving drinking and frats (assaults, rapes)
—"Dry" fraternities

Make a brainstorming list. As you read, generate ideas for your writing.

Once you have narrowed your topic, you can formulate a **research question**. Having a specific research question helps make your research efficient. It also allows you to enter into research with an open mind, genuinely seeking answers to a question you find interesting. A good research question might be, "What has led fraternities to go dry and ban alcohol?" Another is, "Can fraternities survive if they go dry?" If you begin to research without a question, you might spend a lot of time going in too many different directions. Even with a question in mind, you might start with one idea, begin reading and researching, and find that it is not interesting to you. You can always go back to your preliminary brainstorming and narrow your search to another branch of the topic and another question.

Someone writing an editorial about a town that is discontinuing a curb-side recycling program, for example, might begin by asking, "Is recycling useful?" Someone researching the phenomenon of exercise addiction might ask, "What causes addictive behaviors?" Narrowing a topic and clearly defining a research question allow you to focus your research effectively. You will not be overwhelmed with too much information (if your topic is too broad) or discouraged by finding too little (if your topic is too narrow). Looking up "exercise," for example, probably won't help you research exercise addiction because the topic is too broad. Likewise, trying to find information about exercise addiction only as it has been reported in women between the ages of eighteen and twenty-one might be too narrow.

A good research question is in-depth enough to help you formulate a thesis—the main argument or point of your paper—and narrow enough to fit the parameters of your assignment. Your thesis probably won't be fully refined until you do your research and see where you want to go with an idea. Though following a single research question helps lead you to information, you should always be flexible in your researching. If you bump into another interesting trail of information, follow it. A solid thesis might

RESEARCHING · IN · THE · REAL · WORLD

Dave Metzler

Television Producer and Director

Dave Metzler is coexecutive producer for *Queer Eye for the Straight Guy.* **He has also produced other documentary/reality projects for VH-1 and Bravo. His research ranges from examining trends in clothing and design to break dancing, disco, and fast-food. For a project on the history of supermodels, Metzler says his research began, as most research projects do for him, with a quick Internet search using Yahoo! or Google. He says he often uses Amazon.com to find books on a topic, but is more likely to call experts in a field he is researching, although not before gathering information to fuel the interview. His research question was, "What was the first use of the word** *supermodel*?" **Online he found a listing of** *Sports Illustrated* **swimsuit models and statistics on their height and weight from 1970 through 2000. He also found information about the hourly rates models were paid through those years.**

He looked at the connection between models and designers, and then "I hit the Internet to figure out whom to call."

Metzler says the limitation of the Internet is too much information. "Weeding through the fake sites takes too long," Metzler says, and he often makes the mistake of looking for the one right site with all the answers. "Nobody has the whole answer. You need to pick up many clues in many places," Metzler says. His best research tool, he says, is talking to people. "I'm always surprised by how many people have specialized knowledge. I often work with researchers who work for Errol Morris [the independent filmmaker], and they know every weird character with every weird expertise in the US. But what surprises me most is that everything has been documented somewhere, and my research is about finding it."

occur to you after you follow different research paths and try several times to formulate a research question.

Your library may have a number of good ways to help you begin your reading and formulate your research question. Most libraries have research tools ranging from online catalogs to special databases available through computer terminals at the library or through "proxy" or home computer connections. Your library may pay fees to link to these databases. Most will provide citations for articles. You can then track the articles down on microfilm or microfiche or even in back copies of journals at the library. Others provide full text of sources.

Some common databases are Ebscohost, CQ Researcher, and Twayne Series. Others include the following.

WorldCat

WorldCat lists and describes books and holdings from libraries in forty-five countries. The database includes journals, musical scores, video recordings, maps, magazines, newspapers, computer programs, manuscripts, sound recordings, visual materials, and websites.

InfoTrac

InfoTrac is a searchable online library containing full-length articles, abstracts, and bibliographic citations from scholarly and popular periodicals, including a broad range of journals, magazines, encyclopedias, and newsletters.

LexisNexis

LexisNexis provides legal, news, public record, and business information, including tax and regulatory publications, in online, print, or CD-ROM formats. The database is searchable by field of interest, like news, business, medicine, and law.

Readers' Guide Full Text

Readers' Guide Full Text, produced by the H. W. Wilson Company, offers index listings—with full citations—and abstracts of the most popular general-interest periodicals published in the United States and Canada. You can get the full text for articles written after 1994. Some libraries also have Readers' Guide Full Text available in bound book and CD-ROM formats.

ISI Web of Science

The ISI Web of Science links to the Science Citation Expanded, Social Sciences Citation Index, and Arts and Humanities Citation Index. It provides access to multidisciplinary information from research journals, including full-text articles.

Proquest

Proquest provides full text of current periodicals and newspapers and is updated daily, dating back to 1986. You can also link to e-journals and get information about dissertations. "Back files of record" pages from Proquest Historical Newspaper Collection show the pages exactly as they appeared to the original readers.

CREATING A WORKING BIBLIOGRAPHY

Keep track of all your sources, even if you are not certain you will use them in your writing. Careful record keeping will ensure that citations and quotations are accurate. Noting the title, author, publisher, date of publication, volume and page numbers, and webpage addresses while you are researching will make it unnecessary to retrace your steps after you decide which sources to include.

One useful way to create your working bibliography is to write all the information for each source on a separate index card. Using the correct documentation style when you write the information (see Chapter 15) will make it easy to type the Works Cited page when you have completed your paper: simply alphabetize the cards and copy the information. You might also want to make notes about the usefulness of the source or about what information it covers right on the card. Then, when you review your sources, you will know which source to consult for which information.

Another timesaving strategy researchers use is to give each source a code letter. If you put the letter on each note card you make from the source, you won't have to write all the bibliographic information on each card, but you will still keep your material organized efficiently.

A card might look like this.

Kauffman
Kauffman, Stanley. Regarding Film. Baltimore: Johns Hopkins University Press, 2001.
Compilation of his reviews from The New Republic, 1993–2000.

READING WITH FOCUS: TAKING USEFUL NOTES AND AVOIDING PLAGIARISM

Accuracy is essential when taking notes—and so is focus. As you read through your sources, look for ideas that support or refute your thesis. If you encounter ideas you have not considered, do not ignore them; read them and allow them to refine or qualify your original thinking. On the other hand, do not feel that you need to write down every fact, every example, or every quotation that you find. Keep focused on your topic, and skip sections in your sources that are tangential or irrelevant to your concerns.

The most useful note cards tell you three things at a glance.

1. They tell you the source from which you got the information by including the code letter of the source or the last name of the author.

2. They tell you the page number(s) for a written source, the URL of an electronic source, or the date and time at which an interview was conducted.

3. They tell you the general topic of the information on the card.

Try to create topic headings that are consistent. For example, do not write "film reviews" on one card and "movie criticism" on another.

The information you write on a card should be either a summary or a paraphrase of the material or a direct quotation. Take the time to put quotation marks around every phrase or sentence as you take it from a source, so that you won't have to rely on your memory about which words are yours and which

RESEARCHING · IN · THE · REAL · WORLD

Jean Trounstine
Professor and Writer

Jean Trounstine teaches writing at a community college and to prison inmates. She became aware that you can make connections across the globe through the Internet and cites prisonactivist.org as an example.

For her current writing project, a memoir about growing up German-Jewish in Cincinnati, Trounstine has used the Internet to check out factual information like "When was Feinberg Synagogue founded?" She is also using Archive Libraries, reading through original documents and newspapers like the *American Israelite*.

Sometimes this kind of research involves travel. Trounstine points out that regional libraries have certain collections that relate to the people or culture of the place. She found a book, *The Jews of Cincinnati* by Jonathan Sarno, especially useful, but what has fascinated her most was old newspaper articles she found archived. "I found a small article about one of my relatives. And I came across the announcement of someone's Bar Mitzvah I went to, a letter against Zionism, ads for bakeries I went to, names of people and their businesses—the Weil Funeral Home, Hahn's meat packing company."

come from the source. Using more than three words from a source without quotation marks or attribution is considered **plagiarism.** Passing off a source's original thinking as your own is also considered plagiarism. When you are working on a long-term project, even if you have the best of intentions, you will not remember whose words you are copying by the time you write the first draft. Most unintentional plagiarism can be avoided by being careful and accurate at this point in the research project. (See pages 575–578 for more on plagiarism.)

A note card might look like this.

Kauffman   Themes
Review of Eyes Wide Shut, August 16, 1999
—"Every married person has within himself or herself a
secret cosmos of sexual imaginings, longings, fantasies,
and perhaps extramarital actions."
—Original story written in 1926 by Arthur Schnitzler

p. 145

Key each note card to a main topic in your outline as this one does with "Themes"

Taking notes on cards is a good way to organize your material, but many people use photocopies to keep track of their sources. They print out copies of citations and full-text articles, and even e-mail themselves notes and copies. Whichever method you use, make sure to keep track of the origin of the ideas. Tracking down a source again to get the publication date or correct spelling of the author's name can waste a lot of your time. A quick notation of the full source will save you time later.

EVALUATING YOUR SOURCES

Libraries all over the world share so much information that finding the few sources that are just right for your inquiry may be a daunting task. One online search for "the space program in the 1960s" returned 58,260 results or "hits." A library search was equally comprehensive, linking to sources covering rocket science and planet exploration, among others. Knowing how to evaluate your sources will save you time and will help you eliminate irrelevant information and focus on the information most useful to your research project. Evaluating sources involves critical thinking and a system or set of criteria for judging their usefulness.

Evaluate a source by answering questions based on authorship, scholarship, bias, and currency.

Authorship   Finding out about the person who researched and wrote the information is key in evaluating books, articles, and Web material. What are the author's credentials? For example, has the author shown up in bibliographic lists you have found at the ends of articles, or in textbooks or other books? Has the author written other books on the subject? Is the author connected to a school or organization? Connections to advocacy groups—groups that take positions on issues—can shape an author's point of view and make it closer to opinion than fact.

Scholarship   Quoting from works with good research makes your writing credible. Does the writing cite other sources? Does it offer depth, or is it an overview? Are claims explained and documented? Does the work include a list of sources, links, or a bibliography that leads to other information? Is it well written and free of typographical, spelling, grammatical, or other mistakes that bring its accuracy into question?

Bias   What is the purpose of the work: to argue, to report, to sell, to entertain? Who is the audience? Is the audience a specialized group with shared values? Is the audience general? How do the author's credentials imply a possible point of view in the writing? Is bias apparent? A source with a clear bias can be useful when you want a strong position on an issue, rather than a balanced view. A researcher must understand the bias of a source in order to use the source well. In general, sources with the least amount of bias offer more reliable factual information than do biased sources. Quoting facts from sources that argue for a special point of view can make you seem like a spokesperson for the viewpoint, rather than an objective writer.

Currency   When was the book published, and by whom? Has the material been updated? Asking these questions is particularly important with sources that report new information—scientific publications, for example. Your research is fundamental to making your writing credible. Quoting outdated sources may show your reader that you do not understand the subject you are writing about.

Answering these questions can help you understand whether you want to use the source in your writing, though they don't necessarily eliminate a source. At times you may want to show an extreme viewpoint—in making a counterargument in an editorial, for example. You may want a historical perspective you can get only from information that is clearly out of date to show the context of a social movement, for example, or thinking that has now changed.

For example, the following book, published in 1953, might be useful to a researcher looking at women and society, even though the thinking about women and sexual behavior has changed since its publication date. Starting with an outdated notion that was considered state-of-the-art thinking in 1953 might make a really interesting—and creative—opening for an argument. Likewise, citing a well-accepted theory about women and behavior that has not changed since the 1950s might also make a thought-provoking opening.

Author Kinsey, Alfred C. (Alfred Charles), 1894-1956
Title Sexual behavior in the human female, by the Staff of the Institute for Sex Research, Indiana University: Alfred C. Kinsey [and others]

Whatever you read, evaluate it in terms of its authorship, scholarship, bias, and currency. These criteria can help you decide what is useful and reliable; they can also help you narrow and refine your search by helping you select material.

THE SEARCH

The best researchers use multiple avenues of investigation. They consult a range of already published sources (secondary sources) and conduct surveys, polls, and conduct interviews (primary sources).

Using Books

Though books are not the first choice of research source material for many students today, they are not just charming relics of a bygone past. Books are edited, reviewed, and selected by librarians for inclusion on the shelves. This screening process means that the books on library shelves, if not too old, tend

R E S E A R C H I N G · I N · T H E · R E A L · W O R L D

Andrew Hosier
Library and Information Science Student

Andrew Hosier's work in information science leads him daily to electronic databases like WorldCat, which he recommends as a starting place for searches. Since they require users to be subscribers, these databases aren't available on the free Web. Hosier emphasizes how much material is hidden from conventional search engines. "For example, I once looked for foundations or charities that might make grants to an equine rescue organiza-tion. The listing on the 'Net was only a quarter of the ones I was able to find easily in a proprietary data-base—admittedly not available to the general public."

Hosier also warns that it can be "difficult to gauge the validity and reliability of information on the Web, especially if the supporting sources are not cited." And the abundance of results can make narrowing the list from five thousand to the ten best results difficult.

to have some merit and reliability—not always, but usually. Most material on the Web, on the other hand, has not been screened. Anyone can post anything, so Web material ranges from worthless to exceptionally valuable. Sometimes the Web can be the place to find facts fast or do general reading. Other times, books are the right place to go for research. For example, if you are researching the life of a slave in Georgia in 1860, books would probably offer more depth than webpages.

Always evaluate your sources, even when using books. Some books may have the same problem that some websites have: too much bias. Reading the bibliographies in your textbooks, in general reference books, and in prominent books about the subject will help you become familiar with the main texts and with some of the prominent writers who are experts in the field. An author's name or a book title that appears in several bibliographies might make a good source for your research.

How to Find Books on Your Subject All libraries have catalogs, now mostly online versions rather than drawers of cards. Library catalogs make it possible to print out a list of a library's holdings. You can search a catalog by title to find a particular book or by author's name to find works by an expert, someone a professor has mentioned, or someone whose name shows up in several bibliographies. Most catalogs include subject headings under the book's bibliographic information. Use subject headings to get ideas of other places to find information related to your topic.

Catalog entries list author, title, publisher, and call number. Other information that might be helpful in assessing the source are number of pages, the presence of a bibliography and index, and a list of subjects related to the material in the publication.

RESEARCHING · IN · THE · REAL · WORLD

Estelle Belisle

Translator for the Organization of American States

As a foreign-language translator, Estelle Belisle finds some limitations in using the Internet. It is good for giving her a general understanding of subjects she might be working with—technical aspects of mine clearing, for example—and for specific information—such as the correct title of a treaty. But, she says, she finds that weeding through irrelevant material and bad translations can take up a lot of her time. She likes a site that identifies acronyms (www.acronymfinder.com), and she often uses the State Department site for the Summit of the Americas. Still, Belisle admits, her top reference tools are monolingual and bilingual dictionaries.

What a Catalog Tells You You get a great deal of information from a catalog entry, including the basics of author and title. The following entry came up in a keyword search on "children and television viewing."

Author Anderson, Daniel R., 1944–
Title Early childhood television viewing and adolescent behavior: the re-contact study / Daniel R. Anderson . . . [et al.] ; with commentary by Reed Larson.

You find out who published the work and what type of source it is—a book, a study, a thesis, or a dissertation, for example.

Imprint Boston: Blackwell Publishers, 2001.

You get information about the location of the book—in which library and where it is shelved, and whether the book has been checked out.

Location Mugar
Call No. LB1103 .F35 v. 66 no. 1
Status Available

The catalog entry will contain other information—length of publication, a brief description of the publication (sometimes with chapter headings or section titles), and subject headings covered in the publication.

Descript viii, 158 p.; 23 cm.

Series Monographs of the Society for Research in Child Development; serial no. 264, v. 66, no. 1
Monographs of the Society for Research in Child Development ; v. 66, no. 1.

Note Includes bibliographical references.

Contents Abstract—[ch.] 1. Introduction—[ch.] 2. Method overview—[ch.] 3. Media use in adolescence—[ch.] 4. Academic achievement—[ch.] 5. Creativity—[ch.] 6. Aggression—[ch.] 7. Extracurricular activities—[ch.] 8. Health behaviors—[ch.] 9. Self-image : role preference and body image—[ch.] 10. Summary and conclusions—References—Acknowledgments—Commentary. **Children** and adolescents in a changing media world / Reed Larson.

Subject Television and children.
Social interaction in adolescence.
Child development.

Alt author Larson, Reed, 1950–

Practice 14.1
Reading a Catalog Entry

Compare the following entry to the previous one on page 545. How do these sources differ? How are they alike?

> *Author* Menzigian, Margaret H
>
> *Title* A study of the leisure time activities, television viewing habits, and the expressed interests of a selected population of fifth grade children in connection with their studying of natural science by television, by Margaret H. Menzigian [and] Ellen Marion Shepherd
>
> *Imprint* 1960
>
> *Location* Mugar
>
> *Call No.* EdM 1960 me
>
> *Status* Available
>
> *Descript* v, 65 p., 66 folded insert., 67–72 p. illus. 30 cm
>
> *Note* Thesis (M.A.)—Boston University, 1960
>
> *Alt author* Shepherd, Ellen Marion, joint author

Practice 14.2
Evaluating a Catalog Entry

Evaluate this source based on the information from a library catalog.

1. Describe the bias you can detect from the catalog entry.

2. Would you eliminate this book as a source for information about bias in media? Why?

> *Author* Goldberg, Bernard, 1945–
>
> *Title* Bias: a CBS insider exposes how the media distorts the news / Bernard Goldberg.
>
> *Imprint* Washington, DC: Regnery Pub.; Lanham, MD: Distributed to the trade by National Book Network, c2001.
>
> *Location* Mugar
>
> *Call No.* PN4784.O24 G65 2002
>
> *Status* Available
>
> *Descript* 232 p.: ill.; 24 cm.
>
> *Contents* Introduction: They think you're a traitor—News Mafia—Mugged by the Dan—Emperor is naked—Identity politics—How Bill Clinton cured homelessness—Epidemic of fear—I thought our job was to tell the truth—How about a media that reflects America?—Targeting men—Where thieves and pimps run free—Most important story you never saw on TV—Liberal hate-speech—Ship be sinking—Connecting the dots … to terrorism—Newzak.
>
> *Isn/music #* 0895261901 (alk. paper)
>
> *Subject* Journalism—Objectivity.
>
> Television broadcasting of news—United States.

Evaluating Books Use the questions about authorship, scholarship, bias, and currency to help you narrow your book choices. Look at the title, author, and date of publication. The title could provide a good sense of whether the source is right for your purpose.

Using Periodicals: Academic Journals, Trade Journals, and Popular Magazines

Periodicals of all types are available both online and in print. Some are exclusively online, and others have not made it into electronic formats. You can find journal articles by searching through indexes on library databases such as the *Reader's Guide to Periodic Literature*. As with books, you can usually search these indexes by subject, author, title, or keyword. The databases may include the full periodical article or just a citation listing the journal name, article title, date, volume, and page numbers. You might be able to retrieve articles through online archives, on microfilm or microfiche, or in print copies.

Academic journals like the *Journal of Finance*, *Social Work: The Journal of the National Association of Social Workers*, *American Literature*, and *Circulation: The Journal of the American Heart Association* announce and explain new findings in their specialty fields. They are usually not written for the average reader but rather for people with special training or interest in the field. Nevertheless, they can be useful to you because they are reliable and current. Journal articles are juried—that is, they are reviewed and chosen by scholars or experts in the field. Therefore, the articles are usually in-depth, with footnotes and detailed bibliographies. In other words, the conclusions the authors have reached are clearly documented.

R E S E A R C H I N G • I N • T H E • R E A L • W O R L D

Nancy Schachter

Founder of Jupiter Group, a Design Firm Based in San Francisco and Hong Kong

Since she works in graphic design and marketing, keeping up with trends in the marketplace, stores, and magazines is essential to Nancy Schachter . She reads the *Wall Street Journal* daily and browses through bookstores, where she looks "in unsuspecting sections for a different twist on a subject." She says she is always looking through trade journals and magazines like *How, Communicative Arts*, and *Graphis* in order to stay current.

One thing Schachter has learned from doing research is "to follow up and find out who the so-called expert being cited is." She says good sources are sometimes too busy to talk to you when you need them, and she finds that junior staff members are sometimes great sources—well informed in the details and eager to talk.

Trade journals, too, have specialized audiences, but they can be useful in your research. Trade journals help professionals in specific fields keep up with current trends, new products, and other up-to-date information. Article authors are practitioners in specialty fields, and they are writing for other experts. They are often writing to report trends and new findings, just the information you may be looking for. Studies in the *Journal of the American Medical Association*, for example, often announce new theories or counter conventional medical thinking. Other useful trade and professional publications include *WWD: Women's Wear Daily, Nutrition Today, Adweek,* and *Editor and Publisher.*

While some popular magazines like *Time, Scientific American, Discover,* and *Smithsonian* might not have the authority and depth of academic journals, they are usually reliable, cover a wide range of topics, and are highly readable because they are written for a general audience. Though they quote sources, they do not include bibliographies. They can be good sources for up-to-date news and current reporting on trends and events.

Be especially alert for bias in periodicals because it can be difficult—especially when you search electronically and do not see all the articles in a particular publication—to judge whether an article is fair and reasonably objective. Since popular magazines do not include bibliographic citations or footnotes, you must look carefully at the way the writers cite sources within the text. Their sources might be worth checking. For example, if you find census data that reveal a significant population decrease in a particular state, you might go directly to the most recent census data—either through an online or library search of government documents—to confirm those figures for yourself before you cite them as factual in your paper.

Sometimes you will consult periodicals that have a distinct point of view. Trade journals, for example, report news from within a certain industry. You will not find criticism of the industry in such publications, but you will find a particular perspective. Being aware of bias proves to your readers that your research is thorough and that your writing is trustworthy.

Using Newspapers

You can search most large daily newspapers through their online archives by going directly to their websites, though the online archives probably will not date back much farther than 1975. Some newspapers will charge you for the full text of an online article, though you can often get copies of articles for free through libraries that subscribe to databases. Some newspapers, like the *New York Times,* are available on microfilm and microfiche. To find newspaper articles before 1975, you can search databases like Dow Jones Interactive, InfoTrac, and LexisNexis, if your library subscribes. You can also phone newspapers and request older material.

Ask yourself whether the news source is a well-known paper with an established record of reliability. In reliable newspapers, the opinion pieces are labeled and separated from the news stories, and advertising is set apart from news articles by appearance and by content. You should not be confused about whether you are reading an advertisement or a news report. Contemporary news sources should be free of personal bias and opinion and should make clear where they got their information—by either providing attribution following quotations or making clear references to the source in the text ("according to a report released by the NRA today," "according to a company statement released today"). If you are reading excerpts of news accounts that were printed in other sources first, go to the original publication and verify the accuracy. You could easily lose your credibility by citing inaccuracies and misquotes.

Using Surveys and Polls

Data gathered from surveys and polls can be useful to writers, especially writers trying to prove a trend in behavior or establish a new wave of current thinking about an issue. In general, though, you should be very wary of citing surveys and polls. If you do cite one, carefully evaluate the origin of the study. The U.S. census, for example, is a good source. But a quick newspaper opinion poll might not reveal much about public opinion. A poll conducted by a company might be designed to solicit attention for a product rather than to provide information.

Conducting objective and reliable surveys and polls is a job for trained professionals—people who know how to write questions and how to combine them so the survey solicits clear, valid data from which you can extract meaning. These professionals also know how to administer a survey to a wide enough variety of people so that the answers represent a cross-section of the group. If a survey or poll is not conducted according to rigorous standards, results can be invalid or twisted to "prove" the point that someone wants to advance.

Always examine the source of polling and survey data to evaluate their usefulness. A polling organization should be unbiased so that you can trust that the questions were not written in order to solicit a certain response. It is not hard to write a survey that gets you the results you want. For example, you might ask people on your street if they watch Home Box Office (HBO) at least once a week. Negative replies do not necessarily mean that people do not like the network. What if cable is not available in the area, or if the cost of a premium channel is prohibitive? Similarly, think of all the times you have been watching television and the station flashes a number to call and express an opinion on an issue. Consider all the people who might be hitting the redial button, voting over and over, skewing the results—and all those

**Practice 14.3
Detecting Bias**

1. Take a look at the following book titles. What might be the author's bias?

   a. *Rush Limbaugh Is a Big Fat Idiot: And Other Observations* by Al Franken
   b. *Fast Food Nation: The Dark Side of the All-American Meal* by Eric Schlosser
   c. *Nickel and Dimed* by Barbara Ehrenreich

2. Visit the library or a bookstore or go to http://www.amazon.com, and look at the tables of contents and excerpts from these books. Does getting more information further reveal the writers' biases?

3. Visit the following websites to see if you can discover a political bias from looking at the titles of pages and articles.

   a. The Drudge Report at http://www.drudgereport.com
   b. The New Republic Online at http://www.tnr.com

who do not call at all. You can see that some polls and surveys do not give you valid data.

Likewise, you might be tempted to write your own surveys. It is more difficult than you imagine to create, administer, and analyze a survey. You might poll a variety of people on campus about their opinions on a school issue, then use that information in a story for your school newspaper. However, a survey of opinion on your campus is not a sampling of national opinion. Making a generalization about the way American college students feel about a issue would require responses from a cross-section of students in many places and in different socioeconomic situations. Remember, too, that the way you arrange and phrase questions can alter the results. To show public opinion, consider using interviews and quotations as well as survey results from reliable sources.

Using Interviews

Many researchers in academia, in the media, and in business do field research. They interview experts for background information and current thinking. Using quotations from these primary sources enlivens writing and makes it convincing and professional. Consider using interviews for news and technical reports, editorials and speeches, proposals, profiles and trend stories, and academic papers.

You may decide to conduct informal interviews, collecting background material to help you understand topics before you start to write about them. You may also conduct more formal interviews, collecting quotations from people who are expert on subjects you are writing about. If you are unaccustomed to using interviews to research a topic, be assured that they have great advantages. The people you interview can offer insights and up-to-date infor-

R E S E A R C H I N G · I N · T H E · R E A L · W O R L D

Robin Pitman
Real Estate Developer and Former Domain Name Mediator

Robin Pitman helped settle disputes over who had the right to domain names involving the legendary home of Santa and the king of Thailand. She says she was amazed at how she could get so many facts online. Through e-mail she was even able to find an expert on the culture of Lapland to answer her questions.

Currently, she works in real estate development and finds that the Internet gives her an instant connection to legislation, laws, maps, and even phone numbers (she recommends http://www.switchboard.com) for projects. Sometimes, instead of doing a search, "I often guess at the likely URL to see if I can get some place directly and save a little time." The limitations of relying on the Internet have, at times, led to problems. "Occasionally the Internet can't keep updated on changes in streets, or relocations of businesses."

mation you would have no other way of gathering, as well as stories, anecdotes, and even tips about books you should read and other people to contact.

If you are nervous about interviewing a scholar or an expert in a field, remember that most people enjoy being interviewed. They like to talk about their work, research, and fields of expertise, and they enjoy expressing their opinions.

The art and craft of interviewing consists of two parts: asking good questions, and listening carefully to the answers. Listen not just for what is said but also for what goes unsaid, what people avoid discussing. If you have ever witnessed a press conference, especially a political one, you have a good idea of how artfully people can avoid answering questions that make them uncomfortable.

The more people you interview, the more you will learn about the issue and the more useful quotations you will gather. Of course, you will not be able to use everything you collect, but it is better to harvest too much than too little.

Here are some useful interviewing tips.

Make a Contact List Figure out who the main sources might be: names of experts, organizers, advocates, witnesses, and people central to your writing project. If you are writing a profile, you should interview your subject several times. You should also interview people who know your subject and people who know about issues discussed in the profile. People who have lived in a time period or place you are writing about can also be excellent sources. Interview people considered experts on issues related to your project. On a college campus you have ready access to scholars and experts in many different fields. If you are looking for explanations of a trend, you would seek out people directly involved with the trend, or people who keep track of the trends like sociologists, teachers, parents, and psychologists.

When you go to observe something related to your writing, talk to as many onlookers as possible. Do not forget to talk with people whose views differ from your notion of the story. Find out what they are thinking, too. They may direct you to surprising sources and revise your thinking about the subject.

Get Advance Materials before the Interview Go into the interview informed. If your source is an expert, he or she may have written books or articles. Read these publications for background on the person and the topic. If your source works in an organization or company, contact the publicity department to get biographical information. If you are attending an event, see if you can get a press kit from the publicity department. Publicity departments usually issue press releases or press kits well in advance of events. You can call the organization or check out its website. Press releases always come with a contact name, which is a good starting point for your list. Any reading you can do ahead of time—old news stories about related issues, brochures—will make your interviews more focused and more productive.

Set Up the Interview Allow lots of time for phone tag. Do not wait until the last minute to schedule interviews. Once you contact a source, identify yourself immediately and explain exactly what you are requesting: "I'm a student at Central University, and I'm writing an editorial about the ban on jet skis in state waterways. Could I have a half hour of your time to find out more about your views on the proposed legislation?"

Make sure to leave your telephone number, your e-mail address, and a good time to reach you in case your source needs to change plans. It is best to interview in person so you can observe the source's nonverbal mannerisms (as well as interesting details of the setting). A telephone and e-mail interview is better than no interview, however.

Prepare for Your Interview Look over your background research. What questions do you still have about the topic? If you do not understand something, you will not be able to explain it to your readers. Generate a list of questions pertaining to the topic. Figure out what you want to know and how you can use your source's expertise. Know what that expertise is, first of all. Prepare

R E S E A R C H I N G · I N · T H E · R E A L · W O R L D

Maire Messenger Davies
Professor of Mass Communication, Cardiff, Wales

A self-described "old-fashioned scholar and teacher," Maire Messenger Davies calls books her main source for research. "I like books, and I like reading," she says. "I don't like sitting at a computer for hours on end." Davies relies on library staff to help her find books, but she says she likes just browsing through bookshelves at the library and in bookstores.

It seems only a little ironic that she teaches a class on media and culture and that she had trouble using the Internet to research a project on *Star Trek*. "The *Star Trek* pages are enormously cluttered up," Davies says, "with lots of useless material." She gets reliable information on education sites, finding people who are doing research similar to hers. "Good websites list the research that people are doing with references and links to other

pages." Her most surprising research opportunity came as a result of an interview with Patrick Stewart, who plays Jean Luc Picard in *Star Trek, the Next Generation*. She got to interview people who work on producing the television program at Paramount Studios, and had the opportunity to do some audience research while traveling around with Stewart as he toured with stage plays in New York and Yorkshire, England.

"I must admit," Davies says, "finding myself on the Paramount lot in Los Angeles standing next to Deanna Troi, Data, Captain Picard and Geodi LaForge all in full makeup and costume, and chatting about our local football team in London was overwhelming. This ranks as pretty much the most surprising research outcome that has ever happened to me."

your questions ahead of time, but do not stick to the script if the conversation takes an interesting turn.

Have your tools ready: paper, pens, a tape recorder if you have received permission to tape the interview. If you are using a tape recorder, check to see that it is working, bring extra batteries, and always make backup notes in case the recorder fails.

Conduct the Interview Introduce yourself and announce your agenda, just as you did in your initial contact. Aim for an informal and easy tone. The most productive interviews are conversations, not question-and-answer sessions. Make eye contact.

Follow up on brief yes-no type answers. Ask your source to explain or elaborate. Take good notes. Jot down observations and descriptive details that might help set a scene or show character.

Do not forget to ask your source about other sources: other people to interview, something to read, a place to visit. Make sure you have the proper spelling of your source's name and title. Thank your source, and ask if you can call with follow-up questions.

Try to avoid letting the source review the article and approve it prior to publication. Needing to get a source's approval will tie your hands and bias your story. Most sources do not get to see a story until it is published.

Transcribe Your Notes As soon as possible after the interview, transcribe or rewrite your notes. Add details of physical appearance or setting that might later be useful. This is a time-consuming process, but do not put it off. The sooner you rewrite your notes, the more you will remember.

Read Your Notes Critically Annotate your notes as you read through them. Underline important information. Make stars next to or highlight good quotations that are particularly well said or pertinent to your thesis. Cross out irrelevant information so you will not have to reread it, but do not delete it totally in case your focus changes.

What Constitutes Plagiarism of Internet Sources?

Plagiarism is defined as "the use of a source without giving credit to the author."

Online plagiarism includes cutting and pasting sections, paragraphs, and even phrases from online sources *without* using quotation marks or other indications that the material was written by someone else.

Plagiarism also includes taking ideas from sources without noting the original source of the ideas.

Even if you rephrase an idea or put it into your own words, always cite the source.

You can find more on how to attribute Internet sources in Chapter 15, Documentation.

A Guide to Research on the World Wide Web

"On the internet, nobody knows you're a dog."

Using the Web

For people who know little or nothing about Web research, getting started can seem like trying to get a drink from a hose that is turned on full blast. Some good resources on getting started are available on the *Writing in the Works* website, including links to sites that teach you how to use sources available on the World Wide Web.

Because you may search the Web as a first step in getting information, this section covers the basics of how search tools work, including

- How to read a URL (a website address)
- How to evaluate websites and webpages
- How to choose a search tool for getting information on the Web
- How to find "hidden" information on the Web

Understanding a URL

A URL (universal resource locator) is a webpage's address. It appears in the location field at the top of the browser window. Each of the Web's millions of sites has a different URL.

A URL has four parts that are joined together: *protocol://domain name/pathway/ type of file*.

http://www.cdc.gov/ncidod/dvbid/westnile/index.htm

Protocol http:// The protocol gets you access to a server and allows you to download information. The protocol *http:*, for example, is used to download webpages. Another protocol, *ftp:*, is used to download software programs and files to a specific location on the server.

Domain name www.cdc.gov This part of the address tells you whether the site is on the World Wide Web or elsewhere (such as on an FTP site) and what type of website you are looking at. The end of the domain name, *.gov*, indicates the type of domain, in this case a government site. The domain name is useful in evaluating a site.

Pathway /ncidod/dvbid/westnile/index This sequence of characters indicates the pathway: the specific page and the folders in which the page is located. If you have all this information, you can type it right into the location field and go directly to the webpage, which is part of a larger site.

Type of file .htm The final sequence usually describes the type of file, such as picture files (*.gif, .jpeg*), sound files (*.wav, .au,. aif*), or video files (*.mov, .avi, .mpg, .qt*). If you are trying to open a file that requires special software that you do not have, a message or warning will pop up on your browser. You may be linked to a site from which you can download and install the necessary tools, often at no cost. The most common sequence is .htm or .html, which indicates "hypertext markup language."

■ Quick Evaluation of Websites

Use the type of domain in the domain name to help you evaluate Web sources and their likely usefulness.

.com business or marketing site, news site

.gov government site

.edu educational site

.mil military site

.org noncommercial site

Some new domain names are starting to pop up on the Internet. Though still not commonly found, you may see the following:

.aero air-transportation industry

.biz business site

.coop cooperatives

.info all use

.museum museum

.name individual, personal site

.pro profession

Use the same type of questions you would use to evaluate print material. In evaluating webpages, you need to be especially alert for bias and timeliness. Remember that Web material, for the most part, is unevaluated.

Here are some questions to help you evaluate webpages.

Authority The person or group responsible for the website is not always apparent.

- Is there a clear statement of whose site it is and who is responsible for the content? Have you heard of the organization before? Are the articles signed? Is there a print version?

- Does the homepage include a phone number or postal address that indicates that the company is legitimate?

- Can you find a link to information about the identity of the company, such as "About Us"?

- Is the formality of the writing or graphics appropriate to the subject matter?

- Is the material being provided as a public service?

Scholarship What looks like a fact on a webpage might not be.

- Does the site include sources to document claims?

- Does any material that seems like a claim have a citation, so that you can check the source directly? Does the site link to sources?

- If the site includes excerpts from other published sources, are the sources complete? Have they been altered or shortened?

- Can you find errors in grammar or spelling that may indicate incorrect information?

- Does the site include a bibliography?

Bias   Expect promotional sites to present one side. Noncommercial sites might also be posted by advocacy agencies, so be aware of the purpose of the site. Some websites conceal their purpose. Some might seem to be offering information but instead make sales pitches or arguments. Others lure you in with the promise of one thing and then switch to another topic, or to a specific view of a topic.

- Is the purpose of the site to sell or promote a product or service?
- Is the information aimed at promotion of a specific point of view?
- Does the site link to other sites that espouse a distinct point of view?

Currency   Check dates of posting and most recent updates. This is especially important with news sites, the best of which are updated frequently, sometimes hourly.

- Do the links work?
- Are the links current?

These questions were based on checklists from the Widener University Library website and the University of California/Berkeley Library websites. For slightly different and more in-depth checklists, consult **http://muse.widener. edu/Wolfgram-Memorial-Library/webevaluation/news.htm** and **http://www. lib.berkeley.edu/TeachingLib/Guides/Internet/Evaluate.html**.

Search Tools

Your Internet search will be more efficient and effective if you know how to use the right search tools—a good search engine or directory—and how to make the search as broad or as limited as you want it to be. Most people have a favorite search tool. The best tool for you is the one you are most comfortable with and best at using. Try out a few listed on the next page, become accustomed to specialized searches on several, and see which one is a good fit. While most search engines and directories basically work in similar ways, they have subtle differences in organization and language.

Note that both search engines and directories reside on websites. When you find the ones you like best, bookmark them in your browser so you can easily return.

■ Directories

A directory is a searchable listing of websites, not of webpages. This means that a directory will send you to a site on the Web that will be a collection of pages that focus on your topic. Subject directories look at general topics and then further break those down into subcategories. They do not, like search engines, look for specific words on individual pages. This approach offers some advantages, as Chris Sherman and Gary Price, experts on searching the Internet, explain in *The Invisible Web: Uncovering Information Sources Search Engines Can't See*: "Directories are similar to telephone yellow pages, because they are organized by category or topic, and often contain more information than bare-bones white pages listings."

A directory includes a brief overview or description of each website. Directories are compiled and maintained by people, not by computers as search engines are. The editors who put directories together pick the sites based on predetermined criteria, including whether a site is reputable. They then write a brief description of the site. The fact that directories usually come with annotation is an advantage. It frees you from finding home-pages and reading through sites to see what they are about.

Some directories are

- Yahoo! at http://www.yahoo.com
- LookSmart at http://www.looksmart.com
- Open Directory Project at http://www.dmoz.org
- HotBot at http://www.hotbot.com
- Librarian's Index to the Internet at http:lii.org
- About.com at http://home.about.com

Directories are most useful for general research, usually the kind you do at the beginning of a project, when you are trying to understand the basics of a subject. Subject directories like Yahoo! and the Librarian's Index to the Internet can be good starting places for general research. They provide a good general grounding in a topic, but they are not as useful in getting specific pieces of information. For example, a Yahoo! search for the topic "globalism" returned these website matches.

Globalism: <u>The Secret Agenda</u>—features news and opinions on globalisation and the World Trade Organization.
http://www.**globalism.**com.au/
More sites about: <u>Australia > Political Issues > Trade</u>

<u>World — Nationalism: Normative</u> **Globalism** as Pan-Nationalism—posits that a world government has no special ethical value; its supporters should be classified as pan-nationalists of a special type.
http://web.inter.nl.net/users/Paul.Treanor/world.nation.html
More sites about: <u>Political Theory > Nationalism</u>

Globalism <u>Watch</u>—Links UN homepage. UN news site. UN press releases (last 7 days). World Bank. World Trade Organization. Commission on Global Governance....
http://www.geocities.com/geronl/

These results give you a summary overview of the type of sites you might consult to get information about globalism. If you knew nothing about globalism, this Yahoo! search could be a useful starting place. If you are just starting a search, having fewer but better, or at least prescreened, results can make your search more manageable and useful.

■ Search Engines

You reach a point in any research project when your research question becomes more focused and you need access to material that addresses more-specific questions. That is where search engines come in.

While directories send you to websites, search engines will show you webpages, which are embedded inside websites. These webpages have been collected by Web crawlers, also called Web spiders and robots, that roam the Internet, cataloging every word of every page they contact. They move from website to website through the links, recording everything. No human reviews these results, so you can get all kinds of material, much of it not what you are looking for. Weeding through the results can sometimes be tedious.

And search engines can be large. Yahoo! is one of the most popular subject directories and catalogs about 2 million websites; Google, one of the most popular search engines, catalogs 1.5 to 2 *billion* webpages.

Some search engines are

- Google at **http://www.google.com**
- Teoma at **http://teoma.com**
- Lycos (works in conjunction with HotBot) at **http://www.lycos.com**
- All the Web (fast) at **http://www.alltheweb.com**
- MSN Search at **http://search.msn.com**

Some metasearch engines that combine results from several other search engines are

- Dogpile at **http://www.dogpile.com**
- Metacrawler. at **http://www.metacrawler.com**
- Vivisimo at **http://vivisimo.com**
- SurfWax at **http://surfwax.com**
- Ixquick at **http://www.ixquick.com**

Because of their size and way they are assembled, search engines are very effective in providing answers to specific questions or giving you lots of information on a specific topic. Examining the URL of a result might help you select some results. Look at the domain and the type of file you can access.

For example, here is one result from a Google search for "garbage on Mt. Everest," a very specific topic. Note that the URL includes "kidsweb." How useful will this site be to you?

MONTHLY NEWS—July 2000: Japanese Alpinist-Adventurer Cleans **Mt_Everest.**
…in the seven continents by scaling Mount Everest at the age of 25 in May 1999 returned to the world's tallest mountain a year later to clean up **garbage** …
<www.jinjapan.org/kidsweb/news/00-07/noguchi.html—5k—Cached—>
Similar pages

Here are some other Google results.

Planet Ark: Climbers bury bodies, gather **Mt._Everest_garbage**

…Climbers bury bodies, gather **Mt. Everest garbage.** …
www.planetark.org/dailynewsstory.cfm/newsid/ 16156/newsDate/ 28-May-2002/story.htm—23k—Cached—Similar pages

Conquering **Mt._Everest** and Trash
…from here. View the popular Southeast Ridge. Take a look at the **garbage** that exists on **Mt._Everest.** What Is a Sherpa? Although the …
www.riverdeep.net/current/2000/ 04/front.060400.everest.jhtml—37k—Cached—Similar pages

Environment News: Glass Bottles Banned on **Mt. Everest**
…The Everest area is so polluted with **garbage** that a cartoonist some time ago drew an illustration of a heap of **garbage** showing the pile taller than **Mt.** …
ens.lycos.com/ens/nov98/1998L-11-17-01.html—18k—Cached—Similar pages

Nepal sherpas clear 4.3 tons of trash from **Mt._Everest**
…The NMA hauled about 2.2 tons of **garbage** off Everest in 1996 and some American … More than 1,000 people have reached the top of **Mt Everest** since it was first …
www.fatearth.net/news/output/a/enn.news.ft/ 20010525/3b0e7c68.4eec.7/default.php—16k—Cached—Similar pages

[**PDF**]The World's Highest **Garbage** Dump Do you know what it is? If you …
File Format: PDF/Adobe Acrobat—View as HTML
…**Everest.** The commodity (**garbage**) that I constantly think about and which most of you manage in some way as part of your business, at one time or another is …
www.envasns.org/eii/President/Nov.pdf—Similar pages

Garbage <u>on Everest, Problem or Opportunity?</u>
…**Everest** are largely devoid of archeological interest. Aggressive **garbage** collection in recent years by the CTMA (China/Tibet Mountaineering Association) in the …
classic.mountainzone.com/everest/ 99/north/disp4-21simo.html—29k—
<u>Cached</u>

Unlike directories, search engines do not give you descriptions of what is on a site. The text under these results shows you where your search words appear on various pages, which may be deep within websites.

You can get hundreds of thousands of results with a search engine and even more with a metasearch engine, which offers your request for information to several search engines at the same time. A search for "vegetarian" harvested 211,000 results. This number of results is overwhelming, not helpful. Knowing how to limit a search can help you control the power of a search engine, making your search easier and better. Here are examples of results from Yahoo! (a directory) and from Google (a search engine) on a search for "urban sprawl."

Yahoo! Website Matches

<u>Limitless City:</u> <u>A Primer on the</u> **Urban Sprawl** <u>Debate</u>—Oliver Gillham book on the issue of American **sprawl.**
http://www.limitlesscity.com/
More sites about: <u>Shopping > Social Science Books</u>

Sprawl <u>Watch Clearinghouse</u>—provides information, advice, and referrals on issues related to **sprawl,** smart growth, and livable communities.
http://www.**sprawl**watch.org/
More sites about: **Urban** <u>Studies ></u> **Urban Sprawl**

<u>Smart Growth Network</u>—encourages development that is environmentally, fiscally, and economically smart and helps create national, regional, and local coalitions to support smart growth.
http://www.smartgrowth.org
More sites about: **Urban** <u>Studies ></u> **Urban Sprawl**

<u>Scenic America</u>—nonprofit organization dedicated to preserving and enhancing the scenic character of America's communities and countryside.
http://www.scenic.org/
More sites about: **Urban** <u>Studies ></u> **Urban Sprawl**

Sprawl <u>City</u>—focusing on consumption and population growth and their roles in **urban sprawl** and its effect on natural habitat and farmland around U.S. cities.
http://www. **sprawl**city.org/
More sites about: **Urban** <u>Studies ></u> **Urban Sprawl**

Reproduced with permission of Yahoo! Inc. Yahoo! and the Yahoo! logo are trademarks of Yahoo! Inc.

Practice 14.4
Selecting good websites
Compare the results from a search for "urban sprawl" on Yahoo! to those returned from Google. Look at the type of information you get about the sites you are being offered. Which sites in the matches would you try first? Why?

Sprawl Net, The attempt to collect information, ideas, and opinions about the contemporary **sprawl**ing landscape, and to encourage interested people from a wide variety of fields to work together.
http://riceinfo.rice.edu/~lda/**Sprawl**_Net/Home.html
More sites about: **Urban** Studies > **Urban Sprawl**

Sierra Club: **Sprawl** Campaign—includes a overview of the topic, reports, and more.
http://www.sierraclub.org/**sprawl**
More sites about: **Urban** Studies > **Urban Sprawl**

International Bulldozer Blockade—fighting to save communities from **urban sprawl.**
http://www.norfolk-county.com/users/claytons/main.html
More sites about: **Urban** Studies > **Urban Sprawl**

GSA Center for **Urban** Development and Livability—endeavors to leverage federal real estate actions in ways that bolster community efforts to encourage smart growth, economic vitality, and cultural vibrancy.
http://goodneighbor.gsa.gov/
More sites about: **Urban** Studies > **Urban Sprawl**

Sprawl Resource Guide—looks at the roots of **sprawl,** its problems, and strategies for dealing with it.
http://www.plannersweb.com/**sprawl**/home.html
More sites about: **Urban** Planning and Design Journals > Planning Commissioners Journal

New Urbanism Resource Index—resources for downtown revitalization, suburban **sprawl,** new urbanism supporters and critics, and more.
http://bradley.bradley.edu/~ajh/nu.htm
More sites about: **Urban** Planning and Design > New Urbanism

Dal Tokyo—ongoing comic strip narrative set in a spectacular **urban sprawl** sometime in the future.
http://www.daltokyo.com/
More sites about: Comics and Animation > Comic Strips

Google's Webpage Matches

Sustainable Minnesota's **Sprawl** Resources
. . . NON MINNESOTA RESOURCES. GOVERNMENTLATED SITES. Legislation: **Urban Sprawl** and Smart Growth Study Act (HR 1739)—introduced by Rep. . .
.

Description: Links to information and resources related to **sprawl** issue (both in Minnesota and nationally)
Category: Society > Issues > . . . > Growth and Sprawl > Resource Directories
www.me3.org/projects/sprawl/—68k—Cached—Similar pages

Courtesy of Google.

Urban Sprawl @ nationalgeographic.com
…Voice your opinion. Special, To see what some planners prescribe for the ills of **urban sprawl,** visit our virtual "smart growth" suburb.…
B5-EXend:magma.nationalgeographic.com/ngm/data/
2001/07/01/html/ft_20010701.3.html—83k—Cached—Similar pages

Urban_Sprawl
…Group Says NAACP Must be Aware of the Impact of **Urban Sprawl** on Blacks Sociologist preaches 'smart growth'—For a civil rights organization steeped in the …
Description: 4000 articles about the history of **urban sprawl** in Arizona.
Category: Regional > North America > …> Society and Culture > History
www.goldcanyon.com/us/urbansprawl.html—28k—Cached—Similar pages

Indicators of **Urban_Sprawl**
Indicators of **Urban Sprawl.** Prepared by Oregon's Department of Land Conservation and Development May 1992 * From 1970 to 1990, the …
end:www.uoregon.edu/~pppm/landuse/sprawl.html—6k—Cached—Similar pages

Metropolis St. Louis: Suburban **Sprawl**
…Concerns). The more than 60 congregations have spent the last year studying and acting on our concerns regarding **urban sprawl.** In …
www.mstl.org/focus/sprawl/—12k—Cached—Similar pages

Urban Sprawl: Good for Minorities?
…**Urban Sprawl:** Good for Minorities? By Leonard C. Gilroy. Published Exclusively on Reason Public Policy Institute .org on October 26, 2001. Leonard C. Gilroy.…
Description: Leonard C. Gilroy
Category: Science > Social Sciences > …> Publications
www.rppi.org/opeds/102601.html—58k—Cached—Similar pages

…1991. **Urban Sprawl.** "Critiquing **Sprawl's** Critics," by Peter Gordon and Harry Richardson, Policy Analysis no. 365, January 24, 2000.…
Description: The leading Washington think tank and policy institute's special division for environmental protection …
Category: Society > Issues > Economic > Environmental
www.cato.org/research/natur-st.html—75k—Cached—Similar pages

Note that search tools, including their advantages and limitations, change daily. Many are becoming hybrids, part directory and part search engine. Yahoo! now incorporates some search technology from Google. If you type in a search inquiry that appears too long and detailed—"What was Buddha's name before he became enlightened?"—Yahoo! will tell you that it is switching out of directory mode. You will see a notation on the screen—

"search powered by Google"—and you will get webpages, not websites. Though directories are starting to pair up with search engines more and more, not all directories offer this kind of search. And most search engines will not offer you directory material, so understanding the difference between the two is still important.

■ Refining a Search

Any search should begin with keywords or phrases. Experienced researchers suggest imagining the words that would appear on an ideal webpage for your search. Sometimes keywords can send you to unwanted sites. Take the example of the student trying to find information about a meat-eating marsupial, the Tasmanian devil, who kept getting results about the Warner Brothers cartoon character. Typing in the keywords "Tasmanian devil" didn't work for her search. Thinking about the ideal webpage led her to incorporate "height" and "weight" in her search.

Search engines have ways to specialize or limit searches. Usually you can do this by clicking "advanced searches." Every search engine has a different preference for advanced searches. Some teach you how to use Boolean operators, which are words such as *and*, *not*, and *near*, to combine words you want to be included in a result. To get more information about specializing your searches, go to your favorite search engine. The *Writing in the Works* website links you to user guides for the big search engines and directories.

A good, simple, and fast way to limit searches is called "Search Engine Math" on searchenginewatch.com at http://searchenginewatch.com/facts/math.html. According to the writer of this site, Danny Sullivan, all you really need to know is how to add and subtract to refine your searches.

Remember, the more refined your search, the better. Some researchers say that an initial search should be so narrow that it yields no results. Start as narrowly as possible, and expand a little at a time.

The Plus Symbol Use the plus symbol (+) to add words that you imagine would appear on the webpage, similar to using *and* to limit a search. You could search for

> +seat belts +school buses

Pages that have both terms would be the only ones in your results. Say you are investigating a specific state, Oregon. Search for

> +seat belts +school buses + Oregon

This search would be limited to pages that have these three terms—a fairly narrow search.

The student searching for information about the Tasmanian devil might predict the words that would appear on a useful page and search for

+Tasmanian +height +weight

The Hyphen Another way to control the information you retrieve on a search is to exclude certain words from the search. If you want to eliminate a certain part of the information that you will probably pull up, you can use a hyphen (-). This is like using *not* in a Boolean search. You could search using a hyphen this way.

Tasmanian devil-Looney-Tunes

Or you could search for information about the Buddha statues of Afghanistan without being deluged by references to the Taliban, the group that destroyed the ancient statues, like this.

+Buddha+Afghanistan-Taliban

Quotation Marks Typing several words into a search engine ensures that the words are on the same page, but not in the same phrase. Use quotation marks to connect the words. If you wanted to know more about right brain intelligence, you could use

"right brain intelligence"

Other Search Methods You can find other methods of power searching in the next section, Deep Research: Using the Invisible Web. One quick way to include or exclude information is to omit results from a particular site by typing in a phrase like -site.org. For example, say you want information about abortion rights, but you do not want any advocacy groups. You can block results from certain host sites by typing

abortion-**host:org** OR abortion-**site:org**

You could limit your search about abortion to just government documents.

abortion +**host:gov** OR abortion +**site:gov**

Many search engines allow you to limit a search to a domain through the advanced searched option. You could combine a series of commands to control results as well. You might be looking for information about health care advocates in Pennsylvania, but also want to eliminate business or marketing sites. On Google, you could type

"health care advocate" +Pennsylvania –**site.com**

Practice 14.5
Comparing Results from Search Engines and Directories

Do a search for one of the following on a search engine and on a directory. Compare your results.

1. What is homeopathy?

2. What is the Second Amendment to the U.S. Constitution?

3. Who is the founder of Montessori education?

4. What is the difference between psychosis and neurosis?

Deep Research: Using the Invisible Web

Not everything available on the World Wide Web can be found by using search engines and directories. Though estimates vary, search engines and directories include only 20 percent to 50 percent of all the material available on the Web. Often, high-quality information does not appear in the results of the search tools we have discussed. This material makes up the part of the Internet called "the invisible Web," or "the deep Web." Information on such websites is invisible to search engines because of the way search engines collect data—by using computer robots or Web crawlers. The crawlers might be blocked from getting information inside a website for several reasons.

1. Access to the site might require a password or registration. The databases you can get into through your membership in a library, for example, are not available to most search engines. These are called proprietary databases. LexisNexis is an example.

2. The user must type in questions or fill out an electronic form to retrieve information. All the information about books and music easily accessible through Amazon.com, for example, does not appear in search engine results. You need to go directly to the Amazon.com database and fill out the fields requesting information.

3. The files are not text (non-HTML), but are picture, film, or music files. Web crawlers, though becoming better at collecting these files, favor easily archived text files.

4. The databases offer too much information. Government documents are often in this category; they include huge quantities of information that most users of search engines would not find useful. This excluded material can be very useful to academic researchers, though.

Currently you can get access to many high-quality sources through your home or library computer, but not by using a search engine alone. Some of the material that will be most useful to you as a researcher will be contained in documents generated by governments, organizations, and research institutes—sources considered authoritative and reliable. These groups care about accuracy and are unbiased.

When should you turn to sources on the invisible Web? The answer is when you know a good bit about your topic and are seeking specific information. Since the invisible Web is a huge digital library, you could spend hours wandering around it if you do not have a specific idea of what you are looking for. Clearly, this is not the place to start your research. You will also find that knowing something about your topic and the special terminology of the field will prove invaluable in searching databases.

www.invisible-web.net

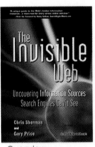

About the Site
About
FAQ
Suggest a Site

About the Book

Overview
Contents pdf
Introduction pdf
Chapter 12
About the Authors
Buy the book

Related Sites
SearchDay
Virtual Acq. Shelf

The Invisible Web Directory

Art and Architecture

Bibs/Library Catalogs

Business and Investing

Computers and Internet

Education

Entertainment

Government Info

Health and Medical

News and Current Events

Public Records

Real-Time Information

Reference

Science

Searching for People

Social Sciences

Transportation

To get to places the search engines can't see, you need gateways. One guide, *The Invisible Web: Uncovering Information Sources Search Engines Can't See*, by Chris Sherman and Gary Price, explains the hidden resources on the Web, and its companion website at http://www.invisible-web.net offers a list of sites that, when linked to directly, provide an enormous amount of reliable information.

Generally, you will find the material on the invisible Web by going to sites that catalog and describe databases and collections of documents. The catalog sites will link or direct you to the database sites, but it is important to know what you are looking for and to have a clear research question. Once you are on a gateway site, you will find search devices that will help you find what you need.

For instance, if you go to http://www.invisible-web.net, you will find these and other databases.

Folger Shakespeare Library Online Catalog (HAMNET)
The Folger Shakespeare Library® is an independent research library… A major center for scholarly research, the Folger houses the world's largest collection of Shakespeare's printed works, in addition to a magnificent collection of other rare Renaissance books and manuscripts on all disciplines— history and politics, theology and exploration, law and the arts. The collection, astonishing in its range and variety, consists of approximately 280,000 books and manuscripts; 27,000 paintings, drawings, engravings and prints; and musical instruments, costumes and films.
Note: B
Search form: http://shakespeare.folger.edu

National Geographic Society Publications Database
The NGS Publications Index includes broad subject indexing to magazines, books, films and videos, educational products, map products, interactive features, and newsletters produced by the Society.
Note: B
Search form: http://www.nationalgeographic.com/publications/index.html

HazDat (Hazardous Substance Release/Health Effects Database)
HazDat, the Agency for Toxic Substances and Disease Registry's Hazardous Substance Release/Health Effects Database, is the scientific and administrative database developed to provide access to information on the release of hazardous substances from Superfund sites or from emergency events and on the effects of hazardous substances on the health of human populations.
Search form: http://www.atsdr.cdc.gov/hazdat.html
Related resource 1: GATHER (Health Issues Spatial Data)
Resource ID: 345

Bill Tracking Database
The full text of bills, resolutions, and constitutional amendments, and their status, history, votes, analyses, and veto messages are available.
Note: California
Search form: http://www.leginfo.ca.gov/bilinfo.html
Related resource 1: (Michigan) Bill Tracker
Related resource 2: (Virginia) Legislative Information System
Resource ID: 510

Some directories of searchable databases are

- Direct Search at <http://www.freepint.com/gary/direct.htm
- Invisible Web Catalog at <www.invisibleweb.com
- IncyWincy at <http://incywincy.com
- Complete Planet at <http://www.completeplanet.com

Research Scenario

To get a better idea of how to use the invisible Web as a resource, follow the path in this scenario. You are a student at the University of Nebraska at Lincoln. At lunch one day, your friends observe that crime on campus seems to be rising, based on conversations with other students.

Since you have a trend article due soon, you decide to look at the question of whether the crime rate at the University is rising, and you wonder how this shift may or may not compare with other four-year colleges in Lincoln and what all of this says about student safety on campus. Your subject is so specific that you probably will not have much luck finding a book or website specifically on the topic of crime on colleges in Lincoln, but you think the data must be compiled somewhere.

This appears to be a problem whose solution can be found on the invisible Web. You begin your search at one of the most popular invisible Web directories, www.invisible-web.net, and among the search subjects you find Legal/Criminal. You select that general subject area and then select the subcategory of Crime and Criminals. There you find a database compiled by the U.S. Department of Education's Office of Postsecondary Education on campus crime reports.

The database allows you to set a series of search criteria for your data: geographic region, state, city, type of institution (two- or four-year; public, not-for-profit, for-profit), and number of students enrolled.

You select the fields that allow you to search for all public and private four-year colleges of any size in Lincoln, and the database returns four results: Bryan LGH Medical Center School of Nurse Anesthesia, Nebraska Wesleyan University, Union College, and University of Nebraska at Lincoln.

At the University of Nebraska, reports of nonforcible sex offenses fell from two in 1999 to zero in 2000, the most recent figures available. Burglaries rose from twenty-four to forty-two; motor vehicle theft rose from two to five; and arson declined from nine to six reported cases. There were no cases of murder and one case of a forcible sex offense in the two-year period.

Generally, crime at the college appears to be rising slightly, but it might also be interesting to see how the school compares to other four-year schools in Lincoln. A quick check of the database tells you that in the same period there were no reported crimes at tiny (student population fourteen) Bryan LGH Medical Center School of Nurse Anesthesia.

There were also no crimes reported in that period at small (student population 742) Seventh Day Adventist-affiliated Union College. At

Methodist-affiliated Nebraska Wesleyan (student population 1,741), the only reported crimes were four burglaries in 2000, down from six in 1999.

Compared to those other schools, it would appear that the University of Nebraska was nearly plagued by a crime wave over that two-year period. But considering that the university, with an enrollment of 22,408, is so much larger than the other colleges, it would appear that the campus crime rate is relatively modest.

If you decided to broaden the scope of your research, you might also try going back to the database to compare the crime statistics at the University with those of other comparably sized public Midwestern colleges. Such a comparison would give you a better sense of just how big the problem is, or is not, at the school, and could also give you a springboard to a broader story about campus policing policies and student safety.

While all this information is on a website that catalogs invisible sites, some of the larger search engines, like Google, are starting to include databases. Search engines are now increasingly able to find caches of gov-

Practice 14.6   Research Treasure Hunt

Find information that will help answer the following research questions. Make note of your research path: which books, periodicals, and/or websites and webpages you consulted. Make note of where you started and how many sources it took to get to the answer.

1. For an explanation of a trend: Are teens smoking more now than they were ten years ago?
2. For a profile on a local rap artist: What are the roots of rap?
3. For an editorial on schoolyard bullies: Find an expert to interview.
4. For a technical report: Explain the migration of butterflies.
5. For a historical profile: Get the weather in Dallas on the day John F. Kennedy was assassinated.
6. For a proposal: Get statistics on the number of dogs euthanized in your state last year.
7. For a news report: Find the number of registered independent voters in your state.
8. For a report on globalism and commerce: Get information about commercial trademarks found on Mount Everest.
9. For a film review: How many films has Steven Soderberg made?
10. For a trend article: How many McDonald's restaurants are in China?
11. For a sidebar to a news report on domestic terrorism: Can you really make a nuclear bomb at home?
12. For a proposal involving conserving fossil fuels: What was the top-selling car in the United States last year, and what kind of gas mileage does it get?
13. For an editorial: Should Puerto Rico be a state?
14. For an editorial: How did sixteen become the minimum age for drivers?
15. For a trend article about compulsive gambling: Why can you gamble on Indian reservations?

ernment documents, though sometimes the Web crawlers get only to the webpages fronting various databases.

You can find a database on Google by typing in a subject name and the word database.

"campus crime database"

While such changes are making search engines ever more useful, it is unlikely that search engines will ever catalog all or even most of the continuously growing body of information on the Web. But, as you can see, mastering some of the techniques of mining the digital gold in the invisible Web can pay handsome dividends by putting a virtual Library of Congress on every Web user's desktop.

15. DOCUMENTATION

The outer surface of truth is not smooth,
welling and gathering from paragraph to
shapely paragraph, but is encrusted with a
rough protective bark of citations.

— Nicholson Baker

An Israeli archeologist magnifies the inscription on an ancient Hebrew tablet to document its authenticity.

DOCUMENTATION

Many of the writing assignments you do in college and at work require you to become knowledgeable about topics that are new to you. Becoming expert enough to write with some authority about a historical era, a scientific discovery, a film theory, or a leading philosopher is one reward of research. To be a credible and reliable researcher trusted by your readers, you must clearly document all the sources that you consulted. The conventions of research writing are specific, and it is important to attend carefully to all the details.

OBJECTIVES

In this chapter you will learn to

▶ attribute sources

▶ avoid plagiarism

▶ integrate sources by quoting, paraphrasing, and summarizing

▶ document papers in MLA and APA styles

ATTRIBUTING SOURCES

Attributing your sources—an essential part of research writing—means honestly acknowledging the books, periodicals, experts, and websites you consulted. Attributing sources gives you credibility. If your points are backed up by reliable and valid research or acknowledged experts in a field, your reader trusts what you have written. Clear attribution also allows readers to find your source and read in more depth about your topic. For each source that you use in your paper, even if you do not quote directly from it, you need to provide information that will allow a reader to find and examine the same material that you did.

You have to be scrupulously honest about acknowledging your sources, whether you are using other writers' language or ideas in your work. You must give them credit; if you do not, you have, in effect, plagiarized—stolen from them. The consequences of plagiarism, as you assuredly know, are serious. Students and professors found guilty of plagiarism are often suspended or dismissed from the institution. In the professional world, people who plagiarize often lose their jobs. However, most plagiarism in student papers is unintentional, due to lack of knowledge or information, rather than a result of dishonesty.

AVOIDING PLAGIARISM

The best way to avoid plagiarism is to keep careful notes as you do your research. Immediately put quotation marks around any words that you take from a source, and write down the name of the author, the title of the source, and other publication information. Here is the essential information you need for citing books, articles, and websites.

Books	Articles	Websites
Author(s) or editor(s)	Author(s)	Author(s)
Title	Title	Title
Edition	Periodical	Publisher
Place and date of publication	Volume and issue	Date of electronic publication
Name of publisher	Date of publication	Date you accessed the source
Page numbers	Page numbers	Web address

The ease of cutting and pasting information from websites into your notes makes it especially important to be careful when you use Web sources. As you write your notes, be sure to indicate any direct information you paste in from websites, either by highlighting the information in another color or by inserting quotation marks around it. Follow the material immediately with information from the chart above.

The ethics of research demand absolute honesty in reporting information from your sources. As careful as you are in documenting sources, be equally careful not to twist someone's theories or ideas to fit your thesis. Even adding a word to a quotation without noting that you have added it violates the unspoken compact you have made with your reader to be a reliable and credible researcher.

What to Document

Just as a car or a stereo belongs to you, so does your original thinking. If an author has developed a theory or an insight after studying a subject, that theory or insight is his or her intellectual property, and you cannot use it without giving credit to the source. This rule applies to speech, visuals, music, computer programming code, and mathematical notations as well as to words. If you use someone's original thinking, you have to attribute it to that person by means of a clear citation.

However, you do not have to give a citation for a fact or observation that is general knowledge. If you read in three or four sources that Ronald Reagan was elected president in 1980, you do not have to provide citations stating where you read that fact. It is considered common knowledge. Common knowledge includes

▶ Historical facts that you can find in many reference books (George Washington was the first president of the United States)

▶ Commonly accepted opinions (children should be protected from viewing extreme violence or explicit sex)

▶ Information that appears in many reference books (the boiling point of water, the colors of the rainbow)

▶ Commonly known proverbs or quotations (idle hands are the devil's workshop)

On the other hand, if you read a political analyst's theory about the impact of the fall of communism in 1989, you have to attribute that theory to the analyst, even if you do not quote his or her exact words. If you were writing for a history course and using MLA style, you would cite the author's name in the text, giving a brief explanation of the his or her expertise.

Historian and scholar Timothy Garton Ash, after witnessing the collapse of communism in Eastern Europe, believes that the free market of capitalism will be embraced by Eastern Europeans and regarded as a panacea for economic ills (152).

This in-text reference keys the reader to the full citation on the Works Cited page.

Ash, Timothy Garton. *The Magic Lantern: The Revolution of 89*. New York: Random House, 1990.

INTEGRATING SOURCES: QUOTING, PARAPHRASING, AND SUMMARIZING

When you take material directly from a source, you have three possible ways of using it in your paper: you can quote it, paraphrase it, or summarize it. As you write your paper, you have to make decisions about which and how much material you will use. Too many citations or many long citations make a reader feel as though you have done no original thinking about the topic but have merely strung together the work of others. Choose your quotations because of how authoritative they are and how well they are phrased, and use them to support or illustrate *your* points. Likewise, use summaries sparingly to condense important information, but be assured that your reader does not want to read a whole paper of summaries of other people's ideas. (See Chapter 2 for more discussion of this topic.)

Quoting

When you quote directly, you copy the words you are citing—carefully and accurately—into your text, and you enclose them in quotation marks. If you are using MLA documentation style and the material is fewer than four typed lines, enclose it in quotation marks. Be sure to introduce the quotation clearly, attributing the words to the writer. If you quote a passage of five lines or more, indent the material farther than the paragraph indentation (usually another 1/2 inch, or five more spaces), and leave off the quotation marks. The indentation and this block format, as well as the page reference at the end, inform your reader that it is quoted material.

In-Text Citation

In her interview with Christopher Scanlan, editorial writer Dianne Donovan says, "For an editorial writer, reading is just extremely important because you have to know about so many things" (298).

Block Form In her interview with Christopher Scanlan, editorial writer Dianne Donovan says:

> For an editorial writer, reading is extremely important because you have to know about so many things. You have to have a breadth of knowledge, if not of experience, which most of us don't. That allows you to be able to see a lot of different viewpoints and also to be able to come up with a lot of different things to write about. (298)

Different style manuals have different requirements for numbers of spaces to indent and numbers of lines to include in a block quotation. See pages 611–612 for guidelines for quoting material using APA style.

Using Ellipses, Brackets, and Single Quotation Marks

SIDEBAR

If you intentionally leave out some words in a quotation, use ellipses (…) to indicate the omission.

> As Dianne Donovan says, "You have to have a breadth of knowledge … which most of us don't."

If you add a clarifying word or phrase, put it in brackets to show that it is your language.

> Dianne Donovan says, "[Editorial writers] have to have a breadth of knowledge, if not experience, which most of us don't."

If you incorporate a quotation within your quotation, use single quotation marks to set off the incorporated quotation.

> Discussing how the editorial conference works, Donovan says, "I'll pitch something. 'Here's the issue and here's what I think we should say about it,' and you make your argument."

Paraphrasing

When you paraphrase material, you put it into your own words, but you cover all the same material as the original. The length of your paraphrase should be roughly the same as the original. Even though you are using your own phrasing and wording, the ideas are not yours, so you still must attribute the passage to the author. You might paraphrase the Christopher Scanlan interview this way.

> In her interview with Christopher Scanlan, Donovan says that because editorial writers have many different topics to write about, they have to read widely and deeply. Most editorial writers cannot know everything about the topics they have to write about, and they have to come up with new topics and be able to see them from multiple perspectives (298).

Summarizing

Summarizing is a way to condense lengthy material. In summarizing, you convey the highlights of someone's ideas, but you do not usually include the details or illustrative examples. One trick in summarizing a long section is to look for the topic sentence in each paragraph. If you put these topic sentences in your own words, you can usually accurately summarize a long piece of writing. Again, if you are summarizing or paraphrasing someone else's ideas, you have to give them credit in the form of a clear citation.

The first three pages of Dianne Donovan's interview with Christopher Scanlan might be summarized this way.

> In her interview with Christopher Scanlan, Dianne Donovan talks about her craft as an editorial writer. She has always enjoyed writing and began writing editorials in high school. She believes that a good editorial writer has to read widely and deeply. She also believes that writing editorials is a craft, not an art. Her beat originally was family issues, but soon she became interested in welfare reform and juvenile justice. She has written fourteen or fifteen editorials about the juvenile justice system in Chicago (298–312).
>
> —Christopher Scanlan, "A Conversation with Dianne Donovan"

DOCUMENTATION GUIDELINES

Different fields of knowledge have developed different conventions and rules for citing sources within a paper and at the end of a paper in a Works Cited or a References section. Documentation styles vary in terms of where you place the date of publication within a citation, whether to use a comma after the name of an author, and so on. The differences might seem arbitrary, but they provide important information to readers and signal that you have been careful with details. No one expects you to memorize these conventions, but you are expected to consult the appropriate style manual when citing sources and to apply the guidelines accurately.

The two most common documentation styles in academic writing are MLA style and APA style. Modern Language Association (MLA) style is used primarily for writing in the humanities and is described fully in Joseph Gibaldi's *MLA Handbook for Writers of Research Papers*, now in its sixth edition (New York: MLA, 2003). American Psychological Association (APA) style is used primarily for writing in the natural and social sciences and is described fully in *Publication Manual of the American Psychological Association*, currently in its fifth edition (Washington, DC: American Psychological Association, 2001). Some specialized fields use their own documentation forms. A few of these other forms are listed here.

▶ **AP style** Norm Goldstein, ed., *Associated Press Stylebook and Briefing on Media Law*, 35th ed. (New York: Associated Press, 2000).

▶ **CBE/CSE (previously Council of Biology Editors, now Council of Science Editors) style** *Scientific Style and Format: The CBE Manual for Authors, Editors, and Publishers*, 6th ed. (New York: Cambridge University Press, 1994).

▶ **CGOS style** Janice Walker and Todd Taylor, *The Columbia Guide to Online Style* (New York: Columbia University Press, 1998).

▶ **Chicago style** *The Chicago Manual of Style*, 15th ed. (Chicago: University of Chicago Press, 2003).

Ask your teacher or editor what style you should use, and then stick to those conventions. Many websites, especially sites of university writing centers, contain guides to the major documentation forms. And, of course, each of the listed groups publishes its own manual that gives complete, specific, and clear rules for creating in-text citations and Works Cited or References pages. The following overviews of MLA and APA style will give you the information you need for most of your academic writing assignments.

Overview of MLA Style

The *MLA Handbook for Writers of Research Papers* is the authoritative source for documenting research papers in English and the humanities. You can consult the handbook or the website at http://www.mla.org for more detailed information. The following overview provides information on

▶ Formatting the manuscript

▶ Citing sources in the text

▶ Creating a Works Cited list

At the end of this section is a student paper in MLA style that you can use as a model.

■ Formatting the Manuscript (MLA)

Presentation is important, and the *MLA Handbook* specifies these conventions for preparing a paper for submission. Also see the model paper on pages 603–610.

Paper Use good quality 8 1/2-by-11-inch paper. Fasten the pages with paper clips; avoid both staples and binders, which make it harder for your professor to read and comment on your work.

Title Page Title pages are not required in the MLA format, though your professor might require one. If you do not use a title page, set up the first page with your name, the professor's name, the course name and number, and the date in the upper left corner, with all lines double-spaced. Leave a 1-inch margin from the top and the left side. Double-space, center the title, double-space again, and begin typing your paper.

Margins, Spacing, Font, and Indenting Leave 1-inch margins on all four sides, and double-space the entire paper. Use an easy-to-read font; 10-point to 14-point Times and Times New Roman are the most commonly used. Indent ½ inch at the beginning of each paragraph. When you use a quotation of more than four lines of prose or three lines of poetry, indent 1 inch, and do not use quotation marks around the indented quotation. Double-space within the quotation.

Paging Put your last name and consecutive page numbers in the upper right corner of the paper, about ½ inch from the top. Use Arabic numerals (1, 2, 3) for page numbers, and do not use punctuation or the word *page* or its abbreviation.

Headings Headings are optional in MLA-formatted papers. If the material is complicated and would benefit from being subdivided, create headings that are brief and parallel in phrasing, and be consistent in the font you use for them.

Visuals If you include graphs, tables, maps, charts, illustrations, or photographs, place them directly after you introduce them in the text. Identify a table with a table number and title above the table (Table 1 Album Titles and Release Dates). Label each figure with a number and a caption below the visual (Fig. 1. Album revenues.). Cite the source underneath the table or visual.

Works Cited The final section of your paper is titled Works Cited. Begin a new page, and center the title 1 inch from the top. Use regular type for the title, avoiding quotation marks, boldface, italics, and so on. Alphabetically list all works you cited in the text. Runover lines should be indented ½ inch (word processing software calls this a "hanging indent").

■ Citing Sources in the Text

The MLA format requires citing sources in the text, usually by placing the author's last name and the page number in parentheses after the quoted or paraphrased material. The citation should be brief but complete enough to lead your reader to the full citation in the Works Cited section at the end of the paper. For example, if you mention the author's name in the sentence, you can simply enclose the page number(s) in parentheses after the quotation. The following list shows how to cite sources in the text of your paper.

Author named in text

> Graff defines his recent book, *Professing Literature*, as "a history of academic literary studies in the United States" (1).

Author not named in text

> Several scholars have studied recent developments in academia in the context of the history of university teaching (e.g., Graff).

> Modern literary studies have their origin in classical studies (Graff 19-35).

Reference to entire book When you cite an entire work by the name of the author alone or by author and title, you do not need a parenthetical reference. A reader will be able to find bibliographical information by looking up the author's name in your list of works cited.

> Slade's revision of *Form and Style* incorporates changes made in the 1999 edition of the *MLA Handbook* and the 1998 edition of the *MLA Style Manual*.

Work with four authors When a work has four or more authors, you may list all four authors or give only the last name of the first author followed by et al. (the abbreviation for *et alii*, "and others").

> The authors of *Women's Ways of Knowing* make a distinction between "separate knowing" and "connected knowing" (Belenky et al. 100-30).

> (Belenky, Clinchy, Goldberger, and Tarule 100-30).

Use the same form of reference you choose for the text in the list of works cited.

More than one author with the same last name When you have more than one author with the same last name, include the first initial in subsequent references. Subsequent references to Helen C. White's *The Mysticism of William Blake* and E. B. White's *Charlotte's Web* would read as

> (H. White 75) (E. White 67)

If the first initials are identical, spell out the first names.

When the two authors are father and son, with the son designated as Jr., include the designation *Jr.* in the reference, preceded by a comma.

> That book chronicles visionary experiences in early modern Spain (Christian, Jr.).

Reference to a hypothetical author with the designation III or IV after his name would also include the number in Roman numerals, preceded by a comma, if one or more of his predecessors were also represented in the list of works cited. In the list of works cited, these suffixes are included whether or not works by the namesakes also appear.

List the names of editors, compilers, or translators without the accompanying abbreviation that appears in the list of works cited.

> Many of the articles in *Research on Composing* advocate further exploration of the motivation for writing (Cooper and Odell).

Work listed by title only For a work listed only by title in your list of works cited, use the title in parentheses, shortening it to two or three words. Your abbreviated title must include the word by which the title is alphabetized in your list. You would not want to abbreviate the title in the example below to "Pharaoh," for example, because the entry should be alphabetized by "Ancient."

> Due to air pollution, Egypt plans to move the statue of Ramses II from the main railroad station in Cairo to the west bank of the Nile ("Ancient Pharaoh Statue").

Corporate author For a corporate author, use the name of the organization (abbreviated if it is lengthy, after the first citation) in place of the name of the author.

> The annual report revealed substantial progress in fundraising (American Museum of Natural History 12, hereafter AMNH). . . . (AMNH 15).

Multivolume work To cite an entire volume of a multivolume work, use the author's name and the abbreviation *vol.*

> This valuable reference work surveys the major operas of Mozart and Puccini (Newman, vol. 2).

To cite a portion of a volume of a multivolume work, use an Arabic numeral to indicate the volume, followed by a colon and the page number(s).

> Newman discusses the controversy about the quality of Mozart's *The Magic Flute* (2: 104-05).

If the author's name were not in the sentence, the parenthetical reference would read

> (Newman 2: 104-05)

Two or more works by same author When you have two works or more by the same author, use a shortened version of the title in each reference.

> Shaughnessy points out that "the beginning writer does not know how writers behave" (*Errors* 79).

> Teachers applauded Shaughnessy's assertion that "teaching them [beginning writers] to write well is not only suitable but challenging work for those who would be teachers and scholars in the democracy" ("Diving In" 68).

Material cited in another source When you quote material from a source other than the original, introduce the name of the source with *qtd. in*. The author and title of the source you actually consulted appear in the list of works cited.

> Goethe wrote that "it takes more culture to perceive the virtues of *The Magic Flute* than to point out its defects" (qtd. in Newman 2: 104).

Multiple citations When you need to include more than one work in a parenthetical citation, separate entries with a semicolon.

> (*Errors* 79; "Diving In" 68; Brooks and Warren 5)

Literary works Because works of literature, particularly pre-twentieth-century works, usually can be found in numerous editions, provide a section or chapter number, introduced with a semicolon and the appropriate abbreviation, after the page number so that your reader can locate the passage in another edition.

> Margery Kempe relates the details of her journey to Constance with pilgrims headed for Jerusalem (96-98; bk 1, chap. 26).

For drama and poetry, omit the page number and cite the work by act, scene, line, or section, as appropriate. MLA prefers Arabic numerals in such citations.

> In an aside, Claudius informs the audience that the queen has drunk from the poisoned cup he intended for Hamlet (5.2.274).

Electronic and Internet sources Material accessed electronically, or by computer, may not have any page numbers or it may appear in differing page configurations on different terminals. To give your reader the best possible opportunity to locate the material, you need to compensate for the variability of appearance. It is also advisable to provide more information about the author, particularly when he or she may not be known to your readers, than you would for a printed source.

If the electronic source provides paragraph numbers, use them in place of page numbers.

> Mike Sosteric, editor of an online journal of sociology, estimates that publishing a 60-page paper electronically costs less than a penny more than publishing a paper half that length (par. 17).

> The editor of *EJS (Electronic Journal of Sociology)* boasts that he can publish a refereed scholarly article within two days (Sosteric, par. 22).

If the source does not designate either page or paragraph, cite the name of the author only and provide some additional identification, such as the title or the qualifications of the author in your text. In the following example the forum in which the talk was given serves to identify the otherwise unidentified speaker as a person thought, by at least the organizers of the meeting, to have relevant knowledge about electronic publication.

> In after-dinner remarks at the 1994 American Psychological Society, Paul Ginsparg estimated the cost of electronic storage at $700 per gigabyte.

Because this source is not paginated, all identifying information appears within the text.

■ Placement and Punctuation of Parenthetical Documentation

Parenthetical references should generally be placed at the end of a sentence. Quotation marks, if any, precede the reference; end punctuation, commas, colons, and semicolons follow it.

> Tannen argues that "men and women have different assumptions about the place of talk in relationships" (85).

> "Men and women have different assumptions about the place of talk in relationships," according to Tannen.

> What changes in behavior could result from the assumption that, as Tannen puts it, "men and women have different assumptions about the place of talk in relationships" (85)?

If confusion might result about the distinction between your own conclusions and an idea from a source, place the parenthetical reference within a sentence, generally at the end of a clause or phrase.

> Understanding that "men and women have different assumptions about the place of talk in relationships" (Tannen 85) might help teachers understand their students' comments.

The sentence itself represents the writer's conclusion, which is stated in part with a quotation from Tannen.

For an ellipsis at the end of a sentence, the parenthetical reference follows three points indicating the omission and precedes the period.

> Schele and Freidel explain that for the Mayas "the Underworld was sometimes called Xibalba . . ." (66).

A parenthetical reference at the end of a set-off quotation follows the period. One space separates the period from the reference, which is not followed by a period.

> According to Schele and Freidel, the Maya represented each point of the compass with a different color.

> East was red and the most important direction since it was where the sun was born. North, sometimes called the "side of heaven," was white and the direction from which the cooling rains of winter came. . . . West, the leaving or dying place of the sun, was black. South was yellow. (66)

■ Creating a Works Cited List

The last page of your paper will be titled Works Cited. All the parenthetical citations you inserted in your paper refer your reader to the complete entry in this final list. Include each work you have cited in your paper, but not works you read but did not cite. Alphabetize your list by last name of the author or, in the case of an entry without an identified author, the first word of the title, excluding the articles *A, An,* and *The.*

● BOOKS

The bibliographical listing for a book includes the name(s) of the author(s) or of the editor(s), compiler(s), or translator(s), as appropriate for the particular book; the title of the book with any subtitle; and the facts of publication, which include the city of publication (and, if needed for clarification, the state), the publisher, and the date of publication. Each portion ends with a period followed by one space. Invert the first author's name, placing a comma after the surname and a period after the first name(s), which should be spelled out in their entirety unless the title page displays initials; the names of any additional authors are not inverted. Underline the complete title and subtitle, but not the final period. Take the facts of publication from the title page or the copyright page. Abbreviate the publisher's name. If several cities are listed, cite only the first. If the state is needed for clarification, use U.S.

Postal Service abbreviations, and if the country or province is needed, include a standard abbreviation, available in most dictionaries.

Book by a single author

Winfield, Richard Dien. *Law in Civil Society*. Madison: U of Wisconsin P, 1995.

Book by two or three authors

Simonds, Wendy, and Barbara Katz Rothman. *Centuries of Solace: Grief in Popular Literature*. Philadelphia: Temple UP, 1992.

Book by four or more authors You may include the names of all authors if you have some reason to do so, but the abbreviation et al., meaning "and others," is preferred.

McPherson, William, et al. *English and American Literature: Sources and Strategies for Collection Development*. Chicago: ALA, 1987.

McPherson, William, Stephen Lehmann, Craig Likness, and Marcia Pankake. *English and American Literature: Sources and Strategies for Collection Development*. Chicago: ALA, 1987.

An edited, compiled, or translated volume The name of the person(s) responsible for the book go(es) in the author's position, followed by an abbreviation for the function—ed. for *editor*, eds. for *editors*, comp. for *compiler*, comps. for *compilers*, or trans. for *translator(s)*.

Baum, Robert, ed. *Reform and Reaction in Post-Mao China: The Road through Tiananmen*. New York: Routledge, 1992.

When the person(s) have more than one function, include all of them.

Vaughan, James H., and Daryl M. Hafter, eds. and trans. *The Diary of Hamman Yaji: Chronicle of a West African Muslim Ruler*. Bloomington: Indiana UP, 1995.

Group or corporate author

Bicycling Magazine. *Reconditioning the Bicycle*. New York: Rodale, 1989.

American Museum of Natural History. *Annual Report 1993–1994*. New York: American Museum of Natural History. 1995.

Anonymous work

Times Atlas of the World. 8th ed. London: Times, 1990.

If you know the name of the author, provide it, but do not use *Anonymous*, even if it appears on the title page.

Scarborough, Dorothy. *The Wind*. New York: Harper, 1925.

Work in an anthology, particular selection singled out The title of the anthology or collection follows the title of the particular work you used, and its inclusive page numbers follow the entire entry. The name(s) of the editor(s) are not inverted. Underline or quote the title of the individual work as MLA format would require in any other situation.

> Burghardt, Gordon M. "On the Origins of Play." *Play in Animals and Humans*. Ed. Peter K. Smith. Oxford: Basil Blackwell, 1984. 5-42.

> Wilson, August. *Ma Rainey's Black Bottom*. *Modern and Contemporary Drama*. Ed. Miriam Gilbert, Carl H. Klaus, and Bradford S. Field, Jr. New York: St. Martin's, 1994.

Previously published article in a collection Begin with the original publication information and introduce the collection with Rpt. in for *Reprinted in*.

> Ten, C. L. "Mill on Self-Regarding Actions." *Philosophy* 43 (1968): 29–37. Rpt. in John Stuart Mill, *On Liberty*. Ed. David Spitz. Norton Critical Edition. New York: Norton, 1972. 238–46.

Reprinted work assigned new title Begin with the publication information for the edition you used and introduce the initial version with Rpt. of for *Reprint of*.

> Matthews, Gareth. "Ritual and the Religious Feelings." In *Explaining Emotions*. Ed. Amélie Oksenberg Rorty. Berkeley: U of California P, 1980. 339–53. Rpt. of "Bodily Motions and Religious Feelings," *Canadian Journal of Philosophy* 1 (1971): 75–86.

Entry in a reference book Treat entries in a reference book like articles in a collection.

> "Vicksburg Campaign." *Encyclopaedia Britannica*. 1973 ed.

> "World Climatology." *Times Atlas of the World*. 1990 ed.

For less well-known reference works, provide full publication information.

> Brasingly, C. Reginald. "Birth Order." *Encyclopedia of Psychology*. Ed Raymond J. Corsini. New York: Wiley, 1984.

Introduction, preface, foreword, afterword

> Howard, Maureen. Foreword. *Mrs. Dalloway*. By Virginia Woolf. New York: Harvest-Harcourt, 1981. vii–xiv.

Multivolume work, inclusive reference to all volumes If you use more than one volume in a multivolume work, cite the entire work. If the volumes were published over a period of years, give the first and last years.

> Wellek, René. *A History of Modern Criticism, 1750–1950*. 8 vols. New Haven: Yale UP, 1955–92.

Multivolume work, reference to one volume To cite one volume of a multivolume work with all volumes bearing the same title, provide the number of the one you used.

> Wellek, René. *A History of Modern Criticism, 1750–1950.* Vol. 8. New Haven: Yale UP, 1992.

You may also choose to include publication information for the entire multi-volume work.

> Wellek, René. *A History of Modern Criticism, 1750–1950.* Vol. 8. New Haven: Yale UP, 1992. 8 vols. 1955–92.

When each volume has a separate title, you may cite the work without referring to the other volumes, or you may include the title of the particular volume along with that of the complete volumes.

> Freehling, William W. *The Road to Disunion.* New York: Oxford UP, 1991.

> Freehling, William W. *The Road to Disunion.* New York: Oxford UP, 1991. Vol. 1 of *Secessionists at Bay, 1776–1854.* 2 vols. 1991–92.

Book in a series When the title page indicates that a book is part of a series, give the series title and number before the city of publication.

> Eiser, J. Richard, ed. *Attitudinal Judgment.* Springer Series in Social Psychology 11. New York: Springer-Verlag, 1990.

Publisher's imprint If the book is part of an imprint, a name given to a group of books within a company's publications, the name of the imprint comes first, followed by a hyphen and the name of the publishing company.

> Bell, Derrick. *Faces at the Bottom of the Well: The Permanence of Racism.* New York: Basic-Harper, 1992.

Reprinted work Cite the original date of publication if it differs from the date of any particular edition, as with a paperbound edition of a hardcover book or a work brought back into print after a number of years.

> Jamieson, Neil L. *Understanding Vietnam.* 1993. Berkeley: U of California P, 1995.

> Markham, Beryl. *West with the Night.* 1942. Berkeley: North Point, 1983.

Edited work When an editor has prepared a version of a text by another author, supply the editor's name preceded by the abbreviation Ed. for *Editor*.

> Conrad, Joseph. *Lord Jim.* Ed. Thomas C. Moser. Norton Critical Edition. New York: Norton, 1968.

Translated work

> Appelfeld, Aharon. *Katerina*. Trans. Jeffrey Green. New York: Random House, 1992.

To emphasize the name of the translator, place that name in the author position of the entry.

> Green, Jeffrey, trans. *Katerina*. By Aharon Appelfeld. New York: Random House, 1992.

Work with multiple publishers

> Shelley, Percy Bysshe. *Selected Poems*. Ed. Timothy Webb. London: Dent; Totowa: Rowman, 1977.

Published conference proceedings Treat the proceedings like a book, but supply information about the conference if it is not included in the title.

> Eble, Connie C. "Etiquette Books as Linguistic Authority." *The Second LACUS Forum, 1975*. Ed. Peter A. Reich. Columbia, SC: Hornbeam, 1976. 468–75.

> Glasscoe, Marion, ed. *The Medieval Mystical Tradition in England*. Papers read at Dartington Hall, July 1984. Cambridge, Eng.: Brewer, 1984.

Article in collection of proceedings Treat a paper within the proceedings like an article in a collection.

> Bradley, Ritamary. "The Speculum Image in Medieval Mystical Writers." *The Medieval Mystical Tradition in England*. Papers read at Dartington Hall, July 1984. Ed. Marion Glasscoe. Cambridge, Eng.: Brewer, 1984. 9–27.

Book in a foreign language If you wish to clarify any portion of the entry with an English translation, place it in brackets immediately following the original language version, which should be punctuated and capitalized according to rules for the particular language.

> Buendia, Felicidad. *Libros de caballerías españoles* [Spanish Novels of Chivalry]. Madrid: Aguilar, 1960.

Pamphlet Government publications The entry for a pamphlet follows the rules for a book. When the author of a government publication is identified, list it like a book.

> Gates, Jane Potter. *Educational and Training Opportunities in Sustainable Agriculture*. U.S. Department of Agriculture. Beltsville, MD: National Agricultural Library, 1991.

Otherwise, list the document by the government agency that produced or sponsored it, using the following abbreviations:

Cong. for Congress

Dept. for Department

sess. for session

Cong. Rec. for *Congressional Record*

S. Rept. for Senate Report

H. Rept. for House Report

S. Res. for Senate Resolution

H. Res. for House Resolution

GPO for Government Printing Office

When used as an author entry, as in the entry below, United States is spelled out; otherwise it is abbreviated as U.S., as in the entry immediately above.

United States. Cong. Senate. Committee on Environment and Public Works. *Construction and Repair Programs to Alleviate Unemployment.* Hearing 97th Cong., 2nd sess., 1 Dec. 1982. Washington: GPO, 1983.

United States. President. Proclamation. Martin Luther King Day. 15 Jan. 1988.

Cong. Rec. 17 Nov. 1980: 3852.

Titles within titles When the interior title would normally be italic, leave it roman, but italicize punctuation that is part of the longer title.

Doris Lessing's The Four-Gated City: *The Summer before the Dark*

The Plays of Samuel Beckett: Waiting for Godot *and* Endgame

When the interior title would normally be in quotation marks, underline the entire title.

Coleridge's "Kubla Khan" and "Rime of the Ancient Mariner"

Book with unspecified publisher, place, date, or pagination Use the following abbreviations for missing information at the appropriate place in the entry: n.d. for no date, n.p. for no place, n.p. for no publisher, n. pag. for no pagination.

Eliot, George. *Felix Holt.* Edinburgh: William Blackwood, n.d.

Eliot, George. *Felix Holt.* N.p.: William Blackwood, n.d.

Eliot, George. *Felix Holt.* Edinburgh: n.p., n.d.

Eliot, George. *Felix Holt.* Edinburgh: William Blackwood, n.d. N. pag.

Unpublished dissertation The title of an unpublished dissertation should be placed in quotation marks (not underlined), and should be identified with the abbreviation Diss., the name of the institution, and the year.

> Virgili, Carmen. "Literature of the Spanish Civil War." Diss. New York U, 1990.

Published dissertation Underline the title of a dissertation published on microfilm, identify the institution and date, and supply publication information for University Microfilms International, abbreviated as UMI.

> Moskop, William W. *The Prudent Politician: An Extension of Aristotle's Ethical Theory.* Diss. George Washington U, 1984. Ann Arbor: UMI, 1985. 85-13289.

• ARTICLES IN PERIODICALS

Citations for articles include (1) the name(s) of the author(s) or editor(s); (2) the full title of the article within quotation marks; and (3) the facts of publication, which usually include the name of the periodical (underlined), the series name and number if any, the volume number (for a scholarly journal only), the date of publication followed by a colon, and the inclusive page numbers on which the article appears. Omit any introductory article in the periodical title (*Los Angeles Times*, not *The Los Angeles Times*). When an article does not appear on consecutive pages, but rather is dispersed throughout a publication, MLA uses only the first page number followed by the symbol +, as in 67+ for an article appearing on pages 67–79 and 84, 85, and 89.

Article in a scholarly journal

> Gaunt, Simon. "The Significance of Silence." *Paragraph* 13 (1990): 202–16.

Article in a journal paginating each issue separately

> Gardner, Thomas. "An Interview with Jorie Graham." *Denver Quarterly* 26.4 (1992): 79–104.

Journal using only issue numbers When a journal numbers by issue rather than by volume, treat the issue number like a volume number.

> Nwezeh, C. E. "The Comparative Approach to Modern African Literature." *Yearbook of General and Comparative Literature* 28 (1979): 22.

Article in journal with more than one series Identify the series immediately after the title by ordinal number (2nd, 3rd) or ns for new series and os for old series.

> Klein, Milton M. "The Pleasures of Teaching and Writing History." *William and Mary Quarterly* 3rd ser. 52 (July 1995): 483–87.

> Erickson, Peter. "Singing America: From Walt Whitman to Adrienne Rich." *Kenyon Review* ns 12.1 (1995): 103–19.

Article in a newspaper For an article in a newspaper, use the name of the newspaper as it appears on the masthead, excluding any introductory article, such as *The*.

> Mercer, Pamela. "U.S. Venture Bets on Colombian Coal." *New York Times* 27 July 1995, late city ed.: D7.

When the location of the publication is neither included in the title nor widely known, include it within brackets after the title without underlining.

> "Unknown Author of *Wind* Answers Crane Criticism." *Sweetwater Daily Reporter* [Texas] 15 Dec. 1925: 6.

> *Observer* [London] 17 Oct. 1990, sec. 2: 5+.

When a particular edition of a newspaper is specified, include its designation, abbreviated, after the date (natl. for national, intl. for international, and so on).

> Donnelly, John. "Unrest in Iraq May Be a Mirage." *Miami Herald* 22 July 1995, intl. ed.: 1A+.

Article in a magazine For a weekly magazine, give day, month, and year; for a monthly, give the month and year only. Abbreviate all months except May, June, and July.

> Kinoshita, June. "The Mapping of the Mind." *New York Times Magazine* 18 Oct. 1992: 44+.

> Brody, Howard. "How Would a Physicist Design a Tennis Racket?" *Physics Today* Mar. 1995: 26–31.

Anonymous magazine article

> "Weather Satellite Finally Fit for Work." *Science News* 18 Mar. 1995: 171.

Editorial

> "Potomac Yard Decision." Editorial. *Washington Post* 16 Oct. 1992: A24.

Letter to editor

> Lightfoot, Frederick S. Letter. *New York Times* 21 Oct. 1992: A22.

A response to a letter to the editor should be so designated.

> Fleishman, Avrom. Reply to letter of David E. Johnson. *College English* 57 (1995): 224–26.

Review of a book Give the reviewer's name, if any, followed by the title of the book introduced with Rev. of, the name of the author, and the facts of publication.

> Moore, Walter. "Great Physicist, Great Guy." Rev. of *Genius: The Life and Science of Richard Feynman*, by James Gleick. *New York Times Book Review* 11 Oct. 1992: 3.

> Kienitz, Gail M. Rev. of *Tennyson and the Doom of Romanticism*, by Herbert F. Tucker. *Religion and Literature* 24 (Spring 1992): 87–90.

Review of a performance Include information identifying the performance after the title of the review.

> Hassell, Graham. "Sometimes Excess Isn't Enough." Rev. of *The Grand Ceremonial*, by Fernando Arrabal. Lyric Studio, Hammersmith, Eng. *Times Literary Supplement* [London] 14 July 1995: 20.

Review of a film or video

> Rickey, Carrie. "Disney's *Pocahontas*: Is It Fact or Fiction?" Rev. of *Pocahontas*, dir. Michael Gabriel and Eric Goldberg. *Philadelphia Inquirer* 18 June 1995: H1+.

Titles within titles Change double quotation marks to single quotation marks when they appear within another quoted title.

> "A Reading of Coleridge's 'Kubla Khan.'"

An underlined title appearing within a title in quotation marks remains underlined.

> "A Principle of Unity in *Between the Acts*"

Serialized article Cite a series of articles published in more than one issue of a periodical under the same title in one entry.

> McPhee, John. "Annals of the Former World." *New Yorker* 7 Sept. 1992: 36+; 14 Sept. 1992: 44+; 21 Sept. 1992: 39+.

If the articles have different titles, enter each one separately with a brief description of the series. Alphabetize the entries by the names of the authors, or, if the authors are the same, by title.

> Kolbert, Elizabeth, and Adam Clymer. "The Politics of Layoffs: In Search of a Message." *New York Times* 8 March 1996: A1+. Pt. 6 of a series, The Downsizing of America, begun 3 March 1996.

> ———. "The Price of Jobs Lost: A National Heartache." *New York Times* 3 March 1996: A1+. Pt. 1 of a series, The Downsizing of America.

Abstract in an abstracts journal

Moskop, William W. "The Prudent Politician: An Extension of Aristotle's Ethical Theory." Diss. George Washington U, 1984. *DAI* 45 (1984): 4445B.

Dyson, Anne Haas. "Writing Children: Reinventing the Development of Childhood Literacy." *Written Communication* 12 (1995): 527–47. *Current Index to Journals in Education* 28 (1996): item EJ251057.

Microform collection

Nicoll, Allardyce, and George Freeley, eds. *American Drama of the Nineteenth Century.* New York: Readex Microprint, 1965-. Micro-opaque.

• ELECTRONIC SOURCES

Electronic sources can be divided into two types, depending on whether or not they utilize the Internet.

Electronic Sources on the Internet

The citation for an electronic source on the Internet should provide information sufficient to permit your reader to locate the exact same material you used. Because sources on the Internet can be easily altered or erased, meeting this criterion often requires more information than is normally needed for print sources.

The minimum information for an electronic source includes

1. The author, editor, or translator of the source (as available and relevant), reversed for alphabetizing and, in the case of an editor or translator, followed by the appropriate abbreviation

2. The title of the section you used, in quotation marks or underlined, as MLA style would require in any other context

3. The title of the entire source, in italics, whether it is a book, a website, or a scholarly project

4. A description of the source (if it has no title) in Roman, as in: Home page

5. The name of the editor or translator (if not cited at the beginning of the citation) preceded by the appropriate abbreviation, such as Ed. or Trans.

6. Publication information for a print version of the source (if one exists)

7. The date of the electronic publication or the latest update

8. The number of pages, paragraphs, or other sections, if they are numbered (but not the number of pages in your printed copy of the source)

9. The date you accessed the source (*not* followed by a period)

10. The electronic address of the source, surrounded by angle brackets and followed by a period. If the URL is long or complicated, provide enough detail to enable your reader to get to the search page

If you need to break an electronic address, split it only after a slash mark.

Book

Johnstone, Catherine Laura. *Winter and Summer Excursions in Canada.* London: Digby, Long, 1894. Early Canadiana Online. 2 Nov. 2001 http://www.canadiana.org/cgi-bin/ECO/.

Book, published simultaneously in print form

Audi, Robert. *Moral Knowledge and Ethical Character.* New York: Oxford UP, 1997. Electronic Text Service, Columbia University. 1 Nov. 2001 https://www1.columbia.edu/sec/dlc/oup/audi/.

Book with author, editor, and translator

Merriam, Brian. *The Midnight Court [Cúirt an Mheádhon Oídhche].* Trans. and ed. Noel Fahey. 1998. Noel Fahey. 26 Oct. 2001 http://www.homesteader.com/merriman/welcome.html.

Book with editors emphasized

Kerst, Friedrich, and Henry Edward Krehbiel, eds. *Mozart, the Man and the Artist, As Revealed in His Own Words.* By Wolfgang Amadeus Mozart. Project Gutenberg Release #4042. 1 Nov. 2001 ftp://ftp.ibiblio.org/pub/docs/books/gutenberg/etext99/swnsg10.txt.

Article accessed electronically, with print equivalent

Campbell, James. "Alfred Nobel and His Prizes." *Boston Review* 26.5 (2001): 27–30. *Boston Review.* 29 Oct. 2001 http://bostonreview.mit.edu/BR26.5/Campbell.htm.

Article in an online journal

Readings, Bill. "Notes from the Electronic Underground." *Surfaces* 4 (1994): 53 pars. 14 Nov. 1998 http://tornade.ere.umontreal.ca/boudreaj/vol4/readings.htm.

Article in an online magazine

Church, Sue. "Irish Expatriate Keeps in Touch via the Web." *Computer Mediated Communication Magazine* Aug. 1996. 30 Nov. 1998 http://www.december.com/cmc/mag/1996/aug/church.html.

Newspaper article, electronic version

Schiff, David. "Leonard Bernstein: The Man Who Mainstreamed Mahler." *New York Times* 4 Nov. 2001. 6 Nov. 2001 http://www.nytimes.org/ 2001/11/04/arts/music/04SCHI.html.

Document online

Calahan, Margaret, et al. *Fall Staff in Postsecondary Institutions, 1993.* Washington: GPO, 1996. NCES 96-323. Natl. Center for Educ. Statistics, 30 Nov. 1998 http://nces.ed.gov/pubsearch/pubsinfo.asp?pubid= 96323XXXXX.

Poem online

Pinsky, Robert. "Ginza Samba." *Internet Poetry Archive.* 16 Sept. 1997. U of North Carolina P and North Carolina Arts Council. Internet, RealAudio. 25 Nov. 1998 http://www.sunsite.unc.edu/ipa/pinsky/ginza/html.

(Without print equivalent)

Pinsky, Robert. "The Tuning." *Atlantic Monthly.* Apr. 1995. *Atlantic Unbound.* 30 Dec. 1998 http://www.theatlantic.com/unbound/poetry/ antholog/tuning.htm.

(With print equivalent)

Play online

Chekhov, Anton. *The Swan Song.* Trans. Marian Fell. Project Gutenberg Release #1753. 5 Nov. 2001 ftp://ftp.ibiblio.org/pub/docs/books/gutenberg/ etext99/swnsg10.txt.

Scholarly project

Internet Medieval Sourcebook. Ed. Paul Halsall. 8 Jan. 2000. Fordham U. 1 Nov. 2001 http://www.fordham.edu/halsall/sbook.html.

Professional site

Center for Creative Photography. 11 Oct. 2001. U of Arizona and U of Arizona Main Library. 1 Nov. 2001 http://dizzy.library.arizona.edu/branches/ ccp/home/main.html.

Personal site

Smith, Michael W. Home page. 15 Oct. 2001 http://www.gse.rutgers.edu/ people/mws.htm.

Document created by a private organization, no date

Oxfam International. *Towards Global Equity: Strategic Plan Summary 2001–2004.* 20 Oct. 2001 http://www.oxfam.org/strategic_plan/equity.htm.

Online review, editorial, abstract, or letter

Cupples, Douglas W. Rev. of *The Lost Colony of the Confederacy*. By Eugene C. Harter. 30 Nov. 1998 http://www.h-net.msu.edu/reviews/index.cgi.

Article in a reference database, accessed on Internet

"Fermi, Enrico." *Britannica Online*. Vers. 98.1.1. Nov. 1998. Encyclopaedia Britannica. 30 Nov. 1998 http://www.eb.com:180.

Online posting on a discussion list

Franklin, Phyllis. "Climbing Mt. Everest." Online posting. 10 June 1977. E-GRAD. 15 Sept. 1998 http://www.reg.unci.edu/UCI/HUMANITIES/ENGLISH/egrad.html.

Personal e-mail message

Bell, Gordon R. "More Descendants of Benjamin Hooke." E-mail to the author. 28 Nov. 1998.

Electronic Sources Not on the Internet

Some materials, such as computer software and CD-ROMs, are accessed electronically but in themselves are not electronic. In addition to the information you would include for an electronic source on the Internet, you may need to provide a description of the medium (CD-ROM, diskette, etc.); the name of the database or vendor; and the date of electronic publication.

Computer program

Adobe Acrobat. Ver. 5.0.5. CD-ROM. San Jose, CA: Adobe, 2001.

Material from a database accessed electronically Identify the medium of the database you used: CD-ROM, diskette, videodisc, magnetic tape, and so on.

When you cite only part of a database, identify the title of that part within quotation marks.

Guerrini, Anita. "The Ethics of Animal Experimentation in Seventeenth-Century England. *Historical Abstracts on Disc, 1982–1995. Spring 1995 Update*. CD-ROM. Retrieval Software, 1992. 15 Aug. 1995.

Underline or quote the title of the entry as MLA format would require in any other context.

Gainsborough, Thomas. *The Morning Walk. Microsoft Art Gallery: The Collection of the National Gallery, London*. CD-ROM. Redmond, WA: Microsoft, 1994.

When the material requires or includes more than one electronic medium, name all of them.

> *Perseus 1.0: Interactive Sources and Studies on Ancient Greece.* CD-ROM, videodisc. New Haven: Yale UP, 1992.

● OTHER SOURCES

For a wide range of other sources, provide some equivalent of author, title, and facts of publication. Because such sources usually have many persons identifiable as author in the broadest sense of the word, you will have to select those you consider necessary for locating the source and those important for your purpose in citing it. Include any information about writers or performers before or after the title with these abbreviations: Prod. for *Producer* or *Produced by*, Writ. for *Writer* or *Written by*, Dir. for *Director* or *Directed by*, Perf. for *Performer* or *Performed by*, Narr. for *Narrator* or *Narrated by*, Adapt. for *Adapter* or *Adapted by*, and Cond. for *Conductor* or *Conducted by*. Entries for the same source in two papers with different emphases, one on writers and the other on directors, would be constructed differently and would most likely provide different information. In either case, however, the reader should be able to identify and locate the material.

Television or radio program   An entry for a television or radio program includes the following information, if available and appropriate in a particular instance: title of the episode, in quotation marks; title of the program, underlined; title of the series; name of the network; call letters and city of the local station; and date of broadcast.

> *Jonathan: The Boy Nobody Wanted.* Perf. JoBeth Williams and Chris Burke. WNBC, New York. 19 Oct. 1992.

> "Some Can Sing." *The Language of Life.* Writ. and narr. Bill Moyers. Perf. Robert Hass, Claribel Alegría, and Carolyn Forché. PBS. WNET, Newark, NJ. 9 July 1995.

> "Hiroshima: Why the Bomb Was Dropped." Narr. Peter Jennings. *Peter Jennings Reporting.* Prod. David Gelber and Martin Smith. ABC. WLOV, Columbus, MS. 27 July 1995.

Sound recording   For a recording of music or voice, underline the title of the complete work and place any segment of it within quotation marks. After the title, identify the medium (unless it is CD), the producer or publisher, and the date. The entry may begin with any of the composers, authors, or performers you wish to emphasize, identifying their function if it is not obvious. You may include identifying numbers or letters at the end of the entry.

> Handel, George Frideric. *Water Music/Wassermusik.* Cond. Neville Marriner. Academy of St. Martin-in-the Fields. London: EMI, 1989.

Do not underline a musical composition identified by form, key, or number even when it is the title of a recording.

> Brahms, Johannes. Symphony no. 3 in F major, op. 90. Cond. Sir Georg Solti. Chicago Symphony Orchestra. Rec. in Medinah Temple, Chicago, May 1978. Musical Heritage Society, 1989. 11170X.

Enclose a selection within quotation marks. If the name of the songwriter is given, include it.

> The Beatles. "The Long and Winding Road." By John Lennon and Paul McCartney. <u>Let It Be</u>. LP. Apple, n.d.

> Dave Brubeck Quartet. "Far More Blue." *Time Further Out*. Audiocassette. New York: CBS, n.d.

Treat a spoken recording like a sound recording.

> Thomas, Dylan. "Fern Hill." *Dylan Thomas Reading*. Vol. 1. LP. Caedmon, n.d.

> *Family Counseling*. Narr. K. Hunter. Audiocassette. Washington, D.C.: American Psychological Association, 1989.

Performance A performance, such as a concert or play, usually begins with the title of the work. If you wish to emphasize any of the persons involved, place that person's name in the author position.

> Molnar, Frederic. *The Play's the Thing*. Adapt. P. G. Wodehouse. Dir. Gloria Muzio. Roundabout Theatre Company. New York. 15 July 1995.

> Close, Glenn, perf. *Sunset Boulevard*. By Andrew Lloyd Webber. Minskoff Theatre, New York. 1 Apr. 1995.

> Beatty, Talley, chor. *Come and Get the Beauty of It Hot*. Perf. Marilyn Banks. Prod. Glory Van Scott. Symphony Space Theater, New York. 12 Sept. 1995.

> Schwarz, Gerard, cond. Piano concerto in F major, K. 459. By Wolfgang Amadeus Mozart. Perf. Cecile Licad. Mostly Mozart Festival Orchestra. Avery Fisher Hall, New York. 28 July 1994.

Film or videotape The basic form for a film entry begins with the title, underlined, and includes the director, the distributor, and the year. You may also include the names of writers or performers, as relevant.

> *Country Life*. Writ. and dir. Michael Blakemore. Perf. Sam Neill, Greta Scacchi, John Hargreaves, and Kerry Fox. Miramax, 1995.

> Costner, Kevin, perf. *Waterworld*. Writ. Peter Radar and David Twohy. Prod. Charles Gordon and John Davis. Universal, 1995.

When a videocasette has a date different from that of the film, include both dates, as illustrated below.

> Gilliam, Terry, dir. *The Fisher King*. Writ. Richard LaGravenese. Perf. Robin Williams and Jeff Bridges. 1991. Videocassette. Tristar, 1993.

Musical composition An entry for a musical composition begins with the name of the composer, followed by the title of the piece. When the work is identified only by type or key, that identification is not underlined. When the composition goes by another title, that title is underlined.

> Beethoven, Ludwig van. Sonata no. 19 in G minor, op. 49, no. 1.

> Bach, Johann Sebastian. *Brandenburg Concertos*.

If you refer to the score in published form, cite it as a book, underlining and capitalizing principal words, even those for number and form, and providing the city of publication, publisher, and date.

Works of art When referring to the actual work of art, provide the place where it can be found in addition to the artist and the title, underlined.

> Gainesborough, Thomas. *The Morning Walk*. National Gallery, London.

When you use a reproduction of the work, provide the information in the entry above followed by publication information for your source. If you wish to provide the original date of the work, place it after the title, followed by a period.

> Vallayer-Coster, Anne. *The White Soup Bowl*. 1771. Private Collection, Paris. *Women Artists*, 1550–1950. By Ann Sutherland Harris and Linda Nochlin. New York: Knopf, 1977. Plate 52.

Published letter To cite a published letter, give the name of the writer, the name of the recipient and the date, followed by the facts of publication for the source.

> Crane, Stephen. "To Lily Brandon Munro." March 1894? Bradley, Sculley et al., eds. *The Red Badge of Courage*. 2nd ed. Norton Critical Edition. New York: Norton, 1976. 129.

Unpublished letter Identify letter(s) you received as Letter(s) to the author and give the date(s). If the credentials of the letter writer require mention, place that information in the body of your text.

> Mazzeo, Joseph A. Letters to the author. 8 Aug. to 31 Dec. 1996.

If the unpublished letters reside in an archive, provide the name of the collection and full information about the location.

> Cockburn, Robert. Letter to Lord Melville. 17 May 1819. Manuscript Collection. Group 125. Rutgers U, New Brunswick, NJ.

Interview Identify a published interview according to the format, whether book, television program, or radio broadcast.

> Lipkowitz, Ina, and Andrea Loselle. "An Interview with Julia Kristeva." *Critical Texts* 3.3 (1986): 3–13.

> Warner, Margaret. Interview with John Kenneth Galbraith. *The News Hour with Jim Lehrer*. PBS. WGBH, Boston. 5 Dec. 1995.

For an interview you conducted, identify the medium of communication, as for example, Personal interview for face-to-face communication, Telephone interview, E-mail interview. Place any identification of the person interviewed in the body of your text.

> Jones, Tom. Personal interview. 26 May 1995.

Map or chart

> *World Climatology*. Map. *Times Atlas of the World*. 1990 ed.

Cartoon

> Schoenbaum, Bernard. Cartoon. *New Yorker* 2 Nov. 1992: 82.

> Watterson, Bill. "Calvin and Hobbes." Comic strip. *Miami Herald* 22 July 1995, intl. ed.: 9A.

Advertisement For an advertisement, use the name of the company as the author and identify the publication in which it appeared.

> Infiniti. Advertisement. CBS. 10 Sept. 1995.

> Tiffany and Co. Advertisement. *New York Times* 27 July 1995, late city ed.: A3.

Lecture or speech If a lecture has a title, place it in quotation marks, followed by the name of the conference, the place, and the date.

> Jochens, Jenny. "Gender Equality in Law? The Case of Medieval Iceland." Center for Medieval and Early Renaissance Studies, 26th Annual Conference. Binghamton, NY. 15 Oct. 1992.

For a classroom lecture or informal meeting, designate the nature of the remarks after the name of the speaker.

> Rittner, Robert. "The Great Awakening." Lecture to History 101. State University of New York. Buffalo, NY. 25 Apr. 1995.

> Randall, Emily. Speech at student council meeting. Ventura County Community Coll. Ventura, CA. 15 Sept. 1996.

Manuscript or typescript Identify a manuscript or typescript with the appropriate abbreviation, ms or ts, and identify the location for unpublished material or the means of publication.

> Scarborough, Dorothy. *The Wind*, ms. Dorothy Scarborough Papers. Texas Collection, Baylor U, Waco.

Legal sources Cite legal sources according to the *Uniform System of Citation*, but place them in the reference list, rather than in footnotes (as they appear in legal documents and periodicals).

■ Model of Student Paper in MLA Style

Eóin O'Carroll's paper, "Unchained Melodies," uses the MLA documentation style that is appropriate for an English course. By comparing this paper with the version on pages 631–642, you will see the differences between the MLA and APA styles of documentation.

Eóin O'Carroll

Professor Blau

ENG 201

12 March 2004

Unchained Melodies:

Music and Innovation in the Digital Age

In the early 1980s, the record industry was experiencing a sharp decline in sales. Falling revenues, they claimed, were the fault of the blank audiocassette. "Home taping is killing music" was the industry slogan at the time. Today, with sales slumping again, the record industry is making the same dire predictions. The bugbear of the Recording Industry Association of America (RIAA) this time is not audiocassettes and home tapers, but peer-to-peer networks and mp3 file sharers. On September 8, 2003, the day that the RIAA launched its first round of lawsuits against file sharers, the association issued a press release quoting president Cary Sherman: "We simply cannot allow online piracy to continue destroying the livelihoods of artists, musicians, songwriters, retailers, and everyone in the music industry" (RIAA).

It is hard to say, however, to what extent digital music is responsible. If file sharing is cutting into album sales, it is not necessarily a bad thing—after all, people who make CD burners have livelihoods, too. Moreover, cutting into album sales is not necessarily the same thing as "killing music." Rather, many of the record industry's practices are killing music. Digital music is more likely to rescue it.

To review some background to present events, in the late 1970s, the record industry saw a looming crisis. After hitting an all-time high in 1978, album sales were declining precipitously. Between 1978 and 1982, sales dropped more than forty percent, with revenues falling from $6 billion to about $3.5 billion (Liebowitz 7).

Identifying information should be flush left and double-spaced.

The title is centered and double-spaced with no extra space above or below.

The text begins two lines (one double-space) below the title and is double-spaced.

Eóin spells out the name of the organization and gives the abbreviation in parentheses.

The author of this press release is unnamed, so the organization's name is given in parentheses. This quotation comes from a website, so no page number is given. Note that the period goes after the citation information here.

The author's name is followed by the page number. Do not write *p.* before the page number. Note that the period goes *after* the citation information here.

604

The writer's last name appears in every header and is followed by the page number (without a comma).

The cause? According to the RIAA, which represents the five largest record labels, the blame fell squarely on the blank cassette tape, and the fans who were using it to copy tracks from vinyl LPs that they would then mix, catalogue, and swap. The RIAA demanded congressional hearings, and the international recording industry began placing on records a skull-and-crossbones logo—the skull was shaped like an audiocassette—with the slogan "Home Taping Is Killing Music" (Brown).

Of course, nothing of the kind happened. Album sales began to climb steadily over the eighties. This increase was in part due to the advent of the compact disc, but was also a result of the audiocassette, which helped bring music out of the home and into people's Walkmans, boom boxes, and car stereos (Liebowitz 6). The ominous slogan and logo now appear only on ironic T-shirts. Despite the industry's prophesies, home taping did not kill music.

In 1999, when nineteen-year old Northeastern University dropout Shawn Fanning wrote a program that allowed users to scan the hard drives of other users for music files, he threatened to upend a dynamic that had existed for decades between those who sell the music and those who consume it. For users, Napster combined radio-on-demand with the world's largest record store, all free of charge. For the record labels, it augured a disturbing future, a world in which there was no need for those who manufactured, packaged, distributed, and promoted musical recordings.

Recording artists themselves were split on Napster's impact. In April 2000, San Francisco heavy metal band Metallica, a band that had first established itself through allowing fans to trade concert bootlegs, launched a lawsuit against Napster copyright violations (Alderman 110–11).

The author's name is followed by the page numbers. Do not write *p.* before the page numbers.

O'Carroll 3

"At the end of the day, this is about control," said drummer Lars Ulrich in an interview with *Business Week* a month after the lawsuits. "We feel that this is our music, that we own the rights to it, we pay for it, we have the right to do with it what we want, where we want, and how we want."

In the same article, rapper Chuck D defended Napster, calling it "a new form of radio, of global exposure." Chuck D, a harsh critic of the record business, argued that labels had been deliberately jacking up CD prices and treated recording artists as "a disposable commodity." But with file sharing, he said, "you can have as many as a million people operate within the music game and change the whole process of how the money is going to be distributed" (Berman).

When this article ran, there was no evidence that Napster was actually cutting into album sales. Indeed, some argued that the opposite was occurring. According to entertainment attorney Ken Hertz, "'N Sync, Britney Spears, and Eminem were the three most heavily trafficked artists at Napster the week before their records came out, and those records were the fastest selling records of all time." Hertz speculated that record executives deliberately "seeded" Napster with these albums as a way of promoting them (Alderman 117).

After Napster's free file sharing shut down in the summer of 2000, a host of other programs—KaZaa, Gnutella, Morpheus, iMesh and Limewire, to name a few—immediately rose to take its place, and file sharing continued nearly unabated. According to the Associated Press, users swap more than 150 million songs each month (Straziuso).

But it is still an open question whether file sharing is harming recording artists. Stan Liebowitz, an economist at the University of Texas at Dallas, analyzed thirty years of sales figures in an attempt to measure file sharing's impact. Using figures provided by the RIAA, he

Citation information appears at end of the article.

This statement is common knowledge and therefore requires no citation.

606

When appropriate, use figures to illustrate your argument.

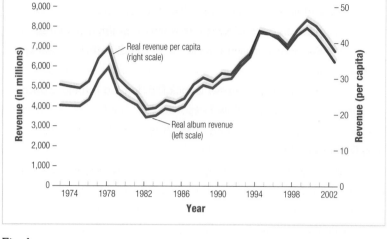

Fig. 1.

Album sales over the past three decades (Liebowitz 7)

showed that there have been several dips in sales in the past and that they have always been followed by further increases (see Fig. 1).

Nonetheless, Liebowitz concludes that the steep decline that began in 2000 is partly a result of file sharing. "No other explanations," he writes, "that have been put forward seem to be able to explain the decline in sales that have occurred since 1999." He calls the harm "significant" (29). "Still," he writes, "it is not clear that the harm will be fatal" (29). Liebowitz does add, however, that the rise in sales during the first year of Napster can be attributed to the increased exposure of albums that resulted from file sharing.

Others disagree. In a 2002 article in *Slate*, Mark Jenkins blamed the slump in sales on the poor quality of the music. Most CDs come from five companies. MTV dominates the music video business and Clear Channel dominates both radio and concerts. The result is a

Since the author has already been identified, only the page number is necessary.

Italicize names of magazines, even online ones.

O'Carroll 5

stultifying homogeneity of dance pop and boy bands, a musical landscape that Jenkins says is much like that of 1978.

> [T]he music of 'N Sync and Britney Spears is not unlike disco: Both are intellectually underachieving, cookie-cutter styles that have made stars of performers not known primarily for their skills as singers, songwriters, or musicians. (Jenkins)

In other words, listeners turn to the Internet because that is where the good music is.

Many recording artists feel compensated for any loss in album sales by the added exposure they gain from having more people listening to their music. Like many up-and-coming bands, the Valhalla Kittens offers mp3s on their website for users to download free of charge.

"[P]eople who might not come see the band otherwise can be swayed after hearing the mp3s on our website," writes Courtney Naliboff, a vocalist for the glam/cabaret rock act, in an e-mail interview.

For others, free music downloads can actually boost album sales. Singer/songwriter Janis Ian also offers free mp3s on her website. "Every time we make a few songs available on my website," she writes in an article posted on her site, "sales of all the CDs go up. A lot."

Ian scoffs at the record labels' argument that downloads are killing sales and taking money out of the pockets of recording artists.

> Costing *me* money? I don't pretend to be an expert on intellectual property law, but I do know one thing. If a music industry executive claims I should agree with their agenda because it will make me more money, I put my hand on my wallet . . . and check it after they leave, just to make sure nothing's missing. (Ian, italics in the original)

The brackets in the first word in this quotation indicate that Jenkins lowercased the letter *t* in the word *the* and that Eóin capitalized the *t*.

Long quotations should be indented 1 inch. Note that there are no quotation marks, and that the citation information goes after the period.

If you put italics into a quotation for emphasis, you should indicate this at the end of the quote. If the italics were in the quotation to begin with, you should say so too.

Many musicians share the perception that record labels are ripping off recording artists. In a speech to the Digital Hollywood online entertainment conference in 2000, rocker Courtney Love criticized the practice, known as recoupment, in which musicians pay costs for recording, marketing and promotion, tours, and music videos out of their royalties. In her speech, which was reprinted on *Salon*, Love described how this practice has forced some artists, such as Toni Braxton and TLC, into bankruptcy, despite having sold millions of CDs. "The system's set up so almost nobody gets paid," she said. What's more, even if the royalties are paid off, the record label retains the rights to the album: "[The band] can pay the mortgage forever but they'll never own the house." Love claims that selling mp3s online would cut out the middleman, saving the consumer money and allowing the artist to sell more albums. "Major labels are freaking out because they have no control in this new world. Artists can sell CDs directly to fans. We can make direct deals with thousands of other websites and promote our music to millions of people that old record companies never touch" (Love).

Apple iTunes, the most popular legal model for online music sales, fails to live up to Love's vision. When a record company produces physical CDs, it deducts from the artist's royalties charges for packaging, shipping, breakage, and returns. The same is true for songs sold over iTunes. But of course, digital music can't be packaged, shipped, broken, or returned. The artist should be getting a bigger cut, but they're not. The labels are pocketing the difference.

Activists and legal scholars have come up with many alternative systems of compensating recording artists for downloaded music. The Electronic Frontier Foundation proposes several models, such as a tax on CD burners, a revenue-sharing system from advertisements displayed in file-swapping software, or an added

---

Eóin added the phrase "The band" to make the quotation clearer. He used brackets to indicate that he did so.

charge on Internet bills that would grant a license to share music (Electronic Frontier Foundation). Any of these models could provide greater payments to recording artists while providing fans with a broader range of music at a much lower price.

Lawrence Lessig, a professor of law at Stanford University, compares the current debate over file sharing with one that happened over a century ago. At the beginning of the twentieth century, sheet music composers were outraged about the proliferation of player pianos. Manufacturers were creating piano rolls—rolls of perforated paper that would fit inside the pianos—from sheet music without paying the composers. Congress resolved the debate by striking a balance. They did not ban the technology outright, nor did they allow the companies to continue to profit at the composers' expense. Instead, they created a "compulsory licensing right." Once a composer granted permission for someone to create a piano roll, any manufacturer could pay a flat rate (two cents a copy) to the composer for each copy (Lessig, 108–09). This compromise allowed companies to continue to develop new technologies while protecting artists from exploitation.

The point is that it can be done—we can create a system in which listeners have access to a broad range of inexpensive music, and in which recording artists are paid fairly. With mp3 technology, artists no longer need a big company to manufacture, package, store, ship, and promote their craft. It is this possibility—not slumping album sales—that really worries the record companies. Just as the radio made carrier pigeons obsolete, and the refrigerator made milkmen obsolete, digital music has the potential to make record companies obsolete. And far from killing music, file sharing might give it some life.

Works Cited

Alderman, John. *Sonic Boom: Napster, MP3, and the New Pioneers of Music*. Cambridge: Perseus, 2001.

Berman, Dennis. "Lars Ulrich vs. Chuck D: Facing Off over Napster." 2000. *Business Week*. 25 May 2000 http://www.businessweek.com/ebiz/0005/0525ulrich.htm.

Brown, Dan "Home Taping Did Not Kill Music." 2003. CBC News Viewpoint. 23 Oct. 2003 http://www.cbc.ca/news/viewpoint/vp_browndan/20031023.html.

Electronic Frontier Foundation. "Making P2P Pay Artists." 11 March 2004 http://www.eff.org/share/compensation.php.

Ian, Janis. "The Internet Debacle: An Alternative View." 2002. 10 March 2004 http://www.janisian.com/article-internet_debacle.html.

Jenkins, Mark. "Hit Charade: The Music Industry's Self-Inflicted Wounds." 2002. *Slate*. 20 Aug. 2002 http://slate.msn.com/?id=2069732.

Lessig, Lawrence. *The Future of Ideas*. New York: Random House, 2001.

Liebowitz, Stan. "Will MP3 Downloads Annihilate the Record Industry? The Evidence So Far." 2003. University of Texas at Dallas School of Management. 21 July 2003 http://wwwpub.utdallas.edu/~liebowit/intprop/records.pdf.

Love, Courtney. "Courtney Love Does the Math." 2000. *Salon*. 14 June 2000 http://archive.salon.com/tech/feature/2000/06/14/love.

Naliboff, Courtney. E-mail to the author. 13 March 2004.

Recording Industry Association of America. "Recording Industry Begins Suing P2P File Sharers Who Illegally Offer Copyrighted Music Online." 2003. 8 September 2003 http://www.riaa.com/news/newsletter/090803.asp.

Straziuso, Jason. "Music Piracy Activity Slows." *Detroit Free Press*. 23 February 2004 http://www.freep.com/money/business/bnews23_20040223.htm.

Overview of APA Style

The *Publication Manual of the American Psychological Association* is the authoritative source for documenting research papers in the sciences and social sciences. You can consult the handbook or the website at http://www.apastyle.org for more detailed information. You will get an overview here of

- Formatting the manuscript
- Citing sources in the text
- Creating a References page

At the end of this section is a student paper in APA style that you can use as a model.

■ Formatting the Manuscript (APA)

APA style has somewhat different requirements for formatting than MLA style, but presentation is just as important. See the model paper on pages 631–642.

Paper   Use good quality 8½-by-11-inch paper. Fasten your manuscript with paper clips; avoid both staples and binders because they make it harder for your professor to read and comment on your work.

Title Page   APA style calls for a separate title page, numbered as page 1. A title—or a shortened title, if yours is long—and page number go against the right margin, about ½ inch from the top of the paper. This running head should appear on all the pages of your paper.

Though APA does not specify how to format the title page, the usual format is to center your title about a third of the way down the page. Use regular type and the same font as in the rest of the manuscript (do not use all capital letters, italics, boldface, or the like). Double-space the title if it is longer than one line. Double-spaced and centered under the title, type your name. Double-spaced under your name, type your course number; then, after another double space, type the date.

Abstract   The second page of your paper is the abstract, a brief (no more than 120 words) summary of your paper. Center the word *Abstract* about 1 inch from the top of the page, and double-space the text.

Margins, Spacing, Font, and Indenting   Leave 1-inch margins on all four sides. Double-space your entire manuscript. Use easy-to-read fonts; 10-point to 14-point Times and Times New Roman are most commonly used. Indent ½ inch, or between five and seven spaces, at the beginning of each paragraph. When you use a quotation of more than forty words, indent ½ inch, or five to seven spaces, and do not use quotation marks. (Check with your professor; some will ask you to indent 1 inch or ten spaces in academic papers.) Double-space within the quotation.

Paging Begin your paper on page 3.

Headings Headings are encouraged in APA-formatted papers. If your material is complicated and would benefit from being subdivided, create headings that are brief, parallel in phrasing, and consistent in the font you use. Use no more than two levels of headings, if possible.

Visuals If you include graphs, tables, maps, charts, illustrations, or photographs, place them directly after you introduce them in the text. Label the table at the top with the table number and title (Table 1 Album Titles and Release Dates). Label each figure below the image with a number and a caption that identifies it (Figure 1: Album revenues). Cite the source underneath the visual.

References The final page of your paper is called References. Center the title about 1 inch from the top of the page. Do not add quotation marks, boldface, italics, and so on. Alphabetically list all works you referred to in the text of your paper, double-spaced with a hanging indent.

■ Citing Sources in the Text

The APA format requires you to cite at least the author and the date in the parenthetical citations within the text of your paper. Sometimes you will add the page reference as well. A citation should be brief but complete enough to lead your reader to the full citation in the References list at the end of the paper.

Author named in your text If you mention the author's name in your text, cite only the date of publication in parentheses, immediately after the author's name.

> Gould (1989) attributes Darwin's success to his gift for making the appropriate metaphor.

Subsequent citation in same paragraph When another sentence in the same paragraph refers to the same author, the parenthetical material, if it remains the same, need not be repeated. In any subsequent paragraph, however, you would need to provide the parenthetical information again. Use the last name only in both first and subsequent citations, except when two authors have the same last name.

Author not named in your text When you do not mention the author's name in your own text, that name, followed by a comma and the date of publication, appears in parentheses at the end of your sentence or, if you have referred to more than one source, at the end of the relevant clause.

> As metaphors for the workings of nature, Darwin used the tangled bank, the tree of life, and the face of nature (Gould, 1989).

Citation of parts of sources To indicate a precise location within the source, whether or not you quote from it directly, add the page or chapter number preceded by the appropriate abbreviation: p. for page, pp. for pages, chap. for chapter, *pt.* for part. In citing electronic sources in which portions of the document are numbered or designated in some other way, use an abbreviation for the marker used in the document, such as *sec.* for section and *par.* for paragraph.

> (Gould, 1989, p. 14) (Gould, 1987, chap. 2) Tiihonen, 2000, sec. 3)

Author and date cited in text If you use both the name of the author and the date in the text, a parenthetical reference is not needed.

> In a 1989 article, Gould explores some of Darwin's most effective metaphors.

Direct quotation with name of author When your sentence contains a quotation and includes the name of the author, place the publication date and page number in parentheses. Abbreviate the word *page* or *pages* (p. or pp.). The publication date follows the name of the author; the page number follows the end of the quotation.

> Gould (1989) explains that Darwin used the metaphor of the tree of life "to express the other form of interconnectedness—genealogical rather than ecological—and to illustrate both success and failure in the history of life" (p. 14).

Direct quotation without name of author When you use a quotation but do not identify the author in the sentence, the name of the author, date of publication, and page number appear in parentheses at the end of the sentence, followed by the period for the sentence.

> Darwin used the metaphor of the tree of life "to express the other form of interconnectedness—genealogical rather than ecological" (Gould, 1989, p. 14).

Work by two authors When you refer to a work by two authors, cite both names each time the reference appears. Within the parentheses use an ampersand (&), but within your text spell out the word *and*.

> Sexual-selection theory has been used to explore patterns of insect mating (Alcock & Thornhill, 1983). . . . Alcock and Thornhill (1983) also demonstrate . . .

Three, four, five, or six authors For a work by more than two authors but fewer than seven, cite all names in the first reference. In subsequent references, cite only the name of the first author and use et al.

> Scientists have isolated a gene connected to circadian rhythms in plants (Millar, Straume, Chory, Chua, & Kay, 1995, p. 1163). . . . They identified the mutations that activated light-dependent pathways (Millar et al., 1995, p. 1165). . . .

Seven or more authors For a work by seven or more authors, give only the last name of the first author followed by et al. in both first and subsequent references.

> Scientists have constructed a deletion map of the human Y chromosome (Vollrath et al., 1992). . . . Their studies resolved a region of the chromosome into ordered intervals (Vollrath et al., 1992) . . .

Distinguishing entries with multiple authors When two entries with multiple authors shorten to exactly the same form, cite as many names as you need to distinguish the two parenthetical references. If in addition to the article above with Vollrath as first author followed by Foote, you had another in which the name Smith followed Vollrath, the two shortened references would appear this way:

> (Vollrath, Foote et al., 1992) . . . (Vollrath, Smith et al., 1992).

If these two articles were published in different years, the second name would not be necessary to distinguish them:

> (Vollrath et al., 1992) . . . (Vollrath et al., 1993).

Authors with the same last name When you cite works by two or more authors with the same last name, use initials to identify the authors in the text even if the dates of publication differ.

> R. Dawkins (1986) and M. S. Dawkins (1980) have contributed to an understanding of consciousness in animals.

Work cited in another work When the source of a direct or indirect quotation is a secondary source, refer to the source you actually used within parentheses and in the reference list.

> Darwin's metaphors (as cited in Gould, 1989) . . .

If you use a direct quotation from the secondary source, the parenthetical reference reads (as quoted by Gould, 1989).

Work identified by title When a work is noted in the reference list by title alone, a shortened version of the title is used to identify the work parenthetically in the text. Within the text, whether in parentheses or not, titles are presented differently from the way they are in the reference list. All words are capitalized, except words of four letters or more; the title of a book, report, brochure, or periodical is underlined; and the title of an article or chapter appears within quotation marks.

> The National Endowment for the Humanities supports "theoretical and critical studies of the arts" but not work in the creative or performing arts (*Guidelines*, 1994, p. 1).

> Changes in the Medical College Admissions Test to begin in 1991 are expected to encourage more students to pursue general studies in the humanities, natural sciences, and social sciences ("New Exam," 1989).

Corporate author When you cite a work by a group author, use the name of the corporation or organization as the author.

> Retired officers retain access to all of the university's educational and recreational facilities (Columbia University, 1995, p. 54).

You may use well-known abbreviations of the name of a corporate author in subsequent parenthetical references or in the text itself. For example, you might use NSF for National Science Foundation, NIMH for National Institutes of Mental Health, and ERIC for Educational Resources Information Center. In this case, your first reference to the group or organization should include the abbreviation you intend to use.

> The *Guidelines* (National Endowment for the Humanities [NEH], 1994) specify . . . The NEH gives block grants to states. . . . It funded a study of . . . (*Guidelines*, 1994)

Work explicitly identified as anonymous If the title page actually gives the author's name as "Anonymous," use that word for the author and omit the title: (Anonymous, 1925). You will find few such instances, particularly among recent works.

Classical work For a classical work, or any work so old that it was not published in the modern sense, cite the date of the translation you used: (Aristotle, trans. 1985). If the date of authorship is relevant, include it in your text. For identifying specific parts of a classical work, use conventional line, book, or section numbers, as appropriate for each particular case. The entry for the *Nicomachean Ethics* would read: (Aristotle, trans. 1985, 1123a34).

Bible or other sacred writing Refer to passages in the Bible with citations of book, chapter, and verse and place the translation you used within parentheses, but not in the reference list: Jeremiah 48.18 (New Revised Standard Version). APA uses a period rather than a colon between chapter and verse: 2 Cor. 15.2.

Reference to more than one work Parenthetical references may mention more than one work. Multiple citations should be arranged as follows:

List two or more works by the same author in order of date of publication: (Gould, 1987, 1989).

Differentiate works by the same author with the same publication date by adding an identifying letter to each date: (Bloom, 1987a, 1987b). The letters also appear in the reference list, where the works are alphabetized by title.

List works by different authors in alphabetical order by last name and use semicolons to separate the references: (Alcock & Thornhill; Gould, 1989).

■ Creating a References Page

The last page of your paper will be titled References. All the parenthetical citations you inserted in your paper refer your reader to the complete entry in this final list. Include each work you have cited in your paper but not works you read but did not cite. Alphabetize your list by last name of the author or, in the case of an entry without an identified author, by the first word of the title, excluding the articles *A, An,* and *The.*

● BOOKS AND CHAPTERS OF BOOKS

Basic Form The entry for a book begins with the last name of the author, followed by a comma and the initials of the author's first and middle names, followed by periods. The date of publication appears in parentheses, followed by a period. Only the first word of the book title, the first word of the subtitle, and proper names within both are capitalized. The entire title and the end period are italicized. Facts of publication include the city of publication and, if the city might be unfamiliar to readers or confused with another location, the name of the state. Use U.S. Postal Service abbreviations for states. The name of the location is followed by a colon and the name of the publisher. The entry ends with a period. The names of university presses are spelled out.

Nagel, P. C. (1992). *The Lees of Virginia: Seven generations of an American family.* New York: Oxford University Press.

Two or more authors For a book by more than one author, invert and list the names of all the authors. Use commas to separate surnames and initials. Place an ampersand (&) before the name of the last author.

Forsyth, A., & Thornhill, R. (1983). *The evolution of insect mating.* Cambridge: Harvard University Press.

Brochure Treat a brochure like a book, but designate it as a brochure within brackets.

Edition other than the first Identify an edition other than the first within parentheses following the title without any intervening punctuation. The number of the edition should be in serial form (2nd, 3rd, 4th, etc.) or, if it is a word, abbreviated (Rev. ed.).

> Dreyfus, H. (1989). *What computers can't do* (2nd ed.). New York: Harper & Row.

Reprinted work The entry for a reprinted work indicates the original date of publication within parentheses.

> Darwin, C. (1964). *On the origin of the species: A facsimile of the first edition.* Cambridge: Harvard University Press. (Original work published 1859)

The parenthetical reference in the text includes both dates: (Darwin, 1859/1964).

Treat a paperbound book issued in a year other than that of the hardcover edition as a reprinted work.

> Jamieson, N. L. (1995). *Understanding Vietnam*. Berkeley: University of California Press. (First published in hardcover 1993)

The parenthetical reference in the text includes both dates: (Jamieson 1993/1995).

Edited volume Indicate that a book is an edited volume by placing the abbreviation for editor (Ed.) or editors (Eds.) within parentheses in the author position.

> Stanton, D. C. (Ed.). (1987). *The female autograph: Theory and practice of autobiography from the tenth to the twentieth century.* Chicago: University of Chicago Press.

Chapter or article in edited book In a reference to a chapter or article in an edited book, place the name of the author of the chapter in the author position. The second part of the entry identifies the book in which the article appears. The name(s) of the editor(s) is (are) not inverted when not at the beginning of the entry. The page numbers for the individual chapter or article appear in parentheses after the title of the book.

> Burghardt, G. M. (1984). On the origins of play. In P. K. Smith (Ed.), *Play in animals and humans* (pp. 5–42). Oxford: Basil Blackwell.

For two or more editors, use the abbreviation Eds.

> Dubin, F., Eskey, D., & Grabe, W. (Eds.). (1986). *Teaching second language reading for academic purposes.* Reading, MA: Addison-Wesley.

When the author of the article and the editor of the book are the same, but the book includes articles by other authors, list the name in both author and editor positions.

> Olney, J. (1980). Autobiography and the cultural moment: A thematic, historical, and bibliographical introduction. In J. Olney (Ed.), *Autobiography: Essays theoretical and critical* (pp. 3–27). Princeton: Princeton University Press.

When all the chapters in a book are by the same author and you wish to cite one of them by title, place the word In before the book title. The example below indicates that Finke is the author of both the chapter and the book.

> Finke, L. (1992). The rhetoric of desire in the courtly lyric. In *Feminist Theory, Women's Writing* (pp. 29–74). Ithaca: Cornell University Press.

Reprinted article When an article in a collection was published previously, list the version you actually used, but give the original citation in parentheses.

> Howarth, H. L. (1980). Some principles of autobiography. In J. Olney (Ed.), *Autobiography: Essays theoretical and critical* (pp. 84–114). Princeton: Princeton University Press. (Reprinted from *New Literary History*, 1974, 5, 363–381.)

The parenthetical citation in the text includes both publication dates: (Howarth, 1974/1980)

Works without designated author Enter and alphabetize a book or brochure without an author or editor by title alone.

> *Guidelines and application form for directors, 1996, summer seminars for school teachers.* [Brochure] (1994). Washington, DC: National Endowment for the Humanities.

Author as publisher When you consider the publisher as the author, replace the name of the publisher with Author.

> Teachers Insurance and Annuity Association, College Retirement Equities Fund. [Pamphlet]. (1995). *The participant.* New York: Author.

Multivolume works For a multivolume work published over several years, place in parentheses the year of publication of the first volume and that of the last volume, separated by a hyphen.

> Ripley, C. P. (Ed.). (1985–1992). *The black abolitionist papers* (Vols. 1–5). Chapel Hill: University of North Carolina Press.

When referring to the entire multivolume work within the text, cite it as (Ripley, 1985–1992).

To refer to a single volume in a multivolume series, include only the relevant date, and place the volume number after the title without any intervening punctuation.

> Ripley, C. P. (Ed.). (1987). *The black abolitionist papers* (Vol. 2). Chapel Hill: University of North Carolina Press.

When each volume has an individual title, provide both the multivolume and the volume titles, underlined continuously.

> Freehling, W. W. (1992). *Secessionists at bay, 1776–1854: Vol. 1. The road to disunion*. New York: Oxford University Press.

Translated work Indicate the name of a translator within parentheses after the title by the initials of the first name(s) and the full last name. If you have used only the English translation, you do not need to include the original title. If you wish to do so, place it within brackets.

> Derrida, J. (1976). *Of grammatology* (G. Spivak, Trans.). Baltimore: Johns Hopkins University Press. (Original work published 1967)

The parenthetical reference in the text should indicate the original date of publication as well as the date of the translation: (Derrida, 1967/1976).

Book in a foreign language When you cite from a book in a foreign language, supply an English translation of the original title within brackets. If the work has not been translated, use your own translation or the English title by which the work is known. The bracketed title is not underlined or italicized.

> Kristeva, J. (1983). *L'Histoires d'amour* [Tales of love]. Paris: Denoël.

Work in a series The entry for an individually titled work in a series provides both the volume and the series titles.

> Eiser, J. R. (Ed.). (1990). *Attitudinal judgment*. Springer Series in Social Psychology, no. 11. New York: Springer-Verlag, 1990.

● PERIODICALS

Basic entry The basic entry for an article in a periodical begins with the last name(s), followed by the initials (not the entire first names), of all authors. The year of publication follows in parentheses; for magazine and newspaper articles, give the month and day (if any) or the season (capitalized). Next come the title of the article, not enclosed in quotation marks; the title of the periodical, including the article *the*, italicized through the end punctuation mark, if any; the volume number, underlined or italicized through the end punctuation mark, if any; and inclusive page numbers. A period follows the author, the date, the title of the article, and the end of the entry. The name of the periodical, the volume number, and the page numbers are separated by commas. Only the first word of the article title, the first word of the subtitle, and proper names within both are capitalized. All words except articles and prepositions are capitalized in the title of the periodical, and the title is underlined or italicized. The abbreviation *p.* or *pp.* is used in references to daily newspapers but not to journals or magazines. Both numbers in inclusive pages include all digits.

Article by one author

> Smith, J. (1995). The title of the article. *The Title of Journal, 1*, 101–105.
> Simon, G. (1990). The significance of silence. *Paragraph, 13*, 202–216.

Article by two authors For an article by two authors, invert the names of both authors, using a comma to separate surnames and initials. Place an ampersand (&) before the name of the second author.

> McLaren, P., & Estrada, K. (1993). A dialogue on multiculturalism and democratic culture. *Educational Researcher, 22*, 27–33.

Article by three to six authors List the names of all authors up to six, separating surnames and initials with a comma and placing an ampersand (&) before the name of the final author.

> Dornbusch, S. M., Carlsmith, J. M., Bushwall, S. J., Ritter, P. L., Leiderman, H., & Hastorf, A. H. (1985). Single parents, extended households, and the control of adolescents. *Child Development, 56*, 326–341.

Seven or more authors For an article with seven or more authors, list the first six names and use et al. to refer to the rest, no matter how many.

> Vollrath, D., Foote S., Hilton, A., Brown, L.G., Beer-Romano, P., Bogan, J.S., et al. (1992, October 2). The human Y chromosome: A 43-interval map based on naturally occurring deletions. *Science, 258*, 52–60.

Names with suffixes For names followed by a suffix such as Jr. or III, place the suffix after the initials for the first name, preceded and followed by a comma.

> Harper, C. L., Jr., Nyquist, L. E., Bansal, B., Wiesmann, H., & Shih, C.-Y. (1995, January 13). Rapid accretion and early differentiation of Mars. *Science, 267*, 213–216.

When the name appears in regular rather than inverted order, no punctuation separates the name and the suffix: C. L. Harper Jr., Charles S. Levings III.

Journal paginated by issue If each issue of a journal begins with page 1, give the issue number in parentheses after the volume number. The issue number is not italicized.

> Brunsdale, M. M. (1991). Stages on her road: Sigrid Undset's spiritual journey. *Religion and Literature, 23*(3), 83–96.

Magazine article The entry for an article in a magazine or newsletter with a volume number includes the month and day (if any), as well as the year, the volume, and the pages.

> Osborn, M. (1994, March 11). Status and prospects of women in science in Europe. *Science, 263,* 1389–1391.

Most magazines have volume numbers, although in popular publications they are often not featured prominently. If you ascertain that the magazine has no volume number, follow the format for a newspaper article. If no author is given, begin the entry with the title of the article.

Newspaper article Entries for articles in newspapers are constructed according to the principles for magazines, except that the volume number is omitted and the abbreviation p. or pp. is used to indicate page(s).

> Morain, D. (1993, June 7). Poor countless hit hardest by budget cuts. *The Los Angeles Times,* p. A1.

Newspaper article, unsigned An entry for a newspaper (or magazine) article without a byline or signature begins with the headline or title in the author position without italics, or quotation marks.

> New exam for doctor of future. (1989, March 15). *The New York Times,* p. B10.

Newspaper article, discontinuous pages When a newspaper article appears on discontinuous pages, give all page numbers and separate the numbers with commas.

> Broad, W. J. (1989, March 14). Flight of shuttle begins flawlessly. *The New York Times,* pp. A1, C7.

Newspaper article in designated section When you cite a newspaper article with a special designation, indicate its nature in brackets following the title.

> Williams, R. L. (1992, May 13). National university is an outmoded idea [Letter to the editor]. *The Chronicle of Higher Education,* p. B4.

Special issue of a journal In an entry for a special issue of a journal, identify the editors (if any) of the issue and the title of the issue. If the issue does not specify its editors, the title of the issue occupies the author position.

> Political and social issues in composition [Special issue]. (1992). *College Composition and Communication, 43*(2).

Monographs In an entry for a monograph, identify the nature of the material within brackets if the series or journal title does not, and give the volume number of the issue. Place additional identifying numerals, such as issue and serial (or whole) numbers, in parentheses after the volume number without an intervening space.

> Hinde, R. A. (1990). The interdependence of the behavioral sciences [Monograph]. *Philosophical Transactions of the Royal Society, 329,* 217–277.

> Kreutzer, M. A., Leonard, C., & Flavell, J. H. (1975). An interview study of children's knowledge about memory. *Monographs of the Society for Research in Child Development, 40* (Whole No. 1).

Abstract or synopsis If you wish to cite the abstract of a published article rather than the article itself, provide a complete entry for the published article and cite the source of the abstract, if it is different, in parentheses. Place the designation Abstract within brackets after the title and before the period.

> Dorin, J. R., Inglis, J. D., & Porteous, D. J. (1989). Selection for precise chromosomal targeting of a dominant marker by homologous recombination. [Abstract]. *Science, 243,* 1357–1360. Abstract obtained from *Science Abstracts,* 1989, 75, Abstract No. 1153.

Article in press When an article either is being considered or has been accepted for publication, the phrase in press takes the position of the date, and the name of the journal follows, but no volume or page numbers are given.

> Smith, S. (in press). An experiment in bilingual education. *Journal of Bilingual Education.*

Two such articles by the same author should be identified with lowercase letters preceded by a hyphen: (in press-a, in press-b).

● ELECTRONIC SOURCES

The citation for an electronic source should provide information sufficient to permit your reader to locate the material that is identical to the source you used. Because electronic sources can be easily altered or erased, meeting this criterion requires more information than is needed for print sources. Before submitting an article to an APA journal, you need to check all the URLs (electronic addresses) in your references for currency and to eliminate any citations that are no longer available. In the case of academic or work-related research papers, you might want to include printouts of some of your electronic sources in an appendix.

Electronic sources can be divided into two types: those available through the Internet and those not on the Internet.

Sources on the Internet

Entries for materials from the Internet should include the same facts of publication necessary for print sources: last name of the author followed by the initial(s) of given names; the date of publication within parentheses; the title of the section you used; the title of the database, project, or site, italicized. In addition, citations for electronic sources include the date you accessed the site and the URL. You may break a URL only after a slash. Do not insert a hyphen into a URL and do not follow it with a period. You may also include, as appropriate, information such as the date of the latest version of the site; the number of pages, paragraphs, or sections; and the e-mail address of the Webmaster maintaining the site. To locate some of this information, you may have to explore the entire site carefully. Also, some of the copyright information may be on the homepage from which the site branches: to find this page, remove the final segments of the address until you reach the homepage or click the appropriate link on the site. If you cannot find some of the required information, cite anything you have that will be useful to readers.

Internet articles identical to a print source

Corbett, K. J. (2001, Winter). The big picture: Theatrical moviegoing, digital television, and beyond the substitution effect. [Electronic version]. *Cinema Journal, 40,* 17–32.

When the electronic and print versions are identical, only the bibliographic information for the print source is required.

Article in an Internet-only periodical

Youngblood, G.M. (1999, Summer). Web hunting: Design of a simple intelligent web search agent. *ACM Crossroads, 5.* Retrieved October 15, 2001, from http://www.acm.org/crossroads/xrds5-4/webhunting.html

Provide the URL that links directly to the article. An Internet-only periodical does not usually have page numbers.

Newspaper article, electronic version

Chang, K. (2001, October 19). Precursor to tiniest chip is developed. *The New York Times.* Retrieved October 19, 2001, from http://www.nytimes.org/pages/science/html

Document created by a private organization, no date

The Literacy Volunteer Connection (n.d.). *Tips for volunteer tutors.* Retrieved October 17, 2001, from http://literacyvolunteer.homestead.com/TipsForTutors.html

When an individual is not identified as the author, use the name of the organization in place of the author.

Document, no author identified, no date

Advice for job hunters. (n.d.). Retrieved October 1, 2001, from http://www.howard.dowding.ukgateway.net/

When neither an individual nor an organization is identified as taking responsibility for creation of the site, place the title of the document at the beginning of the entry. Use the abbreviations n.d. (no date) for undated documents.

Chapter or section in a document, no page numbers

Stone, G. (2000, March). Lead length and voice in U.S. newspapers (conclusions and readability). *Web Journal of Mass Communication Research, 3.* Retrieved October 10, 2001, from http://www.scripps.ohiou.edu/wjmcr/vol103/3-2a.htm

Cite the entire document when pages or sections are not marked.

Report on government agency Website, no date

United States Senate. (n.d.). *Senate oral history program.* Retrieved October 19, 2001, from http://www.senate.gov/learning/learn_history_oralhist.html

Private organization report on organization Website

Oxfam International. (n.d.). *Towards global equity: Strategic plan summary 2001-2004.* Retrieved October 20, 2001, from http://www.oxfam.org/strategic_plan/equity.htm

Organization document, from Website of a different organization

American Council of Learned Societies. (2000, November). *Report on history e-book project.* Retrieved October 25, 2001, from Columbia University, Center for Comparative Literature and Society Website: http://www.columbia.edu/cu/research/

For a document accessed from the website of an organization other than the one that produced the document, identify and cite the URL of the provider you used.

U.S. government report online

Department of Energy. (2001, March 13). *Protection of human subjects.* Retrieved October 26, 2001, from http://www.access.gpo.gov/nara/cfr/waisidx_01/10cfrv4_01.html#706

Paper presented at a virtual conference

Mackieh, A., & Cilingir, C. (1996). *Effects of performance shaping factors on human error.* Paper presented at the CybErg 96 virtual conference. Retrieved October 26, 2001, from http://www.curtin.edu.au/conference/cyberg/centre/paper/mackiehpaper.html#

Because a virtual conference takes place online, no place can be specified.

Message posted to a newsgroup

Stonehouse, R. (2001, October 25). Did the Trojan War occur? Message posted to newsgroups://soc.history.ancient.humanities.classics

When you have other relevant sources, avoid referring to newsgroups because the messages usually do not remain online very long, and the origin of the message is not verifiable. Provide the precise date of the posting; the subject heading, not italicized; and the address of the newsgroup.

Message posted to online forum or discussion group

Adams, E. (2001, October 4). Question to Martha Nussbaum. Posted to http://chronicle.com/colloquylive/s002/1/10/nussbaum/chat

Electronic Sources Not on the Internet

Some materials, such as computer software and CD-ROMs, are accessed electronically but in themselves are not electronic. In addition to the information you would include for an electronic source on the Internet, you may need to provide a description of the medium (CD-ROM, diskette, etc.); the name of the database or vendor; and the date of electronic publication.

Journal article retrieved from an electronic database

Robinson, D. T., & Smith-Lovin, L. (2001, September). Getting a laugh: Gender, status, and humor in task discussions. *Social Forces, 80,* 125–158. Retrieved October 19, 2001, from http://muse.jhu.edu/journals/social_forces/v080/

Encyclopedia or dictionary entry

Sobel, Robert D., ed. (1900). *Smith, Charles Emory.* Biographical directory of the United States executive branch. Retrieved October 25 from http://lexisnexis.com/hisuniv/

Abstract obtained from a database

Brown, L., & Halweil, B. (2001, May). Virtual water. *Canada and the world backgrounder, 66.* Abstract retrieved October 25, 2001, from Readers Guide Abstracts: http://firstsearch.oclc.org

Electronic version of U.S. government report available from GPO access database

U.S. Senate (2001, October 22). Joint Committees of the Congress. *Senate Calendar of Business, 107th Congress.* Retrieved October 29, 2001, from Senate Calendar Online via GPO Access: http://www.access.gpo.gov/congress/browse-sc.html

Data file, available from NTIS Website

North Atlantic Treaty Organization. (1990, May). *NATO Thesaurus Project* [Data file]. Available from National Technical Information Service Website: http://neptune.fedworld.gov/

Computer software

In an entry for computer software, include the name of the author or producer; the year of development or publication; the title, not italicized; immediately after the title, a description of the material in brackets; the facts of publication; and any additional information necessary for locating and running the program.

> Interactive Physics II [Computer software]. (1992). San Francisco: Knowledge Revolution.

> Quotation Reference Collection [Computer software]. (1995). Reno: AAPEX Software.

• OTHER SOURCES

Technical and Research Reports

Basic entry Entries for technical and research reports should follow the basic format for a book entry. The identifying title, series, or number of the report, if any, should be placed in parentheses immediately after the title. The name of the agency publishing the report should not be abbreviated as an acronym, even if it is well known.

> Gates, J. P. (1991). *Educational and training opportunities in sustainable agriculture.* Beltsville, MD: National Agricultural Library.

Report from an information service For a report that comes from an information service, such as the National Technical Information Service (NTIS) or Educational Resources Information Center (ERIC), identify the service and document number in parentheses at the end of the entry.

> Groak, J. J. (1974). *Utilization of library resources by students in non-residential degree programs.* Washington, DC: U.S. Government Printing Office. (ERIC Document Reproduction Service No. ED121236)

Report from a university When a university (as opposed to a university press) is the publisher, provide the name of the university, followed by the name of the specific unit or department.

> Carter, G. E., Parker, J. R., & Bentley, S. (Eds.). (1984). *Minority literature and the urban experience.* LaCrosse: University of Wisconsin, Institute for Minority Studies.

Report from corporation or organization

> American Museum of Natural History. (1995). *Annual report, 1993–1994.* New York: Author.

Proceedings of Meetings

When a presentation at a meeting appears in book form, the entry follows the format for an article in an edited book.

> Eble, C. C. (1976). Etiquette books as linguistic authority. In P. A. Reich (Ed.), *The Second LACUS Forum, 1975* (pp. 468–475). Columbia, SC: Hornbeam.

Unpublished paper presented at meeting For an unpublished paper presented at a conference or symposium, indicate the date of the presentation within parentheses after the name of the author and identify the conference as fully as necessary after the title. If the name of the city is well known, the name of the state may be omitted; otherwise, include both city and state.

> Jochens, J. (1992, October). *Gender equality in law? The case of medieval Iceland*. Paper presented at the 26th Annual Conference of the Center for Medieval and Early Renaissance Studies, Binghamton, NY.

Poster session

> Gilbert, D. R. (1995, August). *Investigations into low temperature and low pressure deposition of diamond thin films*. Poster session presented at the Applied Diamond Conference 1995, National Institute of Standards and Technology, Gaithersburg, MD.

Dissertations and Theses

Microfilm of dissertation When you use a microfilm of a dissertation as the source, give the microfilm number, as well as the volume and page numbers in *Dissertation Abstracts International*.

> Baker, C. A. (1985). Multiple alliance commitments: The role of the United States in the Falklands war. *Dissertation Abstracts International, 45*, 4445B. (UMI No. 85–77, 123)

Typescript of dissertation When you use the typescript copy of a dissertation, give the university and year, as well as the volume and page numbers in *Dissertation Abstracts International*. If the dates are different, provide the date of the dissertation after the name of the university.

> Moskop, W. W. (1995). The prudent politician: An extension of Aristotle's ethical theory (Doctoral dissertation, George Washington University, 1984). *Dissertation Abstracts International, 45*, 4445B.

When the years are different, list then chronologically, separated by a slanted line, in the parenthetical reference: (Moskop, 1984/1985).

Unpublished dissertation or thesis Treat a dissertation or thesis that does not appear in *Dissertation Abstracts International* as an unpublished work. Italicize the title and identify the university, the city, and, if necessary for identification, the state.

> Peters, B. (1995). *The biographer as autobiographer: The case of Virginia Woolf.* Unpublished master's thesis, Pace University, Riverdale, NY.

Unpublished Materials and Works of Limited Circulation

Completed material not submitted for publication When unpublished material is in completed form, italicize the title and indicate the unpublished status at the end of the entry.

> Johnson, S. J. (1992). *The teaching of twelfth-grade advanced placement mathematics.* Unpublished manuscript, University of California, San Diego.

Manuscript submitted or accepted for publication When an unpublished manuscript has been submitted or accepted for publication, designate it as in press.

> Little, C. A. (1992). *Forms of childhood autism.* In press.

Draft material When you refer to unpublished material in unfinished form, such as a rough draft or unorganized tabular data, put the name of the topic in brackets in the title position without underlining or italics. Indicate the status of the material at the end of the entry. Use the date you consulted the material.

> Jensen, H. C. (1992). [Settlement patterns for Norwegian immigrants, 1890–1920]. Unpublished raw data.

Publication of limited circulation When a work, although published, probably will not be available in most libraries, give the address at which a copy might be located or obtained.

> Inouye, L. (1993, April). GECA—The organic agriculture training school, El Salvador. *Oxfam American project report,* pp. 1–4. [Brochure]. (Available from Oxfam America, 26 West Street, Boston, MA 02111-1206)

Reviews and Published Interviews

Book review Provide the title of the book under review within brackets following the title.

> Moore, W. (1992, October 11). Great physicist, great guy [Review of the book *Genius: The life and science of Richard Feynman*]. *The New York Times Book Review,* p. 3.

If the review does not have a title, use the material within brackets as the title, retaining the brackets.

> Kienitz, G. M. (1992). [Review of the book *Tennyson and the doom of Romanticism*]. *Religion and Literature, 24*(1), 87–90.

Film or video program review Provide the title of the film or video program under review within brackets following the title. If the review does not have a title, use the material within brackets as the title, retaining the brackets, as shown above for a book.

> Canby, V. (1992, May 22). Cruise and Kidman in old-fashioned epic [Review of the motion picture *Far and Away*]. *The New York Times*, p. C10.

Published interview Follow the basic format appropriate for the book or periodical in which the interview is published. The name of the interviewer occupies the place of the author, and the person interviewed is identified by both first and last names within brackets.

> Jahanbegloo, R. (1992, May 28). Philosophy and life [Interview with Isaiah Berlin]. *The New York Review of Books*, pp. 46–54.

Unpublished interviews, conducted through media such as telephone or e-mail, are cited parenthetically within the text as personal communications but are not listed as references.

Audiovisual media In entries for audiovisual media, place the name of the principal organizer or creater in the author position, and in parentheses identify the person's function. The nature of the medium should be indicated in brackets immediately after the title. Enter the place and date of publication as for a book. If a work has limited circulation, provide an address from which it can be obtained.

Film

> Eastwood, C. (Director). (1992). *Unforgiven* [Motion picture]. Hollywood: Warner Brothers.

> Batty, P. (Producer). (1987). *The Divided Union* [Video]. Tinley Park, IL: Fusion Video.

Television broadcast

Entries for television series place the name of the producer in the author position. For an individual episode of a series or a single program, place the name of the writer or reporter in the author position and place the name of the producer in the position of the editor.

Television series

> Moyers, B. (Writer and producer). (1995). *The language of life.* [Television series]. Newark, NJ: WNET.

Single episode from series

> Jennings, P. (1995), July 27). Hiroshima: Why the bomb was dropped. [Television series episode]. In D. Gelber and M. Smith (Producers), *Peter Jennings reporting.* New York: ABC.

Individual program

> Lacy, M. D. (1995, September 4). *Richard Wright: Black boy* (G. P. Land and J. Judin, Executive Producers, Independent Television Service and Mississippi Educational Television). New York: WNET.

Recording

Entries for recordings begin with the writer of the composition, followed by the original date.

> Handel, G. F. (1771). Suite no. 1 in F major [Cond. N. Marriner, Academy of St. Martin-in-the-Fields]. On *Water music/Wassermusik* [CD]. Hayes, Middlesex, England: EMI. (1989)

> Williams, M. (1971). Katydid's ditty [Recorded by Mannheim Steamroller]. On *Classical gas* [CD]. Omaha: American Gramaphone Records. (1987)

Cassette When you have a number for a cassette or other material, include it with the description enclosed by parentheses.

> Hunter, K. (Speaker). (1989). *Family counseling* (Audiocassette Recording No. 1175). Washington, DC: American Psychological Association.

> Westen, D. (Author and speaker). (1995). *Is anyone really normal? Perspectives on abnormal psychology* (Videocassette No. 658). Springfield, VA: The Teaching Company.

■ Model of Student Paper in APA Style

This version of Eóin O'Carroll's paper, "Unchained Melodies," uses the APA documentation style that is appropriate for a communication or sociology course. By comparing this version of the paper with the version on pages 603–610, you will see the differences between the APA and MLA styles of documentation.

The title of the paper appears in the header, followed by five spaces and the page number.

Unchained Melodies: Music and Innovation in the Digital Age

Eóin O'Carroll

ENG 201

The title, writer's name, and class go in the center of the title page, double-spaced.

The abstract should be single-spaced and no more than 120 words. It should outline the paper. (See more about writing abstracts on the *Writing in the Works* website.)

Abstract

Record companies are claiming that free mp3 downloads are killing music, but it is really the labels, not the consumers, that are killing music. Even if digital music is hurting album sales—and experts disagree over whether they do—many recording artists are embracing free mp3s for the increased exposure they offer. At the same time, recording artists are complaining that they are being harmed by the labels' business practices. Digital music potentially allows the musician to make a fair wage while providing a broader range of music to the consumer for less money. And they do not need the record labels to do it.

Unchained Melodies: Music and Innovation in the Digital Age

In the early eighties, the record industry was experiencing a sharp decline in sales. Falling revenues, they claimed, were the fault of the blank audiocassette. "Home taping is killing music" was the industry slogan at the time. Today, with sales slumping again, the record industry is making the same dire predictions. The bugbear of the Recording Industry Association of America (RIAA) this time is not audiocassettes and home tapers, but peer-to-peer networks and mp3 file sharers. On September 8, 2003, the day that the RIAA launched its first round of lawsuits against file sharers, the association issued a press release quoting president Cary Sherman: "We simply cannot allow online piracy to continue destroying the livelihoods of artists, musicians, songwriters, retailers, and everyone in the music industry" (RIAA, 2003, ¶ 4).

It is hard to say, however, to what extent digital music is responsible. If file sharing is cutting into album sales, it is not necessarily a bad thing—after all, people who make CD burners have livelihoods, too. Moreover, cutting into album sales is not necessarily the same thing as "killing music." Rather, many of the record industry's practices are killing music. Digital music is more likely to rescue it.

To review some background to present events, in the late 1970s, the record industry saw a looming crisis. After hitting an all-time high in 1978, album sales were declining precipitously. Between 1978 and 1982, sales dropped more than forty percent, with revenues falling from $6 billion to about $3.5 billion (Liebowitz, 2003, p. 7).

The cause? According to the RIAA, which represents the five largest record labels, the blame fell squarely on the blank cassette tape, and the fans who were using it to copy tracks from vinyl LPs that

---

The paper begins on page 3.

The title is centered and double-spaced.
The text begins two lines below the title and is double-spaced.

Eóin spells out the name of the organization and gives the abbreviation in parentheses.

This press release is from a webpage and doesn't have a page number. When citing quotes or facts from webpages without page numbers in APA style, give the paragraph number.

This internal text citation gives the author's last name, the year, and the page number. The citation is surrounded by parentheses and followed by a period. Note the *p.* before the page number.

they would then mix, catalogue, and swap. The RIAA demanded congressional hearings, and the international recording industry began placing on records a skull-and-crossbones logo—the skull was shaped like an audiocassette—with the slogan "Home Taping Is Killing Music" (Brown, 2003).

Of course, nothing of the kind happened. Album sales began to climb steadily over the eighties. This increase was in part due to the advent of the compact disc, but was also a result of to the audiocassette, which helped bring music out of the home and into people's Walkmans, boom boxes, and car stereos (Liebowitz, p. 6). The ominous slogan and logo now appear only on ironic T-shirts. Despite the industry's prophesies, home taping did not kill music.

In 1999, when nineteen-year old Northeastern University dropout Shawn Fanning wrote a program that allowed users to scan the hard drives of other users for music files, he threatened to upend a dynamic that had existed for decades between those who sell the music and those who consume it. For users, Napster combined radio-on-demand with the world's largest record store, all free of charge. For the record labels, it augured a disturbing future, a world in which there was no need for those who manufactured, packaged, distributed, and promoted musical recordings.

Recording artists themselves were split on Napster's impact. In April 2000, San Francisco heavy metal band Metallica, a band that had first established itself through allowing fans to trade concert bootlegs, launched a lawsuit against Napster copyright violations (Alderman, 2001, pp. 110–111).

"At the end of the day, this is about control," said drummer Lars Ulrich in an interview with *Business Week* a month after the lawsuits. "We feel that this is our music, that we own the rights to it, we pay for

Since this citation is from a website and doesn't include any quotes or specific facts, no page or paragraph information is given.

The year of this publication is given earlier, so it is not cited again.

For multiple pages, use *pp*.

it, we have the right to do with it what we want, where we want, and how we want" (Berman, 2000, ¶ 12).

In the same article, rapper Chuck D defended Napster, calling it "a new form of radio, of global exposure." Chuck D, a harsh critic of the record business, argued that labels had been deliberately jacking up CD prices and treated recording artists as "a disposable commodity" (Berman, 2000, ¶ 43). But with file sharing, he said, "you can have as many as a million people operate within the music game and change the whole process of how the money is going to be distributed" (¶ 47).

When this article ran, there was no evidence that Napster was actually cutting into album sales. Indeed, some argued that the opposite was occurring. According to entertainment attorney Ken Hertz, "'N Sync, Britney Spears, and Eminem were the three most heavily trafficked artists at Napster the week before their records came out, and those records were the fastest selling records of all time." Hertz speculated that record executives deliberately "seeded" Napster with these albums as a way of promoting them (Alderman, 2001, p. 117).

After Napster's free file sharing shut down in the summer of 2000, a host of other programs—KaZaa, Gnutella, Morpheus, iMesh and Limewire, to name a few—immediately rose to take its place, and file sharing continued nearly unabated. According to the Associated Press, users swap more than 150 million songs each month (Straziuso, 2004, ¶ 5).

But it is still an open question whether file sharing is harming recording artists. Stan Liebowitz, an economist at the University of Texas at Dallas, analyzed thirty years of sales figures in an attempt to measure file sharing's impact. Using figures provided by the RIAA, he

The author and year were just given, so only the paragraph number is needed.

This statement is common knowledge and therefore requires no citation.

showed that there have been several dips in sales in the past, and that they have always been followed by further increases (see Figure 1).

Nonetheless, Liebowitz concludes that the steep decline that began in 2000 is partly a result of file sharing. "No other explanations," he writes, "that have been put forward seem to be able to explain the decline in sales that have occurred since 1999." He calls the harm "significant" (2003, p. 29). "Still," he writes, "it is not clear that the harm will be fatal" (p. 29).

Others disagree. In an article in *Slate*, Mark Jenkins (2002) blamed the slump in sales on the poor quality of the music. Most CDs come from five companies. MTV dominates the music video business and Clear Channel dominates both radio and concerts. The result is a stultifying homogeneity of dance pop and boy bands, a musical landscape that Jenkins says is much like that of 1978: "[T]he music of 'N Sync and Britney Spears is not unlike disco: Both are intellectually underachieving, cookie-cutter styles that have made stars of performers not known primarily for their skills as singers, songwriters, or musicians" (¶ 5). In other words, listeners turn to the Internet because that is where the good music is.

Many recording artists feel compensated for any loss in album sales by the added exposure they gain from having more people listening to their music. Like many up-and-coming bands, the Valhalla Kittens offers mp3s on their website for users to download free of charge.

"[P]eople who might not come see the band otherwise can be swayed after hearing the mp3s on our Web site," writes Courtney Naliboff, a vocalist for the glam/cabaret rock act, in an e-mail interview (personal communication, March 13, 2004).

Italicize names of magazines, even online ones.

In APA style, the year of the publication usually goes after the name of the author.

The brackets in the first word in this quotation indicate that Jenkins lowercased the letter *t* in the word *the* and that Eóin capitalized the *t*.

Personal communications, including e-mail, are considered "nonrecoverable." They are cited only in the text and not on the reference page.

For others, free music downloads can actually boost album sales. Singer/songwriter Janis Ian also offers free mp3s on her website. "Every time we make a few songs available on my Web site," she writes in an article posted on her site, "sales of all the CDs go up. A lot" (2002, ¶ 14).

Ian scoffs at the record labels' argument that downloads are killing sales and taking money out of the pockets of recording artists.

> Costing *me* money? I don't pretend to be an expert on intellectual property law, but I do know one thing. If a music industry executive claims I should agree with their agenda because it will make me more money, I put my hand on my wallet . . . and check it after they leave, just to make sure nothing's missing. (Ian, 2002, ¶ 9, italics hers)

Many musicians share the perception that record labels are ripping off recording artists. In a speech to the Digital Hollywood online entertainment conference in 2000, rocker Courtney Love criticized the practice, known as recoupment, in which musicians pay costs for recording, marketing and promotion, tours, and music videos out of their royalties. In her speech, which was reprinted on *Salon*, Love described how this practice has forced some artists, such as Toni Braxton and TLC, into bankruptcy, despite having sold millions of CDs. "The system's set up so almost nobody gets paid," she said (2000, p. 2). What's more, even if the royalties are paid off, the record label retains the rights to the album. "[The band] can pay the mortgage forever but they'll never own the house." Love claims that selling

Long quotations should be indented five to seven spaces or 1/2 inch. No quotation marks are used, and the citation information goes after the period.

If you add italics into a quotation for emphasis, indicate this at the end of the quote. If the italics were in the original quotation, say so.

Salon is a website, but it has page numbers.

Eóin added the phrase "The band" to make the quotation clearer. He indicated that he did so by using brackets.

mp3s online would cut out the middleman, saving the consumer money and allowing the artist to sell more albums.

Major labels are freaking out because they have no control in this new world. Artists can sell CDs directly to fans. We can make direct deals with thousands of other websites and promote our music to millions of people that old record companies never touch. (p. 5)

Apple iTunes, the most popular legal model for online music sales, fails to live up to Love's vision. When a record company produces physical CDs, it deducts from the artists royalties charges for packaging, shipping, breakage, and returns. The same is true for songs sold over iTunes. But of course, digital music can't be packaged, shipped, broken, or returned. The artist should be getting a bigger cut, but they're not. The labels are pocketing the difference.

Activists and legal scholars have come up with many alternative systems of compensating recording artists for downloaded music. The Electronic Frontier Foundation proposes several models, such as a tax on CD burners, a revenue-sharing system from advertisements displayed in file-swapping software, or an added charge on Internet bills that would grant a license to share music. Any of these models could provide greater payments to recording artists while providing fans with a broader range of music at a much lower price.

Lawrence Lessig (2001), a professor of law at Stanford University, compares the current debate over file sharing with one that happened over a century ago. At the beginning of the twentieth century, sheet music composers were outraged about the proliferation of player pianos. Manufacturers were creating piano rolls—rolls of perforated paper that would fit inside the pianos—from sheet music without paying the composers. Congress resolved the debate by striking a balance. They did not ban the technology outright, nor did they allow the companies to continue to profit at the composers' expense. Instead, they created a "compulsory licensing right." Once a composer granted permission for someone to create a piano roll, any manufacturer could pay a flat rate (two cents a copy) to the composer for each copy (pp. 108–109). This compromise allowed companies to continue to develop new technologies while protecting artists from exploitation.

The point is that it can be done—we can create a system in which listeners have access to a broad range of inexpensive music, and in which recording artists are paid fairly. With mp3 technology, the artists no longer need a big company to manufacture, package, store, ship, and promote their craft. It is this possibility—not slumping album sales—that really worries the record companies. Just as the radio made carrier pigeons obsolete, and the refrigerator made milkmen obsolete, digital music has the potential to make record companies obsolete. And far from killing music, file sharing might give it some life.

References

Alderman, J. (2001). *Sonic boom: Napster, MP3, and the new pioneers of music*. Cambridge: Perseus.

Berman, D. (2000). Lars Ulrich vs. Chuck D: Facing off over Napster. *Business Week*. May 25, 2000. Retrieved March 11, 2004, from http://www.businessweek.com/ebiz/0005/0525ulrich.htm

Brown, D. (2003). Home taping did not kill music. CBC News Viewpoint. October 23, 2003. Retrieved March 11, 2004, from Canadian Broadcasting Company website: http://www.cbc.ca/news/viewpoint/vp_browndan/20031023.html

Electronic Frontier Foundation. Making P2P pay artists. (n.d.). Retrieved March 11, 2004, from http://www.eff.org/share/compensation.php

Ian, J. (2002). The Internet debacle: An alternative view. Retrieved March 10, 2004, from http://www.janisian.com/article-internet_debacle.html

Jenkins, M. (2002). Hit charade: The music industry's self-inflicted wounds. *Slate*. August 20, 2002. Retrieved March 11, 2004, from http://slate.msn.com/?id=2069732

Lessig, L. (2001). *The future of ideas*. New York: Random House.

Liebowitz, S. (2003). Will MP3 downloads annihilate the record industry? The evidence so far. Retrieved March 9, 2004, from University of Texas at Dallas website: http://www.pub.utdallas.edu/~liebowit/intprop/records.pdf

Love, C. (2000). Courtney Love does the math. *Salon*. June 14, 2000. Retrieved March 12, 2004, from http://archive.salon.com/tech/feature/2000/06/14/love

Recording Industry Association of America. (2003). Recording industry begins suing P2P file sharers who illegally offer copyrighted

Heading is centered.

Indent the second line of the citation five spaces.

No posting date was available on this site.

If you must break a Web address into two lines, put the break after a period or slash. Never hyphenate a Web URL.

If a page is part of a large and complex website, such as that for a university or a government agency, identify the host organization before URL. Precede the URL with a colon.

music online. Retrieved March 9, 2004, from the RIAA website: http://www.riaa.com/news/newsletter/090803.asp

Straziuso, J. (2004). Music piracy activity slows. *Detroit Free Press.* February 23, 2004. Retrieved on March 13, 2004, from *Detroit Free Press* website: http://www.freep.com/money/business/ bnews23_20040223.htm

Figure Captions
Figure 1 Album sales over the past three decades (Liebowitz, 2003, p. 7)

When appropriate, use figures to illustrate your argument.

Figure 1

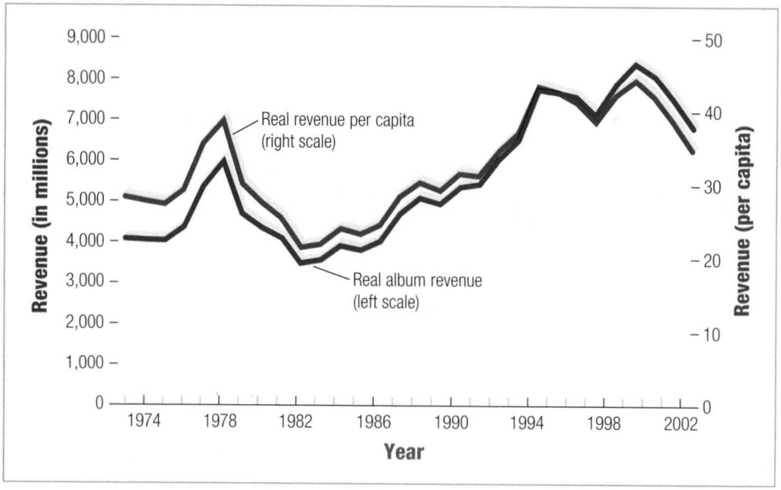

PART IV
GRAMMAR HANDBOOK

It was an instinct to put the world in order that powered her mending split infinitives and snapping off dangling participles, smoothing away the knots and bumps until the prose before her took on a sheen, like perfect caramel.

—David Leavitt

643

WHY STUDY GRAMMAR?

Some people believe that grammar is a set of ironclad rules they must memorize. Others believe that grammar describes a constantly shifting system of conventions, ways to communicate clearly and predictably within a community of people who speak and write in that language. Our view is this: rules exist; some may seem confusing at first, but the purpose of learning grammar is to understand the basic patterns of the language in which you are writing. In a very real sense, when you are engaged in the act of writing, grammar describes the tools of your trade. Understanding grammar allows you to write more precisely, more elegantly, and even more creatively.

On the practical side, in college, at work, and in your community, your ideas will be considered more or less seriously depending on how well you use the conventions of standard, written grammar. Poor grammar creates a kind of static between you and your reader, making it hard for the reader to "hear" what you are saying. Good grammar skills give you another real-world advantage. You can accomplish the basic work of writers: refining, editing, and proofreading your own writing, so that you can say exactly what you mean to say the way you mean to say it. When you learn grammar for a reason—to edit your own work, to write with clarity, to improve your style—it may make new sense to you, perhaps in a way it never has before. To ensure that your good ideas will be read with the interest they deserve, learn the rules and play by them. Later on, perhaps, you can break them.

The next four chapters provide an overview of grammar. Chapter 16 will guide you through a review of the basic vocabulary of grammar, and Chapter 17 is a review of punctuation rules. Chapter 18 will help you identify and avoid common grammatical errors. Chapter 19 provides some grammatical tips specific to the challenges of writing English as a second, third, or sometimes fourth language.

You can use these chapters in a number of ways.

▶ You can read each chapter sequentially, first building a grammar vocabulary, and then using that vocabulary to identify and correct common errors. At the end of each major point is a practice exercise that you can use to test your understanding of that grammatical point and reinforce its concept.

▶ You can use the chapters as a reference handbook, looking up the conventions of punctuation (17b-f), for example, or the rules governing subject-verb agreement (18b-1).

▶ Each topic is keyed to one of the numbers and letters in the outline printed at the beginning of each chapter as well as in the index.

- ❯ You can use the practices to test your skills in identifying and fixing errors in a text, and then review the points you do not understand.

- ❯ You can keep a grammar log of the errors you make in your papers and key them to the sections that address those issues.

WHAT IS STYLE?

Good writing begins with knowing what you want to say, then communicating those ideas as clearly and correctly as possible. Built onto that foundation are the elements of style: the word choices, sentence patterns, and syntax of your writing. Although grammar comes with a set of rules, writing well goes beyond adhering to the conventions of standard grammar. Writing with style and voice results from the deliberate choices you make to use a particular word, sentence, or grammatical construction instead of another. The style chapter on the website provides you with a host of strategies to help you make those choices wisely.

"And remember—no more subjunctives where the correct mood is indicative."

16. GRAMMAR REFRESHER

This chapter can help you review

▶ Parts of speech

▶ Parts of sentences

▶ Sentence types

16a Parts of Speech

Knowing the basic parts of speech gives you the vocabulary to talk about grammar and gives you an important understanding of how each part of speech functions. The following is a brief overview of the eight parts of speech.

16a-1 Nouns

Nouns name people, places, things, or abstract concepts: *daughter, city, pencil, hope*.

■ **Countable Nouns** Countable nouns name countable things and have a plural form: *book (books), child (children), friend (friends)*.

■ **Noncountable Nouns** Noncountable nouns name things that you cannot count, so they do not have a plural form: *courage, advice, information* (see 19a).

■ **Proper Nouns** Proper nouns name specific persons, places, organizations, months, and days of the week. Proper nouns are capitalized: *Mother Jones, Central College, Fridays*.

■ **Common Nouns** Common nouns name general persons, places, things, or abstract concepts: *parent, school, weekdays*.

■ **Collective Nouns** Collective nouns name groups but are usually referred to as single entities: *a committee, an audience, a community*.

Practice 16.1   Nouns

Check your understanding of the types of nouns by identifying the boldfaced words in the following sentences as proper nouns (PN), common nouns (CN), or collective nouns (COLL). Circle all noncountable nouns.

1. Ancient **astronomers** saw only twelve **constellations** in the **sky**.
2. A **theory** put forth by **Aristotle** included the **idea** of feeling **pity** and **fear** for the tragic **hero**.
3. In 1988 George **Eastman** invented a **camera** that revolutionized **photography**.
4. A large **community** of Old World **monkeys** sits on the tree **branches** for most of the **day**.
5. **Starfish** live in the shallow **waters** of the **coast**.

16a-2 Pronouns

Pronouns substitute for or refer to nouns, noun phrases, or other pronouns. The noun that the pronoun refers to is its **antecedent**.

Professor Garcia read from *her* new book. [*Professor Garcia* is the antecedent of *her*.]

Travel is *its* own reward. [*Travel* is the antecedent of *its*.]

■ **Personal Pronouns** Personal pronouns refer to specific persons, places, or things. Personal pronouns can be subdivided by their function in a sentence, whether they substitute for nouns that function as subjects (see 16b-1), substitute for nouns that function as objects (see 16b-2), or show ownership or possession (see 17e-1).

Subject Pronouns (SP)	Object Pronouns (OP)	Possessive Pronouns (PP)
I	me	my, mine
you	you	your, yours
he, she, it	him, her, it	his, her, hers, its
we	us	our, ours
they	them	their, theirs
who/whoever	whom/whomever	whose

SP   PP
She talked about *her* travels in Asia.

SP   OP
We gave *her* a standing ovation.

■ **Indefinite Pronouns** Indefinite pronouns refer to nonspecific persons, places, or things and do not need antecedents: *all, any, anybody, anyone, anything, both, every, everybody, everyone, everything, few, many, most, none, no one, nothing, somebody, someone, something, several, some.*

Everyone was fascinated by Professor Garcia's adventures.

No one stirred as she talked.

■ **Reflexive Pronouns** A reflexive pronoun refers back to the subject or to another noun or pronoun in the sentence.

Singular	Plural
myself	*ourselves*
yourself	*yourselves*
himself	
herself	*themselves*
itself	

Megan traveled for six months by *herself*.

Megan saw the other students starting off by *themselves*.

■ **Intensive Pronouns** Intensive pronouns emphasize nouns and use the same forms as reflexive pronouns.

Megan *herself* made all the arrangements.

We *ourselves* decided it was the right time to travel.

■ **Relative Pronouns** Relative pronouns introduce dependent clauses (see 16b-4): *who, whom, whose, whoever, whomever, whichever, whatever, that, which, what.*

Professor Garcia was the professor *who* influenced me the most.

Biology class was the one class *that* I never missed.

■ **Interrogative Pronouns** Interrogative pronouns begin questions: *who, whom, which, what, whose.*

Who went with you?

Whose car did you take?

■ **Demonstrative Pronouns** Demonstrative pronouns point back to their antecedent nouns, noun phrases, or clauses: *this, that, these, those.*

Amy got an interview with the lead singer of her favorite band. *That* was the highlight of her year.

She wrote these two articles for her school paper. *This* is better than *that*.

Practice 16.2   Pronouns

Identify the boldfaced words in the following sentences as personal pronouns (PP), indefinite pronouns (IP), reflexive pronouns (REF), intensive pronouns (INT), relative pronouns (REL), interrogative pronouns (INTER), or demonstrative pronouns (DP).

1. Colonel Mustard **himself** put the coded message in **its** secret hiding place.

2. Anyone can collect stamps by ordering **them** on the Internet. **Who** wants to order stamps?

3. The architect **who** put the Arts and Crafts detail on **your** front door was a genius.

4. Give the mitten to **whoever** needs warm clothing for the camping trip.

5. Five years ago, **someone** left a mysterious message on **my** phone. **That** was weird.

16a-3   Verbs

Verbs express action (*read, love, study*) or a state of being (*is, seem, appear*).

■ **Auxiliary Verbs** Some auxiliary verbs are forms of *to be, to do,* and *to have* that help the main verbs.

> Frida *was* painting in her studio. (*be, am, is, are, was, being, been*)
>
> Frida *does* paint well. (*do, does, did*)
>
> Frida *has* painted beautiful landscapes. (*have, has, had*)

Other auxiliary verbs, called **modals**, express probability, such as *may/might, can/could, will/would, shall/should, must, ought to,* and *have to.*

> Frida *ought to* contact a gallery.
>
> She *might* become as famous as her namesake, Frida Kahlo.

■ **Transitive Verbs** Transitive verbs (VT) show action and transfer that action from the subject to the receiver of the action, which is called the **direct object (DO)**. The direct object answers the question *what?* or *whom?* after the verb.

$$\text{VT} \xrightarrow{\text{what?}} \text{DO}$$

> Frida *paints* abstract *landscapes.*

$$\text{VT} \xrightarrow{\text{whom?}} \text{DO}$$

> She *asked Pablo* to critique her art.

■ **Intransitive Verbs** Intransitive verbs (VI) may express an action, but there is no receiver of that action, no direct object. Common intransitive verbs are *lie, sit, sleep, occur, die, fall, walk, go,* and *come.*

> VI
>
> Frida *sat* on a stool while she painted.

> VI
>
> When she finished her work, Frida *slept* soundly.

■ **Linking Verbs** Linking verbs (LV) , also known as state-of-being verbs, link the subject to a word after the verb. The word can either describe the subject (an adjective) or rename the subject (a noun). The most common linking verb is the verb *to be* in any of its forms: *am, are, is, was, were.*

LV
Frida **is lovely.** [*Lovely* describes Frida.]

LV
Frida **is my cousin.** [*Cousin* renames Frida.]

Other linking verbs that can express a state of being are *feel, seem, look, taste, smell,* and *appear,* depending on how they are used in the sentence. The verb *feel,* for example, can be either a transitive verb, taking a direct object, or a linking verb, connecting an adjective to the subject.

I *feel* **the material between my thumb and index finger.** [*Feel* is transitive; it takes the direct object *material.*]

I *feel* **sad today.** [*Feel* is a linking verb, expressing a state of being and linking the adjective *sad* to the subject *I.*]

■ **Verb Tenses** Verb tenses change to indicate the time of an action or process, often relative to the time of the writing.

	Present	Past	Future
Simple	*I paint*	*I painted*	*I will paint*
Progressive	*I am painting*	*I was painting*	*I will be painting*
Perfect	*I have painted*	*I had painted*	*I will have painted*

Verbs in the **progressive tense** use a form of *to be* plus the *-ing* form of the verb to show actions that continue for a while.

This morning I *am painting* **the third in my landscape series.**

Yesterday I *was painting* **my second landscape.**

Verbs in the **perfect tense** express actions completed by the present, past, or future time.

I *have painted* **my series, and I am ready for the show.**

I *had painted* **my second landscape before I fell asleep.**

I *will have painted* **the entire series when the show opens.**

■ **Verb Moods** Verbs express three **moods.** Verbs in the **indicative** mood make statements or ask questions.

I *will paint* today.

Will you *join* me?

Verbs in the **imperative** mood issues commands.

> *Come* in here!
>
> *Do not make* a mess.

Verbs in the **subjunctive** mood express wishes in conditional terms or hypothetical conditions.

> I wish I *were* as good a painter as Frida.
>
> If I *had taken* lessons when I was young, I *might be* an artist today.

Practice 16.3   Verbs

Identify the verbs in the following sentences as transitive verbs (VT), intransitive verbs (VI), or linking verbs (LV).

1. The night sky **seemed** luminous.

2. Joe **slept** past noon every day on his vacation.

3. Leah **ran** the marathon in record time.

4. We **felt** the first stirrings of love that night.

5. Ethan **felt** strong after his workout.

Choose the correct verb tense or mood in the following sentences.

1. Before Zachary (**made/had made**) plans, he (**checked/had checked**) online for the movie times.

2. When Kayla (**ran/ is running**) fast, she always wins the race.

3. If Mac (**was/were**) in charge, things would be different around here.

4. Yoshi made the changes to the proposal that she and Mac (**discussed/had discussed**).

5. When Ben (**was/were**) younger, he was always in trouble.

16a-4

■ **Adjectives** Adjectives modify, describe, identify, or give information about nouns and pronouns. Adjectives can be placed before the nouns or pronouns they modify or after linking verbs. Adjectives placed after linking verbs are called **predicate adjectives**. (*Predicate* refers to the part of a sentence or clause that includes the verb and objects or phrases connected to the verb. See 16b-1.)

The *fresh* breeze blew past Joel's head. [*Fresh* modifies *breeze*.]

The breeze felt *fresh*. [*Fresh* is a predicate adjective and modifies *breeze*.]

Adjectives show degree or intensity. The suffix *-er* or the use of the adverb *more* makes an adjective comparative, and the suffix *-est* or the use of the adverb *most* makes the adjective superlative.

Positive	Comparative	Superlative
fresh	*fresher*	*freshest*
independent	*more independent*	*most independent*

■ **Articles** A, *an,* and *the* are sometimes classified as adjectives because they modify the nouns they precede. The more common term for them is **article**. (See also 19a.) *A* and *an* are **indefinite articles** because they describe one of a number of things.

> Give Becca *a* book to read, and she is happy.

> *A* library can be *a* sanctuary.

The is a **definite article** because it describes only one thing or class of things.

> Give me *the* book on the shelf.

> *The* local library is her sanctuary.

16a-5   Adverbs

Adverbs modify or give information about verbs, adjectives, other adverbs, or entire clauses or sentences. They often explain *how, when, where, why,* or to *what extent* something happens. They convey manner, time, frequency, place, direction, and degree.

> The thief ran *quickly* down the alley. [The adverb *quickly* modifies the verb *ran.*]

> The *very* fast thief jumped the fence. [The adverb *very* modifies the adjective *fast.*]

> The thief climbed the ladder *extremely quickly*. [The adverb *extremely* modifies the adverb *quickly.*]

> *Unfortunately,* the thief escaped. [The adverb *unfortunately* modifies the entire sentence.]

■ **Conjunctive Adverbs** A **conjunctive adverb** modifies a clause or sentence while connecting that clause or sentence to the previous one.

Some conjunctive adverbs are *consequently, however, moreover, therefore, thus,* and *for example.*

> The thief escaped. *However,* he turned himself in the next day.

> He was filled with remorse; *moreover,* he returned the money he stole.

Practice 16.4   Adjectives and Adverbs

Identify the boldfaced words in the following sentences as adjectives (ADJ) or adverbs (ADV). Draw an arrow to what each word modifies.

1. The **fastest** runner was **unfairly** eliminated due to **new** rules about eligibility.

2. The **intense** odor of **noxious** fumes seeped **quickly** from under the **locked** garage door.

3. An **attentive** audience **closely** watched the **unusual** dance program **yesterday**.

4. Although Martin was **picky**, he gave the hotel at the **busy** seaport his **highest** recommendation.

5. Flood water surged **violently** over the **small** bridge; **however**, the bridge held **fast.**

16a-6   Prepositions and Prepositional Phrases

Prepositions are often short words like *of, by, for, to, in,* and *around* that begin prepositional phrases. They often show relationships of time and space. Some common prepositions are *about, above, across, after, along, around, before, behind, below, beneath, beside, between, by, except, for, from, in, into, like, near, of, on, through, to, under,* and *with.* (See also 19d-2.)

Around the block

In the air

Down the street

Across the avenue

To the meeting

At one o'clock

A **prepositional phrase** is made up of the preposition and the words that follow it. The noun or pronoun after the preposition is called the object of the preposition.

| PREPOSITIONAL PHRASE | PREPOSITIONAL PHRASE |
| PREP.   OBJECT | PREP.   OBJECT |

Ben went *around the neighborhood on his new bicycle.*

| PREP. PHRASE | PREPOSITIONAL PHRASE |
| PREP.   OBJ. | PREP.   OBJ. |

At dusk he went *into his house.*

16a-7 Conjunctions

Conjunctions join two or more similar sentence parts, such as words, phrases, and clauses.

■ **Coordinating Conjunctions** Coordinating conjunctions (CC) link two or more parallel words, phrases, or clauses. The seven coordinating conjunctions are *and, but, for, or, nor, so,* and *yet.*

> CC
> The baker made tarts *and* pies. [The coordinating conjunction *and* connects the two words *tarts* and *pies.*]

> CC
> He couldn't decide whether to make a crust *or* to buy one. [The coordinating conjunction *or* connects the two phrases *to make a crust* and *to buy one.*]

> CC
> He made the pie crust, *but* he bought the tart shell. [The coordinating conjunction *but* connects the two clauses *He made the pie crust* and *he bought the tart shell.*]

■ **Subordinating Conjunctions** Subordinating conjunctions (SC) introduce dependent clauses and connect them with independent clauses (see 16b-4). A subordinating conjunction establishes a relationship between dependent and independent clauses, usually telling *when, why,* or *under what conditions.* Some of the many subordinating conjunctions are *after, as, as soon as, because, before, even if, if, since, unless, when, while,* and *why.*

> DEPENDENT CLAUSE
> SC
> *When* he ran out of cherries, the baker started making apple pies. [*When he ran out of cherries* is a dependent clause. *When* is the subordinating conjunction.]

> DEPENDENT CLAUSE
> SC
> Our mouths watered *while* the pies cooled. [*While the pies cooled* is a dependent clause. *While* is the subordinating conjunction.]

■ **Correlative Conjunctions** Correlative conjunctions (COR) appear in different parts of the sentence but work together to join the two sentence parts. Common correlative conjunctions are *both/and, just as/so, either/or, neither/nor, not only/but also,* and *whether/or.*

> *Either* cherry pie *or* apple pie is fine with me.

> *Not only* does he love baking them, *but* he *also* loves eating them.

16a-8 Interjections and Expletives

Interjections are emotional exclamations and are often punctuated by the exclamation mark if they stand alone.

Eureka!

Ouch!

Wow!

Interjections can also be incorporated into sentences.

> I smiled at him, but, *oh*, he made me mad.
>
> *Darn*, he missed the bus.

Expletives are words that are place markers. Since they are introductory words and are often followed by a form of *to be*, they are often mistaken for subjects of sentences. Expletives never function as subjects.

There are

Here is

It is

Expletives tend to be overused and can cause confusion with subject-verb agreement. When possible, limit your use of expletives.

Use of Expletive: *There* are two reasons for us to go: economy and efficiency. [The subject is *reasons*.]

Omitted Expletive: Two reasons for us to go are cost and efficiency.

Use of Expletive: It is a good deal that we should take advantage of. [The subject is *deal*.]

Omitted Expletive: We should take advantage of this good deal.

Practice 16.5   Prepositions, Conjunctions, Interjections, and Expletives

Identify the boldfaced words in the following sentences as prepositions (P), coordinating conjunctions (CC), subordinating conjunctions (SC), correlative conjunctions (COR), interjections (I), and expletives (EX).

1. The Industrial Revolution began **when** steam-powered machines started spinning cotton thread.

2. The construction crew identified contaminated soil yet failed to report it **to** the Environmental Protection Agency.

3. "**Never!**" we answered **after** Coach asked when we would be willing to give up.

4. **Either** I will major in math, **or** I will go into engineering.

5. Bats are scorned and treated as pests, **but** they are useful in controlling mosquito populations.

6. There are compelling reasons to study biology, **and there** are equally good ones to specialize in mammals.

Practice 16.6   Parts of Speech

In the passage below, identify each boldfaced word as a noun (N), pronoun (P), verb (V), adjective (ADJ), adverb (ADV), preposition (PR), conjunction (C), interjection (I), or expletive (EX).

Watching a **film** is an experience like no other **that** I have had. **When** the **velvety darkness surrounds** me, I am **literally** transported **to** another **world.** Nothing exists **except** the screen and **me.** The **music** begins; the credits **roll; and** I **am completely hooked. Anyone who** knows me **knows** well **neither** to offer me a handful of popcorn **nor** to talk to me. I am by **myself in** my own world, apart from **everyday** reality. **Hush! It** is magic.

16b Parts of Sentences

16b-1 Subjects and Predicates

Sentences have two parts: subjects and predicates. The **simple subject** is the agent of the action, *who* or *what* the sentence is about, and the **simple predicate** expresses the action or, in the case of linking verbs, the state of being. (See also 19c.)

SUBJECT   PREDICATE

The *senator voted.* [*Senator* is the subject; *voted* is the predicate.]

SUBJECT PREDICATE

The *bill passed.* [*Bill* is the subject; *passed* is the predicate.]

Most sentences are more complicated than a simple subject and predicate and include other words, phrases, and clauses that modify or complement the subject and predicate, forming the complete subject or the complete predicate.

SUBJECT   PREDICATE

The angry senator in the first row voted vehemently against the motion. [The complete subject is *The angry senator in the first row*, and the complete predicate is *voted vehemently against the motion.*]

SUBJECT   PREDICATE

The appropriation bill passed by a slim margin. [The *appropriation bill* is the complete subject, and the complete predicate is *passed by a slim margin.*]

Practice 16.7   Subjects and Predicates

Identify the complete subject and the complete predicate in the following sentences.

1. Life is good.

2. Our lives are sometimes easy and sometimes difficult.

3. I spent an exciting three weeks trekking through the rain forests of Costa Rica.

4. I hiked up mountains and through forests thick with vegetation.

5. Six of us who had taken a course in rock climbing went on a separate adventure.

16b-2 Complements

A word or group of words that completes a predicate is called a complement. Complements can be direct objects, indirect objects, object complements, and subject complements. Four common sentence patterns show how these complements are used. (See also 19c-1.)

■ Subject + Transitive Verb + **Direct Object** (S + VT + **DO**): The **direct object** answers the question *what?* or *whom?* after a transitive verb.

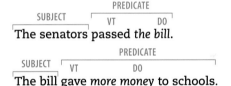

■ Subject + Transitive Verb+ **Indirect Object** + Direct Object (S + VT + **IO** + DO): The **indirect object** answers the question *to whom?* or *to what?* after a transitive verb.

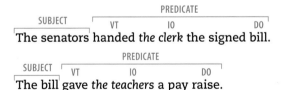

■ Subject + Transitive Verb + Direct Object + **Object Complement** (S + VT + DO + **OC**): The **object complement** describes (adjective) or renames (noun) the direct object.

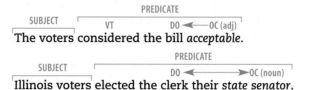

PREDICATE

SUBJECT | VT | DO ◄——OC (adj)

The voters considered the bill *acceptable.*

PREDICATE

SUBJECT | DO ◄————►OC (noun)

Illinois voters elected the clerk their *state senator.*

■ Subject + Linking Verb + Subject Complement (S + LV + SC): The **subject complement** describes or renames the subject after a linking verb (*be, become, appear, feel, seem*). (See 16a-3.)

A complement that describes the subject is called a **predicate adjective (PA)** .

A complement that names the subject is called a **predicate noun (PN)** .

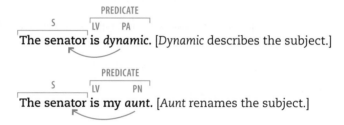

PREDICATE

S | LV | PA

The senator is *dynamic.* [*Dynamic* describes the subject.]

PREDICATE

S | LV | PN

The senator is my *aunt.* [*Aunt* renames the subject.]

USAGE TIP When you substitute a pronoun for a predicate noun, use the subject form of the pronoun: **The senator is *she.*** It is I.

Practice 16.8   Complements

Show your understanding of complements by writing sentences in the following patterns.

1. Write a sentence with a transitive verb and a direct object.

2. Write a sentence with a transitive verb, an indirect object, and a direct object.

3. Write a sentence with a linking verb and a predicate adjective.

4. Write a sentence with a linking verb and a predicate noun.

5. Write a sentence with a transitive verb, a direct object, and an object complement.

16b-3 Phrases

A phrase is a group of words that lacks a subject or a verb; it never expresses a complete thought by itself but instead modifies a noun or a verb. Four categories of phrases are prepositional phrases, verbal phrases, appositive phrases, and absolute phrases.

■ **Prepositional Phrases** A prepositional phrase contains a preposition with its object, which is the noun or pronoun in the phrase.

PREP. PHRASE		PREP. PHRASE		PREP. PHRASE	
PREP.	OBJECT	PREP.	OBJECT	PREP.	OBJECT

Over the river and *through* the woods, *to* grandmother's house we go.

■ **Verbal Phrases** Verbal phrases are formed from verbs but function as nouns or modifiers. Three types of verbal phrases are infinitives, gerunds, and participles.

Infinitives Infinitives are formed by adding *to* in front of the verb (*to pass*, *to run*, *to love*). An infinitive phrase includes the infinitive and its modifiers.

Jon gave himself a huge party *to celebrate his birthday.* [infinitive phrase]

He invited all his family, friends, and colleagues *to dance at a club.* [infinitive phrase]

Gerunds A gerund is formed by adding *-ing* to a verb, and they function as nouns in sentences. For example, a gerund could be the subject of a sentence or its direct object. A gerund phrase includes its modifiers.

GERUND AS SUBJECT
Passing the age of twenty made Jon feel old. [gerund phrase as subject]

GERUND AS DIRECT OBJECT
He loved *celebrating with his friends.* [gerund phrase as direct object]

Participles Participles are formed by adding *-ing* in present tense or *-ed* in past tense to verbs, and they function as adjectives that modify nouns or pronouns. A participial phrase includes its modifiers.

The boy, *passing Micha on the street,* broke into a run. [present participle modifying the noun *boy*]

Running fast, he looked back over his shoulder. [present participle modifying the pronoun *he*]

Exhausted, Ed slowed to a walk. [past participle modifying the noun *Ed*]

■ **Appositive Phrases** Appositive phrases modify the nouns or pronouns they follow by describing them in different words. An appositive phrase consists of the appositive (the word that describes the noun or pronoun) and its modifiers.

Jack, *my best friend from high school,* broke into a run. [appositive phrase describes *Jack*]

The appositive, *the word that describes the noun or pronoun,* often appears between commas. [appositive phrase describes *appositive phrase*]

■ **Absolute Phrases** An absolute phrase modifies a whole sentence or clause and consists of a noun plus a participle with its modifiers or complements. Absolute phrases can be placed anywhere in the sentence.

Noah tiptoed into the room, *his eyes squinting in the sudden light.*

Noah, *his eyes squinting in the sudden light,* tiptoed into the room.

His eyes squinting in the sudden light, Noah tiptoed into the room.

Practice 16.9   Phrases

Identify the boldfaced phrases as prepositional (P), infinitive (I), gerund (G), participial (PL), appositive (APP), or absolute (ABS).

1. Shooting a film is Emma's ambition, but, *Finding Remo,* **her student film,** was terrible.

2. The animation came out jumpy, and no one wanted **to sit through the hour-long film.**

3. Shooting their film, Emma and Jesse felt totally confident.

4. Sweat running down her face, Jesse yelled, "It's a wrap."

5. Making films is truly all they want **to do**.

16b-4   Clauses

A clause is a group of words that includes both a subject and a verb. Clauses may be **independent clauses** or **dependent (subordinate) clauses**.

■ **Independent Clauses** Independent clauses (IC) express complete ideas. They can stand alone as complete sentences or be part of longer sentences.

INDEPENDENT CLAUSE

The film was tasteless.

INDEPENDENT CLAUSE

The film was tasteless because it showed violence only to gross out the viewer.

■ **Dependent Clauses** Dependent clauses (DC) (also called subordinate clauses) cannot stand alone. As all clauses do, a dependent clause has a subject and a verb, but it does not express a complete thought by itself. A dependent clause has to be linked to an independent clause for the meaning to be clear. The signal of a dependent clause is that it begins with a subordinating conjunction (SC), such as *if, when, because,* or *while,* or a relative pronoun (RP), such as *who, whom, which,* or *that.* (See 16a-7.)

DEPENDENT CLAUSE

INDEPENDENT CLAUSE   SC

The film was tasteless *because it showed violence only to gross out the viewer.*

DEPENDENT CLAUSE

SC   INDEPENDENT CLAUSE

If I could have gotten my money back, I would have left in the middle.

DEPENDENT CLAUSE

IC   RP   IC

My friends, *who do not usually mind violence,* had to cover their eyes.

■ **Noun Clauses** Dependent clauses can function in sentences as nouns, adjectives, or adverbs. **Noun clauses** function as subjects, objects, complements, or appositives, and they begin with relative pronouns such as *that, who, whom,* or *whoever* or with subordinating conjunctions such as *how, why,* or *whatever.*

SUBJECT

Whatever Jay decides to do will make him successful. [noun clause functions as subject]

DIRECT OBJECT

We know *why he works so hard.* [noun clause functions as direct object]

■ **Adjective Clauses** Adjective clauses, sometimes called relative clauses, modify nouns or pronouns, and they begin with relative pronouns such as *who, whose, whom, which,* or *that* or subordinating conjunctions such as *how, when,* or *where.*

His father, *whom Jay greatly admires,* set the standard. [adjective clause modifies *father*]

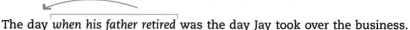

The day *when his father retired* was the day Jay took over the business. [adjective clause modifies *day*]

■ **Adverb Clauses** Adverb clauses modify verbs, adjectives, other adverbs, or whole clauses, and they begin with subordinating conjunctions such as *before, because, if, when,* and *while.*

DEPENDENT CLAUSE   INDEPENDENT CLAUSE

SC

When he took over the business, Jay wrote a note to his father. [adverb clause modifies the independent clause]

INDEPENDENT CLAUSE   DEPENDENT CLAUSE

SC

Jay said he would keep all his father's traditional values *as he updated the business.* [adverb clause modifies the independent clause]

Practice 16.10   Clauses

Identify the boldfaced clauses as either dependent or independent. Identify each dependent clause as a noun clause (NC), adjective clause (ADJ), or adverb clause (ADV).

1. Anne Bradstreet was a remarkable poet **who wrote in the seventeenth century**.

2. She came to America **when she was only sixteen**.

3. Even though she was so young, **she was already married to Simon Bradstreet**.

4. **Simon Bradstreet became governor** soon after they arrived from England.

5. Anne, however, retired to the wilds of Andover and wrote poetry.

Practice 16.11   Phrases and Clauses

Show your understanding of phrases and clauses by writing the following sentences. Identify each of the elements with a label.

1. Write a sentence that includes a prepositional phrase and an infinitive phrase.

2. Write a sentence that includes a gerund phrase.

3. Write a sentence that includes a participial phrase.

4. Write a sentence that has a subordinate clause that functions as a noun.

5. Write a sentence that has a subordinate clause that functions as an adjective.

6. Write a sentence that has a subordinate clause that functions as an adverb.

7. Write a sentence that has an infinitive phrase, a prepositional phrase, and a subordinate clause. Label each phrase or clause.

16c Sentence Types

With an understanding of phrases and clauses, you can build interesting and varied sentences. The three essential types of sentences are simple, compound, and complex. These three types are the patterns on which all sentences are built.

16c-1 Simple Sentences

A **simple sentence** has one independent clause (IC). It can be a two-word sentence, with one subject and one verb, or it can be longer, including many modifiers and phrases but no other clauses. Both of the following sentences are simple sentences.

INDEPENDENT CLAUSE
SUBJECT   VERB
Kim studied.

                                                                         SUBJECT
PREP. PHRASE   PREP. PHRASE   PARTICIPLE PHRASE
On Tuesday evening between ten and midnight, Kim, hoping to ace the
VERB   PREP. PHRASE   PREP. PHRASE   PREP. PHRASE
course, studied hard for her midterm exam in history on the causes
PREP. PHRASE
of the Vietnam War.

A simple sentence can have great power. After a long, explanatory paragraph, a simple sentence can emphasize or clarify a point.

> "At that moment, I saw her as I'd like to hope she saw herself, despite those summers of my poorly concealed embarrassment, condescension, and disdain. She *was beautiful.*"
>
> —Karlene Barrett, "Vacation"

16c-2 Compound Sentences and Coordination

A **compound sentence** has at least two independent clauses connected by the coordinating conjunction (CC) *and, but, for, or, nor, so,* or *yet* followed by a comma. Two independent clauses may also be connected by a semicolon.

INDEPENDENT CLAUSE   CC   INDEPENDENT CLAUSE
Kim studied for the exam, and *then she slept soundly.*

INDEPENDENT CLAUSE   INDEPENDENT CLAUSE
Kim studied for the exam; then she slept soundly.

INDEPENDENT CLAUSE   CC   INDEPENDENT CLAUSE   CC   INDEPENDENT CLAUSE

Kim studied for the exam, and *then she went to bed,* but *she slept fitfully.*

Too many compound sentences can create the rhythm of the breathless narratives of unsophisticated writing (*And then I went to the store, and I saw this man, and he had a big moustache, and I asked him if he saw my pet frog*).

Avoid too many compound sentences in a row, but a few well-constructed ones can be used to good effect to create a sense of **coordination**. Since compound sentences have independent clauses on either side of the conjunction, they can be used effectively to create a sense of balance in your writing. If you want to show two equally attractive alternatives or give equal emphasis to two ideas, the compound sentence is a good stylistic choice.

> "We had not spoken a word to each other, but I knew I was forever tied to this girl. Her wide eyes stared into mine, and I saw the dreams she held for what she could become."
>
> —Stephanie Sheen, "African Eyes"

16c-3   Complex Sentences and Subordination

A **complex sentence** has one independent clause and at least one dependent clause (DC). The dependent clause begins with a subordinating conjunction such as *although, because, if,* or *when* or a relative pronoun such as *which, who,* or *that.*

DEPENDENT CLAUSE   INDEPENDENT CLAUSE
SC

Although Kim studied hard, she slept fitfully.

DEPENDENT CLAUSE   INDEPENDENT CLAUSE   DEPENDENT CLAUSE
SC   SC

Although Kim studied hard, she slept fitfully because she was nervous.

The idea of one clause being dependent or subordinate should give you a clue about how to use the complex sentence most effectively in your writing. When one idea is less important than another or when one idea depends on another, you can use the structure of the complex sentence to subtly suggest this sense of **subordination**.

> "Their adventures, *while tinged with the fatalism that attends any crime spree,* have the thrilling, life-affirming energy for which the best road movies are remembered."
>
> —Janet Maslin, "On the Run with Two Buddies and a Gun"

Practice 16.12   Sentence Types

Test your understanding of sentence types by identifying the sentences below as simple, compound, or complex.

1. When the stock market crashed, I thought I would not be affected.

2. I knew a few families that had invested their life savings.

3. They had worked hard, and they felt safe.

4. They had made some bad choices, but it was not out of ignorance or greed.

5. Everyone at that time was in the same situation.

6. When classes were over for the semester, Jeff went straight to bed.

7. He slept for two days in a state of complete exhaustion.

8. Jeff had hoped to spend the rest of the break relaxing; however, his empty bank account suggested otherwise.

9. Within a week he had one part-time job at the mall and one at a restaurant.

10. Jeff will finally be able to relax when classes begin again.

17. PUNCTUATION

Punctuation is a set of conventions used to clarify your meaning. Punctuation marks have two main purposes: to end sentences and to show grammatical relationships within sentences.

17a Proofreading Symbols

Copyeditors, writers, and writing teachers often use a shorthand method to indicate corrections they make while proofreading. Most proofreading symbols are easy to understand, and they give you a convenient way to make corrections when you proofread your own work or a writing partner's work during peer revision. The most common proofreading symbols are in the following chart.

Symbol	Example (change marked)	Example (change made)
ˆo	Correct a typo.	Correct a typo.
⁻r⁻/ m⁻ /⁻o	Correct more than one typo.	Correct more than one typo.
t	Insert a leter.	Insert a letter.
	Make a deletion.	Make a deletion.
	Delete and close up space.	Delete and close up space.
#	Insertproper spacing.	Insert proper spacing.
# / ͜	Inserts pace and close up.	Insert space and close up.
tr	Transpose letters indicated.	Transpose letters indicated.
tr	Transpose as words indicated.	Transpose words as indicated.
tr	Reorder shown as words several.	Reorder several words as shown.
⌐	⌐ Move text to left.	Move text to left.
⌐	⌐Move text to right.	Move text to right.
¶	Indent for paragraph.	Indent for paragraph.
no ¶	No paragraph indent.	No paragraph indent.
run in	Run back turnover lines.	Run back turnover lines.
⌠	Break line when it runs far too long.	Break line when it runs far too long.
⊙	Insert period here.	Insert period here.
ͱ	Commas commas everywhere.	Commas, commas everywhere.
⌄/ ⌄͟	Its in need of an apostrophe.	It's in need of an apostrophe.
	Add quotation marks he begged.	"Add quotation marks," he begged.
;	Add a semicolon don't hesitate.	Add a semicolon; don't hesitate.
:	She advised "You need a colon."	She advised: "You need a colon."
?	How about a question mark.	How about a question mark?
⁻=⁻	Add a hyphen to a bill like receipt.	Add a hyphen to a bill-like receipt.
(/)	Add parentheses as they say.	Add parentheses (as they say).
lc	Sometimes you want Lowercase.	Sometimes you want lowercase.
caps	Sometimes you want upperCASE.	Sometimes you want UPPERCASE.
ital	Add italics instantly.	Add italics instantly.
rom	But use roman in the main.	But use roman in the main.
bf	Add boldface if necessary.	Add boldface if necessary.

17b Periods, Question Marks, Exclamation Marks

17b-1 Periods

Periods (.) are used at the ends of sentences and in abbreviations, decimals, initials, and inside Internet addresses.

■ **Sentences** A period is placed at the end of a declarative sentence or a mild command or request.

> The latest virus disabled my computer.

> Show me your paper.

■ **Abbreviations** Periods are also used after most abbreviations: Dr., Ms., Ph.D., a.m.

> Mr. Carter won the Nobel Peace Prize in 2002.

> I will get my B.A. in three years.

Exceptions to this rule are names of organizations, countries, agencies, and U.S. Postal Service abbreviations of state names.

> CBS, USA, FBI, ME (Maine)

USAGE TIP If you end a sentence with an abbreviation that has a final period, do not add an end period: **In three years I will get my B.A.**

■ **Decimals** Periods are used in decimals and fractional amounts of money.

> My GPA is 3.5.

> You owe me $3.50.

■ **Initials and Internet Addresses** Periods are used with initials and computer addresses.

> You can buy F. Scott Fitzgerald's books on Amazon.com.

17b-2 Question Marks

A **question mark (?)** ends an interrogative sentence.

■ **Direct Questions** Place a question mark after a direct question.

> Is this lecture confusing?

■ **Direct Quotations** When used in direct quotations, question marks go inside the quotation marks when the quotation asks the question, and outside the quotation marks when the full sentence poses the question.

Who said "Two paths diverged in a yellow wood"?

I asked him, "Who wrote the poem?"

■ **Other Kinds of Questions** Place a question mark after a question that might appear within a statement or in a series of phrases that ask questions.

Madame Helen—does anyone remember her?—will be available for consultations after nine o'clock.

Do you believe in psychic occurrences? Extrasensory perception? Unidentified flying objects?

17b-3   Exclamation Marks

An **exclamation mark (!)** ends an urgent sentence or a sentence that shows emotion or excitement.

Bring me a bandage immediately!

I won!

USAGE TIP Limit your use of exclamation marks in formal writing. Try to find a verb that expresses excitement or emphasis rather than using punctuation to signal excitement. **Okay: Schuyler was curious! Better: Schuyler bombarded me with questions.**

Practice 17.1   Periods, Question Marks, and Exclamation Marks
Proofread the following short passage. Add periods, question marks, and exclamation marks where necessary. Practice using the appropriate proofreading symbols from the proofreading chart.

Yesterday morning around five a m , two masked men robbed a jewelry store at 51 Main St in St Paul, MN and shot a bystander C B S and N B C had camera crews on the spot within the hour One eyewitness, Maria L Gonzalez, M D , asked the police how she could feel safe going on calls at night knowing she might bump into a thief She exclaimed, "I'm terrified" Then she asked, "How can I protect myself" You can follow the story on CNN com

17c Semicolons and Colons

17c-1 Semicolons

A **semicolon (;)** joins elements in a sentence in specific ways.

■ **Independent Clauses Without Conjunctions** Use a semicolon to join two independent clauses that are not joined by coordinating conjunctions. Using a semicolon instead of a period is a stylistic decision that conveys that the ideas in the clauses are closely related.

> Zoe laughed at his joke; she did not think it was funny. [closely related]

> Zoe laughed at his joke. Conversation shifted to a new topic. [not closely related]

■ **Independent Clauses with Conjunctive Adverbs** Use a semicolon between independent clauses joined by a conjunctive adverb, such as *however, nevertheless, moreover, therefore,* or *thus,* or a transitional phrase such as *for example.*

> Zoe laughed at his joke; however, she was offended.

> She tried to change the subject; for example, she asked him where he went to school.

■ **Items in Long Lists** Use a semicolon to separate items in a long list, especially to avoid confusion if some items in the list are already separated by commas.

> Tamar was at the party with her oldest friends, Marlene and Doug; her twin brothers, Caleb and Jacob; and Cindy and Peter, her coworkers.

Usage Tip Always place semicolons outside quotation marks: **At the party he asked, "Do you want to hear this joke?"; I said "No."**

17c-2 Colons

A **colon (:)** presents specific details.

■ **Before a List, Series, or Quotation** Use a colon to introduce a list, a series, or a formal or long quotation.

> I did all my work: a history report, an article about cloning, a take-home exam, and math homework.

All term my professor repeated this message: "If you manage your time well, you will be able to do all your work and have some time to relax."

■ **Between Independent Clauses** Use a colon to connect two independent clauses when the second one illustrates or explains the first.

Ellen completed her work early and could do the one thing she had wanted to do all term: She slept for twelve hours straight.

■ **Before an Example** Use a colon after a clause to provide a one-word example.

I completed my work early and could do the one thing I've wanted to do all term: sleep.

■ **Other Uses** Some other common uses of the colon are as follows.

▶ After a salutation in a formal letter or memorandum

Dear Professor:

To: Ben Gould

▶ In a book title, to separate the subtitle from the title

The Fourth Genre: Contemporary Writers of/on Creative Nonfiction

▶ In citations from the Bible or in bibliographic sources

Judges 11:3

Hunt, Douglas. *The Dolphin Reader*. 6th ed. Boston: Houghton Mifflin, 2003.

▶ In divisions of time

I get up at 6:05 every day.

Practice 17.2 Semicolons and Colons

Proofread the following short passage, and add semicolons and colons where necessary. Practice using the appropriate proofreading symbols from the proofreading chart.

Dear Town Official
At 530 yesterday evening, I went to return *The Flight of the Iguana A Sidelong View of Science and Nature* to the library on Main Street however, I was unable to cross the street. The traffic was so fierce that I waited for a solid forty minutes then I returned to my home. It is time for this town to take its head out of the sand and install that newfangled modern convenience a traffic light.

17d Commas, Dashes, and Parentheses

17d-1 Commas

A **comma (,)** clarifies relationships within a sentence.

■ **Lists** Use commas between items in a list.

Mia's progress has been slow, steady, and significant.

USAGE TIP Academic writers use a comma before the conjunction in a list; writers in journalism and media often omit the last comma before the conjunction. Whichever style you choose, be consistent.

■ **Coordinate Adjectives** Use a comma between coordinate adjectives. (Coordinate adjectives each modify the same noun.)

Mia has shown a slow, steady improvement.

■ **Introductory Phrases or Clauses** Use a comma after an introductory phrase or dependent clause.

To improve over such a short time, **Mia had to have worked hard.** [introductory phrase]

DC   IC

Since she worked so hard, **Mia improved significantly.** [introductory dependent clause]

If the independent clause comes before the dependent clause, do not use a comma.

IC   DC

Mia improved significantly since she worked so hard.

■ **Coordinating Conjunctions** Use a comma before a coordinating conjunction (*and, but, or, for, nor, so, yet*) in a compound sentence.

Mia's improvement was significant, but she was still not happy.

If the conjunction is not followed by an independent clause, do not put a comma before the conjunction.

PA   PP

Mia's improvement was significant but *unsatisfying to her.* [The expression *unsatisfying to her* is a predicate adjective and a prepositional phrase, not an independent clause]

■ **Inessential Clauses** Use commas around inessential (nonrestrictive) dependent clauses. Do not put commas around essential (restrictive) clauses.

A clause is **inessential or nonrestrictive** if it can be taken out of the sentence without changing the basic meaning of the sentence. Commas around the clause signal that the enclosed idea is additional information, not essential to the meaning of the sentence.

An **essential** or **restrictive** clause cannot be taken out of the sentence without altering the meaning of the sentence. The lack of commas signals that the clause is essential to the meaning of the sentence.

> Mia, *who is almost twenty,* improved significantly in her work. [provides additional but not essential information]
>
> The student *who worked so hard* is named Mia. [provides essential information]

USAGE TIP The relative pronoun *which* always introduces an inessential clause, so commas always go around a *which* clause. The relative pronoun *that* always introduces an essential clause, so commas never go around *that* clauses.

> The exam, *which I found challenging,* was the final graduation requirement. [provides additional but not essential information]
>
> The exam *that I passed* allowed me to graduate. [provides essential information]

■ **Participial and Appositive Phrases** Use commas around participial phrases (verbal phrases that function like adjectives) and appositive phrases (noun phrases that modify nouns or pronouns by describing them in different words). (See 16b-3.)

Modifies

> Mia, *having worked as hard as she could,* took a break. [participial phrase]

Renames

> Mia, *the most diligent student in the class,* finally earned her A. [appositive phrase]

■ **Attributions and Interrupters** Use commas around attributions in quotations and around phrases that interrupt a sentence.

> "I'm proud of Mia," *he said,* as he looked over her work. [attribution]
>
> Other teachers, *however kind they may be,* don't see her improvement. [interrupter]
>
> Show me her scores, *please.* [interrupter]

■ **Clarity** Use commas to help your reader avoid confusion.

To Mia, Anne was the role model of a hard worker.

■ **Other Uses** Commas are also used in the following situations.

▶ In addresses and names of geographical places

Becca lives at 81 Main Street, Madison, Wisconsin.
Last year she traveled to Florence, Italy.

▶ In openings and closings of letters

Dear Professor Lopez,
Sincerely,

▶ In direct address

Michael, do you hear me?

▶ In inverted names in bibliographies, indexes, and other reference lists

Lazlo, Ernestine

▶ To separate a name from a title or degree and with *Jr.* and *Sr.*

My internist is Ernestine Lazlo, M.D.
Frank Sinatra, Jr. was never as famous as his dad.

▶ In dates

October 22, 1968

▶ With figures that have more than four digits

$1, 250
1, 000,000 burgers sold

17d-2 Dashes

Dashes (-- or —) are used in certain situations instead of commas. A dash creates a less formal tone in a piece of writing.

■ **Surprise and Irony** Use a dash to create a sense of surprise or signal an ironic comment.

Professor Tsao told us to read all of Chapter 8, to write out four exercises, to complete our research papers—and to have a good weekend. [sets off an ironic comment]

■ **Parenthetical Comments** Use dashes to set off a parenthetical comment in a sentence.

> Professor Tsao—a teacher who loves to challenge students—told us to read all of Chapter 8, to write out four exercises, and to complete our research papers by Monday morning. [sets off a parenthetical comment]

■ **Lists and Explanations** Use a dash to introduce a list or explanation at the beginning or end of a sentence.

> Tonight I have a huge amount of homework—all of Chapter 8, four exercises, and a research paper.

17d-3 Parentheses

Parentheses (( )) are used in the following cases.

■ **Asides** Use parentheses around asides or incidental information.

> Professor Tsao *(my workaholic economics teacher)* piled on the homework.

■ **Explanatory Material** Use parentheses around explanatory material.

> I finished all the work *(Chapter, 8, four exercises, the research paper)* at midnight on Sunday.

■ **Lists within Sentences** Use parentheses around letters or numbers in a list within a sentence.

> I finished the three assignments: *(1) Chapter 8, (2) the exercises, and (3) the research paper.*

Practice 17.3 Commas, Dashes, and Parentheses

Proofread the following passage, adding commas, dashes, or parentheses where necessary. Practice using the appropriate proofreading symbols from the proofreading chart.

Lance Armstrong who some people call the best athlete in America won the Tour de France this year. Although fans wondered whether he could come back after his bout with cancer they had no doubts after watching his impressive some even said "superhuman" performance. Armstrong's feats were astonishing sprinting up hills sliding around hairpin curves and crossing the finish line minutes before his closest rival the cyclist from Germany.

"He won" said a long-time fan "and he deserved to win."

This fan who cheered and pumped his fist in the air has been following Armstrong's career for many years.

"Whether or not Armstrong won the race he would be a hero in my book," the jubilant exhausted fan concluded.

Armstrong will be signing autographs for fans tomorrow in two locations: 1 the bookstore at 29 Rue d'Orly Cannes and 2 the bookstore on the Champs Elysee Paris.

17e Apostrophes and Hyphens

17e-1 Apostrophes

Apostrophes (') are used in possessives and contractions.

■ **Possessives** Use an apostrophe to indicate that a noun or indefinite pronoun is possessive.

Singular Nouns Use -'s with singular nouns or pronouns.

Professor *Johnson's* class is hard but interesting.

Everyone's workload is lighter than mine.

Use -'s with most singular nouns ending in s. If the noun ends with a z or *eez* sound, use the apostrophe alone.

The *dress's* hem was dragging on the ground.

Ray *Charles'* performance was mesmerizing. [noun ends with a z sound]

Plural Nouns Use -s' with plural nouns that form the plural by adding an s.

I attended both *professors'* classes.

My workload is heavier than all the *bosses'* workloads put together.

Use -'s with irregular plural nouns that do not use -s to form the plural.

Put the cheese next to all the *mice's* holes.

Children's games are often more fun than adults' games.

Compound Nouns Use -'s on the last word of a compound noun.

My *sister-in-law's* mother visited yesterday.

Two or More Nouns Use -'s on each noun to show individual ownership, but only on the last noun to show joint ownership.

John and Susan's new house required a huge mortgage. [joint ownership]

John's and Susan's studios needed serious renovations. [individual ownership]

USAGE TIP Since possessive pronouns already show possession, they never use apostrophes: *his, hers, its, yours, theirs, whose*: **The line snaked its way around the block.**

■ **Contractions** Use an apostrophe to replace the letter or letters deleted in a contraction.

do not	don't
that is	that's
Madam	Ma'am
forecastle	fo'c's'le
it is or it has	it's

17e-2 Hyphens

Hyphens (-) are used as follows.

■ **Compound Modifiers** Use a hyphen to punctuate compound modifiers that work together to modify nouns.

> Miles gave me *second-hand* information. [*Second* modifies *hand*, not *information*; together *second* and *hand* modify *information*.]

> Hannah is a *three-year-old* terror. [The words *three, year,* and *old* work together to modify *terror*.]

Generally, when the modifier follows the noun, do not hyphenate it.

> I received the information *second hand*.

When the modifier is preceded by an adverb that ends in *-ly* or by the adverb *very*, omit the hyphen.

> Kristen is an *extremely bright* child.

> Greg is a *very kindhearted* guy.

■ **Compound Words** Use the hyphen to form a compound word—a word made up of more than one word that functions as a single word.

> My *brother-in-law* is a *happy-go-lucky* guy.

Make a compound noun plural by putting -s at the end of the main noun.

> I have two accomplished *brothers-in-law*.

Since conventions vary widely about using compound modifiers, it is a good idea to check your dictionary.

■ **Prefixes and Suffixes** Use the hyphen to link some prefixes and suffixes to words. The most commonly hyphenated prefixes are *ex-*, *pro-*, *self-*, and *neo-*, and a common suffix is *-elect*. Do not use a hyphen with the common prefixes *anti*, *co*, *non*, *post*, *pre*, and *un*.

The *governor-elect* tried to be both *pro-choice* and *pro-life*.

Check a dictionary or style guide to determine whether to hyphenate a word with a prefix or suffix.

■ **Other Uses** Following are additional uses of hyphens.

▶ At the end of a line to divide a word between syllables

▶ In written fractions

one-tenth

▶ In numbers from *twenty-one* to *ninety-nine*

▶ In numbers and dates that indicate a span

1946-2000

Practice 17.4   Apostrophes and Hyphens

Proofread the following passage, and insert the apostrophes and hyphens where necessary. Practice using the appropriate proofreading symbols from the proofreading chart.

I observed Mrs. Jones fifth grade class yesterday afternoon. In my preobservation conference in the teachers lounge, Mrs. Jones asked if I could help with the antismoking campaign she planned to launch in Mondays assembly. Although Im extremely happy to be useful, I wonder if its an appropriate job for a well intentioned exsmoker like me. I asked my master teacher. She told me that over two thirds of the teachers had been smokers, and she was sure that my expertise would be convincing to the eleven year old children in all the fifth grade classrooms.

17f Ellipses, Brackets, and Quotation Marks

17f-1 Ellipses

Ellipses (. . .) have the following uses.

■ **Intentional Omissions** Use ellipses to tell your reader that you have intentionally omitted a word or phrase in quoted material.

In despair Hamlet cries, "O that this too, too sullied flesh would melt . . . How weary, stale, flat, and unprofitable seem to me all the uses of this world!" [The writer has omitted three lines of Hamlet's speech that are not pertinent to her point.]

■ **Hesitancy** Use ellipses to indicate a speaker's hesitation or uncertainty.

Veronica said, "I can't quite remember . . . well . . . maybe a few lines from *Hamlet* have stayed in my head."

If the ellipses end the sentence, add the period to make four dots.

Veronica said, "I just can't remember. . . ."

17f-2 Brackets

Square brackets ([ ]) and angle brackets (< >) are used in these situations.

■ **Quotations** Use square brackets to indicate that you have added clarifying material to quoted passages.

The governor said, "I will be glad to give her [*his opponent, Senator Reo*] a chance to debate me in a public forum."

Use square brackets to insert words that are necessary to make a quotation grammatical or comprehensible.

The governor said he would be glad to "debate [*Senator Reo*] in a public forum."

■ **Internet Addresses** Some teachers may ask you to use angle brackets in e-mail addresses and Web URLs.

You can find the news at <http://www.cnn.com> or by e-mailing me at <kbaruk@hotmail.com>.

17f-3 Quotation Marks

Quotation marks (" ") have the following uses.

■ **Direct Quotations** Use quotation marks around all material that is directly quoted from other sources or to indicate someone's spoken words in dialogue.

Hamlet's most famous speech begins, "*To be or not to be—that is the question.*" [quotation from other source]

Senator Reo replied, "*I would love to debate the governor.*" [dialogue]

Do not use quotation marks around indirect quotations.

Senator Reo replied that she would love to debate the governor.

USAGE TIP In a quoted sentence within a sentence, do not use a period: The line "Show me the money" became popular last year.

■ **Titles** Use quotation marks to set off titles of magazine articles, television episodes, poems, short stories, songs, and other short works. Titles of longer works such as newspapers, magazines, novels, films, television shows, and anthologies are italicized.

I read "The Good Doctor" in the *New Yorker*.

"The Pine Barrens" was my favorite episode of *The Sopranos*.

■ **Single Quotation Marks** Use single quotation marks (' ') to set off quotations inside quotations.

The governor announced, "Senator Reo said, 'I accept,' so the debate is on."

■ **Other Punctuation** Follow these rules for using quotation marks with other punctuation marks.

Commas and Periods Commas and periods always go inside quotation marks.

"Well, then, it's all set," said the governor, "and I'm happy."

Question Marks and Exclamation Marks Question marks and exclamation marks go inside the quotation marks when the quoted material is a question or an exclamation, and outside the quotation marks when the whole sentence is a question or an exclamation.

Who said, "I accept"? [whole sentence is the question]

The senator asked, "When do you want to debate?" [quoted material is the question]

He said, "Eureka!" [quoted material is the exclamation]

"I am elated," he yelled! [whole sentence is the exclamation.]

Practice 17.5   Quotation Marks and Accompanying Punctuation

Proofread the following dialogue, adding all necessary commas, periods, question marks, exclamation marks, and quotation marks. Practice using the appropriate proofreading symbols from the proofreading chart.

1. Quiet she commanded

2. What's wrong he asked Do you hear something

3. What I hear is you talking she answered so stop talking

4. I'm scared he cried

5. Then go home she growled You asked Can I come and I said Yes you can

6. Well you should have said No way he said and ran home.

17g   Capital Letters, Numbers, and Italics

17g-1   Capital Letters

Capital letters are used at the beginning of sentences, in titles, for proper nouns, and for adjectives derived from proper nouns.

■ **Proper Nouns**   Use capital letters to begin specific names of people, races, titles, geographical locations, regions, historical eras, months, seasons, organizations, and institutions, but not general names of the same.

> *Georgetown High School* [specific name] **was the best** *high school* [general name] **in the area.**

> **I shook** *President Zeroff's* [specific title and name] **hand; she was the fifth** *president* [general title] **of** *Central College* [specific institution].

■ **Adjectives from Proper Nouns**   Use capital letters to begin adjectives made from proper nouns.

> **The best ethnic food in London is** *Indian* **food.**

> **Most Londoners prefer crumpets to** *English muffins.*

■ **Sentences and Quotations**   Use capital letters to begin sentences and quotations. Do not use a capital letter if the quotation is the continuation of a sentence or an excerpt that is a word, phrase, or dependent clause.

> **"I tried to run," she said, "but my feet wouldn't move."** [quotation is continuation of a sentence]

> **She felt "awkward, clumsy, and stupid," but it turns out that she was suffering from hypothermia.** [quotation is an excerpt]

■ **Titles** Use capital letters to begin all words in titles except for articles (the/a), short prepositions, and conjunctions, unless they are the first word in the title.

"The Pine Barrens" is my favorite episode of *The Sopranos*.

"The Good Doctor" was first published in the *New Yorker*.

■ **Other Uses** Other examples of the use of capital letters include the following.

▶ Nations: *England, Turkey, Japan*

▶ Planets: *Mercury, Mars, Venus*

▶ Stars: *Perseus, Sirius*

▶ Public places: *Times Square, Fisherman's Wharf, the Chicago Loop*

▶ Names of streets: *Beacon Street, Oak Lane, Allen Road*

▶ Days of the week and month: *Friday, November*

▶ Holidays: *Thanksgiving, Bastille Day, Fourth of July*

▶ Religions, deities, sacred texts: *Buddhism, Zeus, The Upanishads*

▶ Languages: *Hindi, Swedish, Vietnamese*

▶ Names of ships and aircraft: *Queen Mary, Enola Gay*

▶ The first-person pronoun: *I*

Check a dictionary if you are not sure whether a word or phrase should have an initial capital letter.

17g-2 Numbers

Numbers can appear as numerals or as words.

■ **Academic Writing** Spell out numbers from *one* through *ninety-nine* in academic writing.

It rained for forty days and forty nights.

Use numerals for 100 and higher.

Archeologists discovered 5,000 bones at the site.

■ **Media Writing** Spell out numbers from *twenty-nine* through *ninety-nine* for media writing.

The census showed fifty single-parent households in this village.

Use numerals for 1 through 28 and 100 and higher.

> The police counted 10 members of the clergy and 120 protesters at the sit-in.

■ **Beginning Sentences** Spell out numbers that begin sentences.

> Two hundred people attended the council meeting.

■ **Page and Chapter Numbers** Use numerals for page and chapter numbers.

> Read pages 3–30 in Chapter 9.

■ **Fractions and Percentages** Use numerals for percentages.

> The polls showed a 75 percent approval rating.

■ **Addresses and Dates** Use numerals for addresses and dates.

> On January 5, 2006, I will move to 29 Packard Road.

17g-3 Italics

Italics (*italics*) or underlining (<u>underlining</u>) are used in the following situations.

■ **Titles** Use italics (on the computer) or underlining (in handwriting) to set off titles of long works such as books, newspapers, magazines, journals, movies, and plays.

> I read a review of *The Taming of the Shrew* in *Entertainment Magazine.*
> I read a review of <u>The Taming of the Shrew</u> in <u>Entertainment Magazine</u>.

■ **Foreign Words** Use italics (on the computer) or underlining (in handwriting) to set off foreign words.

> Jacques called his grandmother "*grand-mére* ."

■ **Words, Letters, Numbers** Use italics (on the computer) or underlining (in handwriting) to set off words, letters, and numbers when referring to themselves.

> How many *3*s are in *9*?
> Spell *quick* with a *q* not a *kw*.

Practice 17.6   Capital Letters, Numbers, and Italics

Proofread the following passage, adding capital letters, numbers in their correct form, and italics where necessary. Practice using the appropriate proofreading symbols from the proofreading chart.

> 4 years ago I had no idea that college was even in my future. I lived in a small town, population twenty thousand, in the southwest. Only fifty percent of our graduating class went on to college. One day in english class I read a novel by the portugese writer Jose Saramago. The novel was called blindness, and it is about White Blindness that causes everyone in an unnamed european City to go blind. We discussed the Novel in class, and I realized that I loved talking and thinking about Books and Movies. It was then that I decided that College was indeed what I wanted, and I went to my Guidance Counselor that very day.

"I'll have the misspelled 'Ceasar' salad and the improperly hyphenated veal osso-buco."

18. COMMON ERRORS

Once you understand the parts of speech, parts of sentences, and sentence types reviewed in Chapter 16, you know the basic concepts that will allow you to make sense of grammatical rules. In this section you will learn to identify and avoid making errors in

▶ Sentence structure

▶ Agreement

▶ Verb tense

▶ Parallelism

▶ Modification

▶ Frequently confused words

18a Sentence Structure Errors

18a-1 Fragments

A sentence written in standard English has a subject and a complete predicate (a verb and its modifiers or complements). (See 16b.) A **fragment** is missing one of its parts, either the subject or the verb. Sometimes writers use fragments intentionally for emphasis or to dramatize thinking that is confused.

> **I love you. A lot.** [emphasis]

> **She ran through the corridors.** *Where to go? In a room? In a closet?* [confusion]

Using intentional fragments is a stylistic choice. When fragments are unintentional, they are considered sentence structure errors. Learn to identify and correct the following kinds of fragments.

■ **Omitting the Verb** A fragment may be caused by the omission of a verb.

FRAGMENT: *Isabel running down the corridor into rooms and closets.* [*Running* (a participle) describes Isabel, and the subject *Isabel* has no true verb.]

COMPLETE SENTENCE: **Isabel ran down the corridor into rooms and closets.** [*Ran* is the verb.]

■ **Omitting the Subject** Not including a subject also causes a fragment.

FRAGMENT: **Isabel ran down the corridor.** *And looked into rooms and closets.* [The verb *looked* has no subject.]

COMPLETE SENTENCE: **Isabel ran down the corridor and looked into rooms and closets.** [*Isabel* is the subject; *ran* and *looked* are compound verbs describing what she did.]

COMPLETE SENTENCE: Isabel ran down the corridor. She looked into rooms and closets. [*She* is the subject of the second sentence.]

■ **Using Dependent Clauses Alone** A dependent (subordinate) clause contains a subject and a verb, but it cannot stand alone. It must be connected to an independent clause to form a complete sentence.

Dependent clauses begin with subordinating conjunctions such as *although, because, if,* and *when* or relative pronouns such as *who, which,* or *that.* (See 16b-4.)

FRAGMENT: *Although she was initially scared and confused.* [Even though this group of words has a subject *she* and a verb *was,* it is a dependent clause and a fragment. It does not express a complete thought and cannot stand alone.]

COMPLETE SENTENCE: Although she was initially scared and confused, Isabel finally figured out where she was. [The dependent clause *Although she was initially scared and confused* is now connected to the independent clause *Isabel finally figured out where she was.*]

COMPLETE SENTENCE: She was initially scared and confused. [Dropping the subordinating conjunction *although* makes this a complete sentence.]

18a-2 Fused Sentences and Comma Splice Errors

Fused sentences and **comma splice errors** occur when two complete sentences are run together. A fused sentence has no punctuation between the two complete sentences.

FUSED: *Isabel ran down the corridor she did not know where she was going.*

A comma splice error has a comma between the two complete sentences.

COMMA SPLICE: *Isabel ran down the corridor, she did not know where she was going.*

To correct the errors, first identify the two complete sentences. Then you can fix them in one of four ways.

1. Add a period.

   Isabel ran down the corridor. She did not know where she was going.

2. Add a semicolon.

   Isabel ran down the corridor; she did not know where she was going.

3. Add a comma and a coordinating conjunction.

   Isabel ran down the corridor, but she did not know where she was going.

4. Add a subordinating conjunction to one sentence.

> **Although** Isabel ran down the corridor, she did not know where she was going. [If you introduce the sentence with a dependent clause, put a comma after the introductory clause.]

Practice 18.1   Fragments, Fused Sentences, and Comma Splice Errors

Identify and correct the sentence structure errors in the following passage. Mark all fragments (frag), fused sentences (FS), and comma splice errors (CS).

Isabel never forgot her car keys, they were always clipped securely to her belt. Always handy. She was surprised and annoyed that she had lost them, moreover, she was late for her practice. Isabel, not believing she was in such a crunch. She checked the ground near her car, then she bolted for the building. As she ran down the corridor, checking the floors and looking into classrooms. She heard the clanking of metal on metal. In front of her was her little sister Molly, Molly had a grin on her face as she jangled the keys. "I guess you can give me that ride now," Molly said, "Let's go, you don't want to be late for practice."

18b Agreement Errors

In English grammar, subjects agree with their verbs and pronouns with their antecedents.

18b-1 Subject-Verb Agreement

Subjects and verbs agree in number; a singular subject takes a singular verb, and a plural subject takes a plural verb.

SINGULAR SUBJECT AND VERB: *Chris runs* three campaigns at the same time.

A verb agrees with the subject of the sentence, not with the noun in an intervening prepositional phrase.

One of the boys *runs* the antismoking campaign. [The subject is *one*, not the noun *boys* in the prepositional phrase *of the boys*.]

PLURAL SUBJECT AND VERB: *Chris and Jason run* three campaigns together.

■ **Compound Subject** A verb that agrees with a **compound subject** joined by *and* is usually plural.

S ————————————— V
Christopher and Jason run the campaign. [The compound subject is *Christopher and Jason*.]

A verb agreeing with a compound subject that is preceded by *each* or *every* is singular.

S   V
Each boy and girl *is* a good organizer.

When a compound subject is joined by *or* or *nor*, the verb agrees with the subject closest to it.

S   S   V
Neither Christopher *nor* the other *boys run* the campaign in a vacuum. [*Boys* is the subject closest to the verb, so the verb is plural.]

■ **Collective Noun** A verb agreeing with a **collective noun** (a noun that represents a group but functions as a single entity) is singular. Some examples of collective nouns are *audience, committee, jury, family,* and *group.*

S   V
The antismoking *committee runs* a fundraiser each year.

■ **Indefinite Pronoun** Agreement of verbs with **indefinite pronouns** can be confusing. These three rules govern the agreement of indefinite pronouns and verbs.

1. Some indefinite pronouns always take singular verbs; *each, everyone, everybody, everything, either, neither, anyone, anybody, anything, one, no one, nobody, nothing, someone, somebody,* and *something* act as third-person singular pronouns.

   S   V
   Someone has to run this campaign.

   S   V
   One of the boys *is* going to be the high school liaison.

2. Some indefinite pronouns always take plural verbs; *many, most, both, few,* and *several* are plural in meaning and thus take plural verbs.

   S   V   S   V
   Many are go-getters, but *few are* as enthusiastic as they.

   S   V
   Several are extraordinarily talented.

3. Some indefinite pronouns can be either singular or plural, depending on the context. These indefinite pronouns include *all, any, none,* and *some.*

> S   V
>
> **All of the boys** *are* **qualified to run the campaign.** [In this case, *all* refers to *boys,* which is plural.]

> S   V
>
> **All the pie** *has* **been eaten.** [In this case, *all* refers to *pie,* which is singular.]

18b-2 Pronoun-Antecedent Agreement

Pronouns must agree in person (first, second, third), gender (male, female), and number (singular, plural) with the nouns or other pronouns they refer to in the sentence. (In pronoun use, **person** refers to the use of *I* or *we* for first person, *you* for second person, and *he, she, it,* or *they* for third person.)

The nouns or pronouns that pronouns refer to are called their **antecedents.** The general rule is that pronouns refer to the closest already-named noun. As a writer, you have to be sure that the pronoun reference is both unambiguous and in agreement.

■ **Ambiguous Pronoun** An ambiguous pronoun reference confuses the reader as to whom or what the pronoun refers.

AMBIGUOUS: When Christopher asked Jason to run the campaign, *he* blushed. [Since *he* could refer to either man, it is not clear who blushed.]

CLEAR: When Christopher asked Jason to run the campaign, *Jason* blushed.

Ambiguity also occurs when pronouns do not refer to anything that has been named in the sentence. Usually the ambiguous pronouns are *it, this, that,* or *which.* In these cases, substitute clear nouns for the ambiguous pronouns.

AMBIGUOUS: The campaign was funny and irreverent. *They* hung *it* in the student union and put *it* on the campus radio station.

CLEAR: The campaign was funny and irreverent. *The committee members* hung *a poster* in the student union and put *an ad* on the campus radio station.

■ **Agreement in Person** Make sure the pronoun agrees in person (first, second, or third) with its antecedent. Do not, for example, mix a third-person antecedent with a second-person pronoun.

Incorrect: *Students* should bring *your* good ideas to the meeting.

Correct: *Students* should bring *their* good ideas to the meeting.

■ **Agreement in Gender and Gender-Equal Pronouns** Pronouns and their antecedents have to agree in gender. Male antecedents require *his* as the pronoun referent; female antecedents require *her.* This rule does not usually pose a problem unless you get into the tricky area of deciding whether to refer to a mixed-gender group as male or female. Since you want to be both clear and accurate, the most sensible way to solve this problem is either to change the pronoun and its antecedent to their plural forms or to use the slightly longer, but equally acceptable, *his or her*.

PLURAL: *People* brought *their* best ideas.

GENDER EQUAL: *Each person* brought *his or her* best idea.

INCORRECT: *Each person* brought *their* best idea.

■ **Agreement in Number** Make sure a singular pronoun agrees with a singular antecedent and a plural pronoun with a plural antecedent. If the antecedent is a compound subject joined by *and*, the pronoun will be plural.

Christopher and Jason did *their* work well.

If the antecedent is a compound subject joined by *or*, the pronoun will agree with the antecedent closest to the pronoun.

Either Christopher or *Jason* did all *his* work.

If the antecedent is an indefinite pronoun, the pronoun is usually singular. (See the rules for subject-verb agreement in 18b-1 for indefinite pronouns that are singular, plural, or both.)

Either can do the work as long as *he* is willing.

Ask *both* to bring *their* best ideas.

Practice 18.2 Agreement

Identify and correct the agreement errors in the following passage. Mark and correct all errors in subject-verb agreement (s-v agr) and pronoun-antecedent agreement (p-a agr).

Today, a collegewide coalition of student activists meet to launch their antismoking campaign. The two organizers, one a sophomore and one a junior, speaks at noon. The event is open to anyone who are students at this college.

Each committee member have created a public awareness poster or radio spot that best expresses his position on the antismoking issue. It should be relevant and appeal to students. Some students have written radio spots; others have drawn posters; someone have even created a television storyboard.

After the presentation, they will vote for the best one. Either one student or two has a chance to win a $50 prize. The best reward, of course, is a heightened awareness of its dangers.

18c Pronoun Case Errors

Pronouns change forms depending on whether they are used as subjects or objects in a sentence or show possession.

Subject Pronouns (SP)	Object Pronouns (OP)	Possessive Pronouns (PP)
I	me	my, mine
you	you	your, yours
he, she, it	him, her, it	his, her, hers, its
we	us	our, ours
they	them	their, theirs
who/whoever	whom/whomever	whose

18c-1 Subject Pronouns

Subject pronouns (also known as **nominative pronouns**) substitute for nouns that are subjects in clauses and sentences, are appositives of words in the subject case (16b-3), or are subject complements (nouns that come after linking verbs and rename the subjects). (See 16b-2.) A pronoun can be the subject of the sentence.

He **plays lead guitar in the band.** [*He* is the subject of the verb *plays*.]

They **are booked for the next three weekends.** [*They* is the subject of the verb *are*.]

The pronoun can serve as an appositive.

We **fans go to all of the shows.** [*We* is the appositive of the subject noun *fans*.]

The pronoun can be used as a predicate noun.

The most ardent fan is *she*. [*She* is the subject complement of the noun *fan*.]

It was *they* **who began the new sound in popular music.** [*They* is the subject complement of the pronoun *it*.]

18c-2 Object Pronouns

Object pronouns substitute for nouns that are direct or indirect objects, the objects of prepositions, or appositives of nouns in the objective case. Pronouns can be direct or indirect objects.

> IO
> The usher gave *us* our programs. [*Us* is the indirect object.]

> IO   DO
> The usher gave it to *us*. [*It* is the direct object.]

A pronoun can serve as the object of a preposition.

> My little sister sat *between* my friend and *me*. [*Me* is the object of the preposition *between*.]

An object pronoun can be an appositive.

> The lead guitarist sang directly to *us* fans. [*Us* is the appositive of the noun *fans*.]

18c-3 *Who* and *Whom/Whoever* and *Whomever*

Knowing that the pronouns *who* and *whoever* are subject pronouns and *whom* and *whomever* are object pronouns should help you figure out how to use these pronouns correctly.

> Greg is the drummer *who* plays with the band. [*Who* is the subject of the verb *plays*.]

> The manager hires *whoever* has talent and drive. [*Whoever* is the subject of the verb *has*.]

> Greg is the drummer *whom* Tess loves. [*Whom* is the direct object of the verb *loves*.]

> Greg is the drummer to *whom* Tess wrote a fan letter. [*Whom* is the object of the preposition *to*.]

> Tess contacts *whomever* she admires. [*Whomever* is the direct object of the verb *admires*.]

Sometimes the choice between *who* and *whom* can be confusing when words or phrases come between the subject pronoun *who* and its verb.

> PARENTHETICAL
> Tess is the fan *who* we all agree is most knowledgeable about the music. [The words *we all agree* form a parenthetical expression that interrupts the sentence. *Who* is the subject of the verb *is*.]

Choosing between *who/whoever* and *whom/whomever* in prepositional phrases can also be tricky. Most of the time, a pronoun in a prepositional phrase takes the object form.

> To *whom* should Tess give the tickets? [*Whom* is the object of the preposition *to*.]

However, when the prepositional phrase includes a clause, the rule changes. The pronoun after the preposition becomes the subject of the clause, and the entire clause functions as the object of the preposition. The correct pronoun form should be *who* or *whoever*.

OBJECT OF PREPOSITION

PREP.   S   V

> Tess wanted to speak with *whoever* could get her an autograph. [*Whoever* becomes the subject of the verb phrase *could get*. The entire clause *whoever could get her an autograph* becomes the object of the preposition *with*.]

OBJECT OF PREPOSITION

PREP.   S   V

> The band gave autographs to *whoever* waited at the stage door. [*Whoever* becomes the subject of the verb *waited*. The entire clause *whoever waited at the stage door* becomes the object of the preposition *to*.]

18c-4 Possessive Pronouns

Possessive pronouns, like possessive nouns, show ownership.

> Coach *Brown's* team was not ready for the game. [*Brown's* is a possessive noun.]

> *His* team was dispirited because of *its* losses. [*His* and *its* are possessive pronouns.]

When they show possession, personal pronouns and the relative pronoun *who* do not use apostrophes. *My, mine, our, ours, your, yours, his, her, hers, its, their, theirs,* and *whose* are already in the possessive form. (See 17e-1 for apostrophe use with possessive nouns and indefinite pronouns.) Be careful not to mix up the possessive form of these pronouns with contractions of pronouns and verbs:

it + *is* = *it's*	*you* + *are* = *you're*
who + *is* = *who's*	*they* + *are* = *they're*

Possessive Pronoun: Give the team *its* due.

Pronoun-Verb Contraction: *It's* time to look at the bright side.

Possessive Pronoun: This is the team *whose* efforts have been greatest.

Pronoun-Verb Contraction: Jake is the player *who's* most improved.

Possessive Pronoun: *Your* hard work has paid off.

Pronoun-Verb Contraction: *You're* to be congratulated.

POSSESSIVE PRONOUN: *Their* teamwork has been exemplary.

PRONOUN-VERB CONTRACTION: *They're* proud of all the players this season.

USAGE TIP   Be careful not to confuse *their* and *they're* with the expletive *there*: *There* are many reasons that *they're* proud of *their* efforts.

Use the possessive case when a pronoun modifies a gerund (a verbal formed by adding *-ing* to a verb that functions as a noun). (See 16b-3.)

Their running has been superb. [*Their* modifies the gerund *running*.]

No one can fault *his* coaching. [*His* modifies the gerund *coaching*.]

Practice 18.3   Pronoun Case

Choose the correct pronoun case from the boldfaced words in the following sentences.

1. (**We/Us**) students decided to hike for a week during the break.
2. The seniors gave the job of organizing the equipment to (**we/us**) sophomores.
3. Graham gave us a lecture about (**his/him**) hiking.
4. The most enthusiastic hiker is (**he/him**).
5. The student (**who/whom**) was the most experienced will be the leader for the first day.
6. Most of us will follow (**whoever/whomever**) we respect.
7. The job of cook will go to (**whoever/whomever**) can boil water.
8. Hikers (**who/whom**) Graham says are fit can begin (**their/they're/there**) trek tomorrow.
9. Helena will be one of the hikers (**who/whom**) Graham will train tonight.
10. ("**Your/"You're**") ready to start whenever (**your/you're**) group is ready," he said.

18d   Verb Tense Errors

Sometimes verbs can trip you up if you are not careful about the time relationships among events in your writing. Two problem areas are maintaining the correct verb tense progression and using the correct verb tense consistently.

18d-1   Verb Tense Progression

Verbs change tense in order to show time relationships among events. The principal verb tenses are listed on this chart.

	Present	**Past**	**Future**
Simple	*I run*	*I ran*	*I will run*
Progressive	*I am running*	*I was running*	*I will be running*
Perfect	*I have run*	*I had run*	*I will have run*

Simple tenses show events occurring in the present, the past, and the future.

PRESENT: Chris *runs* a good campaign.

PAST: Chris *ran* a good campaign.

FUTURE: Chris *will run* a good campaign.

Progressive tenses show an action in progress.

PRESENT: Chris *is running* a good campaign.

PAST: Chris *was running* a good campaign.

FUTURE: Chris *will be running* a good campaign.

Perfect tenses show an action completed prior to another action.

PRESENT: Chris *has run* a good campaign when he hits a snag.

PAST: Chris *had run* a good campaign when he hit a snag.

FUTURE: Chris *will have run* a good campaign when he will hit a snag.

Practice 18.4   Verb Tense Progression

Choose the correct verb tense for each sentence below.

1. After the success of the campaign, Chris (**will run/will have run**) for office in his public relations organization.

2. Jason (**was/had been**) an officer the year before they mounted the campaign.

3. Right now, Chris and Jason (**are speaking/speak**) to students in the Student Union.

4. In high school Chris and Jason (**belonged/had belonged**) to a PR club.

5. Before they (**graduated/had graduated/were graduating**), they (**had won/won/were winning**) a prize for creativity.

18d-2 Verb Tense Consistency

To maintain verb tense consistency, do not shift verbs from one tense to another unless you are indicating a time change. Once you choose a verb tense in which to report an event or tell a story, be consistent.

INCORRECT: When the campaign *was* over, they *feel* satisfied.

CORRECT: When the campaign *is* over, they *feel* satisfied.

CORRECT: When the campaign *was* over, they *felt* satisfied.

Three conventions of verb tense use are as follows.

1. In discussing literary works, use present tense.

   Jonathan Franzen *writes* about the Midwest state of mind.

2. In reporting a story for a newspaper, use past tense.

   Jonathan Franzen **explained** his perspective in a reading last night.

3. In making a generalization, use present tense.

   Jonathan Franzen **writes** postmodern fiction.

Practice 18.5 Verb Tense Consistency

Choose the correct verb tense for the boldfaced verbs in the following sentences.

1. Three students (**worked/work**) for Habitat for Humanity over spring break, according to the Office of Student Services.
2. Community service (**is/was**) an important part of an education at our college.
3. Erica (**teaches/had taught/taught**) school kids in Ecuador last year.
4. The plot of the book (**centers/centered**) around three students who wandered into the rain forest.
5. When they returned from spring break, they (**write/wrote**) a report to put on file.

18e Parallelism

To maintain parallelism or parallel structure in your writing, keep words, phrases, and clauses in the same grammatical form when they are in a series or connected by a coordinating conjunction.

PARALLEL NOUNS: Dana does not eat *candy, cake,* or *pasta.*

PARALLEL ADJECTIVES: Dana is *strong, healthy,* and *athletic.*

PARALLEL VERBS: Dana *rides* horses, *plays* basketball, and *swims.*

PARALLEL PHRASES: Dana loves *riding horses, playing basketball,* and *swimming laps in the pool.* [parallel gerund phrases]

PARALLEL CLAUSES: *Dana loves to ride horses,* and *she loves to play basketball.* [parallel independent clauses]

FAULTY PARALLELISM: Dana loves *to ride, play,* and *swimming.* [*to ride* and *play* are infinitives; *swimming* is a gerund]

Maintain parallel structure in comparisons using *as* or *than.*

NONPARALLEL STRUCTURE: *Eating healthfully* is as important as *to play sports.*

PARALLEL STRUCTURE: *Eating healthfully* is as important as *playing sports.*

NONPARALLEL STRUCTURE: Dana's *sports equipment* is better than *Louise.* [comparing sports equipment to Louise]

PARALLEL STRUCTURE: Dana's *sports equipment* is better than *Louise's.* [correctly comparing Dana's equipment to Louise's equipment]

Maintain parallel structure with correlative conjunctions (see 16a-7).

NONPARALLEL STRUCTURE: *Not only* does Dana love to swim *but* she *also* is running every day.

PARALLEL STRUCTURE: *Not only* does Dana love to swim *but* she *also* runs every day.

> **USAGE TIP** Use parallel structure to achieve a sense of balance and elegance in your writing. Many memorable lines in literature or speech use this kind of parallel structure or balance: "*Ask not what your country can do for you; ask what you can do for your country.*"—John F. Kennedy. "*I have nothing to offer but blood, toil, tears and sweat.*"—Winston Churchill.

Practice 18.6   Parallelism

Correct any errors in parallelism in the following sentences.

1. The benefits of exercise—improved health, you may lose weight, feeling fit, and you look good—are convincing reasons to work out.
2. Either Hank is running every day or he works out three times a week.
3. A penny earned is a penny well worth putting in the bank.
4. Benjamin Franklin not only wrote aphorisms but he also was becoming the American ambassador to France.
5. Franklin was a statesman, writer, flew kites, and an inventor.

18f Modification Errors

Modifiers are words, phrases, or clauses that qualify or limit. Modifiers function as adjectives or adverbs (see 16a-4 and 16a-5). Errors occur when modifiers are misplaced or positioned so that they do not clearly refer to the word or phrase they modify.

18f-1 Misplaced Modifiers

Modifiers should appear next to the word(s) they modify. Misplaced modifiers often create confusion and sometimes even unintentional humor.

MISPLACED: I rented a movie at the video store *starring Tom Hanks*. [*starring Tom Hanks* incorrectly refers to the video store, not the movie]

CORRECTLY PLACED: At the video store, I rented a movie *starring Tom Hanks*.

MISPLACED: My friend gave me four dollars to rent the *movie in quarters*. [*in quarters* incorrectly refers to the movie, not the four dollars]

CORRECTLY PLACED: My friend gave me four dollars *in quarters* to rent the movie.

Modifiers like *only, frequently,* and *sometimes* can be confusing if they are placed in the middle of a sentence; such placement can cause confusion about whether these adverbs are modifying the words that precede them or follow them.

AMBIGUOUS: Tom Hanks plays roles *frequently* portraying a hero. [*Frequently* can refer to how often Hanks plays roles or to how often he portrays a hero.]

CLEAR: Tom Hanks *frequently* plays roles portraying a hero.

CLEAR: Tom Hanks plays roles portraying a hero *frequently*.

18f-2 Dangling Modifiers

Dangling modifiers dangle because they have nothing in the sentence to modify. Often, dangling modifiers are introductory participial phrases like *seeing the movie* or infinitive phrases like *to see the movie*. Grammatically, the phrase should modify the noun or pronoun that immediately follows it.

DANGLING MODIFIER: *Seeing the movie,* Tom Hanks was extraordinary. [*Seeing the movie* dangles. This phrase incorrectly modifies *Tom Hanks*.]

CLEAR: *Seeing the movie,* Gus thought Tom Hanks was extraordinary. [*Seeing the movie* modifies *Gus*.]

DANGLING MODIFIER: *To see the movie clearly,* glasses had to be worn. [*To see the movie clearly* dangles. The phrase incorrectly modifies *glasses*.]

CLEAR: *To see the movie clearly,* Gus had to wear his glasses. [*To see the movie clearly* modifies *Gus*.]

Practice 18.7   Dangling and Misplaced Modifiers
Rewrite the following sentences, identifying and fixing the dangling modifiers (DM) and misplaced modifiers (MM).

1. Seeing the film for the first time, Tom Hanks was perfect in the role.

2. When finding himself alone, a soccer ball became his surrogate friend.

3. Hanks's character dined on fish and coconut milk that he speared in the ocean.

4. After being rescued, raw fish turned his stomach.

5. The camera focused on the lavish buffet of lobster, crabs, and sushi in a tight shot.

6. I eat fish frequently getting an allergic reaction.

18g   Frequently Confused Words

Some pairs of words sound enough alike or have such similar spellings or meanings that they may be confusing. This list explains some word pairs that are frequently confused.

- **advice, advise**   *Advice* is a noun, and *advise* is a verb.

   My counselor *advised* me to listen to his good *advice.*

- **affect, effect**   Most of the time *affect* is a verb meaning "to influence."

   How much will that C *affect* my final grade?

Most of the time *effect* is a noun meaning "the result."

   What is the *effect* of that C on my final grade?

Used as a verb, *affect* means "to put on a false show."

   He *affected* an air of boredom.

Effect can be also a verb, meaning "to cause."

   He *effected* the change of mood by laughing loudly.

- **among, between**   Generally, use *among* when referring to many things and *between* when referring to two things.

   Kenza divided the candy **between** *the two kids; they divvied it up* **among** *their friends.*

- **anxious, eager**   Use *anxious* to suggest worry and *eager* to suggest anticipation.

Isabella is *eager* to start her new job but *anxious* about making a mistake.

■ **as, like**   As is a subordinating conjunction. It introduces a subordinate clause.

Jose looks *as if* he saw a ghost.

Like is a preposition. It is followed by the object of a preposition.

He looks *like* a ghost.

■ **bad, badly**   *Bad* is an adjective, and *badly* is an adverb. Use the adjective form *bad* after a linking verb and the adverb form *badly* after a transitive verb.

Scott felt *bad because he had the flu.* [*Bad* describes his state of being.]

Scott felt *badly* because he burned his finger tips. [*Badly* describes his inability to feel sensations.]

■ **beside, besides**   *Beside* means "next to." *Besides* means "also" or "other than."

I put my book *beside* the table.

Besides, I wanted to read it before I went to sleep.

Nothing *besides* a nap would do.

■ **censor, censure**   Both words can be nouns or verbs. As a noun, *censor* names the person who deletes objectionable material, and as a verb *censor* is the act of deleting that material.

The *censor censored* my mail

As a noun, *censure* means "disapproval," and as a verb it means "to disapprove."

The student body *censured* Gene for plagiarism.

Gene took the *censure* seriously.

■ **continual, continuous**   *Continual* means "repeated often," while *continuous* means "ongoing."

Shane had *continual* run-ins with his professor.

Their *continuous* argument about grades gave us all headaches.

■ **different from, different than**   Generally speaking, use *different from.*

This movie is significantly *different from* the book.

■ **disinterested, uninterested** A *disinterested* person is impartial; an *uninterested* person is bored.

> Fatima was *uninterested* in the lecture, but she wanted a *disinterested* person to judge whether the professor was boring.

■ **elicit, illicit** *Elicit* is a verb that means "to draw out"; *illicit* is an adjective that means "illegal."

> The detective *elicited* a confession from the crook, but since his words were recorded on an *illicit* wiretap, the confession was inadmissible in court.

■ **farther, further** In formal writing, use *farther* to suggest distance and *further* to suggest degree.

> Augie lives *farther* from school than you.

> Callie has *further* research to do on her paper.

■ **fewer, less** Use *fewer* with countable items and *less* with quantities or amounts.

> The store sold *fewer* quarts of milk this week.

> They now have *less* milk in stock.

■ **good, well** Generally speaking, *good* is an adjective and *well* is an adverb.

> This is a *good* time to study *well*. [*Good* modifies the noun *time*; *well* modifies the verb *study*.]

After a linking verb, use the predicate adjective *good*.

> Although I have attended only one lecture, Professor Bloom seems *good*.

When referring to health, *well* functions as an adjective.

> Although she was ill for a while, now Professor Bloom seems *well*.

■ **hanged, hung** Use *hanged* with bodies (executions) and *hung* with objects (curtains).

> In old westerns, murderers were *hanged* at dawn.

> We *hung* our clothes in the closet.

■ **imply, infer** Both words are verbs, but *imply* means "to suggest" and *infer* means "to deduce" or "to draw a conclusion."

I *implied* that we should be friends, but he *inferred* that I never wanted to see him again.

■ **irregardless, regardless** *Irregardless* is considered nonstandard usage in all situations. Always use *regardless*.

I want to see you *regardless* of the consequences.

■ **its, it's** *Its* is a possessive pronoun, and *it's* is a contraction of *it* and *is*.

The clock had a smudge on *its* face.

It's time to go.

■ **lay, lie** *Lay* is a transitive verb that takes a direct object. It means to put something down. *Lie* is an intransitive verb that means to recline.

I *lay* the book on the table.

When I am tired, I *lie* down.

The two verbs use the following forms (see 18d-1).

Present	Past	Perfect	Progressive
Lay	laid	laid	laying
Lie	lay	lain	lying

■ **lend, loan** Use *lend* as a verb and *loan* as a noun.

Jacob had to take out a *loan* because Tony would not *lend* him a dime.

■ **media, medium** *Media* is the plural form of *medium*.

The film *medium* is the most dynamic, but all the visual *media* interest Vassili.

■ **prejudice, prejudiced** *Prejudice* is a noun; *prejudiced* is an adjective.

Jonah had a great deal of *prejudice* against *prejudiced* people.

■ **principal, principle** Use *principal* for a person who is the head of an organization, such as the principal of a school. When used as an adjective, *principal* also means the main or most important element. *Principle* is a truth, a tenet, or a belief.

Mr. Leavy is the *principal* of my sister's high school. [head of school]

The *principal* crop is wheat. [main]

The university's hiring policy is based on the *principles* of diversity and equality. [tenets]

■ **proved, proven** Use *proved* as the past participle form of *prove* and *proven* as the adjective form.

His *proven* [adjective] record of support for tax cuts *has proved* [past participle] that he is the best candidate for mayor.

■ **quote, quotation** *Quote* is a verb, *quotation* a noun.

Always *quote* accurately from all *quotations*.

Media writers sometimes use *quote* as a noun.

The reporter got some good *quotes* for her article.

■ **raise, rise** *Raise* is a transitive verb, so it always takes a direct object. It means "to cause something to move upward" or to "bring up." *Rise* is an intransitive verb that means "to move upward."

Mama *raised* her kids to *rise* when grownups entered the room.

■ **sit, set** *Sit* is an intransitive verb meaning "to take a seat." *Set* is a transitive verb that takes a direct object and means "to put something down."

When you *sit* on your chair, please *set* the teacup on the table.

■ **than, then** Use *than* with comparisons and *then* to indicate time.

She is taller *than* her mother.

She grew as tall as her mother, and *then* she grew taller.

■ **their/there/they're** Each of these homonyms has a different meaning. *Their* is a pronoun that indicates possession. *There* is an adverb that indicates place. *They're* is a contraction of *they* and *are*.

The children have *their* father's eyes.

Put the book down *there*.

They're free to leave whenever they desire.

■ **to, too, two** Each of these homonyms has a different meaning. *To* is a preposition (to the store). *Too* is an adverb meaning "also" or "many." *Two* is the number after *one*.

We went *to* the all-you-can-eat buffet.

We ate *too* much.

Two of us had to lie down for an hour.

■ **who, whom** Use *who* or *whom* when referring to people; use *that* or *which* when referring to objects.

Who functions as a subject in a sentence or clause, and *whom* functions as an object in a sentence or clause.

Who is this masked man? [*Who* is the subject of the sentence.]

He is the masked man *who* saved your life. [*Who* is the subject of the dependent clause.]

Whom do you trust? [*Whom* is the direct object.]

He is the man *whom* I trust with my life. [*Whom* is the direct object in the dependent clause.]

■ **who's, whose** *Who's* is a contraction of *who is*, and *whose* is a possessive pronoun.

Whose turn is it to see the man *who's* so ill?

■ **your, you're** *Your* is a possessive pronoun; *you're* is a contraction of *you are*.

You're a person who likes *your* food prepared well.

Practice 18.8 Frequently Confused Words

To review confusing word pairs, choose the correct word in the following sentences.

1. (To/too/two) often we are so (eager/anxious) to begin a new adventure that we forget to (sit/set) for a while and think about (its/it's) possible outcomes.

2. (There/their/they're) are many questions to (rise/raise) before (your/you're) able to choose wisely.

3. For example, (who/whom) do you want to accompany you when you (sit/set)off?

4. (Who/Whom) is your choice of companion when you feel (bad/badly) or when things don't go (well/good)?

5. I would want to be with someone with a (proved, proven) track record, someone (who/whom/that/which) would rather be safe (than/then) take risks (regardless/irregardless) of the consequences.

6. I don't mean to (imply/infer) that I am (prejudice/prejudiced) against risk-takers. I just feel (like/as if) I want to have a cool head around me when I'm about to (lay/lie) my life on the line.

7. My (principal, principle) goals are to experience life, to go (further, farther) than people expect, and to make (fewer/less) mistakes than those who have gone before me.

19. TROUBLE SPOTS FOR NONNATIVE SPEAKERS OF ENGLISH

If you are not a native speaker of English, you have undoubtedly grappled with the thousands of ways that English differs from your language in vocabulary, syntax, punctuation, and grammar. Many comprehensive handbooks and websites exist for learning English and the rules that govern its grammar. One of the best handbooks is *Universal Keys for Writers* by Ann Raimes (Houghton Mifflin, 2004). Two good websites are http://www.eslcafe.com and http://www.owl.english.purdue.edu.

This chapter will help you identify and correct the most common problems that nonnative speakers encounter.

▶ Nouns and articles

▶ Verbs and verbals

▶ Sentence structure

▶ Idioms

19a Nouns and Articles

19a-1 Countable and Noncountable Nouns

Countable nouns are specific things that can be counted (one, two, three) and can take a plural form.

Singular	Plural
one girl	two girls
one room	three rooms
one book	four books

Some quantifiers used with countable nouns are *many, few,* and *a few.*

Noncountable nouns or **mass nouns** cannot be counted and do not have plural forms.

Correct	Incorrect
advice	advices
gasoline	gasolines
information	informations
wheat	wheats
courage	courages

Some quantifiers used with noncountable nouns are *much*, *little*, and *a little*. Other noncountable nouns are *furniture*, *electricity*, *excitement*, *jewelry*, *homework*, *blood*, *education*, *fun*, *faith*, *soccer*, and *zoology*.

Some nouns can be either countable or noncountable, depending on their context. When a noun is used in a specific sense, it is countable. The same noun used in a general way is noncountable.

Countable	**Noncountable**
The perfume comes in three *fragrances*.	The roses have a lovely *fragrance*.
Three *hairs* turned gray overnight.	Sena's *hair* is short and black.
Boiling and freezing are two specific *temperatures*.	The *temperature* outside is freezing.

Practice 19.1   Identifying Countable and Noncountable Nouns

Identify the boldfaced words in the following sentences as countable nouns (CN) or noncountable nouns (NCN). Look at the context for nouns that could be either.

1. All my **money** is in **euros**.

2. After Josh saw the **movie**, he decided to major in **film**.

3. Marie watched the **scenery** go by as she traveled across the **country**.

4. The **heat** on the **bus** was set far too high.

5. Claudia packed her **clothing**: **dresses**, **skirts**, and **sweaters**.

19a-2 Articles

To figure out whether to use an **article**—*a*, *an*, *the*—in front of a noun, follow these guidelines.

Generally speaking, use *a* or *an* with a nonspecific reference and *the* with specific references.

A *firefighter* **has a dangerous job.** [refers to any firefighter]

***The** firefighter* **suffered from smoke inhalation.** [refers to a specific firefighter]

Use *a* or *an* for nonspecific references to singular count nouns. Use *a* before words that begin with consonant sounds: *a bird*, *a dog*, *a plane*. Use *an* before words that begin with vowel sounds: *an eagle*, *an insult*, *an airplane*, *an hour*.

Kirsten should buy *a dog* **to keep her company.**

Brendan bought *an angora scarf* **to keep him warm.**

Use *the* in these cases.

▶ A specific reference to a noun previously mentioned

Kirsten bought a dog. She named *the dog* Fergie.

▶ A specific reference to a noun known by the writer and reader

Brendan put *the scarf* around his neck.

▶ A reference to an entire class of things

***The clothing industry* is suffering from the recession.**
***The boxer* is a noble breed of dog.**

▶ An adjective in the superlative

That line of clothing is *the warmest*.
My dog Otis was *the best* in the litter.

▶ A reference to a noun followed by a modifying phrase or clause

***The clothing* that is sold here is made of natural fibers.** [*That is sold here* is a clause modifying *clothing*.]

Holly is *the dog* down the street. [*Down the street* is a prepositional phrase modifying *dog*.]

▶ A reference to a plural proper noun (a noun that names a specific person, place, or organization)

Kirsten memorized *the U.S. presidents*.

Brendan took Otis hiking in *the Rocky Mountains*.

Use no article at all in these cases.

▶ A nonspecific reference to a plural countable or noncountable noun

Susan and Rebecca bought *camping supplies: raisins, protein bars, and freeze-dried apricots*. [All nouns are plural countable nouns.]

Susan and Rebecca bought *camping equipment: tents, poles, stoves, and sleeping bags*. [*Camping equipment* is a plural noncountable noun.]

▶ Most proper nouns

***Lettie* gave the book to *Mother*.**

***Habitat for Humanity* will be building houses in *Central America*.**

▶ A generalization about a plural countable noun

***Books* are my passion.**

***Trousers* are warmer than *skirts*.**

Practice 19.2   Articles

In the following blanks, put in the correct article: *a, an,* or *the*. If an article is not needed, put an X in the blank.

1. _____ English professor gave me _____ grammar lesson about _____ use of _____ articles.

2. _____ old proverb says, "_____ beauty is in_____ eye of _____ beholder."

3. Rick purchased _____ new notebook for class, but then he discovered that he had bought _____ wrong size.

4. Julie gave _____ ticket to the show to _____ Mother.

5. My adviser gave me _____ useful advice about _____ field I want to study.

19b   Verbs and Verbals

You might want to review the sections on transitive verbs, intransitive verbs, linking verbs, verb tenses, predicates, verb moods (see 16a-3), and verbal phrases (see 16b-3).

19b-1   Verb Complements

A complete predicate consists of a verb and its complements. **Complements** are nouns or adjectives that can function as direct objects, indirect objects, object complements, or subject complements (see further discussion in 19c-1).

> **Hector *recommended going to the theater tonight*.** [*Recommended* is the verb; *going to the theater tonight* is the complement of the verb.]

Verb complements can be

▶ Gerunds (verb + *-ing*): *running, laughing, jumping*

▶ Infinitives (*to* + verb): *to run, to laugh, to jump*

▶ Infinitives with the *to* omitted: *run, laugh, jump*

Gerunds and infinitives are not true verbs but are instead verbals created from verbs that function as other parts of speech (nouns, adjectives, or adverbs). The following guidelines will help you decide when to use each form.

Use the gerund form but not the infinitive form as verb complements after these verbs:

acknowledge	delay	imagine	regret
admit	deny	insist on	resist
advise	depend on	keep	risk

appreciate	detest	miss	suggest
avoid	discuss	postpone	talk about
be	dislike	practice	tolerate
can't help	enjoy	quit	
consider	escape	recall	
consist of	finish	recommend	

CORRECT: Jean *avoids running* in the dark.
CORRECT: She *considers going* to the gym at night.
INCORRECT: Jean avoids *to run* in the dark.
INCORRECT: She considers *to go* to the gym at night.

Use the to + verb infinitive form, not the gerund form, as verb complements after these verbs.

afford	demand	need	threaten
agree	expect	offer	venture
ask	fail	plan	wait
attempt	hesitate	prepare	want
beg	hope	pretend	wish
bother	intend	promise	
choose	learn	refuse	
claim	like	seem	
consent	manage	struggle	
decide	mean	tend	

CORRECT: Max *demanded to go* with his cousins.
CORRECT: Jack *begged to join* them also.
INCORRECT: Max *demanded going* with his cousins.
INCORRECT: Jack *begged joining* them also.

Use the to + verb infinitive form or the gerund form as verb complements after these verbs.

begin	like
cannot stand	love

continue   start

dread   try

hate

Correct: Fwar began *to cook* the dinner.

Correct: Fwar *began cooking* the dinner.

Correct: David *tried to help*.

Correct: David *tried helping*.

Use the infinitive form without the *to* as a verb complement after these verbs only when the verb is followed by a noun or pronoun.

have   help   let   make

Correct: Lucia *let* all the kids *cook* a dish.

Correct: Hank *helped* Lucia *set* the table.

Incorrect: Lucia *let* all the kids *to cook* a dish.

Incorrect: Hank *helped* Lucia *to set* the table.

Practice 19.3   Verb Complements

Fill in the blanks with the correct form of the verb: gerund *(-ing)*, infinitive (with *to*), or infinitive (without *to*).

1. When her family arrived for a visit, Maria wanted (take) _____ them to a wonderful restaurant.

2. Traveling by train across the country, Thom appreciated (see)_____ the vastness of the plains.

3. Nicole could not begin (understand) _____ what I was saying until she took off her headphones.

4. Jacques let his sales clerk (take) _____ a day off from work.

5. The dog threatened (bite)_____ José if he did not back off.

19b-2 Modal Auxiliary Verbs

Modal auxiliary verbs are *will, would, can, could, shall, should, may, might,* and *must*. These verbs are used to show conditions such as possibility, ability, permission, assumption, necessity, and obligation.

> *can:* ability
>
> *could:* polite question or conditionality
>
> *may:* permission or possibility
>
> *might:* permission or possibility

must: necessity or logical assumption

shall: polite question or intention

should: advisability or expectation

will: intention

would: polite question or conditionality

Modal auxiliary verbs do not change form and are always followed by the simple form of a verb.

CORRECT: Mac *may go* to the movies.

INCORRECT: Mac *may to go* to the movies.

INCORRECT: Mac *may going* to the movies.

Use only one modal at a time. To combine modals with other words that express conditions, use phrases such as *be able to*, *be allowed to*, or *have to*.

INCORRECT: If they are good, the children *might could* get a treat.

CORRECT: If they are good, the children *might be allowed* to get a treat.

Use *will* or *shall* in the present tense and *would* in the past tense to indicate intention.

> We *will* finish our work quickly.

> We said that we *would* do it quickly.

Shall is usually used in polite questions.

> *Shall* we go?

Use *can* in the present tense or *could* in the past tense to indicate ability.

> If we hurry, we *can* make the show.

> We *could* not go because the car had broken down.

Use *may, might, can,* or *could* in the present tense and *could* or *might* in the past tense to indicate permission or possibility.

> You *may* go only if the weather holds.

> The girls *might* go together, or they *might* go separately. [present]

> The girls *might* have gone if the weather had been good. [past]

Use *would* or *could* to ask a polite question or to indicate conditionality.

> *Would* you be able to attend my dinner? [question]

> *Could* you let me know as soon as possible? [question]

> Erin *would* go if Amy went with her. [conditionality]

> Sue *could* go also to make it more fun. [conditionality]

Use *should* to indicate advisability or expectation.

> **John thought that they *should* all go together to save money.** [advisability]
>
> **They *should* all arrive momentarily.** [expectation]

Use *must* to indicate necessity or to make a logical assumption.

> **John thought that they *must* all go together to save money.** [necessity]
>
> **They *must* have all left together since they are all here now.** [logical assumption]

Practice 19.4   Modal Auxiliary Verbs

Rewrite the following sentence using the appropriate modal auxiliary verb for the conditions listed below: Jesse rides horses.

> Example: Indicate that Jesse has permission from her mother to go riding this afternoon.
> Her mother says that Jesse *may* go riding this afternoon.

1. Indicate that Jesse expects to go riding this afternoon.

2. Indicate that Jesse asked permission to go riding.

3. Indicate that Jesse has the ability to ride horses.

4. Indicate that Jesse's horseback riding depends on whether her mother can take her to the stables.

5. Indicate that it is necessary for Jesse to ride today if she wants to be in the show.

19b-3 Phrasal Verbs

Some verbs combine with prepositions or adverbs to create new meanings. When combined in this way, prepositions and adverbs are called **particles**, and they no longer function as prepositions or adverbs. These two- or three-word verbs can be confusing since their meaning is often very different from the meaning of the original verbs. For example, as a transitive verb *look* means *to gaze*. However, when you add the preposition *over* to form *look over*, the meaning changes *to review*.

> **Larry is going to *look over* his notes before the test.**

When *for* is added to *look*, it creates *look for*, which means *to seek*.

> **Larry will *look for* an easy way to memorize the equations.**

The following list shows some of these two- and three-word verbs.

Verb	Phrasal Verb	Example
break	break up (separate)	Donald and Daisy *broke up* last night.
	break down (cry)	Daisy tried to be brave, but she *broke down*.
	break down (fail to function)	I guess their communication *broke down*.
bring	bring up (mention)	Fred *brought up* a problem.
come	come across (discover)	Elisa *came across* those old photographs.
	come over (visit)	We plan to *come over* tonight to see them.
	come up with (develop)	They want to *come up with* a way to preserve the photographs.
hang	hang on (persist)	I am sure I can *hang on* until summer.
look	look for (seek)	The police *looked for* a solution to the crime.
	look over (examine)	They *looked over* all the evidence.
	look up to (admire)	The officers *looked up to* their chief.
	look down on (scorn)	They looked *down on* lawbreakers.
put	put on (don)	Izzy *put on* her dancing shoes.
	put off (postpone)	Unfortunately, they *put off* the show.
	put up with (endure)	She *put up with* our teasing.
run	run across (encounter)	Cindy *ran across* her cousin Lionel.
	run out of (use up)	Soon she *ran out of* things to say.

Phrasal verbs can be transitive and take a direct object, or they can be intransitive and not take a direct object (see 16b-3).

Put on is a transitive phrasal verb.

Isabella *put on* a dress. [*Dress* is the direct object of the verb *put on*.]

Come over is an intransitive phrasal verb.

Isabella plans to *come over* tonight. [no direct object]

When a phrasal verb is transitive, the particle can sometimes be placed after the direct object, separated from the verb.

Isabella *put* a dress *on*.

They *looked* all the evidence *over*.

Practice 19.5   Phrasal Verbs

Identify the complete phrasal verbs—the verbs and their particles—in the following sentences. Note whether the phrasal verb is transitive (takes a direct object) or intransitive (does not take a direct object).

1. Although he wanted to study in India, Francisco had to turn the offer down.

2. He looked up the information about the university, but the book had left out some steep costs.

3. Since he hated to call his farewell party off, however, Francisco told all his friends to come over.

4. In the middle of the party, Francisco broke down and told his friends the truth.

5. "I will get over this disappointment," he said, "because I really did not want to give up so many good friendships."

19c   Sentence Structure

English sentences have a great deal of variety, but most begin with one of the five basic sentence patterns. By adding words, phrases, and clauses, you can modify these basic patterns.

19c-1   Basic Sentence Patterns

English sentences have both subjects and predicates. The subject is the agent of the action, the person or thing acting in the sentence. The subject can be a single word, a phrase, a clause, or a string of these elements. The predicate is an assertion about what that subject does and always includes a verb.

SUBJECT   PREDICATE
Students study. [The subject is *students*; the predicate is *study*.]

SUBJECT   PREDICATE
All the *students* in my class *study* extremely hard for tests. [The complete subject is *all the students in my class*; the complete predicate is *study extremely hard for tests*.]

Subjects and predicates combine to form sentences that fit into a number of predictable patterns.

■ **Subject + Intransitive Verb**   An intransitive verb does not transmit action to an object or a person: *sleep, fall, go*.

   S   VI
We *went*. [*We* is the subject; *went* is the intransitive verb.]

       S   VI
Our whole family *slept* at Grandmother's house. [*Family* is the subject; *slept* is the intransitive verb.]

■ **Subject + Transitive Verb + Direct Object** A transitive verb transmits the action of the subject to an object or person. The direct object is a noun, pronoun, or noun phrase that receives the action of a transitive verb. It often answers the question *what?* or *whom?* after the verb.

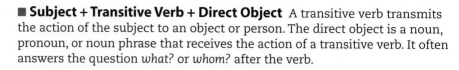

We *brought* a *pie* for dessert. [*Brought* is a transitive verb; *pie* is the direct object that tells *what* we brought.]

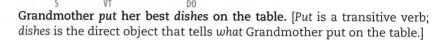

Grandmother *put* her best *dishes* on the table. [*Put* is a transitive verb; *dishes* is the direct object that tells *what* Grandmother put on the table.]

■ **Subject + Transitive Verb + Indirect Object + Direct Object** The indirect object is a noun, pronoun, or noun phrase that tells *to whom* or *for whom* the verb acts.

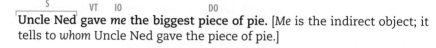

Uncle Ned gave *me* the biggest piece of pie. [*Me* is the indirect object; it tells to *whom* Uncle Ned gave the piece of pie.]

I gave the large brown *dog* the rest of my food. [*Dog* is the indirect object.]

■ **Subject + Transitive Verb + Direct Object + Object Complement** The object complement describes or renames the direct object.

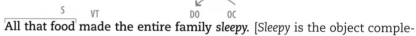

All that food made the entire family *sleepy*. [*Sleepy* is the object complement; it describes the direct object, *family*.]

Grandmother called us *couch potatoes*. [*Couch potatoes* is the object complement; it renames the direct object, *us*.]

■ **Subject + Linking Verb + Subject Complement** The subject complement describes or renames the subject after a linking verb. Linking verbs connect subjects to complements. The most common linking verbs are *be*, *became*, *appear*, *feel*, and *seem*.

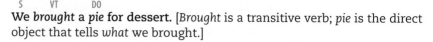

Uncle Ned became *cranky*. [*Cranky* is the subject complement; it describes Uncle Ned after the linking verb, *became*.]

My brother Don is his *favorite nephew*. [*Nephew* is the subject complement; it renames *Don* after the linking verb, *is*.]

Usage Note The verb comes before the subject in a question or when a sentence begins with *there* or *here*:

    S   LV
Gina is a good athlete. [subject + verb]

    LV   S
Is Gina a good athlete? [verb + subject]

    V   S
There are many good athletes on the team. [verb + subject]

Practice 19.6   Basic Sentence Patterns

Identify the sentences below as one of these patterns:

    S + VI (subject + intransitive verb)
    S + VT + DO (subject + transitive verb + direct object)
    S + VT + IO + DO (subject + transitive verb + indirect object + direct object)
    S + VT + DO + OC (subject + transitive verb + direct object + object complement)
    S + LV + SC (subject + linking verb + subject complement)

1. John rode his new motorcycle carefully in the traffic.

2. He is a very cautious rider.

3. John gave Fritzi a ride on the back of the motorcycle.

4. Fritzi fell off.

5. Luckily, Fritzi was unhurt.

19c-2 Modifying Sentence Patterns

Once you know these five sentence patterns, you can modify the sentences by adding words, phrases, and clauses. A few guidelines will help you modify the sentences clearly. Since adverbs can be placed in different parts of sentences, they can cause some confusion.

■ **Adverbs** Adverbs and adverb phrases that express time (*today, next week, at four o'clock*) and place (*in the room, outside, in the country*) are placed at the beginning or end of a sentence but not between a verb and direct object.

Correct: The blues singer gave a wonderful performance *yesterday*.

Correct: *Yesterday* the blues singer gave a wonderful performance.

Incorrect: The blues singer gave *yesterday* a wonderful performance.

Correct: The fans bought her CDs *at the performance*.

Correct: *At the performance*, the fans bought her CDs.

Incorrect: The fans bought *at the performance* her CDs.

Adverbs of frequency (*always, sometimes, never*) are placed right before the verb they modify.

CORRECT: We *always* go directly home after the concert.

INCORRECT: *Always* we go directly home after the concert.

Some adverbs of frequency (*often, many times*) can be placed at the end of a sentence.

CORRECT: We have been to the concert hall *often*.

CORRECT: We have been to the concert hall *many times*.

Adverbs that modify adjectives or adverbs are placed directly before those adjectives or adverbs. Adverbs that modify sentences or clauses are placed directly before those sentences or clauses.

CORRECT: Marlene is *extremely* interested in child-care issues. [modifies the adjective *interested*]

CORRECT: She works *very* intensely at her job. [modifies the adverb *intensely*]

CORRECT: *Fortunately,* she manages her time well. [modifies the entire sentence]

Some adverbs that modify sentences can be placed after the subject or at the end of the sentence.

> Marlene, *fortunately,* manages her time well.

> Marlene manages her time well, *fortunately.*

■ **Adjective Phrases** Adjective phrases are placed after the nouns they modify.

CORRECT: The museum *recommended by my friend* had a fascinating exhibit.

INCORRECT: The *recommended by my friend* museum had a fascinating exhibit.

CORRECT: The dinosaurs, *extinct for centuries,* seemed real.

INCORRECT: The *extinct for centuries* dinosaurs seemed real.

■ **Indirect Objects** Indirect objects are placed after the verbs and before the direct objects.

CORRECT: **The guide gave** *me* **a wonderful tour.** [The indirect object *me* goes after the verb *gave* and before the direct object *wonderful tour.*]

CORRECT: **The audio guide showed** *visitors* **the major exhibits.** [The indirect object *visitors* goes after the verb *showed* and before the direct object *major exhibits.*]

■ **Pronouns** Pronouns that restate the subject should be omitted.

CORRECT: **Doug and Alex love baseball.**

INCORRECT: **Doug and Alex** *they* **love baseball.**

CORRECT: **Erica is a football fan.**

INCORRECT: **Erica** *she* **is a football fan.**

■ **Subordinating Conjunctions** Subordinating conjunctions (*although, after, since, if*) are not used with coordinating conjunctions (*and, but, for, nor*).

CORRECT: **Although the storm was over, the waters were still rising.**

INCORRECT: *Although* **the storm was over,** *but* **the waters were still rising.**

CORRECT: **Since the streets were flooded, the rescue workers rode in boats.**

INCORRECT: *Since* **the streets were flooded,** *and* **the rescue workers rode in boats.**

Practice 19.7   Modifying Sentence Patterns

Using the guidelines for modifying sentence patterns, write the following sentences.

1. State when you went to bed last night. Use an adverb of time.

2. State how often you phone your friends. Use an adverb of frequency.

3. Describe your room. Use an adjective phrase.

4. State to whom you gave a gift. Use direct and indirect objects.

5. Explain when you will visit home. Use a subordinate clause.

19c-3   Reported Questions and Quotations

Questions and quotations can be direct (reported firsthand) or indirect (reported secondhand). The sentence structure changes in these two modes. (See 17f-3 on the punctuation of quotations.)

■ **Quotations** Direct quotations report a speaker's exact words. The words are enclosed in quotation marks. Indirect quotations do not use quotation marks, and the pronouns, verb tense, and time markers shift.

DIRECT QUOTATION: Joe asked me, "*Are you ready to party?*"

INDIRECT QUOTATION: Joe asked me if *I was* ready to party. [The pronoun shifts from *you* to *I*; the tense shifts from *are* to *was*.]

DIRECT QUOTATION: The bandleader said, "*We will give* a great show *tomorrow night*."

INDIRECT QUOTATION: The bandleader said that *they would give* a great show *the next night*. [The pronoun shifts from *we* to *they*; the tense shifts from *will give* to *would give*; the time marker shifts from *tomorrow night* to *the next night*.]

■ **Questions** Reported direct questions use the inverted pattern, verb + subject. Reported indirect questions use the standard subject + verb pattern but omit the question mark.

DIRECT QUESTION: Ingrid asked Carlos, "Are your parents coming to visit this winter?"

INDIRECT QUESTION: Ingrid asked Carlos whether his parents were coming to visit this winter.

DIRECT QUESTION: My parents asked me, "Will we stay with you?"

INDIRECT QUESTION: My parents asked me if they would stay with me.

Practice 19.8   Reported Questions and Quotations

Change the following direct questions and quotations to indirect questions and quotations.

1. Senator Lopez asked us, "How many of you will vote for me?"

2. The reporter from the *Daily News* said, "The crowd went wild."

3. The police officer told the crowd, "Settle down, or we will ask you to disperse."

Change the following indirect questions and quotations to direct questions and quotations.

4. We told the police that we had just come to see Senator Lopez that evening.

5. The reporter said that he had never seen such an unruly crowd.

19d Idioms

An idiom is a common expression whose meaning cannot be understood from the meaning of its individual words. Expressions like *watch your back*, which means "be careful," and *keep an eye on*, which means "watch something," cannot be figured out by looking up each word. Many phrasal verbs (see 19b-3) and prepositional phrases are idiomatic expressions.

To master the idioms of English, you have to learn them in context. As you talk with people, listen to the radio, watch films and television, or read, be alert for these expressions and write them down. Many websites and handbooks contain lengthy lists of English idioms, and you can look up their meanings or add them to your personal list. A few websites you might want to visit are http://www.caslt.org/research/esllinks, http://www.eslcafe.com, and http://www.comenius.com/idiom/index.

19d-1 Some Common Idioms

This list explains a few of the hundreds of idiomatic expressions in English.

Idiom	Definition	Example
at this point	at this time	At *this point,* he stopped his lecture.
be broke	lack money	Gail could not go to the movies because she *was broke.*
brush up on	review	Steve will *brush up* on verbs before the test.
cut down on	decrease	Hector has to *cut down on* sweets.
drop off	deliver	Kris *dropped off* the sweater you left in her car.
foot the bill	pay	Mike got a raise and will *foot the* bill at the restaurant.
go to pieces	lose emotional control	Olivia *went to pieces* when she lost her wallet.
lose one's temper	get angry	Bad drivers make me *lose my temper.*
mixes up	confuses	Petey always *mixes up* the twins.
on second thought	thinking again	*On second thought,* Rebecca decided to go.
out of the question	not possible	Going out on a school night is *out of the question.*
take turns	alternate	Lily and Cate *took turns* crying.

19d-2 Idiomatic Prepositional Phrases

Prepositional phrases are difficult to learn because the same preposition can have different meanings. The phrases *on the boat*, *on time*, and *on the menu* all use the preposition *on*, but in slightly different ways. It is best to learn prepositional phrases as you learn all idiomatic expressions: as a whole and in context. A few common prepositional phrases will give you a sense of their usage.

at	at noon, at the dance, at home, at a glance, at peace
in	in the box, in April, in Asia, in love, in time, in the airplane
on	on top of, on time, on Sunday, on the bed, on Main Street
to	to the store, to bed, to the bottom, to the city, face to face

Practice 19.9   Idiomatic Prepositional Phrases

Fill in the blanks with the correct preposition: *at, in, on,* or *to.*

1. Yesterday _____ noon, I met my friend Anne _____ a restaurant _____ the new mall.

2. We did not like anything _____ the menu, so we called the server _____ the table.

3. One of the cooks _____ the kitchen said she could make us a special meal _____ one o'clock.

4. We left the restaurant and went _____ some of the stores _____ Elm Street. _____ one o'clock we returned _____ the restaurant and ate _____ style.

Credits

Chapter 7

Page 235: "A Blackout for the Blind," *Boston Globe*, Editorial, October 9, 2003. Copyright 2003 by Boston Globe Newspaper Company. Reproduced with permission of Boston Globe Newspaper Company in the format textbook via Copyright Clearance Center.

Page 242: Paul Mulshine, "End the Hands-Off Policy on Cell Phones," (Newark) *Star-Ledger*, July 5, 2001. © 2000 by The Star-Ledger. All rights reserved. Reprinted with permission.

Page 245: Cynthia Tucker, "The 'Quota' Cry Doesn't Faze Me," *Atlanta Journal-Constitution*, June 29, 2003. Copyright © 2003 by the Atlanta Journal-Constitution. Reproduced with permission of Atlanta-Journal Constitution in the format Textbook via Copyright Clearance Center.

Page 247: Lisa Wehran, "Economic Status, Not Race, Should Be the Basis of College Admissions," *Columbus Dispatch* (Ohio), 2 August, 2003. Reprinted by permission.

Page 250: Sally Jenkins, "As Many Soldier On, Athletes' Relevance Fades Away," *Washington Post*, October 14, 2001. © 2001 by The Washington Post, reprinted with permission.

Chapter 8

Page 267: Susan Kellam, "Give 'Em Shelter," 1999, http://www.connectforkids.org.

Page 270: Jessica Hollander, "Stopping Teen Dating Violence," *Boston Globe*, October 3, 2003, copyright 2003 by Boston Globe Newspaper Company. Reproduced with permission of Boston Globe Newspaper Company in the format textbook via Copyright Clearance Center.

Page 274: Karen Lee, Proposal from Foster Parrots, Ltd.

Page 292: Interview with Garland Waller, "The Silent Screams: Court Ordered Abuse of Children," Proposal.

Page 278: 911 Bears Program Proposal by The Pine Tree Neighborhood Group.

Chapter 9

Page 333: Big Brothers Big Sisters of the Tri-State, Mission Statement.

Page 324: 911 Bears Program Proposal by The Pine Tree Neighborhood Group.

Page 327: Reprinted by permission of Spay USA.

Page 333: Website for Tri-City Family Housing, including Intro Flash Movie.

Chapter 10

Page 353: Google Search page. Courtesy of Google.

Page 358: Children's Literature Web Guide Home Page. Reprinted by permission of David K. Brown.

Page 360: Densho: The Japanese American Legacy Website, What Does an American Look Like? and Wartime Hysteria, Project Seattle, Washington. Reprinted with permission.

Page 361: Densho: The Japanese American Legacy Website, What Does an American Look Like? and Wartime Hysteria, Project Seattle, Washington. Reprinted with permission.

Page 362: Densho: The Japanese American Legacy Website: What Does an American Look Like? and Wartime Hysteria, Project Seattle, Washington. Reprinted with permission.

Chapter 11

Page 382: Thomas Doherty, Review of *Fargo*, *Cineaste*, 22, no. 2, 1996, p. 47.

Page 382: Richard Corliss, review of *Fargo*, *Time*, March 18, 1996, p. 91. © Time Inc., reprinted by permission.

Page 386: Mark Caro, Review of the movie *O*, *Chicago Tribune*, November 30, 2001, reprinted by permission.

Page 387: Jeffrey M. Anderson, "Clint's Wild *River*," *San Francisco Examiner*, October 8, 2003 (www.examiner.com). Reprinted by permission.

Page 395: Ann Homaday, "*Whale Rider*: This Girl, She Goes!" *Washington Post*, June 20, 2003, p. C5. © 2003, The Washington Post, reprinted with permission.

Page 399: Janet Maslin, "Such a Very Long Way from Duvets to Danger," *New York Times*, October 15, 1999. Copyright © 1999 by The New York Times Co. Reprinted with permission.

Page 402: Roger Ebert, *Fight Club* movie review, from the Roger Ebert column by Roger Abert, copyright © 1999 The Ebert Company, distributed by Universal Press Syndicate, reprinted with permission. All rights reserved.

Chapter 12

Page 431: David Maloof, Notes for "Pan Music," published in *Hampshire Life Magazine* section of the *Daily Hampshire Gazette*, June 27, 1997.

Page 434: Edgar Allen Beem, "Cutting Edge or Over the Line?," *Boston Globe Magazine*, December 30, 2001. Copyright 2001 by Boston Globe Newspaper Company. Reproduced with permission of Boston Globe Newspaper Company in the format textbook via Copyright Clearance Center.

Page 435: Judith Newman, "Running for Office, Running for Life," from *Self*, reprinted in *Reader's Digest*, October 2001. Reprinted with permission from the October 2001 Reader's Digest.

Page 443: Jack Falla, "The Top Drill Instructor in Boot Camp 101," *Campus Voice*, August/September 1984.

Page 448: Stephen Magagnini, "Hmong Teen Builds Future in Two Conflicting Worlds," *Sacramento Bee*, September 12, 2000.

Page 456: Susan Orlean, "Show Dog," from *The Bullfighter Checks Her Makeup*, copyright © 2001 by Susan Orlean. Used by permission of Random House, Inc.

Page 464: Notable Writer: Susan Orlean.

Page 468: Mike Sager, "The Marine," first appeared in *Esquire*, December 2001, vol. 136, issue 6. Reprinted by permission of the author.

Chapter 13

Page 485: David Abel, "Male Call on Campus: Enrollment Trends Widen Gender Gap, Upset Social Scene," *Boston Sunday Globe*, November 5, 2000. Copyright 2000 by Boston Globe Newspaper Company. Reproduced with permission of Boston Globe Newspaper Company in the format textbook via Copyright Clearance Center.

Page 486: Anne Driscoll, "Giving Girls a Sporting Chance," *Boston Globe Magazine*, November 24, 1999. Copyright 1999 by Boston Globe Newspaper Company. Reproduced with permission of Boston Globe Newspaper Company in the format textbook via Copyright Clearance Center.

Page 503: Emily Nussbaum, "My So-Called Blog," *New York Times Magazine*, January 11, 2004, pp. 33–37. Copyright © 2004 by the New York Times. Reprinted with permission.

Page 478: Bella English, "Old Game, New Players," *Boston Globe Magazine*, February 19, 1999. Copyright 1999 by Boston Globe Newspaper Company. Reproduced with permission of Boston Globe Newspaper Company in the format textbook via Copyright Clearance Center.

Page 510: Camille Rodriquez, "M.D. Realities: Medical Schools Take on Decade-Long Applications Slump as Prospective Students Face Doubts."

Page 482: AIDS Map, from Strong, Sayad, and Yarber, *Human Sexuality: Diversity in Contemporary America*, 5th edition, © 2005, McGraw-Hill. Reproduced with permission of The McGraw-Hill Companies.

Page 483: Number of Brands Used in Past Year by Twelve- to Fifteen-Year-Olds, Hoyer/MacInnis, *Consumer Behavior*, 3rd edition, p. 361. Copyright © by Houghton Mifflin Company. Reprinted with permission.

Page 483: Adolescent Health Status.

Chapter 14

Page 558, 561: Yahoo! search for "globalism" and "urban sprawl." Reproduced with permission of Yahoo! Inc. Yahoo! and the Yahoo! logo are trademarks of Yahoo! Inc.

Page 533: Reprinted with permission from *Encyclopaedia Britannica*, © 2004 by Encyclopaedia Britannica, Inc.

Page 567: Chris Sherman and Gary Price, *The Invisible Web: Uncovering Information Sources Search Engines Can't See*. Cyber Age Books, 2001. Reprinted by permission.

Chapter 15

Carole Slade, *Form and Style*, 12th edition. Copyright © 2003 by Houghton Mifflin Company. Reprinted with permission.

Page 606: Album sales over the past three decades. Adapted from Stan Liebowitz, "Will MP3 downloads Annihilate the Record Industry? The Evidence So Far," University of Texas at Dallas School of Management, 21 July 2003, http://www.pub.utdallas.edu/ ~liebowit/intprop/records.pdf.

PHOTO CREDITS

Chapter 1

Page 2: Denis Boulanger/Vandystadt/TIPS Images.

Page 9: From *The Journals of Dan Eldon: The Journey Is the Destination*, edited by Kathy Eldon, 1997. Cover image by Dan Eldon. Chronicle Books, San Francisco, CA, chroniclebooks.com.

Page 15: © The New Yorker Collection 1976 George Booth from cartoonbank.com. All rights reserved.

Page 19: Excerpt "An American Daughter" by Wendy Wasserstein, *The Paris Review* no. 142 (Spring 1997), page 164.

Page 23: *Breezing Up (A Fair Wind)* by Winslow Homer, 1873–1876. Gift of the W. L. and May T. Mellon Foundation, image © 2004 Board of Trustees National Gallery of Art, Washington, DC.

Page 23: Infrared assembly of *Breezing Up (A Fair Wind)* by Winslow Homer, 1873–1876. Gift of the W. L. and May T. Mellon Foundation, image © 2004 Board of Trustees National Gallery of Art, Washington, DC.

Chapter 2

Page 44: American Science & Engineering Inc.

Page 54: Thinkstock/Getty Images; Page 55: Thinkstock/Getty Images.

Page 56: *Free at Last*, collage portrayal of Nelson Mandela by Jeremy Sutton (www.jeremysutton.com).

Page 57: With permission Universal Studios Media Licensing, Matte World Digital and Amblin Entertainment.

Page 57: With permission Universal Studios Media Licensing, Matte World Digital and Amblin Entertainment.

Page 64: The Everett Collection.

Chapter 3

Page 68: Enrique's Journey © 2002 Los Angeles Times. Photos by Don Bartletti.

Page 75: Enrique's Journey © 2002 Los Angeles Times. Photos by Don Bartletti.

Page 75: Enrique's Journey © 2002 Los Angeles Times. Photos by Don Bartletti.

Page 78: Enrique's Journey © 2002 Los Angeles Times. Photos by Don Bartletti.

Page 78: Enrique's Journey © 2002 Los Angeles Times. Photos by Don Bartletti.

Page 89: Enrique's Journey © 2002 Los Angeles Times. Photos by Don Bartletti.

Page 81: Shepard Sherbell/Saba/Corbis.

Page 93: PictureNet/Corbis.

Page 99: W. Marc Bernsau.

Page 89: Enrique's Journey © 2002 Los Angeles Times. Photos by Don Bartletti.

Page 315: The Ad Council and America's Second Harvest/ ConAgra's Feeding Children Better Foundation. Photo by Oliver Jiszda.

Page 319: Produced by Royal Typewriter Company for U.S. Civil Service Commission. Photo: NARA Still Picture Branch.

Page 321: U.S. Department of Transportation and The Ad Council.

Page 321: U.S. Department of Transportation and The Ad Council.

Page 322: The Ad Council and America's Second Harvest /ConAgra's Feeding Children Better Foundation.

Page 324: © 2004 The Pine Tree Brook Neighborhood Associations. Courtesy, Dick Russell.

Page 324: © 2004 The Pine Tree Brook Neighborhood Associations. Courtesy, Dick Russell.

Page 326: The Ad Council and the Coordinated Campaign for Learning Disabilities.

Page 329: Courtesy, Unitarian Universalist Urban Ministry.

Page 331: Credit: Eric Green (www.civildefensemuseum.com).

Page 330: U.S. Department of Homeland Security and The Ad Council. Photo courtesy Kenryk Kaiser/Stock Photo/Picture Quest.

Page 332: South Short Women's Center.

Pages 333, 334: Tri-City Housing.

Chapter 10

Page 345: Paul Bergen/Redferns Music Library.

Chapter 11

Page 370: Reuters/Corbis.

Page 374: Warner Bros. Pictures/Zuma Press.

Page 375: Focus Films/Zuma Press.

Page 375: Andrew Cooper/Miramax Films/Zuma Press.

Page 380: Metro-Goldwyn-Mayer/Photofest.

Page 380: 20th Century Fox.

Page 383: Gramercy Pictures/Everett Collection, Inc.

Page 396: South Pacific Pictures Ltd.

Page 400: Kobal Collection/The Picture Desk.

Page 407: PACHA/Corbis.

Chapter 12

Page 412: *Judy Remains Resilient* by Daphne Confar. Courtesy of the artist.

Page 419: *Andy Warhol* by Jamie Wyeth. Photo: The Collection of Cheekwood Museum of Art, Nashville, Tennessee.

Page 425: NARA Still Picture Branch.

Page 422: *Head of a Girl (Girl with the Pearl Earring)* by Jan Vermeer. Photo: Scala/Art Resource.

Page 440: *One Girl Child* by Daphne Confar. Courtesy of the artist.

Page 433: Pam Berry.

Page 467: Peter Doyle.

Page 464: Bucci/Getty Images Entertainment.

Page 428: Photo and text by Allison Roberts.

Page 458: Courtesy John Shane.

Chapter 13

Page 470: Erik Sumption.

Page 477: Elliott Erwitt/Magnum Photos.

Page 484: Text and graphic by Thomas Starr, *Boston Globe*, Opinion, September 14, 2004. Thomas Starr is a graphic designer and an associate professor at Northeastern University.

Page 479: Courtesy, Brookhaven National Laboratory.

Page 481: Bridal Row, 2000 by Amie Potsic.

Page 497: Wisconsin Historical Society. Photo by J. Robert Taylor.

Page 498: Hulton-Deutsch Collection/Corbis.

Page 499: Bettmann/Corbis.

Page 500: Bob Martin/Allsport/Getty Images.

Page 501: AP Photo/Kathy Willens.

Page 482: Map from Strong et al., *Human Sexuality: Diversity in Contemporary America*, 5th edition, The McGraw-Hill Companies.

Chapter 14

Page 528: Digital Vision Photography/Veer Inc.

Page 554: "On the Internet, no one knows you're a dog" © The New Yorker Collection 1993 Peter Steiner from cartoonbank.com. All rights reserved.

Chapter 15

Page 572: David Silverman/Getty Images

Chapter 16

Page 646: © The New Yorker Collection 2001 Peter Steiner from cartoonbank.com. All rights reserved.

Chapter 17

Page 668: "The Importance of Punctuation" © Dan Piraro 2002/King Features Syndicate.

Chapter 18

Page 688: "I'll have the misspelled 'Ceasar' salad the improperly hyphenated." © The New Yorker Collection 2002 Jack Ziegler from cartoonbank.com. All rights reserved.

Index